U.S. SURGEON GENERAL C. EVERETT KOOP AWARDS THE SURGEON GENERAL'S MEDALLION TO JAMES L. REPACE "FOR HIS ROLE AS A CO-BELLIGERENT IN THE FIGHT AGAINST TOBACCO," WASHINGTON, DC, JULY 10, 1989.

D1088646

ENEMY No.1
WAGING THE WAR ON
SECONDHAND SMOKE

By James L. Repace

Publisher: Repace Associates, Inc.

© 2018 James L. Repace, All rights reserved.

Cover Art: *Vapors*, Purple and Gold Smoke by Bob Cornelis (Getty Images, by permission).

All rights reserved.

Repace Associates, Inc.
3479 Monitor Court, Davidsonville, MD 21035

ISBN: 978-0-578-19702-9

Interior design by booknook.biz

JIM REPACE DEPLOYING TWO MONITORING PACKAGES CONTAINING MONITORS FOR FINE PARTICLES, CARCINOGENS, AND ENVIRONMENTAL MEASUREMENTS IN AN OTTAWA PUB IN 2002 WITH KEN JOHNSON OF HEALTH CANADA.

TABLE OF CONTENTS

TABLE OF ILLUSTRATIONS

PREFACE

"As the following facts disclose, despite some rising pretenders, the tobacco industry may be the king of concealment and disinformation.

[Judge H. Lee Sarokin, Haines v. Liggett, U.S. District Court, New Jersey, 1992].

On Monday, April 27, 1998, *The Wall Street Journal* reported that Big Tobacco had long regarded me as one of their worst enemies. Located on the front page of the Journal's MARKETPLACE section above the fold, a lengthy article, *"Tobacco Memos Detail Passive-Smoke Attack,"* reported the disclosure of hitherto secret tobacco industry internal memoranda. The lede announced, "Determined to keep reports about secondhand smoke dangers from mushrooming, the tobacco industry mobilized a counterattack in the mid-1980's to systematically discredit any researcher claiming perils from secondhand smoke."

A sidebar graphic, emblazoned Smoke and Mirrors, featured a February 25, 1985 memo from the Director of RJ Reynolds' Smoking and Health Division, to RJR's Director of Public Affairs: *"As I am sure you are aware, Repace and Lowrey will soon have their analyses published... We anticipate that if Repace runs true to form there will be a good deal of media copy written about their analyses and thus we should begin eroding confidence in this work as soon as possible."*

In a second memo, an RJR consultant warned, "Reynolds cannot ignore this issue and stay in business." Another quoted a Brown and Williamson tobacco attorney complaining to a high-level colleague that, "We're becoming the industrial equivalent of South Africa ... the lowered social acceptability of smoking is tied directly to the secondhand smoke issue ...". One particularly revealing memorandum, dated March 27, 1991, noted "Philip Morris had divided the universe of its potential opponents into 'battlefields' that included science, litigation, media, government, employers/insurers and transportation/public places."

"When asked for comment, an industry spokesman refused to discuss the substance of files that the companies regarded as 'privileged,' asserting: '... the tobacco wars have been heated, ... there is no shortage of strong views both within the industry and outside.'" The *Journal* article continued: "On the issue of passive smoke, James Repace ... loomed as enemy No. 1. Dr. Repace, along with a naval researcher, Alfred Lowrey, published landmark studies that helped support a Surgeon General's 1986 report concluding that secondhand smoke causes disease" [WSJ, 1998].

Enemy #1 is the inside story of the secondhand smoke wars that have been waged in local, state, national and international arenas for more than four decades beginning in the latter part of the 20th Century and extending to the present day. A brief bit of background on the guy who became Big Tobacco's "Enemy No. 1." From 1968 to 1979, I worked as a physicist at the Naval Research Laboratory (NRL) in Washington, DC, performing radiation effects research. During this period, I became involved in several battles over outdoor air pollution from smokestacks which introduced me to the world of public interest science, and led to a change of career. From 1979 to 1998, I served as an air pollution policy analyst at the Environmental Protection Agency (EPA) Headquarters in Washington DC. My research papers on air pollution from secondhand smoke and its risk to nonsmokers were published as works of public interest science and were not commissioned by NRL or EPA. Since 1998, I've been an international secondhand smoke consultant based in the Washington DC metropolitan area, doing business as Repace Associates, Inc. [www.repace.com].

In the mid-1970's, I attacked the problem of secondhand smoke using the tools of experimental physics, developing a hypothesis of the determinants of tobacco smoke air pollution in buildings, and measuring the concentration of its most prominent atmospheric marker, particulate tobacco tar, in restaurants, bars and other microenvironments to verify it. I discovered that tobacco smoke pollution of commercial and residential buildings exposed nonsmokers to levels of air pollution far in excess of that on busy commuter highways. With my long-time friend and co-author, Dr. Alfred Lowrey, we published that work in the journal *Science*. At the EPA, I became a pioneer in the emerging field of indoor air pollution. I was also an outspoken and effective scientific advocate for smoke-free indoor air. Judging by its virulent response, the tobacco industry fully realized that both this new field and I had the potential to inflict major damage to its profits.

In the early 1980's when the first studies implicating passive smoking as a lung cancer risk for nonsmokers began to appear, Lowrey and I estimated the number of nonsmokers who died from secondhand smoke exposure each year using a process known as quantitative risk assessment. Our approach involved quantifying the health impact of secondhand smoke on nonsmoking building inhabitants in the two most-frequented microenvironments, the home and the workplace. This was a challenging multi-disciplinary problem, involving elements of air pollution physics, ventilation engineering, epidemiology, medicine, risk assessment, and sociology. To accomplish this, I had to teach myself the rudiments of several of these arcane fields from scratch. This effort resulted in the development and validation of mathematical models to predict exposure, dose, dose-response, risk, and control of secondhand smoke.

Although I did not realize it at the time, I was an early practitioner of both of the new disciplines of exposure science and environmental epidemiology. And I would soon learn the hard way that a scientist working in either of these fields would run afoul of big polluting businesses whose economic interests were threatened. As Richter et al. (2002) aptly stated, "In most scientific fields, the rewards go to investigators who report positive findings. But in the environmental sciences, the situation is the opposite. In environmental and occupational medicine, and in epidemiology and related disciplines, 'positive' findings about hazards and risks are threatening to powerful interests. Investigators who study or report these risks are therefore at increased risk for harassment by the very nature of their work. … Environmental scientists and occupational health and safety professionals measure and report health risks from exposures to toxic and physical agents so that preventive measures can be put into effect. As a result of their work, they may be subjected to harassment, lawsuits, ostracism, job loss, loss of funding, intimidation, abuse, threats, or even force after reporting such risks, or are prevented from investigating or reporting risks altogether." Today, climate scientists can regrettably be included in this infamous list [Mann, 2016; Hansen, 2009].

The tobacco industry's response to my work was classic: publishing slick brochures questioning it, hiring "white-coats" (moles) to discredit it, lobbying journal editors to reject my papers, barraging EPA with a plethora of Freedom of Information Act Requests about my work, travel, and leave records, and employing powerful tobacco state congressmen in attempts to get me fired from my government job and discredited in the eyes of EPA management.

Adept in navigating the swamp of Washington politics, I fired back with every tool at my disposal. I enlisted pro-bono public interest law firms and sympathetic journalists in my defense. The incessant barrage of industry attacks energized my scientific efforts to quantify secondhand smoke air pollution, and its effects on lung cancer and heart disease rates in nonsmokers. Over the years, I managed to measure exposure to secondhand smoke in offices, factories, restaurants and bars, in homes, on aircraft, on cruise ships, and in casinos. This body of evidence helped build a scientific consensus that secondhand smoke pollution of indoor air dominated human exposure to fine particle air pollution, that it sickened and killed nonsmokers in massive numbers, and that it could not be controlled by ventilation absent tornado-strength levels of air exchange. Policy makers in the U.S. and abroad took notice.

I responded to the world-wide interest in my research by outreach to universities, scientific groups, medical groups, voluntary health organizations, NGO's, federal, state, and local policy-makers and legislators as well as the media. From 1980 to 2015, I lectured in more than two-thirds of U.S. States, in nearly two-thirds of the Canadian Provinces, and in Australia, New Zealand, Hong Kong, Chile, Spain, Greece, Portugal, Italy, Ireland, England, and Norway. I also consulted for the World Health Organization, the Pan American Health Organization and The Netherlands. I testified four times before the U.S. Congress.

In addition to my work at EPA, I became involved in a whirlwind of activities with many other federal agencies, including The National Cancer Institute (NCI), The National Heart, Lung, and Blood Institute (NHLBI), The Centers for Disease Control and Prevention (CDC), The Surgeon General's National Advisory Committee on Smoking and Health, The National Institute for Occupational Safety and Health (NIOSH), The Occupational Safety and Health Administration (OSHA), The Departments of Energy (DOE), Transportation (DOT), and Health (DHHS), the National Institute for Environmental Health Sciences (NIEHS), The National Security Agency (NSA), and the Pentagon, as well as many state, provincial, and local governments in the U.S. and Canada. I discussed the lung cancer risks to nonsmokers from secondhand smoke on television, appearing on The CBS Evening News, ABC's Good Morning America, 60 Minutes, NOVA, CNN, and PBS. And I gave interviews to many major and minor newspapers, magazines, and TV and radio stations in the U.S. and abroad. This sustained public outreach had its impact.

As Bertrand Russell (1960) wrote:

> The knowledge that the public possesses on any important issue is derived from vast and powerful organizations: the press, radio, and, above all, television. The knowledge that the governments possess is more limited. They are too busy to search out the facts for themselves, and consequently they know only what their underlings think good for them unless there is such a powerful movement in a different sense that the politicians cannot ignore it. Facts which ought to guide the decision of statesmen—for instance, as to the possible lethal qualities of fallout—do not acquire their due importance if they remain buried in scientific journals. They acquire their due importance only when they become known to so many voters that they affect the course of the elections . . .

In recognition of my efforts (or trouble-making, depending on whose ox was being gored), I received a Special Achievement Award from EPA (1984), was awarded The Surgeon General's Medallion from Dr. C. Everett Koop (1989), Certificates of Appreciation from the US Departments of Transportation (1989) and Health and Human Services (1990), OSHA's Impact Award (1994), The Secretary of Labor's Excellence Award (1994), Certificates of Appreciation from Action on Smoking and Health (1998), and Americans for Nonsmokers' Rights (1998), A Lifetime Achievement Award from the American Public Health Association (1998), The American Lung Association of Maryland's Distinguished Service Award (1998), the Prince Georges' County Maryland Civic Federation President's Award (1998), the Flight Attendant Medical Research institute's Distinguished Professor Award (2002), the Robert Wood Johnson's Innovators Combating Substance Abuse Award (2002), A Certificate of Recognition for Excellence in Smoke Studies from The National Cancer Institute of Milan [Italy] (2003), the Constance L. Mehlman Award for exposure science contributions influencing public policy from the International Society of Exposure Science (2015), and The Albert Nelson Marquis Lifetime Achievement Award (Marquis Who's Who, 2017).

Between 2003 and 2012, I served as a Visiting Assistant Clinical Professor at the Tufts University School of Medicine, and as a Consultant to the Stanford University Department of Civil and Environmental Engineering. Over a period of about 35 years, I published 87 papers on secondhand smoke in scientific, medical, engineering, and legal journals (55 of them peer-reviewed), as well as 10 peer-reviewed papers in physics and electrical engineering. This book draws on my research work published in scientific, engineering, medical, and legal journals, that I strove to make accessible to policy-makers at every level of government, the media, and to the public as well.

It also draws on the litigation I have been involved in as an expert witness. I testified for the nonsmoking plaintiffs as an expert witness in five-dozen mostly successful toxic tort legal cases involving morbidity and mortality due to chronic secondhand smoke exposure. Taking advantage of the legal discovery process, I developed insight into the factors affecting secondhand smoke concentrations in workplaces and the sociology of workplace management of workers' health and welfare, as well as exposures in homes. The plaintiffs included a nurse, railroad workers, flight attendants, office workers, casino workers, teachers, prisoners, children in child custody cases, and occupants in multi-unit housing. By year's end of 2017, I had given 48 scientific conference presentations, 58 invited talks before medical and scientific groups, gave 121 television, radio, newspaper and magazine interviews, authored about ten dozen reports for various legal clients and residents of multi-unit dwellings, and testified 155 times before international, federal, state, and local policy-making bodies.

I have enhanced my tale using the industry's own contemporaneous internal documents, unknown to me at the time, and largely discovered after I began to write this book. It was akin to a peek into the unholy archives of the Nazi High Command in the wake of WWII. This is not hyperbole. According to the American Cancer Society and the World Lung Foundation, "globally, tobacco use killed 100 million people in the 20th century, much more than all deaths in World Wars I and II combined. Tobacco-related deaths will number around 1 billion in the 21st century if current smoking patterns continue" (Tobacco Atlas, 2015).

These formerly hidden industry documents are posted online on the *Truth Tobacco Industry Documents* [TTID] website (formerly known as the Legacy Tobacco Documents Library). The TTID archive was established in 2002 by Prof. Stanton A. Glantz, of *The Cigarette Papers* fame, at the University of California, San Francisco (UCSF), and hosted by the UCSF Library and Center for Knowledge Management (Glantz, et al., 1996; TTID, 2018). A former president of Californians for Nonsmokers' Rights, Stan Glantz is a prominent cardiac researcher, statistician, and pre-eminent anti-tobacco activist who himself has long been a top industry target. The tobacco industry, through front organizations, sued the University of California (unsuccessfully) twice in an effort to halt Glantz's work (SF Examiner, 1997).

TTID presently has become an archive of nearly 15 million tobacco industry documents. They concern Big Tobacco's fraudulent advertising, manufacturing, marketing, licit and illicit scientific research, dirty legal tricks, and corrupt political influence. TTID was built to house and provide permanent access to tobacco industry internal corporate documents produced during litigation between US States, the Department of Justice, and the seven major tobacco industry organizations as well as other sources. These internal documents expose the machinations of one of the most malevolent and heartless industries in the world.

In the 20th Century, they included powerful corporations like Philip Morris, RJ Reynolds, Brown & Williamson, Lorillard, Liggett, and British American Tobacco. In the 21st Century, the top 5 largest companies are China National Tobacco Company, Philip Morris International (Altria Group, Inc.), Japan Tobacco International, British American Tobacco, and Imperial Tobacco Group, with combined revenues of a third of a trillion dollars, and reaping annual net profits of $31 billion (Tobacco Atlas, 2015). This kind of income enabled them to buy immense political influence, and the ability to delay or prevent meaningful regulation.

Industry lawyers, including company lawyers and external counsel, played a key role in waging this campaign. As Guardino and Daynard (2007) wrote, tobacco company lawyers and external counsel have been involved for decades in nefarious activities having little or nothing to do with legitimate legal practice. To the contrary, they employed underhanded tactics that impeded the flow of information about the dangers of both smoking and secondhand smoke to the public and the medical community. Internally to the industry, these tactics encompassed assessing and attempting to influence company scientists' beliefs, whitewashing in-house scientific research intended for publication, and preventing in-house scientists from publishing potentially damaging results. Moreover, industry lawyers manufactured phony attorney-client privilege and work-product to conceal sensitive documents from disclosure in litigation, among numerous other dirty tricks.

As an index of how seriously the industry was concerned about my activities, an unrestricted September 2017 query of TTID using the search term, "Repace," yielded an astounding 26,968 documents, including a nearly 800-page dossier. To winnow down this plethora of paper pollution, I used search terms compiled from my curriculum vitae, research publications, and presentations, as well as news stories, scholarly books, and important events and persons as I recall them. To be clear, most references labeled TTID are tobacco industry internal documents documenting their tactical and strategic war plans, few of which I knew about until I began research for this book in 2013.

The modern nonsmokers' rights movement began around 1970, coinciding with the emergence of the Clean Air Act and Earth Day, and really began to take off after 1980. The rise of this phenomenon can be assessed by the contemporary appearance and relative popularity of the terms *environmental tobacco smoke (ETS), passive smoking, secondhand smoke (SHS), and involuntary smoking.* Environmental tobacco smoke was originally a disinformation term promoted by tobacco industry publicists to make tobacco smoke pollution appear like a natural and harmless part of the environment. Nevertheless, it was adopted by many researchers and in several authoritative government reports. For a time, I used it myself to convince turf-conscious skeptics at EPA that ETS was an environmental issue and properly within the province of EPA, and not exclusive to the Public Health Service. Involuntary smoking has been a term primarily used in Surgeon General's Reports, while passive smoking tends to be used by medical researchers, but secondhand smoke is the currently preferred term used by many researchers, by nonsmokers' rights groups, and by the media.

Figure 1 shows the historical frequency of use of these competing terms for tobacco smoke pollution in various books. It mirrors the rise of the nonsmokers' rights movement by the frequency of appearance of the words environmental tobacco smoke, secondhand smoke, passive smoking, and involuntary smoking appearing in Google Books from 1965 to 2008 [Google, 2017]. In an effort to combat the grave threat to its profits posed by independent scientific research on secondhand smoke, the tobacco industry, armed with junk science and using high-priced legal, scientific and medical mercenaries, attacked its real or imagined enemies on a variety of fronts, targeting research, researchers, professional societies, public health officials, journalists, news organizations, federal workers, and federal agencies in a massive campaign of influence, disinformation, fraud, and intimidation. The purchase of the best congress that money could buy through copious campaign contributions proved to be one of the most effective weapons in the tobacco industry's arsenal.

Although it may be hard for many Millennials to believe, for most of the past century, nonsmokers were second-class citizens when it came to secondhand smoke exposure in the workplace and public places. As a researcher, activist, and author of early scientific papers on the exposure, dose, risk and control of secondhand smoke, I became a contributor to public policy on smoking restrictions in restaurants, bars, and other workplaces for nearly 40 years. I was motivated first by outrage at being forced to breathe secondhand smoke, then by scientific curiosity, and finally by the barrage of venomous counterattacks from a rogue industry and its running dogs hell-bent on defending the pollution of buildings, public transportation, and workplaces with tobacco smoke by the users of its highly addictive products, using any means, fair or foul. Mostly foul.

As Princeton Professor Harry G. Frankfurt wrote, "One of the most salient features of our culture is that there is so much bullshit" (Frankfurt, 2005). On smoking and secondhand smoke, the tobacco industry turned bullshit into an art form. In characterizing the practices of sociopathic tobacco industry executives, the machinations of its shyster lawyers, bent scientific consiglieri, oleaginous PR flacks, corrupt congressmen, industrial-strength moles, and the industry's fellow travelers in the commentariat, as well as the so-called "smokers' rights" groups with their online tobacco trolls, I have let their words and actions speak for themselves. Readers of this book can form their own judgement.

This book is dedicated to nonsmokers the world over who have suffered from secondhand smoke, and to those who will suffer no more. And to my family, Hilarine, Justine, Max, Nick, Paul, Alex and Jon.

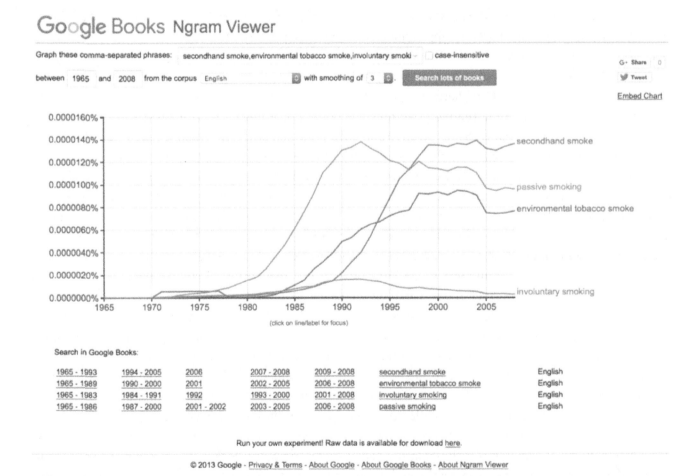

FIGURE 1A. DESCRIPTIVE TERMS CORRELATING WITH THE RISE OF THE NONSMOKERS' RIGHTS MOVEMENT, 1970-2008 [GOOGLE N-GRAM VIEWER, 2017].

The Dean's Lecture

James Repace, MSc., Biophysicist
Visiting Assistant Clinical Professor, Tufts
Univ. School of Medicine, and
REPACE ASSOCIATES, Inc.
Secondhand Smoke Consultants

**The Secondhand Smoke Wars:
Battles on the Road from
Science to Policy**

April 19th, 2006
11:30 Reception in Room 105
12:00 Lecture in Winslow Auditorium

REPACE ASSOCIATES, Inc.

FIGURE 1B. THE TALK AT YALE UNIVERSITY THAT INSPIRED THIS BOOK, WITH GRATITUDE TO PROF. BRIAN LEADERER.

PART ONE

THE EARLY YEARS

CHAPTER 1

WHEN SMOKING WAS KING

Where do they go, the smoke rings I blow each night?
Oh, what do they do, those circles of blue and white?

Smoke Rings, © EMI Music Publishing, The Mills Brothers, London Sessions 1934-1939

On the Ides of March 1965, 14 months after the 1964 Surgeon General's Report proclaimed that cigarette smoking was a cause of lung cancer in men, Nick Repaci, my 59-year old father, drowned in a sea of blood after a lung tumor moled into his aorta. He had been smoking for 45 years. With his passing, the wages of tobacco became personal. I had long noticed that whenever he lit up, it triggered a liquid smoker's cough. He would wheeze after climbing two flights of stairs. In the 1950's, when I was in my mid-teens and my father was in his mid-40's, I had intuited that cigarettes were injuring his health, and asked him why he didn't quit. He replied, "I can't."

Dad died at home in the arms of my brother Bob, who was then 21 years old. By 1965, I had become acutely aware that cigarette smoking was responsible for the growing epidemic of lung cancer. I had read the medical literature on lung cancer intensively in an effort to help him seek the best medical treatment. His tumor was inoperable, and radiotherapy only palliative. Once The Big C bites your lungs, you buy the farm. The 5-year survival rate for lung cancer in that era was a mere five percent. Sixty years later, despite advances in treatment, more than half of the better than 220,000 annual victims of lung cancer in the U.S. still died within a year of diagnosis (ALA, 2016).

A BRIEF HISTORY OF SMOKING IN THE 20TH CENTURY

Historian Allen Brandt aptly labeled the 20th Century *The Cigarette Century* in his book by that name. J.A. Bonsack invented the first cigarette-rolling machine in 1880. Prior to that time, commercial cigarettes had been rolled by hand. A skilled worker could roll but four cigarettes per minute, insufficient to satisfy popular demand in the 1870s. In 1875, the Allen and Ginter Company in Richmond, Virginia, offered a prize of $75,000 for the invention of an automatic cigarette rolling machine. Bonsack's patent was granted in 1881. It could produce 200 ready-made cigarettes per minute, revolutionizing the cigarette industry [Wikipedia, 2016]. The rapid expansion of the American cigarette industry in the late 1880s alarmed temperance workers, religious leaders, health reformers, businesspeople, educators, eugenicists, and even some pipe and cigar manufacturers who resented the competition. From 1893 to 1921, fifteen states enacted prohibitions on cigarettes [Goodman, 2005]. Prior to World War I, smoking of tobacco had been largely the province of men, who embraced the rituals of pipes, cigars, and hand-rolled cigarettes. Very few women smoked. Smoking indoors was mainly confined to saloons, smoking cars, private clubs, and sporting establishments, while some hotels and homes provided smoking parlors where men could repair for post-prandial cigars and brandy (Speer, 1968).

At the turn of the 20th century, per capita annual consumption in America was just 54 cigarettes. Then in 1913, R.J. Reynolds Tobacco developed Camels, a flavored imitation Turkish cigarette, packaged to make smoking more convenient. It was a major success: first year sales totaled 425 million packs, increasing annual per capita cigarette consumption by 60% to 87 sticks. Camels were soon trailed by Lucky Strike (American Tobacco) and Chesterfield (Liggett and Meyers) brands. During the First World War, the alternating boredom and tension of military service recruited a new generation of male cigarette smokers, whose tobacco consumption became 60 to 70 percent higher than in civilian life. Post war, prohibitionist groups became preoccupied with ratification and enforcement of the 18th Amendment to the U.S. Constitution, which prohibited the sale of alcohol, and lost interest in tobacco control. [Goodman, 2005].

In the 1920's, bolstered by less harsh blends of cigarette tobacco, coupled with slick advertising campaigns targeting women, cigarette smoking soon became broadly accepted, even acquiring a patina of chic. By 1922, trend-setting New York women brazenly smoked in public, and by 1927, 14 of the 15 state cigarette prohibition laws had been repealed. In 1934, even First Lady Eleanor Roosevelt smoked cigarettes in public. Polite customs were soon discarded, with smokers no longer feeling the need to seek permission before lighting up indoors. Smoking indoors became pandemic (Speer, 1968).

By 1935, American per capita consumption of cigarettes had increased 27-fold from fin de siècle levels to 1450 cigarettes annually. With the onset of World War II, consumption among men accelerated; in 1944, better than 25 percent of U.S. cigarette production was diverted to the troops abroad, typically for free or at low cost, addicting many millions of new smokers. President Franklin D. Roosevelt jauntily sported his trademark cigarette holder. As women poured into the wartime labor market, their smoking rates also rocketed upward.

During the post-war period, the deadly toll exacted by smoking became apparent. As the cohorts of cigarette smokers aged, their vastly increased mortality rate relative to nonsmokers became blindingly apparent to medical researchers. The lung cancer deaths of actor Humphrey Bogart in 1957, and broadcaster Edward R. Murrow in 1965, each at the age of 58, personified the early onset mortality due to smoking, as had the death of chain-smoking Franklin D. Roosevelt from a stroke at the age of 63 in 1945.

Appallingly, from March 1952 until at least May 1956, the so-called Micronite Filter in Lorillard's Kent cigarettes was made of blue needle-like crocidolite asbestos fibers, the most lethal variety. Note that asbestos-related inflammatory pulmonary disease and bronchogenic carcinoma were well-established by the mid-1950's and asbestos-caused malignant mesothelioma was recognized by the 1960's. Senior scientists and executives of the tobacco companies already knew about the cancer risks of smoking in the 1940's and were aware that smoking could cause lung cancer by the mid-1950's [Cummings, et al., 2002]. Between 1952 and 1956, smokers inhaled asbestos fibers coupled with tobacco smoke carcinogens from 13 billion cigarettes (Mintz, 2016), increasing their fatal lung cancer risk by 10-fold relative to non-asbestos filtered cigarettes, and 90-fold relative to that of a nonsmoker.

Lung cancer had been a very rare disease prior to the advent of cigarettes. By the mid-1960's, nearly 70 million Americans were smoking regularly. Lung cancer deaths exploded exponentially, from less than 3,000 in 1930, ascending to 18,000 by 1950, rising to 27,000 in 1955, and blowing past 41,000 by 1962. In 1964, Surgeon General Luther Terry, himself a cigarette and pipe smoker, issued his landmark report, *Smoking and Health*, sounding the first major U.S. public health alarm. Dr. Terry's Report concluded that cigarette smoking caused lung cancer, outweighing occupational exposures in the general population and all other causative factors by far. Smokers' risk of developing lung cancer increased both with the duration of smoking and the number of cigarettes smoked daily, and decreased after quitting smoking, prima facie evidence of causality. Relative to nonsmokers, the average male cigarette smoker had ten-fold the risk of lung cancer, and heavy smokers had twenty-fold the risk, while co-exposure to asbestos and other workplace lung carcinogens synergistically increased that risk much further.

The Surgeon General had also concluded that cancer of the lung, head, and neck for pipe and cigar smokers who mostly took the smoke into their mouths, although less than for cigarette smokers, was much greater than for nonsmokers. No safe level of smoking had ever been discovered. The Surgeon General also noted that deaths from arteriosclerotic, coronary, and degenerative heart disease rose from 273,000 in 1940, to 300,000 in 1950, jumping to 578,000 by 1962, while reported deaths from chronic bronchitis and emphysema soared from 2,300 in 1945 to 15,000 in 1962. All were diseases linked to smoking. Dr. Terry, a cardiologist, had quit smoking when his report was issued. It was too late; he would die from congestive heart failure in 1985 at the age of 73.

In the wake of the 1964 Surgeon General's Report, U.S. smoking prevalence began a slow decline; in 1966, prevalence had decreased to 52 percent of men and 34 percent of women, averaging 42.4% of the population. But two thirds of American children still grew up in households with one or more smokers, suffering increased rates of asthma, SIDS, low birth weight, middle ear infections, pneumonia, and impaired lung growth. I was among these; as a child I had suffered from multiple asthma attacks and middle ear infections, and my tonsils and adenoids had to be cut out. After the surgery, I returned home for Christmas, suffered a throat hemorrhage, passed out from the loss of blood, and was re-hospitalized. My family had no clue that my malady could be caused by secondhand smoke.

Big Tobacco Begins a Fifty-Year Campaign of Deception

In 1950, fourteen years before the 1964 Surgeon General's Report, medical studies had begun to implicate smoking as a cause of disease. In England, Richard Doll and Bradford Hill published a preliminary report in *BMJ* suggesting that smoking was linked to carcinoma of the lung. This was echoed in the U.S.: Evarts Graham and Ernst Wynder, in a 1950 *JAMA* article, also implicated smoking as the cause of the massive 20th Century epidemic of lung cancer. They concluded that excessive and prolonged use of tobacco, especially cigarettes, seemed to be an important factor in the induction of bronchogenic carcinoma. And in 1953, Wynder and Graham showed that cancer could be induced experimentally by painting tobacco smoke condensate (tar) on the backs of mice. (Ironically, Graham, a heavy smoker, would himself die in 1957 of lung cancer at the age of 74.) This study was followed by a second *BMJ* report by Doll and Hill in 1954, of forty thousand doctors over a 20-year period that confirmed their earlier findings. The British Doctors Study persuaded the British government to advise the public that smoking and lung cancer rates were related.

Alarmed by this major threat to their profits, in 1954, the U.S. tobacco industry reacted with the first of many decades of disinformation campaigns designed to reassure smokers that smoking was safe, and that the industry could be relied upon to protect the health of smokers. This flagrant lie was entitled *"A Frank Statement to Cigarette Smokers."* Blowing smoke on the damaging Graham and Wynder mouse-painting experiment, it stated in part that,

> "Recent reports on experiments with mice have given wide publicity to a theory that cigarette smoking is in some way linked with lung cancer in human beings. Although conducted by doctors of professional standing, these experiments are not regarded as conclusive in the field of cancer research. However, we do not believe that any serious medical research, even though its results are inconclusive should be disregarded or lightly dismissed. At the same time, we feel it is in the public interest to call attention to the fact that eminent doctors and research scientists have publicly questioned the claimed significance of these experiments. Distinguished authorities point out:
>
> 1. That medical research of recent years indicates many possible causes of lung cancer.
> 2. That there is no agreement among the authorities regarding what the cause is.

3. That there is no proof that cigarette smoking is one of the causes.
4. That statistics purporting to link cigarette smoking with the disease could apply with equal force to any one of many other aspects of modern life.
5. Indeed, the validity of the statistics themselves is questioned by numerous scientists. We accept an interest in people's health as a basic responsibility, paramount to every other consideration in our business. We believe the products we make are not injurious to health. We always have and always will cooperate closely with those whose task it is to safeguard the public health." [ALA archive, 2000].

The Frank Statement was a slickly-worded piece of propaganda designed to obscure the obvious fact that lung cancer was overwhelmingly a disease of smokers; it still remained rare among nonsmokers. The Frank Statement was packed with weasel-words conveying uncertainty: "not regarded as conclusive; many possible causes; no proof; statistics purporting; validity questioned; we believe the products we make are not injurious to health." The unidentified "Distinguished Authorities" from "medicine, science, and education" would soon be recruited and form the so-called Tobacco Industry Research Committee, a propaganda machine designed solely for the purpose of defeating any effective efforts to reduce smoking. These "Authorities" were the first in a long succession of industrial-strength tobacco moles whose sole function was to blow smoke on the science implicating smoking as a cause of lung cancer. So much for "Cooperating closely with those … who safeguard public health."

Cityscapes and countryside alike became awash in billboards promoting the safety of cigarettes. Radio, television, magazines, and newspapers barraged the public with a blend of bogus health claims and pure hogwash. A sampling of these includes those by Camels: "More doctors smoke Camels than any other cigarette;" Old Gold: "Not a cough in a carload;" Lucky Strike: "20,679 Physicians say Luckies are less irritating;" Kools: "Doctors … agree that Kools are soothing to your throat;" Kent: "No other cigarette approaches such a degree of health protection and taste satisfaction;" L&M: "Just what the doctor ordered;" Chesterfield: "Nose, throat, and accessory organs not adversely affected by smoking Chesterfields;" Philip Morris: "Medical authorities recognize Philip Morris proved less irritating to the smoker's nose and throat," and "When smokers changed to Philip Morris every case of nose or throat –due to smoking- either cleared completely or definitely improved;" Viceroy, "Gives double-barreled health protection" [tobacco.stanford. edu]. And later cigarette marketing began to avoid any mention of health whatsoever by using simplistic slogans such as, "Come to Marlboro Country;" and "I'd walk a Mile for a Camel." Smokers realized too late that Marlboro Country was the cancer ward, and it was hard to walk across the street for a Camel while dragging an oxygen tank. This slick advertising campaign was in part successful in retarding the public's recognition that smoking caused lung cancer (Proctor, 2012).

The industry had been well aware of this for a long time and had an amazingly cynical view of its customers. In an Opinion piece for the *New York Times* in 1993, Bob Herbert wrote that a few years earlier, he had interviewed a former cigarette model, David Goerlitz, who had appeared in ads for R.J. Reynolds Tobacco. "Goerlitz described an outdoor photo session in which several cartons of Winstons were scattered around. A number of Reynolds executives were at the session and Mr. Goerlitz asked if it would be all right if he took a few cartons for himself. One of the executives said, sure, take them all. Mr. Goerlitz, surprised, said, 'Don't any of you smoke?' The executive shook his head. *'Are you kidding?'* he asked. *"We don't smoke that shit. We just sell it. We reserve the right to smoke for the young, the poor, the black and the stupid."* [DLPA, 2016; Herbert, 1993].

GROWING UP IN A WORLD OF SMOKE

The frenetic smoking of the wartime years produced a super-abundance of smoking role models for the children of America. Mine included my father, four of my uncles by marriage, my barber, doctor, and dentist, not to mention most of the actors on the silver screen. But none of my mother's seven sisters and four brothers smoked. On the radio, the personable Arthur 'Buy 'Em By the Carton' Godfrey, whose show I enjoyed regularly, praised Chesterfield cigarettes and Lipton Tea, an odd combination. I recall smoke-filled theatres where we watched double features on Saturday afternoons. Smoking was routine on public transportation, in retail stores, and even in the homes of nonsmokers, ashtrays were routinely put out to accommodate smoking guests.

Growing up in Mt. Vernon, New York, on the northern edge of The Bronx during the war years, I remember ration coupons for sugar and meat, air raid sirens, blackout curtains on the windows, whistle-blowing air raid wardens, half-moon car headlights, buildings with coal-burning furnaces, the air filled with fly-ash, pictures of planes, tanks, and ships in the papers, and four uncles in the uniforms of the Infantry, Air Force, Seabees, and the Coast Guard. On the day that the War ended, on September 2nd 1945, I recall church bells ringing for hours. For most of the 1940's my parents labored in the garment industry, my father wielding a steam iron that pressed finished women's dresses, and my mother working as a seamstress sewing the dresses in the same factory. Like many blue-collar children of our generation, Bob and I were latchkey kids.

Our neighborhood echoed with the shouts of rambunctious free-range boys and girls. We played stickball in the street, touch football using stale cabbages tossed out by the local grocer, pitched pennies, had cap-gun and water-pistol fights, played hopscotch and handball, built wagons with repurposed baby carriage wheels, lumber scraps purloined from building sites, and milk crates that "fell off the truck." We flew kites with time-wicked firecrackers from the roof of the factory building across the street, bombarded hapless pedestrians with water balloons, and shot off illegal fireworks on the Fourth of July.

In the early 1950's, my parents went into the dress business, opening a small factory employing about twenty seamstresses, two pressers, and two finishers. It was a union shop, and all of the workers belonged to the International Ladies Garment Workers Union (ILGWU). Dad would solicit work from the wholesale jobbers in Manhattan, bring bolts of cloth and patterns up from the City in his station wagon, spread layers of cloth on a fifty-foot table, cut out the dress patterns using a fine circular saw, assemble the pieces in rolls of work, and distribute them to the workers. Weekly, he would transport the finished dresses back to the jobbers, who would market the dresses to department stores. My mother managed the factory and refused to permit smoking on the premises. Even my father and the other presser, Nick Stabile, had to go out on the roof to smoke. The ILGWU rep told Mom that it was the only smoke-free factory he had ever heard of.

When I was twelve, under the pervasive influence of cowboy movies, I bought a 14-ounce can of Prince Albert pipe tobacco, a packet of paper wrappers, and a cigarette-rolling machine at the local cigar store. A large wooden Indian guarded the door. I hand-rolled a hundred cigarettes and eagerly lit one up. After filling my mouth with the acrid foul-tasting smoke – I found it impossible to inhale – it took me three days to cleanse the toxic waste absorbed into my palate, despite repeated tooth, tongue, and palate brushings laved with liberal doses of mouthwash. I vowed to never again repeat that revolting experience. From that moment on, I viewed smoking as something poisonous. Asthmatic as a child, I would routinely get carsick, likely from breathing secondhand smoke in the backseat of our 1946 Dodge. I suffered breathing problems every Fall, when nearby homeowners would rake enormous heaps of fallen leaves into the gutters and burn them; the suffocating smog lingered for hours trapped beneath the nighttime atmospheric inversions. In the spring pollen season, I sneezed until I thought my head would fly off. I became convinced that I had been born on the wrong planet.

Born in 1938, I was a charter member of the generation born between 1925 and 1942. In 1951, a *Time* magazine article caustically characterized children of my generation as "unimaginative, withdrawn, unadventurous, and cautious," and branded us "The Silent Generation." Our parents had suffered through the Great Depression, and afterward times remained hard and money was scarce. Dad said that "your best friend is $5 in your pocket." During the early 1950's, conformity, conservatism, and McCarthyism reigned; it was dangerous to express contrary political opinions. We were expected to work hard, keep quiet, and conform. I often failed to meet those expectations.

I Become Interested in Science

As an adolescent in the early 1950's, I found books on astronomy, rocketry, and nuclear fission spellbinding. I built model rockets and made gunpowder – in those days even a 13-year old boy bent on no good could buy the necessary ingredients from any pharmacy: potassium nitrate, flowers of sulfur and powdered charcoal. Imagine that. A library book described the manufacture of black powder by the Krupp Works in Germany. When I came to the part about breaking up the dried gunpowder cake with wooden mallets in a shed far removed from the main factory in case of explosion, I enlisted Bob to do that part on our fire escape. We fabricated our own fireworks, selling them to neighborhood kids. I often carried a jar of gunpowder around in my back pocket. I carefully concealed these lunatic activities from my parents. The culmination of these dangerous stunts occurred when was when I was 14. I built a rifle out of an old car antenna, filled the barrel full of match heads, with a pencil stub for the bullet. When I test fired it up on the roof, it blew up in my face, blinding one eye. I became significantly risk averse after this major folly.

I was not the only one of my friends to do outré things. My best high school friend, Gary "Moon" Goodman, got his nickname from his obsession with building telescopes and stargazing in the winter cold at four in the morning. He lived on the upscale side of town and had a stay-at-home Mom; his Dad was a book publisher who owned a private plane. One day, Moon synthesized nitroglycerine in his basement using a fancy chemistry set. To test out the product, he whacked a drop with a hammer. The hammerhead blew right through the cellar ceiling into the kitchen above. Although his face was blackened and blistered, Moon's thick glasses enabled him to escaped serious injury. He went on to Cal Tech to study astronomy. Another childhood friend, Jimmy Farrington, whose dad was a house painter, built a neat replica civil war cannon out of an old lock, a metal tube, and a couple of toy wheels, loaded it with a firecracker, and fired a lead slug through a plaster wall in his house. He later became a skilled machinist.

My best neighborhood friend, Jack Armstrong, worked in the radio and TV sales and repair shop on the ground floor of my building. Bob Badie, a larger than life Persian immigrant who owned it, made house calls carrying a large toolkit that he affectionately called his "swindle box." He did very well and moved with his Italian wife and infant son into a large house on Grandview Boulevard in neighboring Yonkers. After school, I loved hanging around the shop while Jack worked learning the trade. I sometimes helped him carry heavy TV sets, and became fascinated with the complex tangle of wires, vacuum tubes, and circuits that comprised the innards of radio and television sets. Jack went on to a career with the telephone company.

The Challenges of High School and College

In middle school, influenced by the glamor of nuclear power and rocketry, I decided to become a scientist. My idol was Albert Einstein. However, during my first two years in high school, I paid scant attention to assigned homework, preferring to spend my time on my personally-designed curriculum, which consisted primarily of reading public library books of my own selection, both fiction and non-fiction. Mt. Vernon had a large and wonderful walnut-paneled library built by Dale Carnegie. A voracious reader, I consumed a book per week, including the 720 page *Moby Dick*, with a dictionary by my side. I was enthralled by Chesley Bonestell's space art illustrating Willy Ley's book, *The Conquest of Space*. My middle school had very useful practical courses in wood and metal-working, which I also enjoyed. Although I acquired a large vocabulary, ignoring my schoolwork was not a useful recipe for passing my courses. I flunked Latin and Algebra in my 9th year, and Plane Geometry and English in my 10th; I was summarily punished with summer school in both years. Finally, reality set in. Realizing that my poor grades would preclude admission to college, I decided to take a serious interest in studying in my junior and senior years of high school. I achieved high grades in English, Advanced Algebra, Trigonometry, Introductory Calculus, and Physics. One of the most useful courses was one in touch-typing. I was the only boy in the class, and by far, the worst typist. On the other hand I can still type with all ten fingers, and am comfortable with composing text on a keyboard. Very useful, since my handwriting today is like a doctor's – illegible.

In 1954, when I was sixteen, I built a radio in a cigar box based on an RCA circuit diagram with resistors, capacitors, and vacuum tubes bought in Radio Shack, when it actually catered to experimenters. I finished it one morning at 3 AM, and foolishly turned it on without double-checking the connections. It sparked and a plume of foul-smelling smoke erupted. I had hooked the selenium rectifier in backwards. It taught me to always check my work. In the 9th grade, after reading about Albert Einstein and nuclear power, I aspired to become a nuclear physicist. With a busload of other high-school kids, I visited the Brookhaven National Lab on Long Island and was fascinated by the big cyclotrons that accelerated charged particles and the bubble chambers that detected their collision tracks. I imagined becoming a high-energy physicist.

In my senior year, I applied to Columbia, NYU, and the Polytechnic Institute of Brooklyn. I was accepted by NYU and Brooklyn Poly, and opted for the latter. According to Poly's guidance counselor, I scored the highest grade ever recorded up to that time on the English part of the entrance exam, a legacy of my insatiable reading. In the math part, however, I was just average, although average for Poly was pretty good. In those chauvinistic days of the 1950's, almost all of Poly's 40,000-strong day and night-school student body was male, with the exception of about 50 or so female graduate students. At the beginning of his introductory lecture to our freshman English class, Prof. Obermeyer, an expat South African, got our all-male class to pay rapt attention with the crack, "So just because you guys have a penis and a beard, you all think you're Jesus Christ." That pretty much summed up male attitudes in the 1950's.

I was 17 years old when I started college in 1956. I majored in physics and minored in mathematics. My required undergraduate courses included Engineering Mechanics, Theoretical Mechanics, Electrical Engineering, Electricity and Magnetism, Electromagnetic Theory, Thermodynamics, Atomic Physics, Abstract Algebra, several courses in Calculus, Inorganic and Organic Chemistry, Technical Drawing, Instrument Drawing, Experimental Physics Lab, English, and German. My only electives were History of Science, and Fine Arts. I bought foot-long egg salad, tuna salad, or salami and mozzarella sandwiches on Italian bread for lunch at a local deli and washed them down with chocolate milk. Brain food for the budding physicist.

When I studied Organic Chemistry, I became fascinated with synthesizing bizarre chemicals such as Congo Red, and I dyed my handkerchief crimson; luminol, which is the spectacular substance which energizes firefly tails; and best of all, fluorescein, a dye which glowed a brilliant green with reflected light as if it contained a light source. I made a small vial of it in the lab, and as a practical joke, I surreptitiously dumped it in the pool at the Brooklyn YMCA where we had bare-assed swimming class. The pool, which must have contained at least 10,000 cubic feet of water, soon fluoresced with a brilliant green glow from a few milliliters of fluorescein, almost as if it were radioactive. I was never fingered as the culprit. I got an "A" in my Organic chem lab. By contrast, I found Inorganic Chemistry less inspiring, except when we synthesized nitrogen tri-iodide, a contact explosive, which we would sprinkle on the lab floor where it would explode when walked on (this was not one of the department-approved syntheses).

In our experimental physics lab in my junior year, we were tasked with coming up with our own hypothesis for an experiment, then designing and building an apparatus to test it using lab machinery, explaining the physics behind the results, and writing it up as a final report. I loved this class. I built a device called a Hilsch

Tube, which utilized a T-shaped tubular structure where high pressure air was shot up the leg of the T, whirled around in a spiral chamber which had a large hole at the wide part of the spiral, opening into one arm of the T, and a small hole in the center opening into the other arm. Both arms of the T had valves to regulate the airflow. The air coming out of the outer part of the spiral into one arm was hot, while frost built up from the air leaking through the center hole into the other arm. I measured the temperature difference with chromel-alumel thermocouples which I fabricated in the lab and measured the thermocouple output voltage using a galvanometer. It was a spectacular device, and the lab professor kept it for future demonstration in his lectures.

Brooklyn Poly did not have dorms, so all students commuted from home. I traveled to Grand Central Station daily via the New Haven Railroad and later the New York Central line, and then by subway to the Borough Hall stop in Brooklyn. During my rail commute, I avoided the smoking cars, which were like gas chambers. If I had to walk through one to a nonsmoking car, I held my breath as long as possible. Fortunately, with passengers crammed in like sardines, the New York subways did not permit smoking.

When I started college in September 1956, two out of three men and one out of three women smoked in America. By the time I graduated in 1963, per capita cigarette consumption had climbed to a historic annual peak of 4336 cigarettes. The custom of smoking typically began in one's teens, sparked by imitation of peers or adult role models, and was sustained by profound nicotine addiction. Cigarettes, like alcohol, became a quintessential social lubricant. In the face of such widespread popularity, it became virtually impossible for the now bare majority of nonsmokers to avoid exposure to secondhand tobacco smoke.

In the late 1950's, Brooklyn Poly's socials, filled with cigarette, cigar, and pipe smoke, were aptly advertised as "Smokers." They were disgusting. I attended only one, which was so smoke-filled that the air had turned blue and reeked with unbearable fumes; I left after ten minutes with burning eyes and a scratchy throat. Although smoking in my college classrooms was usually rare, during exams many students would light up, filling the room with smoke that made me dizzy and unable to concentrate, so I worked as fast as possible, before my brain quit functioning normally. In winter I would sit in the back of the room and open a window behind me, igniting complaints by the smokers who objected to the cold draft.

It took me nearly seven years to graduate because I cut down each semester's credit hours to a manageable 11 instead of an enervating 19. I emerged with 136 credits, sixteen more than required, with a B.S. in Physics in 1963. I decided to become an experimental physicist, and imagined I would go immediately to graduate school, but paying for it was a problem. My parents' limited resources were now devoted to brother Bob, who was majoring in Applied Math at NYU. When I finally graduated, I felt mentally exhausted. My mother asked what my plans were. "I'm going to graduate school in the fall, and I'm planning to take the rest of the summer off and go to the beach." She shouted, *Oh, no, you're not, bum!"* A little while later, Mom stormed into my room carrying a copy of the Yonkers, NY, *Herald Statesman's* Help Wanted section with several job openings circled. "You are not going to sit around here all summer without a job! Start looking!" I eyed the circled postings skeptically. However, one caught my eye: it was an ad for a summer job as a senior laboratory technician in the laboratory for nuclear medicine and thyroid studies at Grasslands, Westchester County's Hospital in Valhalla. It looked really cool. I called and made an appointment the next day.

I Become a Health Physicist

The nuclear medicine lab was at the ground floor basement level of the TB building and held a variety of interesting looking medical equipment. A tall, powerfully built man with thick glasses and a cultivated Boston accent greeted me with a smile. "Hi, I'm Dr. Arthur Bauman, and this is my lab and clinic; I see patients with thyroid problems and do medical research using radioactive tracers. Tell me about yourself." I related my education and told him I was very interested in nuclear physics. He gave me a technical medical paper that he had co-authored with the well-known medical physicist Rosalind Yalow, who would win the Nobel Prize in

1977. Their paper concerned the use of radioactive iodine 131 (isotope symbol, I^{131}) to study the uptake and excretion of iodide by thyroid glands to determine if they were euthyroid (normal), hyperthyroid (overactive), or hypothyroid (underactive). He asked me to take my time reading it, and then explain to him what I thought the paper meant. It contained some differential equations that I recognized immediately; the paper was utterly fascinating, and I explained it back to him. After the interview he showed me around the lab and told me what the duties of his lab assistant would be: assisting with the dosing and administration of radioactive drugs to patients, analyzing the data collected according to a set protocol, presenting the results to him, and general care of the instrumentation and cleaning the lab. He asked me if that appealed to me. I nodded enthusiastically. I went home on a high.

The next morning Dr. Bauman called and offered me the job. I started the following day. My first duties involved cleaning up the mess of test tubes containing old samples of radioactive blood and familiarizing myself with the ordering and storage of radioactive iodine and cobalt. Radio-cobalamin, tagged with radioactive Cobalt-57 (Co^{57}), was used to study pernicious anemia. I had to titrate a set dose of this agent and give the patient an "atomic cocktail." Pernicious anemia involves an inability of the intestine to absorb vitamin B-12 (cobalamin), due to a lack of a substance called *intrinsic factor* in the bloodstream. Intrinsic factor is an important protein that allows the body to absorb vitamin B12, which is required for red blood cells to form and grow. Abnormally low levels of B12 can cause a range of symptoms including fatigue, shortness of breath, diarrhea, nervousness, numbness, or tingling sensation in the fingers and toes. Severe deficiency of B12 causes nerve damage. The test involved collecting 24-hour urine output, usually about 1 to 1½ liters, and if the body absorbed the tagged vitamin, the urine would emit gamma radiation. If it was not radioactive, the patient was in trouble.

To evaluate the thyroid, I would titrate a given dose of radioiodine, tagged with I^{131}, which was both a gamma- and beta radiation emitter; this was administered intravenously. I also did some brain scans, and Dr. Bauman trained me to draw blood from patients so I could test it without him being there. He saw private patients daily at his home office, which he shared with his wife, Dr. Caroline, a pediatrician, in a leafy part of the City of White Plains and would arrive only in the afternoon. Soon I was running the lab by myself and used one of the medical residents to inject the radio iodide, as only physicians were allowed to inject patients due to the potential for anaphylactic shock, a life-threatening medical emergency. Dr. Bauman also asked me to lecture once a week to the medical resident staff on radiation physics and elementary calculus. I loved it, although most of the residents were not enamored of calculus, to Dr. Bauman's consternation. By summer's end, Arthur and I had become lifelong friends.

Later that summer, a health physicist, Richard (Dick) Mooney, arrived to calibrate our radiation detectors. Mooney worked at Delafield Hospital, a city-owned hospital in New York that treated indigent cancer patients jointly with Columbia University medical school whose resident physicians would train on them. He said that Delafield had a full-time competitive opening for a junior health physicist, and if I decided not to go back to school in the fall, I should give him a call. At summer's end, I decided that working for a year to earn tuition for my master's study was essential and called Mooney. The interview went well, and I was hired to work in the Medical Physics Laboratory of the City of New York, run by Carl Braestrup. Braestrup was one of the first American physicists to warn of the hazards of radiation; he studied the safety of X-ray and Cobalt radiation therapy facilities as director of the Physics Laboratory in the New York City's Department of Hospitals. During WW II, Braestrup had served as Surgeon General of the Army, publishing more than 50 articles on radiation protection, and worked with a Columbia University research team on radiological aspects of the Manhattan Project. Carl had developed various devices to measure the dose and type of radiation exposure, including the well-known film badge worn by radiation workers, which he had been using since the 1930's. [It was adapted by Ernest Wollan at Oak Ridge Labs in 1943 to improve its accuracy by adding a cadmium filter.] He was the co-author of a 3-volume series of books on Radiation Protection, the first major work on the subject. I bought and read these; they were fascinating and highly instructive; I subsequently developed considerable expertise in radiation dosimetry.

I was soon running the film badge service for the City of New York by myself (there were roughly a dozen city-owned hospitals) and measuring the radiation dose to patients in the operating room (OR) during radium implants for uterine carcinoma. Radium is a powerful and dangerous gamma radiation emitter. My job in the OR was to ensure that the patient's healthy tissues were not overdosed with radiation, as well as to ensure that the physicians performing the procedure were properly protected from ionizing radiation – using the well-established principles of time (minimize) and distance (maximize); the third principle, shielding, was not feasible in the OR, since the docs needed to work on the patient. They often got careless, and I would periodically attempt to scare them by turning up the volume on my Geiger counter and holding it in front of them to get them to conduct their medical conferences in the corner of the operating room, instead of leaning on the patients with their elbows.

The most appalling episode I ever witnessed was when a medical resident worked on a super-obese female patient with terminal cancer on whom he had to perform a caudal block. This medical procedure involves inserting a large caliber needle, like a veterinarian might use on horses, into the base of the patient's spine and threading a fine catheter through it to deliver a continuous dose of anesthetic. As he was an advanced medical resident, the supervising physician left him alone in the OR. I was there setting up my monitoring equipment. Because of the enormously thick layer of fat on her back, he had great difficulty locating the right insertion point, and after about 15 minutes of trying and numerous needle stabs on the weeping patient who was in great pain, I couldn't bear to watch anymore and walked out into the hall. I peeked through the glass into a neighboring OR, watching a breast cancer operation in awe as the surgeons peeled back the surface layers to get at the tumor. When I returned to the OR about 10 minutes later, I was revolted to see that the hapless resident was still stabbing the fat lady in the spine with the horse needle. The poor woman was now loudly wailing in agony. Alerted by her cries, a few minutes later, his surgical supervisor returned. She stormed up to him, placed both hands on his chest, and without a word, shoved him bodily out of the way. She slid her finger down the patient's spinal column, and in one shot, stuck the needle and catheter in, making a perfect insertion, and stormed out, leaving the red-faced resident to finish his botched job. Fledgling doctors learned their craft by treating the City's charity cases.

I learned to calibrate the big 2 million-volt therapeutic X-ray machine, the small lower voltage diagnostic X-ray machines, and the cobalt therapy machines. Carl told me he once watched in horror as an electrician who was working on one of the diagnostic machines accidentally touched a live wire and got electrocuted. Once a week, I would lecture the medical staff on radiation physics. After about three months, Dick Mooney announced that my job, which was a temporary appointment, was being advertised as open to all applicants. He told me that it was competitive – the City administered a technical test of radiation physics knowledge; as long as I finished in the top three, I could retain my $5000/year job permanently. I was appalled to learn that *fifty* applicants had applied. However, I managed a third-place finish and kept my job.

This was especially rewarding because at the end of my first day on the job, I had wandered out the side door of the hospital into a small park on the grounds, overlooking Riverside Drive in Manhattan, and spotted a very attractive young woman sitting on a park bench. She was on the last chapter of Ayn Rand's novel, *The Fountainhead*, which I had also read. I struck up a conversation, and she gave me a nice smile. I learned her name, Hilarine, and discovered that she was a Hunter College grad, a zoology major who worked with mice in the cancer research laboratory of the City of New York. We saw each other every day and soon were dating on weekends. Thirty-nine days later, I proposed marriage and she accepted. It was the day after President Kennedy was shot. Hilarine was born and raised in the New York City borough of Staten Island, in the small town of Princess Bay, in a Sears-built prefab home on a large lot where her father, a bridge tender for the City of New York, raised vegetables and chickens. We were married the following year. I moved into her 5-flight walk-up apartment at 530 West 163rd street, two blocks from Delafield Hospital. Living and working in Manhattan had its good, bad, and ugly moments.

The good parts were living two blocks from work, being able to attend Broadway plays, visit New York's many museums and living close to great bakeries and delis. The bad part included the City's alternate side of the street parking rule for street cleaning, which meant that I had to move my car and hunt for a new and scarce parking space on the other side of the street at 8 AM every weekday morning before work. The ugly part was the outdoor air pollution in the City, caused by a combination of heavy street traffic, apartment house incinerators, and toxic air pollution blowing across the Hudson River from Northern New Jersey's petrochemical refineries. In the summertime, Delafield Hospital was not air conditioned, and the heat and humidity were often unbearable. We had large windows that were open to the outside air, and industrial strength floor fans to keep us cool. Moreover, the outdoor air pollution drifting in through those open windows was so bad that my eyes would sting and water.

By 1964, Bob had grown into a handsome, muscular six-footer who excelled in collegiate track and field sports. He won a dozen medals in cross-country and javelin, was a cracker-jack chess player, and was widely admired by the co-eds. I taught Bob to play chess when I was 12 and he was 7. I beat him the first thousand games we played. And insufferable big brother that I was, I kept detailed records of my great victories on the side of the wooden chess box. He lost every game until he was 15 years old, and soon became so good that I couldn't beat him at all. At that point, I lost interest in playing him. Bob breezed through NYU as a math major and earned his Master's in Applied Math before entering the Information Technology profession. He got a Masters rating in chess as well. He had a long and successful career in IT, despite developing a near-fatal case of Hodgkin's Disease in the 1960's, part of a cancer cluster of five victims within a six-month period among his Kappa Sigma fraternity brothers at NYU. I learned a lot about Hodgkin's disease, from reading medical textbooks and research papers. I kept a copy of the *Merck Manual of Diagnosis and Therapy* in the john. With the aid of a medical dictionary, I learned a lot of medical terminology and gained some valuable insight into the practice of medicine and human physiology.

After two failed courses of radical radiotherapy, which left his arms permanently disabled, ending his college sports career, Bob's disease appeared intractable. However, he was successfully treated with MOPP, an experimental chemotherapy then newly developed by NIH. The "O" in MOPP was Oncovin, made from vincristine, an extract of the periwinkle flower. It was a sobering illustration of the ephemeral nature of good health and the consequences of disease even to supreme physical specimens like Bob. Despite his handicap, he was able to drive his car with certain modifications and steered his yacht with his feet. He lived life to the full until age 60, when he passed away in 2004 from scarring to his heart, an unfortunate consequence of high-level radiation exposure. My background in Health Physics and my familiarization with medical terminology and the medical literature would prove vital backgrounding when I became interested in air pollution physiology and epidemiology in the ensuing years.

The decade of the 1960's was pandemic with oppressive tobacco smoke indoors. Nonsmokers were essentially second-class citizens. Secondhand smoke permeated retail stores and public buildings, workplaces, meetings, lodge halls, and theaters, restaurants, bars, and nightclubs. It contaminated the air at sporting events, in college classrooms, locker rooms, on buses, trains, ships, and planes, in taxis, carpools, and at social gatherings. The waiting rooms of medical offices and hospitals were filled with smoke. Smoking in most workplaces was ubiquitous unless there was danger of fire or explosion. If you were a nonsmoker, the only way you could breathe smoke-free indoor air in workplaces and on most public transportation was by wearing a gas mask. I recall once taking a bus from Penn Station in New York City to New Brunswick, New Jersey, a trip of about an hour's duration. After the bus took off, numerous smokers lit up, filling the bus cabin with smoke. It aggravated my asthma, and I couldn't breathe. In frustration, I yelled at the smokers to have some consideration. I was ignored. I kept a handkerchief over my nose the whole way, and never rode an interstate bus again.

In 1968, Fredric Speer, a physician researching nonsmokers' reactions to secondhand smoke, observed that exposure could readily produce itching, tearing, burning or swelling of the eyes; sneezing, blocking, running, itching, or dryness of the nose; headache, dizziness, nausea, hoarseness, sore throat or wheezing, and that nonsmokers with allergies reacted two-and-one-half times as frequently as non-allergic nonsmokers (Speer, 1968). I was far from atypical in my sensitivity to secondhand smoke.

FIGURE 2. THROUGHOUT MOST OF THE 20TH CENTURY, SMOKING IN HOMES, WORKPLACES, BARS, AND RESTAURANTS, AS WELL AS BUSES, TRAINS, AND PLANES, WAS WIDELY TAKEN FOR GRANTED.
Artwork credit: Dr. P. Ole Fanger, University Professor, International Centre for Indoor Environment and Energy, Technical University of Denmark, Lyngby, Denmark (Presented to the Author).

CHAPTER 2

THE BRASS KNUCKLE SCHOOL OF PHYSICS

"Every Friday morning researchers gathered to present their work, and heated arguments were typically the result. 'I always think back on it as the 'Brass Knuckle School of Physics,' "Repace says."

[Jean Kumagai, CAREER CHOICES, Exposing the Dangers of Tobacco Smoke. Physics Today, 48:59-60 (1995).]

Justine, our first child, was born in Manhattan on Thanksgiving Day, 1964, and with Hilarine no longer working, our income was cut in half. So I applied for a job at Columbia University, and was offered a new position at a paltry 10% increase in pay, plus all the prestige I could eat. I turned it down. Perusing the want ads in the *New York Times*. I saw an interesting solicitation for B.S. level physicists to work at a "large national company" in New Jersey. My preliminary interview with a headhunter sent me to RCA's corporate laboratory, The David Sarnoff Research Center in Princeton NJ. I landed two back-to-back interviews with two PhD physicists in the lab's general research laboratory, one in the laser research group, and the other in the insulator physics group. I received job offers from each at a 30% increase in pay. While both groups performed very interesting research, I resonated more with Joseph Dresner, chief of the group, and his office mate, Peter Mark. Both men were in their 30's. Joe was born in Belgium, and Peter in Germany; both had come to America as the children of immigrants. Both Joe and Peter had been graduate students at NYU under the German-born physicist Hartmut Kallmann, the inventor of the photomultiplier scintillation counter for ionizing radiation.

Joe had previously worked in health physics, and in my interview, he asked me an arcane question concerning the conditions under which the roentgen, a measure of radiation exposure, is defined. I gave a spot-on scientific explanation. Peter queried me about voltages in connected and disconnected electrical circuits; I gave him a correct but incomplete answer. He then proceeded to give me an erudite two-minute chalk-talk explaining it fully. The job involved being Joe's support scientist and inventing one-of-a-kind scientific apparatus. As an aspiring experimental physicist, this was my cup of tea.

A bit of background on America's great industrial research laboratories. The General Electric Research Laboratory founded in the U.S. in 1900 was directed by the famous "Wizard of Schenectady," the German-born American mathematician and electrical engineer Charles Steinmetz, who developed theories of alternating and direct current that made possible the electrical power industry so essential for modern civilization. The nation's adoption of industrial research and development was influenced by German and European practices, that valued industrial research and support for university research and graduate training.

In the 1930's, The Philips Laboratory in the Netherlands favored an interdisciplinary industrial research by hiring a mixed group of physicists, chemists, crystallographers, and electrical engineers. Philips took on intelligent young researchers with some experience in scientific research, gave them liberty in choosing their research subjects, significant budgetary freedom, and avoided the micromanagement of research details while remaining mindful of company goals. The Lab encouraged publication in peer-reviewed journals and presentations at international scientific meetings. Most importantly, it allowed research management to arise out of competence. Philips Labs invented the compact disk and the DVD; today it remains one of the few remaining consumer electronics companies still supporting large scale multidisciplinary R&D.

The great expansion of U.S. industrial research occurred in the wake of World War II, which saw the formation of Dupont Labs in Wilmington, Delaware, IBM's Watson Lab in Yorktown Heights, New York, AT&T's Bell Labs in Murray Hill, New Jersey, and Xerox's Palo Alto Research Center in what is now called Silicon Valley (NAS, 2005).

Organized along the lines of Philips, RCA Laboratories was founded in 1942, and was situated a few miles from Princeton University, within commuting distance of RCA's main New Jersey factories at Camden and Harrison, as well as its corporate headquarters in New York City. During the war years, the lab's staff concentrated on war-related work. Its engineers and scientists developed improved radar antennas, radar-jamming systems, and acoustic depth charges to combat Axis submarines. They also continued to develop television systems.

Post-war, RCA continued military R&D, but began to emphasize basic research. By the 1950's, its research staff had doubled its wartime size. The lab then pioneered the development of color television, high-fidelity phonographs and tape recorders, transistors, lasers, computers, integrated circuits, advanced vacuum tubes, and videodisc players. The facility was eponymously renamed the David Sarnoff Laboratories in 1951, after RCA's iconic founder [Wikipedia, 2016].

At first, I commuted to the Sarnoff lab starting on the "A" train from the 168th Street Station in Manhattan to Penn Station on 34th Street, then rode the Pennsylvania Railroad to Princeton Junction, New Jersey. At that point, I'd either take the shuttle to the lab, or in good weather, spend a delightful 15 minutes walking paths through the lab's extensive park-like campus of woods and fields. Later that year, Hilarine, Justine, and I moved to a one-bedroom ground-floor garden apartment in Highland Park New Jersey, a welcome change from our five-flight Manhattan walk-up apartment. Highland Park, with a substantial Sephardic population, sported a great bagel bakery, as good as any in Manhattan. We lived about 25 miles from Princeton, which was far too expensive for us even on my new annual salary of $6500.

The Raritan River divides the town of Highland Park from the city of New Brunswick. One day I strolled across the connecting bridge and stared down into the brown, murky, oily depths of the river. It looked and stank like used crankcase oil. I asked a passerby how the local people put up with it. He said, "It's been like that since the 1920's." When we travelled on the Jersey Turnpike back to Staten Island and Westchester to visit our families on weekends, we had to pass through the petrochemical refinery belt of Northeastern New Jersey. The stench from their uncontrolled emissions was unbearable. Used to breathing the much cleaner air of Westchester County, New York, I could not understand how the local residents could tolerate it.

There were several hundred research scientists and engineers on staff at the Sarnoff lab, plus a large support staff of highly skilled machinists and glass-blowers, and it sported a country-club-like atmosphere. Mid-morning and mid-afternoon, uniformed waitresses would ring a cowbell in the hallway as they made their rounds, serving up excellent freshly-brewed coffee, tea, and delicious Danish pastries, which fostered close social and intellectual interaction among scientists in different groups. Even the spoke-and-hub layout of the buildings was designed to foster this exchange.

I look back upon this time and place as my apprenticeship where I absorbed the mores and self-reliant work habits of the professional scientist in the office and the lab I shared with Joe and Peter. Like the rest of the scientists and engineers in the General Research Lab, they worked solo rather than in teams. They spent time in the Sarnoff Center's extensive research library searching the scientific literature, performing mathematical calculations, discussing their work, and planning experiments. Those experiments usually required custom-built apparatus, which they sometimes designed and built themselves. Other equipment was designed and fabricated by professional support staff like myself. The Lab located self-service machine shops on every floor. This gave staff access to drill presses, lathes, glass-blowing equipment, metal-bending presses, plus an abundant supply of materials plus a skilled model maker who worked on more complicated jobs beyond our skill levels. He was also on call to advise us on the intricacies of the equipment we used. Bigger jobs were performed by the model-makers in a large well-staffed machine shop on the ground floor, who would also assist with design. I learned a great deal about practical experimental physics in this hands-on fashion and delighted in inventing specialized one-of-a-kind apparatus. I had a company credit card to purchase the electro-mechanical equipment I needed to fabricate the apparatus I designed to carry out my research tasks. I generally worked on my own.

My work was mainly to serve as Joe's support scientist. Joe would tell me the sort of apparatus he needed to perform his experiments and leave me to work out the details. For example, his experiment used an alloy composed of three elements (selenium, tellurium, and arsenic) with different melting points that he needed to evaporate in a high-vacuum chamber in such a matter that the alloy would maintain its fixed chemical composition (the technical term is stoichiometry). I invented a clockwork-driven left-handed spring device to drop bits of the alloy into a hot crucible under very high vacuum (10^{-12} torr) to flash-evaporate thin film layers onto quartz substrates with evaporated gold-film electrodes to be used in experimental vidicons (television camera tubes). My device worked perfectly, and Joe was quite pleased – and he was not easily satisfied. We developed a close working relationship. I became crackerjack at thin-film deposition.

The purpose of our applied research project was to build a TV camera tube from this selenium alloy, allowing RCA to compete with rival Philips Laboratories lead-oxide-based Plumbicon ©. The "Selenicon" camera tube incorporated a photo-conducting thin film insulator deposited onto a transparently thin gold layer, which in turn was deposited on a transparent quartz disk the size of a silver dollar. The electron beam formed one electrode, and the conducting gold film was the other. When objects were imaged on the bottom layer of the insulating film through the quartz glass substrate, the photo-electric effect would discharge the illuminated areas of the thin film, and by scanning the electron beam across its surface in a "raster," a grid of finely-spaced parallel lines, the optical signal was transformed into an electrical one.

Joe's device worked fine at room temperature or below but had one fatal flaw: the thin insulating film would crystalize at elevated temperatures, becoming a conductor, which ruined its electro-optical properties. Because TV cameras were often left out in the hot sun, Joe's Selenicon turned out to be not commercially viable. This was disappointing. But doing science involves dealing with failure. Failures are part and parcel of the research process. Good scientists learn from their failures and are not discouraged by them.

Scientists in RCA's general research lab were allowed to spend half time on whatever research took their fancy, keeping in mind the imperative to publish. I had many illuminating conversations with Peter and was fascinated by his chalk-talks on the blackboard with other scientists who would visit our office frequently to work out solutions to research problems. I admired the way he explained the workings of electrical current injection in solids in a lucid way. Peter read a new technical book cover-to-cover every year, to keep learning new things.

Joe's basic research focused on trying to make solid-state blue light. My role in this project was to melt elemental lithium, sodium, and potassium onto vacuum-etched anthracene crystals. These flammable alkali metals were kept stored in jars of oil, as they could react with oxygen in the air and burst into flame. To accomplish this task, I worked in a nitrogen-filled glove bag to prevent fire and loaded pieces of the metals into a surgical syringe heated by a nichrome coil, like the kind used in toasters. This worked extremely well. I point this out because it was necessary to become expert in the hazardous properties of industrial materials to avoid getting injured or even killed in the physics lab. I had worked with high levels of ionizing radiation in nuclear medicine, as well as infectious blood products, and was already well attuned to the necessity for lab safety. This familiarity with medicine, industrial hygiene, and radiation dosimetry would help me immensely in my later career involving air pollution from secondhand smoke.

One of the most valuable lessons I learned from working alongside Joe and Peter was that the fundamental difference between school and the research lab was that as a student you learned how to answer questions posed by your professors, whereas the research scientist first had to discover the right questions to ask. I learned that scientific expertise and reputation are built by serial peer-reviewed research publications, paper-by-paper. The scientific role models I worked with instilled in me the free-spirited independence, self-confidence, pride in accomplishment, ability to tolerate criticism, persistence in the face of adversity, and love of intellectual adventure essential to scientific inquiry as well as the imperative to publish.

Another virtue of working closely with professional physicists of high caliber was to learn how to think critically. I learned the interdependent relationship between theory and experiment. I learned how to adapt to making mistakes and learning from them, and to value constructive criticism. Most importantly, I absorbed the techniques of presenting one's work to peers and engaging in reasoned scientific argument. The ethic of the research scientist is a curious mind, intense concentration on problem definition and problem solving, tenacity, self-motivation, and the ability to work alone for long periods. I learned how to recognize bullshit masquerading as science, which would turn out to be an essential skill in dealing with tobacco-industry funded research by its scientists and consultants.

One of the best features of working at the Sarnoff lab was absorbing the give and take of the brass-knuckled encounters of the Friday afternoon seminars. Every week, a staff member who was ready to submit his or her work to a journal for publication had to present it first to an audience of peers for constructive criticism. The researcher would stand at a podium and using overhead slides and a blackboard, present it to an audience of 50 to 100 other researchers. Scientific disputes inevitably occurred and given the large egos of PhD scientists and engineers, tempers sometime flared. I recall one engineer whose lecture was interrupted by a shout by a member of the audience that he had made a critical mistake. The engineer disputed that. "Write down the integral," said his critic repeatedly, "it's obvious." Others in the audience piled on.

Another amusing instance involved Murray Lampert, a former high-energy physicist, who morphed into a pre-eminent solid-state theoretician specializing in the electronic physics of insulators. Murray was a friend of Joe's. But that did not spare Joe from Murray's criticism. Joe was an experimental physicist. He emphasized to me that an experimental physicist had to be great at experimentation and very good at theory. Of course, being very good at theory wasn't the same as being great at theory. For most physicists, it was rare to be both.

One Friday seminar, as Joe presented his work on the photo-hall effect in vitreous selenium, Murray took exception to Joe's interpretation of the results. Another theoretician disagreed with both Murray and Joe, chiming in with a third interpretation. The two theoreticians began an esoteric heated argument that went way over my head. It continued for perhaps ten minutes while Joe stood patiently listening. Finally he interrupted, reiterating his own interpretation. Murray barked, "Shut up, Joe, you don't know anything about this!" The two theoreticians then continued their dispute for another extended period, neither giving an inch. Finally, they agreed to disagree, and Joe unflappably continued his talk to the end. These disputatious encounters were not limited to seminars. During one of Peter's chalk talks in his office, both Peter and a gray-haired scientist began contesting a point at the same time. Neither would yield to the other and both continued to talk over each other for several minutes. Finally, Dr. Grayhair interrupted: "shut up, Peter, I'm older than you." Peter reluctantly complied. I came to think of these debates as the "Brass Knuckle School of Physics." In the fall of 1966 both Peter and Murray departed RCA labs to accept tenured positions on the faculty of electrical engineering at Princeton. In 1970, they co-authored *Current Injection in Solids,* which became the definitive book in its field.

Escape From The Nazis

I was inspired by the travails encountered by Peter's father, Hermann Mark, which took major ingenuity and courage to surmount. Reflecting on it would provide a sense of perspective during a low point in my life two decades later. Peter regaled us with stories about his father, Dr. Hermann Mark, a world-renowned polymer chemist who was a professor at Brooklyn Poly while I was a student there. Peter would often telephone the old man from our office at RCA and converse in fluent German. Peter and his brother Hans, also a physicist who later became Secretary of the Air Force under President Carter, referred to their father as the "*Geheimrat*," or Privy Counselor. Isidore Fankuchen, my favorite professor at Brooklyn Poly, who taught a brilliant and highly entertaining course in X-Ray Crystallography in Poly's Graduate School, said of Hermann Mark that "he was the nicest guy who never won a Nobel Prize." This he said, was because the Nobel Committee viewed Mark's seminal work on polymers as "too applied." Hermann Mark's escape from the Nazis is a stellar example of scientific ingenuity when Shit Happens. I have added additional details to Peter's account from the American Chemical Society's website (ACS, 2014).

Hermann Mark was born in Vienna in 1895, son of a Jewish convert to Lutheranism. After earning his PhD at the University of Vienna, Mark joined the Kaiser Wilhelm Institute, (now known as the Max Planck Institute), where he worked on the molecular structure of fibers, using the new tools of X-ray diffraction and ultramicroscopy, becoming an expert crystallographer. He later authored more than fifty papers on the structure of metals, organic and inorganic compounds, and polymers. Linus Pauling learned X-ray diffraction from Mark, which enabled Pauling's seminal work on the structure of proteins. Mark had become acquainted with Albert Einstein, a frequent visitor to the Institute. Einstein asked Mark to verify the Compton Effect describing one of the three major forms of interaction of radiation with matter (whereby an incident X-ray photon induces electron scattering and increases its own wavelength, i.e. losing energy in the process). This became the strongest confirmation of Einstein's quantum theory of light that would earn him the 1921 Nobel Prize in Physics.

In 1926, Mark departed Max Planck for the manufacturer I.G. Farben to begin investigating synthetic fiber technology. In 1932, the plant's managing director warned him that since Hitler would soon take power in Germany, Mark's position as an Austrian-born foreigner and the son of a Jew would make him persona-non-grata. He suggested that Mark would be prudent to immediately seek a job outside of Germany. Mark soon accepted a position as professor of physical chemistry at the University of Vienna, where he designed a curriculum in polymer chemistry. However, Austria proved to be only a temporary haven. When Austrian Nazis began to prevent Jewish professors from teaching courses, to burn the cars of Jews, and engage in running street battles with opposition Socialists, Mark realized he was in dire jeopardy.

Then a bolt of lightning struck: in 1937, the Canadian International Pulp and Paper Company (CIPPC) offered Dr. Mark a position as research manager for its Canadian operations. In early 1938, Mark, who had become a wealthy man, began preparing to flee Austria. But even if he could get out, he knew the Nazi authority would not permit him to emigrate with his fortune. In a brilliant stroke, using his own ample savings, he clandestinely stockpiled spools of platinum wire, ostensibly for use in the chemistry department of the university. The Mark family then fashioned the wire into coat hangers, and Frau Mark knitted covers for them, so that the wire could be smuggled out of the country in their steamer trunks full of clothes.

Mark's elder son, Hans, later estimated the value of the platinum at roughly $50,000, a fortune in the 1930s. The equivalent in 2017 would be nearly $800,000. When Hitler's troops invaded Austria in March 1938, declaring *Anschluss*, the political union of Germany and Austria, the Mark family's refuge became completely unsafe. Mark was arrested, thrown in a Gestapo prison, stripped of his passport, and interrogated. After a time, he was released with a stern warning "not to contact anyone Jewish" (ACS, 2014).

Upon his release, Mark fled to the Canadian Embassy and cabled CIPPC that he was ready to come. He then paid an enormous bribe equal to a year's salary to retrieve his passport from the Nazi bureaucrats. The Embassy issued Canadian visas to the Marks, as well as transit visas to allow them to pass through Switzerland, France, and England. At the end of April 1938, Mark cleverly draped a Nazi flag on the radiator of his car, strapped ski equipment on the roof, and drove his family across the border, finally reaching Zurich with his steamer trunks full of platinum wire hangers. From there, they transited through France and on to England. Mark and his wife and two young sons then travelled to Canada. Mark later immigrated to America to take a post as an adjunct professor at the Brooklyn Polytechnic Institute, where he subsequently established the Polymer Research Institute, which still endures (ACS, 2014).

ESCAPE FROM THE NAZIS *AND* THE COMMUNISTS

Menachem Simhony, another physicist I met at the lab, had a far darker tale of survival in the face of adversity than Hermann Mark. His story offered an insight into life in an authoritarian regime. For a year, I car-pooled with Simhony, an Israeli physicist who lived nearby in Highland Park. He worked at RCA as a Fulbright Fellow from August 1966 to December 1967, part of his three-year sabbatical leave from the Hebrew University in Jerusalem where he was a professor. During our commutes Menachem related the tragic story of his early life in Eastern Europe. He had been born in 1922 into a family of Polish Jews. After the Nazi invasion of Poland in 1939, Menachem's entire family was arrested and slaughtered in the Holocaust. Then in his late teens, he alone managed to escape the savage clutches of the Gestapo by fleeing across Poland's border into Soviet Russia. He then managed to obtain a job in an electrical factory, where he became a valued worker.

One day there was a fire in Menachem's communal apartment, which burned up his *only* pair of pants. It took him several hours to borrow another pair, and he arrived very late for work. In the Stalin era, being late for work was a "crime against the state." He was immediately placed under arrest for "unexcused absence," hauled before a judge, and summarily sentenced to six months in jail. His boss intervened on his behalf, getting Menachem's sentence reduced to six months at half-pay. Later, he was accepted to university as a graduate student and lab technician, but he had to purloin lab alcohol and sell it just to get enough money to eat. Menachem related that stealing goods from work and selling them in the underground economy was the norm for many workers just in order to survive. Only Party Members were paid enough money to live on. The authorities knew this, and if an average person came into conflict with the authorities for any reason, the very fact of your survival meant that they could easily uncover a ready-made charge against you. This was the Potemkin façade of the "workers' paradise" under Soviet Communism.

Menachem earned his Master's in physics but was prevented from continuing on to his doctorate because the anti-Semitic Stalin did not believe that Jews should have PhDs. After Stalin died in 1952, Menachem earned his PhD, and became a senior lecturer at the Velikiye Luki Pedagogical Institute in the Department of Physics and Math from 1954 to 1957. However, the Russian social climate remained hostile to Jews. Eventually, refugee Poles were allowed to repatriate back to Communist Poland. Menachem obtained a position as a Senior Assistant in the Physics Department of Warsaw University from September 1957 to December 1959. However, he found that the Communists would permit Jews to emigrate to Israel, provided they took no money with them, a lesson apparently learned from the Nazis. Despite this Menachem and his wife departed Poland and he became a physics professor at The Hebrew University of Jerusalem in 1960. Retiring in 1983, he remained Professor Emeritus until his death in 2015. In 1994, he authored a theoretical text, *Invitation to the Natural Physics of Matter, Space and Radiation*, offering an explanation of why physical realities such as the inertia properties of mass occur.

THE SAGA OF THE RED BARON

There were also some great moments of levity at the lab. Foremost among these were the madcap exploits of Albrecht Fischer, a crystallographer who worked across the hall from our lab. Scientific research is a demanding game, so hobbies and distractions become important stress relievers. For example, the Lab purchased several croquet sets for the use of staff during lunch breaks and manicured a large patch of lawn to provide a perfect playing surface. I loved the game, becoming a one-eyed croquet shark, often earning my lunch money from my fellow players. While playing, I noticed that some of the staff were flying big radio-controlled model airplanes on the expansive grassy fields surrounding the lab. Al Fischer became one of these model airplane aficionados. Born and raised in Germany, Fischer had been drafted into the Wehrmacht in his late teens during WWII. Managing to survive the war unscathed, he later earned his doctorate and went to work for RCA's Zurich Labs in Switzerland. Subsequently he transferred to the Sarnoff Lab in Princeton. Fischer worked across the hall from our lab. He was friendly and personable and would often visit our office during morning or afternoon coffee breaks to schmooze with Joe and Peter.

One summer, Al built a radio-controlled model airplane with 6-foot wingspan. He painted it a garish red and equipped it with a powerful Italian-made engine equipped with a large three-bladed wooden propeller. While learning to fly, Al would routinely crash his plane spectacularly on takeoff. Bystanders thronged the field to watch. His battered craft soon became quilted with patches. But persistence paid off. After dozens of crashes, Al finally learned to fly, and became quite adept. I nicknamed him "The Red Baron," a sobriquet that caught on with my amused fellow observers.

That summer, one of the model shop machinists, Walter Valentine, one of the highly skilled craftsmen called model-makers, painstakingly built a classic Piper Cub with a six-foot wingspread, taking special pains painting the trim as he sat there in the field. It took him all summer. The Baron would tease him while passing by: "Trim Doesn't Fly, Wally." After months of work, Wally produced an exquisite work of art. However, so afraid of wrecking it, he asked a fellow craftsman from the Model Shop, a crackerjack model airplane flyer, whom I dubbed "Eddie Rickenbacker," after America's most successful flying Ace in WWI, to pilot Wally's plane in its first flight.

On the day of the maiden flight of Wally's Piper Cub, The Red Baron and Eddie Rickenbacker are engaged in solo aerobatics, maneuvering in great arcs, high in the crisp autumn air. Back-to-back they stand, oblivious to each other, hundreds of yards apart under a cloudless sky of cerulean blue. Suddenly, it appears to us observers that these arcs will intersect. But surely the odds that the craft will cross at the same altitude at the same time must be vanishingly small. Nevertheless, the dozens of onlookers become spellbound with anticipation. Suddenly, both craft improbably collide in mid-air! The Baron's plane with its powerful 3-bladed prop rams Wally's Work of Art mid-fuselage, chopping it in two in a spectacular burst of flinders! Engine still running full bore, the front half of Wally's plane nosedives, plummeting into the earth in an enormous burst of balsa! A stricken Wally runs across the field to see what might be salvaged from the wreckage. The Red Baron, focused only on a safe "dead stick" landing of his powerless plane, fails to see Wally. Wally in his anguish, appears unaware of the Baron's rapidly descending plane. Unbelievably, the Baron's plane whacks Wally smack in the side of his head! Wally whacks the plane back! Curse You, Red Baron! The crowd roars! I am laughing so hard that tears are running down my cheeks. The Baron runs over and apologizes profusely to Wally. The Baron's notoriety spreads rapidly throughout the lab.

But wait – it gets better! The Baron loses his taste for ersatz flight. He develops a yen for the real thing and buys a Benson Gyrocopter. This bizzaro Rube-Goldberg contraption is basically a flying chair, driven by a lawnmower engine mounted under the seat, driving a shaft behind the pilot that ends in an overhead propeller. It is thoroughly insane. The Baron flies it over the company picnic and bombards the crowd with Hershey's Kisses. I am not making this up. He gets banned from Lawrenceville Airport as a "hazard to aviation."

Becoming eager for a change of venue, Al returns on sabbatical to RCA Zurich, where he buys a used powered single seat glider, which at least has the virtue of wings. It has a small pull-start gasoline engine allowing it to take off from a runway to gain altitude, whereupon the engine is stopped, whence it transforms into a pure glider. The Baron sends us a postcard describing the "phantasmagoric experience" of gliding silently among the Alps. One day, he becomes so enraptured by this experience while far from the airport, that he becomes inattentive to his altitude, and glides too low. He repeatedly pulls the lanyard in a futile attempt to restart the engine. It is too late, and he crashes into a farmer's stone wall, breaking his leg. A year later, he returns to the Sarnoff Lab.

Undaunted by his Alpine crash, the Baron buys a brand-new German-made power-assisted glider. It costs $8000. He successfully test-flies it from the privately-owned Twin Pines Airfield in Pennington, New Jersey, to Elmira, New York, and back. A local Princeton newspaper describes the subsequent debacle. A week later, on the 25th of July 1968, in the midst of a sharp turn above a wooded area in Hopewell, New Jersey, the Baron's new flying machine spins out of control and he plunges about 250 feet down into the woods near a road. Fortunately, while driving by, New Jersey State Trooper John Logan witnesses the crash. The 40-year old Baron is taken to Mercer hospital where he is treated for a possible concussion and cuts to his head and right leg. (GLIDER PILOT INJURED, Princeton Periodicals, Town Topics, 25 July 1968). He survives his latest airborne folly (hey, you have to give the guy credit for persistence!) and moves back to Germany, where he takes a professorship at the University of Dortmund. He becomes emeritus in 2008, ending his successful career in flat-screen technology.

In a footnote to the Baron's Day Job, a complacent RCA corporate management foolishly failed to see the promise of flat-screen technology, preferring to keep manufacturing the then profitable bulky picture tubes. The Japanese were more far sighted. As we gaze into our flat screen computer monitors and TV sets today, we know how that story ended. RCA sold the Sarnoff lab to Westinghouse around 1970, and it later became a contract research organization.

I Depart RCA for Greener Pastures

In mid-1966, our second child, Maxwell, was born. When he was about 14 months old, Hilarine took a part-time job in a local chocolate shop while I baby-sat. By 1967, I had just spent nearly six years as a part-time graduate student at Brooklyn Poly pursuing my Masters in Physics, while working full-time. Joe had generously approved an RCA Assistantship grant of tuition and books, plus one day a week off to study. I wrote a 100-page expository report on the operation of a solid-state radiation detector for ionizing particles in fulfillment of the final requirement for my Masters' in Physics, scoring a gratifying A+ for my efforts. After I got my MSc., I asked Joe for a promotion. However, he told me I was near the top of my paygrade and would never really succeed professionally at RCA unless I got my PhD. With two small children at home, going further in my studies felt impossible. So, while grateful to Joe for his support, I decided to move on. Accordingly, I took out a 1-page ad in the American Institute of Physics placement service. Astonishingly, I soon landed *six* interviews, and received *five* job offers. It was the halcyon days for physicists. The most lucrative – and least desirable – offer was from Standard Packaging, a company that evaporated aluminum onto Mylar sheeting; it was a local Jersey company, whose executives treated me to a fancy luncheon, while proffering a whopping 56% increase in pay, but it was a grubby factory job. I turned it down.

Two handsome offers came from Westinghouse Nuclear Power labs in Pittsburgh. I flew out there and from the taxi on the way to the lab from the airport, I observed red smoke, orange smoke, black smoke, and white smoke emanating from factory chimneys, and the air reeked with pollution. The jobs were really interesting, and the salary would have yielded a very respectable 40% increase in pay, but Pittsburgh's pollution was a complete turn-off. So, no sale there too. The fourth offer came from the well-known physicist Samuel

Goudsmit, who was editor of *Physical Review Letters*, for an editorial position on Long Island, a very desirable place to live, but it was a non-research position. I turned that down, too. The fifth job offer was from the Naval Research Laboratory in Washington, DC, and while it offered only a 25% increase in pay, the lowest of the lot, it was a wonderful opportunity to work in applied physics research as a professional. I accepted immediately, and after my secret security clearance was approved by the FBI, I went to work at NRL in early 1968, moving my family to suburban Maryland, where I still live.

On my last day on the job at RCA, the guys take me out for a nice lunch, and I imbibe a couple of adult beverages. When I return, as my last official act, I decide to clean up my syringe furnace, which has some sodium metal left in it. The normal procedure is to dissolve the sodium slowly in alcohol. However, in my wine stupor, I commit a massive folly. I forget whether the appropriate alcohol solvent is ethanol or methanol. I pick up the wrong alcohol, and worse, I compound my error by pouring it directly from the 4-liter jug instead of into a small beaker. I pour the liquid into the syringe through a funnel, and the liquid sloshes over, pooling in the sink. The sodium metal bursts into flame, igniting the alcohol. A foot from my face, a huge sheet of flame soars five feet above the sink into the fume hood exhaust! Even worse, a jet of flame 3 inches long emanates from the top of the nearly full alcohol jug that I am holding in my hands. Instantly, I realize that if I drop it, I will likely be burnt to a crisp; if I continue to hold it, it might explode. Although I am in deep shit, I don't panic. I quickly put the jug down, cap it with a Petri dish and slam down the glass face of the fume hood. Then Bill S., a ceramic engineer who works in that bay, arrives with a fire extinguisher and puts out the fire. By the time the fire crew arrives a few minutes later, the flames are out. It is a damned close call.

Bill himself had an even more terrifying experience earlier that year. He is working with a beaker of bromine solution and suddenly it foams up into his face. He is not wearing safety goggles, and his eyes are drenched with the corrosive liquid. In blind panic, he fails to remember where the eyewash fountain is a few feet away, nor does he recall the shower each bay has installed over its entrance doorway ten feet away but manages to recall the one in the corridor fifty feet down the hall. Groping blindly along the wall, Bill manages to blunder his way there, grabs the big ring at the end of the shower chain, and yanks it violently, snapping the chain. He then leaps up and grabs the pipe with a strength born of desperation, ripping it right out of the wall, and the resulting jet of water into his face saves his eyesight. It also creates an enormous flood that cascades down the stairway like a waterfall. Another very close call.

Working in a research laboratory is dangerous and requires *constant vigilance*. There are corrosive acids and bases, toxic chemicals, flammable substances, carcinogens, high voltage, radioactive materials, laser radiation, explosive substances, and poisonous gases. I always kept a copy of Sax's *Dangerous Properties of Industrial Materials* on my desk and referred to it constantly. I familiarized myself with standard industrial hygiene practice. My familiarity with the hazards of toxic substances would prove enormously valuable in the future.

On Monday August 21st, 1967, *The New York Times* carried a long front-page story by Jane Brody, entitled *"New U.S. Smoking Report Warns of Cigarette Peril,"* reporting on a Public Health Service panel's report based on 3000 published studies, implicating cigarette smoking as a probable "cause of death from coronary heart disease, 11 million cases of chronic illness in the country, 77 million days lost from work and 306 million days of restricted activity each year. And, it added, the cigarette habit is associated with deaths from peptic ulcers, stroke, aortic aneurism, and cancer of the larynx, mouth, pharynx, esophagus and bladder, as well as the lungs." The article concluded with the sentence, "The new report also confirmed the association between smoking during pregnancy and low birth weights, but added it was still not known whether this effect was harmful." I clipped the article, adding it to my background knowledge. It gave me many more reasons to reaffirm my revulsion to cigarette smoke.

United States Naval Research Laboratory

The **US Naval Research Laboratory** (NRL) is the corporate research laboratory for the United States Navy and the United States Marine Corps and conducts a broad program of scientific research and advanced development. NRL has existed since 1923, when it opened under the Office of Naval Research at the instigation of Thomas Edison. "The Government should maintain a great research laboratory.... In this could be developed...all the technique of military and naval progression without any vast expense."

Bust of Thomas Edison at the front gate of the Naval Research Laboratory.

Naval Research Laboratory complex on the Potomac River in Washington, DC.

NRL's accomplishments range from the development of Gamma-ray Radiography and radar to the Large Angle and Spectrometric Coronagraph Experiment (LASCO) and Dragon Eye (a robotic airborne sensor system). The Laboratory first proposed a nuclear submarine in 1939, and developed over-the-horizon radar in the late 1950s. The details of Grab I, deployed by NRL as the nation's first intelligence satellite, were recently declassified. The Laboratory is responsible for the Identification friend or foe (IFF) system. In 1985, two scientists at the Laboratory, Herbert A. Hauptman and Jerome Karle, won the Nobel Prize for work in molecular structure analysis. The projects developed by the laboratory often become mainstream applications without public awareness of the developer; an example in computer science is Onion Routing.

A few of the Laboratory's many current specialties include plasma physics, space physics, materials science, and tactical electronic warfare.

FIGURE 2. A SCREENSHOT FROM THE NRL WEBSITE IN 2006.

CHAPTER 3
THE BLUE PLAINS SLUDGE WAR

"Will the lungs of Washington Area residents be the final stage for the treatment of sewage?"

Thomas Grubisich, The Washington Post, March 29, 1973.

My initial involvement in public interest science came by the force of circumstances. Since 1968, I had been working at the Naval Research Laboratory (NRL) in Washington, DC. It is the corporate research laboratory of the U.S. Navy, inspired by Thomas Edison in 1923. NRL comprises a campus-like complex with a staff of more than 2,500 researchers, engineers, technicians and support personnel. It is led by a commanding Naval officer, usually a captain or an admiral in his last posting, and a civilian research director who manages the laboratory. NRL conducts multi-disciplinary research in the physical, engineering, space, and environmental sciences. Figure 2 shows a snapshot of the NRL website in 2015.

During 1968 and 1969, I worked in what was then NRL's Ocean Sciences Division, in the Nuclear Oceanography Branch on a project whose object was to determine the salinity of the Paleolithic seas from the ratio of trace elements in fossil and extant barnacles. My part of the effort to accomplish this was to use nuclear activation analysis to make precise measurements of the half-lives of radioisotopes of calcium, magnesium, and potassium. These elements formed salts which could be activated radioactively to determine the salinity of the Paleolithic seas by comparing the activity of the shells of fossil barnacles harvested from buried strata in seacoast deposit to those of extant barnacles. These isotopes were produced variously by bombardment with high energy protons from cyclotrons, high-energy x-rays from linear accelerators, and neutrons from nuclear reactors. I had previously worked with X-ray and gamma radiation, was an expert on radiation dosimetry, and of course I was familiar with semiconductor nuclear particle detectors (Repace, 1969). Our lab contained racks of nuclear radiation detectors and pulse-height analyzers. My large private office was located on the top floor of the five-story nuclear physics building. It had operable windows and a pleasant view of NRL's central tree-lined grassy mall. I got along well with my two co-workers in our tiny branch, Tom Gordon, who was my immediate boss, and Bud Larson, my other co-worker, and initially with the branch chief, Jack Hoover.

I BECOME A TOASTMASTER

Soon after I came on board, Tom Gordon introduced me to Toastmasters, a speaking club, of which NRL possessed three. Scientists are required to do presentations of their work at annual meetings, so the clubs were blessed by the Navy and were common among federal agencies. [By 2016, Toastmasters International would have more than 332,000 members belonging to 15,400 clubs in 135 countries.] The famous comedian, George Burns, had been a member. I had long realized that public speaking was an important skill that I sorely lacked, and I enthusiastically joined. Meetings would run like this: after an "icebreaker" speech introducing ourselves, at their convenience, club members would volunteer to deliver a set of a dozen 5-minute speeches guided by a manual published by Toastmasters International. After that, we spoke when we had something to say. We met during our lunch hour, brown-bagging our lunches. At each meeting, which usually incorporated three five-minute speeches, a member would be assigned on the spot to deliver a three-minute constructive critique of one of the speeches, counting the number of "ahs," or "whiskers" as they were called in Toastmaster parlance, discussing the best and worst aspects of the presentation, including such factors as eye contact, posture, facial expressions, pitch, pacing, power, pauses, as well as the use of props and other visual aids.

Our program of speeches included ones such as the Icebreaker, the Persuasive Speech, the Inspirational Speech, and the Humorous Speech. It proved to be a seminal experience. The Thomas Edison Club's specialty, and my forte, was the humorous speech. When I joined, all members of Toastmasters International clubs had to be male. In 1973, these anachronistic rules were changed, and women began to join our club. This forced us to clean up our language a bit, but our humor remained. Doing a humorous speech was difficult, like doing standup comedy: if the audience remains silent when you crack a joke, you immediately know you have bombed. If you hit it just right, someone in the audience will begin to roar with contagious laughter. With a gift for foreign and domestic accents, and a warped sense of humor, I hit more often than I missed.

In graduate school, I had been a cotton-mouthed bumbler in front of a large group, but under the influence of Toastmasters, I evolved into an articulate and fearless public speaker. A well-developed sense of humor is vitally important for anyone who speaks in public. I made many friends through Toastmasters. Tom Gordon, Joe Aviles, Clancy Sheppard, Jerry Hannan, Hal Eaton, "Ott" Ottenstrauer, and Al Lowrey, among many others in our club, were all accomplished speakers with a finely-honed sense of humor. I learned much about public speaking from these peers, and later went on to win several humorous speech contests. During this era, Lowrey and I became lasting friends, and he introduced me to jogging, which became a lifelong pursuit. We jogged four days a week at lunchtime, with Fridays reserved for pizza and beer. Al and his wife, Barbara, who worked at NASA doing orbital calculations, lived in a neighboring development, a couple of blocks from NASA's Goddard Space Flight Center in Greenbelt.

My best contest speech was *The Great Beer Hall Putsch*, a spoof of former German rocket scientists then working in the US space program, delivered with a faux German accent. (My two years of college German was finally put to good use). I used a toothbrush head dyed black as a prop Hitler mustache, affixed to my lip with double-sided tape. "Vunce ze rockets are upp, who cares vere zey come down? It's not my department, says Charley Von Braun." (With apologies to Tom Lehrer). It won our club contest, the Area contest, and the District 36 Speech Contest, a competition among well over 100 clubs, covering the Washington Metro Area.

My second-best humorous speech (and my all-time favorite) was my parody of Sherlock Holmes, *The Theatre of the Absurd,* which I narrated in a faux English accent. It won the Area Speech contest, which included six clubs, conjuring a tale of Holmes as he rode in a "horse-drawn carriage careening madly through the streets of London, while consulting street-maps baked into fortune cookies," and fighting the coach driver, an accomplice of the Mad Fiend, Moriarty, eventually toppling him into the road, where "he was run over by a manure-spreader, poor devil." In February of 1969, I lampooned smoking in a humorous speech entitled *Tobacco Road,* which parodied the ubiquitous cigarette commercials on TV and in the newspapers and magazines. It totally bombed, getting no laughs and winning no contests.

The most important lesson I learned at Toastmasters, is that no matter the subject, if the speaker is entertaining, the audience will pay attention. I was a natural at subitizing the next sentence in the text of my prepared speech and looking the audience in the eye as I spoke. I never kept my head down while I read. That's one of the hallmarks of a boring speaker. And I became adept at extemporaneous speaking. (This would prove to be an essential skill for doing the live radio and television interviews that lay hidden in my future. Taped interviews for TV news were actually harder than live, as newscasters would often ask you to repeat in one minute what you just took three minutes to say on camera. That's doing the editors' work for them.)

In 1968 Hilarine and I decided to have one more child. By March of 1969, Hilarine, who normally weighed 115 pounds, had gained 65 pounds and her belly had grown so large she could scarcely stand up. Seven and one-half weeks before her due date, her obstetrician decided to hospitalize her. This was fortuitous, as soon after her arrival at Holy Cross Hospital in Silver Spring, her water broke. A half hour later, she gave birth to three identical baby boys. Paul and Alexander weighed over four pounds each, and Nicholas, the largest triplet, weighed over five pounds, and was able to come home within a week. Since they were so premature, this was an amazingly high weight. Paul and Alexander were incubated and came home two weeks later when they reached five pounds, as preemies typically lose weight for a period after birth and then regain it if they survive. If a preemie's weight drops below two pounds, survival becomes marginal.

For the first several weeks, each triplet required feeding every three hours. By the time one infant had been breast-fed, cleaned, and diapered, it was time to do the next. This would have required Hilarine to be on-call 24/7. Fortunately, Prince Georges' County provided a practical nurse to help with minor chores for six weeks, and Hilarine's mother came to stay another month afterward. After that it was Cold Turkey. My mother had a business to run so she couldn't take much time off. Although we lived in a pleasant two-bedroom apartment with a balcony in a leafy garden apartment development, we began to make plans to buy a single-family home.

DOING SCIENCE IN THE PUBLIC INTEREST

In late 1969, Congress passed the National Environmental Policy Act (NEPA). No longer was government to be merely the conservator of wilderness, it now became the protector of earth, air, land, and water. NEPA declared the intent of Congress was to "create and maintain conditions under which man and nature can exist in productive harmony," and to "assure for all Americans safe, healthful, productive, esthetically and culturally pleasing surroundings." It mandated that henceforth all federal agencies planning projects bearing on the environment were required to submit Environmental Impact Statements, reports accounting for the likely consequences for human health and the environment. Secondly, NEPA directed the President to form a Cabinet level Council on Environmental Quality to assist the President by preparing an annual Environmental Quality Report to Congress, gathering data, and advising on policy. On April 22nd 1970, America had its first Earth Day, a celebration of clean air, land, and water in which millions participated. I was oblivious to this; we were in the midst of purchasing our new home on three quarters of an acre on a dead-end street in the outskirts of the Prince Georges' County City of Bowie. We moved in on June 1st and began planting trees, shrubs and a large vegetable garden.

On December 2, 1970, the United States Environmental Protection Agency (EPA) was established to consolidate in one agency a variety of federal research, monitoring, standard-setting and enforcement activities to ensure environmental protection. And on New Year's Day 1970, President Richard M. Nixon signed NEPA into law, observing that "the 1970s absolutely must be the years when America pays its debt to the past by reclaiming the purity of its air, its waters, and our living environment. It is literally now or never." (Imagine any Republican saying that in 2018, in today's anti-science, anti-regulatory, anti-EPA GOP). This brand-new federal agency, led by its first administrator, William Ruckleshaus, began a series of public hearings around the country to get public comment on its proposed regulations to control air pollution. My good friend and fellow Toastmaster, Jerry Hannan, a supervisory research chemist at NRL, had volunteered to attend the EPA hearing being held in Washington DC as a rapporteur for the American Chemical Society. However, Jerry's brother, the Archbishop of New Orleans, was visiting him, creating a conflict. Jerry asked me if I could attend the hearing in his stead and take notes. I was happy to do this.

Late on the following Friday afternoon, I show up at the Air and Space Museum auditorium in downtown Washington. The auditorium is packed, and I take a seat in the rear. One after the other, a procession of polluters, coal-fired power plant operators, oil refiners, incinerator manufacturers, and the like, testify that the pollution from their industries is insignificant and does not deserve stricter regulation. One commenter outrageously asserts, "since nobody makes a fuss over the disposal of old tires and television sets, why should a few hundred thousand tons of smoke-stack emissions that are quickly diluted in the huge volume of the atmosphere be of any public concern?"

At that moment, I experience a flashback to November 24th, 1966, a Thanksgiving Day I shall never forget. New York City was in the grip of a notorious three-day episode of killer smog. One hundred twenty luckless souls died from the pollution [Davis, 2002]. Thousands more were sickened. I was one of them. That afternoon, while journeying alone from Staten Island to Westchester, I get stuck in a bumper-to-bumper traffic jam on the then elevated West Side Highway in Lower Manhattan. I sit immobilized for at least two hours in the middle lane, high above the street below, enveloped by the choking fumes and surrounded by idling 1960's era cars belching pre-catalytic converter carbon monoxide emissions. I become dizzy and breathless and feel like I am slowly suffocating. There is no fresh air to breathe, nowhere I can go to escape. As I linger on the verge of collapse, finally the traffic begins to move and there is fresher air to breathe. I have managed to survive, but I can never forget.

Back in the Air and Space Museum after reflecting on that life-threatening Thanksgiving Day air pollution episode, I build up a full head of steam, as industry after industry denigrates the proposed air pollution control measures. I realize that in an effort to maximize profits, industry would do what it had always done: foist the pollution on the public, which would bear both the health penalties and economic costs. At the end of the scheduled testimony, the hearing examiner asks if there is anyone in the audience not signed up who wishes to testify. Without consciously thinking, I spring out of my seat and stride down to the podium. In the best tradition of Toastmasters, I deliver a fiery extemporaneous speech denouncing the polluters. This provokes the audience into a standing ovation. Caught up in the flare of emotion, I undergo an epiphany: *I am an environmentalist.*

GASSED BY CIGARS

Meanwhile, at work, I continued to measure the half-lives of radioactive calcium (^{49}Ca), magnesium (^{27}Mg), and potassium (^{38}K). Transforming a stable isotope of potassium into a radioisotope of potassium required high energies, which I supplied using X-rays from a powerful a linear accelerator (Linac) in the basement of the nuclear physics building. The Linac accelerated electrons with 22 million electron volts of energy (22 MeV) into a tantalum metal target, producing *Bremsstrahlung*, i.e., X-ray photons of sufficient energy to knock a neutron out of the stable Potassium (^{39}K) nucleus in what is known as a γ-n (gamma-n) reaction, transforming it into unstable radioactive potassium (^{38}K). The gamma rays emitted by the subsequent radioactive decay were measured using a Lithium-drifted Germanium semiconductor radiation detector, known as a Ge(Li) ("jelly") detector.

Making magnesium and calcium radioactive in quantities sufficient to make accurate determinations of half-life required a substantial neutron flux, whereby stable ^{48}Ca and ^{26}Mg captured slow neutrons and were made radioactive. The neutrons were supplied either by the National Bureau of Standards research reactor in Gaithersburg, MD, or the NRL swimming pool reactor. The swimming pool nuclear reactor has a core (fuel elements and control rods) immersed in a deep pool of ordinary water, which acts as a combination neutron moderator (slowing down the neutrons to increase their capture cross-section), cooling agent, and radiation shield. This has the dual advantages of low operating temperatures and pressures, unlike the high flux commercial power reactors designed to generate electricity. One can stand safely right above the pool without getting exposed to dangerous levels of nuclear radiation. While in operation, it's a magnificent sight to behold. The pool glows with the spectacular electric blue light of Cherenkov radiation; I would gaze into the pool enthralled while my samples were being activated. After nine months of research, I submitted my very first scientific paper, "Precision Measurements of the Half-lives of ^{27}Mg, ^{38}K, and ^{49}Ca" for publication in the journal *Radiochimica Acta.* It survived peer-review and was published later that year. Invited by my good friend from college, John Zukas, who was an Army Captain, I gave my first scientific presentation, a well-attended talk on the semiconductor detector for nuclear radiation at the Army's Aberdeen Proving Ground in 1969.

Prior to the time Lowrey and I met, I played cards at lunchtime with the guys in my branch. Actually, it appeared to be one of the unstated requirements of my new job. I was expected to be the bridge partner of our branch chief, Jack Hoover, and the other physicists, Tom and Bud, were the other pair. I had no problem with learning and playing the game. But I had a major problem breathing the insufferable smoke of the stinking cigars the three of them smoked incessantly during the game. My co-workers took my passive smoking for granted, and as a new employee, I was initially reluctant to buck the culture, and I tried to avoid the worst of the smoke. In those bad old days, smoking was permitted everywhere at NRL except in areas where there was danger of fire or explosion. The NRL personnel office, located outside the gate next to the credit union, had nicotine-stained walls, and reeked like an ashtray. However, after six months I became totally gassed out by the toxic cigar smoke and told Hoover I could not play bridge any longer. This put me on the irascible Hoover's shit list. Soon afterward, Hoover let me know just how pissed off he was. He stormed into my office one morning to remind me that my first year was probationary, and then informed me that my work was unsatisfactory, so I should expect to lose my job when my one-year probationary period ended. I sat at my desk all morning staring at the wall, stupefied. I had already produced a publishable manuscript as expected and required. We now had five small children and we had just bought a house with a large mortgage. Later that afternoon Hoover withdrew his threat, saying that maybe he had acted hastily, but it was too late. I had already concluded that he was unstable. I couldn't risk our livelihood with such a lunatic boss. He had lost my trust. And I had breathed enough of his stinking cigar smoke to last a lifetime.

I immediately began to network with friends and acquaintances who worked in other NRL branches to effect a transfer. One of these was Bruce Faraday, a nuclear physicist, who as it happened, had previously left the branch over conflicts with the eternally foul-mouthed Hoover, making space for my hire. Bruce, who worked in our building, was delighted to stick it to Jack Hoover, whom he loathed. He related a story where what he termed the "Hoover-treatment" was given to a glass-blower, Mort Fink, whom Hoover had supervised for a time. The vindictive Hoover took a dislike to Fink and reportedly told him that "Fink, you'll always have a job, here, even if it's at the end of a broom." Bruce said he'd gladly help me find another post at NRL. He had good contacts in the Solid State Devices Branch of NRL's Electronics Division who were looking to hire new staff; they needed somebody with experience in both radiation and electronics. I had both. I told Bruce that I had worked at RCA's Sarnoff Research Lab in solid state physics research before coming to NRL, so I had the requisite electronics background, and worked with radiation in my current NRL job, as well as in two New York hospitals as a health physicist.

And I was also an expert in the esoteric field of radiation dosimetry. I demonstrated this during my interview with Franklin Harris, an electrical engineer, and one of the two section chiefs in the Solid State Devices branch. He demonstrated his current research, which involved irradiating silicon chips with a 5000-volt electron beam to study the effects of radiation damage. I looked skeptically at his bench-top apparatus and warned, "Frank, your setup is hazardous. That 5 kilovolt electron beam will scatter soft x-rays all over the lab when it impinges on the target, exposing you to the risk of cataracts and skin cancer. You need to cover it with a lead-glass bell jar to absorb the radiation." He gaped at me in astonishment. I recommended that he summon the Health Physics Branch in to investigate, and later that week, their measurements confirmed both my diagnosis and my remedy. The following week, Frank offered me a job.

In the wake of my departure two weeks later, Jack Hoover's branch was dissolved, and he took retirement. I felt sorry for Tom and Bud, whose company I enjoyed. However, they managed to land on their feet and transferred to suitable positions elsewhere in the Oceanography Division. As for the bully Hoover, he got what he deserved. Anyway, retirement gave him more time to spend on his stock investments; he kept a bookcase filled with a variety of stock prospectives in his office and took pride in his substantial portfolio.

In 1971, our sixth and last child, Jonathan, was born. My uncle, Frank Palladino, a homebuilder, and my brother Bob drove down from Westchester, and in three days that winter, converted our screened porch into an extra bedroom. Frank, a former Seabee during the War, worked all day like a machine. Bob and I kept him supplied with lumber; he worked so fast we could barely keep up. Hilarine fed him steaks and chops for dinner and he slept at night in front of the fire. When it was done, I did the finish carpentry, installed the closet doors, painted the room and had it carpeted. Max and Jon slept in that new room until they left home. I then converted it into a home office.

In 1971, I was accepted into the graduate physics program at Catholic University in Washington, DC, and the branch approved an NRL Thomas Edison Fellowship, including full tuition and books, which would allow me to pursue my PhD half time. Life got even better. In 1973, I successfully completed my course studies, but our new branch chief, John Davey, requested I return to work full-time without writing a thesis. Citing Cold-War exigencies, he promised it wouldn't hurt my chances for promotion, but if I really wanted to write a thesis, I'd have to do it on my own time and my own nickel. I reluctantly capitulated.

MY FORAY INTO INDUSTRIAL HYGIENE

John Davey, as branch chief, also was the branch safety officer, a duty he disliked. He directed me to perform that additional task, a responsibility I willingly embraced. As I previously emphasized, in a physical research laboratory environment, there are many hazards that often are not taken seriously enough by researchers and support staff: toxic chemicals, including gases, liquids, and solids, high voltage, ionizing and non-ionizing radiation, explosion, and fire. For this reason, NRL supplied its staff with fume hoods, fire extinguishers, negatively pressurized lab spaces, safety goggles, eye-wash fountains, ear protectors, rubber gloves, lead-brick shielding, and the like. Nevertheless, most staff had little training in lab safety. I attended the monthly meetings that the NRL Safety Branch conducted. However, Branch Safety Officers were trained, and expected to be proactive. Accordingly, in a search of the Electronics building for potential hazards, I soon discovered the widespread use and misuse of asbestos.

Several ignorant co-workers made fun of me after my warnings by appallingly slapping asbestos gloves together under my nose and slamming the drawers of asbestos-lined file cabinets. One day, two Navy industrial hygienists visited and asked me, as the branch safety officer, about any known hazards in the Electronics Building. I promptly pointed out that the entire attic floor contained piping sheathed with asbestos and the glass shop had large sheets of asbestos blankets hanging from the ceiling as heat shields. The Navy soon ordered it removed, and workers dressed in moon suits arrived to remove it. The head of the glass shop went nuts, and wrote a vituperative memo to Davey, complaining about my unwarranted interference in his operations, despite the fact that my intervention may have prevented the glass shop workers from developing mesothelioma; yet another illustration of the Richter principle. Davey ignored the memo.

In another illustrative episode, I had some samples irradiated using a miniature Linac located in a small unvented chamber. Afterward, I detected the telltale sweet burning odor of toxic ozone permeating the space after the Linac had been operated. It had been generated by the high voltage electrons impinging on atmospheric oxygen. I warned the Linac technician to wear a gas mask to prevent ozone-induced lung damage when he operated the machine. He expressed skepticism, saying he had done this for years without any problem. Sadly, not long afterward, he had to retire on disability with a lung ailment. Yet another illustration of the widespread ignorance of health and safety measures among people who should have known better. I began to realize that most people, even otherwise well-educated professionals, were often astonishingly clueless about health and safety hazards.

Pollution also affected electrical equipment, as well as people. Our section had a circuit-testing computer run by an otherwise competent electrical engineer, George N., who was an inveterate chain smoker. The computer repairman was in there almost weekly due to breakdowns. I commented to Hap Hughes, our new section chief after Frank Harris retired, that it was likely that George's smoking was causing the frequent breakdowns, not faulty equipment. Hap took my advice and asked George not to smoke in the computer room. After that, the breakdowns ceased. A few weeks later, I opened up the top of a crab-pot sized apparatus I had designed to make surface state measurements on silicon chips. The inside was full of reeking stale cigarette butts and ashes. Since I was measuring the effect of surface impurities on chip performance at an extremely sensitive level of detection, I had to disassemble the entire apparatus, and have it acid cleaned at considerable expense. This was no simple matter, as it chamber contained gas and electrical connections, plus a nichrome heater and liquid nitrogen piping to vary the temperature from very hot to very cold in a controlled dry atmosphere. Not being able to smoke while he worked evidently made George a bit crazed. Such are the wages of nicotine addiction.

My main research effort involved investigating how nuclear radiation affected the performance of the silicon-on-sapphire chips that were the heart of military (and domestic) electronics and computers. Driven by the Cold War, in the early 1970's several new electronic research problems emerged: one of which was how to prevent ionizing radiation from the Van Allen Belt from frying a space satellite's computer, another involved preventing a high altitude anti-missile nuclear burst from instantaneously knocking out the electronic circuits of a ballistic missile or that of a SAC bomber bearing down on a Soviet target. At the altitudes that these planes and missiles flew, blast was a minor problem due to the thin air. But weapons tests showed that the megarad radiation dose would instantly fry the plane's electronic circuitry. Medical experts felt that fatally-dosed bomber crews could survive long enough to reach their targets if the plane's electronics survived the ionizing radiation pulse.

My research aimed at discovering how to prevent high-level radiation-induced positive charge from building up at the silicon-sapphire interface of the chip, altering its electrical properties. Using high-voltage ramp techniques and laser scanning, I found that this could be achieved by building in a negative charge layer by controlling the growth rate of the epitaxial silicon layer on the sapphire (aluminum oxide) substrate. I tested my circuits using bremsstrahlung from a gigantic Van de Graaf generator that served as a nuclear weapon effects simulator. I got four research papers in two years and a promotion to a PhD-level GS 13 out of this.

One additional responsibility Hap gave me was monitoring the performance of a contract researcher. One contract had been awarded to a Princeton University professor of electrical engineering, which also involved studying radiation effects on computer chips. In perusing his quarterly progress report, I noticed his assertion that he had dosed the chips to megarad levels of radiation, comparable to what one would get in a nuclear burst or prolonged flying of a space satellite in the Van Allen Belt. But nowhere was there a discussion of how he had measured the radiation dose. This raised a red flag. I phoned him and asked how he had calibrated his X-ray machine. There was a long silence at the other end of the line. This signaled a silent "Oh, Shit!" moment. Incredibly, this goon had no clue whatsoever that he even needed to calibrate the exposure level! This made his research reports just so much bullshit. After some further questioning, he disclosed that he used a surplus x-ray machine. I said, "OK, why don't we make the best of this. I'll calibrate some thermoluminescent crystal dosimeters in my lab, bring them up to your lab, and you can expose them in your machine in the same way you did before, so we can salvage your experiment."

I traveled up to Princeton and performed the experiment the way he should have, salvaging his data and the Navy's investment. During lunch at the faculty club, he complained that if the Department "didn't have an informal quota on admissions, all of the Electrical Engineering students would be Orientals." Coming from a family of immigrants, I felt offended. When I got back to Washington, I recommended that his contract with the Navy be terminated. And so it was. Professor So and So had exceeded my informal quota on incompetents.

DOING SCIENCE IN THE PUBLIC INTEREST

One day early in 1973, an event occurred that would alter the arc of my career. Woody Anderson, one of the physicists in our branch, and a close friend, walked into my office with a worried look on his red-bearded visage. "Hey Jimbo, did you know that Blue Plains is going to build a dozen sludge-burning incinerators next door, and that the Lab was planning to endorse it?" I was stunned. NRL's next-door neighbor, along the banks of the Potomac, was metropolitan Washington's Blue Plains Sewage Treatment Plant. Thus began our involvement in a heated and highly public dispute over the air pollution impact of incinerating the hundreds of tons of sewage sludge that metropolitan Washington DC generated every day. The sludge war that resulted would thrust me headlong into the heady and highly contentious world of public interest science.

What happens when your toilet waste is flushed down into a hole in the planet? Unless you live in a rural area with septic tanks, the effluent flows or is pumped downhill into a body of water. In the primitive days of the 1970's, a number of cities in the U.S. pumped their untreated raw sewage right into the rivers, bays and oceans. This was also true abroad. And as recently as 2000, I visited certain coastal cities, Viña Del Mar in Chile and Oporto in Portugal, where signs in the hotel bathrooms admonished guests to deposit their soiled toilet tissue in covered crocks, to prevent it from washing up on the beaches.

In the early1970's, in Washington, DC, the state of the art in the Blue Plains sewage treatment plant consisted of a primary settling tank to remove rocks, roadkill, and other insoluble objects washed into the storm sewers that were interconnected with sanitary sewers. In the next stage of treatment, the sewer water flowed into a secondary digester tank where anaerobic bacteria would biodegrade the raw sewage. The resulting sludge would be de-watered by being vacuumed up on the surface of giant cylindrical sieves, then scraped off by blades onto conveyer belts leading to dump trucks and thence to a D.C. landfill. As long as it worked as advertised, this was deemed adequate treatment at that time. However, a major deficiency with the Blue Plains plant was that its maximum holding capacity during a rainstorm was less than the combined influx of raw sewage and storm water. The plant could contain sewer water up to a maximum of 300 million gallons per day (MGD) and was running daily at peak capacity. However, because Washington's sewers were inter-connected with Washington's storm drains, in a cloud-burst, an additional 200 million gallons could flow into the plant. Thus, on a rainy day, as much as 500 million gallons of storm and sewer water could inundate the plant, exceeding its holding capacity, and the overload of 200 MDG of untreated sewage would flush straight into the Potomac River, enough to make the river one-third sewer water at times of low flow.

This putrid effluent made the Potomac unswimmable, unfishable, smelly, and unsightly – not just due to the floating turds and condoms – but because algae fed on the phosphorus and nitrogen in the sewage, causing the growth of massive algal blooms that covered the Potomac River downstream of the plant with a blanket of lurid green slime. Signs posted on the riverbanks in Maryland, DC, and Virginia warned that the water was unsafe for swimming or fishing. This enraged a lot of influential conservationists. Feeling the heat, local officials imposed a highly controversial moratorium on new sewer hookups. This triggered a concatenation of unfortunate events. It stopped new home building dead in one of the top ten trading markets in the U.S, infuriating the area's influential building developers, who bankrolled the local politicians who appointed the commissioners who oversaw the Washington Suburban Sanitary Commission (WSSC). The WSSC is the umbrella agency that controls the sewer permits for Washington, Northern Virginia, and DC's Maryland suburbs. The politicians, fearful of losing lucrative campaign contributions, in turn pressured the fledgling Environmental Protection Agency (EPA), which regulated water pollution, to fund new sewage treatment construction in Washington and upgrade the plant to end the moratorium.

EPA responded favorably to these demands in November 1972, circulating a telephone-book-thick draft environmental impact statement (EIS) for public comment as NEPA required. EPA offered to contribute a billion dollars to upgrade the plant to handle the 500 million gallons of effluent daily. Further, wrote the EPA, this would generate one dewatered ton of sludge per million gallons of effluent, and since the District didn't have the capacity to landfill 500 tons of sewage sludge daily, EPA proposed building a dozen incinerators to burn it on site instead. As the next-door neighbor of Blue Plains plant, one of the recipients of the EIS was NRL, and it became the responsibility of the Lab's Environmental Chemist, Victor Piatt, to make recommendations on the EIS to Navy management. Vic's office was in my building. I knew him as a polished speaker from the rival Forum Toastmasters club. He was a good-natured man who wore wire-rimmed glasses and sported a fringe of gray hair around his balding pate. He readily agreed to loan me a copy of the EIS.

As I perused the voluminous EIS, it appeared that a large part was devoted to cataloging the flora and fauna of the Potomac River Valley that might be impacted. This was irrelevant. The only part that concerned me was EPA's estimate of the air quality impact. This was laid out in a 60-page chapter on the air pollution from the incinerators. There were a number of very troubling things in it. First, because there was a height-limitation imposed on the incinerator chimneys due to their proximity to National Airport across the river in Arlington, Virginia, the design omitted any smoke stacks; the smoke and fumes from a dozen incinerators would simply belch out from holes in the two-story high roof. I thought this was totally insane, a prescription for aerodynamic downwash of the plume in the wake of the building, which would inevitably fumigate NRL whenever the winds blew from the South, which was a typical summer condition.

Second, EPA's pollution calculations were based on average atmospheric conditions instead of worst-case. On average, said the EPA, the air quality impact of incineration was "minor," adding "only" 2% to the air pollution emitted daily for the entire Washington metropolitan area. This rang a false note. Diluting the incinerator emissions over the entire air volume over Washington DC was highly misleading. Why not take a dilution area twice as large, then the impact would halve to just 1%! This was thinly disguised sophistry – an attempt to minimize the apparent air pollution impact just to placate the howling politicians and braying developers at the expense of the NRL workforce. I thought, *over my dead body will they burn that shit.*

I rushed over to Vic's office in alarm: "Vic, we'll be less than a kilometer downwind of a dozen incinerators belching sludge smoke!" He replied, "Oh, no, Jim, the air quality impact will be minor, and we won't have to put up with the smells anymore." The awful stink from the plant was the one drawback of working at NRL, especially during the summer when the prevailing winds blew from the South, towards NRL. One of Vic's most unpleasant jobs was to rush over to Blue Plains whenever the stench became intolerable and demand that the inattentive sludge workers hose off the smelly scum from the surface of the holding tanks. I suspected this was the major reason that caused Vic to be a passionate advocate of incineration at Blue Plains. I tried in vain to persuade him to see reason, but he remained adamant. I realized that in any disagreement with the Lab's Environmental Officer, his professional opinion would trump mine with NRL management.

Driven by apprehension over the prospect of working downwind from the suffocating smoke of a dozen incinerators, I set out to learn everything I could about air pollution and incineration. I studied EPA Criteria Documents on the health effects of the acid gases sulfur dioxide and oxides of nitrogen, and the respirable particulate matter released during combustion. I read the physicist S.J. Williamson's illuminating 1973 textbook, *Fundamentals of Air Pollution,* cover-to-cover. I borrowed EPA audio tapes on air pollution dispersion and control.

Williamson's book made it clear that aside from its irritating effects, air pollution in sufficient amounts could kill. I learned about the air pollution disaster in Donora Pennsylvania in 1948 in the bowl-shaped Monongahela River Valley. The smog began on October 27 with a temperature inversion confining the smoke in the valley, and it lasted until October 31. It sickened more than a third of the town's 14,000 residents and killed 20 outright. Another 50 residents died of respiratory causes within a month. It was caused by air pollution from the Donora Zinc Works smokestacks and led to the enactment of major federal clean air laws.

I mused over the notorious London smog episode which began on December 5, 1952, when an inversion settled over the city, and smoke from a million coal stoves and fireplaces cooled and settled like a blanket over the city. Visibility dropped to near zero. The sulfurous smoke and fog finally cleared on December 9, after about 4000 metric tons (tonnes) of smoke particles, 480 tonnes of hydrochloric acid, and 3200 tonnes of sulfuric acid had belched into the stagnant air. Ultimately nearly 13,000 Londoners died from the pollution. However, the government stopped counting the air pollution deaths at 4000. The fearful British government lied, attributing the remaining 9000 deaths to "influenza" to avoid a shift from soft to hard coal, which would have slowed the impecunious Britain's war recovery efforts. However, this tragedy ultimately led to the UK Clean Air Acts of 1956 and 1968 [Davis, 2002; Met Office, UK, 2015].

I pored over EPA air pollution modeling methodology (my bible was Bruce Turner's *EPA Workbook on Atmospheric Diffusion Estimates*). I talked to experts, studied textbooks of air pollution physiology and obtained chemical analyses of Blue Plains sludge. After several months of intensive study, by April 1974, I felt competent enough to write a counter-EIS on the environmental impact of sludge incineration at Blue Plains. I produced a 100-page document titled *Air Pollution from Sludge Incineration, An Analysis of the Environmental Impact of the Proposed Sludge Incinerators at The Blue Plains Sewage Treatment Plant, Washington, DC*. In it, I discussed the uncontrolled substances that made their way in to sewage effluent the chemical analysis of Blue Plains sludge done by EPA, and most importantly, the emissions of toxic metals in the smoke plumes, especially mercury and beryllium, as well as total particulates, acid vapors, and radioactive pollutants from hospital waste. I performed atmospheric dispersion calculations incorporating scrubber efficiencies, plume rise, wind velocity, atmospheric stability, and terrain topography to estimate the downwind ground-level pollutant concentrations at NRL, the Navy's adjacent Bellevue enlisted men's housing, as well the nearby Hadley hospital and Wingate House, a high-rise apartment building on a nearby hill.

Salient among my conclusions were (1) that, based on EPA's own analysis of mercury in Blue Plains Sludge, the proposed incinerators would emit 60% more toxic mercury, a cumulative poison whose vapors were long known to cause Mad Hatter's Syndrome, than EPA regulations would allow a mercury smelter to emit; (2) because there were no stacks, just holes in the roof, the smoke would be subject to aerodynamic downwash, and be essentially a ground level release of the plume that would fumigate NRL; (3) The estimated health impact of particulate matter on the nearest neighbors of the plant would increase the risk of respiratory disease mortality between 15% to 250%, and respiratory disease morbidity by 65% to 1100% among NRL personnel and military families living at Belleview, the adjacent Naval housing development to the north, and the more distant Bolling Air Force Base, where a number of Navy Admirals and Army and Air Force Generals had large brick riverside homes and the Presidential helicopters were based. Lowrey and I would run shirtless through the lawn sprinklers in front of the Top Brass's homes on very hot summer days to keep cool during our six-mile noontime run. We avoided running on days when the smog was so thick that it obscured the Washington Monument. On such days, we devoured hot pizza and washed it down with cold beer.

When I was done, I presented Vic with a copy of my Blue Plains analysis, firmly convinced that my careful calculations would persuade him to change his mind. But Vic rejected it out of hand. Each of us became frustrated with the other's intractable position, and our vocal disagreement grew increasingly heated. We both became red in the face and began to bellow at each other. Abruptly, Vic raised his hand and shouted,

"Stop! Look, Jim, we belong to rival Toastmasters clubs. Why don't we have a formal debate on this?" This immediately appealed to me as a brilliant suggestion. We were both scientists; it would be a civilized duel of the minds, reminiscent of the Brass Knuckle School of Physics. Best of all, it would broadcast my findings to a wide audience of potential victims. I loved it.

We shook hands amicably, agreeing to hold a formal Thomas Edison vs. Forum Toastmasters Club debate in NRL's big auditorium a couple of weeks later on a Friday afternoon in the summer of 1973. We sought to advertise our debate in *NRL Labstracts*, the Lab's weekly newsletter for the staff, which all three of NRL's Toastmasters clubs routinely utilized as a regular vehicle for publicizing Toastmasters events. However, Navy military management, who no doubt was anxious to head off a potential labor-management dispute with several thousand nervous scientists, engineers, and support staff, stonewalled us. They abruptly refused to print our debate notice.

To Burn Or Not To Burn, That Is The Question

However, Woody Anderson and Jim Comas, another physicist friend from our branch, quickly organized an informal publicity network, and we soon had every doorway entrance in dozens of lab buildings plastered with a flyer announcing: **An NRL Toastmasters Debate, To Burn or Not to Burn – Sludge Incineration at Blue Plains.** Jerry Hannan, an excellent speaker, volunteered to be my second. Jerry performed research on algae in NRL's Ocean Sciences Division. Vic chose another good speaker, Don Hammond, an engineer from his club, as his second. I approached the debate with some trepidation. On the plus side, I had been in Toastmasters for 5 years, had held all of the leadership positions, and was an accomplished public speaker with a number of trophies to show for it. On the downside, I had no formal training in air pollution, and Vic was an environmental professional. I knew that I had to convey my findings in a clear, concise, and persuasive way to a professionally skeptical audience of scientists and engineers, and to mount a reasoned and temperate rebuttal of the opposition's arguments.

We chose a Friday afternoon lunch hour for the debate. The auditorium, located about 50 yards from the Potomac River, had a capacity of 500 persons. It was packed with an overflow crowd of NRL staff who filled all the seats plus a large number of standees lining both walls. We mounted our respective daises and debated, pro and con, over the safety of sludge incineration for an hour, with Jerry and I hammering home our major arguments: • the proposed incinerators would emit more mercury, a cumulative poison that caused brain damage, than EPA regulations would allow a mercury smelter to emit on the same site, • the patent inability of air pollution scrubbers to remove gaseous mercury, • and the propensity of mercury, a heavy metal, to condense and precipitate out within a short distance from the stacks, poisoning the air and the ground, based on studies around chlor-alkali plants in Sweden. We showed slides to emphasize our points.

Vic and Don countered with an argument first based on authority: summarizing the EPA EIS, they noted that EPA had concluded that the air pollution impact was minimal, and emphasized that EPA's conclusions could be trusted. Then they asserted that burning the sludge would eliminate the offensive odors. We rebutted their first point by observing that the health-based mercury emission limitation for chlor-alkali plants should apply independent of whatever source generated the pollution, and that the health of the staff was in jeopardy from mercury pollution, emphasizing that mercury was a well-known cumulative poison, like lead. As for the second point, we countered that this was a specious argument, since the primary source of the odor was from scum accumulating on the surface the settling tanks, which could be readily handled by enforced hosing off of the surface. At the end, the moderator asked for a show of hands: all in favor of incineration? A smattering of hands went up: All opposed to incineration? A forest of hands was raised! The crowd went wild, cheering, stomping their feet, whistling and breaking out in boisterous applause. Jerry and I were elated. I felt totally vindicated.

Woody, Comas, and I then decided our next step should be to take our case to the public. I sought advice from Julian Holmes, an NRL space scientist and colorful local environmental activist often quoted in the local press and radio. Julian regularly railed against the corrupt politicians whom he derided as "thugs who served the interests of the bulldoze-and-build developers who were despoiling our lands and rivers." Julian gave me a lot of good tips on how to develop media interest in environmental stories. He taught me a vital lesson that would serve as battle armor in the future Tobacco Wars: the power of the press: *Sunlight is the best disinfectant.*" Woody, Comas and I managed to interest a Washington Post reporter, Thomas Grubisich, into doing a feature story. Soon, a 47-column-inch article illustrated by a large picture of a 19-foot incinerator, appeared on page 1 of *The Washington Post's* Metro section on March 29, 1973 and ran for several pages inside. The three-column caption read, "Whither Sludge From Sewage?" The brilliant and incendiary lede said it all: "**WILL THE LUNGS** OF **WASHINGTON AREA RESIDENTS BECOME THE FINAL STAGE OF TREATMENT FOR SEWAGE?**" We three musketeers were identified as "concerned NRL scientists." The next day, a Channel 5 TV crew interviewed us outside the front gate of NRL, pouring still more gasoline on the fire. I followed this up with a 17 column-inch letter to the editor, which the *Post* printed in full on April 29, replete with a big picture of a revolting looking sludge-settling tank.

Woody then suggested what was to prove to be an enormously fateful step: "Jim, I think you should take your report to the Natural Resources Defense Council (NRDC)." He explained that NRDC was a public interest environmental action group organized and run by lawyers. NRDC fought for clean air and clean water. Woody was a member. He gave me their phone number. I was put through to a sharp young NRDC attorney, David Hawkins. Hawkins had joined NRDC in 1971, working on industrial air pollution control and attainment of air quality standards. He invited me to his downtown DC office, listened attentively to my story, and glanced through my report. He appeared very knowledgeable about air and water pollution. A few days later, he called me: "Mr. Repace, we've decided to endorse your report. We'll send a letter to William Ruckleshaus, the EPA Administrator, with your report appended." This chance meeting would have a profound effect on national environmental health policy in the next decade. Later the Environmental Defense Fund, a sister environmental organization organized by scientists, took up the case, and I worked with them as a co-plaintiff in a citizen's lawsuit against EPA.

In May 1974, EPA issued its Final Environmental Impact Statement on Blue Plains. Its preface stated: "On April 19, 1973, a highly technical and very serious critique of the proposed incinerators was submitted to the Regional Office by the Natural Resources Defense Council. Accordingly, EPA is holding the comment period open until it can study the health aspects of incinerator emissions." This was a tremendous validation of my calculations. Subsequently, EPA issued a report titled, *Evaluation of Potential Mercury and Beryllium Emissions from Proposed Sludge Incinerators to be Located at the Blue Plains Waste Treatment Facility in Washington, DC.* It asserted EPA's belief that "while the emissions should not pose a health threat, there was a specific lack of information concerning the composition of the sludge and the fate of materials processed in sludge incinerators." Then EPA dropped the other shoe: it warned the District government not to proceed with installation of the incinerators until it received explicit EPA authorization, and mandated that the sewer authority investigate alternatives to incineration. EPA also stated that it would produce a supplement to the Final EIS reporting on recent developments on sludge disposal alternatives to incineration. This sounded to me like an augury of victory.

In October 1974, as a result of the legal Petition For Review filed against EPA by the Environmental Defense Fund, EPA issued a proposal to include sewage sludge incinerators under the National Emissions Standards for Hazardous Air Pollutants (NESHAPs), based on the mercury content of sewage sludge. I received a letter from EPA soliciting further comment on its new proposal. I provided EPA an analysis of the energy costs of incineration vs. other means of disposal and observed that incineration merely reduced

500 tons of dry sewage solids to 200 tons of toxic ash, which still had to be disposed of in a landfill every day of the year.

Finally, in a press conference on February 12, 1975, Dan Snyder III, the administrator of EPA Region III, dropped a bomb on the Washington Suburban Sanitary Commission (WSSC): In a 180° about-face, he announced, "Environmentally, sludge incineration degrades air quality." Furthermore, Snyder elaborated, "sewage sludge contained nutrients that could partially replace fertilizers, and contains organic soil builders, benefits that would be lost if sludge were incinerated," that "such alternatives were less costly than incineration," and finally, that at a time of energy scarcity, "incineration would consume 14 million gallons of fuel oil and 45 million kilowatt hours of electricity per year." This effectively sounded the death knell for sludge incineration at Blue Plains. "*There is a tide in the affairs of men, Which, taken at the flood, leads on to fortune.*"

Lowrey's boss, Jerry Karle, shook my hand and thanked me for my efforts. In an amusing postscript, the manufacturer of the 12 incinerators that had been destined for Blue Plains wrote a furious letter to NRL management, filled with invective complaining about "NRL scientists meddling into things that were none of their business," and singling out Woody, Comas, and me. In an ironic turn of events, NRL management gave his letter to none other than my friend and debating partner, Patrick Jeremiah Hannan, to draft a reply for management's signature… . It doesn't get any better than that.

ENVIRONMENTAL SCIENCE BECOMES MY AVOCATION

Our victory in the Sludge War whetted my appetite for using physics to help solve vexing environmental problems. My notoriety led Rhea Cohen, an articulate former Greenbelt, MD, City Council member and ardent environmentalist, to approach me to run for president of the Prince George's Environmental Coalition, a local activist environmental group. I immediately agreed and was soon elected. Rhea and her husband Lenny, a NASA physicist, became good friends of ours. One of my first tasks was to team up with Woody to take on the problem of the District of Columbia's Incinerator Number Five. What we accomplished together was written up in the June 1974 issue of *Physics Today*, the monthly news magazine of the American Physical Society. The entire issue was devoted to public interest science. There were four articles: Public-Interest Science, An Overview – How Scientists Advise The Congress; Scientists In State Government; and Working With Citizens' Groups (which featured Woody and me).

The latter article reported three examples of what scientists can accomplish when they enter the arena of public-policy debate. It noted, "The demand for scientists to help citizen-action groups has expanded enormously during the past decade, partly because of increased awareness of consumer and environmental-protection issues, and partly because of new legislation that requires in-depth consideration of the social costs of proposed federal programs." The article discussed ways in which physicists could work with environmental groups to help solve environmental problems. The article was illustrated with a photo of the two of us standing in front of two giant incinerator smokestacks (Figure 3). The photo caption read: "Mercury and other pollutants are emitted from the stacks of this municipal refuse incinerator in Washington D.C. recently constructed in an inner-city residential neighborhood. The incinerator is located near an elementary school and playground. Physicists James Repace and Gordon Wood Anderson, in conjunction with the Environmental Coalition in Prince George's County, Maryland, calculated the amount of mercury emitted … which came remarkably close (within 1%) to the physicists' calculations. As a result, the City Council ordered the District Department of Environmental Services to monitor mercury in the stack gases."

The overview article observed that "it was not until the 1960's that a renewed public understanding of the insensitivity of governmental and industrial bureaucracies led to a substantial commitment in the legal profession to public-interest law. It appears that the scientific community may now have reached a similar point; a growing awareness of the dangers of leaving the exploitation of technology to special industrial and governmental interests has led to an increased readiness among scientists to undertake work in public-interest science." I read these articles with growing excitement: I was actually on the cutting edge of the new wave of science in the public interest.

During these years, when I got home from the lab, I would lie down on the living room carpet in front of the fireplace and read Edith Hamilton's *Mythology: Timeless Tales of Gods and Heroes,* to the children. Until they got too big, the triplets would crawl up on my back and the singlets would gather round to listen. The children were fascinated by these strange tales from Greek and Roman mythology. I would also teach them science and math fundamentals. We did not have a television until 1973, when my mother bought us one over my protest, so that the triplets, who had formed their own language, could watch and listen to Sesame Street. I capitulated, but it was the only TV program they were permitted to watch. I strictly rationed TV time by installing a keyed on-off switch to lock the TV and kept the key on my key ring. No boob-tubing cartoons for the kids. They could play outdoors – we lived on a dead-end street with two houses, bordering on Highbridge Park – and read books, which were plentiful in our home.

FIGURE 3. JIM REPACE AND WOODY ANDERSON IN FRONT OF DC INCINERATOR #5, *PHYSICS TODAY* JUNE, 1974 (AUTHOR'S PHOTO).

When we worked together on the DC incinerator issue, Woody would drive out to my home in suburban Maryland from his townhouse on North Carolina Avenue in DC, and we would work together on my dining room table. His wife, Gillian, a gifted musicologist and conductor, worked as a music librarian at the Library of Congress, where she restored the musical scores to silent films, and conducted them with an orchestra. Hilarine would bake a batch of cookies and Woody was allowed to devour as many as he wanted. Our six small children (Figure 4), Justine (10), Maxwell (8), Nicholas (5), Paul (5), Alexander (5), and Jonathan (3), who were permitted only 2 cookies each per day, eyed him enviously. They dubbed him the "The Cookie Monster." With his full red-gold beard, I imagine he did resemble Sesame Street's Cookie Monster in the children's eyes. One day, Justine baked a jumbo chocolate chip cookie the size of a dinner plate for Woody and displayed it before dinner. He was delighted. After dinner, Woody asked, "Justine, where's my cookie?" She smiled guilelessly, replying, "We ate it."

When Woody had his 40th birthday, Gill hired a belly dancer to perform at his party. When she had her 40th, she demanded equal treatment. Since there were no male belly dancers available, Woody asked our mutual friend and co-worker, Arrigo Addamiano, who had a PhD from the University of Rome and another from Oxford, along with a wicked sense of humor, to do the honors. In turn, Arrigo told Woody that he would do it only if I agreed to join him. I immediately got the idea for a great practical joke, and readily agreed. At the party, Arrigo appeared in a grass skirt and I wore two bathing suits; stuffed between them was one of Hilarine's old nylon stockings filled with pieces of sponge. As I danced, I slowly pulled off the outer bathing suit in a strip-tease, and the two-foot-long nylon stocking phallus sprang out to the raucous laughter of the guests.

A DISCIPLE OF THE MOST DESTRUCTIVE INFLUENCE

There was one more sludge battle to be fought. About 15 miles south of DC lay the upscale riverfront community of Piscataway, named after the Indian tribe who had once inhabited the area. At the foot of the hillside on which the homes were perched, sat the Piscataway sewage treatment plant, which housed a brand-new $2 million dollar sludge incinerator which was about to go operational. In the wake of the Washington Post article, I received a call from the president of the Piscataway Hills Citizen association. He invited me to make a presentation on the hazards of sludge incineration. I gave an educational slide show to over 100 attendees, emphasizing the unfavorable topography, which would place the homes directly in the plume. Following the Q & A, the Association asked me to testify at an upcoming public hearing on their behalf before the Prince George's County Council. In July 1974, I spoke in opposition to a triumvirate of local developers, plus Dan Geller, an apparatchik from EPA's Region III based in Philadelphia, as well as representatives of the Washington Suburban Sanitary Commission (WSSC). Afterward, the head of the County Health Department was asked for his opinion; he responded, "I cannot guarantee the safety of the citizens if the incinerator is allowed to operate." The County Council promptly voted to close down the incinerator, to the raucous applause of the audience. This stuck in the craw of both the WSSC and the local Pols.

One of these Pols, The Hon. Gladys Noon Spellman, chair of the County council (and later a US Congresswoman), caustically denounced me in the *Prince George's Journal*: "Repace is a disciple of the most destructive influence in Prince George's County." Puzzled, I phoned the *Journal* reporter to inquire who this "most destructive influence" was. He confided that it was none other than my old friend and mentor, NRL space physicist Julian Holmes! I learned a valuable lesson: helping citizens solve environmental problems would make political enemies. Little did I know: the local Pols would be featherweight adversaries compared to Big Tobacco's congressional allies. *Morturi te salutamus*.

The shut-down of the Piscataway sludge incinerator before it ever operated sent shock waves through the WSSC, and its Board of Commissioners invited me to repeat my presentation at their headquarters in Hyattsville, MD. Following my slideshow, they barraged me with questions. One of these changed the course of my life: "Why don't you concentrate your efforts on highway traffic pollution, or smoking? They cause a great deal more pollution than our small incinerator." I replied that I already had commented on the regional transportation plan, and that smoking was a separate issue outside the purview of our organization. However, as I left the building, I had an epiphany: *I had never seen the air outdoors as polluted as the indoor air in bars and restaurants was from tobacco smoke.*

FIGURE 4. OUR CHILDREN IN 1974: TRIPLETS, NICK, PAUL, AND ALEX WITH THEIR EASTER BASKETS, AND JUSTINE, JON, AND MAX.

PART TWO

THE BATTLES BEGIN

CHAPTER 4
WHERE THERE'S SMOKE, THERE'S IRE

"On the occasion of Abraham Lincoln's Birthday, 'Mr. Lincoln' will proclaim the liberation of nonsmokers in a ceremony on the West Front Steps of the U.S. Capitol. Sponsored by GASP, the (Group Against Smokers' Pollution), the ceremony will focus on the freedoms nonsmokers are entitled to: ... to breathe clean air free from tobacco smoke; ... to voice their objections to smoking; ... to take action to restrict smoking in public places."

Press Release, Group Against Smokers' Pollution, P.O. Box 632, College Park, MD, February 12, 1975

Up until 1980, the paucity of scientific research underpinning the notion that the breathing of secondhand smoke could induce any of the diseases of smoking in nonsmokers impeded the understanding of the nature of the threat to nonsmokers' health. Despite this, by the early 1970's, the little there was had been enough to raise the concern of Surgeon General Jesse Steinfeld. He issued a prescient warning in the 1972 Surgeon General's Report, *Public Exposure to Air Pollution from Tobacco Smoke:*

SUMMARY: 1. An atmosphere contaminated with tobacco smoke can contribute to the discomfort of many individuals. 2. The level of carbon monoxide attained in experiments using rooms filled with tobacco smoke has been shown to equal, and at times to exceed, the legal limits for ... ambient air quality ... and can also exceed the occupational Threshold Limit Value for a normal work period ... . This would be particularly significant for people who are already suffering from chronic bronchopulmonary disease and coronary heart disease. 3. *Other components of tobacco smoke, such as particulate matter ... have been shown ... to affect adversely animal pulmonary and cardiac structure and function. The extent of the contributions of these substances to illness in humans exposed to the concentrations present in an atmosphere contaminated with tobacco smoke is not presently known* [Italics mine].

Discomfort was hardly the right term. The reality was that for many nonsmokers, exposure to secondhand smoke in the workplace induced fear, loathing, frustration, and misery. The experience of Donna Shimp, a service representative for Bell Telephone in New Jersey in 1976 was a prime example. Ms. Shimp's workplace was so smoky that she suffered severe abrasion of her corneas; she wrote that she "felt like a piece of meat thrust into a smoke-house for curing" (Shimp et al. 1976). When Shimp complained to her management, she was callously offered a Hobson's Choice: "You can either be fired to protect your health or take a lower-level job with a pay-cut in a smoke-free area designed to protect sensitive telephone switching equipment." The company took better care of the health of its electro-mechanical equipment than the health of its staff. The reality of that era was that most smokers took for granted that they were entitled to use the common indoor air that they shared with nonsmokers as a sewer for their smoke. This was the rule followed by management in white collar and pink collar workplaces, not the exception. In blue collar workplaces, smoking was banned only in areas where it posed a danger of fire or explosion.

Outraged at her cavalier treatment, Ms. Shimp filed suit against the New Jersey Bell. Prevailing against all odds, she slapped the uncompromising company with a court injunction requiring her accommodation. She wrote a book about her experience, entitled "*How to Protect Your Health at Work: A Complete Guide for Making the Workplace Safe.*" (Shimp D, et al., 1976). Several years later, Donna and I corresponded and we became lifelong friends.

Donna Shimp's success in court proved to be an anomaly. The experience of a group of nonsmoking federal workers typified the legal zeitgeist. Labor-management strife over smoking in the workplace was rife at the Social Security Administration (SSA) offices in Baltimore, MD. In April 1978, social science researcher C.B. Barad surveyed all 21,366 SSA employees, both smokers and nonsmokers, with a 70% response rate. Barad circulated a questionnaire asking workers whether they would prefer special smoking areas, separation of smokers and nonsmokers, or total prohibition of smoking at work. About 31% of SSA staff admitted to smoking on the job, equally divided between men and women. More supervisors smoked (41%) than non-supervisors. Unsurprisingly, less than 3% of the smokers said they were bothered by secondhand smoke. By contrast, Barad found that more than 50 % of the nonsmoking workforce complained that ambient tobacco smoke impaired their work efficiency. In fact, 36 % of the nonsmokers complained that they had been forced to move away from their workstations to avoid tobacco smoke. Their complaints included eye, nose, and throat irritation, or coughing, and 25% said they had a respiratory condition aggravated by tobacco smoke exposure (Barad, 1979).

Twenty percent of the nonsmokers reported difficulty in concentrating on work due to passive smoking, and the 14 % of the nonsmokers who suffered most from inhaling the irritating and debilitating fumes of found it difficult to produce any work at all. Nearly 25 % of the nonsmokers expressed feelings of frustration and hostility toward both smokers and management. Moreover, 52 % of nonsmokers who tried informally to get smoking coworkers to refrain from smoking in the office met with failure and another 34 % got mixed results.

An overwhelming majority, 87% of the 6,623 smokers, opposed a total prohibition of smoking at work. Fiftyfive percent rejected special designated smoking areas away from the workstation, as well as separation of smokers and nonsmokers into different work areas. By contrast, 51% of the nonsmokers, i.e., 7518 persons, preferred restricting smokers to designed smoking areas, while a total smoking ban was favored by a third of the nonsmoking workers but by only 13% of the smokers. The 41% of the supervisors who smoked were the root of the problem, leading to a frustrating inability of nonsmokers to obtain any relief through appeals to management. Upon exhausting their administrative remedies, a cadre of frustrated workers sued the SSA, asserting that the federal government had a common-law duty to protect the health of its employees. They were joined by GASP, ASH, and Federal Employees For Non-Smokers' Rights (FENSR).

The Social Security workers ultimately failed to succeed in litigating a smoke-free workplace. Nearly two years later, U.S. District Court Judge C.R. Richey dismissed the SSA case with prejudice, stating that health protection of employees was not appropriately a part of the common law, and that the Court lacked jurisdiction. The workers appealed, but the Court of Appeals upheld the trial court's dismissal. They then appealed to the U.S. Supreme Court which affirmed the appellate courts' opinion in October 1979. This decision by the High Court was a clear signal that legal efforts to obtain smoke-free workplaces were doomed.

The travail of Lanny Vickers, a 39-year old purchasing agent for the Veterans Administration (VA) Hospital in Seattle, further exemplified the brutal futility of litigation in this smoky era. Vickers suffered from headaches and severe eye, nose, and throat symptoms from secondhand smoke allegedly caused by his work environment. On July 15, 1977, he filed suit against the VA [*Vickers vs. Veteran's Administration, 1982*]. Vickers sued for unspecified monetary damages and demanded that the VA be forced to provide him a working environment free of smoke. It was to no avail; he won neither damages nor an order for the VA to accommodate him. Moreover, Vickers' suit had burdened him with substantial legal expenses. In his ruling, the judge noted that Vickers' chief and coworkers had voluntarily agreed not to smoke around him at work. However, Vickers had argued that his supervisor, one David R. Radke, a cigarette and pipe smoker, had discriminated against him by giving him undesirable work assignments because of his complaints. The trial Judge, Donald S. Vorhees, unsparingly ruled that the Veterans Administration could not be forced to provide Vickers with a smoke-free working environment. Judge Vorhees, who piously stated that he had never smoked himself, ruled that smokers in Vickers' workplace "have certain rights which must be balanced against Vickers' desires. Until and unless Congress enacts a statute banning the smoking of tobacco in Government offices or the Veterans' Administration promulgates a policy against smoking in its offices, the desires of those employees who wish to smoke cannot be disregarded" (NY Times, 1982). The judge further ruled that it was *Vickers'* responsibility to avoid tobacco smoke (Repace, 1985). How was he supposed to effect this secondhand smoke avoidance in his work environment? Was Lanny Vickers supposed to wear a gas mask at all day at work?

Subsequently, in 1981, Vickers appealed the ruling to the Employees' Compensation Appeals Board at the U.S. Dept. of Labor. Its three-judge panel was more sympathetic, accepting Vickers' claim on the basis of "temporary aggravation of chronic rhinitis, pharyngitis and laryngeal tracheitis." The Board also accepted Vickers' claim of intermittent periods of disability from March 8, 1978 to February 10, 1983 and noted that he had transferred to a new position within the VA in November 1983. Then on August 20, 1984, Vickers filed a second occupational disease claim, alleging that he had become depressed due to unfair treatment received since he raised the issue of a smoke-free work environment. Tragically, he was hospitalized on July 25, 1984 for depression and suicidal ideation. The Appeals Board subsequently accepted his claim for temporary depression on May 29, 1985. Vickers continued to have ongoing problems relating to his workplace exposure lasting as long as 1999, which led to his being unable to work, and the Board sustained his award of compensation for work-related depression (USDOL, 2001).

The flight attendants' union had been fighting in vain for an in-flight smoking ban since the late 1960s, in the face of antipathy from the airline industry, as well as fierce tobacco industry opposition. One flight attendant, Sara Nelson, recalled, "It was a real uphill battle… for us it was a workplace issue; we had members who were experiencing shortness of breath and all of the problems created by secondhand smoke, up to and including deadly diseases like lung cancer … the smoke would hang in the cabin right at about face level, so the whole time you are working on the flight you were breathing in smoke" (Sharkey, 2015). In the 1960's, the airlines aggravated the problem of smoking on aircraft by distributing free cigarettes to the smokers with their meals (Szabo, 2014).

Like Lanny Vickers, nonsmokers could only experience smoke-free workplaces, retail stores, hospitals, buses, trains, taxis, planes, restaurants, bars, theaters, or social events if they wore gas masks. Smokers often took high umbrage at nonsmokers' complaints, regarding polluting the indoor air with their smoke as an inalienable "right." With the exception of the very few activists at the time, nonsmokers marginalized by smokers felt impelled to suck it up and refrain from complaining.

By 1969, Hilarine and I simply avoided dining in smoke-polluted restaurants and prohibited smoking in our home. We posted a small No Smoking sign on the front door of our house to ensure that visitors, including my father-in-law, got the message loud and clear. He was not happy having to smoke outside. A Herblock cartoon in 1976 expressed our feelings vividly: it pictured a miserable nonsmoking couple dining in a restaurant surrounded by smokers emanating plumes of smoke that wafted in their faces. The man said to the woman, "I heard the food here is very good. Maybe we can take some home and taste it" (Repace, 1985). Our social life revolved around bi-monthly meetings of our two Gourmet Clubs in private homes. One club was comprised of young non-smoking couples from the baby-sitting co-op in our garden apartment complex in Greenbelt, Maryland, a few blocks from NASA's Goddard Space Flight Center. The second one was composed of nonsmoking couples whose husbands worked at NRL. It had been started by Al Lowrey, who loved to cook (Figure 3). So once a month we dined out in smoke-free comfort in the homes of our friends.

I had been fortunate at work; at Grasslands and Delafield Hospitals, no one I worked with smoked. At RCA, neither Joe nor Peter smoked, and when Peter departed for Princeton in 1966, his replacement, Kris Wronski, an expat Brit who was a light smoker, agreed for a time to smoke outside in the hall. After he got busy with his research he changed his mind, so I found things to do outside the office in the lab or library while he had his nicotine fix. Workers in occupations with "normal" (or worse) levels of smoking did not have this luxury. Among nonsmokers in general, there was considerable suppressed discontent with the pandemic pollution by cigarette, pipe, and cigar smoke in workplaces, retail stores, bars and restaurants, the cinema, and in transportation. And yes, let's not forget breathing the smoke blown on you by some asshole next in line during the hours-long waits at the MVA to renew one's license or registration. Yes, my dear Millenials, in those days you had to actually show up in person. There was no internet, no on-line convenience, no click-and-pay, no credit cards, no cell phones, no computers. Any geezer who's nostalgic for those days must be senile.

GASPing For Air

Finally, a great awakening began to take place in the early 1970's. A smoke-free air crusader, Betty Carnes, of Scottsdale, Arizona, pioneered Arizonans Concerned About Smoking, beginning her smoke-free advocacy way back in 1964. By 1972 she was laying siege to the Arizona legislature, resulting in the enactment of state laws that restricted smoking in government-owned buildings and health facilities. In 1974, Garfield Mahood, in Toronto, Canada, became the Executive Director of the Non-Smokers' Rights Association (NSRA) and its sister charity, the Smoking and Health Action Foundation (SHAF). Gar then began his decades-long campaign for a smoke-free Canada.

In Maryland, Clara Gouin founded the Group Against Smoker's Pollution (GASP) in 1971, a year after her 58-year old father, a life-long smoker, died of lung cancer. She reminisced about the Bad Old Days in a poignant speech in 2006 that reflected the angst of many nonsmokers in the Smoky Seventies:

"Missing him was all the more painful because it seemed that there was nothing anyone could do to end the public scourge of smoking. People smoked everywhere ... at work, at home, in stores, in restaurants, at meetings, at parties ... it was the 'social' thing to do. ... I felt so futile trying to stand against a hurricane of smoke. To make matters worse, my little daughter would get horribly congested whenever we took her anywhere — restaurants were out of the question — but she was fine inside our home. The smokier the situation, the worse she became. It suddenly dawned on me that tobacco smoke was the culprit. In those early years, no one talked about the effect of smoke on nonsmokers. All the research had been directed at the health effects on smokers. The Surgeon General's first report on the hazards to smokers had been published only a few years earlier, and the public was just beginning to realize that smoking was harmful.

It did not enter anyone's mind that it could harm nonsmokers too. My nonsmoking friends and I had often groused (among ourselves) about having to put up with tobacco smoke everywhere we turned. We complained about needing to air out our coats and jackets after attending meetings, of needing to shampoo our hair immediately after attending a smoky social event, of reeking ashtrays on restaurant tables, of ashes being dropped on our furniture and rugs. Why in the world were we putting up with this imposition? ... We were putting up with discomfort, inconvenience, and even physical symptoms from tobacco smoke, and we weren't doing anything more than discreetly waving it away from our noses.

… It was one thing to try to get smokers to quit — that was impossible. But it was another thing altogether to keep smoke out of our own lungs. We had a right to breathe! After a sleepless night, I resolved to start an organization of nonsmokers" [C.Gouin, personal communication, 2006].

GASP's first newsletter, *The Ventilator,* went out in March of 1971, and Clara Gouin soon emerged as a soft-spoken but determined spokesperson for the nascent nonsmokers' rights movement. GASP was one of the first organizations of its kind. Clara soon was making appearances on national TV and radio shows and being interviewed for stories in national magazines. GASP spread like wildfire throughout the US, taking root in California, and soon expanding to 45 local chapters nationwide. The Lung Association of Southern Maryland and GASP joined hands and announced that their aim was to begin "a new strategy in our battle against smoking: we began to champion the rights of the nonsmoker, who is affected in much of the same way as the smoker, albeit second-hand. Our immediate goal is to eliminate smoking in public places; our larger aim is to undercut the social acceptability of smoking. … We have promoted legislative restrictions on smoking in public places; to this end we have testified at public hearings in Annapolis [the State capital] and elsewhere." … "We have sponsored nonsmokers' activities, such as a 'Nonsmokers' Night in dinner theaters, in an effort to persuade restaurant owners to provide smoke-free facilities" [Lung Association, 1975].

In March of 1974, National GASP issued a booklet, "The Nonsmokers' Liberation Guide, A Manual of Revolutionary Tactics and Strategies to Secure the Breathing Rights of Nonsmokers Everywhere!" GASP sold lapel buttons proclaiming GASP/NON-SMOKERS HAVE RIGHTS TOO. I wore one of these to a party in the early 1970's, and a woman came up to me, and after reading my button, smiled and blew smoke into my face. A cartoon of the era expressed the zeitgeist: It showed a smoker surrounded by a cloud of smoke speaking to a nonsmoker wearing a respirator: "It's equal rights – I have a right to smoke and you have a right to wear a mask" (Repace, 1985).

One GASPer wrote an essay in which he related the following anecdote:

"I vividly recall a train trip with a now deceased colleague who suffered from pulmonary emphysema. We boarded a one-car train that was marked "No Smoking" at the front end. We did not know that at the rear end there was a "Smoking Permitted" sign. By the time we got to our destination, my friend was in agony; his situation had been aggravated by a standing-room-only crowd, and the smokers were ignoring the "No Smoking" sign in the front by simply facing the rear of the car" [Garfield, E, 1973].

On January 11, 1975, the first U.S. Nonsmokers Rights Summit Conference was held at the University of Maryland; 67 attendees came from as far away as Texas, Florida, Michigan and Canada; most paid their own way. They included homemakers, physicians, legislators, volunteer agency staffers, all dedicated to the proposition that the right to breathe clean air supersedes the right to smoke. It was co-sponsored by the Lung Association of Southern Maryland and the National Interagency Council on Smoking and Health. Clara Gouin was the Keynote Speaker. In conjunction with this, GASP staged a major protest demonstration on the steps of the U.S. Capitol, to call attention to nonsmokers' rights. Bill Wall, an Abe Lincoln doppelganger, read "An Emancipation Proclamation for Nonsmokers." The protest was publicized and was covered by local news organizations. (C. Gouin, B. Morris, personal communication).

LEGAL ACTIVISM, A NEW TOOL FOR NONSMOKERS' RIGHTS

In the late 1960's, John Banzhaf, a pit-bull professor of law at George Washington University in the District of Columbia, had formed ASH, Action on Smoking and Health, which rapidly became a nationally prominent advocacy organization. Banzhaf played a key role in getting rid of cigarette advertising on television. In the late 1960s, Banzhaf and ASH were already working against passive smoking. In 1969 Ralph Nader joined in, petitioning the Federal Aviation Administration (FAA) to ban smoking on all flights, while Banzhaf petitioned the FAA to require separate smoking and nonsmoking sections on domestic flights. Neither the Nader nor the Banzhaf petitions were successful in changing FAA policies. In 1972, Nader and Banzhaf changed tactics by filing petitions with the Civil Aeronautics Board (CAB). Both were demanding segregation of smokers and nonsmokers on passenger flights. Citing polls reporting that 60% of airline passengers were bothered by smoke in the cabin, the CAB issued a rule requiring airlines to provide separate sections for smokers and non-smokers. However, many airlines failed to fully comply with the regulations. In 1976, ASH successfully petitioned the CAB to ban cigar and pipe smoking on aircraft [Holm & Davis, 2004].

FIGURE 5. AL LOWREY ATTENDING A HAWAIIAN LUAU AT THE REPACE'S, 1970 (AUTHOR'S PHOTO).

Nonsmoking sections on aircraft were a major symbolic step forward in acknowledging that smoking on aircraft (or in any enclosed space) caused discomfort and worse for nonsmokers (Figure 6). However, airline staff found it difficult to enforce the rule, resulting in complaints about lack of sufficient nonsmoking seating. Smoke-sensitive passengers could wind up being seated in the smoking section. Even worse, nonsmoking sections failed miserably to protect flight attendants who had to work in smoking sections. In response to a Cigar Association petition in 1978, the CAB flip-flopped, amending its rules yet again, to reinstate limited cigar and pipe smoking on passenger aircraft. Dissatisfied with this state of affairs, in 1979, ASH sued the CAB, claiming that legally mandated enforcement was inadequate. When the anti-regulatory Reagan administration came into office in 1981, it further weakened enforcement of the previous CAB rules [John Banzhaf III, Wikipedia, 2016].

In March 1976, for the first time, the entire American Lung Association Bulletin [Vol 62, No 2], was devoted to an article by Clara Gouin and Bill Morris, reporting that Lung Associations around the country were taking up the cause against public smoking, and noting that "in most places today you still see smoking in the supermarket, in hospitals and clinics, in cultural centers, in public transportation, in elevators, in restaurants." It featured a picture of a stop sign with the message: "**LUNGS AT WORK NO SMOKING.**" Their article compared the new campaign against public smoking to the successful campaign by the National Tuberculosis Association against widespread public spitting, three-quarters of a century earlier. However, most other local voluntary health organizations, except for a few aggressive chapters around the country, gave short shrift to nonsmokers' rights, focusing their efforts mainly on smoking cessation. Moreover, during the 1970s, with the exception of a few outspoken public health individuals such as Surgeon General Jesse Steinfeld, most government officials failed to recognize that smoking in public and on transportation needed to be regulated.

An additional significant obstacle to public and workplace smoking restrictions was that many of the people with the power to make change were themselves smokers, and thus part of the problem; they strove to preserve the privilege of smoking anywhere with impunity, as was the case at the SSA. In fact, until about 1979, even The National Cancer Institute (NCI), the federal government's leading cancer research arm, focused its research efforts primarily on studying potentially "less hazardous cigarettes." NCI's misbegotten "safe-cigarette" program was led by Gio Batta Gori, an epidemiologist who would later become a consultant for Brown and Williamson Tobacco and the Tobacco Institute when NCI abandoned the safe cigarette program under DHHS Secretary Joe Califano [Wikipedia, 2016].

In 1973, California lawyer and legal editor Peter Hanauer went to a meeting of Berkeley GASP; two of the founders, Irene and Dave Peterson, had created a foundation to provide legal representation to people who were affected by secondhand smoke in the workplace. They were joined by Paul Loveday, another attorney. Loveday became president of Berkeley GASP. Loveday and Hanauer became the backbone of the nonsmokers' rights movement in California [Glantz and Balbach, 2000]. The group later became Californians for Nonsmokers' Rights (CNR), and a then obscure UCSF cardiology professor, Stanton Glantz, became its president. CNR later morphed into a national organization, Americans for Nonsmokers' Rights (ANR).

In 1975, Minnesota became the first state to enact a Clean Indoor Air Act, requiring the creation of "Smoking Permitted" and "No Smoking Areas." In 1976, local chapters of GASP in Northern and Southern California merged into California GASP. Working to pass local legislation modeled after the Minnesota Clean Indoor Air Act, CalGASP launched Proposition 5, a statewide initiative that would be enacted by a direct vote of the people. The Tobacco Industry spent $6 million in defeating the Prop 5 campaign, leaving just a single local law remaining in April 1977 in the Town of Berkeley. Between 1977 and 1980, the tobacco industry spent more than $10 million opposing a resurgence of these efforts in California. Grass-roots activists, recognizing that they could not prevail in the state legislature or win an expensive state initiative campaign, shifted their efforts towards enacting local ordinances. The organization they created took the lead in grass roots organizing against the tobacco industry. The activist nonsmokers, sick and tired of breathing irritating secondhand smoke everywhere, began to speak out. It became clear that legislated local smoking bans were a viable remedy.

A few outspoken physicians began to focus on the industry itself as a disease vector. In 1977, a family physician, Dr. Alan Blum, founded DOC (Doctors Ought to Care). DOC organized physicians and other health professionals to take action on smoking in the clinic, classroom, and community. This was not much appreciated by the directors of the American Medical Association at that time. Similarly in Australia, a movement known as Billboard Utilizing Graffitists Against Unhealthy Promotions (BUGA-UP) sprang up in Sydney in October 1979, later spreading to Melbourne, Hobart, Adelaide, and Perth. The movement targeted cigarette and alcohol advertising, altering the billboard ads by clandestinely painting over some letters and adding others to convey the point that the product is unhealthy. [Wikipedia, 2016]. Many of BUGA-UP members came from professional and university-educated backgrounds and quite a few were young doctors, such as Arthur Chesterfield Evans, an occupational health physician, who later became a member of parliament in New South Wales. Together, its leaders, Bill Snow, Ric Bolzan, and Geoff Coleman, coined the BUGA-UP acronym and began adding it to the defaced billboards, to link its graffiti to a movement rather than the random activity of individuals. One example of the genre showed the Marlboro man lighting up with the words "BUTTS to BUTTS, ASHES to ASHES spray-painted in white over the western scenery. Another displayed a decrepit man in a wheelchair instead of a cowboy on a horse (BUGA-UP.org). And on a billboard in Arizona in the 1970's, Dr. Leland (Lee) Fairbanks, an Indian Public Health Service (IPHS) physician, began a paid advertising campaign for smoke-free IPHS hospitals, finally succeeding in 1983 on the Hopi Reservation. Lee Fairbanks later became president of ACAS and a close friend.

In the country at large, since the early 1970's, evolving public attitudes had inexorably led nonsmokers to become progressively less tolerant of public smoking, and the fledgling nonsmokers' rights movement emerged and spread. It had become abundantly clear to nonsmokers' rights groups that legislated smoking bans, as opposed to litigation, were the key to solving the problem of indoor public smoking. Alarmed by these developments, in 1978, the Tobacco Institute commissioned a poll by the Roper Organization to take the pulse of nonsmokers' changing attitudes toward public smoking. The industry's worst fears were confirmed: The Roper Report concluded that, *the passive smoking issue is the most dangerous development to the viability of the tobacco industry that has yet occurred.* Significantly, it recommended "Developing and widely publicizing information emphasizing that passive smoking is not harmful to nonsmokers' health." The industry adopted this recommendation with a vengeance, and in doing so, would set a high-water mark in the annals of corporate crime.

FIGURE 6. SMOKING AND NONSMOKING SECTIONS ON U.S. PASSENGER AIRCRAFT WERE MANDATED IN 1972 AND WOULD ENDURE UNTIL 1989. SEATS FORWARD OF THE NONSMOKING SIGN WERE NONSMOKING, BUT THAT DID NOT KEEP SECONDHAND SMOKE FROM DRIFTING FORWARD, NOR DID IT PROTECT FLIGHT ATTENDANTS FROM BEING GASSED (AUTHOR'S PHOTO).

THE BEST CONGRESS THAT MONEY CAN BUY

To stave off restrictions on their poisonous products and their toxic emissions, as a new generation of environmental and health and safety laws became enacted, Big Tobacco successfully lobbied Congress to proscribe regulation of tobacco products under every conceivable federal statute. These laws included: the *Federal Hazardous Substances Act*, the *Consumer Product Safety Act*, the *Fair Packaging and Labeling Act*, the *Controlled Substance Act*, and the *Toxic Substance Control Act*. Adding to the damage, a tobacco-friendly federal court ruled that tobacco products could not be regulated under the *Food, Drug, and Cosmetics Act*. Moreover, because federal law is pre-emptive, individual States were also precluded from regulating tobacco products. Because EPA had initially *interpreted* the term "ambient air" in the Clean Air Act of 1970 to mean outdoor air (although the Act actually did no such thing), and since OSHA was mainly focused on health and safety in the dangerous and heavily polluted industrial trades, occupational and environmental health research by these Agencies avoided investigating secondhand smoke. In 1978, when Joe Califano became Secretary of the Department of Health, Education, and Welfare under the incoming Carter Administration, a strong antismoking campaign finally became a federal priority. Califano branded cigarette smoking "Public Health Enemy Number One." The following year, Califano was fired by President Carter, allegedly because of his outspoken stand against tobacco [Goodman et al., 2005].

These failures created a climate in which tobacco industry propaganda and disinformation could flourish and be deployed to defeat smoking ban legislation. Without a scientific base, in the minds of policy makers, many of who were smokers themselves, passive smoking could easily be cast as a minor annoyance among many others too trivial to bother with, outweighed by the demands of business owners, who feared economic losses from smoking bans. They were joined by vocal libertarians who resented government regulation of any kind. However, with sufficient public demand, even annoyances such as noise pollution and public dog defecation, have given rise to noise ordinances and pooper-scooper laws. In this vein, a few politically savvy nonsmokers around the country began to lobby legislatures for legislation to restrict smoking in certain indoor public spaces, especially restaurants.

I JOIN THE BATTLE FOR NONSMOKERS' RIGHTS

In the aftermath of my Piscataway incinerator presentation at the WSSC, I became flushed with enthusiasm over a new public interest scientific problem to solve. I decided to attempt to estimate the level of smoke particulate pollution from cigarettes in a restaurant. My initial back-of-the-envelope calculation suggested that this pollution exceeded the level of EPA's health-based air quality standards. It was destined to change how society perceived secondhand smoke. A couple of years later, I received a flyer in the mail advertising the "First National Conference on Nonsmokers' Rights," organized by former Surgeon General Jesse Steinfeld, a Nixon appointee whose term in office had ended in January 1973. The conference convened at Essex Community College in Baltimore, Maryland. The flyer encouraged attendees to bring posters illustrating their environmental tobacco smoke concerns. Recalling my earlier calculation of the estimated level of air pollution from smoking in a restaurant as a function of time, I decided to graph it on a 2-foot by 3-foot poster board to make a dramatic display. I hung it from a table in the lobby alongside several other posters. My graph suggested that within a half hour in a typical restaurant, the level of EPA's 24-hour outdoor air pollution standard for airborne particulate matter (TSP) would be exceeded due to smoking.

Near the end of his rousing speech, Dr. Steinfeld commented, "I haven't heard a cough from the audience all morning. I guess there aren't any smokers present;" the energized audience laughed, whistled, cheered, and stomped their feet. When he was done, I returned to the lobby to man my poster, full of enthusiasm. A wiry man with piercing blue eyes approached and perused my poster. He introduced himself as Dr. John O'Hara. John described himself an engineering physicist. John was fascinated by my graph, and we struck up a lively conversation. It developed that we had a lot in common: we both had attended graduate school in physics at Catholic University in Washington DC; we both lived in the Maryland town of Bowie, only a few miles apart, and we both worked for the federal government. John related that he suffered from chronic blephoritis, an affliction of the eyes that was greatly aggravated by exposure to tobacco smoke when he dined out.

John was also exposed to secondhand smoke every day at work. This of course, was not unusual in itself. In the 1970's, most workplaces were polluted with secondhand smoke. However, John's work environment was like few others: it was at the heavily-guarded super-secret National Security Agency (NSA) at Fort Meade, Maryland, where he spent much of the day working on top-secret projects in sealed vaults with poor ventilation, surrounded by heavy smokers. I recalled from my work at NRL designing a space-radiation dosimeter for a Navy navigational satellite, that classified work on so-called "Black Satellites" was done in poorly ventilated super-secret sealed vaults. With smokers puffing away in such confined spaces, they were akin to working in a gas chamber.

O'Hara's difficulty with secondhand smoke at work was a further illustration of the problems nonsmokers encountered from smoking in the federal workplace during this era. From the NSA's beginnings in 1952, the Agency's facilities were enveloped in a blue haze of tobacco smoke. On April 13, 1975, O'Hara, then chief of R242 [don't ask], wrote the NSA Director, Lieutenant General Allen, suggesting that Allen issue a memo to the workforce stating the adverse impact that environmental tobacco smoke could have on people with health problems, prohibiting smoking in conference rooms, and establishing nonsmoking areas in the cafeteria and executive dining room. However, John J. Connelly, the NSA Assistant Director of Personnel and Security (ADPS), responded that "the Agency had no authority to prohibit smoking, and that it had to rely on common courtesy and the consideration of one's co-workers to solve the problem." This approach, of course, would accomplish zilch in eliminating secondhand smoke generated by nicotine-addicted smokers. But O'Hara persisted, and in the spring of 1976, the ADPS created a committee to study the problem and make recommendations. However, O'Hara got stonewalled; the committee met only once and resolved nothing. Most NSA smokers and managers felt that environmental tobacco smoke (ETS) was simply just a trivial nuisance, not to be taken seriously [NSA, 2002].

John never described what he did at NSA, and I knew better than to ask. Answers to those kinds of questions were limited to those with both the appropriate security clearance plus a "need to know." In a prior incarnation, he had served as a bombardier on an Air Force B-47, and later had attended college on the GI Bill. Recently, NSA declassified one of O'Hara's early achievements: On February 3, 1966, the USSR shocked the world by making the first soft lunar landing and transmitting signals from its Luna 9 spacecraft. O'Hara built a "black box" to decode the transmissions from Luna 9, and bootlegged an informal arrangement with Honeywell Corporation swapping a high-speed NSA video recorder with an experimental slow-speed Honeywell device, one of only three in existence, to display Luna 9's pictures with the proper aspect ratio. The pictures were on the President's desk that afternoon. But as the saying goes, no good deed goes unpunished. O'Hara was called on the carpet by NSA's nitpicking lawyers for "exceeding his authorities," as he had not first consulted either Legal or Purchasing in arranging the swap. An appalled senior executive in charge of the Director's Advisory Group on Electronic Reconnaissance quickly intervened and the charge was dropped. Results counted at NSA. The declassified pictures may be viewed at NSA's National Cryptologic Museum at Fort Meade, Maryland [J.H. O'Hara, personal communication].

I empathized with John's complaint about irritation from secondhand smoke. I related to him that acute exposure to tobacco smoke had caused my eyes, nose, and throat to be irritated, and prolonged exposure resulted in chest pain and dizziness. These had been especially bothersome during exams in college, in theaters and bowling alleys, or on a bus ride. As a result, I said, I avoided such places and surface transportation as much as I could. On the job – so far – working in hospitals and research laboratories, I had, with the notable exception of Jack Hoover's smoky card game, encountered minimal secondhand smoke exposure, mainly because few scientists or physicians smoked. Nevertheless, this always remained a concern whenever I changed jobs.

John and I decided to form a chapter of GASP. Fortuitously, Clara Gouin, the national founder of GASP, lived nearby in Prince George's County. Moreover, Clara was a friend and board member of the Prince George's Environmental Coalition, which I headed. With Clara's guidance, the three of us worked in O'Hara's kitchen laboring to establish Bowie GASP. John's wife, Merrily, kindly kept us fueled with tea and cookies. John assumed the presidency of the new organization, and I became the vice-president. The newly-formed Bowie GASP took on its first challenge: getting non-smoking sections in restaurants in Prince George's County, our larger political jurisdiction, home to about 700,000 people. This was a priority for John because he and Merrily liked to dine out regularly, but the smoke caused his eyes to sting and water, often ruining his meal. We soon attracted dozens of local non-smoking members who were also fed up with drifting smoke ruining their dining experience. We held our meetings in a conference room in the Bowie Public Library. Figure 7 shows a GASP booth in a local Mall in Bowie, attended by Yours Truly in a then trendy powder blue leisure suit, with my 12-year old daughter, Justine, assisting. GASP members took turns at the booth at the local health fairs for a couple of hours at a time, handing out literature, and soliciting membership and support for smoking sections in restaurants.

John, a great organizer and an indefatigable campaigner, arranged for us to visit the Environmental Matters Committee of the Prince George's County Council in Upper Marlboro, the county seat. One of Upper Marlboro's notable buildings was a large tobacco barn where local farmers auctioned off their crops, for Prince Georges was then a tobacco-growing county in a tobacco-growing state. The head of the Environment committee was a portly black-bearded genial bear of a man, Francis B. 'Frank' Francois, an engineer and patent lawyer by trade. He would prove to be a vital ally. O'Hara made the initial presentation, saying he represented a group of citizens who wanted to enjoy a restaurant meal without inhaling irritating tobacco smoke plumes wafting from a table of smokers a few feet away, and therefore was petitioning for legislation to establish nonsmoking sections in county restaurants. He emphasized that trying to enjoy a meal with cigarette, pipe, or cigar smokers a few feet away on adjacent tables blowing smelly irritating smoke on you was a nightmare. It is a measure of the tenor of the times that we believed that a totally smoke-free restaurant law did not have the remotest possibility of being enacted. The best we could hope for was simply for legislation mandating separate sections in restaurants for smokers and nonsmokers, so the worst of the drifting tobacco smoke would be kept out of our faces. This eminently reasonable step was condemned by local restauranteurs as a radical idea in the mid 1970's. Their objections were vigorously supported by the potent tobacco lobby, who turned out representatives of the Chamber of Commerce, the Bakery, Confectionary and Tobacco Workers' Union, as well as local tobacconists, local tobacco farmers and individual smokers.

County legislators paid close attention to the desires of the business community. Anticipating this, I sought to overcome the predictable opposition using science. In the hearing before the Environmental Matters Committee, I presented my calculations of cigarette smoke pollution for a hypothetical 2000 square foot restaurant, occupied by a full-house of 140 persons, based on the local building code's default occupancy. I assumed that a third of those occupants would be smokers, based on the U.S. smoking prevalence in 1979. My calculations incorporated two intuitive assumptions for which I had no actual data at the time but seemed reasonable first approximations. First, that the secondhand smoke particulate emissions were identical to the average mainstream tar levels of a cigarette. Secondly, that 14% or 20 smokers might be actively smoking at any one time in a restaurant containing 140 persons. I calculated the ventilation rate from the local building code at 8 air changes per hour. I displayed my graph of the estimated respirable particulate (RSP) pollution levels from secondhand smoke overlaid with EPA's outdoor air quality standards for total suspended particulate matter (TSP). The plot showed that tar particles from smoking would exceed EPA's 24-

hour Air Pollution Emergency level of 500 micrograms per cubic meter of total suspended particles (TSP), within a half-hour.

After I finished, Councilman Francois only had one insightful and devastating question for me: "Do you have any measured data to support your calculations, Mr. Repace?" I was too embarrassed by this now glaringly obvious flaw to answer it honestly. So seduced by the elegance of my calculations, I hadn't even considered it. I responded by "Toastmastering" him with the glib reply, "Well, we're just in the process of collecting that data." Then he politely delivered the coup de grâce: "Fine, "please come back when you've done that."

Actually, I had no clue at the time of how to make such measurements. However, I thought, after all, I *am* an experimental physicist, and now it is time for me to prove it. Later that day, I decided to convert a smoke detector to measure the pollution. At work the next day, I went over to Vic Piatt's office, to discuss this idea with Aris Stamulis, an environmental chemist who worked with Vic and shared the office. Vic was a nonsmoker, while Aris was a chain-smoker whose fingers, mustache, and office wall were yellowed with nicotine stains. Nevertheless, Aris was only too eager to help, and spoke the magic words: *"you don't have to modify a smoke-detector, Jim, portable particle detectors have already been invented; in fact, I got a flyer last week advertising a really interesting one."* He rummaged through the huge stack of papers on his desk and pulled out a glossy brochure for something called a "Piezobalance," sold by a company called TSI in Minnesota. I excitedly perused the brochure, profusely thanked Aris, hastened back to my office and immediately rang them up.

FIGURE 7. JUSTINE AND JIM REPACE, TENDING A GASP BOOTH IN FREE STATE MALL IN DOWNTOWN BOWIE, MD, IN 1976. THE POSTER IN FRONT WAS COMPOSED OF CIGARETTE ADS CLIPPED FROM SEVERAL MAJOR MAGAZINES, OVERLAID WITH A BUMPER STICKER FROM JOHN BANZHAF'S ASH – CAUTION: YOUR SMOKING IS HAZARDOUS TO MY HEALTH (AUTHOR'S PHOTO).

After requesting information on the Piezobalance and identifying myself as an NRL staff physicist, I was transferred to Gilmore Sem, one of the developers of the Piezobalance. In 1975, Sem and Tsurubayashi introduced the device, promoting it for "(1) industrial hygiene to locate industrial areas requiring better dust control or compliance measurements; (2) measurements in offices, stores, restaurants, arenas and other public buildings to assist in the adjustment of ventilation systems for control of tobacco smoke; and (3) outdoor measurements to characterize human exposure to respirable aerosol while engaged in activities such as walking down the street, riding in an auto or subway train, barbequing dinner in a backyard, or camping in a remote wilderness." Sem even had calibrated the device using the gold-standard gravimetric method on outdoor and indoor aerosols, welding fumes, and best of all, tobacco smoke, showing all data fell with plus or minus 10% with the gold standard (Sem, 1976).

Gil Sem proved to be a godsend. He explained that the device was portable, battery powered, and depending upon the particle size filter (called an inertial impactor) selected, could measure particles either in the size range of total suspended particles (TSP), i.e., everything that can float in the air (up to 50 microns), or respirable particles (RSP), i.e., only those particles which can be inhaled through the nose into the lung (3.5 microns or less). He said his machine displayed the measured values digitally as two-minute averages that could then be recorded by hand on a data sheet. TSI developed and marketed it to industrial hygienists for occupational health protection of workers in industry. Then he said, "if you're interested in evaluating it, we have a sales representative, Gans & Pugh, in Alexandria, Virginia who can demonstrate it for you."

This was getting better and better: Alexandria was smack across the Potomac River from my office. I thanked Sem and quickly phoned the TSI rep, who promptly offered to come over to NRL to demonstrate it. The next day Mr. Pugh arrived and demonstrated the workings of this new device. It was everything I had hoped for: It had only one really significant drawback. The damned thing cost $3000! There was no way I could afford to buy it. However, I had an inspiration; "Can you loan it to me for a few days, so I can evaluate it?" "No problem at all," said Pugh, "keep it for a week or two if you like." A tremendous bonus was that Gans & Pugh were also sales representatives for 40 other products, and they forgot that I had the loaner instrument, so I was able to keep it for *seven months*. I would treat it as seriously as any scientific project I researched for NRL. Collecting the data I needed to support GASP's efforts with the County Council was now a viable possibility, but I had to move fast. And that required a Partner-In-Crime.

ADAPTING INDUSTRIAL HYGIENE TO INDOOR AIR POLLUTION

So, I immediately called up Al Lowrey, my best friend and jogging partner, fellow toastmaster, fellow gourmet clubber, and go-to-guy for Friday afternoon pizza and beer. Al was a Yale-trained PhD who worked at NRL's Laboratory for the Structure of Matter, which was led by Dr. Jerome (Jerry) Karle. Jerry Karle would win the Nobel Prize in Chemistry with mathematician Herbert Hauptman in 1985 for their work determining the molecular structure of crystals using x-ray diffraction. Jerry's wife, Isabella, a fine self-taught crystallographer in her own right, also worked in the same group as head of the X-Ray Diffraction Section. Her X-ray diffraction experiments elucidating molecular structure were crucial to Jerry's Nobel, and Isabella herself would receive several prestigious scientific awards. Many scientists in that community, including her husband, believed that she should have shared the prize for laying the foundations for Jerry's work (CE&N, 2017).

Al was a theoretician who did computational chemistry for this high-powered group. His arcane computer programs, compiled in trays full of decks of punched cards as long as his leg, took so much computing time that they had to be run overnight on NRL's mainframe CDC 3800 computers, which occupied a huge frigidly air-conditioned room in a dedicated building. Al recruited John Konnert, a crystallographer in Jerry Karle's lab who ran with us every day, to assist by smoking pipes and cigars for our controlled experiments. John refused to smoke cigarettes. So Al, a nonsmoker, volunteered. He barely managed to smoke one cigarette for our experiments, but nearly barfed in the process. I wore a gas mask to avoid breathing the fumes during our study. Together, we performed a series of controlled experiments measuring the growth, equilibrium, and decay of secondhand smoke from cigarettes, pipes, and cigars smoked in a mechanically ventilated vacant office we commandeered in NRL's computer building. We followed up with additional controlled experiments in a naturally ventilated den in Al's basement to see how rapidly smoke dissipated by absorption on room surfaces and airflow through the building envelope.

John Botkin, an NRL ventilation engineer, proved indispensable. His advice opened up a whole new world to us, by explaining how ventilation systems worked. He emphasized the importance of ASHRAE, the American Society of Heating, Refrigerating, and Air Conditioning Engineers. ASHRAE was the professional organization of mechanical engineers that prescribed the ventilation rates that were the basis for the building codes used for designing the ventilation systems in commercial buildings. Botkin was an absolute gold mine of information; he introduced me to what later became my bible: *ASHRAE Standard 62-73, Standards for Natural and Mechanical Ventilation,* which was then the prescriptive basis for design procedures and guidelines for ventilation rates in "all indoor or enclosed spaces that people may occupy, except where other applicable standards and requirements dictate larger amounts of ventilation than this standard." Standard 62 was, and remains in its subsequent iterations, the basis for ventilation requirements for building codes for commercial, institutional, and residential buildings in North America when adopted by ANSI, the American National Standards Institute. In addition, Standard 62-73 specified maximum default occupancies for each building type (e.g. commercial, industrial, and government). This proved to be invaluable for modeling purposes.

Section 1.0 of ASHRAE 62-73 stated its purpose and scope: *"This standard [replacing the ventilation section of ASA Standard A53.1 dated May 23, 1946] defines ventilation requirements for spaces intended for human occupancy and specifies minimum and recommended ventilation air quantities for the preservation of the occupants' health, safety, and well-being. Good ventilation practice exists when clean ventilation air is provided in sufficient quantities to maintain the required oxygen, carbon dioxide, and other air quality levels in the space under consideration."* Section 3.3 specified in part that, *"AIR shall be considered unacceptable for ventilation use in accordance with this standard if it contains any contaminant in a concentration greater than one tenth the Threshold Limit Value (TLV) currently accepted by the American Conference of Governmental Industrial Hygienists."* Table 1 specified the acceptable level for "Particulates: 60 $\mu g/m^3$, annual average, and 150 $\mu g/m^3$ short-term level, not to be exceeded more than once per year." The basis for this acceptable level was otherwise unspecified "Federal criteria for U.S. by 1975," for outdoor air. So here we had ASHRAE applying the criteria for outdoor air for judging the acceptability of indoor air.

ASHRAE later became so important for indoor air pollution control that it would become a major target of disruption by the tobacco industry's lawyers and its moles. ANSI/ASHRAE Standard 62-1973 presented minimum and recommended ventilation rates for 266 building types and became the default basis for most state ventilation codes. ANSI oversees the creation, promulgation, and use of thousands of norms and guidelines that directly impact businesses in nearly every sector, and its endorsement was vital for Standard 62's widespread adoption nationally. The 1973 standard would be updated in 1981; an unholy alliance of the Tobacco Institute and the Formaldehyde Institute concerning the way the standard treated tobacco smoke and formaldehyde vapor prevented the 1981 standard's endorsement by the ANSI (Jansson, 1999). To mollify these obstructionists, ASHRAE eventually caved in, raising the minimum ventilation rate so that these conflicts disappeared in the 1989 revision. Standard 62-1989, *Ventilation for Acceptable Indoor Air Quality* became widely used until its revision in 1999, when ventilation rates designed to "accommodate smoking" would be finally and irrevocably abandoned. As we shall see, the road to that signal achievement would be marked by sustained brutal interference with the ASHRAE 62 committee by Big Tobacco.

Because ventilation systems are mainly the arcane province of mechanical engineers, let me explain, as simply as possible, a few basics. There are two common types of system in common use: the first is the constant flow type, in which intake fans pull in a fixed volume of outdoor air per hour into the building (designed to dilute indoor air contaminated by carbon dioxide and odors from human metabolism), with part of the ventilation air being recirculated (for energy conservation) and part being pumped outdoors by exhaust fans (to remove air contaminants). A thermostat in the room sets the air temperature. A damper inside the ductwork controls the relative amounts of fresh and recirculated air supplied to the conditioned space. It is supposed to be set to provide a recommended minimum of outdoor air to dilute carbon dioxide from human metabolism. Under this system, the airflow remains continuous. This type is typically used in restaurants and bars.

The second type is the variable air volume (VAV) system, whereby the volume of supply air is governed by the same thermostat that monitors room temperature. This type is most often used in office buildings to conserve energy. Under VAV, ventilation air is also comprised of mixed outdoor air recirculated air. However, if heating or cooling is not called for by the thermostat, the airflow will diminish to a preset minimum. I have observed in many low budget buildings I have visited that the preset was dialed down by building management such that the room airflow goes to zero. This leads to periods when the space is not being ventilated, and pollution levels will spike accordingly.

In 1979 there were three regional building codes in use by localities in the U.S.: BOCA (East Coast and Midwest), ICBO (West Coast & Midwest), and SBC (Southern). While a non-industrial building's design ventilation rate at installation had to comply with minimum flows specified by the local building code, these code-specified rates were not (and still are not) enforced after occupancy. So in practice, design outdoor air supply rates in buildings were actually upper limits, complied with at the whim of building owners and operators for whom energy conservation was often more important than fresh air, to the great detriment to the health and comfort of commercial building occupants.

ASHRAE Standard 62-1973 specified the design occupancy in persons per thousand square feet of floor area and recommended outdoor air ventilation rates for an enormous variety of commercial and industrial buildings, including offices, restaurants, bars, theaters, hospitals, auditoriums, bowling alleys, retail stores, factories, and the like. This default design information was absolutely vital for our mathematical modeling since these buildings were all places where people then smoked freely. To the extent that the building was not in compliance with the code-specified rates, the theoretical model would tend to under-predict the concentration. Few building owners would deliberately choose to over-ventilate their buildings because heating or cooling fresh outdoor air costs money in most climates in most seasons.

By 1979, while smoking prevalence had declined from its peak of 42% in the 1960's to 33% of the U.S. adult population (38 percent of men and 30 percent of women), because both the population and cigarette marketing had increased, there were still 51 million smokers, who smoked ever more fiercely, consuming an all-time high of 620 billion cigarettes, equal to 12,000 cigarettes per smoker per year, or 33 cigarettes per smoker per day. With the typical smoker smoking two cigarettes per hour during a 16-hour waking day, at ten minutes per cigarette, a single smoker would spend a third of every waking hour smoking. So, on the assumption that in a group, smokers smoked randomly, for every three smokers in any workplace, restaurant, or bar, one cigarette would always be burning, generating a constant stream of secondhand smoke (Repace, 1980, 1985, 2007).

The less technical reader might want to skip this paragraph. Thus, in our approach to analyzing or predicting secondhand smoke measurements, our model assumed, as a default, that one third of building occupants were smokers. And a restaurant at full design occupancy according to ASHRAE Standard 62, would hold a maximum of 70 persons per 1000 square feet (or per 100 square meters). Then, at the population average smoking prevalence in 1979, an estimated one third of 70 persons (mixed smokers and nonsmokers) in a restaurant at full occupancy would be expected to be smokers, yielding about 23 smokers, and each of these would be smoking one third of the time, so theoretically, we should expect an average of 7.7 smokers actually smoking at any instant, or 11% of the total number of occupants present. And since the design ventilation rate for a restaurant specified by Standard 62 was 20 cubic feet per minute per occupant (occ), the constant-volume flow rate of diluting outdoor supply air would be, assuming as a default, a ten foot ceiling [(20 ft^3/minute-occ)

(60 min/hour) (70 occ/10,000 ft^3)] = 8.4 air changes per hour. The density of smokers in such a space at full occupancy would then be 7.7 smokers per 10,000 ft^3, or 2.7 smokers per hundred cubic meters of floor space, in metric units. Based on what is known as the mass balance model for indoor air pollution, and assuming uniform mixing over the time period of interest, the smoke concentration in the air would then be proportional to the ratio of the smoker density to the rate of removal of the pollution, i.e., the air exchange rate, times a factor which incorporated the mass emission rate of the cigarette, pipe, or cigar. Note that the space volume, which appears in both the numerator and denominator, cancels out of this ratio, so the fact that we could only estimate, rather than measure, the ceiling height would not affect the accuracy of the model.

We now had within our grasp the means to predict the concentration of tobacco smoke in any building, by knowing just three things: the design occupancy, the smoking prevalence, and the space volume. The deposition rate of smoke particles on room surfaces, which added to the ventilation rate due to outdoor air exchange, and the particulate emission rates of typical cigarettes, pipes, and cigars, in an Occam's Razor approach, would be incorporated as fixed default parameters in our model, and determined experimentally. Our major controlled experiment was designed to yield this information: we simply needed to measure the smoke generation rate from a number of smokers smoking several of the most popular brands of cigarettes, plus the growth, equilibrium, and decay of tobacco smoke in the room, including the supply air flow rate for a room in a mechanically ventilated building. By adjusting the coefficient of our equation to fit the experimental data, this would incorporate the mass emission rate of the cigarettes as well as the sorption rate of tobacco smoke on the walls, plus the room mixing. We would then have a mathematical model capable of interpreting and generalizing the actual measured smoke concentrations in a wide variety of buildings where people were smoking.

The next logistical problem facing us was finding a ventilated room in an office building and obtaining several volunteer smokers. John Koontz, an environmental engineer who headed the air pollution control section of the Prince George's County Health Department, solved this problem for us. As luck would have it, Koontz was a member of the Prince George's Environmental Coalition, and he and I frequently discussed air pollution issues. I explained to him what we needed, and why we needed it. Koontz not only provided us with access to a county office building conference room in his department, but also – amazingly – recruited seven volunteer smokers from the health department staff! The plan for our experiments sprang fully formed in my mind; I instinctively knew exactly what needed to be done: request the smokers to smoke in a relay such that four were smoking at any one time over the course of an hour, so as to produce a steady generation of cigarette smoke. This would ensure a uniform growth curve readily amenable to curve fitting. Figure 8 shows the author running the controlled experiment with four of seven volunteer smokers from the Prince George's County Department of Health in Greenbelt, MD, in 1978. My shirt reeked so much afterwards I just tossed it out. I employed two box fans to mix the air so that the concentration measured by monitor would be independent of location in the room. This would ensure a smooth increase of concentration with time and a good curve fit to determine the model parameters.

Al and I set up the Piezobalance and recorded the data with a stopwatch over the course of an hour. Clara Gouin volunteered to record the smoking times and cigarette brands for each smoker. In this manner, we generated a data set that could be used to calibrate our theoretical model. We measured the smoking rates, the room size, and the ventilation rate in the room and recorded the mainstream tar levels of each cigarette as reported by the Federal Trade Commission, as well as the butt lengths after smoking.

The fine particle (PM$_{3.5}$) background level in the 22 ft by 22 ft (484 ft^2) conference room (3990 ft^3 or 113 m^3 in volume) prior to smoking was 53 micrograms per cubic meter ($\mu g/m^3$) with two box fans running to ensure thorough mixing. We measured its ventilation rate at 1.2 air changes per hour using an air flow meter borrowed from my lab at NRL. ASHRAE Standard 62-73 recommended from 7 to 15 cubic feet per minute per occupant for conference rooms at a default occupancy of 70 persons per thousand square feet. So, a roughly 500 ft² conference room would have a design occupancy of 35 persons. For 35 persons, the minimum design air exchange rate would be (35 occupants)(7 ft³/min-occupant)(60 min/hour)/3990 ft³ = 3.7 air changes per hour. Predictably in this era of obsessive energy conservation due to the 1973 oil-shocks, this county government-occupied building had a ventilation rate about a third of what it should have been for maximum occupancy. After a half-hour of smoking, the fine particle concentration increased to a whopping 2000 µg/m³, forty times background.

To put this into perspective, 2000 µg/m³ was the same order of magnitude as the particulate pollution that persisted for a week in the deadly London Smog of 1952, slowly suffocating 12,000 persons forced to breathe it round the clock for several days. At the 33% smoking prevalence in 1978, one would expect 11 to 12 regular smokers out of 35 persons. However, there were seats for 50 persons in this conference room. Our model predicted that this much smoke would be expected if 11 ordinary smokers were present in this conference room, smoking at the U.S. average of 2 cigarettes per smoker every waking hour. In other words, the level we measured was indicative of what one might actually encounter as a nonsmoking office worker attending an all-hands meeting in smoke-filled office building conference rooms as of the late 1970's.

FIGURE 8. JAMES REPACE RUNNING A CONFERENCE ROOM EXPERIMENT IN THE AEROSPACE BUILDING IN GREENBELT, MD, WITH 4 VOLUNTEER SMOKERS IN 1978. (AUTHOR'S PHOTO).

The next step was to perform a field study to assess what the particulate levels were in actual occupied public-access buildings under normal conditions, in both smoking and smoke-free buildings. Al, Clara, John, and I conducted field surveys with the Piezobalance in a number of smoking venues. These included restaurants and bars, bowling alleys and bingo games, lodge halls and sports arenas, hospitals, homes, and hotels, at weddings and in waiting rooms, and in dinner theaters and in dives as well as a dinner party in a private home. We recorded the particulate levels and average number of active smokers present and estimated the space volume by pacing. We also made comparison measurements in buildings where smoking did not occur, such as libraries, churches, and nonsmokers' homes, as well as outdoors, at bus stops, and on highways.

REGULATING SMOKE IN MARLBORO COUNTRY

When we had collected sufficient data, I wrote it up, and John, Al, and I returned to the County Council, to demonstrate our results before the Environmental Matters Committee and Chairman Francois. I displayed bar graphs on poster boards that Al and I had made up. We showed that tobacco smoke polluted the air with particulate levels far exceeding those on the busy commuter routes, US 50 in Maryland and US 295/ Kenilworth Ave. in Washington DC during the morning and evening rush hours over an entire week. This comparison placed our measurements into a perspective that could be widely understood by the general public. By contrast, in buildings without smoking, the air quality was little different from the low levels found outdoors away from busy roadways. These science-based arguments impressed Chairman Francois so much that he immediately ordered committee staff to draft a bill. Some days later, the committee held a 2½-hour work session resulting in draft legislation that proposed smoking sections in restaurants and workplaces.

More than 50 persons attended. Local restaurateurs and tobacco lobbyists vehemently denounced the proposed bill as "excessive governmental regulation," a mindless refrain that soon became a hackneyed argument employed by the tobacco industry and business advocates in support of continued tobacco smoke pollution of restaurants, workplaces, and public buildings. The draft bill proposed that most public access places – including workplaces – must have a separate area set aside for smokers. With one exception, the local supermarket chain, Giant Foods, every local businessman attending the hearing opposed the bill. As proponents of the legislation, Clara Gouin, John O'Hara, Bill Alli (representing Federal Employees for Nonsmokers' Rights at the State Department), and Lowrey and I again bombarded the committee with our scientific data and pleas for smoking and nonsmoking sections in restaurants. The Piezobalance proved to be an effective prop to engage the interest of both the legislators and the press.

The following day, on March 31, 1978, an article in the *Prince George's Journal* reported: "the most effective bill proponent was Jim Repace, another representative of Bowie GASP, who brought with him a $3000 machine that measures the amount of smoke and pollutants in the air. Repace said that outside – even in heavy traffic – the machine rarely exceeded 100 micrograms per cubic meter. Indoors, Repace said, he has received readings as high as 700 micrograms per cubic meter in restaurants where smoking was permitted, and 2000 micrograms per cubic meter in office building conference rooms." It helped to have a visual aid for the committee to focus on, a handy technique I learned in Toastmasters. The Piezobalance data carried the day. Councilman Francois, the Bill's sponsor, pronounced the proposed bill to be "a good start, and we now need to go back to the drawing board."

The final hearing on the revised Council Bill CB-26-78 was held on Tuesday, July 25th 1978. It was attended by 100 speakers and many more observers, and lasted for five contentious hours. As described by the *Prince George's Journal* on the 28th of July, the often-raucous hearing "was marked by loud applause, catcalls, and emotional pleas from both friends and foes of the bill." O'Hara did an absolutely magnificent job in organizing the turnout; he packed the council chambers with more than 100 supporters of the legislation using the GASP Newsletter and telephone chains. The bill's proponents included several doctors and Bowie GASP members, as well as asthmatic members of the public, who persuasively argued that smoking in restaurants was a health issue. Our opponents were mostly small businessmen and of course, tobacco industry representatives (including four from the Tobacco Institute), who insisted that passage of the bill would hurt the county's economy, another bogus argument that would come into widespread use.

The final version of the bill proposed banning smoking in public schools, county buildings used for public meetings, health care facilities, theatres, and movie houses, as well as retail stores that employed more than 8 employees. Restaurants seating 75 persons or more, doctors' waiting rooms, hospital lounges and emergency rooms would have to set up separate smoking and nonsmoking areas. Violators of the restrictions would be fined $25, and offending building owners or managers would be fined $50. The bill, embracing the entire county of nearly 700,000 persons, was enacted into law and went into effect in 1979. It was the very first law restricting smoking in restaurants in a tobacco growing state and enacted in a tobacco-growing county with a wholesale tobacco barn a mile away from the county council chambers, in *Marlboro Country*. And it was the first major victory for Bowie GASP.

On September 7th 1978, The Subcommittee on Tobacco of the Committee on Agriculture of the US Congress held Potemkin hearings on the effect of smoking on nonsmokers. The Tobacco Institute published a small five-page fold-out brochure summarizing the hearings, entitled "*Science and Smoke*." It was all smoke and no science. It featured photos of the band of the industry's paid academic consultants who had parroted the industry's propaganda line. They sliced the baloney very thick. Sherwin Feinhandler, a lecturer in anthropology at Harvard, said "There is always a danger in allowing pressure groups to influence legislation restricting individual freedoms simply to alleviate annoyance…". Dr. Kenneth Moser, a professor of medicine at UC San Diego, opined that "there is not now a sufficient body of evidence of hard facts to support the view that public smoking poses a health hazard to the lungs of the nonsmoker." Norman Heimstra, Dean of the Graduate School at the University of South Dakota, stated that, "not allowing smokers to smoke during sustained operation of complex psychomotor tasks will result in poorer performance." Reuben Cohen, president of a survey research organization, reported that "in a survey of 4000 various annoyances in 799 people in 49 different metropolitan areas in the U.S., only two percent were related to smoking."

And the band played on: Theodor D. Sterling, a professor at Simon Fraser University in British Columbia, averred that "A large number of studies have now demonstrated that indoor air in most public and many private structures is polluted with toxic fumes, dusts, and allergens," but that "Smoking is a minor and often insignificant contributor to pollution in buildings." Walter M. Booker, a consulting pharmacologist, said he had "reviewed the published literature for reliable data which demonstrates whether a nonsmoker absorbs tobacco smoke in public places, and whether the amount is sufficient to cause adverse health effects," concluding that it "does not support the theory that a nonsmoker absorbs amounts which can cause harm." Edwin Fisher, M.D., a professor of pathology at the University of Pittsburgh said his review of the literature enabled him to conclude that there was an absence of compelling data. He was quoted saying, "In God We Trust, others must provide data," and that "What we need is good scientific data before I am willing to accept and submit to the proposition that smoking is a hazard to the nonsmoker." Dr. John Salvaggio, a Professor of Medicine at Tulane and Director of the Allergic Disease Center, reported that "very reputable investigators at the Mayo Clinic have strongly suggested that there are no allergens for man in cigarette smoke." The Chairman of the Subcommittee, Rep. Walter B. Jones, summarized: "A good deal of what we have heard constitutes unassailable scientific facts." In today's parlance, Mr. Jones, they would be characterized as "alternative facts."

Meanwhile, back at the NSA, O'Hara briefed the new NSA Director (Vice Admiral Bobby Ray Inman) and other senior staff on March 22, 1979. He presented data suggesting that smoking was costing the Agency 151 person-years of lost productivity annually, plus untold thousands of dollars attributable to premature deaths and disabilities. Added to this were the expense of extra ventilation to purge secondhand smoke from the air, as well as the cost of cleaning tobacco tar deposited on building surfaces. O'Hara authored an article in the *NSA Newsletter* of March 1979, entitled *Tobacco Smoke and Indoor Air Quality*. This had a significant effect: in April 1979, a newly formed NSA task force initiated a five-day "Smoking Education Program" with video presentations, booths providing data on the harmful effects of tobacco smoke, with displays outside of the auditorium, and invited several external health experts as speakers. I was one of those speakers, giving a talk entitled "Health Effects of Tobacco Smoke on Nonsmokers." As I approached NSA's auditorium building at Fort Meade, two marines dressed in combat fatigues and armed with submachine guns took my slides and escorted me into the packed auditorium. The program was a resounding success and led to the identification of hundreds of people who were suffering from tobacco smoke in their workplaces [NSA, 2002]. However, complete relief from secondhand smoke at NSA still remained elusive.

To stave off restrictions on Big Tobacco's poisonous products and their toxic emissions as a new generation of environmental and health and safety laws became enacted, the Best Congress That Tobacco Money Could Buy proscribed regulation of tobacco products under every possible law. These included: the Federal Hazardous Substances Act, the Consumer Product Safety Act, the Fair Packaging and Labeling Act, the Controlled Substance Act, as well as the Toxic Substances Control Act. Moreover, a tobacco-friendly federal court ruled that tobacco products could not be regulated under the Food, Drug, and Cosmetics Act. Worst of all, because federal law is pre-emptive, individual States were precluded from regulating tobacco products (Repace, 1981). Since EPA had *interpreted* the term "ambient air" in the Clean Air Act of 1970 to mean outdoor air (although the Act actually did no such thing), and since OSHA was mainly focused on health and safety in the dangerous and heavily polluted industrial trades, their research arms ignored secondhand smoke studies.

To summarize: as of the late 1970's, there was a dearth of applied research to support the notion that secondhand or environmental tobacco smoke was actually harmful to nonsmokers in the same way that smoking was harmful to smokers, rather than just a nuisance or minor annoyance as the industry insisted. This lack of data had created a vacuum in which tobacco industry propaganda and disinformation flourished and could be employed to defeat smoking ban legislation. Without this crucial scientific base, policy makers, both in government and in business, many of who were smokers themselves, could dismiss passive smoking as a minor annoyance issue unworthy to be regulated.

In this vein, nonsmokers around the country began to lobby legislatures for legislation to restrict smoking in certain indoor public spaces, especially restaurants. In 1979, 38 states introduced 116 nuisance control bills to restrict smoking in various public places. In response, the tobacco industry pushed back hard, flexing its considerable lobbying muscle as states attempted to respond to demands to regulate public exposure to secondhand smoke. This concerted assault largely overwhelmed the efforts of nonsmokers' rights activists. Only seven laws survived in seven states, a 94% success rate for tobacco lobbyists. In 1980, just one out of 49 such bills passed, a 98% success rate for the bad guys. Over this two-year period, Big Tobacco continued to reign supreme in scuttling state clean indoor air laws. During that time I testified in legislative smoking ban hearings in eight jurisdictions in the metropolitan Washington DC area. In each instance, one or more representatives of the tobacco industry and numerous allied business supporters testified in opposition to these bills. Nonsmokers' rights advocates I spoke to in several states confirmed that this was a usual phenomenon. In four of the eight jurisdictions in the D.C. area (where there was a large public turnout in support) most of the legislation was passed, but often only after several tries (Repace, 1985).

Because of the absence of NIOSH, OSHA, or EPA in the debate over secondhand smoke, other than a few sporadic studies by various researchers measuring carbon monoxide in smoking rooms, there had been essentially no significant scientific research to support public policy on workplace smoking bans. Furthermore, indoor air pollution studies were in their infancy in the mid-1970's. What had been missing in the legislative debates over clean indoor air laws was measurement of the actual pollution levels in real-world settings and comparison of those measurements with health-based air quality standards meant for the protection of public health. Word of our success spread rapidly, and I began to be invited to present our results to a wide variety of groups. In 1979, months before our paper would appear in *Science*, I gave a well-received talk, *Total Exposure to Air Pollution*, to the National Commission on Air Quality.

THE NEW SCIENCE OF SECONDHAND SMOKE

The persuasiveness of the data we presented in obtaining CB-26-78 bill's passage inspired me to publish the results of our efforts in a scientific journal. I suggested to Al that our measurements might be useful to others who were attempting to pass similar legislation, and he heartily agreed. We had kept careful records of our controlled experiments and field studies, as well as the derivation and validation of our mathematical model for the prediction and interpretation of indoor tobacco smoke concentrations as a function of smoker density and air exchange rate. I drafted a 100-page paper on my Royal office typewriter in stages, and revised it in concert with Al, whose insights were invaluable. Our manuscript went through 40 drafts, which Al and I cut and pasted and had professionally re-typed several times at $1 per page. Finally, after months of careful crafting, we decided it was ready to submit for publication.

Our measurements encompassed a wide range of smoking prevalence, ventilation rates, and building occupancy in 38 different indoor locations, most of them in the Washington DC metropolitan suburbs, some in Washington, DC, with the bulk located in Prince George's County Maryland, reflecting our need for local data to submit to the county council. The smoking locations included ten restaurants, three cocktail lounges, two bingo games, a dinner-dance hall, a bowling alley, a sports arena, and a dinner party. The nonsmoking locations included two libraries, a church, five vehicles during rush hour carpool commutes, and five residences, as well as five weekday measurements in five different cars in my nonsmoking NRL carpool morning and night for a week. We also had measurements in the smoking and nonsmoking sections of a Denny's Restaurant in Laurel, MD, and the Goddard Space Flight Center cafeteria in Greenbelt, MD. While visiting back home in Westchester, I added a smoke-free bagel bakery for good measure. In sum, we had made $PM_{3.5}$ measurements in a total of 56 different microenvironments, not counting the venues where we conducted our controlled experiments. Outdoor measurements were made for comparison in all cases. These measurements showed that cigarette smoking created levels of fine particle air pollution much higher than in cars on busy commuter highways, and far in excess of levels in similar spaces where smoking did not occur, where pollution levels were little different from outdoors. Our model suggested that the scatter in the data could be explained by the variation in air exchange rates for various buildings per the ASHRAE Standard. [A later statistical analysis of our data (not performed in the original manuscript) shows that 51% of the variation in fine particle pollution data was due to variation in the density of smokers, while only 8% of the variation in that data was explained by the variation in person density.]

Our controlled experiments performed in homes and offices confirmed that the smoking of cigarettes, pipes and cigars rapidly increased particulate pollution ten to fifty times above background. A field study of particle levels during a church bingo game in a 150,000 cubic foot church with 20 active smokers among 150 persons had pollution levels of 279 micrograms per cubic meter, 9 times as high as levels, 30 micrograms per cubic meter, during Sunday services in the same space with 300 persons present, lighted votive candles, and zero smokers. In other words, a hair under 90% of the particulate air pollution in the church during the bingo game was due to smoking. Overall, when 21 of our smoking buildings were compared with our measurements in 17 nonsmoking buildings, the average level of particulate pollution in the smoking buildings was 6.5 times as high as the nonsmoking buildings. Further, with smokers present, all of the spaces we measured were polluted beyond the level of EPA's 1970's-era clean air standards, some dangerously so, whereas none of those levels were exceeded in nonsmoking buildings or outdoors. To put this into additional perspective, EPA's 24-hour average health-based air quality standard for particulate air pollution (TSP) in the 1970's was 250 micrograms per cubic meter; today's standard, a product of a generation of epidemiological research, is 14% as great, at 35 micrograms per cubic meter ($PM_{2.5}$) the most harmful fraction of TSP. And we observed, courtesy of Wayne Ott, my EPA colleague, that the population spent 90% of its time indoors.

I performed a demonstration measurement in a Denny's Restaurant in Laurel, MD, that was taped for television with Clara Gouin of National GASP (Figure 9). O'Hara was with me when we made the original measurements at Denny's, which was the only local restaurant we could find with a nonsmoking section. He had arranged with the manager to do the measurements. Our measurements uniformly demonstrated marked differences in pollution levels between smoking and nonsmoking sections in cafeterias. This provided clear evidence that while nonsmoking sections reduced secondhand smoke exposure, they did not eliminate it.

Now ponder this. The implications of our results for the way society approached public smoking were profound. We showed that the only two variables controlling secondhand smoke pollution of buildings were smoking and ventilation. Our measurements showed that ventilation wasn't working as a control measure. There were limitations on increases in ventilation rates due to the high energy cost and the need for increasing fan power and duct size to accommodate higher flow rates. Moreover, there was no practical way to enforce increases in ventilation rates. This meant that the only viable control measure was to restrict smoking. In other words, it was implicit in our results that all that would take to clean the air was a 25-cent **NO SMOKING** sign.

We wrote that even the very high 30 fresh air changes per hour then extant on passenger jet aircraft such as the Boeing 707, could not remove enough smoke from the cabin air to protect the health of flight attendants. And further, that given its carcinogenicity, "tobacco smoke presented a serious health risk to the health of nonsmokers that deserved as much attention as outdoor air pollution." We concluded, "Clearly, indoor air pollution from tobacco smoke presents a serious risk to the health of nonsmokers. Since this risk is involuntary, it deserves as much attention as outdoor air pollution." Society treats involuntary risk far more stringently than voluntary risk.

After polishing our manuscript, we settled on an appropriate peer-reviewed journal for publishing our work. Al and I were used to publishing in specialized scientific and engineering journals that were unsuitable. I was a subscriber to the widely read weekly journal *Science*, which published scientific articles in a wide variety of disciplines including public health. It had a riveting science news section that I read avidly each week. Al and I decided that *Science* would be our best vehicle for publication, and we hand-delivered the manuscript to its editorial offices in downtown Washington. To put this choice into proper perspective, *Science* magazine was (and remains today) a highly prestigious and influential international forum for reporting ground-breaking scientific research. Moreover, it is highly selective, publishing only a few percent of the most-worthy submissions, favoring those of high impact potential and wide appeal to a multi-disciplinary audience. We marched solemnly in the outer office of Philip Abelson, Science's editor-in-chief, and presented it to his secretary. Afterward, Al and I went running along the Potomac during our lunch hour, our usual daily routine.

To understand the physics behind our mass-balance Habitual Smoker model, let's conduct a thought experiment: In your head, imagine you are filling a bathtub with fresh tapwater. As it reaches the brim, you partially open the drain and adjust the flow such that the amount of water running in and draining out exactly balance. In this case, the tub is full and the water level remains constant. Now imagine pouring a jug of India Ink slowly and steadily into the tub, so that the water turns jet-black. Then, in an effort to clarify the water, you open both the faucet and the drain completely to increase the flow of clean water into the tub to the maximum extent possible, while maintaining the same volume of water in the tub. But all the time you continue to pour in the ink at a steady rate. In this manner, you can visualize that the water will turn from dark black to some shade of gray, but it will never become crystal clear again.

OK. Got that fixed in your mind? Now imagine replacing the tub by a room, the water with air, and the faucet and drain with a mechanical ventilation system. Then imagine replacing the ink with a group of smokers puffing away. Remember that the ventilation rates are designed essentially to control carbon dioxide and body odor, and thus are fixed by building codes. By the same token, the ducts and fans are sized to supply only that amount of air prescribed by code. The room size is of course fixed and cannot be changed. So, it should now be obvious that the only way the level of secondhand smoke in the room can be decreased is by decreasing the amount of smoking. To put it pithily, it has been a long-held principle of ventilation engineering, that ventilation is no substitute for source control. In 1858, the ventilation pioneer Max Von Pettenkoffer said: "If there is a pile of manure in a space, do not try to remove the odor by ventilation. Remove the pile of manure."

In essence, we showed that trying to control secondhand smoke air pollution by ventilation was like trying to eliminate the stink from a pile of horse manure by opening the barn door. This was the threat our research posed to Big Tobacco, and they were well aware of it.

Figure 9. Clara Gouin with James Repace in the nonsmoking area of Denny's Restaurant, 1978 '(Author's photo).

CHAPTER 5

PIONEERING INDOOR AIR POLLUTION AT THE EPA

"Dear Bill: Here is the material on James Repace which I mentioned to you over the telephone – and which you wanted. Please do not do anything with it until you talk to me. I haven't had a chance to talk to Horace about it. I have a plan. I am not in the picture yet regarding Repace's Science Magazine article. However, that particular publication may be the least of our concerns."

Letter from Frederick Panzer, Vice President, The Tobacco Institute, to William Shinn,
Head of Tobacco Unit, SHOOK HARDY & BACON. March 12,1980. [TTID, Bates # TI07391764]

In 1978, we bought a new 9-passenger Chevy Suburban and a camping trailer, plus a 16-foot inflatable boat with a 25-horse Johnson outboard, for our family vacations. Justine was 14 years old, Max was 12, Nick, Paul, and Alex were 9, and Jon was 7. We camped in the Blue Ridge Mountains of Virginia, and at the beachfront campgrounds of Assateague and Chincoteague Islands in the Delmarva. We travelled to the pleasant beachfront campgrounds of the Atlantic and Gulf Coasts of Florida. Every summer we joined my Mom, my brother Bob, his wife, Linda and their friends in rented beach bungalows in the North Carolina Outerbanks for a week. We feasted on seafood, drank wine, played cards and water-skied on the ocean with our inflatable. Life settled into a pleasant routine. My radiation-hardening research was going well. Research staff were required to publish a minimum of one peer-reviewed paper per year; I had published four papers in the previous two years, and was promoted to a GS-12, a PhD-level civil service grade at NRL.

However, my public interest science research on secondhand smoke had instilled in me a burning desire to work in the field of environmental, occupational, or public health. I yearned to transform my avocation into a professional career. In 1977, at the age of 39, I applied for a job as an industrial hygienist at the Department of Agriculture and struck out. Next, I applied to be a health policy analyst at the Department of Health and Human Services. It was located in the Hubert Humphrey Building a few blocks from the U.S. Capitol, one floor down from the office of the Surgeon General. When the hiring manager interviewed me, he announced that I was "the most qualified of 50 applicants for the job," and then invited me to sit down in a chair, a good thirty feet away from his desk in his huge office. This was a subliminal social signal, and I intuited that the right move was to simply pick up my chair and move it in front of his desk. But at that moment, he lit up a cigarette. This was a big turnoff, and so I remained where I was. Unsurprisingly, that opening fizzled out as well. OK, so occupational and public health were out. I kept searching for federal jobs in these fields with no luck.

One day I received an invitation to a meeting on smoking restriction legislation in the Capitol Hill office of Rep. Robert F. Drinan (D), a Jesuit priest who represented Massachusetts during the 1970's. As the attendees introduced ourselves, one announced that he was an NRDC attorney. Later, I asked him if David Hawkins who had intervened with the EPA five years earlier on my behalf over the issue of sludge incineration, was still around. He replied that in 1977, Hawkins had been appointed by President Jimmy Carter to be the Assistant Administrator for Air, Noise, and Radiation (OANR) at the U.S. Environmental Protection Agency and was initiating major new air pollution control programs pursuant to the 1977 Clean Air Act Amendments. This was a welcome surprise.

NRL expected its staff scientists to present papers at scientific conferences at least once a year. Accordingly, I had submitted an abstract to the 1977 SOS technology summer workshop of the Nuclear and Space Radiation Conference of the Institute of Electrical and Electronic Engineers (IEEE). It was held at a resort in Vail high in the Colorado Rockies. My presentation proposed to discuss the effect of ionizing radiation on silicon-on-sapphire (SOS) devices as a function of growth rate of the epitaxial layer of silicon on the sapphire (aluminum oxide) substrate. I had discovered that the growth rate significantly affected the buildup of positive charge in the integrated circuits made from these devices, changing their electrical properties when they were exposed to megarad levels of radiation, such as might be encountered in a nuclear burst or in the Van Allen Belt surrounding the earth.

On the way to Vail from the airport in Denver, I carpooled with Hap and our sponsor from the Defense Nuclear Agency (DNA). Mr. DNA asked me what I was going to present. When I told him, he said, "You can't talk about that, its classified." I was stunned. "What? Who classified it?" He said, "I did, just now." I asked him to show me any objectionable material in my overhead slides. He said I couldn't show anything that disclosed that the growth rate of the epitaxial silicon layer affected the radiation resistance (hardening) of the device. Determined to present something, I negotiated with him and he designated several offending slides to be removed.

At the session, I delivered my bowdlerized presentation in a sour mood. I felt cheated. Afterward, as I sat in the audience, my mind wandered. I began to ruminate over the implications of Hawkins' appointment. I imagined myself working with him at the EPA, solving air pollution problems in the public interest as I had in the Blue Plains, Piscataway and Incinerator #5 affairs. Making the world a safer place for people rather than for ballistic missiles or space satellites. Doing public interest science full time. I blew off the next session, walked into the Lodge's business office, and requested a typewriter. I sat down and composed a letter to Hawkins, summarizing my technical background, especially my familiarity with ionizing radiation. I touted my accomplishments as a public interest scientist with the Prince George's Environmental Coalition, working on sludge and trash incinerators, mobile sources, and of course, my work on environmental tobacco smoke. I suggested that he needed someone like me on his staff to provide him with scientific input on air pollution control policy. I wrote that I would very much like to come to work for him at EPA. I marked the envelope "Personal" and posted the letter. Some weeks later, Mr. DNA changed his mind, and I was allowed to publish (Repace JL, 1978; Repace JL, Goodman AM, 1978).

In addition to the technical program, one afternoon was devoted to fun. I went whitewater rafting down the Colorado River with a bunch of the engineers. That evening, Joe S., a prominent electrical engineer who worked in radiation hardening research for Northrup Grumman on the West Coast, and I went out together to a Greek bouzouki nightclub for drinks. Joe was an amateur magician who became so adept that he had been admitted into the professional magician's society. We went up to the bar and ordered drinks, and after a while, Joe struck up a conversation with a group of a half-dozen rather tipsy young women who were holding a bachelorette party. Joe began to demonstrate his slick magic tricks. One of them involved a couple of sponge balls enclosed in his hand that he would magically make appear and disappear. He asked the bride-to-be to hold the sponge balls, squeeze them tightly and they would turn into "something that she was thinking about." Upon opening her palm, they sprang open into a large pink replica of the male genitalia. The women screamed in delight. Over the course of the evening we had drunk a lot of ouzo. Joe was already three sheets to the wind. The rest of us weren't far behind.

Our group moved over to the lounge area where Joe started performing card tricks with an oversize deck. Suddenly, the gal who was getting married snatched Joe's cards, tossed them in the air and shouted, "We're playing 52-Pickup!" As Joe got down on his hands and knees to pick up his cards, the bride-to-be deftly swiped Joe's sponge phallus, and all the women headed toward the exit. Spotting the theft, I shouted, "Hey, Joe, they're stealing your prick trick!" He shouted, "Damn it, I went all the way to Washington DC to buy that!" With that he sprang up, ran to the doorway and threw out his arms, blocking the exit. The women screamed and, turning back, they ran headlong into the kitchen, creating pandemonium among the chefs. Soon the kitchen staff began pouring out of the kitchen in dismay. The bouncer appeared, restrained Joe, and the manager escorted the tipsy young ladies out the door. The kleptomane still held Joe's sponge phallus in her clutches. As the last one filed out, I asked her, "What will she do with that thing?" "She's getting married tomorrow, and wants to throw it out in her bouquet…".

TAKING ON COAL FIRED POWER PLANT POLLUTION IN ALEXANDRIA, VIRGINIA

My fourth major attempt to limit smokestack air pollution in the Washington Metro Area came on Saturday, September 3rd 1977, when the *Washington Post* published my lengthy Letter to the Editor, which they captioned: "***Warning: Power Plants May Be Hazardous***." Prior to publication, the Post's Fact Checker called, asking me for my references. The text of my letter read as follows:

To The Editor: "I read your Nov. 18 editorial "Pepco and Clean Air" with great interest. It might interest your readers, especially those living within a few kilometers of Pepco's coal-fired Potomac River electric generating plant, to be made aware of some of the other health hazards of such plants.

Pepco station C, as the Potomac River Plant is called, is a 500 megawatt generating plant that burns as much as 1 million tons of coal per year. In doing so, it has polluted the air with as much as 20,000 tons of sulfur dioxide (per year) and 500 tons of ash, according to figures provided by the Alexandria Health Department. Those are gross pollutants that are familiar to everyone. What is not generally known is that coal contains trace elements, present to only a few parts per million (ppm), which become important when the trace element is highly toxic, when the flue-gas cleaners are inefficient for its removal and when large amounts of coal are burned.

Mercury is such a trace element. It is a cumulative poison capable of causing damage to the central nervous system (Mad Hatter syndrome) and of causing birth defects. Mercury in coal has been found to range from 0.18 ppm to above 300 ppm. The efficiency of electrostatic precipitators for mercury is near zero. According to a Pepco official, the Potomac River Plant has burned West Virginia coal. Mercury analyses of West Virginia coals have averaged 7 ppm. This means that this plant has been producing mercury at a rate of 7 tons per year, or more than 17,000 grams per day. A mercury smelter on the same site would be limited to 2,300 grams per day, by federal law.

Published reports on mercury fallout from chlor-alkali plants in Sweden indicate that most of the mercury is dumped within a few kilometers of the stacks. This is also likely to be the case for Pepco's plant, which has substandard stack heights prone to aerodynamic downwash of the plume. Moreover, a high-rise apartment house, Marina Towers, is located right next to this plant.

Recently, while analyzing soil samples of arsenic-contaminated earth from herbicide spills in downtown Alexandria, the Health Department found unusually high mercury levels that could not be explained. I suggested that these might be due to the Pepco plant, and that high levels would probably be found in the soil throughout Alexandria. Subsequent soil tests showed levels as high as 18 ppm.

The background level for a rural area would be expected to be no more than 0.2 ppm. If mercury absorption in Alexandria is a problem, analysis of hair or urine specimens would likely disclose it. I believe this should be done. It would appear that the conventional wisdom, which permits fossil-fuel power plants to be sited in populated areas, or conversely, for areas around such plants to become populated, leaves much to be desired."

James L. Repace
President
Prince Georges Environmental Coalition
Bowie

The Post added a two column-wide (4"x4") photo of smokestacks belching black smoke appearing above the text and enclosed the entire ensemble in a box. There was no response from the Alexandria Health Department. I wondered why public officials who should know better could be so negligent. I had watched this plant for years from my office window at NRL and had often seen its plume fumigating Marina Towers when the winds blew strongly from the South. A few years earlier, I had visited the plant in connection with an APCA meeting, by invitation of Pepco officials. They mentioned that they bought a megaton of coal from West Virginia every year. Huge mounds of the stuff sat outside in the yards. I became privy to the data on the mercury content of coal from an article I read in *Science*. I tried to interest an activist professor of environmental chemistry at the University of Maryland College Park to get some of his graduate students to gather hair samples from Marina Towers residents for mercury analysis. He professed interest, but never acted. Appallingly, this plant remained in operation until December 21st 2012, thirty-five years later.

WHAT WOULD YOU DO IF YOU WORKED HERE?

Not long afterward, I received a call from Paul Stolpman, Director of OANR's Office of Policy Analysis, and chief of staff for Assistant Administrator (AA) Hawkins, requesting an interview. Stolpman, an economist, had previously worked in operations research under former Defense Secretary Robert McNamara. After the interview, I heard nothing for several months. Then he invited me to a second interview. Again, I heard nothing for several months. Finally, one day as I was in my lab at NRL, quietly making capacitance-voltage measurements on irradiated silicon-on-sapphire devices, I received a call from Stolpman requesting a *third* interview. This time, I was not only interviewed by Stolpman, but by three members of his policy staff. I was delighted to discover that all three had highly technical backgrounds: one was a former high-energy physicist, the second was an industrial engineer, and the third was a lawyer with a graduate degree in chemistry. I felt that I would fit in very well with this group.

The engineer, puffing away on his pipe, posed an odd question: "What would you do if you came to work here?" I responded without hesitation: "Well, if I had the freedom to choose what I wanted to work on, it would include radioactive pollutants, stationary source emissions, as well as criteria and hazardous air pollutants." And I recounted my work on incineration. I avoided mentioning my work on secondhand smoke. He puffed on his pipe and nodded at my reply. A few weeks later, Stolpman called with a job offer to transfer at the same GS 12 level which would facilitate my hiring, with a firm promise of promotion to a GS 13 within a year. I immediately accepted, and joined the Office of Policy Analysis, the staff office of Assistant Administrator

Hawkins. O'Hara was thrilled, and Lowrey advised me to adapt to the EPA culture. Ultimately, when it comes to getting an important government job, push is vital, but pull works better than push.

On a Monday morning in February 1979, I reported for work on the second floor of the EPA Headquarters complex at Waterside Mall in Southwest Washington, where Stolpman's office was located. The Assistant Administrator's Office was located on the 9th floor of the West Tower, with a spectacular view of the Potomac. Stolpman had a large office, about 13 feet by 30 feet, with floor-to-ceiling wall of windows on the long side. It was nicely carpeted and was decorated with a large wooden desk, a Scandinavian-style sofa for guests, and a small refrigerator. It opened onto a 70 ft^2 anteroom along the same window-wall, and had a doorway opening into the corridor. This tiny room, not much bigger than a prison cell, was my assigned office space, the smallest among our group of five. Since this area was also the entryway to Stolpman's office, my office was effectively the width of my desk, with just enough room for my chair, plus a wooden credenza behind me. The chair was broken. At Paul's suggestion, I swapped it for a fancy one with wheels covered in burnt orange burlap that I swiped from a conference room down the hall. Then I furnished my miniature office with a coffee maker, a small refrigerator, a desk lamp (I hated fluorescent light), and a short privacy barrier. Although this office space was extremely modest, it could not have been a better strategic location for me. While waiting for Stolpman to receive them, his visitors often struck up a conversation with me, perhaps under the mistaken impression that I was his administrative assistant, and I soon met a lot of important people at EPA. As an added attraction, my office was isolated from the secretarial bay, where our two secretaries puffed away on cigarettes all day long.

Stolpman, as Chief of Staff for the AA, was in the Senior Executive Service, and thus himself a VIP. As such, he was afforded the two secretaries, and his hand-picked staff of five included a lawyer/chemist, George Sugiyama, who functioned as Stolpman's consigliere, and David Horowitz, a former high energy physicist who worked on transportation planning. On the side, Horowitz published arcane theoretical transportation research papers, that involved rotation of vectors in Hilbert Space (don't ask), in obscure journals. The engineer worked on stationary source (smokestack) air pollution. He retired not long after I joined EPA, and his name has faded from my memory. His replacement, Ms. Margaret Kelley, was a chemist.

Horowitz and 'Skip' Luken, one of Stolpman's two economic consultants, frequently traveled abroad to attend international conferences and present papers. I inquired as to the source of their funding, as international travel funds were as scarce as hen's teeth throughout the federal government unless you were at the managerial level. They told me about the German Marshall Fund, a non-profit NGO and a reliable source of international travel funds for scholars wishing to give papers at conferences in Europe. This was a welcome revelation. It became a mainstay of funding for my overseas trips to present at conferences throughout the 1980's and mid-1990's.

At the end of the workday, our staff would usually gather in Stolpman's office and he would open his refrigerator and break out wine and beer while we traded information on the day's events as well as a bit of EPA gossip for a half-hour or so. Paul divided top EPA managers into two categories, the good guys and the assholes. He was seldom wrong. He would often punctuate his pronouncements with a mirthless laugh. I liked his style. In addition to his two consultants, he had a speechwriter, Tom Super, who worked for the AA. Super had a cabin by the Patuxent River in Southern Maryland where we had occasional staff parties. Stolpman informed me that while staff nominally reported to him, we actually served as science policy staff for the Assistant Administrator. He emphasized that, "I expect you to find something you'd like to do and become an expert at it. You can attend all meetings of the Assistant Administrator, whose agenda is published weekly, and your job is to provide him with expert advice. There's only one rule: *Don't Ever Be Wrong*." This came as a very welcome surprise, as it gave me carte blanche to be creative. I didn't waste a single moment.

INDOOR AIR POLLUTION GETS ON THE FEDERAL AGENDA

To get my feet wet, George Sugiyama helpfully volunteered to get me started on 5-day National Environmental Policy Act (NEPA) Reviews of the environmental impact of proposed federal regulations by other federal agencies. This simple act would have far-reaching societal consequences. NEPA Reviews were triggered when a federal agency developed a proposal to take a major federal action. Each agency's response reflected its own unique mandate and mission. The NEPA review process results in one of three possible actions by EPA on sister agencies' proposals: a categorical exclusion from review, a determination of no significant impact, or a finding that the proposal requires an environmental impact statement (EIS) to be prepared by the initiating agency. EPA had just five working days to file any written comments.

The very next day, George dropped two proposals by the U.S. Department of Energy (DOE) on my desk: DOE's Residential Energy Conservation (RCS) Program, and its New Building Energy Performance Standards. This was astoundingly fortuitous. I recognized immediately that both of these proposed rules mandated energy conservation measures that would result in reduced air exchange rates in both residential and commercial buildings. And that reduction would inevitably cause an increase in indoor air pollution unless indoor source emissions were curtailed. I drafted reply comments for the Assistant Administrator's signature. They went out essentially unchanged over Hawkins' signature to Maxine Savitz, DOE's Acting Assistant Secretary for Conservation and Solar Applications. It would provoke an upheaval in federal policy and research both at EPA and DOE concerning indoor air pollution. It would also have ripple effects in a couple of dozen additional federal agencies. An *Environment Reporter Newsletter* dated March 7, 1980, summarized it this way:

> "EPA's major concern, according to a December 19, 1979, letter to DOE from David Hawkins, EPA assistant administrator for air noise and radiation, is that 'decreased ventilation (from energy conservation measures) may significantly increase indoor levels of carbon monoxide, nitrogen oxides, tobacco smoke, respirable particulates, formaldehyde, and radioactive radon and its decay products.' In his letter to Maxine Savitz, DOE acting assistant secretary for conservation and solar applications, Hawkins requested that DOE 'delay implementation of those few elements of the RCS program which would significantly reduce ventilation rates in residences until control strategies for radon and its decay products and other critical indoor pollutants are developed.'
>
> Hawkins and Savitz met on February 27 to discuss the problem of indoor air pollution and reached an agreement that homeowners and other participants in the RCS program would be told about of the effects on air quality of reduced ventilation." … Jim Repace, an environmental protection specialist in EPA's policy analysis office and a negotiator for the agency with the DOE, said on March 3 that the current draft is 'acceptable, except for the radon portion.' He said that DOE has been very cooperative in including information in the RCS material to participating consumers of potential problems associated with reduced air exchange rates and of measures which can be taken to alleviate these problems."

My efforts led to support from a wide variety of staff at EPA and DOE, who rapidly became invested in the new area of indoor air pollution. This included EPA's Office of Radiation Programs, which realized the potential for the build-up of radon gas in tighter homes that would increase occupants' risks of lung cancer. I made important contacts with middle-level managers at DOE, including Howard Ross at DOE HQ, and Craig Hollowell, who ran the Indoor Air Research Program at DOE's Lawrence Berkeley Laboratory in California. Craig was a master political operator, visiting Washington frequently to advance his program's interests. He always dropped by when in town, and we began to cooperate closely in advancing indoor air programs at both agencies.

The *Environment Reporter* article attracted the unholy interest of the Tobacco Institute. A letter from Fred Panzer to Bill Shinn on this article had one of its paragraphs marked for emphasis with a line in the left margin emphasizing Panzer's greatest concern:

Could Become Major EPA Program

"The issue of indoor air pollution could become a major EPA program in the coming decade," Repace said. It is demonstrable that "indoor air quality from major pollutants is grossly inferior to outdoor air quality" in many areas. Repace said The Clean Air Act gives EPA no specific authority for regulating indoor air quality, but Repace said the question of what powers the agency has in this field is "almost irrelevant" until more studies are done.

And another paragraph had a large asterisk in the margin with the provocative phrase underlined:

*Studies Under Way

David Berg, advisor for EPA energy conservation in the Office of Environmental Engineering, agreed with Repace, stating that EPA cannot propose indoor air quality standards until more information is available [TTID TI07391764].

That the industry viewed the prospect of indoor air quality standards as posing a significant threat to the industry's profits suggests it had long been aware that the use of its products polluted the indoor air, no matter what it said publicly. And this prospect would soon provoke the industry into frenetic and sustained opposition, as the letter from Panzer to Shinn indicated (TTID, T107391764).

David Berg proved to be an effective advocate for indoor air within the Office of Research and Development and became involved in interagency talks as well. The negotiation between EPA and DOE, which was initially spearheaded by Howard Ross and me, soon led to the formation of an ad hoc inter-agency working group on Indoor Air Quality, which would be formalized by Congress in 1983 as the Federal Interagency Working Group on Indoor Air Quality. Its mission was to coordinate federal indoor air quality research while facilitating the exchange of information among federal agencies, state and local governments, the research community, the private sector and the general public. The working group was co-chaired by EPA, DOE, the Consumer Product Safety Commission (CPSC), the National Institute for Occupational Safety and Health (NIOSH), and the Occupational Safety and Health Administration (OSHA). This soon nurtured indoor air pollution research at EPA and DOE, supported by Congressional appropriations under SARA, the *Superfund and Related Agencies Act*, Title IV. A number of other federal departments and agencies also participated as members. I was off to a running start.

'THE TOTAL EXPOSURE CABAL'

I joined the Air Pollution Control Association (APCA) in 1979, where I met several other indoor air pioneers, notably John Yocum, who chaired APCA's TT-7 Indoor Air Quality Committee and who I eventually discovered was one of the reviewers of the paper we submitted to *Science*. Another important member was John (Jack) Spengler, a prominent Harvard professor in the Department of Environmental Health who was deeply involved in the famous Harvard Six City Study of indoor and outdoor air pollution (Spengler, et al., 1981). I would subsequently hold the posts of membership chair and secretary in the TT-7 Committee (1981 – 1984). At TT-7, I also met Demetrios Moschandreas, who turned out to be another reviewer of our paper. (The remaining two reviewers were Amos Turk and Helmut Wakeham, who were not members.) All but Wakeham informed me personally long after our paper was published.

At my first APCA conference in Cincinnati in 1979, I was appalled to find the large auditorium filled with clouds of tobacco smoke. After the installation and pep talk by the incoming president, he asked if anyone in the audience had questions or comments. Rather than speak from the floor without a microphone, I ascended to the podium, commandeered the microphone, and spoke plainly to the several hundred attendees: "I'm Jim Repace from EPA's Office of Policy Analysis in Washington. This is my first APCA conference, and I am compelled to say I'm absolutely appalled at the air pollution from tobacco smoke in this space. I think an organization devoted to air pollution control ought to be ashamed of this. I hope that our incoming president will rectify this travesty." The president-elect, plainly taken aback by my challenge, nevertheless rose to the occasion, announcing that he would put the issue on his agenda. The following year, smoking was banned from the meeting hall at APCA meetings.

Later that year, Jack Spengler, who knew of my work from APCA's Indoor Pollutants committee, and whose environmental monitoring program at Harvard was funded by EPA's Office of Research and Development (ORD), mentioned my work to two researchers in ORD, Wayne Ott and Lance Wallace, and recommended that they get acquainted with me. Subsequently, I got a call from their branch chief, Chuck Brunot, and I made a short technical presentation summarizing our forthcoming *Science* paper to Chuck, Wayne and Lance. We turned out to be kindred spirits. Wayne and Lance were two of the most important ORD players in nudging EPA into indoor air quality research under the rubric of measuring total human exposure to environmental pollution (taking into account contaminants in air, water, and food). We became part of a network of respected back-channel insiders with direct access to the top policy makers in OANR and ORD. We collaborated both informally and formally, trading action memos through our respective Assistant Administrators, and were successful in promoting both a policy and research interest in indoor air pollution at EPA.

Subsequently, Wayne introduced me to the concept of time-activity patterns that sociologists use to quantify, inter alia, how much time the population spends in certain microenvironments. Most importantly for indoor air research, since pollutant dose is the product of concentration and exposure duration, Wayne had compiled data showing that people spend nearly 90% of their time indoors, with the home and the workplace being the two most-frequented microenvironments. Wayne, Lance, and I co-authored a paper, *Total Human Exposure to Air Pollution,* which I presented at the Montreal Conference of the Air Pollution Control Association (APCA) in 1980 (Repace et al, 1980). I incorporated this important exposure analysis concept of time-activity patterns in our 1980 *Science* paper. The concept would become essential for our future risk assessment of passive smoking and lung cancer.

By 1984, congressionally-funded indoor air research programs would be firmly established at both EPA and DOE. Later, Lance and Wayne would run EPA's Total Exposure Assessment Methodology (TEAM) studies that developed and deployed methods to measure the total human exposure to carbon monoxide, toxic VOCs, and carcinogenic air pollutants such as benzene, using a probability-based sampling network to estimate the body burdens of U.S. urban populations. The TEAM studies, comprising 800 people in 8 cities representing a statistical sample of 800,000 U.S. residents, would establish that indoor air pollution was the major contributor to population exposure to many pollutants, including carbon monoxide, volatile organic compounds (VOCs) and fine particulate matter. On the other hand, Wayne's personal monitoring study of carbon monoxide exposure of the population showed that motorcycle riders had the highest exposure to CO of any subgroup in the U.S. One of the more interesting findings from Lance's VOC study was the discovery that smokers exhaled more toxic benzene, toluene, xylenes and styrene than nonsmokers, suggesting that these were prominent chemicals emitted by cigarettes. The TEAM study found that homes with smokers had 50% higher levels of benzene, a potent leukemogen, than homes without smokers.

Lance conducted the large-scale personal monitoring (PTEAM) study of people's exposure to fine particulate matter $PM_{2.5}$, which would show the importance of secondhand smoke for actual population particulate exposure. Earlier, the TEAM Study had measured exhaled breath, which is also a biomarker of the blood concentration of various chemicals. At that time, according to Lance, direct blood sampling for these chemicals was too insensitive. When CDC's blood sampling attained a higher sensitivity a decade later, they found the same Dirty Dozen chemicals (BTEX, perc, TCE, chloroform etc.) that TEAM had found a decade earlier in indoor air (L. Wallace, personal communication).

In 1979, I organized and coordinated EPA's Offices of Air Noise and Radiation and Research and Development to submit comment on the revision of ASHRAE Standard 62-1973, *Standards for Natural and Mechanical Ventilation.* Standard 62 had been modified in 1975 by ASHRAE Standard 90-75, *Energy Conservation in New Building Design*, to use the lowest possible outdoor air ventilation rates for energy conservation purposes, in the aftermath of the oil crisis of 1973. EPA's official comments emphasized that the reductions in outdoor air supply would lead to increased indoor air pollution. As a result, ASHRAE renamed the revised Standard, finally published in 1981 as *Ventilation for Acceptable Indoor Air Quality.* This greatly alarmed Big Tobacco, which perceived it as a major threat. And as we shall see, it would lead the industry to attack and seriously disrupt the ASHRAE 62 revision process for many years using a variety of very dirty tricks.

In addition to the Interagency Working Group on indoor air pollution, I quickly became involved in several other high-profile issues, developing expertise in EPA's regulatory programs and policy development. I began to review and comment on EPA's proposed rules on criteria air pollutants such as carbon monoxide, sulfur dioxide, nitrogen dioxide, and particulate matter, as well as its risk-based regulations on the hazardous air pollutants, arsenic, lead, and coke oven emissions. I worked on incineration of hazardous wastes on land and sea, and ionizing radiation. I made frequent trips to EPA's Research Labs in Research Triangle Park, North Carolina to absorb their research and convey headquarters policy guidance from their prime customer. I also managed to piss off several smokers among the lab's management when I objected to their smoking in the conference room during our meetings. After I convinced them to smoke in the hall, I dumped their ashtrays in the corner behind a wastebasket. My days of suffering secondhand smoke in silence were done. Finito.

I vigorously promoted EPA's new policy interest in indoor air pollution, working with outside groups such as ASHRAE, and the Air Pollution Control Association (APCA), as well as various medical groups such as the New York Academy of Medicine, the American Lung Association (ALA), and the American Cancer Society (ACS). I developed vital contacts throughout EPA's policy and research infrastructure. I maintained a close relationship with Don Shopland of the Department of Health and Human Services Office on Smoking and Health, which produced all the Surgeon General's Reports. Don had been there since the landmark 1964 Surgeon General's Report on Smoking and Health, and had an encyclopedic knowledge of the subject that I had drawn upon when drafting our *Science* paper. We often met for lunch and became lifelong friends.

THE GO-TO-GUY FOR IAQ

I soon became known as the go-to-guy for indoor air quality (IAQ) information both inside and outside EPA, and in early 1981, I was invited to present on the subject to the President's Council on Environmental Quality. I recorded a lengthy interview, "Office Hazards," with Dan Zwerdling of National Public Radio about poor indoor air quality in office buildings. I developed a network of contacts with the national press, remaining mindful only to discuss the science, never to advocate any specific policy. I responded to all policy questions with the time-tested response that "that's above my pay grade." In this manner, I came to be trusted as a knowledgeable spokesman who would not embarrass the Agency. I spoke at the American Cancer Society's National Conference on The Changing Cigarette in New York, on the future of indoor air pollution regulation at Argonne National Laboratory and gave a paper on "An Approach to a National Indoor Air Pollution Policy" (which had the appropriate policy disclaimer appended) at the Second International Symposium on Indoor Air Pollution, Health, and Energy Conservation at the University of Massachusetts, Amherst.

Calls to EPA HQ on indoor air issues were routed to me by the AA's secretaries, and I fielded inquiries from personnel in several other federal agencies as well as the public and the press. I dispensed advice on solving a wide variety of indoor air pollution problems. For example, managerial personnel in certain offices at the Library of Congress complained they were sickened by poor indoor air quality. These included a division head; some of the staff appeared to be suffering from chemical sensitivity due to the exposure. I made a site visit to see if I could help; I diagnosed it as a ventilation deficiency problem. This appeared to be a common problem in the low-budget federal, state, and local government buildings of that era, whose managers cut fresh air to save on costs; they were often oblivious to the costs to the health of rank-and-file office workers.

THE ICE QUEEN COMMETH

In the 1980 presidential election, Jimmy Carter went down in flames, a hapless victim of the spectacularly botched attempt to rescue U.S. diplomatic hostages in Iran, which he had foolishly micromanaged. The Iranian hostage crisis had its roots in the CIA-assisted coup in 1953, which overthrew the democratically elected government of Mohammed Mossadegh and replaced him with their stooge, Shah Reza Pahlevi. The Iranians never forgave the U.S. Carter's bungling of the crisis enabled the anti-regulatory Ronald Reagan to ascend to the Presidency. In early 1981, Reagan replaced Administrator Douglas Costle, a Carter Appointee, with the two-pack per day Marlboro smoker and former Colorado legislator, Anne M. Gorsuch, as the new EPA Administrator. Gorsuch, known as one of the "Colorado Crazies" during her tenure in the Colorado State legislature, seized control of the EPA in May 1981.

During her tenure, Gorsuch briefly married a Colorado rancher named Burford, which soon ended in divorce. As the Washington Post (2004) observed, Gorsuch-Burford was "A firm believer that the federal government, and specifically the EPA, was too big, too wasteful, and too restrictive of business, Ms. Burford cut her agency's budget by 22 percent." Gorsuch-Burford's motto was oxymoronic: "Doing More With Less." She approved a Reduction in Force Plan that involved firing 40% of headquarters staff and demoting and exiling others to remote locations. However, because this induced a flood of the best professional staff to leave, few firings were actually necessary to carry out her austere budget; for FY 1983 she proposed an additional 20 percent cut. Former EPA Administrator Russell Train (1973 to 1977) a Nixon-Ford appointee, fumed, in a Washington Post Op Ed, "It is hard to imagine any business manager consciously undertaking such a personnel policy unless its purpose was to destroy the enterprise." [Layzer, 2012]. Of course, this was precisely its purpose.

"DOING MORE WITH LESS"

In 1981, Gorsuch began to reorganize the Agency. She immediately cut EPA's budget for research and planned to virtually eliminate indoor air research by October 1st of 1981. Stolpman was removed as head of the Office of Policy Analysis and unceremoniously booted out of his fine office. Gorsuch appointees descended like vultures, looting every stick of Paul's elegant office furniture. I now reported to Ms. Louise Giersch, another member of EPA's Senior Executive Service who had fallen into disfavor with the Reaganistas. She had been given the "lateral arabesque" treatment, made famous in the 1969 book, *The Peter Principle*. In Louise's case this involved an involuntary transfer from EPA's Region 9 Office in San Francisco to its Washington DC Headquarters, in the expectation that this would force her to retire. Instead, she and her husband defiantly moved to Washington. In 1979, Louise, a chemical engineer by training, and a former City Council member in Antioch, in the San Francisco Bay Area, had been director of the U.S. Environmental Protection Agency's Air and Hazardous Materials Division, Region 9, which includes California, Nevada, Arizona, and Hawaii.

I got along very well with Louise, an intelligent, dignified, and very pleasant person. I never met Louise's husband, whom she described as a reluctantly addicted smoker who had unsuccessfully moved heaven and earth for years, in futile attempts to quit, until in desperation, he succeeded via hypnotism. By that time, I had received my promotion and moved to a large private office, next to George Sugiyama on the second floor of the Mall, with a huge window wall. Louise's office, next to mine, was the same size, about 150 ft², but the ventilation supply duct had never been connected to the ceiling grille when the offices were remodeled. In other words, her unventilated office was a typical half-ass Town Center Management botch.

In consequence, my office had double the ventilation airflow it should have had, creating such a cold draft that I needed to install a home-made baffle to direct the frigid air away from my desk. For good measure, I blocked off the ceiling return flow grille to positively pressurize my office, keeping my door closed to shut out the cigarette smoke generated by our two secretaries puffing away in the bay outside our suite of offices. With the change in administrations, Hawkins departed and returned to NRDC in May 1981. In 1990, he would become Director of NRDC's Air and Energy Program, and in 2001, Director of NRDC's Climate Center. The Climate Center focuses on advancing policies and programs to reduce global warming.

Reagan replaced Hawkins with Kathleen Bennett, a former Director of Legislative Affairs for the American Paper Institute. Paper mills were notorious for their abysmally odorous air pollution. Naturally, in Gorsuch's eyes, this eminently qualified Ms. Bennet for her job. Neither I, nor any of the old Policy Analysis staff were invited to meetings with Bennett, and we soon had little in the way of official work to do. So, I dragged a surplussed word processor into my office, kicked the door shut, and taught myself to use it. Bennett immediately abolished EPA's Noise Office, and the Office of Air, Noise, and Radiation (OANR) became the Office of Air and Radiation (OAR). This was an environmental crime of great magnitude with persistent adverse consequences. The Noise Program was entirely voluntary and worked by persuading manufacturers to make equipment that made less noise; less noise also meant less wasted energy. It also meant fewer hard-of-hearing senior citizens. In the 1970's, heat pumps, pool pumps, air conditioners, jet skis, powerboats, snow mobiles, boom boxes, jack hammers, diesel trucks, and the like made a hell of a racket. So did the engines in lawn mowers, leaf blowers, weed whackers, chainsaws, motorcycles, cigarette boats, and add-on resonant mufflers for cars, as well as the large engines in jet planes. In recent years, jet ski and powerboat manufacturers, threatened with widespread bans of their products from lakes due to the noise, have managed to equip them respectively with quiet modes of propulsion and silent mufflers, provoked by the threat to their bottom lines. Energy-efficient air conditioners, and pumps of all kinds have quieted down as well. As for the others, America remains a very noisy country, a boon to hearing aid manufacturers.

David Mudarri, a GS-15 PhD economist who had headed EPA's Noise Abatement program, was transferred to our staff and also found himself without any work assignments. Meanwhile, many other frustrated EPA staffers had left the Agency in disgust. Anne Gorsuch soon earned the sobriquet "The Ice Queen" as a result of her frigid treatment of EPA professional staff. I, like the remaining Office of Policy Analysis staff, was reduced to drafting replies to routine requests from Congress, attending useless meetings, and other busy work.

If Carter had been re-elected, Hawkins was prepared to request explicit Congressional authority for EPA to regulate indoor air pollution, and he directed me to prepare a position paper for Ed Tuerk, the éminence grise of the EPA air programs who had helped set the first outdoor air quality standards. I had prepared a 50-page position paper for Ed. Ambient Air in The Clean Air Act has been commonly – but incorrectly – interpreted to apply only to air outside of buildings. This was simply how EPA viewed its brief in the early 1970's. However, with the advent of The Ice Queen, these indoor air regulatory plans remained interred in Tuerk's files, like the Noise Program, never to be resurrected. In 1982, I presented a condensation of my position paper at the Second International Conference on Indoor Air Quality, and later published it as a 16-page paper in *Environment International* (Repace, 1982). As of May 2018, it had been cited 54 times, and on Research Gate, it remains one of my most-read papers with more than 600 downloads.

CHAPTER 6

INDOOR AIR POLLUTION, TOBACCO SMOKE, AND PUBLIC HEALTH

"Over a span of nearly two decades James Repace has carved out a career studying the harmful effects of tobacco smoke on indoor air quality. Along the way he has picked up some powerful enemies—among them the Philip Morris Cos, RJ Reynolds Tobacco Co and several members of Congress. These days of course the problem of 'secondhand smoke' is widely recognized and bans on smoking in public places can be found throughout the country. But when Repace began his research, in 1976, people were only beginning to recognize environmental tobacco smoke as a public health hazard."

[J. Kumagai, CAREER CHOICES Exposing the Dangers of Tobacco Smoke, Physics Today 48: 59-60, October 1995].

The Tobacco Institute, the industry's premier propaganda, disinformation, and dirty tricks organ, had been on high alert since the Roper Report was issued. The opening salvos in a new front line of the secondhand smoke war were traded in Washington, DC, in a March 1980 Channel 5 TV panel discussion. The program empaneled both nonsmokers who argued for nonsmoking sections in public places, and representatives of the tobacco industry in opposition. The latter included one Walker Merriman, the ubiquitous mouthpiece for the Tobacco Institute, as well as a local tobacconist, Dan Geller. In an odd coincidence, Geller had worked for the EPA Region III in sewage disposal management in the early 1970's. I had crossed swords with Geller in the P.G. County Council's public hearing several years earlier in the battle over sewage sludge incineration at Piscataway. Geller had defended the practice of sludge incineration. Before we went on, I greeted him in an anteroom, and asked what his role was on the program. He replied that "I am defending the sale of fine cigars and pipe tobaccos." I snarked, "You really know how to pick the losing side, Dan."

As the program began, a nonsmoking panelist led off by complaining about having to involuntarily breathe secondhand smoke pollution, Merriman interrupted, bloviating that "a nonsmoker would have to spend 100 hours in a smoky room to inhale the equivalent of a single cigarette." I fired back: "That's totally wrong and misleading; my research shows that indoor air pollution from tobacco smoke in restaurants and bars and the homes of smokers is far worse than air pollution from cars and trucks in rush hour on the highways of Washington, DC." Merriman retorted, "OK, Mr. Pseudo-Scientist, where is that research published?" I riposted, "In the journal *Science,* in two weeks." Merriman's jaw dropped and he became speechless. During the commercial break, my horns came out and I taunted Merriman. "Fooled you a bit, didn't I?" He glared at me, turned red, leaned into my face and snarled, "FUCK YOU!" Caught with their pants down, the Tobacco Institute would waste no time before translating Merriman's rage into clandestine action.

THE INDUSTRY DELIVERS A PRE-EMPTIVE STRIKE

On April 10, 1980, the Tobacco Institute's Director of Statistics, Marvin Kastenbaum, fired off a 3-page missive to Dr. Philip Abelson, the Editor of *Science*. Kastenbaum asserted that our impending paper – which presumably he had never seen – was 'scientifically faulty,' and implored Abelson *to refrain from publishing it*. Warming up, Kastenbaum played the ad hominem canard that 'Repace advocated violence against smokers.' Referencing a news article from the Fairfax County, Virginia, *Local Star* in 1979; he cited a passage: "After the Maryland House Environmental Committee voted to defeat a bill [advocating smoking sections in restaurants] whose passage he supported, Repace said, 'Now that the facts are clear, you're going to be seeing nonsmokers become a lot more violent, you're going to see fights breaking out all over'" [TTID T109020978].

This quotation, from *The Washington Star*, a conservative daily, clearly suggested that I had advocated violence against smokers. What had actually transpired during my impromptu street-corner interview initiated by the *Star's* reporter? As I passed him on the street, this reporter asked what I thought might happen in the wake of the bill's defeat. I responded with an anecdote: I had eaten lunch that day with a group of the bill's proponents whom I had never before met. Among these was a guy who introduced himself as Bill Wall. Wall, a Lincolnesque nonsmoker, asserted that while dining out, if smoke from a neighboring table drifted in his direction, he would politely request that the smokers extinguish their cigarettes because their smoke affected his breathing. However, if they refused or ignored him, he persisted, standing by their tables politely reiterating his demand over and over. This I thought was over the top. Unsurprisingly, Wall related that one smoker got so enraged that she clocked him in the kisser with her handbag. He pointed to his healing bruises to prove it. He said he did not attempt to fight back. I was shocked by Wall's tale. I had emphasized to the *Star* reporter that the defeated legislation would have obviated such incidents. I observed that it was reasonable to anticipate that as research increasingly showed how much pollution was created by smoking in restaurants, public disputes, even violent ones, between smokers and nonsmokers could proliferate. This was far from advocating or condoning violent tactics.

It was plain and simple yellow journalism. When I read the article in the local *Star* the next day, I was appalled. Foolishly, I failed to demand a correction. The *Star* article then became grist for the Tobacco Industry's propaganda mill that sought to prevent our *Science* paper from being used by nonsmokers as justification for restrictions on smoking in restaurants, by claiming it was zealotry dressed up to look like science. Although I would give hundreds of speeches and media interviews around the world without ever once demonizing smokers, the industry would make this libel a staple of its sub rosa ad hominem attacks on my reputation for years. Ironically, the *Washington Star* went bankrupt a little over a year later, with most of its staff joining the newly formed conservative newspaper, *The Washington Times* (Wikipedia, 2018).

On a roll, Kastenbaum expounded on his theme in an attempt to discredit our research: "[Repace's] personal point of view may interfere with the objectivity demanded by scientific research. Secondly, by publishing Mr. Repace's work, *Science* and the AAAS may become vehicles for a political cause with possible violent implications." Kastenbaum concluded his plea for censorship with this bizarre admission: "Although I do not know the specific comments of his forthcoming *Science* paper, I have assumed that it does not differ from others which he has placed in the public record for the past three years, for example, the submission on August 2, 1979 before the Civil Aeronautics Board…" [TTID T109020978].

How ludicrous Kastenbaum's demand must have seemed to Abelson. He had sent our initial 100-page manuscript to two peer-reviewers in early 1979. After the initial round of review, he sent us a letter stating, "*Science* might be willing to consider this paper for publication – if it is reduced by half." After several weeks of pruning and re-write, we resubmitted a revised manuscript at the requested length. To save time, we hand-carried it again to Abelson's office and delivered it to his secretary. On her desk lay a full ashtray with a smoldering cigarette. Al and I exchanged knowing looks. The office air was so still as a result of the poor ventilation that a thin stream of smoke rose untrammeled like a taut string to the ceiling. This was a poignant reminder of what the historian Allan Brandt aptly called the "Cigarette Century" in his scholarly book, and an illustration of how common smoking was in offices – even those of *Science's* editor.

Abelson then sent our revised manuscript out again for a second review, but unusually in our professional experience, to two *new* reviewers. Years later, through the release of secret industry documents, I discovered Kastenbaum's letter and the identity of one of the two new reviewers. It was none other than Helmut Wakeham, Vice President and Director of Research for Philip Morris. Wakeham first damned us with faint praise, saying "The authors are to be commended for their careful measurements of RSP and the wide variety of situations in which tobacco smoke might be an RSP contributor. Their experimental findings are in close agreement with Turk's equation as modified by all the assumptions that they make. Then Wakeham argued – without foundation – that with respect to our measurements in the church with and without smoking, "Undoubtedly the physical activity of the parishioners in church is not raising as much dust as the participants in the bingo game. One would expect that a considerable part of the RSP measured in the bingo came is due to other factors than smoking." What those "other factors" could be, Wakeham didn't opine.

We easily disposed of Wakeham's fallacious comment. The dust from people is largely large lint particles (>10 microns) that are much larger than the combustion-generated fine particle size fraction of tobacco smoke, as anyone with familiarity with aerosol physics knows. Thus, they would have been filtered out by the 3.5-micron inertial impactor which discriminates against larger particle sizes that we used in the Piezobalance. As for the dry skin flakes (0.5 to 10 microns), why should 150 clothed and sedentary bingo players shed more skin dust from their faces and hands than 300 actively moving parishioners marching to and from communion? Game, Set, and Match, Dr. Wakeham.

Wakeham then betrayed his true concern: "This reviewer recommends that these observations and calculations be published, possibly as a report rather than an article in *Science*, by the elimination of certain speculative material and with inclusion of some corrections as listed below," notably his demand that "*all implications regarding possible impacts of indoor air pollution on health be omitted*" (italics mine). This of course, would have vitiated our paper. What we hadn't seen was Wakeham's Confidential Comment to the Editor: *"Recommend paper not be published without revisions as indicated"* [TTID 10020209945].

Although we adopted those suggestions of Wakeham's that we found reasonable, we rejected outright his outrageous demand to excise our public health discussion, noting that the remaining three reviewers had all supported inclusion of those adverse health implications. In retrospect, getting a peer-review from a top industry scientist was an astute move by Abelson. It would later preclude the industry from complaining that they did not have a chance for input. Our revised paper, along with the editor's decision to publish our manuscript with the health discussion intact, alarmed Philip Morris researchers. In a secret memorandum from Raymond Fagan, a scientist at Philip Morris's research Center in Richmond VA, to Thomas Osdene, the company's Director of Research, Fagan betrayed what their scientists really thought: "I think that Repace and Lowrey did a good job in measuring respirable suspended particulates (RSP). Much of what Dr. Wakeham suggested has been accepted. In spite of that, the current version is damaging to the industry because of the extrapolations that Repace and Lowery [sic] make and then the unwarrented [sic] conclusions they come to." [TTID 504873564]. In order to meet *Science's* word limit, we had to sacrifice much valuable supporting experimental material, which we would publish in the *ASHRAE Transactions* two years later.

On May 2, 1980, our ten-page article, *Indoor Air Pollution, Tobacco Smoke, and Public Health*, was published in one of the world's premier scientific journals, after three years of painstaking work and forty drafts. Lowrey was identified as a research chemist at the Naval Research Laboratory, and I as an environmental protection specialist at the Environmental Protection Agency, as well as a former research physicist at NRL since most of the work had been done while I was there. We noted that *"This work was sponsored by the*

Prince Georges Environmental Coalition and was performed by the authors in their private capacity. No official support or endorsement by the Environmental Protection Agency, the Naval Research Laboratory, or any other federal agency is intended or should be inferred." This disclaimer was routine and required, while conveying that in our day jobs we were federal scientists. This burnished our credentials with an added patina of respectability.

The Abstract of our *Science* manuscript read:

> *"An experimental and theoretical investigation is made into the range and nature of exposure of the nonsmoking public to respirable suspended particulates from cigarette smoke. A model incorporating both physical and sociological parameters is shown to be useful in understanding particulate levels from cigarette smoke in indoor environments. Observed levels of particulates correlate with the predictions of the model. It is shown that nonsmokers are exposed to significant air pollution burdens from indoor smoking. An assessment of the public health policy implications of these burdens is presented" [Repace and Lowrey, 1980].*

A key conclusion of our research was that "Indoor air is a resource whose quality should be maintained at a high level. Smoking indoors may be incompatible with this goal."

Although Lowrey and I were unaware of it then, Earl Lane of *Newsday* had written an article on May 27th 1980, "New study cites hazards of smoky rooms," reporting on our *Science* paper. It was distributed by the L.A. Times-Washington Post News Service, and was reprinted in the *Louisville Courier Journal*. The *Courier Journal* article was copied and distributed to all 17 staff members of the Tobacco Institute by W.W. Wyatt, Jr. Lane's article reported that the Tobacco Institute attacked our work, asserting "They did not perform studies to see whether there would be health effects as a result of exposure to those particles … We think it is important to look at the whole of the evidences [sic] so far" [TTID 680024042].

OUR *SCIENCE* PAPER CHANGES THE DEBATE

In perspective, with the Clean Air Act's establishment of outdoor air quality standards and controls on stationary and mobile sources of air pollution to prevent recurrence of air pollution disasters, people had become increasingly aware of the health consequences of outdoor air pollution. To suddenly discover that many of the familiar smoky places where people lived, worked, and frequented, especially bars and restaurants, were polluted to levels far beyond those air quality standards as a result of smoking indoors came as a tremendous shock. We were gratified that our paper soon aroused enormous interest within the multi-disciplinary scientific community. Within a few months, we received a deluge of 180 postcards bearing reprint requests from all over the world, from Moscow to Papua New Guinea, and included a hand-written letter of praise from Dr. Melvin Calvin, the 1961 recipient of the Nobel Prize for Chemistry.

Despite the fact that our work was bootleg research, eight years later, the Naval Research Laboratory would include it in its list of the *Top 100 NRL Papers Produced from 1973 to 1988*, as judged by the total number of scientific citations, which, according to Google Scholar, had reached 126 by the end of 1988 (*NRL Labstracts*, 1993). To put this into perspective, the cumulative number of cites to Repace & Lowrey's Science Paper between 1980-1988 placed our paper in the top 0.44% of all NRL scientific papers published between 1945 and 1988 (Google Scholar, 2016; Garfield, 1990). In the early 1980's it provided one of the main pillars of scientific credibility for the nonsmoker's rights movement in its drive for clean indoor air laws.

Data from the *Science* paper is plotted in Figure 10, showing the respirable particle measurements we made in 17 microenvironments with smoking, including a house party, a Knights of Columbus lodge hall dinner-dance, 5 bars, 8 restaurants, two bingo games, the Prince George's County hospital emergency waiting room, a bowling alley, a sports arena during a hockey game, comparative measurements with and without smoking in the nave of a large Catholic church during a bingo game and Sunday services. Additional data points, measured in a dinner theater during smoking and nonsmoking nights as well as a wedding reception, from our ASHRAE paper in 1982 are included as well. To convey the data in an air quality perspective, all of the smoking buildings had respirable particle levels ($PM_{3.5}$) exceeding the level of the 1971 Annual NAAQS of 75 $\mu g/m^3$. Many of them exceeded the 260 $\mu g/m^3$ 24-hour average level of the 1971 National Ambient Air Quality Standard (NAAQS) for Total Suspended particles (TSP). While the standards incorporated daily and annual averaging times that were long-term measurements, nevertheless, it was manifest that levels this high amounted to very polluted air. On the other hand, none of the nonsmoking venues, including busy highways, exceeded the level of either measure. Moreover, as Figure 10 shows, there is a strong linear relationship (r = 0.71, with r=1 being a perfect correlation) between active smoker density, D_s, and respirable particle air pollution (RSP).

We attributed the scatter in the data (deviation from the straight line of the curve fit) in Figure 10 for equivalent smoker densities to differences in the effective air exchange rates (removal rates including ventilation plus surface sorption) for each venue. For example, with a ~40 $\mu g/m^3$ background subtracted, the Knights of Columbus lodge hall during a dinner dance had an RSP level of 660 $\mu g/m^3$ attributable to secondhand smoke, while the Reception Hall had a value of 220 $\mu g/m^3$, despite having nearly the same average smoker density, about 1.25 active smokers per hundred cubic meters of space volume. In the case of the Lodge Hall, the calculated effective air exchange rate is 0.98 air changes per hour, while for the Reception Hall, the air exchange rate is essentially triple, at 2.95 air changes per hour.

When we incorporated the averaging times in the air quality standards and made recourse to four hypothetical persons who had lifestyles involving radically different exposures to secondhand smoke, that resulted in dramatically different air pollution burdens for each of the four. For example, we posited that Nonsmoker *A* was a mailman who lived and worked in a totally smoke-free environment, and thus was exposed only to background air pollution indoors and outdoors. At the opposite extreme, Nonsmoker *C* was a musician who entertained in a smoky nightclub and shared an apartment with a chain smoker. *C's* total annual RSP exposure, 93% of which was tobacco tar from secondhand smoke, was more than 15 times *A's* RSP exposure. The other two examples, an office worker and a flight attendant, had intermediate levels of exposure. All except mailman *A* suffered respirable particle burdens that actually violated the annual NAAQS. We were then able to conclude that, "It appears that over the combined practical range of smoker density [D_s] and air exchange rates [C_v], repeated exposure to tobacco smoke can lead to annual RSP burdens that violate the annual NAAQS." In other words, while a short-term exposure for a few hours might not be enough to violate the daily health-based standard the cumulative effect of multiple exposures in multiple microenvironments was. And these multiple exposures were certainly enough to violate the annual standard.

As the health effects of fine particle pollution ($PM_{2.5}$) due to combustion became more intensively studied, health-based federal air quality standards promulgated in 1971 based on TSP were repeatedly tightened as research on the health effects of outdoor air pollution advanced (TSP included all sizes of airborne particles, including those greater than 10 microns that were too large to infiltrate into the lungs). Decreases in the NAAQS occurred in 1987, again in 1997, yet again in 2006, and by 2012, the 24-hour NAAQS had been reduced to 35 $\mu g/m^3$ and the annual NAAQS to just 12 $\mu g/m^3$. The 2012 Annual NAAQS is less than a twentieth of the 1971 NAAQS. In 1978 we had measured RSP ($PM_{3.5}$) and by 1997, EPA began to regulate the closely-related fine particle pollution, $PM_{2.5}$. So, to put our RSP measurements into a current perspective, the 700 $\mu g/m^3$ exposure for 4 hours during the Knights of Columbus dinner dance, averages out to a daily exposure of 166 $\mu g/m^3$, or nearly 5 times the 24-hour NAAQS extant in 2012. Such exposure added to the widespread exposure in other microenvironments on a daily basis as indicated in Figure 10, inevitably leads to increased morbidity and mortality in the population. Keep in mind that all but one of those indoor data points with smoking was someone's workplace. According to EPA, fine particle pollution penetrates deep into the lungs, into the bloodstream, and leads to premature death in people with heart or lung disease, non-fatal heart attack, irregular heartbeat, aggravated asthma, decreased lung function, increased respiratory symptoms, including airways irritation, coughing or difficulty breathing.

THE NAS INDOOR POLLUTANTS STUDY

In 1980, EPA commissioned a study of Indoor Pollutants by the National Academy of Sciences (NAS). I became EPA's liaison to the NAS Indoor Pollutant Committee, contributing materials and attending their meetings. This committee was comprised of academic indoor air researchers and members of ASHRAE. In July 1981, the NAS issued its report, titled *Indoor Pollutants*. With respect to secondhand smoke, the executive summary concluded in part:

"Virtually every member of our society is exposed to tobacco smoke: 33% of the population smokes, and the rest are exposed to the smoke released by others. The constituents of tobacco smoke are well documented as hazardous, the prevalence of population exposures is very high, and there is an increased incidence of respiratory tract symptoms and functional decrements in children residing in homes with smokers, compared with those in homes without smokers. These considerations and recent evidence of increased lung-cancer rates among nonsmoking women living with smoking husbands have led us to conclude that indoor exposure to tobacco smoke has adverse effects. Coughing, headache, nausea, and irritation of eyes, nose, and throat are among the reported symptoms.

Although many studies have measured various components of tobacco smoke indoors, total exposure has not been determined. Passive exposure to tobacco smoke may constitute an important exposure to respirable particles, such gaseous compounds as acrolein and formaldehyde, benzo[α]pyrene, and various trace metals. Reduced ventilation increases concentrations of tobacco smoke. As an energy-conserving compromise, smoking could be restricted to zones that are well ventilated. Public policy should clearly articulate that involuntary exposure to tobacco smoke has adverse health effects and ought to be minimized or avoided where possible. Under this framework, the prohibition or restriction of smoking in public buildings, offices, etc., is a control option to be considered with ventilation and air cleaning" [NAS, 1981].

The NAS Indoor Pollutants report dismayed the Tobacco Institute. Several counter-actions were recommended by Fred Panzer to Jack Mills and his other henchmen at the Tobacco Institute in a memo dated Sept. 3, 1981. Chief among these were communicating its displeasure to the new EPA administrator Gorsuch and preparing a pre-emptive public relations campaign to offset the anticipated publicity when the report was released the following month [TTID TI1323-0466]. Pre-empting adverse publicity about the health effects of its products was a long-standing public relations ploy of the tobacco industry.

ESTIMATING RISK USING EXPOSURE SCIENCE AND ENVIRONMENTAL EPIDEMIOLOGY

The worst was yet to come for the industry. In 1980 and 1981, three blockbuster epidemiological studies emerged, providing the missing scientific link implicating secondhand smoke as a cause of disease in nonsmokers. The first blow to Big Tobacco came on March 27, 1980, when White and Froeb, publishing in *The New England Journal of Medicine,* reported that prolonged exposure to secondhand smoke in the workplace over 20 years or more reduced small airways function in the lungs in otherwise healthy exposed nonsmokers. In the same issue, an editorial by researchers in the National Heart, Lung and Blood Institute opined in part that "(the) new evidence is sufficient to initiate new legislative actions that would further restrict smoking in public places... ." An internal memorandum of the Tobacco Institute warned that "On the day the article was published, two major smoking restriction bills passed the lower houses of Illinois and New York. The study was cited by them and has been cited repeatedly since by proponents of smoking restriction legislation and in the preambles of smoking restriction bills at both the state and local levels" [TTID TNWL0053523].

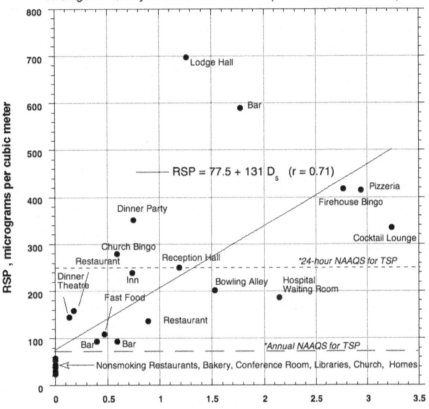

FIGURE 10. GRAPH OF RESPIRABLE PARTICLES (RSP) VS. SMOKER DENSITY, D$_s$, PLOTTING DATA FROM OUR FIELD STUDIES, SHOWING THE 1971 EPA AIR QUALITY STANDARDS FOR TOTAL SUSPENDED PARTICULATE (TSP) (REPACE AND LOWREY, 1980; 1982). THE REGRESSION LINE SHOWS A STRONG CORRELATION BETWEEN RSP AND D$_s$ (R=0.71). OUR MODEL ATTRIBUTED THE SCATTER IN THE DATA (I.E., DEVIATIONS FROM THE STRAIGHT LINE) TO DIFFERENT AIR EXCHANGE RATES. BUILDINGS BELOW THE REGRESSION LINE WOULD HAVE HIGHER AIR EXCHANGE RATES THAN THOSE ABOVE IT.

Then in 1981, Hirayama in the *British Medical Journal (BMJ)* and Trichopoulos in *The Lancet* made back-to-back direct hits. They reported respectively, that in Japan and Greece, the nonsmoking wives of smoking men had nearly twice the rates of lung cancer than the nonsmoking wives of nonsmoking men. The more impressive of these was the 15-year prospective epidemiological study of 91,580 women by Dr. Takeshi Hirayama in *The British Medical Journal*, published on January 17, 1981, entitled "Nonsmoking wives of heavy smokers have a higher risk of lung cancer: A study from Japan." On average, Hirayama found that nonsmoking women whose husbands smoked suffered an increased risk of fatal lung cancer by a statistically significant 78%, relative to nonsmoking women with nonsmoking husbands. Vitally important, Hirayama's study had shown a statistically significant exposure-response relationship between husbands' smoking rate and lung cancer mortality rate. In other words, the more the women's husbands smoked, the greater chance that their wives would die from lung cancer. The study received major international publicity: On January 16, 1981, *The New York Times* reported on Hirayama's research: "The study also strengthens the thesis that the effect of tobacco smoke on the nonsmoker, which has been variously called passive, second-hand or involuntary smoking, may be a cause of lung cancer in the general population."

Two days earlier, a much smaller, but still impressive, case-control study of passive smoking and lung cancer in 302 nonsmoking Greek women by Dr. Dimitri Trichopoulos et al. (1981), had reported an increased risk of lung cancer from spousal smoking which also exhibited a statistically significant exposure-response relationship. Relative to a baseline risk of 1.0 for women whose husbands were nonsmokers, Trichopoulos found a lung cancer risk increase by a statistically significant factor of 2.4 for a woman whose husband smoked, and by a factor of 3.4 if her husband smoked more than a pack per day. These two studies reinforced each other, because they had strikingly similar results despite being from two very different cultures, with different diets and ethnicity. The main similarity between these two racially distinct cultures was a very high male smoking rate coupled with a very low female rate. This was of great epidemiological import, because it minimized the chance of a confounding effect due to active smoking by the subjects, allowing a clear signal to emerge.

This influential new research had two major effects: first, it galvanized the nonsmokers' rights movement. As Richard Kluger would write in his book, *Ashes to Ashes*, in 1996, "In bellwether California, ... the confederation of anti-smoking groups would change its name to Californians for Nonsmokers' Rights drawing sustenance from new data on ETS in studies like those by Repace and Hirayama." Second, it galvanized the tobacco industry to go to war against these new studies. Discerning auguries of smoking bans, Big Tobacco began to wage a no-holds-barred public relations campaign, aided and abetted by their scientific moles, to discredit these three new research studies as flawed by the lack of "sound science," or slanted by "biased researchers" who were "anti-smoker zealots."

What was missing in these two important epi studies by Hirayama and Trichopoulos, which assessed secondhand smoke exposure by its duration and by self-reports (and nearly all others that would follow in the years to come), was quantification of the actual secondhand smoke pollution levels to which these passive smokers were exposed. I thought I could remedy this deficit. Although it was a depressing time for many at the Agency under the repressive Gorsuch regime, the lack of substantive work afforded me with the free time to do some intensive study on the epidemiology of passive smoking. This had been in the back of my mind ever since the publication of our *Science* paper. I realized immediately that, to first approximation, the quantitative lung cancer mortality rates of the Hirayama study could be used as a response rate in an exposure-response relationship between passive smoking and lung cancer. Then, coupled with time budget studies, our models of exposure for the work and home environments, verified by experimental data in real-world settings, could estimate the typical population exposure that caused a given average amount of increased risk of lung cancer in nonsmokers. I believed that by using these quantitative risk assessment techniques, I should be able to estimate the number of Americans who might die each year from passive-smoking-induced lung cancer.

There were two big disadvantages that I needed to overcome. First, I had no formal training in epidemiology, so I had to teach myself its basic principles. On the plus side, I was already familiar with the epidemiological studies of outdoor and occupational air pollutants. Second, I had never performed a risk assessment. However, I had reviewed in depth several EPA draft risk assessments on benzene, arsenic, coke oven emissions and radionuclides and knew the analytical processes employed by EPA. My big advantage was confidence in the maxim of my former NRL branch chief, John Davey, who had opined that, "A good physicist can do anything." While this might sound either like the epitome of arrogance or simple naïveté, I had already had successful professional careers in the disparate scientific fields of nuclear medicine, health physics, solid state physics, nuclear activation analysis, and solid-state electronics. So, I felt this objective was eminently achievable. It seemed to me that the principles of epidemiology and risk assessment were far less complicated than the arcane physics of quantum mechanical scattering. For example, to understand my second paper which dealt with this subject, Phase Shifts of the three-dimensional spherically symmetric square well potential, by PHE Meijer and JL Repace, published in the *American Journal of Physics* in 1975, requires a journey through the looking glass into the esoteric mathematical world of spherical Bessel functions and Neumann functions.

Moreover, I was an expert in radiation dosimetry, whose basic principles are fundamentally similar to the dosimetry of air pollutants. This gave me physical insights into exposure analysis that were quite different from the statistical techniques that professional epidemiologists utilized in their studies of passive smoking that assessed exposure by questionnaire. Accurate exposure assessment was one of the most difficult obstacles for traditional questionnaire-based epidemiology to overcome, and imperfect exposure assessment was responsible for the failure of many an epi study of the general population to produce statistically significant results despite a sound hypothesis. However, it was standard practice in occupational health studies of radiation and chemical workers, whose exposures and doses were measurable and deriving exposure-response relationships was just business as usual.

To proceed, I needed to gain a thorough understanding of classical epidemiological methods. I repaired to Reiter's Technical Bookstore in downtown Washington to purchase a copy of Brian MacMahon's classic text, *Epidemiology principles and methods* (1970). I assimilated it cover-to-cover. I also read works on risk assessment techniques. Drawing on my physics background, I was about to enter the new field of *environmental* epidemiology using highly non-traditional methods involving modeling and measurement of exposure much like that used in *occupational* epidemiology. My impression was that I probably understood exposure assessment of secondhand smoke better than most of the classically-trained epidemiologists of that era whose papers I read. I said to Lowrey, "with these new epi papers, we now have a golden opportunity to perform a risk assessment of passive smoking and lung cancer." Al enthusiastically agreed to a second Repace and Lowrey collaboration. Then I set to work on the risk assessment, taking full advantage of the abundant free time at work made possible by my exclusion from most official EPA business imposed by the profoundly anti-regulatory Gorsuch-Bennett regime.

EPA's engagement with ASHRAE, which I had instigated in 1979, began to bear fruit. The previous edition of ASHRAE Standard 62-1973 had prescribed minimum and recommended ventilation rates for commercial and industrial buildings. However, the new version, ASHRAE Standard 62-1981, *Ventilation for Acceptable Indoor Air Quality,* specified much higher ventilation rates for smoking buildings than for nonsmoking buildings. The minimum rates were designed to control carbon dioxide from human metabolism. For smoking buildings, greater amounts of ventilation air were required to provide an 80% acceptance rate by visitors to a space where smoking was permitted, because occupants suffered olfactory fatigue. In actuality, the odor test panels that were the basis for these rates were comprised of half smokers and half nonsmokers. This failed to compensate for the fact that smokers had far more tolerance to tobacco smoke odor than nonsmokers did, by a factor of three at the critical 80% acceptance level (Cain et al., 1981). Since ventilation economics was a paramount consideration for building owners and managers, this compromise ensured that many buildings would continue to be poorly ventilated and reek of tobacco smoke, despite the new higher rates.

The tobacco industry viewed the higher rates for smoking buildings required by this new standard as a grave threat. The Tobacco Institute compiled an enormous 287-page briefing book on the new ASHRAE standard, documenting the industry's fears. It began with this preamble:

"This summary provides background information on ASHRAE Standard 62-1981, Ventilation for Acceptable Indoor Air Quality. The Standard establishes guidelines for indoor air quality and specifies two separate sets of ventilation rates, one set of rates that are extremely high to be used where smoking is permitted and a second set of much lower rates which may be used if smoking is prohibited. The American Society of Heating, Refrigeration, and Air Conditioning Engineers (ASHRAE) is a professional standards writing organization. Its Standards do not have the force of law. However, ASHRAE Standards are typically adopted by model code organizations and by state and municipal building codes and energy programs.

When adopted by a state or local building code, a Standard becomes law. Adoption of the ventilation rates specified in ASHRAE 62-1981 would be tantamount to a comprehensive public smoking law. Ventilation rate requirements for smoking areas specified in the Standard are from 2 to 5 times higher than for nonsmoking areas. This disparity provides an economic incentive for building designers, owners or managers to design or operate under nonsmoking ventilation rates, and thus save the energy costs of increased ventilation" [TTID TI0043-0795].

TI's Walker Merriman and Elia Sterling lobbied BOCA, one of the three major building-code setting organizations in U.S., in opposition to BOCA's proposal to adopt the new ASHRAE standard [TTID TI0043-0861]. (Elia was the elder son of Ted Sterling – the apple didn't fall very far from the tree). The Tobacco Institute's effort succeeded. Behind the scenes, the industry organized comments in opposition from a number of co-opted ventilation engineers whom it secretly hired as deep-cover moles, coordinated by the giant Washington DC law firm, Covington & Burling [TTID TI00430794]. This was the start of a nasty two-decades-long effort by the tobacco industry intended to subvert the ASHRAE consensus process using both overt and covert means.

The Tobacco Institute disseminated a 2-page propaganda pamphlet, titled, *Consideration for others is a two-way street,* that proclaimed, "First of all, it is important to understand that there is no convincing evidence that tobacco smoke causes disease in nonsmokers. … The temptation is great to correct the bothersome behavior of others by turning to government for rules and regulations. Thus, we can impose legal controls on the occasional errant horn blower, the music listener or the cigarette smoker. But shouldn't we first reflect upon the predictable fate of a society that restricts personal freedom by law? Mutual consideration is and must be the business of people, not of government. Consideration for others is and must be a two-way street."

AN ENIGMA: TWO LARGE STUDIES REPORTING DISPARATE RESULTS

In June of 1981, Larry Garfinkel, chief epidemiologist of the American Cancer Society (ACS), published a very large prospective epidemiological study of passive smoking by 176,739 American women. This cohort was twice the size of Hirayama's. Garfinkel reported an average lung cancer risk increase of only 20%, and it lacked statistical significance; worse, there wasn't a trace of an exposure-response relationship. However, Hammond and Selikoff (1981) were troubled by Garfinkel's analysis, arguing that he had misused the ACS data because it had not been designed as a passive smoking study. Specifically, Cuyler Hammond, Garfinkel's predecessor, who had collected the original ACS data, criticized Garfinkel's study, stating that,

"[I] … would have liked to estimate lung cancer death rates in relation to amount of 'passive' smoking among female subjects who never smoked. [I] refrained from attempting to do so for the following reasons: Since [my] prospective study was not designed for that purpose, no special information on the subject was obtained. Information was available on the smoking habits of the husbands of many of the married women in the study: but not on the smoking habits of the former husbands of women who were widowed, divorced, separated, or married for a second time. More important, in America at that time, women were not generally barred from public and social gatherings where men were smoking; and working

husbands who smoked generally did much if not most of their smoking away from home."
[Hammond & Selikoff, 1981]

However, Hammond's arguments had failed to dissuade Garfinkel from publishing his analysis. On the plus side, one of the most important pieces of data from Garfinkel's study were the actual age-specific lung cancer mortality rates for nonsmoking American women, which were vital for my risk assessment. I was uncomfortable basing my model solely on Hirayama's rates because I didn't have any data to permit modeling the secondhand smoke exposures of Japanese women, such as home sizes and air exchange rates.

Despite Hammond's critique, I realized that any credible risk assessment of passive smoking would have to *explain* Garfinkel's contrary result to be convincing. In physics, an unexpected negative result cannot be dismissed as a fluke. It must be explained. After a careful reading of these three new epi papers and some collateral research, I realized exactly why Garfinkel got different results from Hirayama and Trichopoulos: the Achilles heel of any classical epidemiological study is imperfect exposure assessment. This was not so much of a problem for Hirayama and Trichopoulos, because both of the traditional societies of Japan and Greece in the 1960's and 1970's had high male smoking rates, between 60% and 70%, combined with low female smoking rates, of the order of 5% or 10%. Most importantly, as a result of cultural views that discouraged women from paid work, *Japanese and Greek women had very low labor force participation rates in that era.* I knew this from personal discussions with both Hirayama and Trichopoulos. This meant that in both those societies, spousal smoking was actually a very good surrogate for a woman's total exposure to secondhand smoke. However, in 1960's and 1970's America, Labor Department statistics reported that 40% to 45% of women were participating in the labor force in mostly white and pink collar jobs, and thus be exposed to secondhand smoke at work due to the widespread lack of smoking restrictions. In addition, U.S. female smoking rates approached 30%, so spousal smoking was a comparatively poor surrogate for total exposure to secondhand smoke in America. Workplace exposures, which Garfinkel had ignored, had to be taken into account. Even Hammond and Selikoff had not pointed out this salient fact.

In reaction to Hirayama's study, the Tobacco Institute hired Nathan Mantel, the noted biostatistician, to criticize Hirayama's statistical methods. Mantel responded with a letter, speculating that Hirayama *might* have made an arithmetical error in a standard test for statistical significance. The tobacco industry promptly issued a news release and sponsored full-page ads in national newspapers and magazines trumpeting Mantel's *speculation* without identifying it as such, instead wildly claiming that Mantel had identified a real error in Hirayama's analysis that had "invalidated" the findings. Leaving no stone unturned, the Tobacco Institute also communicated this propaganda line in a letter to the Director of Japan's National Cancer Institute, where Hirayama was on staff in order to discredit him with his management [TI, 1981].

However, in a subsequent interview with *Medical World News (1981)*, Mantel denied ever reaching a firm conclusion. Behind the scenes, as the tobacco industry was publicly attacking Hirayama's article, several of its own experts were privately telling their industry bosses that Hirayama's conclusions were quite valid [Glantz, 1995]. I pondered why Mantel, who had developed a famous and widely cited statistical method, and had authored hundreds of statistical papers, would risk his reputation by taking tobacco money. So, I phoned him to ask why. He wasn't in. Identifying myself as Jim Repace from the EPA, I asked him to return my call and promptly went to lunch. By the time I returned, Mantel had already left several return messages on my voice mail, which I found quite curious. When we finally connected, and before I could begin to ask any questions, Mantel began to complain that he "was losing his office at George Washington University due to lack of funding" and inquired as to whether EPA had any grant money available. I referred him to ORD. No need to inquire further: mystery solved.

Meanwhile, as Lowrey and I labored on our risk assessment of passive smoking and lung cancer, the Tobacco Institute remained busily attempting to discredit our *Science* paper. A memo to Sam Chilcote, President of the Tobacco Institute, from TI apparatchik Jack Kelley, dated November 18, 1981, related the following:

"These are highlights from the Repace file. It took Jim Repace over three and one-half years to work his original proposal into a research project worthy to be published in Science magazine. Over the last five years, Repace has also been quoted in numerous news clips from around the country and has testified at virtually every hearing on smoking restrictions in the metropolitan Washington, D.C. area. At this time it is essential to challenge Repace and his 'science'. At the local hearings, he has a slide show demonstrating the alleged high concentration of particulate matter in the indoor air caused by tobacco smoke. He is in the forefront of the movement to enact federal standards regulating indoor air quality. ... it is imperative that any scientific evidence which would refute Repace be gathered as soon as possible." [TTID TI24162443].

In a highly publicized national ad campaign launched in 1981, The Tobacco Institute published a broadside, *Answers to the most asked questions about cigarettes,* opening fire on both the Hirayama and Repace and Lowrey papers:

"Many people who want smoking banned or restricted in public places say that smoke in the atmosphere can cause disease in nonsmokers. These claims do not, however, stand up before scientific scrutiny. Recently, for example, a Japanese study reporting that nonsmoking wives of smokers have a high risk of lung cancer got a lot of publicity. But the validity of the study was seriously questioned in the medical literature by a variety of experts around the world. Within six months an American Cancer Society study covering 17 years and 200,000 people contradicted the Japanese study. The new research, by the society's statistical director, indicated that 'second-hand' smoke has insignificant effect on lung cancer rates in nonsmokers.

Another study commonly used in support of smoking restrictions involved the measurement of particulate matter in public buildings around Washington, D.C., by two researchers who then claimed that nonsmokers are exposed to 'significant air pollution burdens from indoor smoking.' No definitive piece here, either. Because the investigators measured no substance specific to tobacco smoke—like nicotine, for instance. Nor did they take any readings *before* the introduction of tobacco smoke. Their measurements, therefore, may simply reflect the amount of dust in the air and have little relevance so far as tobacco smoke is concerned. No hard conclusions can be drawn about the effects, if any, of environmental cigarette smoke on the healthy nonsmoker. The issue is an emotional one. And emotion may cloud the perceptions and humors of those who dislike cigarette smoke. Scientific studies on the nonsmoker question continue, as they should."

Al and I decided to poke our long noses into the lion's den: we paid a visit to the Washington headquarters of the Tobacco Institute on fashionable K Street, and discovered a treasure trove: free copies of its weekly newspaper, *The Tobacco Observer*. I put my name on their subscription list. I became an avid reader since it afforded valuable intelligence on our opponents. In 1981, an astonishing photo (Figure 12) of Adolf Hitler reviewing his storm troopers appeared on its front page, the caption noting that he was "history's most famous anti-smoker." It portrayed nonsmokers who objected to breathing tobacco smoke in public places as "Anti-smoker Health Nazis." This became a classic industry propaganda theme that would recur many times over the years as Big Tobacco attempted to silence nonsmokers who vocally objected to breathing secondhand smoke.

In December 1981, the Tobacco Institute sounded the klaxons in a memo circulated to more than a dozen of its minions; it stated in part: …

- "Repace's research on indoor air pollution and ventilation began at least as early as 1976; TI first obtained one of his early research proposals in 1978.
- With his slide show and local research, Repace has become a credible witness on behalf of local smoking restriction proposals in the metropolitan D.C. area and in the Maryland legislature.
- The Science article by Repace/Lowrey launched Repace into a position of national prominence as a spokesman for the need for indoor air quality measurement, standards and regulation. Note especially Repace's recent and future presentations at symposiums as well as two more articles to appear soon.
- The major thrust of Repace's research, articles and pronouncements is that smoking should be severely restricted in public places, especially the workplace.

Adolf Hitler, reviewing his storm troopers, is history's most famous anti-smoker.

FIGURE 12. PROPAGANDA PHOTO DEMONIZING SMOKING RESTRICTION ADVOCATES. SOURCE: *THE TOBACCO OBSERVER,* THE TOBACCO INSTITUTE, WASHINGTON DC, 1981.

- A coordinated industry strategy must be developed in order to successfully challenge the growing number of workplace smoking restriction proposals. Repace is but one part of the problem [TTID TI07391748]. …"

It appears that The Tobacco Institute's spies and informants kept the industry well informed of my research, public speaking and other activities and future plans.

WORKPLACE PASSIVE SMOKING BECOMES A MAJOR BATTLEGROUND

By 1979, annual U.S. cigarette consumption had reached its historic peak of 622 billion, a breath taking 12,300 cigarettes per smoker per year. At the same time, a survey of 3000 US corporations in 1978 showed that 74% of white-collar companies had zero restrictions on smoking in the workplace, while only 31% of blue-collar companies did, largely due fire safety regulations, although it was likely that smoking was allowed in breakrooms. Thus, tens of millions of nonsmoking men and women were forced to breathe secondhand smoke on the job. Secondhand smoke was an annoyance for most nonsmokers, but for some, it had far more severe health consequences. This began to lead to increased litigation. As a result of our *Science* paper, requests for assistance as an expert witness in secondhand smoke litigation began to roll in. Some of the plaintiffs' plights were so compelling that I found them impossible to ignore.

In 1980, in one of my first involvements in workplace smoking litigation, I submitted a pro bono affidavit in support of Plaintiff Paul Smith, in *Smith v. Western Electric*. His plight was similar to Donna Shimp's. In 1975, Smith, a St. Louis, Missouri communications engineer, had experienced severe respiratory tract irritation from passive smoking on the job. His physician advised him to avoid contact with secondhand smoke. In 1980, Western Electric had adopted a draconian policy of "protecting" nonsmokers from secondhand smoke at work. The company bluntly informed Smith of his options: he could either continue working *while wearing a gas mask,* or he could apply for a lower-paying job in a smoke-free location. Smith responded by filing a declaration that he should be accommodated because he was handicapped, but his plea failed at trial. He successfully appealed, with the appellate court reversing the trial court's decision in 1982.

In 1981 I testified in support of Adele Gordon, an EPA contract computer programmer, who was fired for complaining to her management about secondhand smoke symptoms on the job. A trial, *Gordon v. Raven*, was held in Washington DC Superior Court. Ms. Gordon did not prevail. It was the first of more than five-dozen cases (litigation and arbitration) in which I would provide expert testimony from 1981 to 2013. Many of the early workplace passive smoking cases were lost due to the lack of the authoritative scientific support on the health issue. However, this would change in 1986, courtesy of major reports of the Surgeon General and the National Research Council.

A Blondie cartoon of the times pithily illustrated the problem of workplace smoking in those dark years. Dagwood complained to his irascible boss, Mr. Dithers: "Boss, a lot of offices don't allow smoking." Dithers replies, "Well if it bothers you, go to the nonsmoking section." Dagwood: "Where is it?" Dithers jibes, as he lights up a cigar: "Down at the unemployment office" (Repace, 1985).

These cases provided a wealth of practical insight into the kind of suffering and injuries that were incurred by nonsmokers who worked in smoky workplaces. The rules of discovery in litigation permitted an expert witness to obtain inside information concerning the determinants of workplace exposures such as space volumes, numbers of smokers, and ventilation practices. These allowed me to estimate the magnitude and duration of plaintiffs' workplace secondhand smoke exposures and relate them to their adverse health effects. This was case-study occupational epidemiology performed using the forensic tools of litigation.

In May of 1981, The New York Academy of Medicine invited me to participate in a *Symposium on the Health Aspects of Indoor Air Pollution*. My lecture was published as a paper in the Academy's journal (Repace, 1981). I noted that those nonsmokers who were injured on the job by passive smoking had to resort to litigation to gain their right to a smoke-free work environment: cases I mentioned included a bank teller, a social services worker, and a flight attendant. These cases suggested that passive smoking was at bottom really an issue of an employer's failure to maintain a safe and healthy workplace, a violation of a fundamental tenet of the 1970 Occupational Safety and Health (OSH) Act.

I included results from measurements of relative $PM_{3.5}$ levels in smoking and nonsmoking sections in the State Department cafeteria in Washington. I had been invited by Bill Alli, a friend and fellow Bowie

GASP member who worked at the Agency for International Development as a manpower development planner and management analyst. Bill had previously served as a foreign service officer in Pakistan. Alli had been instrumental in organizing State Department employees to form FENSR in the late 1970's. He was an economist by profession, an ex-marine who had endured heavy winter combat in Korea and survived a walking artillery barrage. He wrote a book about his wartime experiences (Alli, 2009). State Department nonsmokers had run into the same secondhand smoke problem that nonsmokers had at SSA. Accordingly, Bill invited me to State to make secondhand smoke measurements in the smoking and nonsmoking sections of their cafeteria, and outdoors.

My measurements read 170 µg/m³ in the cafeteria's smoking section, 110 µg/m³ in the nonsmoking section, and 30 µg/m³ outdoors, demonstrating that the air in State's cafeteria was quite polluted with secondhand smoke irrespective of section (Repace 1981). His embarrassed management rewarded him with a stern rebuke. Once again, no good deed went unpunished. A decade later, following developments at EPA in 1993, FENSR changed its name to Federal Employees for a Smokefree Workplace (FESFW). Then, working through the American Federation of Government Employees (AFGE), FESFW adopted a far more aggressive stance. Skillfully utilizing the Union, and aided by the earlier cafeteria measurements, Bill finally succeeded in gaining full workplace protection for nonsmokers at State.

From 1981 on, I felt that the passive smoking problem was quintessentially a workers' rights issue. Workers had a legal right to a safe and healthy workplace under the Occupational Safety and Health Act signed into law by President Nixon on December 29, 1970. This Act was intended to prevent workers from being killed or seriously harmed at work. The law required employers to provide their employees with working conditions that were free of known dangers. Clearly, workplaces contaminated with the dozens of carcinogens and toxins in secondhand smoke placed workers' health and very lives in jeopardy. Outdoor air pollution was well known to produce morbidity and mortality. Our measurements made clear that ambient levels of secondhand smoke far exceeded levels of outdoor air pollution in the U.S., except during major air pollution episodes, which had become increasingly rare. The Surgeon General's reports on smoking indicated that inhalation of tobacco smoke caused the premature deaths of hundreds of thousands of smokers annually. Because there were no known thresholds for any of its toxic effects, obviously there *must* be adverse health effects in nonsmokers in smoky workplaces where the population spent large portions of its time.

In early 1982, I co-chaired an ASHRAE Symposium on Ventilation and Indoor Air Quality in Houston, Texas, and presented a second Repace and Lowrey paper entitled *Tobacco Smoke, Ventilation and Indoor Air Quality,* which contained much of the information that we had pruned from our 1980 *Science* manuscript. It contained two new controlled experiments comparing the emissions of cigarettes, pipes, and cigars, and three additional sets of field measurements, in a church bingo game, a wedding reception, and a dinner theater on smoking and nonsmoking nights. The dinner theater in Prince Georges' County, MD, on the smoking night had particulate levels triple that of the nonsmoking night. The particulate pollution in the smoky wedding reception in Rockland County, NY, was ten times that measured outdoors in the parking lot. The church bingo game in Bowie, MD, was so polluted with secondhand smoke that if the outdoor air had been polluted to the same level, it would have constituted an air pollution emergency (Repace and Lowrey (1982).

Our new controlled experiments comparing cigarettes, pipes and cigars showed that while the pipe and cigarette emitted about the same level of fine particles, a small cigar emitted twice as much. Moreover, the carbon monoxide emissions of the cigar were a whopping 25 times that of the cigarette. Our comparison of the particulate emissions of low, average, and high tar cigarettes manifested little difference between the low and average tar cigarettes, but the high tar unfiltered cigarette had double the emissions of either.

In addition, we compared our model predictions with fine particle concentrations from secondhand smoke from four smokers measured in the Pierce Foundation Laboratory's exposure chamber at Yale University by

Brian Leaderer, who was doing experiments involving the measurement of secondhand smoke over a variety of smoking and ventilation rates. Over a range of 4 to 16 cigarettes smoked per hour, and ventilation rates ranging from 2 to 14 air changes per hour, our active smoker model fit Brian's data with excellent agreement. We emphasized the patent inability of ventilation to control environmental tobacco smoke as demonstrated by our controlled and field experiments to this audience of ventilation engineers.

At the end of my presentation, in the question-and-answer period, a member of the audience, Prof. Theodor "Ted" Sterling, of Simon Fraser University in British Columbia, got up and asserted that he had "severe reservations" about my presentation, that in his experience "very few air quality problems could be related to tobacco smoke," and that he "had prepared a critique of my work that he hoped I would accept." When I queried him for details, he promptly sat down. This turned out to be a clever ploy by Sterling to avoid an embarrassing public debate. Later, his written critique was appended to our published paper, followed by our rebuttal, which hammered Sterling. A second commenter, L.G. Spielvogel, questioned whether we measured the outdoor airflows in the experimental buildings where we conducted our experiments and whether they might have had no outside air whatsoever. I found out 25 years later that Spielvogel was funded out of a secret account directed by tobacco lawyers [TTID 2505624133]. And as for Ted Sterling, stay tuned.

OF MOLES AND MEN

We didn't have to wait long for our next encounter with Professor Sterling. Although I strongly suspected that he was connected to the tobacco industry, at that time I had no understanding of just how important he was to them. I later learned that Sterling was in fact a long-time and highly paid consultant for the tobacco industry and its stable of outside law firms, who carried out much of the industry's dirty work. In the 1980's Sterling began to concentrate on the secondhand smoke issue, and on me in particular, as documented in a letter from Patrick Sirridge, a lawyer at the industry's go-to law firm, Shook Hardy & Bacon, to executives at Liggett and Meyers, American Tobacco, Philip Morris, Brown & Williamson, Lorillard, and R.J. Reynolds, dated March 1, 1982 [TTID 4]; it stated in part:

"Gentlemen: Dr. Theodor D. Sterling has submitted a request to continue his current project for a two-year period, ending May 1984, with a level of funding for the first year of $377,010 and $430,080 for the second year. We recommend that Dr. Sterling's proposed research be approved and funded as the CTR Special Project. ... The level of funding requested for 1982 is approximately 17.4% over the present level of $321,238 ...

In January 1982, Dr. Sterling prepared written comments (enclosed as Appendix C) in response to a paper presented by James Repace at the ASHRAE [conference] in Houston. Repace has been appearing at legislative and scientific meetings making highly questionable claims about health effects from other people's tobacco smoke. Dr. Sterling's oral presentation at the Houston meeting and the written comments which will be published in the ASHRAE Transactions this summer provide the first public criticisms of the deficiencies in Repace's scientific methodology. Further Dr. Sterling pointed out that Repace's reliance on studies such as Hirayama's was misplaced and that his conclusions were at variance with many published reports and Dr. Sterling's own research on indoor air pollution.

The flexibility inherent in Dr. Sterling's ongoing project enables him to respond within a short time to scientific developments. His willingness to prepare written comments on Repace's paper with only a few weeks' notice is a good example. Dr. Sterling also responded to the publication of Hirayama's article early last year with a highly critical letter to the British Medical Journal, a copy of which is enclosed as Appendix D. Most recently, Dr. Sterling has prepared responsive materials on the scientific aspects of legislative proposals (Waxman and

Hatch bills) pending in Congress. …. We recommend continued support for Dr. Sterling's on-going project and we would appreciate, if possible, receiving your response on or before the next Committee of Counsel meeting scheduled for March 18, 1982."

Shook Hardy and Bacon, headquartered in Kansas City MO, had long defended tobacco's big five companies – American Brands, Brown & Williamson, RJR Nabisco, Philip Morris and Loews Inc. plus the Tobacco Institute, against lawsuits brought by smokers. By 1992, it had prevailed in every single one. In 1992, a federal judge would accuse the law firm of being industry propagandists, apologists and co-conspirators as well as external counsel. Dick Daynard, of the Tobacco Products Liability Project at Northeastern University in Boston, a clearinghouse for plaintiffs' lawyers in smoking litigation was quoted as saying that Shook Hardy "played a central coordinating and enforcing role in the ongoing stonewalling and disinformation conspiracy" (NY Times, 1992).

With respect to Sterling, it became clear that he was willing to say anything, no matter how unscientific, to try to discredit our work. I recall Sterling's effort to deflect attention away from the cigarettes as source of indoor pollution by giving a risible paper, "The Case For Entirely Removing Gas Ranges from Indoors," at the International Symposium on Indoor Air Pollution, Health, and Energy Conservation, University of Massachusetts Amherst, in October 1981. When Sterling concluded, an absolutely livid Bob Macriss of the Gas Research Institute stormed up to a microphone, shouting at Sterling: "What is this? Some kind of Saturday afternoon exercise on the Simon Fraser computer?" And then he proceeded to tear Sterling's presentation apart. Instead of debating Macriss's points, Sterling responded with a passive-aggressive reply: "I'm sorry you feel that way." Later, Bob and I sat down over a few beers. It developed that we each possessed an enormous repertoire of jokes, which we traded for over an hour. We agreed that the best joke of all was Sterling's presentation.

However, the tobacco industry continued to hold old Ted Sterling in very high esteem. A March 11, 1980 document drafted by Max Crohn of Reynolds Tobacco described Theodor Sterling as "one of our industry's most valuable outside assets." In addition to numerous publications and studies, Crohn noted that "[Sterling] has continued to be one of the primary scientists available for consultation with Shook Hardy & Bacon in Kansas City." [USA vs. Philip Morris]. Sterling was so valuable to the industry that between 1973 and 1990, CTR special projects paid him over $5 million, not counting additional funding through Special Account 4.

So apparently our work measuring smoke in public places, demonstrating that it polluted buildings beyond belief, and showing that ventilation was not a viable control measure, was viewed as such a threat to the tobacco industry's viability that they put their biggest hired gun on it. And truth be told, although his antics were often outré, and despite being thoroughly bent, Sterling would prove to be a tenacious and clever adversary, not a lightweight to be easily dismissed like many other industry moles we would encounter.

It had become abundantly clear to us that Ted Sterling was a true industrial-strength Tobacco Mole. In 1993, in response to the enduring barrage of criticism he received from Canadian health and tobacco control groups, he gave them the finger by endowing a $5000 annual *Nora and Ted Sterling Prize in Support of Controversy*" at Simon Fraser University. Our boy Ted wrote the book on unmitigated chutzpah.

"Moles" were our term for tobacco industry consultants whose views on secondhand smoke were dictated by, performed for, paid for, and controlled by the tobacco industry or its external counsel, but promoted as if they were "independent" views. They were funded typically through the industry's outside law firms or laundered through front organizations to conceal their origin. The tactical use of moles was not limited to Big Tobacco. For example, Jack Spengler had co-authored a book, *Health Effects of Fossil Fuel Burning*, published in 1980. He noted that right after the book came out, a very senior Harvard colleague asked to borrow a copy, explaining that he was "being paid to criticize it" [Davis, 2002]. Moles were and continue to be a long-standing staple of polluting industry. Stan Glantz and I kept separate lists of tobacco moles and would periodically trade names to keep them current. Stan was a professor of Cardiology at the University of California, San Francisco, and had been President of Californians for Nonsmokers' Rights (Now Americans for Nonsmokers' Rights) since 1978. We had become close friends soon after publication of my *Science* paper.

THE ICE QUEEN GETS THE AXE

In 1982 Congress charged that the EPA had mishandled the $1.6 billion toxic waste Superfund Program and demanded its accounting records from Gorsuch. She stonewalled and became the first agency director in U.S. history to be cited for contempt of Congress. The EPA turned the documents over to Congress several months later, after the Reagan White House abandoned its court claim that Congress could not subpoena the documents because they were covered by executive privilege. At that point, Gorsuch had become a major liability to Reagan, and he forced her out, ending her destructive 22-month tenure. She stated that her resignation was the result of "pressures caused by the media and the congressional investigation." Critics charged that the EPA was in shambles at this time [Ann Gorsuch, Wikipedia]. Soon the EPA coffee shop began to sell souvenir tee shirts emblazoned with the slogan, "**I Survived the Acid Reign of the Ice Queen**." It was a best-seller. I wore mine while jogging. The Ice Queen's sudden departure proved to be a major disaster for the tobacco industry, for it led to the end of Kathleen Bennett's tenure and the ascendancy of Joseph A. Cannon to run the Nation's air quality programs. Bennett returned to the paper industry in May 1983 as Vice President for Environment, Safety & Health of the James River paper company. Among other fine products, they manufactured toilet paper.

CHAPTER 7

THE PURGE OF THE ICE QUEEN & THE RISE OF JOE CANNON

"Mr. Cannon is the Assistant EPA Administrator for Air Noise and Radiation, nominated a year ago by the President, sworn in by the Chief Justice a year ago December 1, and described by one employee as "member of GASP." Mr. Cannon was the recipient of the September 13, 1984 National Academy of Sciences request for $75,000 to begin a literature review and make research recommendations regarding nonsmoker exposures to tobacco smoke. James Repace is one of his employees. The EPA staff evaluation of Repace's nonsmoker death estimate was addressed to Mr. Cannon. He and the Surgeon General are reportedly in frequent touch."

Memorandum From William Kloepfer, Jr., Senior Vice President, The Tobacco Institute, to John P. Rupp, Esq., Covington & Burling, and Susan Stuntz, Tobacco Institute, Dec. 6, 1984 [TTID T10411-2063].

Joseph A. Cannon, a Washington, DC attorney, a native of Salt Lake City, Utah, was a Mormon who neither smoked nor drank. Cannon had joined the Reagan-Bush Campaign Committee in 1980 and was 33 years old when Anne Gorsuch appointed him as a special assistant for regulatory reform in 1981 after her first choice was rejected. In 1983 she made Cannon an Associate Administrator for Policy and Resources Management. In the wake of Gorsuch's resignation, William Ruckleshaus, the first Administrator of EPA, appointed by President Nixon in 1970, was brought back again by the Reagan Administration to clean house at EPA. In the wake of Gorsuch's firing, Administrator Ruckleshaus promptly got rid of 20 of the 21 top Gorsuch political appointees. The sole survivor of the purge was Joe Cannon, whom President Reagan nominated to be the new Assistant Administrator for Air and Radiation [Kloepfer, 1984].

After Cannon's appointment, Paul Stolpman was soon restored as Director of the renamed Office of Policy Analysis and Review, and Cannon brought in John Topping, also a Washington DC attorney, to serve as his new Chief of Staff. Our remaining staff were also brought back. Louise Giersch returned to her former EPA post in California. I soon established a firm working relationship with both Cannon and Topping, a rapport that would prove enormously significant for the issue of secondhand smoke.

During my tenure with the Office of Policy Analysis, I had become involved in a wide variety of activities. I had joined the Air Hazardous Research Committee in 1980, the Interagency Working Group on Smoking, Heart, Lung, and Blood Diseases in 1982, as well as the EPA working groups on Hazardous Air Pollutants and Radionuclides, and in 1983, I became a member of the Strategy Committee of the Deputy Administrator's Working Group on Risk Assessment. I discovered that many industries paid scant attention to the safe disposal of the gaseous, liquid, or solid waste from their manufacturing processes. If these were not adequately regulated, the general public could suffer sickness or death.

The widespread failure of industry to make health and safety a priority in pursuit of profits or from lack of toxicological expertise produced many environmental disasters. Ethyl Corporation had added tetraethyl lead, a neurotoxic cumulative poison, to gasoline as an anti-knock compound since the 1920's. The lead fumes emitted by vehicular emissions contaminated city air. Air pollution from lead resulted in diminution in children's IQ. Paint manufacturers added lead to interior house paint, and when small children ingested paint chips, they suffered lead poisoning and brain damage. Toothpaste manufacturers even used lead in toothpaste tubes. Shoe stores installed fluoroscope machines that illuminated customers' feet with carcinogenic and teratogenic x-rays which irradiated their bone marrow and gonads, adults and children alike.

Dentists used neurotoxic mercury to make amalgam to fill teeth which leached out into patients' blood (Yin et al., 2016). Mercury emissions from coal-fired power plants and chlor-alkali plants contaminated the air and water. Coal companies dumped mining wastes into local streams and laid waste to mountain tops. The air surrounding early nuclear power plants contained radioactive gases. Hexavalent chromium emissions from industrial electroplating contaminated the air with a potent carcinogen.

Urea formaldehyde foam insulation was introduced into homes causing acute dizziness, rashes, nausea, and nosebleeds for residents. Urea formaldehyde resin in pressed wood products reacted with water vapor to emit free formaldehyde, which caused eye irritation and breathing difficulty especially for residents of mobile homes. Unlike their U.S. counterparts, forest products manufacturers in Scandinavia, responding to their governments' indoor air quality standards, simply changed to phenol formaldehyde resin in their interior wood products, which did not outgas formaldehyde; it has long been used in marine plywood). Carcinogenic asbestos could be found in brake linings, floor and ceiling tiles, and insulation – it was even used in toasters. Industrial effluent poisoned rivers and estuaries, as well as drinking water in wells with toxic VOCs. GE dumped tens of thousands of pounds of toxic PCBs into the Hudson River. In 1980, an estimated 84% of homes used pesticides inside the house; between four and five percent of the residents of such households experienced acute toxic reactions after use.

Self-regulation by industry had failed miserably in protecting the public. This is why Congress had passed laws passed to regulate air pollution, radiation, toxic substances, and pesticides, and EPA had been created to codify, administer, and enforce those laws through regulations. As such, it required a large professional staff of scientists, engineers, toxicologists, and attorneys to function.

EPA's implementation of The Clean Air Act provided for the monitoring and regulation of ozone, sulfur dioxide, carbon monoxide, and particulate matter in the outdoor air from manufacturing processes, power generation, and transportation, as well as radioactivity from mining and nuclear power. In addition, the Clean Air Act provided EPA the authority to control or limit the manufacture and use of hazardous chemical substances such as benzene, vinyl chloride, mercury, beryllium, and asbestos. The Clean Water Act did the same for bays and rivers and streams. The Federal Insecticide, Fungicide and Rodenticide Act (FIFRA) regulated pesticides. And yet all attempts at sensible regulation to protect the health of citizens were vigorously opposed by industry, which sued EPA and engaged in years of obstructive and dilatory litigation. As a result, it usually took an average five to seven years to promulgate a disputed rule, during which the pollution continued unabated.

And for tens of decades, the tobacco industry had marketed a highly addictive product that slowly poisoned its users as well as innocent bystanders with only cosmetic regulation of its advertising as a result of a bought-and-paid-for Congress. However, publicity concerning the dire health effects of secondhand smoke was inexorably leading to local and state clean indoor air laws. That was a horse of a different color.

I TESTIFY BEFORE CONGRESS

From the outset of the Cannon Years, I returned to an active role as an informal spokesman on indoor air for EPA. This attracted notice in Congress. One Sunday evening, on August 2nd 1983, Stolpman phoned me at home, requesting that I report directly to Capitol Hill the next morning to attend a joint hearing of the House Subcommittee on Energy Development and Applications and the Subcommittee on Agriculture Research and Environment of the Committee on Science & Technology. He refused to say what I was expected to do there; "Just show up," he said. The next morning, I sat in the gallery in the hearing room, feeling rather puzzled. As soon as the hearing was gaveled into session, the Chairman, Congressman Jim Scheuer, Democrat of New York, cried out, "Is there a James Repace in the audience?" "Is there a James Repace in the audience?" Surprised, I raised my hand. He said, "Come on up here and sit down, I'd like to ask you a few questions," and he smiled and waved his arm repeatedly in welcome. I proceeded to the witness chair from my perch in the back row of the audience, wondering what the hell was going on. Scheuer announced, "I'd like to know about the effect of smoking on aircraft in restaurants, and other public places; what can you inform this committee about that?" Unexpectedly, it turned out to be an impromptu hearing on indoor air pollution from tobacco smoke. Despite the lack of warning, my Toastmasters experience in extemporaneous speaking kicked in. I launched into a discourse on air pollution from smoking and the inability of ventilation on aircraft or in restaurants to control it, making the point that smoking sections really did little to protect nonsmokers. Scheuer thanked me, and I returned to my seat, a bit stunned, but satisfied. On reflection, if I was surprised, perhaps some members of Scheuer's committee who might not have been so sanguine about my testimony were too.

OUR RISK ASSESSMENT OF PASSIVE SMOKING TAKES SHAPE

Meanwhile, the Tobacco Institute had stepped up its propaganda campaign to deal with the new research implicating secondhand smoke as a major indoor air pollutant that was in all probability capable of causing lung cancer and respiratory impairment in nonsmokers. Figures 11a and 11b show two such ads that ran in Time Magazine. Although the pioneering environmental health group at Harvard in the late 1970's, led by Ben Ferris, Jack Spengler, and colleagues, who directed the Harvard Six City Study, had measured secondhand smoke in homes, there would not be any studies replicating our particulate measurements in public places until 1989, by Spengler's group at Harvard. They reported comprehensive measurements of $PM_{2.5}$ and nicotine in 57 locations, including offices, bars, restaurants, subway and bus stations, grocery stores and laundromats, hospitals and museums, a high school and a library, essentially confirming our results and extending them to report a strong correlation ($SHS\text{-}PM_{2.5} = 0.75 + 14.8 \text{ } SHS\text{-}Nicotine$, $R^2 = 0.78$) between $PM_{2.5}$ in smoking areas and nicotine, in units of $\mu g/m^3$ (Miesner, et al., 1989). Measured particle concentrations ranged from 6.0 $\mu g/m^3$ to about 550 $\mu g/m^3$. Nicotine concentrations were as high as 26 $\mu g/m^3$ in one designated smoking room.

In 1982, Surgeon General C. Everett Koop issued his first report on the Health Consequences of Smoking. The latest in a long line of reports on smoking and health dating back to 1964, this year it zeroed in on cancer. On the subject of involuntary smoking and lung cancer, the Report noted provocatively that:

"In recent months, the popular press has generated interest in the controversy of whether passive or involuntary smoking causes lung cancer in nonsmokers. Three epidemiological studies examined this issue in the past year. Evidence from two of the studies demonstrated a statistically significant correlation between involuntary smoking and lung cancer risk in nonsmoking wives of husbands who smoked. A third noted a positive association, but it was not statistically significant. While the nature of this association is unresolved, it does raise the concern that involuntary smoking may pose a carcinogenic risk to the nonsmoker. Any health risk resulting from involuntary smoke exposure is a serious public health concern because of the large numbers of nonsmokers in the population who are potentially exposed.

Therefore, for the purpose of preventive medicine, prudence dictates that nonsmokers avoid exposure to second-hand tobacco smoke to the extent possible." … "Although the currently available evidence is not sufficient to conclude that passive or involuntary smoking causes lung cancer in smokers, the evidence does raise concern about a possible serious public health problem" [SG, 1982].

EPA had extensive research laboratories in Research Triangle Park (RTP), North Carolina, where I was a frequent visitor, familiarizing myself with the researchers and their research programs. I decided to brief Assistant Administrator Cannon on the desirability of requesting EPA's Office of Research & Development (ORD) to fund a research program on environmental tobacco smoke (ETS) in RTP. I knew ORD would endorse Cannon's request, and Dr. Joellen Lewtas, Chief of the Genetic Bioassay Branch, became the leader of EPA's research on ETS, and a good friend. By this time, I had learned enough epidemiology and risk assessment both from my work at EPA reviewing its risk assessments on the hazardous air pollutants, coke oven emissions, arsenic, and ionizing radiation, and from my own study of scholarly books and papers, to begin drafting a risk assessment of passive smoking and lung cancer. Al Lowrey became a frequent visitor to my private office at EPA, and Al and I had major bull sessions as we reviewed the drafts. Al would make incisive comments, such as "I don't understand what you're saying," or "convince me that what you've written is not bullshit." These sessions sometimes drew in George Sugiyama, who would offer both scientific commentary and encouragement. Ahead lay the boldest work of science I would ever undertake, a work destined to be branded as never-to-be-sufficiently-damned by the tobacco industry, and one that would thrust me onto the national stage.

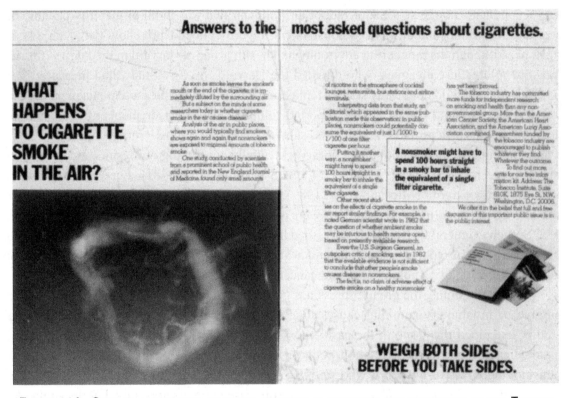

FIGURE 11A. COPY OF A MISLEADING AD WIDELY PUBLISHED IN MAGAZINES AND NEWSPAPERS BY THE TOBACCO INSTITUTE IN THE EARLY 1980'S. (PHOTO COURTESY OF STANTON GLANTZ).

FIGURE 11B. SHORTENED VERSION OF WHAT HAPPENS TO SMOKE IN THE AIR, IN A 1982 TI BOOKLET, *ANSWERS TO THE MOST-ASKED QUESTIONS ABOUT CIGARETTES*, [TTID 03651479]. (PHOTO COURTESY OF STANTON GLANTZ).

The outline of our risk assessment of passive smoking and lung cancer followed the basic guidelines laid down by the National Academy of Sciences: Hazard Identification, Exposure Assessment, Dose-response Assessment, and Risk Characterization, including attendant uncertainty. Using an Occam's Razor approach based on sociological time-activity pattern data, which Wayne Ott had introduced me to in 1979, we adopted the simplifying assumption that the nonsmoking U.S. population was exposed only at work or at home, and that other exposures could be neglected as minor contributors, since this covered 88% of the typical American's time. We used the exposure model developed in our 1980 *Science* paper to estimate the exposure of nonsmokers in a typical office workplace, and in a typical home, weighting the concentrations we calculated for those microenvironments by the probability of exposure from national surveys of smoking policies at work, adult smoking prevalence, and from the percentage of children exposed to smoking at home. We used the ASHRAE Standard to estimate the occupancy, volume, and ventilation rate of our model office, and data from the National Association of Homebuilders to obtain the median volume of a typical single-family home. Data from the literature provided measurements of air exchange rates for such dwellings.

Using these approximations, we modeled the average concentration levels of secondhand smoke particles in a typical office workplace, which covered about 61% of American workers. We modeled the average concentration levels of secondhand smoke particles in a typical single-family home. Our results were comparable to results from the Harvard Six-City Study of 68 homes in six U.S. cities, which had measured both particle concentrations and cigarette consumption. About two-thirds of Americans lived in single-family homes in the late 1970's. So, while this did not encompass the exposure of the entire nonsmoking population, it was a good first approximation. Our modeling yielded a probability-weighted estimate of fine particulate exposure from secondhand smoke for the typical American adult nonsmoker, which we pegged at 1.43 milligrams (mg) of toxic tobacco tar inhaled per day. We estimated that nonsmokers' airborne tobacco tar particle exposures from cigarette smoking ranged from zero to 14 mg daily. The use of exposure modeling was rare in public health epidemiology, although it was extensively used in occupational

101

health epidemiological studies. However, for Al and me, mathematical modeling was a standard tool of the trade. What this permitted us to do that traditional epidemiological studies could not do, was to estimate the range and average levels of air pollution from secondhand smoke experienced by the population in the most frequented microenvironments.

Our next step was to estimate the concomitant range and magnitude of the lung cancer risk to the general nonsmoking U.S. population corresponding to our exposure estimates. This required developing an exposure-response relationship between RSP from secondhand smoke and lung cancer. I knew that we could estimate the numerator of our exposure-response relationship from data in Hirayama's famous 1981 prospective epidemiological study of 91,540 Japanese women [As of Nov. 1, 2017, his paper had 1111 citations (JStor, 2017).] Hirayama had found that those women exposed to their husbands' smoking experienced a statistically significant average annual increase in lung cancer mortality rate of 6.8 lung cancer deaths per 100,000 persons (typically expressed in epidemiological units as person-years), with a range of 5.3 to 9.4 per 100,000 person-years, depending upon the degree of the husband's reported smoking.

I had discussed his study with Dr. Hirayama over dinner after we met at the Third World Conference on Smoking and Health held in Winnipeg, Manitoba, in 1983. He was an engaging personality and quite fluent in English. He shared a draft of a memoir he was writing on the nuclear destruction of Hiroshima, entitled, *The Clouds and The Rain*. It was very poignant; I do not know if he ever published it. Figure 13 is a rare photo of Takeshi Hirayama. A vital insight provided by Hirayama was that Japanese wives typically were stay-at-home moms who were discouraged from paid work and from associating with men outside their family due to Japanese cultural taboos prevalent in the 1960's. Thus, in Japan, her husband's smoking was an excellent surrogate for a nonsmoking woman's exposure to secondhand smoke. However, there was a problem with relying on Hirayama's lung cancer mortality rate in the numerator of my risk model. I had no idea of the sizes or ventilation rates of Japanese homes. Therefore, I didn't know how his cohort's secondhand smoke exposure compared to our estimates of exposure in the U.S.

As for the Garfinkel study, I foresaw a major problem with taking his numerical results at face value, because Garfinkel had ignored the elephant in the room: he had tacitly assumed that his subjects had no secondhand smoke exposure outside the home, a flaw that Hammond and Selikoff had pointed out in connection with social occasions. However, there was a much bigger source of unaccounted-for secondhand smoke exposure for women in the Garfinkel study. I knew from experience that there were few workplaces that were smoke-free in that era. Moreover, the *Statistical Abstract of the United States* showed that the labor force participation rate for U.S. women from 1965 to 1975 ranged from 39% to 44%, and was similar in prior years going all the way back to the 1940's. So, ignoring workplace exposure to secondhand smoke loomed as an obvious error in Garfinkel's exposure assessment. This set me to wondering if there might be a truly unexposed nonsmoking female cohort whose lung cancer rates were published that we could use as baseline controls with which to compare our calculations for women who were exposed to smoking at work or at home. I began an intensive literature search for such a study.

THE SMOKING GUN

If greater exposure to secondhand smoke increases the risk of lung cancer, then lesser exposure to secondhand smoke must decrease the risk of lung cancer. Both Mormons and Seventh Day Adventists shunned smoking, so naturally both groups had very low rates of lung cancer compared to nonsmokers in the general population. It logically follows that lifelong nonsmokers in either religious group were unlikely to be exposed to secondhand smoke at home. Therefore, I painstakingly searched through epidemiological journals in the EPA technical library as well as the National Library of Medicine for a study that compared lung cancer rates among nonsmokers in these religious groups to nonsmokers in the general population. In a magnificent stroke of luck, I discovered two seminal studies published in 1980, reporting on 75,000 nonsmokers, 25,000 Seventh Day Adventists (SDAs) and 50,000 non-SDAs. One was published in the *Journal of the National Cancer Institute* and the other in the *American Journal of Epidemiology*. Both were authored by Prof. Roland Phillips and colleagues at Loma Linda University in Southern California. Phillips had compared lung cancer mortality rates in SDAs to those in non-SDAs. Not only were SDAs unlikely to be exposed to smoking at home, but many SDAs worked for church-run organizations, where they certainly wouldn't be exposed to secondhand smoke, whereas the opposite was true for non-SDAs in the workplace. We were now up and running.

Phillips et al. found that the nonsmoking non-SDAs in the general population had a statistically significant lung cancer mortality rate 2.4 times of the nonsmoking SDAs who strictly adhered to the church's teaching. Moreover, in their papers, Phillips et al. wrote that this lung cancer difference might actually be an effect of passive smoking. I felt sure that they were right. I phoned Phillips and had a long discussion. I emphasized the importance of his data for our work. I asked him if he would share a copy of his computer output with the detailed lung cancer mortality rates for the two groups. He generously agreed to send copies to us. In a lengthy table in the appendix of our manuscript, I calculated the age-specific lung cancer rate difference between the two groups of nonsmokers from Philips et al.'s raw data and using the 1974 Life Tables for U.S. white population, standardized it to estimate the lung cancer death (LCD) rate difference between them. This weighted difference was 7.4 lung cancer deaths (LCDs) per 100,000 person-years.

Gratifyingly, this difference turned out to be within 10% of Hirayama's value of 6.8 LCDs per 100,000 person-years between his exposed and control groups. I was elated. At last I had found the smoking-gun study I needed to accomplish our two goals: first, to estimate the total number of lung cancer deaths among the 100 million adult US nonsmokers due to passive smoking. And second, to derive an exposure-response relationship between nonsmokers' daily average dose of secondhand smoke particles and working lifetime lung cancer mortality risk. This relationship was necessary in order to explain why Garfinkel, by ignoring workplace secondhand smoke exposures of women, had incorrectly placed 38% of his exposed cohort into the "unexposed" category. This was a consequence of using data that had not been collected for the purpose of assessing secondhand smoke exposure. And it was based on an outdated assumption that women did not work outside the home. From my personal experience, I knew this was false. This was an older upper middle-class white male pre-WWII bias. As I knew from living through the decades of the 1940's, 1950's and 1960's, where even doctors' waiting rooms were smoke-filled, such women were highly likely to have worked or be working in white- and pink-collar worksites that were mostly smoke-filled. This of course would have confounded Garfinkel's results, wiping out his study's statistical significance.

Al and I discussed this at length, and we felt confident in using Phillips risk value for the numerator of our exposure-response relationship, and our estimate of the exposure of the average person in the denominator. This yielded an exposure-response relationship, weighted by five-year age groups, of 5 lung cancer deaths per 100,000 persons per year per milligram per day of exposure to tobacco tar from passive smoking. I then multiplied this by the population at risk, U.S. adult nonsmokers aged 35 years and older, to estimate 4700 lung cancer deaths per year among these 100 million U.S. nonsmokers from passive smoking. This turned out to be 65 times as great as all the estimated cancer deaths from all the hazardous air pollutants regulated by EPA at the time. On the other hand, an extrapolation from the risks in smokers, based on the "one-hit" model of carcinogenesis, estimated a lower bound of about 555 deaths per year, but still more than 6 times all the estimated deaths from regulated outdoor hazardous air pollutants.

There was one more crucial step to take: If our exposure-response model had any validity, it should be able to mathematically explain Garfinkel's ostensibly contradictory results compared with Hirayama's study. We knew that Garfinkel's data was clearly confounded by his failure to consider exposure of nonsmoking women to secondhand smoke in the workplace. So, I performed a re-analysis of Garfinkel's cohort assuming our exposure-response relationship with 38% of the women in his control group assumed to be exposed to secondhand smoke in the workplace (these we dubbed "tainted controls").

The 38% figure was based on labor force participation rates of adult women published in the Statistical Abstract of the United States for the period preceding and during Garfinkel's study. Applying this to our model, our exposure-response relationship then accurately predicted Garfinkel's reported risk ratio to within 1%, and his risk rate to within 4%. Moreover, if we recalculated the risk by moving the "tainted controls" into an exposed group, lo and behold, Garfinkel's results differed from Hirayama's by less than 5%! As a finishing touch, we re-analyzed Garfinkel's results using the one-hit dose-response model, which predicted a risk ratio and risk rate results nearly 40% different from his results, lending credence to our SDA model.

FIGURE 13. DR. TAKESHI HIRAYAMA, WINNIPEG, CANADA, 1983; (AUTHOR'S PHOTO).

Al and I polished and re-polished the manuscript and submitted it for publication. It had 86 references, including papers on air pollution epidemiology, medical physiology, ventilation engineering, interactions between tobacco smoke and indoor radon, 27 papers reporting epidemiological studies of passive smoking and lung cancer or respiratory disease, outdoor epidemiological studies of air pollution and cancer, reports on the methodology of risk assessment, papers on the fundamentals of carcinogenesis, including tobacco carcinogenesis, nonlinearity in dose-response relationships, cancer latency, risk assessment of environmental carcinogens, biomarkers of secondhand smoke dose, statistics on labor force participation rates, volumes of homes, studies of human activity patterns, vital statistics of the United States, especially mortality rates by age group in men and women, and regulation of environmental carcinogens. It had been a massive multi-year undertaking involving several scientific disciplines. We decided to submit our manuscript to the *Journal of Occupational Medicine*, which seemed suitable. The editor sent it out to two reviewers who gave it favorable reviews and recommended that it be published with some minor changes. We made them and resubmitted the paper. However, the editor wasn't satisfied, and demanded further changes in the manuscript. We made them and resubmitted the paper. The editor then demanded yet *another* a new set of changes. Al and I began to feel jerked around. We decided that the editor might be wary of the controversy it undoubtedly would provoke, and abandoned *JOM* as a lost cause.

I was aware that Alan Moghissi, an EPA colleague, was the editor of the journal *Environment International*. In 1980, Alan had invited me to lecture on indoor air pollution as a guest lecturer in a course he taught on Indoor Air Pollution and Energy Conservation in the Department of Mechanical Engineering, at Catholic University, where he was an Adjunct Professor. I consulted him for advice. Moghissi, a physical chemist, had served in several positions at EPA since its founding in 1970. Inter alia, he had been Director of its Bioenvironmental and Radiological Research Division, Principal Science Advisor for Radiation and Hazardous Materials, and Manager of the Health and Environmental Risk Analysis Program. Alan asked, "Jim, why not submit it to my journal? I'm the editor and can make a judgment based on the existing reviews; give me all your correspondence with JOM." So, we submitted our revised manuscript, including all of the JOM reviews and written exchanges with its editor, to *Environment International* in May 1984.

In tandem with this, I decided to request an official ORD review of our manuscript through official channels from Joe Cannon to his counterpart, Bernie Goldstein, EPA's Assistant Administrator for Research and Development. It was assigned to a staff epidemiologist, Herman Gibb, in the Carcinogen Assessment Group run by Elizabeth Anderson, Director of the Office of Health and Environmental Assessment. I was not acquainted with him. In his review, Gibb concluded that of our two methods of assessing annual lung cancer risk assessment, the low-end one, using the one-hit model, based on extrapolation of the lung cancer risks in smokers down to the exposure levels of nonsmokers, "was better supported" than the high end one based on the Seventh Day Adventist Study. In her cover letter transmitting Gibb's review to Cannon, Anderson concluded, "It should be noted that even this [low end] risk would, given the size of the population exposed to passive smoking, translate into a significant population risk in comparison to other environmental carcinogens." Although we vehemently disagreed with Gibb's conclusions about the one-hit model being "better supported," we nevertheless forwarded his review on to Moghissi to add to the two others.

ANOTHER BARRAGE BY BIG TOBACCO

In April 1984, The Tobacco Institute had become increasingly apprehensive after the warnings about secondhand smoke in the 1982 Surgeon General's Report on Cancer. Still stinging from the impact of our 1980 Science article and our 1982 *ASHRAE Transactions* paper, they issued a slick 23-page glossy brochure entitled, "*Cigarette Smoke and the Nonsmoker.*" The forward read as follows.

The question of public smoking:

"This booklet focuses on a subject that has become increasingly familiar to many – "public smoking" and the campaign to limit or prohibit smoking in public places.

The crucial question is whether the exposure of nonsmokers to tobacco smoke in normal, everyday situations actually creates a health hazard. We don't think this has been shown. Indeed, many scientists who believe smoking is harmful to smokers have publicly stated there is not sufficient evidence to conclude public smoking is harmful to nonsmokers.

Why, then, is so much emphasis being placed on the subject? A simple answer is difficult, but it seems reasonable to suggest that the failure of the campaign aimed at making smokers stop smoking has resulted in a compensatory effort to make smoking "socially unacceptable."

The campaign for outright bans or restrictions on smoking in public places is noteworthy for its lack of persuasive scientific findings. However, it is breeding discrimination and ill will. Smokers and nonsmokers, friends and neighbors, are being set against each other. Social friction has arisen in many instances. Violence and militancy have been kindled in some cases. And – most seriously– personal freedoms are being attacked and eroded In a democratic society.

There is no need to demand restrictive legislation – to infringe on freedom of choice. Common sense, courtesy and tolerance for the preferences of others are all that is needed to enable smokers and nonsmokers each to enjoy their preferences and to respect those of others. Society is ill-served when its members are subjected to any kind of campaign based on fear or misinformation. No goal can be justified by the use of such expedients or contrivances to attain it. Emotional rhetoric is not a substitute for scientific fact."

The Tobacco Institute
April 1984

The brochure went on to quote the Surgeon General out of context. Under the caption, **The Evidence is not conclusive,** it gave our *Science* paper The Full Monty, quoting the paid criticism of its own moles:

Study design judged to be faulty:

"The 1982 Surgeon General's report, on cigarette smoking and cancer, noted that the available evidence is not sufficient to conclude that other people's smoke causes disease in nonsmokers.

A 1980 study involving measurement of particulates in public buildings in Washington, D.C., is cited frequently to support the claim that cigarette smoke may be harmful to nonsmokers.[10] The authors, James Repace and Alfred Lowrey, reported that in buildings where smoking was permitted levels of respirable particulate matter were far greater than in places where smoking was not permitted.

Serious questions about the study's scientific methodology were raised when Repace presented additional data to a 1982 meeting of the American Society of Heating, Refrigerating and Air-Conditioning Engineers.[11] Questioned from the floor by a consulting engineer, Repace admitted he had not measured the quantity of outdoor air introduced by ventilating systems.[12]

Another critic noted Repace and Lowrey did not measure particulate levels before smoking began, failed to present data on actual ventilation rates and, most importantly, did not determine the specific contribution of tobacco smoke to particulate levels."

Although the industry claimed that there were no health effects from secondhand smoke, it had long funded secret animal studies into this issue that contradicted its public statements. In 1970, Philip Morris had purchased a German research facility, the Institut fur Industrielle und Biologische Forschung GmbH, widely known by its acronym, INBIFO. Philip Morris (PM) arranged this purchase through a Swiss subsidiary, Fabriques de tabac reunites (FTR), and arranged for the appointment of a coordinator, Dr. Ragnar Rylander, a Swedish academic who was retained as a consultant to interface among PM, INBIFO, and FTR. Between 1981 and 1989, INBIFO produced 800 internal reports on ETS. Not a single one was ever made public. Rylander reported the results of these studies orally to Thomas Osdene, who was then the Director of Research & Extramural Studies for Philip Morris, and later became its Vice President for Science & Technology. This ensured that there would be no written record discoverable by inquisitive plaintiff's attorneys who might sue the company. In 1982, Rylander reported to Osdene that INBIFO had found that ETS was four times more injurious in its effects on rats in inhalation studies than mainstream (MS) smoke. PM concealed its knowledge of those studies as well as its own relationship to INBIFO [Kessler, ¶ 305; 2006].

As recently as April 2002, in a disclosure to a U.S. federal court, PM again rejected the statement that ETS causes disease. In 1974, Rylander had chaired an industry-funded workshop in Bermuda that concluded in part, "health effects of active smoking could not be extrapolated to passive smoking." In 1983, one year after reporting the alarming effects of ETS on lab rats to Osdene, Rylander again chaired a Tobacco Institute-funded workshop on ETS, this time at the University of Geneva in Switzerland. The Geneva workshop's conclusions, authored by Rylander, omitted any mention of his rat studies, asserting instead that "the possible health effects of ETS are not significant…" [Diethelm et al., 2004]. Payments to Rylander were routed from the industry via a secret account directed by tobacco lawyers [Kessler, ¶ 305; 2006].

From 1974 to 1989, the tobacco industry sponsored a total of eight so-called "international symposia" on ETS. I had collected the proceedings of every single one. These symposia always arrived at a "consensus" dictated by the tobacco industry's public relations exigencies. The 1989 McGill University conference co-funded by a tobacco industry grant, was typical of the genre. To quote Prof. Donald Ecobichon, of the Department of Pharmacology at McGill, a co-organizer of the McGill conference: "One of the most striking consensus views emanating from this conference is that the published data, when critically examined and evaluated, are inconsistent with the notion that ETS is a health hazard," ... "indoor smoking bans will do little, in the vast majority of circumstances, to ensure meaningful and lasting improvements in indoor air quality." Such symposia, typically organized by academics, were attended and summarized primarily by industry consultants and employees, but a few non-industry affiliated scientists were generally invited to provide a veneer of respectability. Copies of the non-peer-reviewed papers presented at these symposia were sometimes published in obscure journals and have been professionally bound and mailed unsolicited to libraries *gratis* (Repace & Lowrey, 1992). What these mole-infested symposia lacked in quality, they made up for in quantity.

The aim of these by-invitation-only convocations was made crystal clear in an internal memorandum authored and distributed by Donald Harris of PM Asia, on January 24, 1990. Harris set forth the party line: "The Symposium's Proceedings represent the most careful and thorough review of the science on ETS ever conducted and it was done by 82 leading medical and indoor air scientists and researchers from around the world. … Because of the importance of the Symposium's findings – for the industry and PM - *we must use the material wisely and effectively to block attempts by governments to establish public policies against smoking based upon ETS* (italics mine) [TTID 2504042040].

OUR RISK ASSESSMENT LEAKS TO THE PRESS

In September 1984, someone at EPA leaked Gibb's review of our risk assessment to *Inside EPA*, a privately published weekly newsletter. I never discovered who did it. I became alarmed that this leak might jeopardize publication, as some journals had strict policies against pre-publication publicity. I was relieved to learn that *Environment International* was not one of them. Meanwhile, a much bigger leak was about to occur. I had sent a copy of our manuscript for review to Stan Glantz. When I told him about the leak, Stan persuasively argued that since the cat was already out of the bag, and because our risk assessment was so important, he wanted to promote it to his contacts at CBS News in New York so it would reach a wider audience. I knew this would not give Moghissi heartburn, so I agreed. In for a penny, in for a pound. A producer at CBS asked Stan to fax him a copy of our paper.

I soon received a call from the producer requesting an interview with me at my desk at EPA. I certainly was no stranger to interviews with the national press, including television, as I had served as a spokesman on indoor air science issues for the agency since 1981, given interviews to National Public Radio and Canada's CBC on passive smoking in 1982, had been interviewed by *Readers' Digest* on indoor pollution in 1983, appeared on nationally syndicated Metromedia TV in an interview on passive smoking in 1983, gave an interview on indoor pollution on CBS 6-O'Clock news in New York in 1983, and RKO General Radio in 1984. However, I realized that being interviewed at my desk at EPA HQ on such a high profile controversial issue mandated the explicit approval of Joe Cannon, which I requested through Stolpman as a matter of courtesy. Joe quickly approved my request, and on Wednesday, September 26, 1984, our risk assessment garnered a staggering 3 minutes of nationally-broadcast airtime on the CBS TV Evening News With Dan Rather, where it was prominently billed as an "EPA Passive Smoking Study."

Two days after the CBS broadcast, Joe Cannon walked into my office and sat on the corner of my desk. Without preamble, he said, "Jim, I've re-programmed $75,000 from the Radiation Program, and I want you to take it and commission a National Academy of Sciences Report on Environmental Tobacco Smoke." In 1980, the NAS Indoor Pollutants report had cost twice as much. I swallowed that thought and enthusiastically agreed to take on the project. Afterward, I phoned Don Shopland, at the Office on Smoking and Health (OSH), and asked if he could scrape up another $75,000 to help fund the NAS study. He was delighted. Shortly thereafter, Don, his Office Director, Dr. Joanne Luoto, and I jointly met with Devra Davis, a prominent epidemiologist who was Acting Director of the Board on Environmental Studies and Toxicology at the National Research Council, to commission the report and arrange for funding. The Office on Smoking and Health in those days reported directly to the Secretary of Health and Human Services. As a high-status office, it had ample budgetary flexibility.

My instinct to collaborate with the Office on Smoking and Health would result in the issuance, back-to-back two years later, of two major reports indicting secondhand smoke as a cause of lung cancer: one, by the National Research Council, and a second, by the Surgeon General. The contribution of Don Shopland to public health cannot be overestimated: at this stage in his career, he had worked on 20 different Surgeon General's reports from 1964 on, including five for Surgeon General C. Everett Koop, from 1982 thru 1986. Dr. Koop justly honored Don with the Surgeon General's Medallion in 1987. (In later years, OSH was transferred from Washington to Atlanta, to be buried under layers of CDC bureaucracy, no doubt at the behest of tobacco-state congressmen). Shopland then decamped to the National Cancer Institute's Smoking, Tobacco, and Cancer Program, home to NCI's COMMIT and ASSIST tobacco control programs empowering state efforts to eliminate smoking in the USA. These were run by the brilliant Joe Cullen, Deputy Director of the Division of Cancer Prevention and Control.

Several days later, I received a call from Irvin Molotsky, a *New York Times* reporter. He first asked if there had been any press coverage in the wake of the CBS broadcast. I told him I knew of none. He said he wanted to do a story on our study. I decided to clear this with Moghissi. Alan replied with a characteristic twinkle in his eye, "make sure they spell the name of the journal right." On Saturday, November 3rd, 1984, two days after my 46th birthday, an 1160 word article headlined in 26-point boldfaced type, **E.P.A. Study Links Deaths of Nonsmokers to Cigarette** By IRVIN MOLOTSKY, appeared prominently on the back page of Section A of the *Times*. It read in part:

> WASHINGTON, Nov. 2— "A study by the Environmental Protection Agency estimates that 500 to 5,000 nonsmokers die each year of lung cancer caused by others' cigarettes. The study says that 'passive' tobacco smoke is the country's most dangerous airborne carcinogen, even if the lower figure of 500 deaths is used. ... It was conducted over the past three years by James L. Repace, a physicist and policy analyst in the environmental agency's Office of Air and Radiation, and Alfred H. Lowrey, a research chemist in the Laboratory for the Structure of Matter at the Naval Research Laboratory."

The article observed that a debate over whether nonsmokers exposed to secondhand smoke at home, at work, or in public places has been contentious for years. It quoted Dr. Elizabeth Anderson, the director of EPA's Office of Health and Environmental Assessment as saying even at the lower bound this translated into a "significant population risk." William D. Toohey Jr, a Tobacco Institute spokesman disagreed, telling the *Times* that our study: "has a major problem in that it relies on data that have been seriously questioned ... It is totally unsupportable." On the other hand, it quoted accolades from health and anti-smoking group spokespersons, including the American Lung Association. The *Times* article ended with a pithy quote from our paper: "passive smoking appears to pose a public health risk larger than the hazardous air pollutants from all industrial emissions combined" [NY Times, 1984].

The following week a barrage of phone calls and letters that would ultimately exceed 500 bombarded our office with requests for copies of the study. Our two secretaries complained so much that Stolpman issued me a personal answering machine where they could direct callers to leave their names and addresses. Meanwhile, on November 7th, Tom Osdene, the Research Director for Philip Morris, wrote a memo to Mark Serrano, PM's Vice President for Operations, detailing his plans to attack our work:

> "**Subject**: Repace – EPA Validation of Repace Data.
> "Repace and Lowrey have written a paper in which they assess the 'nonsmoker's lung cancer risk from passive smoking.' This paper is based strictly on an exposure model which they use to make a risk assessment in two microenvironments. There is no direct experimental data and they have picked data from a number of epidemiological studies which in themselves are seriously flawed (e.g., Trichopoulos, Hirayama, etc.) They arrive at their Conclusions by a series of complex calculations which according to Tony Colucci (ETS advisory group, Washington Meeting, Nov. 1), may themselves be open to criticism. ... At the meeting in Washington (ETS group), it was stated that John Rupp (Covington & Burling) is working with Dr. Sorell L. Schwartz (Prof. of Pharmacology at Georgetown University) who will provide a detailed critique of Repace's work and may be published. Dr. Colucci will assist Rupp and will meet with Schwartz. This paper also brings up the whole question of risk assessment by EPA and Marvin Kastenbaum feels that the whole question needs to be approached on a fundamental basis" [TTID 201579355].

On November 29, 1984, The Tobacco Institute weighed in with operational plans laid out in a memo from TI Vice President Kloepfer to TI President Chilcote, with cc's to Dave Henderson, Don Hoel, John Rupp, and Susan Stuntz:

TO: SAMUEL D. CHILCOTE, JR.
FROM: WILLIAM KLOEPFER, JR.
SUBJECT: EPA MONITORING STATUS

Here's our EPA status and outlook, following an inventory session
with Susan Stuntz and John Rupp on November 21:

1. John expected to have, this weekend, a critique from Dr. Sorell Schwartz at George Washington University of the Repace estimate. He intended to express it to Dr. Tony Colucci at Reynolds and Mike Davidson, the background smoke specialist at Jacob & Medinger [*], for immediate review. He hopes to have the paper ready for presentation at EPA by the end of this week.

2. We discussed who might visit whom at EPA. We agree Dr. Schwartz should represent us, accompanied by either Stuntz, Ralph Vinovich or myself, and John and possibly another attorney, depending on whether purpose of the visit is to the General Counsel's office or the operating division in which James Repace is employed. Our group will meet in advance.

…

5. We are assembling as much information as we can from public records on the co-authors of the death estimate — Repace and Lowery [sic], who is employed by the Naval Research Laboratory. Attached are notes about Repace, prepared by Katherine Becker. We will ask her for a similar review regarding Lowery. In addition, John will file an FOI request at NRL for documents pertaining to the estimate paper. We are puzzled by the fact that Repace, while employed in several areas of jurisdiction and expertise, appears to confine his numerous public appearances to only one – indoor air and especially tobacco smoke — over which we believe EPA has no regulatory authority. We are taking steps to learn the extent to which these external activities have been supported by EPA in terms of Repace's working time and expenses.

6. We did not discuss, but we must try to follow up on, the matter of how the Repace estimate as a private, unpublished document, reached CBS and the New York Times.

7. We expect to have a further report for you at the end of this week [TTID TI 4599-1675].

*[N.B.: Jacob and Medinger was a law firm used by the tobacco industry to suppress and conceal scientific research. Kessler, 2006].

The tobacco companies were already on red alert. RJ Reynolds had unleashed a pre-emptive strike earlier that year, with a large ad campaign launched in January 1984, which had run in national newspapers and news magazines, under the auspices of RJR's chairman, E.A. Horrigan, Jr. [Pride, 1984; TTID 621508026]. The Reynolds campaign in part, addressed the issue of public smoking: "We believe, for example, that smokers and non-smokers can work out their relationships with each other through mutual cooperation and consideration without legislative interference." In a brochure titled, *An Open Debate*, Corrigan asserted that, "There has been a great deal of overreaction on the issue of smoking in public places. An objective look at all of the evidence available would, the company believes, clearly show a reasonable person there is no reliable scientific proof that cigarette smoke causes disease in nonsmokers, In fact, the weight of the evidence is that it does not." He went on to cite Garfinkel's study as "proof" [TTID TI00430746]. One Reynolds ad stated in part: "There has always been some friction between smokers and non-smokers. But lately this friction has grown more heated. The controversy has been fueled by questionable reports which claim that 'second-hand smoke' is a cause of serious diseases among non-smokers. But, in fact, there is little evidence – and certainly nothing which proves scientifically – that cigarette smoke causes disease in non-smokers" [TTID 51271 6782].

Another read, "Many non-smokers are annoyed by cigarette smoke. This is a reality that's been with us for a long time. Lately, however, many non-smokers have come to believe that cigarette smoke in the air can actually cause disease. But a scientific study by the Harvard School of Public Health, conducted in various public places, found that non-smokers might inhale anywhere *from 1/1000th to 1/100th of one filter cigarette per hour.* At that rate, it would take you at least 4 days to inhale the equivalent of a single cigarette. Often our own concerns about our health can take an unproven claim and magnify it out of all proportion; so, what begins as a misconception turns into a frightening myth. Is "second-hand smoke" one of these myths? We hope the information we've offered will help you sort out some of the realities" [TTID TI 17720302].

Moghissi asked for and received certain changes and additions to our manuscript. Satisfied that the paper was ready for prime time, he informed us that our paper would be accepted for publication. He said that he would even write an editorial about it. In echoes of the approach that the Tobacco Institute had made on our *Science* manuscript, Moghissi added that four tobacco industry representatives had visited him in an attempt to discourage the publication of our paper. He rejected their plea out of hand. He said they would have to settle for sending in a Letter to the Editor.

Meanwhile, British American Tobacco (BAT) in an internal review of the scientific literature in late 1984, feared further increases in public concern over the passive smoking issue. In particular, BAT's review singled out the passive smoking and lung cancer studies of Hirayama, Trichopoulos, and Garfinkel. The publicity surrounding Repace and Lowrey's risk assessment made them very uneasy because the publication of "annual body counts which can then be compared to road accidents, drug deaths, and other statistics of concern to the general public" [TTID 1190964960]. BAT's analysis was spot on: in 1985, I authored a book chapter which contained a table in which I compared the estimated annual lung cancer mortality risk from passive smoking to other causes of death; it was comparable to the annual risk of death by drowning or from fires [CCCP, 1985]. In subsequent years, when cardiovascular deaths from secondhand smoke were added in, the total risk would be comparable to road deaths.

Although print copies were not yet available, the imminent publication of our paper ignited a firestorm of national publicity: On the 10th of January 1985, I gave an interview on passive smoking to INN News, a cable TV outlet. On January 11, a *New York Times* Editorial captioned "Making Cigarettes Pay, stated: "Secondhand smoke also poses a threat. A recent study by the Environmental Protection Agency calls passive tobacco smoke 'the country's most dangerous airborne carcinogen" and the cause of 500 to 5,000 deaths from lung cancer yearly.'" On January 31, in a front-page story captioned "**Smoker's smoke risk to all – study,**" *USA TODAY* reported "Tobacco smoke breathed by non-smokers is the USA's most dangerous cancer-causing air pollutant, killing from 500 to 5,000 people a year, a soon-to be-published government study says. Tobacco Institute spokesman Bill Aylward said it contradicts findings of a 1983 National Institutes of Health panel that passive smoke has a small effect on non-smokers. 'We feel our numbers are virtually ironclad,' said study author James Repace, an EPA policy analyst, 'They present a pretty strong argument'."

Events began to move faster. On the 16th of January, I presented a talk, Risk Assessment of Passive Smoking, to the Interagency Technical Working Committee on Smoking, Heart, Lung, and Blood Diseases, at the National Institutes of Health. On Sunday, the 4th of February, a United Press International wire service story reported: "Scientist says tobacco smoke is one of deadliest indoor air pollutants." That evening, I received a request to appear early the next morning, Monday the 5th of February, on ABC TV's *Good Morning America*; I gave them a five-minute live interview on the risk assessment of passive smoking. Later that morning, I did another live 13-minute interview on CNN. This was a very large amount of national broadcast time. In the wake of my previous September CBS interview at EPA HQ, with minor reservations, I decided not to bother to clear these new interviews with EPA in advance.

On Wednesday the 7th, Bill Toohey at the Tobacco Institute wrote his boss, Susan Stuntz, complaining, "Susan, I have received three calls from State Activities' field staff in the past several days seeking information on the Repace/Lowery [sic] paper. Apparently, they are getting hit with the lousy news stories about it at legislative hearings. Attached, you will find a short piece which essentially outlines what I have told reporters about the paper and its authors. Obviously, it needs to be cleared. In any event, this, or another 'one-pager' on Repace, appears desperately needed" [TTID T1082291158]

Later that week, I received a telephone call from Phil Angell, Administrator Ruckleshaus's chief of staff: He announced that, "we are having difficulty getting this message through the chain of command (meaning Joe Cannon). We (meaning Bill Ruckleshaus) would like you to cool the publicity." I inferred immediately that Ruckleshaus had received complaints from tobacco state congressmen and senators. I promised Angell to cool it, but in any case, there was not much damage left to do: I had already rather thoroughly covered all the major media outlets in the US and Canada.

Two days later, I gave a well-received invited talk to the Interagency Task Force on Environmental Lung Cancer, and on March 15th, I was invited by the National Cancer Institute to review grant proposals as a panelist on a Special Study Section for Passive Smoking Research. This also proved to be a seminal event: I was asked to review, along with Larry Garfinkel, the chief epidemiologist for the American Cancer Society, what proved to be an outstanding grant proposal from Prof. Pellayo Correa at LSU. Dr. Correa proposed an epidemiological study of passive smoking and lung cancer that would later prove to be a crucial paper for EPA in its world-famous 1992 quantitative risk assessment of passive smoking and lung cancer.

Correa's outstanding proposal beat out a competing proposal by Prof. Michael Lebowitz, an epidemiologist at the University of Arizona, who was a prominent indoor air researcher on secondhand smoke, and also an inveterate chain-smoker who had downplayed the risks of passive smoking. I had known him from when he had been on the NAS Indoor Pollutants Committee in 1981. I had long suspected Mike Lebowitz of industry ties but could never prove it. Nevertheless, I made no secret of my suspicions to several of our mutual colleagues. Lebowitz was not unaware of this, and he vehemently denied any industry ties. My bias against Lebowitz's retrograde views led to a long soul-searching conversation with Wayne Ott. Ultimately, I decided I had to grade his proposal on its scientific merit, ranking it against all competing proposals. Ultimately, both Garfinkel and I rated Lebowitz's proposal as "meritorious." Unfortunately for him, it was below NCI's funding cut-off. It simply could not compete with Correa's proposal with the limited funds available. Nevertheless, when Lebowitz found out how I had voted, it earned me his undying enmity. I do not know if he felt the same about Larry Garfinkel. Although we travelled in the same circles and attended many of the same meetings, Mike refused to speak to me ever again.

As I was doing research for this chapter decades later, I uncovered an internal memo written in 1987 by Susan Stuntz, Senior Vice President for Public Affairs for the Tobacco Institute: "Michael Lebowitz of the Univ. of Arizona, has in the past consulted with Shook, Hardy and Bacon on ETS issues" [TTID TI 17720302]. In Judge Kessler's decision in the governments RICO lawsuit in 2006, Lebowitz would be listed as being funded from "Special Account 4," the account that the industry used to fund its tobacco moles. Kessler identified General Counsel from Philip Morris, Reynolds, Lorillard, Liggett, B&W, and American Tobacco and lawyers from Jacob, Medinger & Finnegan and Shook, Hardy & Bacon as in control of the allocation of funds from Special Account No. 4. It appears that my mole sniffer had been up to snuff.

Meanwhile, at the National Security Agency, Dr. Peter Newton had been appointed as an ombudsman with the title of Agency Smoking Policy/Compliance Officer. During the first week in January of 1985, he polled the Agency workforce on smoking in the workplace. Eighty percent of the workforce responded. Newton found that 81 percent of the respondents were nonsmokers and that 34 percent of these nonsmokers said smoking was currently a problem in their work area. Seventy-five percent said that smoking in the workplace had adversely affected their productivity [NSA, 2002].

I GO ON THE LECTURE CIRCUIT

I began to be invited to present talks at national conferences and universities and was noticed by international organizations. I spoke on "The Cancer Risk from Workplace Smoking" at the Society of Occupational and Environmental Health's Conference on Smoking in the Workplace, on the 10th of April. I was asked by the World Health Organization to organize a planning workshop for a research program investigating passive smoking on aircraft, which I carried out in Geneva, Switzerland, on the 17th of April. On the 30th of April, I lectured on the risk assessment of passive smoking before the Bio-Engineering Program at the University of California, Berkeley. The flurry of national publicity for our risk assessment continued to provoke another virulent attack of agita in the tobacco industry. On April 25, 1985, Kloepfer, then the Tobacco Institute's senior VP for public relations, in an 18-page Report on the Public Smoking Issue to the industry's Communications Committee, raged:

> "The nonsmoker battle for smoke-free air – more complicated than fire safety, more damaging than ad restrictions and ultimately a greater bottom-line threat than excises. ... We are defending two fronts – political regulation and private rulemaking. We are fighting legislation, we are confronting research by regulatory agencies such as FAA and EPA. Indoor air quality is a buzz phrase in a dozen other agencies which we must monitor. Workplace restrictions grind on in their course. The focus is dangerously narrow: ambient smoke. Some of our retaliation is working. Some is in the pipeline. We have only begun, however, to take the decisions, make the commitments and exploit the opportunities that can win this battle over the basic social acceptability of smoking.
>
> The Repaces and Lowreys, Whites and Froebs, Hirayamas, Trichopoulos's and countless other anti-smoker scientists have kept refueling the public's paradoxical fear of its environment, to the extent that seventy percent of nonsmokers and a majority of smokers now believe that ambient smoke is probably hazardous and a no-smoking sign will restore health to the indoor air. They have reinforcements on the way.
>
> *Environment International* has scheduled publication of Repace's nonsmoker death estimate for late May. We expect he'll make a new news story out of it. But he may not know that we'll beat him to the media in a series of documented, one-on-one briefings. Repace may not know the journal editor's own skepticism, the editor's warm reception of Sorrell Schwartz' critique, and the editor's eagerness to get and publish the critical scientific responses we're stimulating. We know other scientific hits are going to be needed here" [TTID TIMN 285603].

Our 19-page paper was published in the Volume 11, #1, January 1985 issue of *Environment International*, the print version of which would hit the street in May. It was the lead article. As promised, it was accompanied by an editorial, "Health Risks of Passive Smoking," by A. Alan Moghissi. His editorial noted in part that:

"This issue of *Environment International* contains a contribution on the carcinogenic risk of nonsmokers who are exposed to tobacco smoke. This contribution is coauthored by Repace and Lowrey, who have been active in the study of pollution of indoor air primarily caused by smoking. Due to the controversial nature of the paper by Repace and Lowrey and its significance, added measures were required to assure adequate peer review and the documentation of the underlying information, including assumptions. Despite the efforts by the authors, the reviewers, and the editors, there is no doubt that this paper will be discussed and its conclusions will be disputed by various interested parties." … "*Despite these and other complicating factors, Repace and Lowry make a convincing case for public health hazards of public smoking* [italics mine]. The unquestionable facts are that tobacco smoke exposes nonsmokers to some potent carcinogens. Accordingly, the relevant question is not whether passive smoking poses a carcinogenic risk but what the magnitude of the carcinogenic risk is. Considering the size of the population of passive smokers, the risk could be significant."

Disappointing Kloepfer's eager expectations, Moghissi's editorial supported our major conclusions.

The abstract of our paper, A Quantitative Estimate of Nonsmoker's Lung Cancer Risk From Passive Smoking (J.L. Repace, and A.H Lowrey) *Environment International*, 11: 3-22 (1985) reads as follows:

"This work presents a quantitative assessment of nonsmokers' risk of lung cancer from passive smoking. The estimates given should be viewed as preliminary and subject to change as improved research becomes available. It is estimated that U.S. nonsmokers are exposed to from 0 to 14 mg of tobacco tar per day, and that the typical nonsmoker is exposed to 1.4 mg per day. A phenomenological exposure-response relationship is derived, yielding 5 lung cancer deaths per year per 100,000 persons exposed, per mg daily tar exposure. This relationship yields lung cancer mortality rates and mortality ratios for a U.S. cohort which are consistent to within 5% with the results of both of the large prospective epidemiological studies of passive smoking and lung cancer in the United States and Japan. Aggregate exposure to ambient tobacco smoke is estimated to produce about 5000 lung cancer deaths per year in U.S. nonsmokers aged ≥ 35 yr, with an average loss of life expectancy of 17 ± 9 yr per fatality. The estimated risk to the most-exposed passive smokers appears to be comparable to that from pipe and cigar smoking. Mortality from passive smoking is estimated to be about two orders of magnitude higher than that estimated for carcinogens currently regulated as hazardous air pollutants under the federal Clean Air Act."

ANOTHER PRE-EMPTIVE STRIKE BY BIG TOBACCO

Shortly before the print edition of *Environment International* that contained our article appeared in May 1985, The Tobacco Institute issued a slickly produced glossy 42-page brochure, launching a major attack on our risk assessment. It included a gratuitous ad hominem attack for good measure. It was sent to the industry's publication distribution lists accompanied by a cover memo from TI apparatchik Susan Stuntz that read in part: "The attached 'Situation Report: Tobacco Smoke in the Air,' has been prepared in anticipation of the publication of James Repace's latest attack on environmental tobacco smoke, in *Environment International*" [TTID 541024852].

Situation Report: Tobacco Smoke in the Air

Foreword

"This report focuses on an issue that is receiving increasing publicity – the question of whether exposure of nonsmokers to tobacco smoke in normal, everyday situations represents a health hazard. Most recently, a calculation developed by two government employees, James Repace and Alfred Lowrey, has received a great deal of attention. Repace and Lowrey claim that cigarette smoke in the air is responsible for 500 to 5,000 lung cancer deaths per year among U.S. nonsmokers. They derived these numbers using highly controversial 'risk assessment models,' data from their own questionable 1980 report on particulates in the air in various buildings, and data from other equally questionable epidemiologic studies.

The authors, who prepared their report independently, are long time, highly vocal anti-smoking activists. Repace, for example, testifies frequently as a member of the Group Against Smokers' Pollution (GASP) before legislative bodies considering smoking restrictions. He also has been used as a witness by Action on Smoking and Health (ASH) in several 'nonsmoker's rights' lawsuits. He can hardly be described as an 'unbiased' researcher. The Repace-Lowrey calculation has not yet appeared in print in a scientific journal – it is scheduled for publication in Environment International *in late May. Appearance of the article in print likely will bring a new round of publicity to the claims. This report demonstrates that publicity and attempts at remedial action based upon the Repace-Lowrey calculation, are highly unjustified."*

The Tobacco Institute
May 1985
The opening paragraph spelled out the industry's worst enemies:

"Today, advocates of smoking restrictions promote several highly publicized studies as 'proof' that tobacco smoke in the air represents a health hazard to the nonsmoker. The studies most frequently cited are three highly questionable works by Repace and Lowrey[1], Hirayama[2], and Trichopoulos, et al.[3] These three well publicized studies – two in 1981 and one in 1984-1985 – claim that cigarette smoke in the air increases the risk of lung cancer in nonsmokers."

These lies were getting tedious. Al had never been a member of GASP, and I had abdicated my position as VP of Bowie GASP in 1979. Although I had served as an expert witness in secondhand smoke litigation, I had never served as an expert witness in litigation for Action on Smoking and Health (ASH). Moreover, ASH did not do private lawsuits. But outright fabrications like this had never troubled the Tobacco Institute. Lowrey and I also published another paper that year, in the *New York State Journal of Medicine* (NYSJM). At that time, it was edited by Dr. Alan Blum, the charismatic physician who was very active in opposing the tobacco industry. Alan, who amassed an enormous collection of tobacco advertising, later became a good friend. In our paper, "An indoor air quality standard for ambient tobacco smoke based on carcinogenic risk," we concluded that, "At typical smoking occupancies for an office environment, achieving this standard would require impractical amounts of ventilation or prohibitive costs for air cleaning equipment. It appears that the only practical control measures are complete physical separation of smokers and nonsmokers on different ventilation systems, or prohibition of smoking in the workplace." This statement followed directly from the exposure-response relationship we had derived in our *Environment International* risk assessment paper using the habitual smoker model posited in our *Science* paper.

Why *can't* ventilation control tobacco smoke? The answer derives directly from three considerations. First, on average, all cigarettes have about the same amount of tobacco in them, about ¾ of a gram, and are typically smoked at an average rate of 2 cigarettes per hour. So, the smoke emissions are essentially determined by the number of smokers in the room. The second factor is the room volume, which of course is fixed. The density of smoke in the air is directly proportional to the number of active smokers divided by the room volume, i.e., the density of smokers in the space. The third factor is the ventilation rate. The smoke concentration is inversely proportional to the ventilation rate. Thus, the smoke concentration in the air is determined by the ratio of the smoker density to ventilation rate. Since the room volume appears both in the numerator (smoker density) and the denominator (air flow per unit volume) of the model, it cancels out. The greater the number of smokers in room of a given size, the higher the smoke concentration.

On the other hand, ventilation rates are prescribed by local building codes, which are based on engineering recommendations, and may or may not be attained in practice. The reason for this is that building operators have the ability to close outdoor air intakes to conserve energy. And they often do, especially in the Class C building stock (public buildings, such as courthouses and schools, as well as low-budget office buildings) since heating, cooling, and dehumidifying outdoor ventilation air costs money. Why not use a more powerful fan to increase airflow? The problem that arises is that increasing the ventilation airflow without increasing the ventilation duct diameter and the louver size will create cold drafts and excessive air noise. Further, enlarging the size of the ducts in an existing building involves major reconstruction and expense, is disruptive to building occupants and is therefore highly impractical. Air cleaning devices suffer from the same practical limitation as ventilation: the need for smoke removal rates sufficient to yield acceptable risk.

This raises the question of how high do air flow rates need to be to control secondhand smoke to an acceptable level of risk? And how can we judge the amount of harm caused by chronic exposure to a given concentration of secondhand smoke? Federal decision rules on safe levels of risk from hazardous air pollutants in place in 1980 defined *de minimis* (acceptable) risk, or a risk that's "beneath regulatory concern," as a mortality rate range for involuntary risk varying from 1 death per ten million persons to 1 death per hundred thousand persons per lifetime depending upon the mandate of the federal agency (Repace and Lowrey, 1993). For a population of 100 million nonsmoking office workers at maximum acceptable risk of one death per hundred thousand persons at risk, or 1/100,000, this is equivalent to 1000 deaths per working lifetime of 40 years or 25 deaths per year.

According to our risk model, achieving even this level of acceptable risk for lung cancer from passive smoking for a nonsmoker exposed in an office setting, simply by using ventilation, would require an increase from the ASHRAE-recommended design ventilation rate of 0.84 air changes per hour to a ridiculously high 226 air changes per hour. This is an increase by a factor of 269. To achieve this using air cleaning devices would require an expenditure of $28,000 per smoker in 1985 dollars [Repace and Lowrey, 1985b]. And this is just for lung cancer. It does not even begin to consider the risks posed by the other diseases caused by passive smoking. I would not address that issue until 1998.

Our NYSJM paper raised alarms at the highest levels of the tobacco industry. Our paper thoroughly provoked Hugh Cullman, the Vice Chairman of Philip Morris Incorporated. Following Cullman's command, TI's William Kloepfer Jr., sent out a memorandum seeking comment on our NYSJM paper from industry scientists and lawyers at Philip Morris, Reynolds Tobacco, and Lorillard:

> "Hugh Cullman [Vice Chairman of the Board of Philip Morris] has asked us to challenge the following statement by Repace in a recent news interview: "It would take about two hundred and twenty six air changes an hour to clear the air sufficiently of tobacco smoke under typical smoking conditions in an American office, in order to get what we would call

an environmentally acceptable cancer risk of one chance in a hundred thousand lifetime of contracting lung cancer, and typical ventilation rates in offices are about one air change an hour . It simply isn't economic to do it by ventilation and physically it's practically impossible. You'd create a windstorm" [TTID 504003177].

In August, September, and October, the Tobacco Institute secretly conducted "Repace Briefings" with KOIN-TV and KPTV-V in Portland, OR, ABC News in New York, Knight-Ridder in Washington DC (accompanied by Nancy Balter of Georgetown U.), Business Week (accompanied by Sorrell Schwartz of Georgetown U.), WSOC-TV in Charlotte, NC, and with the editor of the Grand Rapids, MI Press, as well as the Bureau of National Affairs in Washington DC. [TTID TINY 0007635].

ATTACK OF THE INDUSTRY MOLES

The tobacco industry also wasted no time in organizing letters to the editor critical of our risk assessment. *Prior* to our paper being published, three letters to the editor arrived on Moghissi's desk, from M.D. Lebowitz, P.R.J. Burch, and C. S. J. Kilpatrick, followed by one from L.C. Johnson and H. Letzel, that arrived after our paper was published. Johnson and Letzel identified themselves as employees of the German tobacco industry. The only way the first three critics could have obtained pre-publication copies of our paper was from the tobacco industry, who had obtained it from EPA under the Freedom of Information Act (FOIA). But it was very useful intelligence knowing who the moles were, although we did not deign to tar them with this fact in our reply. In fact, Lowrey and I were greatly amused by this orchestrated criticism, which we regarded as great sport. Scientists often can learn more from critics of their work than from supporters; defending one's research broadens one's perspective.

The critical mole letters and our rebuttal were published together in *Environment International* 12: 33-38, 1986. In our 5-page rebuttal, we noted, in part, that "In letters to this journal, Lebowitz, Burch, Johnson and Letzel, and Kilpatrick have suggested respectively, that nonsmokers may not be exposed to sufficient smoke to cause disease, that tobacco smoke may not even cause lung cancer in smokers, that our domestic exposure assessment is overestimated, and that exposure of a nonsmoker requires the presence of a smoker for the duration of the exposure."

Lebowitz disingenuously assailed our model, quoting dosages from secondhand smoke estimated by several workers who were either employed by or funded by the industry, whose estimates were $1/10^{th}$ to $1/100^{th}$ that of our model. Lebowitz failed to mention that these estimates were based on linear extrapolation from nicotine or cotinine dose, *not* on fine particulate exposure from tobacco tar. The threshold argument by Lebowitz at bottom assumed that a proven human carcinogen, tobacco smoke, somehow lost its ability to cause cancer below 0.5 to 2 cigarette-equivalents inhaled per day. This ignored the fact that we did not resort to a cigarette equivalent argument in this paper. Moreover, we noted, a 1984 position paper published by the American Association for Cancer Research concluded that there was a *lack* of an apparent threshold in the dose-response curve between lung cancer death rates and smoking rates.

We estimated that the typical RSP exposure of a US nonsmoker to secondhand smoke at 1430 micrograms per day (the tar equivalent of $1/10^{th}$ of a cigarette), and the most-exposed nonsmoker at an estimated 14,300 micrograms per day (the tar equivalent of a single cigarette). By comparison, the average smoker actually smoked 32 cigarettes per day, amounting to a daily inhalation of 457,600 milligrams of tobacco tar, or 320 times a cigarette-equivalent estimate for the average passive smoker. The flaw in Lebowitz's argument was that it implicitly assumed that there was a linear dose-response relationship between tobacco tar and lung cancer. But there was no evidence to justify such an assumption. [This provoked a literature search, and I would later discover that there were smoking studies that showed substantial non-linearity.]

The arguments by Burch began by shamelessly denying that active smoking caused cancer at all and went downhill from that imbecilic argument to advancing the ludicrous proposition that nonsmokers prone to lung cancer "were prone to marry smokers, while nonsmokers resistant to lung cancer preferentially married nonsmokers." We dismissed Burch's comments as "completely lacking in merit." Under what stone did they dig this guy up?

Johnson and Letzel's critique was at least on point: they asserted that our domestic exposure assessment was overestimated, although they provided no contradictory data. We countered that we had grounded our modeling in the ever-useful Harvard Six-City study, using hard data measured in smoker's homes. We rebutted their other arguments, including charges that we overestimated cigarette smoking rates, that our equilibrium model of exposure was inappropriate, and that we had overestimated exposure probabilities for nonsmokers in the home.

Although our calculations and physical intuition suggested we had made valid estimates of the range of nonsmokers' exposures to ETS, we had no way of comparing these predictions to measured data in the U.S. population in 1985. However, two decades later, based on data reported by CDC in its National Health and Nutrition Survey (NHANES), and development of a pharmacokinetic model, I would validate our RSP exposure estimate for the typical and most-exposed nonsmokers in the population using dosimetric means, by calculating the level of nicotine exposure from the nicotine metabolite, cotinine in blood serum (Repace et al., 2006). More on this later.

As far as Kilpatrick's assertion that nonsmokers could be exposed only during the short time a smoker was actively smoking, he manifested a clear lack of understanding of the persistence of secondhand smoke. The residence time of smoke in the air from smoking a single cigarette in a single-family home with a typical air exchange rate of ¾ of an air change per hour was more than four hours. (Not to mention that over a period of four hours, a typical smoker would have smoked 8 cigarettes). He also suggested that models could not be used to estimate risk because there was no proven relationship between passive smoking and lung cancer, that the absence of a threshold for carcinogenesis had not been proved, and that measurements of ambient tobacco smoke had limited bearing on dose to the target organ. The first two arguments were easily dismissed as mere speculation since he presented no data in support of his claim. Kilpatrick further argued that we should have used a more sophisticated model than the simple one-hit model for extrapolation from the risk in smokers to that of nonsmokers. We parried this by citing a 1984 analysis by Todd Thorslund of EPA's Carcinogen Assessment group who used our exposure model coupled with the very sophisticated EPA multi-stage carcinogen assessment model to extrapolate the risks in cigarette smokers down to the passive exposure of nonsmokers and obtained results similar to ours. [A technical note: the multistage model was based on a Taylor series expansion of the dose-response relationship; the one hit model was simply the first term in the expansion, with the higher order terms dropped. This could be done without significant error if the dose was low.]

Kilpatrick further criticized us for assuming that the entire lung cancer rate difference between SDA's and NonSDAs was due to passive smoking. This criticism had been and would be raised by others, but we had shown in our paper that by using this assumption we were able to predict the risk rate and risk ratio to within 4% in the Garfinkel cohort study. This was our trump card. In science, the acid test of any model is does it accurately predict the results of other research? Finally, Burch accused us of attributing *all* nonsmokers' lung cancer to passive smoking, when our paper clearly stated that we estimated that only *one-third* of nonsmokers' lung cancer was due to passive smoking. He obviously didn't bother to read our paper carefully.

However, the industry was not done with their attacks. The following year, the arch mole Ted Sterling mounted a sophisticated assault on our work in a 25 page article published in *Environmental Carcinogenesis Reviews* (Journal of Health, C4(1), 93-118 (1986) by Arundel, Irwin and Sterling.

They asserted that:

"Repace and Lowrey's phenomenological estimate of lung cancer risk from ETS exposure has been widely accepted in the U.S. and Canada. Yet the estimate is based on several unrealistic assumptions and on unstable data that warrant closer examination. It is the purpose of this review to examine several problems with the phenomenological model and to evaluate the reliability of the lung cancer risk estimates derived from it."

Arundel et al. raised three basic points:
1. The SDA-NonSDAs lung cancer rate difference was based on very few lung cancer deaths and are unstable.
2. The apparent differences in lung cancer mortality between SDA and NonSDAs never smokers may be due to a variety of factors other than ETS exposure.
3. A number of assumptions and calculations are made that are clearly incorrect.

In our 10-page rebuttal invited by the editors [Repace & Lowrey, 1986], the statistical stability issue in Arundel et al.'s first point was the hardest to deal with. We needed professional statistical advice. Wayne Ott introduced me to Steven Bayard, a biostatistician in EPA's Carcinogen Assessment Group who had performed many of EPA's most difficult hazardous air pollutant risk assessments, and who had taught biostatistics at Yale. I asked Steven to explain the concept of stability. He said, "Stability of an estimate in age-specific data depends primarily on the number of person-years of observation. While it is true that the 11,472 SDA women had only 15 lung cancer deaths (LCDs) during the 17-year follow-up period, they contributed a total of 195,015 person-years (PY) at risk. This extrapolates to a crude annual incidence rate of about 7.7 LCDs per 100,000 PY at risk, with a standard error of 0.06 LCDs per 100,000 PY." We used this argument in our rebuttal. I was impressed with Steven's deep understanding of this issue. If the tobacco industry had not hired Sterling to do this hatchet job, I might never have met Steven; we later became close friends. My respect for his talents would have catastrophic consequences for Big Tobacco six years later.

As for Arundel et al.'s second point, Lowrey and I regarded the argument about the SDA-NonSDA LCD difference being due to dietary or occupational differences as just so much hand-waving. We had addressed potential dietary differences between the two cohorts in our paper. It was true that many Seventh-day Adventists were lacto-ovarian vegetarians. For over a century, SDAs had recommended a vegetarian diet that included both milk products and eggs. Despite this, the dietary argument as a significant factor in the observed lung cancer differences between these two groups was very weak. This was because both cohorts of SDAs and NonSDAs studied lived in heavily agricultural California, where fruits and vegetables rich in anti-oxidants were abundant year-round. (Also, it did not escape my notice that the dietary differences between the Japanese and Greek women in the Hirayama and the Trichopoulos studies were profound, and that seemed to make little difference.) Moreover, there was no hard evidence that there were significant occupational differences between these two groups, so that inference was sheer speculation. Although dietary difference was a common criticism of our hypothesis and had been raised by Herman Gibb at EPA and the Office of Technology Assessment in its report on ETS, as well as a pack of industry moles, it didn't actually matter for our model.

To us as physical scientists, what actually mattered was *did our dose-response model make predictions that were consistent with observations?* Even if we had plucked that dose-response relationship from the forehead of Zeus, the model predicted Garfinkel's results accurately and showed that those results were consistent with Hirayama's. Furthermore, the fact that the lung cancer mortality rate difference we had derived from the SDA Study was nearly identical to Hirayama's indicated to us that the risk we had estimated was consistent with observations. None of the early critics of our risk assessment understood this. With the passage of time, however, it would become apparent that our estimates would fall within the same range as that of EPA's professional risk assessors as well as others around the world (Repace and Lowrey, 1990).

To give the devils their due, one of the more interesting criticisms that Arundel et al. leveled against our work was actually a rather good one: they noted that nonsmokers do not have the same age and sex distribution as the general population that includes smokers. This backfired: when we recalculated our results with those suggested corrections, the result was a 5% *increase* in the estimated number of LCDs.

Then they argued that if we made a linear extrapolation from the average smoker's dose of tobacco smoke to the average nonsmokers' dose, the risk would reduce from our estimate of 7.4 LCDs per 100,000 PY to 0.11 LCDs per 100,000 PY. We rebutted this by observing that a linear extrapolation could not possibly be justified due to *the large dose effect,* which can cause a non-linear flattening of the dose-effect curve at high levels. This was a well-known phenomenon observed in radiobiological studies. However, large dose effects were not only limited to ionizing radiation, there was actual evidence of this effect published in the epidemiological literature of smoking and lung cancer. Both Doll and Peto in the UK and Hirayama in Japan had reported highly non-linear dose-response curves for the lung cancer risks in smokers, such that smokers of more than 40 cigarettes per day actually had *lower* lung cancer rates than smokers of 20 cigarettes per day. Epithelial lung cells that died due to an overdose of tobacco smoke poisoning could not become cancerous.

Just placing a ruler on a graph of the lung cancer rate vs. cigarette per day curve clearly showed that a linear extrapolation down to the low doses of nonsmokers overestimated their actual lung cancer rate, indicating that a dose-response relationship derived by linear extrapolation of smokers' exposures to nonsmokers' exposures was inappropriate. In 1992, we published a letter to the editor showing this explicitly (Repace and Lowrey, 1992). Finally, we noted that Arundel et al., in criticizing our sensitivity analysis, blundered by using an improper age adjustment technique in their analysis of Hirayama's data. We relished this major battle with our arch-enemy Ted Sterling and were confident that we had done an excellent job in rebutting his arguments. And we enjoyed playing whack-a-mole.

There is a fascinating footnote to this story. Anthony Arundel, Sterling's graduate student, called to apologize several months later, bitterly complaining that he had felt "used" because Sterling had re-written large parts of Arundel's critique of our work, and regretted "that he had ever chosen Ted as an advisor." This admission was an act of courage on Arundel's part, and I thanked him.

AN EPA-SPONSORED "AGENT PROVOCATEUR"

In a letter dated August 1st 1985, Prof. Richard J. Thompson, at the Department of Environmental Health Sciences of the University of Alabama in Birmingham, wrote a personal letter to his friend, Dr. Anthony Colluci, Director of Scientific Litigation Support for the R.J. Reynolds Tobacco Company. In it, Thompson sympathized with the industry's dismal state of affairs in an enlightening, but not enlightened, commentary. He wrote [TTID 504225137]:

> Dear Tony,
> "Background - On reflecting on the problems you have concerning the issue of environmental tobacco smoke, I am reminded of some of the history of this issue and others which have preceded it or which are current as 'environmental nightmares.' As you know, there is some truth in the observation that the EPA research director is the person who writes the headlines for the Washington Post. (The WP serves as the prime source of 'panic' articles portending environmental doom.) James Repace is known to you as a government (EPA) sponsored agent provocateur who has made control of tobacco smoking as his crusade. ... Although there are

many groups which have assumed a posture of moral righteousness in opposing tobacco, the EPA clique has a long history of sensationalizing the issue. …

Personal monitoring has been the central effort occupying the time and energy of a clique in EPA for a number of years. This group has, with literally millions of public funds, build a power base and gained tremendous visibility. What is incredible to me is that they have been deemed credible by the press and, apparently, by the public. You now have a program based on zeal and pseudo science which is considered hard science and which fills a need for sensational issues the press always has had.

…

Modus Operandi - As an illustration of how the use of soft numbers has been transmuted to hard data to generate public concern (to the point of frenzy in instances), one might note one of the first 'monitoring' efforts carried out by Dr. Lance Wallace in 1978. Dr. Wallace is an astrophysicist by training and a frenetic worker. He 'borrowed' analyzers he caused (by control of funds) to be purchased by a monitoring group for the ostensible purpose of performance evaluation. He used these devices out of the box without calibration and reported levels in commuter vehicles roughly twice the threshold limiting value of 50 ppm. It is on this type of approach this group has functioned.

…

Dr. Wallace serves the group as sparkplug and intellectual gadfly. Mr. Repace has his primary mission as cessation of smoking, and Dr. Wayne Ott serves as consigliore [sic] and modeler. By reinforcement, they have built indoor monitoring - personal exposure - environmental tobacco smoke into an emotional issue with the potential for heavy public funding.

…

ETS, The New Environmental Crisis - In all cases, a particular pollutant and the industry which uses it have been the bad 'thing' and the 'bad guys'. The hour of the tobacco company is nigh. One may note the signs: The Air Pollution Control Association has designated indoor pollution as the primary of four themes for the next (1986) national meeting. Technical committee TT-7, Indoor Air Quality, has been allotted time for eight (8) symposia. With Jim Repace as secretary, the odds are great that passive, sidestream or environmental tobacco smoke will be featured if not a symposium topic. Don Ehreth, Deputy Assistant Administrator of the Office of Research and Development of EPA, was chatting with Repace and Wallace at the APCA meeting. Repace was complimented by Wallace for getting a headline on ETS and congratulated Wallace for making the headlines in Greensboro. Ehreth noted that, 'you guys are doing a great job of making this issue visible. We are going to make this the biggest issue of all and have a gigantic program. We have to have controls'. (Chapter 11 like Johns Mansville?)

At the Technical Council Meeting of TT-7 (indoor air quality), it was noted that TT-7 finally was not only acceptable, but in vogue with the hottest issue in APCA. It was said that Congress will insist that indoor air be given massive funding and the responsibility assigned to EPA (up until now, all agencies have shunned responsibility for non-occupational indoor air). When EPA gets the responsibility, the control process will begin by tenets of the Clean Air Act. (Indoor air quality is 10 to 100 times higher than that of ambient air, for which some standards exist.)

Recommendations - Reynolds cannot ignore this issue and stay in the tobacco business. Reynolds cannot win by attacking public 'Gods' (MD's), or by attacking critics whose coin is emotion.

- promote hard air quality generation (to undercut soft science sensationalism);
- never, never, never make any factual error within the current state of the art in whatever discipline is used;
- provide seed money to promote better monitoring techniques to avoid smearing techniques whereby the thing deemed least defensible morally is the culprit for low air quality;
- promote critiques of questionable work or interpretations, especially in print;
- promote publications of indoor quality assessments of high quality. The ground rules are that a criteria document should only contain published work, and this is beginning to be interpreted as published in a peer-review journal;
- avoid using people who will speak when out of their areas of expertise. It is obvious to me as an outsider that some lawyer(s) wrote the ad attacking the "Mr. Fit Program" which I am sure had no benefit to Reynolds.

This is lengthy, but it is easier to edit than create. I hope there is something useful in this.

Best Regards, Dick
Richard J. Thompson."

There was as much chance of omitting industry lawyers from the ETS issue or getting moles to speak only within their areas of expertise as a snowball not melting in hell. Selling bullshit was their stock in trade. Thompson was correct in certain respects and dead wrong in others: I did chair a session on the Health Effects of Environmental Tobacco Smoke at the APCA meeting in Minneapolis in June 1986. However, it would *not* be RJ Reynolds that would "promote hard air quality generation," or promote indoor air quality assessments of high quality, but EPA's Office of Research and Development. Lance Wallace and Wayne Ott had already long recognized that the early work with borrowed, uncalibrated monitors, while pointing out areas of useful research, was no substitute for an organized indoor air research program with rigorous quality assurance and calibration of monitors, organized around the total exposure concept. This meant measuring the total human exposure to environmental pollutants from all sources, including air, water, and food, and from all modes of entry into the body: inhalation, ingestion, and dermal absorption. This was the genesis of EPA's TEAM studies, which embodied rigorous quality assurance and quality control. However, this did not happen without a struggle. There was a great deal of infighting within ORD over indoor air research. According to Lance Wallace, Courtney Riordan, the head of ORD's Monitoring Division, took control of ORD's Indoor Air project away from Lance at the instigation of David Berg and Don Ehreth, to conduct a "full-scale investigation of IAQ in buildings (hospitals, old-age homes, etc.) at $500K per year. In 1983, Congress pushed EPA (against EPA's wishes) to allocate $2M to the project." Lance strongly differed with Ehreth-Berg approach, and felt the "great need was for collecting monitoring data." I agreed with Lance's broader emphasis. Discouraged, Lance took a two-year sabbatical with Jack Spengler at Harvard to cool off. By the time he returned, said Lance, "David Berg had run the program into the ground, dissension was high, and he was ultimately forced out. I believe Courtney was heard to say it was his worst decision." Ultimately, Lance regained control of the TEAM project in the mid-1980's.

Insofar as Johnson's claim that I made control of tobacco smoking as a personal "crusade," my true motivation was to perform the research that unaccountably nobody else was doing. This had a great deal of resonance among many professional and NGO interest groups, and well as a great deal of public and political support. My efforts did not occur in a vacuum. Keep in mind that right up to the early 1980's, EPA, OSHA and even the Public Health Service, as well as most academic scientists with the expertise, the funds and the budgets to perform secondhand smoke research had failed to do so. Funding for this research simply did not exist. Recall that Lowrey and I had bootlegged our research, funding our efforts out of pocket, and using borrowed equipment and interested citizen volunteers. Like any scientist, I responded to invitations to lecture about my work, and my research clearly met a public need. I was firmly devoted to science in the public interest. Decades of frustration by the nonsmoking workers and hospitality industry patrons certainly qualified as the public interest.

On the 2nd of October 1985, I was invited by Senator Ted Stevens (R) of Alaska to testify on Senate Bill 1440, The Nonsmokers' Rights Act of 1985, before the Senate Committee on Civil Service, on the Health Impact of Tobacco Combustion Products on Nonsmokers. On the 8th of October, Devra Davis invited me to present a talk, "Quantitative Risk Assessment of Lung Cancer Risk from Passive Smoking, before the National Academy of Sciences Committee on Passive Smoking. On the 6th of November, I was invited to present on the Risks of Passive Smoking at Harvard's Institute for the Study of Smoking Behavior and Policy, and on the 4th of December, Ford Motor Company invited me to present on the Health Risks of Active and Passive Smoking at its Joint Annual Health and Safety Conference with the United Auto Workers, in Miami. I had arrived on the national lecture circuit and had developed a limited but bipartisan base of support in Congress, as well as within the EPA.

On November 21, 1985, Anthony Colucci, who had now been promoted to be Director of the R&D Smoking and Health Division of RJR, wrote a confidential memorandum to G.R. Di Marco, RJR's research director, relating the weekly highlights of RJR's Smoking and Health Group. (De Marco had handed over the responsibility of the Research Department in the area of smoking and health to the Law Dept. in 1982 "because RJR's lawyers controlled things in this area" [LA Times, 1998].) Colucci wrote that, "Current plans call for Drs. Nystrom and Green to present a paper to the ASHRAE Committee in June, 1986; and for Drs. Colucci, Viren, and Nystrom to present a paper on the Repace analysis at the Air Pollution Control Association meeting in the summer of 1986. These papers are currently in preparation." ... "The Smoking and Health Group has been requested to review testimony of several scientific witnesses who have been providing health testimony regarding environmental tobacco smoke. The specific witnesses are Dr. Sorrel Schwartz, Professor of Pharmacology at Georgetown University, and Dr. Philip Witorsch, also of Georgetown University. Both Dr. Witorsch and Dr. Schwartz will be at RJRT on December 10, for a mock congressional hearing." ... "A review of microbiological data provided by ACVA Atlantic, Inc. has been completed. These data are the result of a study conducted to ascertain whether or not air handling systems from large buildings are contaminated with allergens or microorganisms which could account for the numerous complaints very often blamed on environmental tobacco smoke" [TTID 50492 1385].

Early the following year, like a bolt out of the blue, the flagship journal of the American Thoracic Society, the *American Review of Respiratory Disease*, published an editorial endorsement of our 1985 risk assessment: Dr. Scott Weiss, an associate professor in the pulmonary unit of the Harvard School of Medicine, who had attended my presentation at Harvard in November 1984, authored a two-page editorial in the January 1986 issue of the journal, entitled "Passive Smoking and Lung Cancer What is the Risk? It was diametrically opposite to Herman Gibb's appraisal of our work. The lead paragraph in Weiss's editorial stated its purpose:

"Repace and Lowrey have recently estimated that approximately 4,700 nonsmoking Americans die each year from lung cancer as a result of involuntary tobacco smoke exposure. The purpose of this editorial is to comment on the association between passive smoking and lung cancer and the biological and mathematical assumptions underlying Repace and Lowrey's assessment of risk."

The concluding paragraph dropped a bomb on the tobacco industry:

"Despite the simplifying assumptions of the risk estimates and the flaws in the epidemiologic data from which they are derived, Repace and Lowrey's figures remain the best current estimates of lung cancer deaths from passive smoking. Current epidemiologic data are sufficiently imprecise to be able to accurately distinguish between the estimate of 500 or 5,000 deaths per year. The higher figure seems a more plausible estimate from the current data. Future epidemiologic studies will allow revision of these estimates but are unlikely to dispute the basic nature of the association" [Weiss, 1986].

SMOKING ON AIRCRAFT

On June 14th, 1985, I had testified at a public hearing on Airliner Cabin Air Quality at the National Academy of Sciences on Indoor Air Quality Problems on Passenger Aircraft. The committee found what I had to say interesting enough that I was invited to present my calculations in detail in at a forthcoming workshop in Woods Hole, Massachusetts on July 25th. My presentation there gave an estimate of secondhand smoke pollution aboard a Lockheed Tristar L-1011-1 jumbo jet with 320 persons aboard, ventilated at the ASHRAE-recommended ventilation rate of 6 air changes per hour. I assumed that ten percent of the passengers were smokers and calculated that the level of fine particulate air pollution from smoking would range between 200 and 300 micrograms per cubic meter. Upon hearing this, Paul Halfpenny, a Lockheed aircraft ventilation engineer on the NAS panel, announced, "we can compare your predictions to data measured by Lufthansa," and he rummaged through a pile of papers and pulled out a file. Every person in the room stared at him in anticipation. I held my breath. Finally, he spoke: "Well, your predictions *are* consistent with Lufthansa's measurements." My stock with the NAS committee went to the moon. Years later, in 1997, giving expert testimony in a lawsuit by flight attendants against the tobacco industry, Halfpenny would testify: "No matter how you ventilate an airplane, smoke concentration is always a problem" [Boca Raton News, 1997].

Satisfyingly, in its 1986 Report, *The Airliner Cabin Environment, Air Quality and Safety*, the NAS Committee recommended a ban on smoking on all domestic commercial flights. Three years later, my work on aircraft would lead me together with Lance Wallace and Margaret Cho of EPA, to serve on a U.S. Department of Transportation Advisory Committee to help design a study to measure indoor air pollution on passenger aircraft. And that in turn would lead to my participation, virtually over the dead bodies of OMB and EPA management, in an historic Congressional hearing to ban smoking on domestic flights.

At the end of 1985, Joseph A. Cannon left EPA to become editor of the *Deseret News* in Utah. At his retirement party roast, I presented him with a rum-soaked cigar.

CHAPTER 8

JUDGMENT DAY FOR ETS

"The judgment can now be made that exposure to environmental tobacco smoke can cause disease, including lung cancer, in nonsmokers. It is also clear that simple separation of smokers and nonsmokers within the same airspace may reduce but cannot eliminate nonsmoker exposure to environmental tobacco smoke."

1986 Surgeon General's Report, *The Health Consequences of Involuntary Smoking,*
U.S. Dept. of Health & Human Services, Washington, DC.

"The most common acute effects associated with exposure to ETS are eye, nose, and throat irritation, and objectionable smell of tobacco smoke. Tobacco smoke has a distinct and persistent odor, making control through ventilation particularly difficult. ... Considering the evidence as a whole, exposure to ETS increases the incidence of lung cancer in nonsmokers."

National Research Council. *Environmental Tobacco Smoke: Measuring Exposures and Assessing Health Effects.* Washington, DC: The National Academies Press, 1986.

The back-to-back 1986 Reports of the Surgeon General, *The Health Consequences of Involuntary Smoking,* and the National Research Council *Environmental Tobacco Smoke - Measuring Exposures and Assessing Health Effects,* declared that secondhand smoke caused lung cancer in nonsmokers (SG, 1986; NRC, 1986). Both also agreed that ventilation could not control secondhand smoke. Their conclusions on causality were far more robust than the International Agency for Research on Cancer's (IARC, 1986) almost reluctant admission that "passive smoking gives rise to some risk of cancer." Neither of the two U.S. reports estimated the magnitude of the mortality from secondhand smoke on nonsmokers. However, the NRC report did include an unofficial appendix that estimated numbers of deaths in passive smokers. It was unofficial because it had not been peer-reviewed for lack of time. Authored by a member of the committee, James Robins of the Harvard School of Public Health, the appendix was simply "presented ... as one possible way to integrate the data contained in the remainder of the report." Robins used three different methods to estimate nonsmokers' lung cancer risk, which yielded estimates ranging from 820 to 3220 annual lung cancer deaths. Robins' estimates overlapped the estimated range of 500 to 5000 annual deaths made by Repace and Lowrey (1985). We searched avidly through both reports to see how well our works had been received by these disparate groups of experts.

The 1986 Surgeon General's report reviewed our 1985 risk assessment in Chapter 2 as follows:

"An alternative method of estimating expected lung cancer rates has been proposed by Repace and Lowrey (1985). They compared the age-standardized lung cancer mortality rates of Seventh-Day Adventists (SDAs) who had never smoked with a demographically comparable group of nonsmoking nonSDAs and attributed the difference in lung cancer deaths solely to involuntary smoking. This analysis was based on the following assumptions: (1) that SDAs had no exposure to passive smoking, whereas all of the non-SDAs were exposed, (2) that men and women had equal lung cancer death rates*, and (3) that there were no other differences between the two groups."

*[N.B., We actually formed a weighted average of male and female SDA lung cancer rates then applied it to the whole group irrespective of gender]

In Chapter 3, our *Science* paper was mentioned:

"Short-term measurements in rooms with smokers can yield respirable particulate concentrations of 100 to 1,000 µg/m³ (Repace and Lowrey 1980). Multihour measurements average out variations in smoking, mixing, and ventilation and yield concentrations in the range of 20 to 200 (µg/m³) (Spengler et al. 1981,1985,1986)."

And later in that chapter, the SG's Report reviewed our exposure model:

"Repace and Lowrey (1980) measured RSP concentration using a Piezobalance in several public and private locations, including restaurants, cocktail lounges, and halls, in both the presence and the absence of smoking. They then developed an empirical model utilizing the mass-balance equation. Using both measured and estimated parameters as input to the model, they validated the model for predicting an individual's exposure to the RSP constituent of ETS. The model takes the form: C_{eq}, $= 650$ D_s/n_v; where C_{eq} equals the equilibrium concentration of the RSP component of ETS (µg/m³), D_s equals the density of active smokers (number of burning cigarettes per 100 m³), and n_v equals the ventilation rate (in air changes per hour). The ventilation rate is a complex parameter that takes into account all the room-specific constants affecting the removal of ETS, such as ventilation, decay, and mixing."

As it turned out, the 1986 Surgeon General's Report had a chapter originally drafted by Michael Lebowitz. Don Shopland, the Report's production editor, told me that the reviewers of Lebowitz's draft "felt it was so biased that it had to be completely re-written," and Lebowitz was not listed in the credits as a contributing author. I was acknowledged as one of the many persons "who lent their support in the development of this Report, by coordinating manuscript preparation, contributing critical reviews of the manuscript, *or assisting in other ways* [italics mine].

Chapter 5 of the NRC ETS report, *Assessing Exposures to Environmental Tobacco Smoke*, also reviewed the Habitual Smoker Model of Repace and Lowrey (1980), concluding:

"The most extensive use of the mass-balance equation for assessing RSP levels due to ETS in occupied spaces has been by Repace and Lowrey (1980). Drawing upon the best available data from several sources, including both measured and estimated parameters, they proposed and applied in field observations a condensed version of the mass-balance equation for estimating RSP exposures due to ETS in a variety of indoor microenvironments. ..."

Although many of the input parameters were estimated from the literature, which is based on limited experimental data, Repace and Lowrey (1980, 1982) applied [various] equations to a variety of situations and found that they produced reasonably accurate estimates in a limited number of occupied spaces with smoking occupancy. Apparently, easy-to-obtain data on building volumes, design occupancy, smoking occupancy, type of ventilation systems, and building standards can improve the prediction of RSP concentrations. In using [their model], the major assumptions deal with mixing, ventilation rates, and sink rates. Additional field testing of the Repace and Lowrey model, as well as a better understanding of the variability of the input parameters, either estimated or measured for use in [the model], is needed."

A DOUBLE-BARRELED BLAST AT BIG TOBACCO

The fruits of the collaboration between EPA and DHHS had resulted in two major reports that placed the problem of passive smoking firmly on the national agenda. As time went on, the agreement of the two authoritative reports from the Surgeon General and the National Research Council fueled a growing public health and scientific consensus that secondhand smoke caused lung cancer. Moreover, there was now a cadre of scientists, led by Jack Spengler at Harvard, Brian Leaderer at Yale, Kathie Hammond at the University of Massachusetts, Jon Samet, MD at the University of New Mexico, Neal Benowitz, MD at the University of California, and Joan Daisey at the Lawrence Berkeley Laboratory, as well as Dietrich Hoffmann and Klaus Brunnemann at AHF, who were early and influential contributors to this new field of secondhand smoke research. And it began to stimulate Stan Glantz to begin research in the field.

On the policy front, these new reports impelled the Department of Defense (DOD) to issue a directive restricting smoking in the workplace. On March 11, 1986, nonsmoking was established as the DOD norm. Although smoking was not totally banned, it was permitted in common work spaces only if it did not adversely affect nonsmokers. However, smoking was still permitted in private offices. At NSA, 60 percent of the cafeteria became a nonsmoking area, smoking and nonsmoking restrooms were designated, and free smoking cessation clinics were conducted during working hours [NSA, 2002]. And it sparked thoughts of enacting smoking restrictions in both EPA and DHHS buildings.

In response to these new developments. Susan Stuntz sent a memorandum to Peter Sparber, Vice President of the Tobacco Institute, discussing the industry's response to the social impact of the reports of Surgeon General and the National Research Council: "The scientific reports of 1986 have meant more than a higher degree of legislative interest in the ETS issue; they also have increased public – and media – attention. As a result, Institute and expert consultant response to public, media and legislative inquiries during the first quarter of 1987 have been stepped up as well" [TTID T107640128].

The twin Surgeon General and National Academy reports also began to stir the hitherto largely somnolent voluntary health organizations (Cancer, Heart, and Lung), as well as provoking fear and anger in the tobacco industry. This in turn led to increased disinformation activity by industry moles. In May of 1986, Shane McDermott, a 'Smoking or Health' staffer for the American Lung Association (ALA), contacted me over ALA's grave concerns about how to deal with the tobacco industry consultants who were members of the "Indoor Air Advisory Group who were travelling around the country testifying against state and local legislation on involuntary smoking at the request of the Tobacco Institute."

McDermott asked me to prepare a white paper rebutting their arguments for the ALA. I did this on my own time. The 13- page white paper, with 26 references, issued on the letterhead of the ALA, was titled: "*A REBUTTAL TO CRITICISMS OF PASSIVE SMOKING RESEARCH BY TOBACCO INDUSTRY CONSULTANTS*," by James L. Repace. It identified me simply as an "environmental scientist who has published extensively in the field of indoor air pollution from tobacco smoke."

The cover memo by McDermott stated that "It is intended to provide background information for Lung Association volunteers to assist them in public testimony on the involuntary (passive) smoking issue." Pulling no punches, I wrote: "Although some of the consultants have extensive publications in other fields, The Indoor Air Advisory Group is notable for its lack of expertise in research in smoking, environmental tobacco smoke, or indoor air pollution, as evidenced by their lack of publications in peer-reviewed scientific journals in these fields. Instead, the group's 'opinion' – not hard research on substantive problems – is advertised as 'currently being prepared for publication.' As a result, the opinions of the Tobacco Institute's Indoor Air Advisory Group (IAAG) are shallow, self-serving, and do not stand the test of scientific scrutiny."

I then proceeded to discredit the industry party line by first pointing out that it was "well-established that inhaled tobacco smoke was a known cause of many fatal cancers, cardiovascular disease, and respiratory disease, and that there was no known threshold for effects. I pointed out the well-known toxicological and chemical similarity between sidestream and mainstream smoke as detailed in the Surgeon General's Reports, and that the consultants "are forced to argue that either sidestream and exhaled mainstream smoke are innocuous substances, or that nonsmokers are exposed to levels of environmental tobacco smoke that are beneath known thresholds for tobacco-smoke-induced disease. In fact, both of these arguments are made by the IAAG, but not a single scientific study is cited in support of this assertion."

The Tobacco Institute had attempted to stem the rising tide of unfavorable reports, and to pre-empt the upcoming 1986 Surgeon General's and NRC reports on ETS by trumpeting yet another slick new pamphlet, *Tobacco Smoke & the Nonsmoker - Scientific Integrity at the Crossroads,* 60-pages in length, summarizing the published lawyer-vetted commentary it had solicited from its own tobacco moles [TTID 2042356366]. Stan Glantz and I read these blivets of industry propaganda with great interest, so that we could keep our lists of tobacco moles current. Naturally, *Crossroads* attacked the work of Repace and Lowrey. In a section titled **Assessing the Literature**, it stated in part:

"Fidelity to the scientific method has not been uniform, and at least a few authors have, in varying degrees, mischaracterized the epidemiologic literature and the conclusions that can legitimately be drawn from it. The mischaracterizations generally have been of two types. The first, and most egregious, involves using a study like Hirayama's, ignoring its fatal vulnerability to misclassification and bias, discounting the criticism to which it has been subjected, and bestowing upon it a spurious validity because of the large number of subjects surveyed. On one occasion, when this approach was carried to extremes, and was combined with certain simplistic assumptions, it was relied upon as support for a controversial 'estimate' to the effect that some 4700 lung cancer deaths per year among nonsmokers in the United States have been caused by environmental tobacco smoke." This assertion has been vigorously and properly rebutted by critics who have concluded, along with Dr. P.R.J. Burch of the University of Leeds, that such estimates 'must be regarded with the utmost suspicion'."

(This was the very same old reliable buffoon P.R.J. Burch who, while twitching his mole's whiskers, had denied that smoking caused cancer three times before the cock crowed). *Crossroads* continued, citing a staff paper by the Congressional Office of Technology Assessment as criticizing our estimates based on the lung cancer rate difference between Seventh Day Adventists (SDAs) and Southern California non-SDAs. *Crossroads* failed to mention that the 1986 Surgeon General's Report on Involuntary Smoking concluded that "Involuntary smoking is a cause of disease, including lung cancer, in healthy nonsmokers." They also managed to ignore Robbin's estimates of mortality from secondhand smoke which overlapped ours.

Crossroads continued with an attack on our field measurements, quoting its consultant Salvatore DiNardi's comments in a January 1986 presentation to the National Research Council (NRC) Committee on Passive Smoking, as "The highly publicized field work of Repace and Lowrey (1980) utilized a clearly inappropriate background (outside air) for comparison, did not include measurements of ventilation rates or relative humidity, and suffered from flaws in instrumentation and technical methodology. Most critically, their conclusions were undermined by their assumption that other indoor sources of RSP-such as heating, air conditioning and ventilation systems, cooking, dusts, fibers, microbial contaminants, human and animal activity, outdoor air characteristics, automobile traffic, and the like – are nonexistent or unimportant" [TTID 80417830].

This was a straw-man argument, as we had not made any such assumptions, had conducted controlled experiments, and had made to the extent possible in that smoky era, comparison measurements in the same venues with and without smoking as well as outdoors. A similar failure to control for non-ETS sources of RSP, DiNardi noted, also diminished the value of a study by Spengler, et al. (1981)." [This was the respected Harvard Six City study]. This critique was incredibly cheeky of DiNardi, considering that his CIAR-bankrolled $688,878 attempt to refute the work of Repace and Lowrey (1980) wound up confirming it, causing it to be quickly deep-sixed by the industry (Kessler, 2006). (So much for Thompson's naïve recommendation, in his missive to Collucci, advising RJR to "promote hard air quality generation.") In any case, the NRC committee found little to like in DiNardi's presentation.

Crossroads also conveniently failed to quote the clear statement in the NRC's 1986 Report that "for the vast majority of conditions, RSP levels due solely to ETS can be expected to equal or exceed levels specified in National Ambient Air Quality Standards for the total suspended particulates," nor did it mention that the NRC considered that model developed by Repace and Lowrey (1980) "produced reasonably accurate estimates in a limited number of occupied spaces with smoking occupancy." Moreover, the NRC Report had given very prominent play to the Harvard Six City Study, which *Crossroads* –unsurprisingly – ignored. *Crossroads* also slammed the comprehensive *National Academy of Sciences Report on Airliner Cabin Air Quality (1986)*, asserting that the NAS was "capable of making policy recommendations based on speculation and convenience rather than objective data and established fact. When asked by Congress to investigate the quality of air within the cabins of commercial airliners, an NAS investigating panel concluded that more research was necessary on a host of potential problems and contaminants, but that despite the absence of scientific support, cigarette smoking on commercial aircraft should be banned." (Perhaps the members of this committee, who had been passengers on commercial aircraft for many years, knew from first-hand experience that these cabins were polluted with tobacco smoke.)

PROJECT DOWN UNDER, DOWN AND DIRTY

In June of 1987, Philip Morris convened a group presentation to senior management concerning "Project Down Under," to brainstorm strategies about combating the growing information that secondhand smoke was harmful, an issue which was strongly felt to be severely damaging to its bottom line (Source Watch, 2014). The presentation summarized the industry's options:

Basic recommendations
1. Big Chill strategy. Do something that, for us, is not different, but for world is different. Advocate accommodation, agree to separation of smokers and non-smokers in public places, but continue to oppose government intervention on this issue.
2. NRA strategy. Put some people out of business who are trying to put us out of business.
3. Find a "rainmaker." Develop a spokesperson who has visibility, respect and impact to carry our message to the press, government and the public.

4. <u>Support dramatic increase</u> in scientific activity on ETS, indoor air pollution and positive sociological and economic aspects of smoking. … The problem, however, needs further action. It is worldwide. Eighty percent of the ETS work is done in U.S., but anti-ETS initiatives are worldwide. We at PM need to speak to each other more closely and coordinate our efforts with the rest of the industry. We need a concomitant increase in scientific activity.

5. <u>Establish CIAR</u> (Center for Indoor Air Research). It is on books, but Barkley situation is holding it up. Need short-term, medium and long-term projects.

6. <u>Current work on ETS needs to be monitored</u> more accurately. CIAR would fund major research. It needs a budget of $3-5 million within five years.

7. <u>Increase the number of consulting scientists</u>. We have 15 now, number should be increased to 50 serving both as spokespersons and researchers. Similar need for overseas increase in consulting scientists because of situations in Scandinavia, Japan, Europe, South America. Begin with 1 or 2 scientists as core and build on them.

8. <u>Establish a genuine scientific journal</u> on indoor air quality. The Repace horror story demonstrates need: it took 20 months for us to get rebuttal letter to Repace study published in journal that published Repace. … *The major body of people affected by ETS question is found in workplace* [italics mine]. Clerical, helpers of industry. We need to focus on this group with messages on right to smoke, slippery slope, drug testing threat." [TTID 2021502671].

It is clear in retrospect that Philip Morris and I were on the same page: *ETS was a major workplace issue*. And – it developed that Philip Morris would opt for the "NRA Strategy," for the Final Solution To The Repace Problem. This would lead to a major public confrontation between me and an influential member of Congress.

EPA's INDOOR AIR PROGRAM BEGINS

As an example of the law of unintended consequences, Dave Mudarri, a senior (GS-15) civil servant made rootless in the wake of the Ice Queen's abandonment of the never-to-be- reconstituted EPA Noise Office, and influenced by EPA's new activities on indoor air, became interested in indoor air pollution, which he saw as a promising new career. Later that year, Dave, who now occupied Louise Giersch's old office, told me that he had decided to form an indoor air staff, and inquired as to my interest. Coincidentally, Stolpman had warned me that my intense focus on indoor air pollution would hurt my chances of promotion to a GS-14. Although I had a great deal of respect and admiration for Paul, the tidal pull of indoor air pollution as a full-time career was too strong. Moreover, I had two kids in college and four more to go, so an increase in salary was especially important. So, I entered into negotiations with Dave, who promised me a promotion within a year. A fledgling Indoor Air Staff emerged in September 1986, consisting of Dave, Betsy Agle, and me. We didn't even have a secretary. The new staff was part of the Office of Program Development, a very low-status part of the Office of Air and Radiation. Our gloomy new "office" was housed in a large windowless warren of mostly empty cubicles poorly lit by flickering fluorescents. Buried in the bowels of Waterside Mall, it was a major change from my former windowed private office on the 9th floor of the West Tower, with its river view, to which I had moved during the Cannon years. Nevertheless, I was excited.

Dave asked me to formulate technical plans for the new program, as the sole scientist on our diminutive staff. I concluded that given the limited size of our staff and our miniscule budget, we should focus on just two major efforts: sick buildings and environmental tobacco smoke. Dave was fine with this, but wisely decided that in view of the high profile of the ETS issue, we needed to gain approbation from the highest echelon of the EPA. He arranged a meeting between the two of us and Deputy Administrator Jim Barnes to lay out our plans for the fledgling indoor air program. Mudarri explained the ramifications of the ETS project to Barnes, who gave us his blessing, but commanded us to "coordinate with the Department of Health and Human Services (DHHS)." I couldn't have asked for a better decision; this meant that Don Shopland and I could work together, with the public health service's involvement taking a lot of heat off EPA. Several years later, this EPA-DHHS collaboration would protect EPA's risk assessment from strenuous efforts by Philip Morris to prevent its release.

As for our indoor air ETS effort, I envisioned four projects: a Fact Sheet explaining the health and control issues, a technical guide written by experts discussing the scientific and engineering issues surrounding ETS, a smoking policy guide for the workplace, and most importantly, an official EPA-sponsored risk assessment of passive smoking and lung cancer. The risk assessment would be funded by us but be performed independently by the Office of Research and Development's Carcinogen Assessment Group, which did all of the hazardous air pollutant risk assessments for the Office of Air and Radiation aside from radioactive pollutants. For indoor air pollution in general, I envisioned a Fact Sheet on Sick Building Syndrome. Dave approved, and we were off and running. Dave, with some empire-building in mind, also suggested that I adopt an informal title: Chief of Technical Services, Indoor Air Staff. This would have most unfortunate repercussions for me.

On September 2, 1986, Susan Stuntz of the Tobacco Institute, in a memo to her boss, Peter Sparber, wrote in part:

"As you know, Nancy Balter [Georgetown University], Gray Robertson [ACVA Atlantic, a ventilation firm in Virginia], Amy Millman (Philip Morris) and I met last Wednesday, August 27, with David Mudarri, who describes himself as a member of the 'outreach and economic incentives staff' — indoor air quality, in the Office of Air and Radiation. Mudarri is a longtime contact of Millman's, who arranged the meeting. … "Mudarri is enjoying something of a rebirth at EPA because Deputy Administrator Jim Barnes has taken a personal interest in indoor air quality. It is an interest shared by the new Assistant Administrator for Air and Radiation Craig Potter. [In May 1986, President Reagan replaced Cannon with J. Craig Potter, who had been Principal Deputy Secretary at the Fish and Wildlife Service.]

Mudarri has worked closely with Potter in the past. Potter has established an indoor air group within EPA to advise the agency on long-range policy and strategy. Mudarri is responsible for coordinating that group; he has informed us that James Repace will play an active role in all deliberations. The policy group will coordinate with the indoor air subcommittee established by the Science Advisory Board to direct indoor air quality research. … Both Robertson and Balter will follow up independently with Mudarri, providing him with additional material. Millman and I will meet with him again following the September 3-4 meetings" [TTID TI4599-1509].

I knew nothing of this meeting, which unfortunately betrayed our plans to the enemy. As for our new Assistant Administrator J. Craig Potter, the only thing I knew about him was that soon after he took office in 1986, he reportedly asked his no-nonsense secretary, a long-time EPA employee, to "cancel all my meetings for the day because I want to go fishing." She replied, "Mr. Potter, you can't do that, a lot of important people are on your schedule." Potter grumbled and repaired to his large office, whereupon he dropkicked his wastebasket right across the room. This bit of juicy gossip spread rapidly through OAR staff and did little to garnish our impressions of our new leader. To be fair, he had been Acting Assistant Secretary for Fish and Wildlife at the Department of Interior, and fishing had been part of his purview. In any case, I found Potter to be a pleasant gentleman and his efforts to promote indoor air do him much credit. When he moved on a couple of years later, the women on his staff serenaded him at his going-away party roasted him with a song parodying him as "Our Air Head." He took it in good grace. He departed to become a lobbyist at the Washington firm of O'Connor & Hannan.

Note that the average life-span of an EPA presidential appointee, most of whom were lawyers, was about 18 months; after they learned the ropes, many went back to the private sector to earn the big bucks as K-Street lobbyists or consultants to industry. Joe Cannon, like David Hawkins, was an exception.

EPA continued to get calls from other federal agencies as well as from the general public, requesting help in solving their intractable indoor air pollution problems. One of these was Justin Dart, Jr., a leader of the international disability rights movement and a wheel-chair-bound polio victim. Dart had been appointed by President Reagan to administer the Rehabilitation Services Administration. Mr. Dart, the scion of the Dart Drug empire, was well-connected, but unlike Reagan's earlier disastrous appointments of the Colorado Crazies, Ann Gorsuch and James Watt, Dart was a truly excellent choice to run his agency. Dart later would be regarded as "Godfather of the Americans With Disabilities Act" of 1990. He had complained to the EPA Administrator that his office was making him sick, and Lance Wallace and I were designated to investigate. As it turned out, the frugal Mr. Dart apparently did not believe in spending the taxpayer's money unnecessarily, and so he had moved into his new office in this Class "C" government building without replacing its old threadbare carpet that had been subject to repeated water leaks, as a result of skimping on maintenance. It was immediately obvious to us that the moldy carpet was a likely explanation for his symptoms, and we recommended it be replaced. Problem solved.

Another day I received a call from a contractor from New Jersey who complained his wife got headaches constantly while at home, but when on vacation, her symptoms would vanish. The man himself had no symptoms. But he suspected some sort of indoor air problem. I carefully questioned him. He told me that he had no water leaks but heated his home with a gas-fired forced air furnace. I had run into a similar problem before with Laird Towle, a member of my old NRL carpool whose wife had similar symptoms when she took long trips to Maine in his station wagon. I had correctly diagnosed it as a leaky muffler coupled with a hole in the chassis. I suggested to the contractor that he might have a cracked heat exchanger in the forced air furnace that could be leaking low-level carbon monoxide into their home. I recommended that he test for that. A few weeks later, he called back with effusive thanks. Another problem solved.

I had developed very good instincts for solving practical indoor air pollution problems. The Jersey contractor was just one of many ordinary citizens with indoor air quality problems that I helped during those years. The AA's secretaries who fielded the calls routinely referred citizens with indoor air quality complaints to me. I regarded such assistance as simply part of my job. After all, I worked for the public and I deeply believed in EPA's mission, which in part states that EPA's purpose is to ensure that "all Americans are protected from significant risks to human health and the environment where they live, learn and work." And I came to distrust anyone in the management chain above me who didn't appear to share that belief. There were some "Schedule Cs" (political appointees) who clearly fell into this category. Some of these had converted to civil service jobs and remained at EPA, often as deadwood, after a change in administration.

By 1987, in the wake of the one-two punch on secondhand smoke by the Surgeon General and the National Research Council in 1986, The July 27, 1987 issue of the news magazine *Business Week* ran a 9-page cover story, captioned NO SMOKING. It described "The Social Revolution Sweeping America," "How Business is Dealing With Smoking Restrictions," "New Ways to Kick the Habit," and "The Impact on the Tobacco Industry." The article opined, "No doubt about it, No Smoking is fast becoming the status quo. Ten states and more than 260 communities already have laws that restrict smoking in public places." The piece noted that "sales of cigarettes have been dropping; they took their most dramatic plunge in 1986: 2%. Today, 32% of the adult population smokes, down from a high of 42% in 1967."

EPA's Indoor Air Staff began to issue a series of five Fact Sheets. All were internally peer-reviewed by various agency offices who had to sign off on them. The first, Indoor Air Facts: #1, titled *"EPA and Indoor Air Quality"* was put out in June 1987. It described the establishment of an Indoor Air Quality Program at EPA designed to address indoor air pollution problems caused by such pollutants as radon, environmental tobacco smoke, asbestos, formaldehyde and other volatile organic compounds implicated in sick building syndrome, as well as biological pollutants and pesticides. It noted that EPA's actions were authorized by Congress under SARA Title IV, the Superfund Amendments and Reauthorization Act, and specifically, the Radon Gas and Indoor Air Quality Research Act, which gave EPA an "explicit mandate to conduct research and disseminate information on indoor air quality problems and solutions." Fact Sheet #1 noted that two manuals, one on the mitigation of environmental tobacco smoke, and one on the diagnosis and mitigation of sick building syndrome, were under development jointly with other federal agencies and private sector organizations.

However, as our plans developed, Eileen B. Claussen was appointed as the new Director of the Office of Program Development. Our program came under her aegis. Ms. Claussen had grown up in South Africa, where she developed an interest in the environment and the natural landscape. She had an MA in English from the University of Virginia. Claussen began her career with positions at Booz Allen Hamilton, Boise Cascade, and the Department of Defense. In February 1987, she hired a new staff person, Robert Axelrad, a brash young man barely in his thirties with a BA in Political Science. He sported a mop of curly dirty blond hair and wore blue jeans. Axelrad had been Claussen's assistant in her previous position in the Office of Solid Waste. This development would bode ill for both Mudarri and me.

JUD WELLS ENRAGES THE INDUSTRY

In 1982, A. Judson Wells, a DuPont executive, and a Harvard-educated physical chemist, retired as director of the fabrics and finishes department of DuPont's industrial products division, after a long and successful career. A tall, trim, distinguished looking and highly intelligent gentleman, Jud Wells looked every inch the commanding executive he had been. After his retirement, Jud became a volunteer for the American Lung Association of Delaware. In the mid 1980's, Jud contacted me, relating that he was interested in the epidemiology of passive smoking, and had become convinced that passive smoking was a significant cause of heart disease in passively exposed nonsmokers. We soon became fast friends and talked often on the phone. I thought his ideas were extraordinarily sound and encouraged him in his pursuits. In early 1986, he presented me with a draft of a risk assessment of passive smoking and heart disease for my comments. I thought it was well done and highly significant. As it happened, I was scheduled to chair a Session on Health Effects of Environmental Tobacco Smoke at the 79th Annual Meeting of the Air Pollution Control Association in Minneapolis in June of 1986. I encouraged Jud to present his work in my session. He agreed and gave an excellent presentation in which he estimated that passive smoking caused about 50,000 deaths per year in the United States, of which about 35,000 were from heart disease and 3000 from lung cancer.

In the Q and A period following his talk, it became evident that our session had been infested with a swarm of nasty tobacco moles whose sole aim was to discredit Wells using ad hominem attacks. One of them savaged Jud with a below-the-belt insinuation that, "as a former DuPont executive, Jud had been responsible for producing jellied gasoline weapons that the American military had deployed in Vietnam," and that as such he was a "war criminal." Since Jud had been director of the Fabrics and Finishings Department, this was the foulest of canards. Other vicious moles in the audience piled on in a tag-team match shouting a barrage of barking mad insults having nothing whatsoever to do with his research on ETS. Jud and I were totally stunned at the virulence exhibited in these unfair attacks. It was clear that the industry regarded his estimates as a major threat. This elevated Jud's work in importance. I urged him to submit his work for publication. In 1988, his peer-reviewed risk assessment, "An estimate of adult mortality in the United States from passive smoking" appeared in *Environment International* [Wells, 1988]. I used a slide of his results in my subsequent presentations on ETS (Figure 14).

Wells was the first researcher to quantify the connection between passive smoking and heart disease as well as a smattering of other diseases. Wells' work resulted in his becoming a major player in the 1992 EPA risk assessment of passive smoking as well as the 1994 OSHA Hearings on Environmental Tobacco Smoke. In addition, his then controversial conclusion that secondhand smoke caused quantifiable heart disease mortality would be endorsed and popularized by Prof. of Cardiology Stan Glantz, in 1991. It would become adopted by the California EPA in 1997, and passive smoking induced heart disease would be a central health conclusion in the 2006 Surgeon General's report 18 years later (Johnson et al., 2008). In the intervening years, Jud published a dozen papers in medical and scientific journals on the health risks of secondhand smoke. In the pantheon of secondhand smoke heroes, A. Judson Wells stands tall. In retrospect, the attack on Wells foreshadowed what was soon to be in store for me. Figure 14 shows Wells' estimates of total deaths from passive smoking in the U.S.

Estimated Passive Smoking Deaths
(U.S. Values from AJ Wells, Env. Internat. 25:515-519, 1999)

Cause	U.S.A.	Canada*[†]
Lung Cancer	3100	350
Heart Disease	47 000	5300
Breast Cancer	8700	990
Cervical Ca.	500	60
Nasal Sinus Ca.	200	20
Brain Cancer, Leukemia, & Lymphoma	1000	110
Total	**60 500**	**6830** Per Year

[†](rounded to 2 figs)

Total 1999 Population   270 million   30.7 million
[scaled from U.S. by relative population size. J.L. Repace, 2000]

FIGURE 14. WELLS' ESTIMATES OF PASSIVE SMOKING FOR THE ENTIRE US POPULATION, ADAPTED TO CANADA BY THE AUTHOR. I USED THIS SLIDE TO MAKE TROUBLE NORTH OF THE BORDER, AIDED AND ABETTED BY GAR MAHOOD OF THE NSRA (Authors' Slide).

CHAPTER 9

THE INDUSTRY STRIKES BACK

"James Repace has been a thorn in the industry's side for years. He has always managed to find a way to take time from his job at the Environmental Protection Agency to present his 'research' linking environmental tobacco smoke to 500-5,000 lung cancer deaths a year in nonsmokers in testimony, in anti-smoking articles, and as an expert witness in lawsuits on behalf of workers. Late last year, however, EPA assigned him to its indoor air quality program team – an assignment that appears to be a direct conflict with his outside activities, for which he has accepted payment. We quietly provided the documentation on Repace's activities to Rep. Don Sundquist of Tennessee. He wrote EPA Administrator Lee Thomas for an explanation, including that documentation in his letter. That request has triggered an investigation of Repace's activities by the Inspector General, and a call from Repace for scientists to send letters to the EPA in his defense.

Memorandum From Susan Stuntz to Peter Sparber, Re: Public Smoking Program,
The Tobacco Institute, May 23, 1987. [TTID, Bates #s TI07640128 - TI07640135].

On the 12th of March 1987, Lee Thomas, the new administrator of EPA, received a letter from Congressman Don Sundquist, Republican of Tennessee, alleging that I had violated EPA's code of ethics by serving for pay as a witness in labor grievance hearings and trials for people with smoking complaints. He complained that I had also testified as a citizen in favor of controls on smoking. This career, according to Sundquist, "conflicts with Repace's public role because it makes him unable to give a fair hearing to the tobacco company side." It was full of half-truths and three outright lies concocted by the tobacco industry and rubber-stamped by Sundquist.

Congress of the United States
House of Representatives
Washington DC 20515
                    March 12, 1987
Mr. Lee Thomas
Administrator
Environmental Protection Agency
Washington, D.C. 20460

Dear Lee:

    As you may know, I serve on the board of the Office of Technology Assessment. In that capacity, I had the occasion last year to review an OTA study related to smoking and its health impact. During the discussion on that study, another related study came to my attention that was written by one of your employees, James L. Repace. Mr. Repace recently became Chief of Technical Services for the Indoor Air Program, Office of Program Development, within the office of Air and Radiation.

At the time, I questioned only the substance of the Repace report, and I asked OTA staff to review it. However, since that time other disturbing information has been brought to my attention regarding Mr. Repace. I will share this information with you because I believe Mr. Repace may have breached a number of regulations governing the ethical conduct of EPA employees. His outside activities raise serious questions about his ability to perform his duties in an independent and unbiased manner.

Specifically, it appears that Mr. Repace's testimony as a paid expert witness on several occasions may have violated 40 CFR, section 3.103(d)(l), which prohibits EPA employees from using their public office for private gain. Moreover, to the extent that Mr. Repace has served as an expert witness in contested litigation involving the issues he apparently has or will be concerned with at EPA, his ability to exercise independent and impartial judgment regarding EPA's indoor air [program] could be impaired. It also seems that Mr. Repace has failed to take appropriate steps to assure that his outside activities do not imply official EPA endorsement.

Mr. Repace's expert witness appearances raise most serious questions meriting immediate review by the Agency. The EPA regulations governing employee conduct prohibit EPA employees from using 'their official positions for private gain or act[ing] in such a manner that creates the reasonable appearance of doing so' (40 CFR, sec 3.103).

It is my understanding that Mr. Repace has testified as a well-compensated expert witness in at least three labor grievance proceedings regarding smoking in the workplace. In February and March, 1984, Mr. Repace was retained to testify in an arbitration in Trenton, New Jersey. The attorney representing the complainants in this case indicated that Mr. Repace charged a premium of approximately $500 per day for his services because he was an employee of the federal government. In May, 1984, Mr. Repace participated as an expert witness in another arbitration proceeding in New York City: According to the attorney representing the complainants in this case, Mr. Repace received $700-1000 per day for his testimony. Most recently, Mr. Repace appeared as an expert witness on behalf of an individual in a proceeding in Ottawa, Canada. The attorney viewed Mr. Repace as an effective witness because of his affiliation with the EPA, and Mr. Repace received approximately $800 per day for his testimony.

Mr. Repace has also testified in connection with two private actions on behalf of individuals claiming hypersensitivity to environmental tobacco smoke. In one of these cases, involving AT&T, Mr. Repace touted his writings, lectures and testimony at public hearings in support of bills seeking to restrict smoking in public and private places. He also claimed that he had been 'retained' by the American Society of Heating, Refrigeration and Air Conditioning Engineers (ASHRAE) as a consultant on the 'interrelationship' between ETS and ventilation. Mr. Repace testified that, as part of his work for ASHRAE, he provided advice ·concerning the development of an ASHRAE Standard on 'Ventilation for Acceptable Indoor Air Quality.'

In addition to his paid expert testimony, Mr. Repace has assisted antismoking organizations such as the Group Against Smoke Pollution (GASP) and the Coalition on Smoking and Health, whose membership includes the American Cancer Society and the American Lung Association. In May, 1986 for instance, Mr. Repace prepared a memorandum to the American

Lung Association entitled 'A Rebuttal to Criticisms of Passive Smoking Research by Tobacco Industry Consultants.' (Attachment A). More recently, in December, 1986, writing in his official capacity as the Indoor Air Program's Chief of Technical Services, Mr. Repace strongly criticized "the inadequate treatment of ETS" in proposed ASHRAE standard 62-1981R, the same Standard on which Mr. Repace worked in his private capacity as a consultant to ASHRAE (attachment B). In addition to his apparent violation of EPA's prohibition against using public office for private gain, Mr. Repace's actions on behalf of these antismoking organizations also would seem to violate EPA guidelines prohibiting conduct creating the reasonable appearances of giving preferential treatment to any organization or person.

Apparently, Mr. Repace's appeal as an expert witness to individuals claiming hypersensitivity to ETS is based, to a large extent, on his position within EPA and his publications and public appearances in support of greater restrictions on the use of tobacco products, which always identify him as an employee of the Agency. These publications often fail to warn readers that his statements and opinions do not carry the official endorsement of EPA. Thus, it would seem that it is not in Mr. Repace's pecuniary interest to take a policy position within EPA that could be perceived as favorable to the tobacco industry and that might reduce his appeal as an expert witness. This situation raises the possibility of a conflict of interest and emphasizes the seeming impropriety of permitting Mr. Repace to remain in a position that demands the ongoing exercise of independent and unbiased judgement.

As stated above, Mr. Repace on a number of occasions may have failed to take appropriate steps to ensure that his publications and speeches are not construed as implying official EPA endorsement, in apparent violation of 40 CFR, sec. 3.500. In numerous publications, Mr. Repace has failed to include a disclaimer adequate to inform readers that 'no official support or endorsement by the Environmental Protection Agency or any other agency of the federal government is intended or should be inferred,' as required by 40 CFR, sec. 3.506. On one occasion, Mr. Repace submitted a letter to the editor of the medical journal Lancet criticizing a December, 1983 article on ETS. Mr. Repace's letter appeared March 3, 1984, and identified his affiliation with EPA's Office of Air and Radiation. The letter contained no disclaimer whatsoever.

These examples suggest that Mr. Repace on some occasions has not taken adequate measures to ensure against his outside activities being construed as implying official EPA endorsement. Rather, Mr. Repace has emphasized his affiliation with EPA in his publications and public appearances. The failure to take steps to ensure that his private opinions are not perceived as official EPA positions, when coupled with his reliance on these opinions in expert testimony, seems improper and requires your immediate attention.

Mr. Repace's policy-related duties as Chief of Technical Services for OAR's Indoor Air Program heightens my concern over his seeming violation of EPA's ethical guidelines. In light of his prior testimony as an expert witness, he will most likely be unable independently to review and analyze EPA indoor air program initiatives. Mr. Repace's apparently inappropriate outside activities should not be permitted to compromise your Agency's independence, and I urge you to review this situation expeditiously.

Sincerely,
D-
Don Sundquist
Member of Congress

My first contact with the investigation was when two agents from EPA's Office of The Inspector General (OIG) showed up one morning in at my cubicle in the bowels of Waterside Mall and flashed their badges. They demanded that I surrender all of my word processor discs and paper files pursuant to investigation of an ethics complaint by a tobacco state congressman. I was simply stunned. Up to this time, I had regarded the attacks on my work by the Tobacco Institute as sort of a game, no more than prima facie evidence of the importance of my work, and my response to those attacks as a legitimate scientific response to criticism. I was right about the latter, but dead wrong about the former: it was no game – it was outright war. This was a vicious personal attack by a tobacco state congressman who was a member of the powerful House Oversight and Investigations Subcommittee. Nevertheless, having gone through the Sludge Wars, I was wise in the ways of Washington, and knew if this matter were hidden from public view, I would be utterly defenseless, despite having done no consulting after joining Mudarri's Indoor Air Staff nine months earlier. Not only did I not have the time or inclination for consulting at that point, I very much doubt that Mudarri would have approved it.

As to the substance of Sundquist's complaints, these were fabricated from whole cloth: my consulting had been approved by Stolpman. I used approved disclaimers in every publication but one, where it was removed without my knowledge by the editor of *The Lancet,* and I had *never* been a paid consultant to ASHRAE. Furthermore, all of the consulting was during my prior position with the Office of Policy Analysis, not my present one with the Indoor Air staff, which was in a different office. And I was picked by plaintiffs' attorneys because of my scientific expertise, not because I was from the EPA, something which I knew better than to tout. I knew the rules. Finally, my official EPA job description was the catch-all category called Environmental Protection Specialist, not the "Chief of Technical Services" of Mudarri's invention.

I recalled that after Ralph Nader published his 1965 book, *Unsafe at Any Speed,* detailing the safety defects of American automobiles, General Motors hired a private eye to investigate him. When this was brought to light, the national press seized upon it as a great David vs. Goliath story, to the considerable embarrassment of the automobile industry. It was the "sunlight is the best disinfectant" defense. I decided that my best course of action was to deploy the Sunlight Defense, and phoned the News Department at *Science* Magazine, which frequently ran stories on political aspects of science, on scientific fraud, and on the travails of scientists. I was put in touch with Elliot Marshall, a prominent writer on their news staff. Vastly exceeding my expectations, Marshall wrote a blistering two-page exposé on April 17, 1987, in *Science's* News & Comment section. It was headlined **Tobacco Science Wars** and was subtitled *The industry has been bullying scientists according to researchers who lead the campaign against environmental tobacco smoke.* It detailed the tobacco industry's efforts to attack scientists and other federal civil servants, including Don Shopland, who was at that time the acting director of the Surgeon General's Office on Smoking and Health. It featured a photo of me in my office at EPA. Marshall had asked me to smile, but I simply couldn't muster one. Marshall also interviewed Stan Glantz. Stan and I were described as "two outspoken scientists [who] accused the tobacco industry of misusing scientific data." Whereas, "Industry representatives meanwhile say their experts have been harassed by anti-smoking 'zealots' and that their right to free expression has been infringed."

Marshall interviewed a Sundquist spokesman, who freely admitted that the tobacco industry had "provided them with information [on Repace] which we sent to the Administrator of EPA." The article also discussed the role of industry consultants from academia, including Sorrell Schwartz, a professor of pharmacology at Georgetown University, and Philip Witorsch, MD, an adjunct professor of pulmonology at George Washington University, who were part of the Tobacco Institute's "Indoor Air Pollution Advisory Group who travelled at industry expense to municipal hearings around the country to point out flaws in Repace's work." According to Marshall, the memo I had done for Shane McDermott of the American Lung Association debunking their moles' activities "truly incensed the Tobacco Institute." The article noted that "Repace, a physicist who runs the technical services office for EPA's indoor air program, wrote some early influential papers linking ambient smoke and cancer [a footnote cited the 1980 and 1985 papers of Repace and Lowrey] most of them on his own time. Glantz, an associate professor of medicine, has published a biostatistics textbook and is chairman of the UCSF graduate program in bioengineering. Both regard cigarette smoke as a toxic pollutant that should be kept out of public places."

The industry took a different view: by this time, it had a substantial war chest for its consultants' efforts to preserve smoking in public places: an internal Tobacco Institute memorandum from TI's vice president, Peter Sparber, to its president, Sam Chilcote, dated March 25, 1987, outlined TI's budget for consultants. Of a total of $1,287,000 for 1987, of which "roughly $720,000 have been spent or committed outright." The breakdown listed $380,000 to Gray Robertson, $270,000 to Sorrell Schwartz and his IAPAG team, with the remainder spread out "across a variety of consultants including Mantel ($32,000), Weeks ($25,000), Sterling ($5000) and Waite ($10,000). … From that amount, we must cover hearings in as many as 15 states, 33 localities and whatever occurs federally. Moreover, we hope to use scientists in at least five legislative briefings, a field staff meeting, the Tobacco College, and two lobbyists meetings. Assuming that the average cost (fees plus travel) for each of these events is about $4,000, continuation of the scientific witnesses in 1987 will be about $250,000" [TTID TI09922106].

As the Office of the Inspector General's (OIG) ethics investigation ground on, one of the two agents informed me of a personal conflict of interest. "I'm a cigarette smoker, is that going to be a problem?" I replied, "Not as long as you don't smoke where I can breathe it." Although there was no chance of that unless we held our interviews in the johns. The unstated subtext to his query was a memo that I had drafted for the AA's signature recommending a ban on smoking in the public areas of EPA buildings in the wake of the Surgeon General's and NAS Reports. In response, Agency management had banished smokers to restrooms located only on every other floor of EPA buildings throughout the entire country. In retrospect, I should have objected to the agent's professed bias. After a six-month long investigation, the investigators arrived at the bizarre conclusion that my EPA-approved paid consulting and litigation during my *past* tenure in the Office of Policy Analysis had relied on my published scientific papers that had been worked on partly on EPA time, so that this created a conflict of interest with my *present* job on the Indoor Air Staff in the Office of Program Development.

OIG informed me that I now had the opportunity to reply in writing to these allegations. It seemed to me that I was being set up for a fall. I quickly decided that I needed outside legal assistance to defend against this twisted reasoning. Washington DC is chock full of public interest legal talent, including lawyers with tobacco smoke expertise. I phoned a friend, Michael Pertschuk, who was co-director of the Advocacy Institute, part of which was the Smoking Control Advocacy Resource Center (SCARC). SCARC's mission was "to provide guides, training, strategic counseling, and other resources to combat the tobacco industry."

Mike Pertschuk had been, inter alia, chief counsel and staff director to the Senate Committee on Commerce, Science, and Transportation from 1965 to 1976, and was instrumental in drafting the landmark legislation requiring cigarette warning labels and banning broadcast advertising of tobacco products. He became chairman of the Federal Trade Commission from 1977 to 1981 and remained as a commissioner until 1984. I asked him for legal assistance in drafting my response to OIG's charges. Mike generously assigned one of his staff attorneys to help me draft my rebuttal. Our rebuttal convincingly made the case that I had neither a real nor an apparent conflict of interest, and the OIG reversed its conclusions.

On June 2, 1988, 68 days after the Sundquist missive, the EPA Inspector General sent his response to Sundquist. It was brief and to the point.

Indoor Air Fact Sheet #3, Ventilation and Air Quality in Offices, which I drafted, was published in February 1988. Among other topics, it discussed ASHRAE Standard 62, Ventilation for Acceptable Indoor Air Quality, and noted that ASHRAE specified 5 cubic feet per minute per person (cfm/person) for nonsmoking buildings and 20 cfm/person for smoking buildings. In the section titled RESOLVING AIR QUALITY PROBLEMS IN OFFICE BUILDINGS, Fact sheet #3 recommended restrictions on smoking. The two-tiered ventilation rates recommended by ASHRAE in 1981 for smoking and nonsmoking buildings had long stuck in the tobacco industry's craw. This provoked it to launch what would become a decades-long abuse of ASHRAE's consensus process, which mandated that the ASHRAE 62 revision committee invite affected industries to designate delegates to the committee so as to arrive at an industry-wide consensus.

I was incensed by this, and at the Healthy Buildings Conference in Stockholm in September 1988, I gave voice to my displeasure. In response to a pointed question from me about nasty industry interference with ASHRAE process at the end of his plenary lecture, Prof. Jan Stolwijk, Susan Dwight Bliss Professor of Epidemiology and Public Health at Yale University. Stolwijk, the imposing gray-bearded chair of ASHRAE's Standard 62 revision committee, conceded that "the influence of various special interest groups, especially the Tobacco Institute and the Formaldehyde Institute, was felt by the committee." Then in blunter terms he was moved to add, "in fact the tobacco industry interfered with the operation of the committee in a most brutal and unfair way." It was now out in the open.

An EPA scientist (I think it was Bob Lewis) who attended some of those Standard 62 meetings told colleagues that, "the representative of the Tobacco Institute repeatedly invoked parliamentary maneuvers that were disruptive and which wore the committee down." In 1989, this war of attrition finally succeeded, and it surrendered unconditionally to the industry's demands. ASHRAE issued a revision of its ventilation standard 62 that abandoned the two-tiered ventilation rate for smoking and nonsmoking buildings. Instead it recommended the same rates for all buildings irrespective of smoking status. And much worse, it relegated smoking to a footnote that informed readers that the recommended rates would *accommodate a moderate amount of smoking.* This was based on the notion of "odor acceptability" by 80% of a test panel of human subjects. However, the olfactory research underlying that had been done by physiologist Bill Cain at Yale in the early 1980's, and as previously mentioned, half of Cain's odor test panel were cigarette smokers whose tolerance for the reek of tobacco smoke was five times greater than it was for the nonsmokers. In other words, if the odor test panel had been comprised solely of nonsmokers, the new 20 cfm/occupant ventilation rate for offices permitting smoking would have been 100 cfm/occupant (B. Leaderer, personal communication).

Fact Sheet #4 dealt with Sick Building Syndrome (SBS). I wrote most of that. Among other causes of this malady, it mentioned that environmental tobacco smoke contributed high levels of irritating volatile organic compounds (VOCs), which were known indoor chemical contaminants. Among other preventive measures, Fact Sheet #4 recommended smoking restrictions. I also had four more projects in the works: a fifth Fact Sheet on Environmental Tobacco Smoke briefly summarizing the knowledge base at that time, an interagency technical compendium of information on secondhand smoke risk and control authored by experts and summarizing the state of the art, a smoking policy guide for managers of workplaces, and most importantly, an official EPA risk assessment of environmental tobacco smoke conducted independently by the Office of Research and Development. Although it was not conceived as such, the policy guide would later raise the issue of smoking in the workplace in a way that would directly confront the industry's status quo strategy of "accommodation" that it promoted world-wide (Repace, 1988).

Fact Sheet #5, Environmental Tobacco Smoke, issued in June 1989, drew heavily from the conclusions of the 1986 *Report of the Surgeon General on Involuntary Smoking,* the 1986 *Report of the National Research Council on Environmental Tobacco Smoke,* and on the Interagency Task Force on Environmental Cancer, Heart, and Lung Disease, noting that these three bodies were unanimous in concluding that passive smoking significantly increased the risk of lung cancer in adults. It noted, in the words of the Surgeon General, "a substantial number of the lung cancer deaths that occur in nonsmokers can be attributed to involuntary smoking." It quoted the Interagency Task Force's conclusions that "the effects of ETS on the heart may be of even greater concern than its cancer-causing effects on the lungs." It reported that studies of indoor air in commercial and public buildings showed that particulate levels were considerably higher when smoking was permitted than not. It observed that "ETS can be totally eliminated from indoor air only by removing smoking, and that separating smokers from nonsmokers in the same room might reduce but would not eliminate nonsmokers' exposure."

This last was a direct quote from the Surgeon General. It noted that research indicated that total removal of tobacco smoke through ventilation was both technically and economically impractical and concluded that "EPA recommends that exposure to environmental tobacco smoke be minimized wherever possible." Finally, it recommended that the most effective way to accomplish this goal "is to restrict smoking to smoking areas that are separately ventilated and directly exhausted to the outside, or by eliminating smoking in the building entirely." On June 21, 1989, Dave Cohen, EPA's media services director, issued a press release on Indoor Air Facts #5, describing environmental tobacco smoke as "one of the most widespread and harmful indoor air pollutants." In sum, Fact Sheet #5 pithily summarized the state of the art on secondhand smoke as reported by federally-issued authoritative reports based on published, peer-reviewed science. It had also been reviewed and approved by reviewers from the Office of Air and Radiation and the Office of Research and Development. At my suggestion, we also solicited and received comments from the Tobacco Institute, which none of the multiple EPA reviewers found to be in any way credible.

Indoor Air Facts #5 provoked a virulent reaction from the Tobacco Institute. In an internal memorandum dated June 21, 1989, to the Executive Committee, Sam Chilcote, Jr. reported in part:

"Enclosed you will find the Environmental Protection Agency's 'Indoor Air Facts (No. 5): Environmental Tobacco Smoke.' This document ignores all of the Institute's substantive comments made in response to an October 1988 draft, as well as a large portion of the scientific literature. The result is a highly inflammatory paper that appears to be designed to further a political agenda, since scientific support is lacking. The Institute has prepared a rebuttal, which also is enclosed."

Their five-page press release (TI, June 22, 1989), led off with a one-page summary. It read in part:

"WASHINGTON, D.C. – In a rebuttal to an Environmental Protection Agency (EPA) 'Fact Sheet' on environmental tobacco smoke (ETS), The Tobacco Institute today provided information from scientific reviews, EPA's own research and other governmental agencies demonstrating that the EPA's document contains inappropriate language and claims that are scientifically unsupportable. In many areas, as The Tobacco Institute's response shows, EPA did not take into account significant portions of the scientific research, including its own findings. …

It went on to claim that the Fact Sheet understated the effectiveness of ventilation in removing ETS. It denied that the Surgeon General and the National Academy of Sciences had reached any firm conclusion that that exposure to ETS is linked to heart disease. It noted that NIOSH found that cigarette smoke was involved in only 2 percent of its sick building investigations. It said that more people were exposed to indoor combustion from cooking and heating appliances than ETS. "The EPA's one-sided fact sheet is inaccurate" said Brennan Dawson, assistant to the president of The Tobacco Institute. 'Clearly, this scientifically deficient document raises questions about the Agency's integrity and credibility. It is regrettable that the Agency has failed to ensure that accurate and balanced information is provided to the public,'" she added. It continued: "The 'Fact Sheet' misstates the health effects of ETS," and asserted that, "viewing the same evidence considered by the NAS and the Surgeon General, the International Agency for Research on Cancer of the World Health Organization concluded, also late in 1986, that the available epidemiological evidence is equally consistent with a finding of an increase in risk or an absence of risk." (IARC Monograph on the Evaluation of the Carcinogenic Risk of Chemicals to Humans: Tobacco Smoking 38, p, 308, 1986)". This was a quote out of context.

The full quote from WHO's IARC Monograph 38 actually stated:

"It is unlikely that any effects will be produced in passive smokers that are not produced to a greater extent in smokers and that types of effects that are not seen in smokers will not be seen in passive smokers. Examination of smoke from the different sources shows that all three types contain chemicals that are both carcinogenic and mutagenic. The amounts absorbed by passive smokers are, however, small, and effects are unlikely to be detectable unless exposure is substantial and very large numbers of people are observed. The observations on nonsmokers that have been made so far are compatible with either an increased risk from 'passive' smoking or an absence of risk. *Knowledge of the nature of sidestream and mainstream smoke, of the materials absorbed during 'passive' smoking, and of the quantitative relationships between dose and effect that are commonly observed from exposure to carcinogens, however, leads to the conclusion that passive smoking gives rise to some risk of cancer.*" [Italics mine.]

This quote out of context was of course a vintage tobacco industry disinformation technique. Of course, what the IARC viewed as a "small" dose was only small in comparison when compared to dose of tobacco smoke inhaled by smokers. More troubling was IARC's tacit assumption that the dose-response curve between exposure to tobacco smoke and lung cancer was linear from the high doses inhaled by smokers to the low doses inhaled during passive smoking. I would rebut this assumption when an industry mole promoted it in 1992.

The Institute's news release continued, attempting to cast Fact Sheet # 5 into disrepute by sounding its enduring clarion call that ventilation could control ETS:

"2) The 'Fact Sheet' Exaggerates the Place of ETS in Indoor Air Pollution and Incorrectly Evaluates the Effectiveness of Ventilation in Removing ETS The 'Fact Sheet' is inaccurate in discussing the contribution of ETS to indoor air pollution. The overemphasis on ETS as a contributor to Indoor air pollution, coupled with the underestimation of the effectiveness of ventilation in removing ETS, results in a misleading presentation of indoor air pollution issues. This could lead people to ignore the more significant contribution of poorly designed and maintained ventilation systems."

This was arrant nonsense. Source control, i.e. preventing smoking in buildings, is far more efficient and enormously less costly to building owners than ventilation or air cleaning in removing indoor air pollution from secondhand smoke. Consider this water pollution analogy: the cost of putting in sewage treatment plants to clean up the Chesapeake Bay runs into the billions for source control; these plants treat the sewage before the polluted water runs into the bay — imagine the cost if you tried to filter the entire bay after the sewage had been dumped into it! In physical parlance, it is easier to capture a low entropy (concentrated) pollutant than a high entropy (diluted) one.

The research of Repace and Lowrey, together with work reported by Leaderer and Hammond at Yale, and that done in the Harvard Six City Study by Spengler and colleagues, showed that the exposure to secondhand smoke particulate air pollution indoors was generally much greater than that from outdoor particulate air pollution. One major problem up to that time is that aside from the work of this handful of researchers, very little effort had been put into the study of indoor air pollution from secondhand smoke.

I had been aware of the utility of cotinine in body fluids as an index of exposure to secondhand smoke due to the work of Martin Jarvis in London in the early 1980's. I had served with Jarvis on an IARC panel chaired by Dietrich Hoffmann at the American Health Foundation (AHF) in Valhalla, NY in 1984, and all of us had authored chapters in IARC Monograph 81, Volume 9, Passive Smoking (1987). In fact, two of the chapters were mine. AHF was a very well-funded research operation and had impressive lab equipment. At that meeting, Hoffmann and his chief tobacco chemist, Klaus Brunnemann, asked me to help plan controlled ETS exposure and cotinine dose experiments they would conduct later that year. Their brilliant work on the chemistry and toxicity of secondhand smoke, particularly on the highly carcinogenic tobacco-specific nitrosamines, informed my understanding of ETS enormously. This was ironic, as Klaus had been formerly employed by Philip Morris in Switzerland and was himself a cigarette smoker (which appalled Jarvis).

AHF was captained by Dr. Ernst Wynder, a darling of NCI for his early seminal work on the carcinogenicity of tobacco tar. I first met Wynder at an ACS meeting in New York at the Waldorf Astoria in 1980. I was aware that he had a reputation as a ladies' man, and I noticed with amusement that he was squiring an elegantly dressed attractive young woman on his arm who appeared to be about 30 years his junior. Wynder was fervent about disease prevention and was one of the early "safe cigarette" advocates, but he, like Richard Peto, had downplayed the notion that ETS was a threat to nonsmokers' health.

In 1987, the Centers for Disease Control, which had been measuring contaminants in human body fluids due to environmental influences, queried EPA to inquire if we had any special requests to add to CDC's national environmental monitoring program. I seized this opportunity to persuade George Provenzano, an economist with EPA's Office of Policy Planning and Evaluation, who was charged with coordinating EPA's response to CDC, to include cotinine monitoring in EPA's recommendations, which included several other pollutants such as blood lead, as well. CDC embraced these, and in 1993, this would bear vitally important fruit as the CDC's future NHANES III national cotinine database.

The Tobacco Institute continued to downplay the utility of cotinine as a quantitative ETS marker either for ETS dose or for health effects. In a memo to its Regional Vice Presidents, the Institute laid down the party line: "The fact that there is cotinine in a person's system doesn't imply any health hazard. And, there are other sources besides tobacco which produce cotinine in body fluids. Dietary sources of nicotine include tomatoes, potatoes and eggplant" [TTID TI2992-1778]. The notion that dietary sources of nicotine were significant compared to passive smoking was Grade A Bullshit. Martin Jarvis and I would later debunk these claims in companion letters published in the *British Medical Journal*. And in 1996, CDC studies of serum cotinine and diet would confirm that we were right on the mark.

Meanwhile, back at EPA, in another regrettable development, Claussen began to give her loyal acolyte Axelrad more and more responsibility despite his manifest deficiency in technical expertise plus a total lack of managerial experience, squeezing Dave Mudarri out of his leadership role. This was manifestly unfair, especially because Mudarri was technically competent, and a very good manager of people and programs. Above all, Dave fostered a collegial work atmosphere. If Axelrad possessed any of these characteristics, I must have missed the memo. However, he was definitely interested in building an empire based on indoor air and ETS. In any case, I had to work with the management I had, not with the management I wished I had. And so, I repeatedly impressed on him the vital importance of an official EPA risk assessment of passive smoking funded by us but conducted by ORD. At first, Axelrad stubbornly resisted expending the funds necessary, instead ludicrously demanding that I produce a brand-new draft risk assessment for the Indoor Air staff in just one month's time. This was impossible and beside the point.

First, Axelrad had no concept whatsoever of amount of work necessary to produce a new risk assessment. It had taken Lowrey and me *four years* of intensive work to produce our original risk assessment (and in fact, starting from scratch, it would also take ORD's Carcinogen Assessment Group four years to produce

air quality, and he is winding up his three-year term as a member of the Environmental Health Committee of the American Society of Heating, Refrigeration and Air Conditioning Engineers (ASHRAE). He is a member of the EPA's Advisory Board on Indoor Air Quality, a member of the National Clean Air Council (an ad hoc group retained by the EPA), and he is on the Board of Editors of Indoor Pollution Law Report. ... More recently, the lead poisoning work he did for HUD from 1976 to 1982 was subsequently used by the EPA to set standards for lead in gasoline.

Billick has a fairly high level of interest in the position at CIAR. He recognizes the need for research in indoor air quality and that to be meaningful and effective, such research would have to be done by private industry. He sees it as a great challenge and the chance to establish an organization such as CIAR very exciting. He is also attracted by the compensation ... and he would welcome the opportunity to return to the Washington area where he still owns a home. On the other hand, he expressed a number of concerns. He will have to be assured that the organization will truly be independent and the findings will be published no matter what the results. He has a real question as to whether any organization supported by the tobacco industry would achieve credibility, even within the scientific community, and he will need to be reassured that the directors would be willing to accept co-sponsors and perhaps even broaden the Board membership to include non-tobacco people.

I have no question that this candidate has the technical skills in the appropriate disciplines, as well as the management experience to carry out the duties of the Executive Director. He certainly has the appropriate contacts in both industry and government, has an open mind about environmental tobacco smoking, and volunteered that, in such sensitive issues, there is only a fine line between science and politics. In a word, he is a tough-minded pragmatist. ... In summary, this bright, highly-experienced, government- and industry-experienced scientist/manager meets most, if not all, the requirements of the idealized specification for Executive Director of the Center for Indoor Air Research, and should be given careful consideration for that position" [TTID TI0199-2176].

So how did being highly qualified for the CIAR director position work out for Billick? Soon afterward, Irv told me that he had met with several tobacco industry executives whom he had favorably impressed. He said that they had promised him a "free hand" in running the organization and were favorably disposed towards making him an offer. [In fact, they had intended to offer him a handsome salary of $120,000 per year; TTID 87824396]. The draft agreement specified that he would report directly to the Board of Directors, which was fine by Billick.

Afterward, Irv told me what happened next. After his meeting with the Board, he was left alone and asked to wait. Suddenly, John Rupp, the external counsel for the Tobacco Institute, entered the room. Rupp clued Billick into what life was really like in the land of Joe Camel and The Marlboro Man: Rupp would be Billick's de facto boss. Billick immediately objected, telling Rupp that the industry execs had promised him that he would have "a free hand in running CIAR." He said that Rupp replied, "I don't care what they said; *I'll* have the final approval on all CIAR decisions." Billick returned to Chicago and on February 4th, wrote a letter to Tom Osdene, chair of the Board of Directors of CIAR, and the Director of Science and Technology for Philip Morris USA. He told Osdene what was wrong with Rupp's proposal:

"... it would be required that when the actual research projects are developed and the investigator selected, a request would be submitted to the Board of Directors for review and funding. It would be possible at that time for any or all of the industry sponsors of CIAR to refuse to support any particular research project. I believe that such a procedure is unworkable if one wishes to attain the industry's goals of objectivity and independence."

Unfortunately for Billick's dashed hopes, "objectivity and independence" were the absolute last things that the industry desired in CIAR's director. Billick was essentially rejecting the notion of tobacco industry control over CIAR. This would never fly. They wanted somebody who would competently administer the organization, but when it came to policy, would be a stooge who would unquestioningly toe the industry line on ETS. Osdene made this abundantly clear in an artfully worded rejection letter, dated February 24, 1988.

"Dear Dr. Billick: On behalf of the directors of the Center for Indoor Air Research ("CIAR"), I want to thank you for the time that you spent considering our offer to serve as CIAR's executive director. I regret that you have declined to accept our offer … It would have been possible, as you suggested, to have organized the CIAR in a manner that minimized the involvement of the Board of Directors in reviewing individual research proposals and in identifying researchers qualified to undertake the projects described in the proposals. But a major deficiency of that approach is that it would not have taken full advantage of the scientific expertise of CIAR's directors … . I certainly wish you continued success in your current position. Thomas Osdene, Ph.D., Chairman, Board of Directors, Center for Indoor Air Research, bc: J. Rupp. A. Spears, M. Ward. [TTID 20233553138]. [Alex Spears was a Lorillard researcher, and Mary Ward was a lawyer in Reynold's R&D division.]

Osdene's letter staggered Billick. In his reply to Osdene, dated March 4, 1988, Billick wrote that he was "mystified" because he "had never declined an offer to serve as executive director," and felt that his February 4th letter was "simply a basis for negotiation." He also noted that he was "never certain what the exact role of Mr. Rupp was" [TTID 2023553132].

I learned volumes from Billick's tale. This, coupled with my reading of the CIAR public prospectus, clearly indicated that the CIAR was clearly intended to be a front organization for Big-Tobacco-directed phony ETS "research" designed solely to serve its public relations needs to preserve smoking in the workplace and protect its profits. And that Attorney John Rupp was involved in this effort right up to his legal eyeballs. Straight-shooter Billick never stood a snowball's chance in Hell.

At that time, I knew Rupp only as this shadowy figure whose job seemed to involve vilification of the industry's targets. I had been subject to a Rupp hatchet job in 1986, at a conference on Indoor Air Pollution in Boston, where I spoke on the risks of passive smoking. His presentation followed mine and began with an announcement that he was external legal counsel for the Tobacco Institute. Rupp devoted his entire presentation to a brutal ad hominem attack on me. It backfired: John Pinney, a friend and former Director of the Office on Smoking and Health at DHHS, and who was now Director of the Smoking Policy Institute at Harvard, was in the audience. Pinney defended me, denouncing Rupp vehemently.

For nearly a decade, the field measurements of public places in our *Science* and *ASHRAE* papers and our *Environment International* risk assessment paper with its quantitative estimate of lung cancer mortality stood virtually alone as examples of their genre with appallingly few exceptions. This was something I could never quite fathom. For a long time with the exception of some very important work by Jack Spengler at Harvard in the Six Cities Study of homes, and with the controlled chamber experiments of ETS particles and nicotine by Brian Leaderer at Yale, and Kathie Hammond at U. Mass., few researchers had pursued secondhand hand smoke exposure research, and no federal efforts had been undertaken to estimate mortality from passive smoking. As such, although we had no way of knowing this at the time, one of CIAR'S several major objectives would be so-called "special projects" whose sole aim was to discredit the works of Repace and Lowrey – by any means, fair or foul. Fair was not an option, so foul it would be. Our battles would extend to the very halls of Congress itself.

In March of 1988, spokespersons for Philip Morris, R.J. Reynolds, and P. Lorillard tobacco companies announced with straight faces that the Center for Indoor Air Research (CIAR), was an organization ostensibly dedicated to funding "objective research in indoor air issues including environmental tobacco smoke" (ETS) was up and running, with its mission "to effectively communicate research findings to the broad scientific community" [CIAR 1989]. In reality, a confidential 1988 industry memo revealed that CIAR was actually part and parcel of an industry strategy to "set up a team of scientists organized by one national coordinating scientist and American lawyers, to ... carry out work on ETS to keep the controversy alive" [ACS, 2003].

The CIAR was particularly important to the industry because while some well-funded university researchers at major research universities had rebuffed direct tobacco company attempts to seduce and neutralize them with lucrative six figure offers for research support [Stolwijk J (Yale); Spengler J (Harvard), personal communications], many legitimate scientists had few qualms about accepting funding from CIAR or serving on its board [Raeburn, 1990]. This lent CIAR a patina of respectability to cover up the dross of corruption laying just beneath the surface. Why was this even possible? CIAR extramural R&D money, reported at $4,000,000 in Fiscal Year 1990, was doubtless the largest source of ETS exposure research funds available in the U.S. at that time in this chronically underfunded area. While NCI funded excellent epidemiological research, they had not hitherto funded exposure studies. OSHA was disinterested in ETS, and NIOSH was starved for funding by Congress, which left only EPA, which had strong support from the public and environmental groups.

EPA's ETS research program, described by the Associated Press as the "largest federal program on ETS" [Raeburn, 1993], had a planned R&D budget for Fiscal Year 1990 of just $230,000 [USEPA, ORD], a mere 5% of what CIAR was prepared to spend. CIAR's solicitation for grant applications carefully noted that biological markers had "limited value" as indicators of ETS exposure or dose, that "inaccurate reports of (ETS) exposure history introduce the problem of misclassification (bias) in epidemiological studies," and that "Important unresolved questions remain about levels of exposure to ETS and possible effects on health," which it deemed, was a reflection of the "contradictory findings among past clinical and epidemiological studies"[CIAR, 1989].

This was by and large following in lockstep the arguments advanced in an internal R.J. Reynolds public relations document marked *Privileged and Confidential for use of attorneys only in smoking and health litigation,* outlining stock questions and answers on ETS and other issues [Mealy, 1988]. Eventually, the industry hired an executive director, Max Eisenberg, PhD, who met their strict requirements. Eisenberg habitually wore a slime-green tweed sports jacket that, coupled with his sallow complexion, gave him a saurian appearance. I always thought of him as "Max The Lizard."

CIAR SPECIAL PROJECTS

As mentioned earlier, one of the "special projects" (i.e., lawyer-directed research) of the ETS Advisory Group of the CIAR was to fund Salvatore DiNardi, then an associate professor at the University of Massachusetts at Amherst to rebut the work of Repace and Lowrey (1980). It blew up in their faces. DiNardi had presented a symposium paper entitled "Conceptual considerations for Monitoring Exposure to Environmental Tobacco Smoke," at an ASHRAE Conference in Atlanta in April 1986. The conclusions of the paper were vague: "Careful evaluation of background exposures to indoor air pollutants is crucial, especially for respirable suspended particles (RSP), where competing sources indoors will always be present," and he did not mention our work.

However, in his research report to the CIAR, tendered in 1988, DiNardi and his graduate student, Susan McDonald, compared three air-sampling methods for measuring RSP in indoor air, a continuous reading TSI Piezobalance, two light-scattering aerosol monitors, the RAM and the HAM, and a gravimetric pump-and-filter method. The 67 sampled sites were selected on the basis that their typical use would be representative of buildings frequented by the public and similar to those measured by Repace and Lowrey (1980). The sites included nightclubs, bowling centers, grocery stores, hospitals, art museums, libraries, offices, fast food and table service restaurants, as well as schools and study lounges, as well as occupied non-smoking areas, unoccupied formerly smoking areas and unoccupied non-smoking areas, food and table service restaurants, schools and study lounges. DiNardi and McDonald found that the mean value for the Piezobalance data in occupied smoking sites was 108 $\mu g/m^3$, triple the 33 $\mu g/m^3$ that they measured in occupied non-smoking sites. Data for the RAM device was similar. Importantly, their comparison with the gold-standard gravimetric method showed that the Piezobalance/Gravimetric ratios were the same within 15% for all but one smoking site, and they found that the Piezobalance actually overestimated the low levels of RSP measured in nonsmoking sites.

After all their careful work, DiNardi and McDonald's results managed to replicate the results we had reported in our *Science* paper. This would have been highly embarrassing for the industry if it had been made public. So CIAR promptly deep-sixed it and wrote it off as a folly [TTID 2021006191]. In his trial testimony in 2004, under close questioning from federal prosecutors, Rupp would misleadingly characterize DiNardi's research as "inconclusive," and "an unfortunate waste of money" DiNardi had received $688,878 in CIAR funding. [U.S. vs. Philip Morris et al., Oct. 2004]. By comparison, in the 1970's, Lowrey and I had funded the research for our *Science* paper out of pocket for perhaps $500, mostly for food and drink in restaurants and bars and to purchase cigarettes and cigars for our controlled experiments in offices and homes and for the professional typing of our manuscript. When our paper was published, Lowrey sprang for a $50 bottle of French wine to celebrate.

At EPA, things were still percolating well for me despite the Sundquist affair. My scientific work coupled with numerous media appearances, congressional testimony, and interviews had bolstered my reputation. One of the most important things that occurred in 1988 was my appointment, with Lance Wallace and Margaret Chu of EPA's Office of Research and Development, to the U.S. Department of Transportation's (DOT) Cabin Environmental Effects Review (CEER) interagency panel to help plan a study, pick the contractor, and review a study of air pollution and other potential health threats to human health in the cabins of America's passenger aircraft. This comprehensive study proposed to measure ETS, ozone, and microbial aerosols, as well as review the existing data on cosmic radiation exposures for a risk assessment of these multiple threats to passengers and crew. My participation would bear fruit in the 1989 Congressional Hearings on renewal of the 1988 bill on the 2-hour smoking ban on domestic flights, which would occur prior to the completion of the DOT report. The DOT project officer was Arnold Konheim of DOT's Office of Regulatory Affairs. A vital sparkplug behind this effort, Arnie Konheim was another of the unsung heroes of the federal bureaucracy, the grease that lubricated the gears of government.

Meanwhile at the National Security Agency, John O'Hara, still the president of Maryland GASP, had become a high-ranking scientist at NSA. He briefed its new Director, Vice Admiral William Studeman, and other senior NSA officials on the persistent problems of smoking in the Agency. Studeman approved O'Hara's recommendations for smoking restrictions over opposition from a couple of the other seniors. On February 21, 1989, Admiral Studeman signed a memorandum stating that as of July 1, 1989, smoking in NSA's common office spaces would be prohibited; nonsmoking areas in cafeterias would be expanded from 60 to 75 percent of the total; the sale of tobacco products in NSA buildings and facilities would be prohibited; and best of all, The Agency would become a totally smoke free workplace as of 1 January 1990. A fifth provision noted that free smoking cessation clinics would be available for anyone wishing to take them.

Although a group of rebellious smokers made a last-ditch effort to overturn the NSA Director's decision, the new policy was implemented with little difficulty. This precipitated a flood of applicants for the smoking cessation clinics [NSA, 2002]. O'Hara recently said: "that was one of the most rewarding days of my life." It took him 25 years of struggling against entrenched smokers. In 1991, John became the Principal Scientist at NSA. As he and I were on our way to a hearing a decade later, he mused cryptically, "If you knew what I know, Jim, you'd be totally amazed." This was the most he ever said to me about his highly classified NSA work, and I knew better than to ask.

By 1989, EPA's in-house research would begin to add significantly to the sparse ETS database. EPA's Office of Research and Development's ETS research program would issue a report, "*Human Exposure and Dosimetry of Environmental Tobacco Smoke,*" by Joellen Lewtas, et al. ORD's research concluded that "Environmental tobacco smoke (ETS) is the largest source of indoor air pollution and is also the major combustion source contributing to total human exposure to mutagens and carcinogens." Further, it reported that "nicotine and its major metabolite, cotinine have been found to be useful quantitative and semi-quantitative measures of human exposure and dosimetry. The relationship between nicotine exposure and urinary cotinine has been studied in pre-school children exposed in their homes and in adults exposed on commercial airline flights. Air monitoring studies in residences and public indoor areas using both nicotine and mutagenic activity have demonstrated that separation of smokers into separate areas does not achieve an ETS-free or genuine nonsmoking area unless there is both physical separation and separate ventilation" (Lewtas, et al., 1989). This ORD research report was a major substantiation of the early work of Repace and Lowrey (1980; 1982) and provided a renewed emphasis on the importance of the nicotine metabolite cotinine as a valid biomarker of ETS exposure. It flatly contradicted CIAR's assertions concerning exposure, dose, risk, and control of ETS.

THE RJR/OAK RIDGE 16 CITIES STUDY BEGINS

Reliable government data based on cotinine dosimetry would not become available from CDC's NHANES study until nearly a decade later. And it would pertain only to the US population as a whole, not to specific occupational groups, such as hospitality workers or construction workers. Reynolds Tobacco scientists immediately seized the opportunity to fill the vacuum by providing their own carefully selected field data. Using the vehicle of the CIAR, Roger Jenkins of Oak Ridge National Laboratories in Tennessee would become the "primary investigator," but in reality, his contribution was confined to the lab, and insofar as the industry was concerned, Jenkins was a valuable figurehead that gave a veneer of respectability to what was actually a clandestine RJR personal sampling project primarily carried out by RJR scientists, and RJR's handpicked survey design firm, Bellomy Research. Bellomy hailed from Winston-Salem, North Carolina, where RJR had a significant research and development facility situated in close proximity RJR's largest tobacco plant, located in a nearby town appropriately named Tobaccoville.

The minutes of the meeting of the Board of Directors of CIAR for Sept. 26, 1989 stated: "Dr. Jenkins of Oak Ridge has begun the laboratory validation of the area and personal monitoring system. The field study details of the project will be discussed with CIAR prior to their implementation. Bi-monthly reports for both Oak Ridge projects are due before October 10, 1989." Jenkins was funded out of Special Account No. 4, directed by the lawyers for Big Tobacco [Kessler, ¶ 305; 2006]. This effort would result in the so-called Sixteen Cities study, which would conclude that "the home, not the workplace was the greater source of ETS exposure for the majority of subjects who either lived or worked in smoking environments" (Jenkins, et al. 1996). This would enable the industry to conveniently argue that OSHA perforce had no business regulating workplace smoking. The 16-City study would feature prominently in the OSHA Hearings on ETS in 1994, and later in the NIEHS hearing in 1998 on whether ETS should be included in its 11th Report on Carcinogens. I will deal extensively with both of these issues later in this book.

As Barnes et al. (2006) later concluded,

"The 16 Cities Study was specifically conceived and designed to forestall regulation of workplace smoking. The extensive involvement of RJR, in particular, in the design and execution of the study, was never clearly disclosed in any of the publications or public presentations of the results. The study authors combined exposure data from restricted and unrestricted workplaces and compared exposure data among study cells in an inappropriate manner. That analysis produced results the industry could cite to support its claim that workplace SHS exposures were low compared with household exposures during its efforts to defeat indoor smoking restrictions. In fact, an alternative presentation of the same data [Figure omitted] demonstrates significant workplace secondhand smoke exposures and supports the need for smoke-free workplaces."

The Four Horsemen of the ETS Apocalypse

On June 29, 1989, the *South China Morning Post* in Hong Kong ran an article entitled, "The Price of Passive Smoking." Reynolds International's Hong Kong apparatchik, R.K. Donner, sent an urgent fax, *Subject Hong Kong / Passive Smoking Article*, to his colleagues, stating, "The attached AP story is very damaging, coming right at the time when we are submitting our rebuttals to the COSH [Hong Kong Council on Smoking & Health] proposals which feature the ETS argumentation. A 'new study' is referred to in the article but is not identified further. Quotes from Ronald Davis [then Director of DHHS's Office on Smoking and Health] and James Repace also get heavy play. Since this is a U.S.-based article, strongly recommend the U.S. Tobacco Institute prepare a letter to the editor rebuttal and DHL [a courier service] to us ASAP. We would then hand-deliver to the Post." ... .

In response, the requested letter from Brennan Dawson of the Tobacco Institute dated July 5th, was received and forwarded on to HKCOSH by Donner. Their missive stated in part that: "A recent wire service story, "Price of passive smoking" (6/29), was an unbalanced article claiming that so-called 'passive smoking' is a significant health risk to nonsmokers. It is important to point out that the article is based solely on a severely flawed and one-sided review of the science on environmental tobacco smoke." ...

In an attachment aimed at HKCOSH, a more detailed commentary appeared. It asserted that:

"The four individuals you have chosen to rely upon – Ronald Davis, James Repace, Stanton Glantz and Judson Wells – have each acknowledged publicly that their ultimate goal is to wipe out cigarette smoking by the Year 2000. They also have acknowledged that their statements and activities relating to ETS have been designed to achieve that goal. The distressing aspect of this scenario is that Messrs. Davis, Repace, Glantz and Wells apparently are prepared to sacrifice scientific truth on the altar of their antismoking agenda. ...Although there may be a place in the United States for statements such as those attributed to Messrs, Davis, Repace, Glantz and Wells – the Four Horsemen of the U.S. Antismoking Apocalypse – we would urge that more attention be paid in Hong Kong to the science than to the politics of ETS."

In particular, the attachment denounced Jud Wells risk assessment as "even less credible than the risk assessment reported by Mr. Repace." [As far as my stating that I wanted to wipe out smoking, that was a lie. I had never said such a thing because my focus was on protecting nonsmokers, not on smoking cessation]. While smoking cessation was a worthy goal, It worked far too slowly to protect nonsmokers, and I regarded it as a waste of time to even mention in my talks. Meanwhile, ORD's Carcinogen Assessment Group had gone into high gear on the ETS risk assessment. Steve Bayard and Jennifer Jinot authored some of the chapters and hired a number of experts to write other chapters, including Brian Leaderer of Yale's Department of Epidemiology, Ken Brown, Neal Simonson, and Jud Wells, all as private consultants (Jud refused any remuneration other than for expenses), plus Dr. Fernando Martinez of the Department of Respiratory Sciences of the University of Arizona to do the chapter on the health effects of ETS on children. As part of the requesting office, I was naturally precluded from playing any role in writing the report. On the other hand, Big Tobacco had been keeping close tabs on ORD's risk assessment and began to employ every weapon in its vast arsenal of dirty tricks to derail it.

In 1989, William Ruckleshaus departed EPA and was succeed by William Reilly, who had been President of World Wildlife Fund until taking over as the head of the EPA. In turn, J. Craig Potter departed to take up his new career with the lobbying firm of O'Connor and Hannan, that provided legal counseling on policy and environmental issues and government relations for clients in a variety of industries. President GHW Bush appointed William Rosenberg, a Michigan businessman and champion of clean fuels, to succeed Potter as the next Assistant Administrator for Air and Radiation. Reilly and Rosenberg would be at the helm during the most critical period for EPA's risk assessment of environmental tobacco smoke.

CHAPTER 10

THE WATERSIDE MALL DISASTER

How did the air at EPA headquarters get so bad, bad enough that hundreds of employees - a fifth of the building's work force, according to the most conservative estimates - became ill? ... As with many office buildings built in the 1970's, when energy conservation was of great concern, the offices and corridors at Waterside Mall EPA headquarters were virtually closed to outside air sources. ... EPA officials placed the number ... at 880 of the 3,700 employees, or 24 percent, based upon their own indoor air quality survey, which they conducted after the unions complained. Either way, prevalence of symptoms was astonishingly high - "higher by an order of magnitude than I expected", according to a letter sent to the National Federation of Federal Employees by Mark Bradley, M.D., an occupational health physician hired by the EPA to determine the extent of illnesses among its work force. Eventually, more than 50 employees became so ill that their physicians said they could no longer work at Waterside Mall.

[Steinman, D. http://www.environmentalhealth.ca/fall93sick.html.] Accessed July 20, 2017.

EPA headquarters, then located at Waterside Mall, was an office building/shopping mall/apartment house complex located a block from the Potomac River in the southwest quadrant of Washington DC, surrounded by a largely residential area. EPA occupied two 12 story towers connected by a ground-floor shopping mall containing retail stores, a supermarket, a pizzeria, and a drug store, above which were two floors of mostly windowless office space. The underground parking garage had additional blue-carpeted windowless offices walled off by cinder block from the parking area. The exhaust fans in this garage appeared to be operated on a hit-or-miss basis. These overflow offices were derisively referred to as "The Blue Lagoon" by those unlucky souls from EPA's TOSCA program who were consigned to work there. Lance Wallace reported that in response to occupants' complaints of various illnesses and sleepiness, he had measured carbon monoxide levels of the order of 20 to 25 ppm, sometimes exceeding EPA's 9 ppm CO standard for 8-hours. Lance was successful in using these measurements to get them moved out (L. Wallace, personal communication, 2018).

There was a child-care center on the main floor of the Mall. On the same site, known as Town Center Plaza, there were two mixed-use five story rental buildings with studio apartments adjacent to the EPA building. Some of these units were lived in. Others were used as cheap office space by private businesses, some of whom were EPA contractors. About 4500 EPA personnel worked in Waterside; the higher status programs had offices in the glass-sided towers or in the windowed areas of the mall. The lower status ones were buried in the windowless interior.

BOMA, the Building Owners and Managers' Association, describes three classes of commercial real estate: Class A structures are the high-end prestige buildings that compete for the well-heeled employers who desire premier office space in desirable locations, and are willing and able to pay rents well above the average for the local area. For example, wealthy law firms and corporate headquarters. Class B buildings compete for a wide range of users with rents in the average range for the area; typically these house general business offices. While Class C buildings are bought for investment, institutional use, or for speculation (BOMA, 2017). Class C buildings are built and run on the cheap and are the most likely to house government offices at the federal, state, county, or municipal level, and often house schools or other low-budget institutions. Class C owners tend to skimp on maintenance and operation; such structures are the most likely become sick buildings.

On BOMA's ABC rating scale, Waterside Mall began as a C and went downhill to D for dump. The two towers and the space above the Mall had not actually been designed as office buildings, but were conversions from what were originally two residential apartment towers separated by a shopping mall above which there was warehouse space. This came about as a result of politics. In 1970, EPA the new Agency established by President Richard Nixon had been ordered to occupy Waterside Mall by GSA in a sweetheart deal engineered by his corrupt Vice President, Spiro T. Agnew, who was caught taking bribes and forced to resign in 1973. Agnew's buddy, Charles Bressler, the owner of Waterside Mall, was a big real-estate developer. Bressler must no doubt have been a big contributor to the Nixon-Agnew campaign, as he sported a pair of Presidential cufflinks. His office was in the ground floor of the Mall, and I met him one day at a meeting after the disaster occurred. He was a short stout man with a mustache who exuded a faintly arrogant affect.

Bressler's company, Town Center Management (TCM), had a checkered reputation; it was accused of racial discrimination in the rental of apartments at three buildings in Washington DC, as well as one in Maryland, in which the company paid a $350,000 settlement to an African-American woman in a bias suit (Washington Post, 1992). In another case, in September of 1969, TCM was sued by a tenant of Town Center Plaza who, among other disgruntled tenants, had withheld a part of his rent due to a failure of the building air conditioning, no small matter in Washington's brutal summer heat and humidity. Playing hardball, TCM locked the hapless tenant out of his apartment and dumped his clothing and personal possessions into a storeroom. He was not allowed to move back and sued. Despite a victory for the tenant in DC trial court, Town Center continued to play hardball, and the litigation dragged on for seven years on appeal. The appellate court ultimately sustained the judgment in plaintiff's favor, awarding him nearly $21,000 in actual and punitive damages (TCM vs . Chavez, 1977).

In 1988 more than 800 employees at EPA headquarters in Waterside Mall signed a petition complaining about the poor indoor air quality in virtually every area of the building. As for the root cause of the indoor air problem, follow the money. Town Center Management Company, the owners of Waterside Mall, signed a contract with the General Services Administration (GSA), which is responsible for the acquisition of federal buildings, at a time when the going rent for DC office space was $5 per square foot. By the mid-1980's, the going rents for office space had quintupled to $25 per square foot. But Town Center Management remained stuck with its long-term contract at the old $5 rate. In an attempt to preserve its profit margin, Town Center began cutting every possible corner in building maintenance and operation, including ventilating the building with enough outdoor air to maintain occupants' health and comfort. The building air quality was stuffy in the mornings, soporific in the afternoon, and sickening on its worst days. In the era when the contract was signed, the energy cost of heating and cooling outdoor ventilation air was $1 per square foot per year. Since Waterside Mall and its twin towers totaled one million square feet, fresh air was obviously a non-trivial cost to the building owners [GAO, 1993].

Whenever maintenance was being performed on EPA's constant-volume ventilation systems, which were closeted behind locked doors, an interested observer could espy the outdoor damper control settings through the open doorways. I looked in as often as possible, and never saw them set above zero. The ASHRAE-recommended ventilation rate for office space was 20 cubic feet per minute per occupant (cfm/occ); however, setting the outdoor damper control to zero meant the dampers would allow only the basic minimum of 5 cfm/occ to enter. Cutting the recommended outside air ventilation rate by 75% was not conducive to occupants' comfort or productivity, and in the presence of strong sources of indoor air pollution, hazardous to health. Typical office building air in the 1980's was a mixture of exhaled carbon dioxide, body odor, secondhand smoke, fart gas, cheap perfume, copying machine ozone, toxic volatile organic compounds from the oil-based paints that were continually being used somewhere in the building, and an assortment of toxic pesticide vapors, smelly restroom disinfectants, cheap glued-down commercial carpets with imbedded dirt and outgassing from poorly cured rubber backing, diesel exhaust from street-level air intakes, and microwave popcorn odors, all combining to form a malodorous chemical brew when coupled with very poor ventilation. All that made for really lousy air quality. Cheap is cheap.

Back in 1981, Daniel Zwerdling, a reporter from National Public Radio, taped a program called "Office Pollution," which featured complaints from workers in various parts of the Waterside Mall complex about symptoms they suffered from poor indoor air quality in the building. Zwerdling interviewed me for that program as well. In those days, the Library of Congress also had significant indoor air quality problems, and I received complaints from several very sick librarians, including a Division Chief, who asked if I could help them out. My diagnosis was a defective ventilation system. I fielded similar complaints from USAID workers when organophosphate pesticides were routinely sprayed in worker's offices, even during work hours, causing one woman such acute respiratory symptoms that she could no longer work in the building. It wasn't only office buildings that had IAQ problems; at USDA's Beltsville Labs, a brand-new lab building sickened workers and eventually had to be closed down when their air-handling system was found to have been installed backwards (H. Repace, personal communication). Incompetent low-bidders were and remain the bane of the federal contracting system. As I said, cheap is cheap.

As for Waterside Mall, by 1988, so many EPA staff, scientists, engineers, lawyers, analysts, secretaries, managers, had become sickened by the foul air in the building, that the agency began to allow them, with a doctor's note, to either work from home or in temporary offices in a neighboring apartment building. I heard that more than 600 workers had signed a petition to Lee Thomas, EPA's Administrator, who had succeeded Anne Gorsuch in 1983, complaining about the poor air quality in the building as a cause of illness, and a number of angry EPA staffers conducted several noisy demonstrations led by the union.

In January 1989, when the Waterside complex was about twenty years old, Lance Wallace and I were asked to assist a joint EPA-NIOSH task force to help investigate the epidemic of sick building illness at EPA. Aside from medical personnel, Lance and I were among the few investigators who interviewed building occupants affected by the toxic air. Lance conducted a statistical survey of symptoms, while I focused on an anecdotal one. I asked injured staffers if they could associate their symptoms with specific causative events such as installation of new carpeting. The EPA/NIOSH indoor air quality investigative team examined the EPA Headquarters building for flaws that might have contributed to the epidemic of sick building syndrome among the employees. Axelrad, although the nominal head of the indoor air staff, did not trouble himself to be included; perhaps he was afraid he might actually learn something.

The Mall's ventilation units were located on its flat roof. To the trained eye, they had many obvious flaws contributing to the poor indoor air quality. For example, the fresh air intakes and contaminated exhausts were located in the same plane, in close proximity. One of the air intakes was located in a confined area near exhausts from the print shop, the supermarket, and several toilet exhausts. Typical of Class C buildings, this was no doubt cheap to install, but was extremely poor construction practice, as it permitted re-entrainment of polluted exhaust air back into the building fresh air intakes. This effectively decreased the net amount of fresh makeup air being supplied to the suffering building occupants by diluting the fresh incoming outdoor air with polluted exhaust air. On the roof of the Northeast Mall, the air-handling units were similarly located such that the air intakes and exhausts were adjacent and in the same plane. When package units such as these were installed, the air intakes and exhausts should have been ducted into different planes to prevent re-entrainment of contaminated exhaust air. But that drives up the capital cost. This poor design and construction practice also extended to the twin East and West Towers, which possessed a raft of other design flaws.

For example, some of the air intakes and exhausts on the roofs of both the East and West Towers were housed in deep narrow wells, ensuring that the trapped contaminated exhaust air would be recirculated back into the buildings. The outdoor air intake wells of those air-handling units also lay in close proximity to the cooling tower wells. This was a risky design, because the roof of the building beneath the cooling tower showed extensive evidence of green algal growth. Thus, there was the potential for entrainment of these potentially allergenic biological organisms into the air-handling units. Figure 15 shows a view of Waterside Mall as it was from the 1970's through the early 1990's.

Located on the periphery of the roof, other West Tower air handling ducts had accumulated dirt and grime on all of the intake louvers. The intake and exhaust ductwork was lined with fibrous material of high surface area. It was blackened with loose soot, also serving as an additional growth medium for microorganisms. There were traces of the same sooty black crud on the supply louvers in many of the offices in the West Tower. The rainwater drains on flat roof of the West Tower had been tarred over in a previous roofing job done by low-bid fly-by-night roofers, allowing a vast lake of water to accumulate on the roof. This water eventually penetrated into the top floor offices and the return air plenums. A maintenance engineer told me that maintenance workers had *deliberately* diverted the roof leak water into the air handling room using buckets and hoses so that it would not leak into the 11th and 12th floor offices of the top EPA political appointees.

Any competent building maintenance worker would recognize that this was a stupendous mind-boggling blunder of epic proportions. The leak should have been diverted into the building toilet piping instead. When our investigation team entered the huge ventilation fan room, we saw that a pool of stagnant water about 4 feet in diameter and about ½ inch deep had accumulated on the floor of the room-sized space. The standing water was a murky dark brown containing a thick sedimentary muck. I photographed it for my report. Oddly, I was the only one equipped with a camera. Allowing stagnant water to accumulate in the ventilation system clearly provided a substantial growth medium for allergenic mold spores that could be dispersed throughout the building by the giant six-foot diameter fans of the building's air handling system.

This in fact would soon actually happen, and it would result in the worst personal health crisis I have ever experienced, then or since. It would take me several years – and consulting ten doctors – before I discovered the true cause. In desperation I finally consulted Dr. Daniel Ein, Chief of Allergy & Immunology at the George Washington University Hospital Center, who diagnosed me as allergic to every mold for which he tested me. It then became clear that I had suffered hypersensitivity pneumonitis due to mold-spore inhalation. It would take me several years to recover.

In 1989, I interviewed eleven other EPA scientists, engineers, and policy analysts who had become ill, most of them reporting symptoms of multiple chemical sensitivity (MCS). Significantly, all of them attributed their illness to a definite exposure event that occurred in the building. Many, but not all, of these persons were atopic. I came into contact with numerous other staffers who complained of MCS or respiratory symptoms related to working in the building; among them were two administrative law judges, and several attorneys, three of whom, significantly, were successive occupants of a single office containing the brand new toxic carpet. One of the worst sources of indoor air pollution was the low-bidder commercial carpeting. The rubberized backing had been improperly cured, and outgassed toxic chemicals. GSA bought it cheap. It was cheap because it stank. Coupled with the toxic glue emissions and the poor-to-nonexistent ventilation, many occupants of the newly-carpeted space experienced severe symptoms, including dizziness, mental confusion, and in the worst cases, brain damage. The first five of the nineteen plaintiffs who were injured by the toxic carpeting sued Town Center Management, and in a jury trial they were awarded $950,000 (Banham, 1995). The toxic carpet was then removed by GSA and, in an appalling feat of gross malfeasance, installed it in the Agriculture Department HQ in Washington, DC (O. Jacykewycz, MD, USDA Health Unit, personal communication, 1995).

FIGURE 15. WATERSIDE MALL COMPLEX AT 401 M ST, SW AS IT WAS IN 1989; THE MALL BUILDINGS ARE IN THE FOREGROUND; ONLY THE PERIMETER OFFICES HAD WINDOWS. THE WEST TOWER LOOMS IN THE CENTER BACKGROUND. ON THE WEST SIDE, AT THE FAR LEFT, IS ONE OF THE TOWN CENTER PLAZA STUDIO APARTMENT BUILDINGS. THE MALL ENTRANCE IS TO THE RIGHT. AT VARIOUS TIMES DURING MY TEN-YEAR TENURE AT THE EPA HQ COMPLEX, I HAD OFFICES ON THE REAR SIDE OF THE SECOND FLOOR OF THE MALL BUILDING, IN THE INTERIOR OF THE SECOND FLOOR, ON THE 7TH AND 9TH FLOORS ON OPPOSITE SIDES OF THE WEST TOWER, AS WELL AS IN THE EAST STUDIO APARTMENT BUILDING (PHOTO COURTESY EPA ALUMNI ASSOCIATION, 2017).

In one of life's bitter ironies, on a Monday morning in early February 1989, just as the new EPA Administrator, William Reilly, took office, I reported for work in my 9th floor office in the West Tower of Waterside Mall, and immediately began to experience a profound irritation of my eyes, nose, and throat. It seemed to me that there were invisible dust particles in the air. However, when I queried several fellow workers as to their perceptions, oddly *none* reported any symptoms. Lance visited me later that morning, and I asked him the same question – with the same result. I couldn't understand it. I went jogging along the Potomac waterfront at lunchtime with my long-time EPA running partner, Jim Stemmle, and found relief in the outdoor air. But when I re-entered the building, my symptoms returned. They abated that night when I returned home. The next morning, when I entered the building the irritation began again immediately. As the days turned into weeks, my symptoms at work progressively worsened, until my lungs felt as if they were on fire. My office-mates continued to report no symptoms whatsoever. I grew more and more fearful of permanent damage to my health.

Finally, as I was driving to work about three weeks later, I realized that my breathing had become so impaired that I needed acute medical attention. I had reached the end of my rope. I drove across the grassy highway median, and headed back East on MD 50, to the Bowie Medical Center emergency room. After being examined in the emergency room, the attending physician referred me to a local pulmonologist, who examined me and prescribed a course of inhaled corticosteroids and a bronchodilator. Then the doctor warned, "If you return to work in the building that's making you sick, your condition will deteriorate." If my condition got any worse, I would need an oxygen tank, like an emphysema patient. I realized that I had waited too long to leave the sick building.

I pondered my options. I recalled that by this time in the rolling indoor air pollution disaster that befell Waterside Mall, EPA had instituted a process to handle the numerous EPA staff who had been afflicted with sick building syndrome (SBS) and much worse, with multiple chemical sensitivity (MCS). EPA had hired an outside medical consultant, Dr. Mark Bradley, an occupational health physician, to examine the affected employees and make referrals to alternative workspace as needed. Many of these wound up working at home. Others were afforded temporary office space in one of the several apartment buildings adjacent to Waterside Mall. Unlike the main buildings, which had sealed windows, these studio apartments had operable 3' x 5' French windows.

Dr. Bradley approved my application for alternative workspace, and I became one of the displaced persons. My new efficiency apartment-office had a large living room, an efficiency kitchen with a stove and refrigerator, parquet floors, and a bathroom. I had an EPA laptop computer but was without a printer. I had to save my work to floppy disk and print out my work later using my home computer and printer. I shared the space with two women, whom I will identify only by their first names, Carol and Becky. Carol was a PhD environmental engineer who was the first occupant of our studio office. She was a single mother with a seven-year-old daughter. It had been her misfortune to have worked in an area with newly-installed toxic carpet, whose rubber backing was found to emit 4-phenylcyclohexene, which is an undesirable byproduct formed during styrene-butadiene copolymerization when curing conditions are not optimum (NIEHS, 2002). In other words, it was typically found in the cheap carpeting commonly installed by low bidders in Class C buildings. A few days later, Becky, an MA policy analyst with the Office of Policy Planning and Evaluation, joined us. She had also been a victim of the toxic carpeting. And like Carol, Becky also had developed symptoms of MCS. She was also single and like all of us, was fearful of losing her income.

Carol and Becky were two of approximately 122 EPA headquarters staff who had worked in areas where new carpet had been installed from October 1987 through April 1988. All of these workers had reported injuries of various degrees of severity. Seventeen were unable to work at their normal duty stations, and at least six appeared to have acquired MCS as a result of exposure. Reports of similar phenomena from the public, structure-activity analyses, and exposure information indicate a causal relationship between MCS and exposure to 4-phenylcyclohexene (4-PC). Hypersensitivity was reported to result from exposure to improperly cured commercial rubber-backed carpeting or toxic carpet glues (Hirzy and Morrison, 1991).

When I arrived, Carol appeared spaced out, and the room was in disarray, with papers spread all over the floor. Carol said she was forced to work with a very old computer, as all the new ones out-gassed vapors that made her dizzy. I knew from my days at NRL that newly fabricated printed circuit (PC) boards were immersed in a bath of organic solvents to remove gummy soldering residue after assembly in clean rooms. Brand new computers were shrink-wrapped and when first turned on, the porous PC boards would outgas volatile organic compounds, some of which were known neurotoxins, as the absorbed liquid heated up and vaporized. Brand new computers could take weeks or even months to outgas completely, aggravating the symptoms of sensitized persons. Fortunately, I had not developed symptoms from my computers.

Carol and Becky had also become sensitive to the odor from the ink in newspapers and to magic markers, symptoms that the three of us had developed in common after our exposures. This suggested that perhaps these exposures may have injured our central nervous systems, despite their disparate causes. The greater the injury, the greater the sensitivity to xenobiotic chemicals. We found that the intermittently operated forced air HVAC system in our office apartment emitted air that was irritating. I repaired to the mall supermarket to purchase rolls of heavy-duty aluminum foil and duct tape. I taped the foil over the air vent supply registers and brought in a space heater to emplace in the French window to heat the fresh but frigid outdoor air. It worked very well, and we immediately experienced a vanishing of irritation, and vast improvement in overall air quality. Carol's mental fog soon dissipated, confirming my intuition. When the weather warmed, I replaced the heater with a box fan.

Despite the lack of file cabinets and office printers, the apartment was a reasonable place to work, except for the roach infestation. These disgusting insects even colonized my telephone console. I took it apart and flushed the roaches down the toilet. I knew better than to use any toxic pesticide that would increase our symptoms. I ran down to the CVS pharmacy, bought a can of boric acid powder, and spread it around the baseboards to repel the roaches. This proved quite satisfactory. We three shared a state of confusion over our futures. Gradually, we began to discuss whether we should pursue legal action. There was already another group of EPA staff who called themselves COPE, an acronym for the "Committee of Poisoned Employees" who had been vocal about pursuing litigation. We decided to join their suit.

In addition to the chemical and biological sources of indoor air pollution in the buildings, these major avoidable deficiencies in the HVAC system design, construction, and operation added to the health problems of EPA staff and were consistent with the multi-etiological health problems reported by affected personnel to the occupational health physician (M. Bradley, personal communication). By 1993, EPA had spent several million dollars in a largely futile attempt to diagnose and fix the air quality problems in the building, and GSA made plans to invest an additional $2 million [GAO, 1993]. Finally, in 1994 GSA caved to the inevitable, and began moving many EPA employees into the new headquarters space in the ironically-named Ronald Reagan building in the Federal Triangle area. The move of all of the now 6800 strong EPA staff out of all of EPA's scattered Washington-area buildings was planned to be completed by early 2001 (EPA, 1997).

Determined to maintain some contact with the indoor air staff, I purchased a particulate and organic vapor gas mask, and wore it to weekly staff meetings at Waterside. By this time, Axelrad had become the de facto head of the indoor air staff, and his rancid nature became manifest. His horns came out, and he began to subject me to constant ridicule. He instituted pizza parties during weekly staff meetings, which of course I couldn't partake through my gas mask, and took malevolent enjoyment at my plight. Unbelievably, he told me that my illness was "all in my head." He even had the cheek to present me with a jar labeled "Clean Air Sponge" at a staff meeting. Two years later, when the division moved offices to a new building in Crystal City, in Arlington, Virginia, I would find yet another jar filled with some sort of sorbent crystals, labeled "Odor Trap," with an unsigned note on it: "Jim – A desk-warming present for you." I felt like clocking this miserable little parvenu in the mouth.

What Axelrad failed to realize was that his profound disrespect was a two-way street. Making me into an enemy was not an astute move. Moreover, I was far from the only one. He openly averred that *everybody* in the building with sick building syndrome was "psychologically disturbed," freely dispensing this ignorant opinion around the agency. Because of his prominent position as acting head of the indoor air staff, Axelrad's boorish behavior became widely discussed and thoroughly despised among employees sickened by the building, among whose ranks were engineers, scientists, lawyers, an administrative law judge, managers, and secretaries, and he earned the undying enmity of EPA's union representatives. Promoted far beyond his level of competence on the basis of his loyalty to Claussen, his callous attitude of indifference to the suffering of his fellow workers betrayed how little Axelrad actually had learned about the adverse health effects of indoor air pollution, and how grossly unfit he was for his managerial position. He was a living embodiment of the Peter Principle: "Employees in an organizational hierarchy will rise until they reach their level of incompetence."

Meanwhile, I continued to vainly strive to discover what could have possibly caused my burning lungs. I queried some of the NIOSH occupational health physicians who were on our investigative team; one of them said, "You have 20th Century Disease." I replied, "I take that to mean you actually don't know." He replied, "That's correct, none of us knows." These were the absolute worst days of my life. I alternated between rage and depression, and my self-confidence was rapidly eroding. I needed to get away. Hilarine and I decided to take a mini-vacation, and we flew to Nassau in the Bahamas for five days. It was cathartic.

In 1989, we had four children still in college who needed our support: our youngest son, Jonathan, was majoring in computer science, and worked at NASA part-time; two of the triplets, Paul, and Alex, majored in microbiology; they were commuting students, as Hilarine and I had been. Nick was a business major at Towson State and lived on campus. Thankfully we no longer had to support our two oldest: Max had a stipend as a doctoral student in physics at UMD, College Park. Justine, a talented artist, had graduated with a BFA from SUNY Purchase, and was working as a commercial artist in Manhattan. Although Hilarine was employed as a horticultural research technician in the Crops Quality Laboratory at the U.S. Department of Agriculture, her pay alone couldn't possibly support our family. I became extremely worried about our financial stability if I lost my job due to disability.

Meanwhile, Eileen Claussen decided to form an official Indoor Air Division; Dave Mudarri didn't even bother to apply for the Division Chief job. Neither did I, for two reasons. First, because I couldn't work in the building, and second, because it was obviously wired for Axelrad. The job clearly required someone with an advanced degree in a technical discipline, which he did not possess. Apparently, what made him Claussen's choice was that he was entirely beholden to her, and therefore was controllable. Axelrad certainly had no independent political base of support or many other friends in the EPA power structure insofar as I could discern. Nor was he scientifically competent. This important post no doubt was advertised nationally, and I'm convinced that many applicants with reputations and stature likely applied. But none made the cut.

So Axelrad emerged as Division Chief. Since he appeared to be interested in pursuing the ETS projects, I decided to hold my nose, ignore the personal slights, the repeated insults, and his sustained admonition that I "should look for another job." I continued to attend the weekly staff meetings while wearing my gas mask, until a few weeks later at our staff meeting, I made what Axelrad agreed was a good suggestion, and then he sneered at me in front of the entire staff, "You're not as stupid as you look." That was the last straw. I would brook no further humiliation. I informed him that I would attend all future staff meetings only by telephone.

Carol, Becky, and I continued working in our studio apartment for nearly a year; then the GSA decided that the building did not comply with its fire safety code for federal workplaces. And so we were re-assigned to a large open 50' by 100' workspace in Crystal City across the Potomac in Arlington Virginia. My new office, set aside solely for the use of persons with medically-approved alternative workspace, had desks for fifty persons, in a brand new building with windows that opened. However, Carol and Becky opted to work from home. My new office space was regularly occupied by only three persons, Kirby Biggs, Steve Shapiro, and Yours Truly. The remaining injured workers also had decided to work at home, and came in to this space infrequently or not at all because they were so sick. On occasion, a few would work at their desks for short periods.

I decorated my office with house plants, installed a coffee maker, and a small refrigerator, and worked happily by an open window. I also traded in my clunky PC for a spiffy little Mac. I used telephone, email and inter-office snail mail to communicate with colleagues and management. I still had no printer at work. During my lunch hour, I jogged along the bike trail that ran from Roosevelt Island to Old Town Alexandria along the Potomac. Life settled into a new routine. I enjoyed the solitude.

THE COMMITTEE OF POISONED EMPLOYEES

Of the approximately 50 persons who developed SBS or MCS, several developed very severe disorders, including anaphylaxis, corneal abrasion, aphasia, loss of peripheral vision, loss of memory, loss of balance, and loss of consciousness. Most of these individuals were forced to work at home due to developing intolerance to environments they normally frequented. Some reported reacting to emissions from magic markers, computers, printing inks in newsprint, and combustion products, reactions that they had never previously experienced.

Most visited as many as a dozen different physicians, seeking a definitive diagnosis and therapy. The most poignant case was the infant child of one of the staff attorneys who had sadly suffered brain damage as a result of the carpet emissions in the day-care center. The attorney herself who had worked in an unventilated office with new carpeting, had suffered a permanent loss of short-term memory. Later when we went to DC court, the carpet emissions in the courtroom caused her to faint, and Kirby Biggs and I helped her to an open window in the hallway until she could recover well enough to leave under her own power (Repace, 1996).

Some of these affected individuals were scientists, highly credible observers with years of previous industrial experience, who were convinced that definite exposure events had induced their injuries. For me and some others, it was mold. For a number of the worst-affected, it was associated with new carpet. Still others worked with stifling lack of ventilation. Many of these articulate and credible victims possessed important staff contacts on Capitol Hill and in the national news media, and the EPA Headquarters at Waterside Mall soon became known as the nation's most notorious sick building, generating more than 160 national news stories. Three years later, *The New York Times* wrote, "Perhaps the best-known lawsuit involves 19 employees of the Federal Environmental Protection Agency, who charge that they suffered a range of neurological, respiratory and immunological illnesses as a result of unhealthy and toxic conditions at EPA headquarters, in the Waterside Mall in Washington, where the agency is a tenant. The employees are suing the landlord and management company. The case may come to trial by the end of the year, said the employees' lawyer, Thomas X. Glancy, of Gordon, Feinblatt, Rothman, Hoffberger & Hollander, of Baltimore" (NY Times, 1992). I was one of the 19. Tom Glancy's prediction proved premature. It would take a decade to be resolved.

Congress soon held hearings at which one affected worker, Bobbie Lively-Diebold, testified articulately before the House Science, Space and Technology Subcommittee on Natural Resources, Agriculture Research and Environment on July 20th 1989. My Crystal City colleague, Steve Shapiro, had testified before the Senate Committee on Environment and Public Works in May of that year. Bobbie appended the anguished personal statements from seventeen other affected workers to her testimony. She was highly critical of EPA's response to the sick building, testifying that "program managers, people sick from indoor air, and various health professionals, and union officials have had a generally frustrating time getting EPA to act responsibly, responsively, and competently."

On June 25th 1989, Dr. Mark Bradley dropped the other shoe, writing a personal letter to Administrator William K. Reilly, a GHW Bush appointee, expressing his deep frustration. Bradley wrote, "During the six-and-a-half month period that I was a consultant at the EPA Health Unit, at least 80% of the individuals who I examined had bona fide medical problems which I believe are caused by working at the Waterside Mall complex. Fifty to sixty percent … had symptoms of … eye and throat irritation, headaches, and so forth. Some of these people were severely affected. Thirty to forty percent of the patients I examined had symptoms and findings of airway hyperreactivity … a form of occupational asthma. Ten percent of patients had evidence of allergic alveolitis, an inflammatory reaction in the alveoli and bronchioles of the lung … This condition can be progressive, leading to progressive pulmonary impairment and death. … A fair number of these patients had more than one process ongoing. I made multiple recommendations for investigative and remedial actions. I got absolutely no response to any of these reports at all, and as far as I can tell, no action of any sort has been taken to rectify this situation."

I, too, felt that EPA's Health and Safety Office bore a heavy responsibility for failure to act more affirmatively. As a recognized EPA expert on indoor air pollution, I remained in great demand for interviews with the national media. I had participated in a TV Interview on Sick Building Syndrome: on PBS's NOVA (US) and BBC's HORIZON (UK), taped at EPA on 10 February 1989. I gave another interview on Indoor Air Pollution and Sick Buildings broadcast on June 11 on the WMCA National Radio Talk Show, and a third interview on effects of sick building syndrome on workers on RCA Cable TV on Nov.15, 1989. As late as

February 7, 1999, the CBS Network TV News Program, 60 MINUTES, would do yet another story on the Sick Building Syndrome. I would be interviewed by the well-known investigative journalist, Morley Safer (his producers asked me not to bring up the subject of smoking, as Safer ironically, was a smoker).

In February 1989, EPA and NIOSH had conducted extensive air quality measurements at 100 sites in Waterside Mall and made an effort to relate those measurements to the health symptoms experienced by EPA staff in the previous year as well as in the week just prior to the survey (Crandall et al., 1990). These air quality tests for volatile organic compounds and molds had been conducted on a bitterly cold day in February. Despite this, the ventilation airflow in the Mall was so vigorous that papers were blowing off workers' desks, and the air even smelled fresh and clean, unlike anything I or anyone else had ever seen or smelled in my previous ten years at EPA. This was an anomaly; the air in the Mall offices normally was stuffy at best and stank at its worst. I immediately called attention to this blatant test rigging to the leader of the EPA research team, but the fix was in. This information went outrageously unreported in the final report of the investigation.

Lance Wallace conducted a preliminary analysis of EPA personnel essay responses to health question-naires administered to occupants of Waterside Mall and two other local EPA buildings used for comparison, Crystal Mall in Arlington, VA, and the Fairchild Building on South Capitol Street in DC who had been at work on that day in February 1989 when EPA and NIOSH made their Waterside air quality measurements. Respondents were invited to describe their experiences with air quality up to and including the day of the measurements. There was a 39% response to the essay question by Waterside personnel (1200 persons) 36% at Crystal, and 26% at Fairchild. The responses differed markedly among the three buildings: At Water-side Mall, essay respondents most commonly emphasized maintenance problems (20%) and health concerns (19%), whereas at the other two buildings, health concerns were ranked first by only 5-10% of responders, and overall ranked no better than fourth.

At Crystal Mall (not my new building), the overriding concern was air circulation, 33% of respondents cited stuffy, stale air as their primary concern. By contrast, at Fairchild, tobacco smoke in the restrooms and at workers' desks (in violation of EPA's smoking policy) was mentioned first by 19% of correspondents. However, Waterside respondents made many more mentions of allergic reactions, headaches, burning eyes, and central nervous system reactions (fatigue, dizziness, and memory loss) than at the other two buildings.

I made sure to mention the test-rigging to the plaintiffs' law firms, Levin Middlebrooks, and Gordon Feinblatt, as well as the abnormal increases in the ventilation rate at the behest of the building owner during the study. We were able to discover the truth during the legal discovery process in our lawsuit [Bahura et al. v. SEW Investors, Inc., DC Superior Court, Civil Action 90-CA-10594; M. Proctor, Levin Middlebrooks et al., personal communication]. I also turned over all the photos I had made of deficiencies in the air handling system. This case would painfully drag on for another decade before arriving at an out-of-court settlement, whose terms I cannot discuss pursuant to the agreement.

CHAPTER 11

THE BATTLE FOR SMOKE-FREE SKIES

WASHINGTON — "Anti-smoking activists, medical experts and several members of Congress called today for a permanent ban of smoking on airliners. Opponents, including tobacco interests and some lawmakers, urged that Congress await the results of a government study before making permanent or expanding the current law that bans smoking on short flights. The differing views came in testimony submitted at a congressional hearing that included a plea from a flight attendant who said her health was ruined from serving smoking passengers and an indoor air expert who said there are worse health hazards – including infectious disease – in an airliner cabin than smoke."

Permanent Ban on Airliner Smoking Urged, June 22, 1989 | From Associated Press

THE AIRLINE SMOKING BAN

In May 1989, the chief counsel for the Subcommittee on Aviation of the Committee on Public Works and Transportation of the U.S. House of Representatives called. She asked me if I'd be willing to testify as a representative of EPA at the Subcommittee's hearing on renewing the two-hour smoking ban on domestic flights, and if so, what would I say. I responded, "Yes, I'd be happy to testify." I then related that I was then serving on the U.S. Department of Transportation's (DOT) Cabin Environmental Effects Review (CEER) Panel, as one of three EPA advisors, along with Lance Wallace and Margaret Chu. The remaining panel members were one each from the NCI, the Army, the Air Force, and two from the FAA. The CEER Panel's charge was to help plan a study of air quality on commercial airliners, pick the contractor from among a number of bidders, review the proposed study design and then peer-review the results of the air quality measurements and risk assessment methodology evaluating the threats to crew and passengers. The contract had been issued to GEOMET Technologies in Rockville, MD. The final report was still being written, with no firm completion date.

I informed her that while I could not publicly discuss the DOT report, I could discuss my own calculations estimating the exposure and lung cancer risk to flight crew and passengers from ETS on aircraft. I emphasized that my calculations suggested that there was a significant cancer risk to flight attendants from passive smoking on aircraft. I noted that I had previously testified before the NAS Committee on Airliner Cabin Air Quality and Environment, as well as the Civil Aeronautics Board. She responded that the committee would very much like to receive my testimony at the hearing. I said that my appearance would have to be cleared by EPA. She said the Committee would handle that end.

This was the beginning of a contentious weeks-long tug of war negotiation between EPA management and the White House's Office of Management and Budget (OMB) on one side, and Subcommittee Chairman James Oberstar (D) Minnesota, on the other. To put the matter plainly, I was one of the Indians at EPA, not one of the Chiefs. It would be very unusual on a high-profile issue like this to have anyone from EPA give official testimony other than a political appointee or at the very least a member of the senior executive service (SES). EPA management first proffered Ken Sexton, a graduate of Jack Spengler's Environmental Health program at Harvard. Ken had become Director of EPA's Office of Health Research and was in the SES. However, Oberstar remained adamant. EPA then offered to have me draft EPA's testimony, and have my second-line supervisor Eileen Claussen, a member of the Senior Executive Service, deliver it, after clearance by the White House via the OMB. EPA further proposed that I would sit in the audience, available to respond to Ms. Claussen for any questions for which she might need technical assistance. Oberstar agreed to this compromise with the proviso that "Repace must sit at the official witness table beside Claussen, not back in the audience." It was tacitly understood by EPA that I would have no speaking role. EPA approved these arrangements. I then drafted Claussen's testimony for agency clearance and White House approval. According to established EPA protocol, I laid out the science and provided several policy options for the decision-makers to choose. These ranged from making no recommendations to a full endorsement of a renewal of the 2-hour smoking ban. Although the science obviously favored the latter, deciding among them was above my pay grade.

I DEFY BOTH OMB AND EPA

In sum, EPA's official testimony wasn't factually bad, but it had two major policy deficiencies: it made no recommendation to renew the 2-hour smoking ban, and there was no explicit recognition of the ETS hazard to flight attendants. I don't know whether Oberstar was aware of this in advance, but as EPA generally leaked like a sieve, he likely did. More importantly, Craig L. Fuller, V.P. George H.W. Bush's chief of staff, had served in the Reagan White House, and was tobacco-friendly. [After serving on Bush's transition, he left government; in 1992 he became a senior vice president at Philip Morris.]

About a week before the Oberstar Committee's hearings, I received a surprise call from the subcommittee's counsel. She informed me that after the federal officials gave their testimony, Oberstar would question each panel member sitting at the table, asking if they had anything to add. I was astonished to learn that this would include me. She then asked, "would you then respond in detail about the cancer risks to flight attendants as you originally proposed?" In other words, she was asking me to testify that I found the cancer risk to flight attendants to be significant by EPA's regulatory benchmarks for hazardous air pollutants. I briefly hesitated, knowing that if I agreed, I would be bucking EPA management and the White House. Then I thought, *what the hell have* I *got to lose?* I responded, "Yes, yes, I will." My father was born in the Italian province of Calabria, and the Calabrese people were notorious for being stubborn, according to my Neapolitan-rooted mother. I clearly had inherited this trait.

On the day of the hearing, the Federal Panel was the first to be heard. The lead speaker was Dr. Ronald Davis, testifying on behalf of the U.S. Public Health Service. He summarized the 1986 Surgeon General's Report and the 1985 NAS Report on the Airliner Cabin Environment, which had recommended a smoking ban on all commercial flights. He also emphasized that "nonsmoking flight attendants have a higher risk of lung cancer because of their exposure to environmental tobacco smoke in the aircraft cabin." Ron reported the results of the 1988 EPA-NCI joint study of nonsmoking Air Canada flight attendants' elevated levels of the nicotine metabolite cotinine in their urine from ETS exposure on aircraft, which showed that nonsmoking sections failed to protect them. He concluded by saying: "A ban on smoking on all commercial aircraft flights would result in greater protection of the health of airline passengers and crew." This was a perfect setup for my commentary.

Ms. Claussen delivered EPA's official White-House-cleared testimony, which reads in part:

"Mr. Chairman and members of the subcommittee, I am Eileen Claussen, Director of the Office of Atmospheric and Indoor Air Programs of the Environmental Protection Agency. It is a pleasure to appear before you today to discuss the problem of environmental tobacco smoke on aircraft. I have brought with me Jim Repace, who works in my office and is an expert on matters of smoking and health." ...

"A significant body of evidence has developed which concludes that environmental tobacco smoke ... poses serious health risks to exposed non-smokers. The Surgeon General concluded in 1986 that ETS is a source of lung cancer in healthy non-smokers and is probably responsible for a substantial number of the lung cancer deaths that occur among non-smokers ... . Additional research is needed in areas such as ETS' possible relationship to heart disease. ...

In a recent study of passive smoking on commercial airline flights jointly conducted by the National Cancer Institute (NCI) and EPA's Office of Research & Development, in-flight exposures to nicotine, urinary levels of its metabolite, cotinine, as well as symptomatic effects, were assessed on four commercial passenger flights. The study found that flight attendants assigned to the nonsmoking section and nonsmoking passengers in that section were not protected from smoke exposure by the separation of the aircraft into smoking and nonsmoking sections. ...

The National Research Council's 1986 report, *The Airliner Cabin Environment – Air Quality and Safety*, [noted] the need for non-smokers to pass through smoking areas to use lavatories on many aircraft also reduces the effectiveness of non-smoking areas and [that] the placement of aircraft galleys often results in increased exposure to ETS by aircraft crew. This report also found that many aircraft do not meet minimum ventilation guidelines recommended by the American Society of Heating, Refrigerating, and Air Conditioning Engineers (ASHRAE) for other enclosed spaces. ...

EPA's ETS research ... taken as a whole, confirms that ETS is a major source of indoor air pollution. It also finds that ETS is the major combustion source contributing to total human exposure to mutagens and carcinogens. ... In conclusion, EPA has found that exposure of non-smokers to environmental tobacco smoke is widespread and that the potential health impacts, although not fully quantified, are significant. As such, the Agency recommends that exposure to environmental tobacco smoke be minimized to the greatest extent practicable. While physical separation of smokers and non-smokers on the same ventilation system may reduce exposures, the most effective way to minimize non-smokers exposure is to restrict smoking indoors to areas which are separately ventilated with direct exhaust to the outside or to prohibit smoking in that space entirely."

So as far as it went, EPA's White House-cleared testimony was fine. The problem was that unlike DHHS, EPA punted on policy, failing to clearly recommend that the smoking ban be continued.

Finally, John Kern, the FAA's Deputy Associate Administrator for Regulation and Certification, wrapped up the federal panel. His testimony was vapid. He referred to the ongoing DOT study of airliner cabin air quality, as well as the earlier NAS study. He noted that the 2-hour smoking ban set in motion by the FAA in April 1988 would expire in April 1990, and that there had been "a high degree of compliance" by the affected air carriers and the flying public, although there had been 100 reports of violations, as well as tampering with the smoke-detectors. FAA also took the Milquetoast Option, making no recommendation on whether the ban should be continued.

After all of the official federal panelists presented their OMB-cleared testimony, Chairman Oberstar began to query each of the official panelists as to whether they had any final remarks. When Ms. Claussen demurred, Oberstar then turned to me and asked: "Mr. Repace, do you have a separate statement?" Bingo! I was off and running. The official hearing transcript of my statement read in part:

> Dr. REPACE. "I am here mainly to answer questions. However, I would like to amplify a few remarks made by Ms. Claussen. As a physicist who has published 23 papers in the scientific, medical and engineering literature, including recent chapters on modeling and field surveys of environmental tobacco smoke contained in the recent monograph, published by the International Agency for Research on Cancer, I have an insight that may be useful. I would like to emphasize in the current EPA fact sheet on environmental smoke [that] environmental tobacco smoke can be removed from indoor air only by removing the source. ... the ventilation systems on aircraft are inadequate to control smoking, and this is because the ventilation rates on aircraft are comparable to ... an office building, but the occupancy of the aircraft in terms of smoker density is far higher."

At this point, Claussen rudely kicked me hard in the leg under the table and whispered furiously: "You're testifying!" I whispered back evenly, "I'm not testifying, I'm just answering his question." Of course I was testifying. What the hell did she think? That I was invited just to sit there like a human version of a potted plant? I blew her off, continuing on for several minutes while Claussen sat there red-faced, fuming in silence. After giving a discourse on ventilation, I reviewed the several published risk assessments of passive smoking and lung cancer around the world. I noted that they averaged 5000 ± 2400 lung cancer deaths per year. This was based on an in-press paper (Repace and Lowrey,1990). Then I got to the heart of my clandestinely-invited testimony:

> "And, finally, in the words of the Surgeon General, as is quoted in [EPA's] fact sheet, a substantial number of the lung cancer deaths that occur among nonsmokers can be attributed to involuntary smoking. I would like to close my remarks and make them personal and not commit EPA to any particular policy, but in the Harvard risk assessment workshop last December, I was asked to present a paper summarizing the risk assessments that were done by independent scientists, including myself, and published in the literature. ... with respect to my own work, which was directed on the aircraft cabin environment, ... the risk of lung cancer to flight attendants based on nicotine exposure, assuming a 20-hour work week, the working lifetime risk for a flight attendant would be three to five per 10,000 at risk, and that can be looked at in two ways: A maximum de minimis risk level for carcinogens in air, water or food is one per 100,000, so we are looking at levels 30 to 50 times the acceptable risk level based on that limited data. We will look forward to more data coming out of the DOT study, which would amplify on that, but based on these levels, I think there is obviously a cause for concern ... ."
> Mr. OBERSTAR. "Thank you, Mr. Repace, for your further amplification of the issues. We appreciate your statement."

At the end of the federal panel's testimony, the Congressmen peppered the panel with questions. Congressman Bud Shuster (R) PA, led off by noting "while I might consider myself anti-tobacco, I am concerned about objectivity or at least the appearance of objectivity, particularly on the part of EPA." Shuster's comment had the tobacco industry's nicotine-stained hands all over it. The ETS Workplace Policy Guide was still a work in progress, and in fact a public review draft would not be released until June 1990. Nevertheless, Shuster proceeded to complain to Claussen about Bob Rosner, Axelrad's handpicked consultant, concerning his role as the author of the ETS Policy Guide, because "Rosner is not an employee of the agency, is not a scientist, but who in private practice runs a smoking-cessation business." Claussen responded by citing EPA's internal scientific review process would handle any potential conflicts. Shuster continued, "My problem is that this person has a conflict of interest, why would we spend the taxpayer's money instead of going out and getting a scientist who has bona-fide scientific credentials who is not operating a for-profit one?" Claussen's response was tepid: "we might have questions about how objective he is, but the work … will be reviewed by … scientists." Shuster admonished, "The product can appear to be tainted if we are not very, very, careful." Of course, the greenhorn Axelrad had not been the least bit careful. Ignoring my advice was coming back to bite him. And it would get much worse.

Shuster then turned his smoking guns on yours truly, segueing into this accusation: "Further the staff tells me, Mr. Repace, with regard to your model, that the EPA has declined to adopt your model as their standard and in fact, has been described [by] EPA as a 'rather crude approach.' Would you defend your position?" I thought, *why thank you, Congressman, for the opportunity to skewer you on the record*. I guilelessly replied, "Well, I think you are referring to an initial review of our risk assessment paper in 1985 by Herman Gibb, who is an epidemiologist with the carcinogen assessment group. I asked for that review before the paper was published so that we could have an independent EPA specialist in cancer risk assessment give us some advice. We took his advice as extra peer review in addition to the rigorous peer-review we got through *Environment International*. We also transmitted it to the editor, and we satisfied the editor that all peer-review comments were met. The paper was then published … Dr. Moghissi, who is the editor, … wrote a favorable editorial on it. There was another favorable editorial in the *American Journal of Thoracic Diseases*, which endorsed our material as the 'best estimates of risks published to date." *Now aren't you sorry you asked, Bud?*

Trying to recover, Shuster turned back to Claussen: "First of all, what is your position with regard to the proposed total ban, Ms. Claussen? Claussen responded, "We do not have an official position." Then it turned into a round robin. DOT's Kern, anxious to avoid controversy, interjected: "Let me say that the FAA is like a fish out of water here in the midst of a panel of technical health experts. Our position right now is we do have a rule that expires next April requiring the two-hour ban. We have endorsed and sponsored [The Airline Cabin Air Quality] study that's going on at OST to help us better understand this very, very complex issue, and we will make a decision at that time. Ron Davis jumped in: "Congressman, I would repeat … 'A ban on smoking on all commercial flights would result in greater protection of the health of airline passengers and crew.' We do not have a specific position on any of the legislation that is being considered by the subcommittee. The Administration does not have any such position to my knowledge."

Rep. Mel Hancock (R) of Missouri took his turn in this tag-team match: "I would just like to see if each of you four can give me an answer. … In your opinion, … do you think smoking should be banned? Dr. Davis: "As a physician, a health official, as someone who wants to see health risks reduced as much as possible, yes, the ban is the preferable approach." Mr. Kern: … "I don't have a professional opinion because … I [don't deal with] public health. I can give you my personal opinion as a life-long nonsmoker that I prefer non-smoking." Ms. Clausen: "I prefer a non-smoking, but I don't think that smoking should be banned everywhere." Mr. Repace: "In 1985, Dr. Lowrey and I addressed this in the *New York State Journal of Medicine*. … We concluded it could be achieved either by separation of smokers from non-smokers by separate ventilation systems or restrictions on smoking in the buildings. That is our position." Then Mr. Hancock began to rant: "Where do we stop? That is my question on the individual rights of the citizens as to doing what they want to do. Once you start, where do you stop? I think, and in fact we are in a well-ventilated room right now. Do I have the right to smoke in this room? There are people here who would deny me that right. I will apologize to the Chairman and the audience if I have offended anybody by smoking. I guess I should have asked ahead of time. … and I think there are other areas that … are more damaging to society than what we are involved in at this time."

There was a great deal more give and take, then Douglas Bosco (D) California opined: "I am convinced that smoking is a carcinogen and to not be around smoke decreases my risk of acquiring lung cancer. But I am not really convinced of the relative risks involved." … "Is an airplane really an unsafe place when people are smoking? Ron Davis responded: "As has been pointed out previously most of the studies of passive smoking show approximately 5000 deaths each year in this country can be attributed to passive smoking exposure, 5000 deaths from lung cancer in non-smokers." … This is a much larger number than the number of deaths attributed to most of the pollutants that we express a great deal of concern about."

Rep. Bob Clement (D), Tennessee: "Mr. Kern, … Northwest and Canada already have a total ban. Why not the airlines making a determination rather than the federal government making that determination about banning smoking on airplanes?" Mr. Kern: "… I guess it is an economic incentive." Mr. Clement: My final question to Dr. Davis. Are we as concerned about other pollutants as we are smoking on airlines?" Dr. Davis: I think we are. And in fact if you look at the money being spent to combat the problems posed by other pollutants, I think you could say that there is much more concern that has been expressed about other pollutants than about environmental tobacco, and perhaps the balance should be redressed the other way." Mr. Clement: "Do you think we can come up with a way of better filtering, better ventilation that will correct the problem for the future? Dr. Davis: "Addressing ventilation and engineering may help somewhat, but as the National Academy of Sciences has concluded, those alterations would be probably economically infeasible; and as Mr. Repace suggested, it makes more sense to control the source of the pollution."

Mr. Clement: "I am a little bit surprised to hear what poor ventilation these aircraft actually have. … But do you run risks of catching other diseases in airplanes because of … poor ventilation systems as well?" Dr. Davis: "There is a risk of transmission of infectious diseases on airplanes but I am not familiar enough with that issue to address it. Perhaps some other Members of the panel … ." Mr. Clement: "Is there someone that could answer that?" Mr. Repace: "Yes. There are a number of bacteria and viruses that can be transmitted by an airborne vector: tuberculosis, rubella, … Cocksackie A27, and certain rhinoviruses, cold viruses. Influenza can be transmitted. In fact [there] was an episode … of influenza on aircraft. If you keep the ventilation rate up, as with other microenvironments, you tend to minimize the risk of those diseases on aircraft. So indeed, even absent tobacco smoke, if you have poor ventilation on aircraft, you are going to expose the passengers to increased risk of contagious diseases. And the practice of turning off the [ventilation] packs in flight to save energy I think is a very poor buy in terms of public health." Mr. Clement: "As I understand it, many of these planes don't take in any fresh air at all, right? They just circulate whatever was there to begin with; is that true? Mr. Repace: "I don't think that is completely true. I think the latest generation of aircraft, the 757's and 767's have very low ventilation rates compared to – Mr. Clement: "In other words the more modern aircraft are doing a poorer job?" Mr. Repace: "That is correct. … Unfortunately there has been a trend in our society since the fuel crisis of the early 1970's – in buildings and extending into the aircraft fleet – there has been a tendency to try to save money by cutting back on ventilation. And unfortunately it has enormous public health consequences."

Mr. Clement: " I wonder if that might be just as much of interest in our focus on health in general as perhaps this other topic. … I think smoking is one area, but if these new ventilation systems are unhealthy in general for any number of diseases that people could contract, than maybe we are looking at really too narrow an issue. Mr. Repace: "I think that the DOT study, the FAA study is looking into these issues as well, and the current sampling on board of aircraft are looking into contagious diseases and spores and fungi … So there will be some effort made to quantify those risks. It is very difficult however, because there are no established exposure-response relationships for viruses and bacteria. In general it becomes very difficult to do a risk assessment on these kinds of things. ... ."

Rep. Pete Visclosky (D) Indiana: "Dr. Davis, ... regarding sidestream smoke, several of the studies that have been undertaken regarding cabin air quality. Would you care to elaborate on that?" Dr. Davis: ... "The last thing that I would say is a concern about long-term health risks from environmental tobacco smoke exposure in flight attendants and in frequent flyers is scientifically plausible." Mr. Visclosky then adjourned the hearing until 5:30 PM. During the break I walked out in the hall into a bank of TV cameras. A reporter asked me, "How can smoking be allowed on aircraft without exposing the passengers and crew?" I replied, "That's for the airlines to figure out."

The Air Transport Association (ATA) submitted a letter outlining the official position of the nations' airlines. Its major positions on all of the legislation included the following. ATA would, in part:

- Support legislation that would make permanent the status quo, in other words, continue indefinitely with the two-hour smoking ban on all domestic flights.
- Would not oppose legislation that would extend the two hour ban, including application to all domestic flights, unless the FAA determines and testifies to, or otherwise states, that such a ban would jeopardize safety. If that occurred, we would then oppose any extension of the smoking ban beyond the period of time that the FAA deems safe.
- Continue to oppose any smoking prohibition that would extend to international operations beyond those currently effected.

So the official position of the airlines was to ignore the plight of those flight attendants exposed to secondhand smoke on flights longer than two hours, worrying more about hypothetical nicotine withdrawal symptoms in pilots.

However, in a spontaneous event, the flight attendants would make their concerns known in such a way that the committee could not possibly ignore. The turning point in the hearing came when the flight attendants testified. Their testimony came very late in the day, at 7 PM, as the federal panel, which led off the testimony, which was originally scheduled for 10 AM, was delayed until 3 PM. I have no doubt that forces inimical to a smoking ban orchestrated this delay to sandbag the flight attendants by preventing their testimony from being broadcast on the evening TV news, as the camera crews habitually would depart by 5 PM to make the 6-O'Clock news deadlines.

At the start of their panel, the first flight attendant to speak broke down in tears at the beginning of her testimony. She announced that she had been diagnosed with cervical cancer the day before. And she attributed that to airliner cabin environmental tobacco smoke exposure. The dozens of female flight attendants sitting in the audience then also broke down and wept in sympathy, and the all-male panel of congressmen looked thunder-struck. Chairman Oberstar spoke with empathy, relating that his own wife had suffered a similar diagnosis and he very much understood what the poor woman was going through. Excerpts from the flight attendants' personal experiences were poignant:

Connie Chalk: "When I began my career as a flight attendant in 1968, I was in perfect health and never smoked cigarettes. After working as flight attendant for two decades, I am no longer in perfect health and I and my doctor blame my physical problems on the years of breathing cigarette smoke. Four years ago, I began to have health problems. I was coughing incessantly and having great difficulty breathing. ... The official diagnosis was chronic inflammation of the lungs. The lung specialist warned me that if I did not stop working smoking flights, I only had five to seven years to live. Even the airline company doctor recommended that I not work on any smoking flights. ... anybody in this room that has ever sat next to a smoker knows you reek, the odor is terrible when you get home. – you take your uniform off and wash it, the water is black, your hose are black, your blouse is black, ... When you wash your hair, it runs a brown, black water. It is terrible ... it has taken its toll on me, and it has taken its toll on many other flight attendants. ... And ... from our passenger counts, we have 25 rows of nonsmoking and four rows of smoking, so that that tells you ... what our passengers want. They want a total smoking ban."

Patricia Young: "... I have been a flight attendant for 23 years. ... Unlike other workers, flight attendants cannot step outside for a breath of fresh air or simply open a window when the air is full of cigarette smoke. ... I suffer from chronic bronchitis and a partial loss of hearing from injuries to my ears while in flight because of cigarette smoke in my work environment. ... I have also interviewed many flight attendants with smoke-related injuries ... some with lung disease and cancer ... the individuals will not talk on the record because they are afraid that their jobs and health benefits will be in jeopardy. ... The ability to remedy the problem rests with you, the Members of Congress. Please be our voice. Let the American public know we, the flight attendants, are not a disposable workforce. Grant the over 100,000 flight attendants in this country the basic right to a healthy and safe work environment." ...

Cathy Gilbert-Silva: ... "I have been a flight attendant for a major airline for 20 years ... and have never been a smoker. ... I can recall being on the sick list as far back as 1972 for blocked ears. As the years went by, I had to take more and more time off work because of a recurring sinus infection, bronchial problems, laryngitis, scratchy throat and blocked ears. In 1976, my supervisor told me either do something about my problems or find new work. ... I was on weekly shots for about five years, I was still getting sick on extremely smoky flights ... while I did feel better with the shots, I would get on the plane feeling perfectly well, ... and by the time we landed my lungs were congested and tight, and my sinuses and eyes burned, my ears were blocked. ... Following an exceptionally smoky flight, I would literally taste cigarette smoke in my mouth for weeks. My husband often complained that my breath smelled like I had been chewing on cigarettes or like an ashtray. ... I had used up all my sick time ... I had no choice but to fly when I was sick. ... I worked with blocked ears. I worked with laryngitis. Only on the occasions when I lost my voice, which happened a couple of times a year, would I take sick leave. ... Finally, in May 1988, I totally lost my voice and could not fly. ... I had surgery on my vocal cords. ... The doctor blamed the dry air in airplanes, speaking above environmental noise ... and bad air quality, especially smoke. I was advised by two doctors and a voice therapist that [unless my work environment changed] I would never get better." ... It is frightening to me that I am no longer a healthy person. ... I am not alone with these problems either. My doctor told me that he is seeing a lot more flight attendants with throat problems. ... It is time that we have a total smoking ban on aircraft."

Several industry moles testified in opposition to the ban; chief among these was Gray Robertson of ACVA Atlantic. His "solution" to the problem was to "double the ventilation rate and add filtration." Oberstar asked him if his recommendations were accepted, would that then mean that cigarette smoking would be acceptable onboard aircraft? Robertson replied, "it is hard to define acceptable. ... but ... there is no doubt that the technology exists today to provide adequate ventilation to dilute all indoor pollutants to minimum levels. ... If you bring it down to an acceptable level there is no question in my mind that can be done with a combination of ventilation and filtration ... and that would apply to tobacco smoke as well." In response to a question by Mr. Visclosky, Robertson grudgingly admitted that "I was paid to do a review of these studies by the Tobacco Institute ... ." And he disclosed that several members of the committee had also requested it. The industry clearly had been trying to drive the outcome.

A number of medical organizations as well as John Banzhaf of ASH testified in favor of a ban. The final panel was allotted to Charles Whitley, Special Consultant to the Tobacco Institute, a former member of congress. He was accompanied by Larry Holcomb, who was described as "an environmental toxicologist and a scientific consultant on issues related to environmental tobacco smoke." Holcomb asserted that an FAA/

NIOSH study "shows us very clearly there were low levels of respirable particulates and very low levels of nicotine." He quoted studies performed by Reynolds scientists as showing "an advantage to seating non-smokers separately in every case." He disparaged the NCI Air Canada study as showing "a miniscule quantity" of nicotine, and as for cotinine, "I don't know if the data is valid or not." Holcomb quoted OSHA standards for respirable particles at 5000 micrograms per cubic meter and nicotine as 50 (actually it was 500) and said "none of the studies done on airlines even begin to approach that figure, none of them. ... They see tobacco smoke. It is the only thing they can see. ... There is no justification for a ban on aircraft on the basis of risk to health of people on those aircraft from a toxicological viewpoint ... so the current practice of separating people with good ventilation, good filtration should do the job."

Mr. Whitley suggested that congress should simply extend the two hour ban until the results of the DOT study were made available, and emphasized that "if the people in the front of the cabin (in the nonsmoking section) are seriously bothered by environmental tobacco smoke, what it means is that the ventilation systems that are on that airplane are just not being operated properly .... Mitigating exposure to smoking contaminants at this time is premature."

All testimony was reprinted in the hearing transcripts (U.S. Congress, 1989).

The Los Angeles Times reported the story as follows:

Permanent Ban on Airliner Smoking Urged

June 22, 1989 | From Associated Press

WASHINGTON — Anti-smoking activists, medical experts and several members of Congress called today for a permanent ban of smoking on airliners. Opponents, including tobacco interests and some lawmakers, urged that Congress await the results of a government study before making permanent or expanding the current law that bans smoking on short flights. The differing views came in testimony submitted at a congressional hearing that included a plea from a flight attendant who said her health was ruined from serving smoking passengers and an indoor air expert who said there are worse health hazards–including infectious disease–in an airliner cabin than smoke. ...

The AP article continued, quoting Representative Dick Durbin (D) IL as saying that only a total ban on airline smoking would "adequately protect the health and safety of airline passengers and flight crews." Durbin was a sponsor of legislation to either make the ban on flights under two hours permanent or expand it to a permanent ban on smoking aboard all commercial flights. Representative Robert Torricelli (D-NJ) argued, "Isn't it time all our domestic flights were smokeless?" On the other hand, Reps. Robert Lindsay Thomas (R) GA and Tom DeLay (R) TX spoke against any anti-smoking bill until the Department of Transportation completed its airliner air quality. Thomas desired 'a solution to this problem which will protect the rights of both those who choose to smoke and those who have decided not to do so.'"

The AP reported that The American Medical Association, the American Association for Respiratory Care and the Association of Flight Attendants all argued for a permanent smoking ban of on all flights. While Gray Robertson, identified as president of "a company that specialized in fighting indoor air pollution," opined that "an airline passenger is more likely to get sick from bacteria, fungi and viruses floating in the poorly ventilated air than from cigarette smoke. Ironically, there has been no evidence of excessive levels of carbon monoxide, airborne particulates or nicotine, all of which have been linked to tobacco smoke as a source."

The next day, Sam Chilcote of the Tobacco Institute reported on the Aviation Subcommittee Hearings to Members of the Executive Committee:

"Eileen Claussen and Jim Repace of the Environmental Protection Agency (EPA) discussed the findings of ETS research conducted by EPA and others, and of the joint EPA-National Cancer Institute airliner study reported earlier this year in the Journal of the American Medical Association. Taking a page from the Fact Sheet EPA released this week, Claussen and Repace also emphasized that separation of smokers and nonsmokers does not prevent nonsmoker exposure to tobacco smoke, and that no amount of ventilation can eliminate tobacco smoke from an indoor environment.

Dr. Ron Davis, Director of the Office on Smoking, and Health, summarized 'the scientific evidence that involuntary smoking is harmful to health.' Emphasizing that his testimony had been cleared by OMB and the White House, he concluded that 'a ban on smoking, on all commercial aircraft flights, would result in greater protection of the health of airplane passengers and crew.'

A panel of flight attendants, providing moving anecdotal testimony, urged the subcommittee to take immediate action to enact a total ban and not to wait for the study. They were accompanied by a representative from Americans for Nonsmokers Rights [who] echoed the call for a total ban. This panel was interrupted by a vote on the House floor and only a few subcommittee members were present for the testimony and the question-and-answer session that followed.

Gray Robertson followed the flight attendants and conducted his full 30-minute slide presentation on cabin air quality. Eight subcommittee members heard all, or part of the presentation, which, on the basis of the question-and-answer session, seemed to spark considerable interest among the members. During the testimony of subsequent witnesses, several members referred to Robertson's presentation in posing questions … While media attendance at the hearings was heavy, coverage appears to have been affected by the delays and interruptions. Most reporters were unable to hear and record the testimony, opting instead to work from press materials being distributed and interviews with various witnesses.

Chairman Oberstar clearly views this as a workplace issue. The panel of eight flight attendants and their representatives, citing chronic illness and urging an immediate and total ban, clearly had the chairman's attention, sympathy, and support. At the end, Chairman Oberstar announced that the subcommittee would act on an (unspecified) airline smoking ban bill 'soon' after the Independence Day Recess (July 1-9)" [TTID 87648759 – 87648763].

The industry achieved a temporary victory in August, when the House voted, 259 to 169, simply to continue the current ban on smoking aboard flights of two hours or less. However, this victory proved to be ephemeral; in September, the Senate voted 77 to 21 to ban smoking on all domestic airlines. House and Senate conferees then reached a compromise in October. And on November 1st, 1989, my 50th birthday, the House of Representatives, on a simple voice vote, overwhelmingly approved a House-Senate conference agreement to ban smoking on *all* commercial airline flights within the continental United States and on most flights to Alaska and Hawaii. President GHW Bush signed the bill into law on Nov. 21, banning smoking on flights of six hours or less. Only longer flights to Hawaii and Alaska could still allow smoking [*NY Times*, Nov. 1, 1989].

A Co-Belligerent In The Fight Against Tobacco

In other developments, I gave a number of invited talks on secondhand smoke that year: to the American Medical Association in January, at Johns Hopkins Medicine in April, as well as interviews in June on tobacco smoke pollution to the Associated Press, USA Today, and the International Herald Tribune. On July 9th 1989, I received a cryptic phone call from Surgeon General Koop's secretary requesting my presence in his office at my convenience the following day. She was unable to say why. I was perplexed but had the strange feeling that I should wear a jacket and tie, something I did not normally do in the heat of a Washington DC summer, and I decided to bring my 35 mm camera along. When I arrived the following day, I was ushered into his office. Dr. Koop walked up to me and hung The Surgeon General's Medallion around my neck, saying, "This is the highest medal it is within my power to give." It came with a parchment scroll signed by Dr. Koop, and the inscription read, "given as co-belligerent in the fight against tobacco." The Surgeon General's Medallion is awarded for actions of exceptional achievement to the cause of public health and medicine. It is typically presented for such actions as medical breakthroughs in public medicine, disease prevention and control, or exceptional service in a senior position in the Department of Health and Human Services.

I had no idea that he held me in such high esteem. I asked Dr. Koop if his secretary might take a picture of the event, and he summoned her in to take the photo. This was the high point of the year for me, and one of Koop's last acts as Surgeon General. Dr. Koop would resign on October 1, 1989. I believe that he was eased out of office by President GHW Bush, who was looking to protect his Southern flank of tobacco states in the next election. Big Tobacco had roundly denounced Koop for years, and the message was clear. Dr. Koop had made a lot of enemies on the right because of his strong stand against tobacco plus his controversial 1986 report on the AIDS epidemic.

I took the medallion and the certificate back to EPA with me and showed it to Axelrad at a staff meeting the next day. In his usual boorish manner, he snapped, "put that away, don't let anybody see that, it's inflammatory!" Really? Eileen Claussen arrived a few minutes later, and she at least had the good grace to congratulate me despite the kick she had bestowed upon me at the Oberstar Hearing. Or perhaps it was just good political sense, as it suggested my efforts had influential support. Unlike his mentor Claussen, despite his minor degree in political science, Axelrad had piss-poor instincts when it came to surviving in the jungle of Washington politics. Whereas the wily operator Claussen, who had acceded to her job as EPA's Director of the Office of Atmospheric Programs in 1987, would ascend to a post as Special Assistant to the President and Senior Director for Global Environmental Affairs at the National Security Council in 1993.

During 1989, I gave a total of 18 talks, interviews, and presentations on ETS, despite my bout of sick building syndrome, and published two papers, one a review, and the other that made the point that workplace restrictions on passive smoking were justified by the risks to nonsmokers, plus a letter to the editor in *JNCI* on smoking on aircraft. These activities kept my sagging spirits up. I was also buoyed by the first published replication of the 1980 work of Repace and Lowrey. After nine long years, Jack Spengler's group at Harvard measured fine particles using next-generation real-time optical aerosol monitors and nicotine filters, deployed in public facilities and offices in 21 buildings in metropolitan Boston. They reported, for 36 nonsmoking areas in public facilities and offices, that fine particulate levels averaged 15 $\mu g/m^3$. While by contrast, in 15 smoking areas, particulate levels averaged 110 $\mu g/m^3$, suggesting that 86% of the pollution was due to ETS. By contrast Repace and Lowrey (1980) had found an average of 38 $\mu g/m^3$ in nonsmoking buildings and an average of 243 $\mu g/m^3$ in smoking buildings, indicating that 84% came from ETS. The Harvard study concluded that "ETS is an important factor in indoor particulate concentrations," and that nicotine concentrations increased with increasing fine particle ($PM_{2.5}$) concentrations, with a high statistical correlation and a particulate-to-nicotine ratio similar to that found by the Yale chamber study of Hammond and Leaderer in 1987.

I was unaware that John Rupp and Bob Lewis [not the same Bob Lewis who worked at EPA] representing the Tobacco Institute had met with Assistant Administrator Rosenberg of the Office of Air and Radiation in June of 1989. Rupp reiterated his client's concerns in a follow-up letter on June 20th, on Covington stationery; Rupp wrote in part [TTID TI08530513]:

"Dear Mr. Rosenberg:

Thank you for the opportunity for Bob Lewis and me to meet with you last week to discuss indoor air quality and environmental tobacco smoke. … Even though EPA's indoor air activities are not denominated as regulatory, they can have a very significant impact. … Although we have been permitted to make written comments on selected draft proposals, at no time has there been an opportunity for a scientific discussion of fundamental issues regarding environmental tobacco smoke. For example, we found the proposed ETS fact sheet to be entirely one-sided as well as inaccurate in a number of critical respects. Anyone reading the fact sheet would naturally assume that there is no dispute as to whether exposure to ETS represents a health risk.

The reason is that only one side of the controversy is presented in the fact sheet. All opposing data and views are simply ignored. We cannot understand how such an approach can be justified. … We do believe, however, that the evidence regarding ETS is – at the very least – sufficiently equivocal to obligate EPA to encourage input and a continuing dialogue on the issue and to refrain from issuing documents that fail even to acknowledge the existence of important opposing views. We would appreciate your consideration of these concerns, which we believe raise questions of fundamental fairness.

Sincerely, John P. Rupp"

Rosenberg's reply, on June 30, was hostile.
"Dear Mr. Rupp:

This is in reply to your letter of June 20, 1989, following up on our earlier meeting to discuss EPA's environmental tobacco smoke activities. I'd like to begin by addressing your point concerning the health effects of exposure to environmental tobacco smoke. At our meeting and in the various letters and comments presented by the tobacco industry, the Tobacco Institute repeatedly makes the point that whether or not there are health effects associated with ETS remains controversial and should be presented as such in all government literature on the subject. The fact of the matter is, we find the Surgeon General and National Research Council reports to be highly credible, a position shared by other government agencies and cleared by the Administration in recent testimony before the House Subcommittee on Aviation.

While we have heard considerable recent criticism of the Surgeon General's report as the bias of a single individual who is vehemently anti-smoking, it is important to note that the Surgeon General's report was actually prepared by a committee and peer reviewed by more than sixty respected scientists. Certainly there are areas of uncertainty concerning some of the health effects (e.g. ETS's contribution to heart disease and pulmonary effects in adults) and the extent of risk from exposures to various concentrations of ETS. However, efforts to discredit the Surgeon General and NRC reports by quoting out of context some of these references – which in our view only serve to highlight the balanced nature of these reports

– does not support your contention that these reports contradict their own conclusions. This view is supported by a careful comparison of your selected quotes with the conclusions of the overall reports and the other evidence considered.

Frankly, the tobacco industry's argument that the basic issue of whether there are any health effects associated with ETS remains highly controversial would be more credible if it were not so similar to the tobacco industry's position on direct smoking, despite the estimated 50,000 studies linking smoking with disease in humans. ...

In the absence of a quantitative lung cancer risk assessment, the recently published fact sheet does not attempt to quantify the extent of the risk to non-smokers. However, given the current state of knowledge concerning the contribution which smoking contributes to indoor air pollution and the health effects associated with ETS, a recommendation to minimize exposure, even in the absence of a formal risk assessment, is not unwarranted. ... If you would like to discuss any of these issues further, please do not hesitate to contact Bob Axelrad, Director, Indoor Air Div., 475-7174.

Sincerely Yours, William G. Rosenberg
Assistant Administrator for Air and Radiation"

So, in retrospect, it appears that Axelrad's hostility to my work was not coming down from OAR's political management, nor was it apparent that it was coming from Claussen. So was Axelrad being influenced by the industry either directly or indirectly? I would not learn the answer to that question until 1995.

Charles Powers, a senior vice president of the Tobacco Institute, reviewed the Rupp-Rosenberg correspondence in a memo to Bob Lewis on July 5th:

7/5/89
Bob,

John Rupp asked me to review his letter to Rosenberg and pass on any comments to you. The letter looks fine to set the record straight with Rosenberg. I suggested to John that maybe some headway can be made with Rosenberg's political assistant, if he has one. One thing that disturbs me is that EPA now says that what they are saying has White House and CM approval. It would be nice to know who is signing off on their testimony as well as Ron Davis' [TTID 10126-0726].

Meanwhile, the tobacco industry cranked its mole machine into high gear, trying to discredit Jud Wells' 1988 paper in *Environment International* estimating 46,000 cardiovascular deaths from passive smoking. The industry solicited comments on the Wells paper from its consultants, Peter Lee, a statistician from England [formerly employed by BAT], and Alan Katzenstein from the U.S. They were sent in as letters to the editor. Lowrey and I counterattacked, defending Wells. This prompted an 18-page crossfire of letters in 1990, among Wells, Hirayama, and Repace and Lowrey on one side, versus Lee and Katzenstein on the other, in *Environment International* Volume 16, #2 (175 – 193), 1990.

Industry consultants Lee and Katzenstein, in their commentaries on Wells' 1988 paper, took issue not only with Wells' estimates of the magnitude of the mortality effect of passive smoking on nonsmokers, but questioned whether mortality occurs at all. Their arguments were based upon the alleged fragility of the epidemiological studies of passive smoking and disease; the potential for misclassification of subjects, disease, or exposure; possible confounding factors; and the lower doses of smoke to which nonsmokers are exposed relative to smokers.

Lowrey and I gleefully took off the gloves to again play our favorite game of Whack-A-Mole. We noted in part that,

> "Hardly an organ system of the human body remains undiseased upon exposure to tobacco smoke. To argue, as do Lee and Katzenstein, that the diseases of smoking are not even plausible in nonsmokers does not give us confidence in their deductive abilities." ... "to be sure, it is possible that thresholds for effect may exist for one or more of the diseases of smoking, but neither Lee nor Katzenstein present any evidence whatsoever that such low dose thresholds exist, let alone that all nonsmokers have exposures and susceptibilities which place them within an adequate margin of safety below such thresholds.
>
> Nonsmokers who report no passive smoking nevertheless possess levels of nicotine and cotinine in body fluids which are significant fractions of those who report a lot of exposure. ... This suggests that there is major misclassification of nonsmoking controls as 'unexposed.' The result of this kind of misclassification of nonsmokers is to cause epidemiological studies to lack statistical significance or to find no effect." ... "we find Wells' predictions of 46 000 deaths per year from passive smoking to be credible, and to indicate, as Wells concluded, that exposure to ETS can have adverse long-term health effects that are more serious than previously thought."

In several papers, Peter Lee had argued for a different kind of misclassification: smokers misclassified as nonsmokers; EPA in its 1992 risk assessment showed that making this downward bias adjustment for individual studies as opposed to pooled studies (as Lee did) results in a very slight downward adjustment (Section 5.2, Table 5-8).

This exchange included a letter-bomb attack on our work by none other than Larry Holcomb, who had now been enlisted as a major player in Big Tobacco's stable of moles, despite the fact that he had never published a single piece of research on ETS, and often didn't know what he was talking about. Holcomb asserted,

> "Wells concludes his report by suggesting that exposure to ETS actually may cause more than 46 000 additional deaths per year. He quotes Repace and Lowrey (1985) and their estimate of 4665 additional lung cancer deaths as support for that suggestion. The Repace and Lowrey estimate scares a lot of people who have not taken the opportunity to review their underlying assumptions. What is overlooked in the emotionalism is what the Repace and Lowrey report really says. Repace and Lowrey start with the assumption that direct smoking and ETS both cause cancer. They do nothing to prove this. They then use a long series of estimates of exposure concentrations and exposure durations to compare ETS exposure to direct smoking. Finally, they calculate the death rate from lung cancer using these assumptions and estimates. What they generate is a calculated guess, not a prediction based on facts. Most of the research done since the Repace and Lowrey study has not supported its findings."

Who were the people who were "scared" by the estimates of Repace and Lowrey other than Holcomb's tobacco patrons?

THE DOT REPORT ON POLLUTION IN AIRLINER CABINS

On December 15, 1989, the U.S. Department of Transportation finally issued its long-awaited final report, *AIRLINER CABIN ENVIRONMENT: CONTAMINANT MEASUREMENTS, HEALTH RISKS, AND*

MITIGATION OPTIONS, Nagda, et al., DOT-P-15-89-5. The DOT study, the largest and best-conducted study of smoking on aircraft ever done, measured pollutants included tobacco smoke, carbon dioxide, microbial aerosols, ozone, and cosmic radiation in a statistical sample of airliner cabins on 92 randomly selected smoking (n=69) and nonsmoking (n=23) flights. Temperature, relative humidity, and cabin air pressure were also monitored. It reported in part that, "RSP concentrations averaged 175 $\mu g/m^3$ in the coach smoking section compared to background levels of 35 to 40 $\mu g/m^3$ on nonsmoking flights. ..." So ~80% of the RSP pollution on passenger aircraft that allowed smoking was due to ETS. Surprise, surprise. "Measured CO_2 levels averaged over 1500 ppm on 87% of flights, well above the ASHRAE comfort criterion of 1000 ppm." This demonstrated that airlines were in fact using substandard ventilation to save fuel and cut costs. ... And undercutting the bogus arguments of Gray Robertson based on his fertile imagination, "measured bacteria and fungi levels were in all cases below the levels generally thought to pose a risk of illness" [TTID PM3006451129].

Interestingly, the report compared the estimates of the lung cancer risk to flight attendants using two published models: those of Armitage and Doll and the phenomenological model of Repace and Lowrey. The estimates of flight attendants' lung cancer deaths for each of the models differed but slightly: for domestic flights, the estimated 35-year exposure lifetime risks respectively ranged between 12 to 14 deaths per 100,000, and for international flights, 13 to 17 deaths per 100,000. While there were an estimated 0.06 to 0.83 deaths per 100,000 nonsmoking passengers." The DOT report estimated that among the 85,000 US flight attendants, with unrestricted smoking, there would be 14 premature deaths due to cancer over a period of 20 years, or about 37 lung cancer deaths for an OSHA-standard working lifetime of 45 years. (At the time that the DOT Report had been issued, fatal heart disease from secondhand smoke exposure was not in the picture. However, if it had, this figure would have been increased to 370 heart disease deaths per 45 years (Repace et al., 1998), for a grand total of over 400 deaths in the flight attendant population of 85,000, or about 5 deaths per 1000 flight attendants per working lifetime. This would be five times the "significant risk" level by OSHA standards.)

By 1990, there were a number of other researchers who had made quantitative risk assessments of passive smoking and lung cancer for populations. Lowrey and I reviewed these in a paper titled "Risk Assessment Methodologies for Passive-Smoking-Induced Lung Cancer," published in the March 1990 issue of the peer-reviewed journal *Risk Analysis* 10 (1): 27-37 (1990). It fleshed out in detail a paper I had presented at the Harvard Workshop on Risk Assessment of Indoor Pollutants in 1988 and had referred to in the Oberstar hearing. Our paper was published in the proceedings of that workshop as one of eight papers. We concluded the following:

> "Nine risk assessments of nonsmokers' lung cancer risk from exposure to ETS have been performed. Some have estimated risks for lifelong nonsmokers only; others have included ex-smokers; still others have estimated total deaths from all causes. To facilitate inter-study comparison, in some cases lung cancers had to be interpolated from a total, or the authors' original estimate had to be adjusted to include ex-smokers: Further, all estimates were adjusted to 1988. Excluding one study whose estimate differs from the mean of the others by two orders of magnitude,* the remaining risk assessments are in remarkable agreement. The mean estimate is approximately 5000 ± 2400 nonsmokers' lung cancer deaths per year. This is a 25% greater risk to nonsmokers than is indoor radon and is about 57 times greater than the combined estimated cancer risk from all the hazardous outdoor air pollutants currently regulated by the Environmental Protection Agency: airborne radionuclides, asbestos, arsenic, benzene, coke oven emissions,, and vinyl chloride."

---

*[The industry-funded paper by Ted Sterling (Arundel et al., 1986)].

We also estimated that at 1986 rates of consumption, smokers emitted nearly 425,000 metric tons of particulate pollution in indoor environments, and increased our mortality estimates to 6700 (range 700 to 7000) nonsmokers' lung cancer deaths per year when passive smoking by ex-smokers was included (Repace and Lowrey, 1990).

Going Down Under

In March of 1990, I was invited to New Zealand by Deidre Kent, Director of ASH of New Zealand, to lecture on passive smoking in the workplace. As Hilarine and I flew over Auckland, a carpet of flowering Jacaranda trees unfolded below us in lavender splendor. I gave several well-received lectures, including one at the University of Auckland Medical School, where I met the passive smoking researcher, Ichiro Kawachi, with whom I would later collaborate in 2000 after he became a professor at Harvard. During our visit, we were invited out on the yacht of Dierdre's husband John, a physician as well as a famous fisherman who had authored several books on trout fishing. We arrived at the dock in Auckland at an amazingly low tide and clambered down a ladder 14 feet to the deck of his ship. Professor Robert Beaglehole, a noted public health researcher at the University of Auckland, greeted us from the deck while sporting a pith helmet, setting the stage for an exotic cruise. Off the coast of Auckland, we sailed around the extinct volcano, Mount Rangitoto, in the middle of the Gulf of Hauraki, and swam in its pristine waters. We dined al fresco on delicious barbequed brook trout caught by Dr. John, accompanied by a zesty chilled New Zealand white wine. I took the helm of the 38-foot yacht for a while, heeling it over until the gunwales were awash. The tipsy crew laughed uproariously.

The following week, Hilarine and I flew to Queenstown in the South Island, an exotic trip full of unforgettable adventure, including white water rafting down the Shotover River. Getting to the river involved a bus ride on a gold miner's trail high in the mountains. The roadway was just wide enough for the bus, which towed a huge pile of rafts behind on a trailer. There was no guard-rail, and a thousand foot drop below. The river seemed tame after that hair-raising experience.

In December of 1990, the New Zealand Parliament passed *The Smoke-free Environments Act 1990* "to prevent the effects of passive smoking on other people by restricting cigarette smoking in places such as workplaces and schools."

The Industry Gets Another Case Of Agita

Apparently the ETS Risk Assessment paper I published in March and the New Zealand trip was brought to Axelrad's attention by the industry, which moved him to issue an outrageous written directive to me on May 18, 1990, which read in part:

> "At the time you begin planning to write a paper which would entail the use of government time, equipment or resources, or which would list or imply any association with EPA, you are to provide me with a written notice about the paper. This written notice shall also include a brief description of the paper, where it would be submitted, and the anticipated date of submission. Prior to submission, a copy of the draft shall be given to me for review to ensure that your association with EPA does not appear and is not communicated in any way in any forum in which you speak or are published on the subject of environmental tobacco smoke unless you are specifically requested or authorized to speak or write on the subject by me."

I was amazed that he would be so utterly stupid as to put such a weapon in my hand. I had no intention whatsoever of obeying his edict, and if he ever came after me for violating this ludicrous order, all I had to do was release it to the press and he would be forced to defend his censorship in public. *This would not have gone well for him.*

The industry was incensed by my New Zealand foray, on top of other grievances dating back to the 1970's. Not content with lobbying Axelrad to terminate my publications on ETS, they decided to escalate their attempt to suppress my work by going to the very top of the Agency. They prepared an amazingly thorough list of my ETS efforts, indicating their unholy fixation on my activities. This annoyance was reflected in a draft letter, dated July 11th 1990, to EPA Administrator William Reilly. The draft, on Covington & Burling stationery, was faxed by John Rupp to Jeff Schlagenhauf, a top Administrative Assistant to Congressman Thomas J. Bliley. Bliley represented the Virginia district around Richmond, which was the home to a large Philip Morris cigarette facility. The fax read in part:

"Dear Jeff:

Attached is a copy of the draft letter that we have discussed focusing on the role played by Jim Repace in the preparation of the EPA documents on environmental tobacco smoke. During the past week, we have had substantial, and I think productive, discussions within the industry concerning the advisability of our sending the attached letter to Bill Reilly [the EPA Administrator]. The letter clearly would move the dialogue you have been having with agency officials to a new level, I am not sure whether up or down. The consensus view that we have come to, and that we offer for your consideration, is that you might most appropriately use the substance of the attached letter to have a conversation with EPA's congressional liaison. You could point out at that time, of course, that you are prepared to proceed by sending a formal letter if officials at EPA are not sufficiently receptive to the concerns you are raising.

The most substantial concern that has been raised about the attached letter in its current form is that, because it focuses on a single individual within EPA, it might cause other agency officials to close ranks to 'protect one of their own.' Reasonable people undoubtedly could differ in that assessment, and certainly have in the discussions to which I have been a party but taking the matter in two steps – may well be the most prudent way to proceed.

My understanding is that Amy Millman [Philip Morris Government Relations] has put in a call to you to discuss this situation. Obviously, I would be more than happy to join in your discussions or to assist in any other way you think desirable.

Best wishes.

Sincerely, John P. Rupp
Attachment [TTID 2026090062-63]

The attachment was a proposed Bliley-to-Reilly letter that read in part:
"… I intend to continue to monitor closely the development of EPA documents relating to ETS and to share with your office any further concerns that arise. At this point, I would like to draw your attention to an additional problem, in relation to the role played in the three ETS projects by Mr. James Repace, an employee in the Office of Air and Radiation with a very extensive history of involvement in antismoking activities. I continue to be of the opinion that involving such obviously biased individuals seriously compromises the objectivity of this project. It has now come to my attention that – despite Mr. David [sic] Axelrad's assurances to the contrary to Mr. Jeff Schlagenhauf of my staff and Mr. Tom Montgomery, Minority Counsel to the Subcommittee on Oversight and Investigations – Mr. Repace is essentially

in charge of the compendium and policy guide projects and from the outset has steered their conclusions in a direction that accords with his own ideology.

In addition, it is clear from the draft ETS risk assessment that was released on June 25, 1990, that Mr. Repace has been intimately involved in that project as well. I note that Mr. Repace is the author of one of the compendium chapters, dealing with 'Exposure Assessment in Passive Smoking.' He also is listed as the individual to contact with regard to this project in Mr. Axelrad's letter of November 27, 1989, transmitting the draft compendium for comment. That Mr. Repace has been more than merely a contact person for the compendium is revealed, however, by the attached memorandum dated June 1, 1987, in which Mr. Repace described the features of the project in its initial stages. ...

Furthermore, I invite your attention to the fact that the draft ETS policy guide accords 'special thanks to Mr. Repace as one of the individuals who provided support and assistance during the development of the report.' Likewise, the guide suggests that readers consult for further information the EPA publication "Indoor Air Facts #5: Environmental Tobacco Smoke" (copy attached), a hopelessly biased and inflammatory document that I understand was largely the responsibility of Mr. Repace. As far as the draft ETS risk assessment is concerned, it likewise explicitly acknowledges Mr. Repace's contribution (at p. xv). ... So far as the three draft documents that we have been discussing are concerned, Mr. Repace's long record of public utterances – including frequent paid testimony in litigation – concerning ETS makes it clear that he is committed to extreme views. With Mr. Repace effectively in charge, EPA's ongoing ETS projects frankly do not have a prayer of turning out objective documents.

Without belaboring the point, I would illustrate the positions that Mr. Repace typically takes on ETS by reference to his recent expedition to New Zealand to provide support for antismoking legislation in that country. Examples of the extensive press coverage given to the visit are enclosed. ... to antismoking activities dates back at least to the 1970s and has involved frequent testimony in support of proposed smoking restrictions before local governmental bodies, appearances in the media, presentations at antismoking conferences, and appearances as a paid witness in lawsuits involving smoking issues. In this regard, I refer you to Mr. Repace's role in a Trenton, New Jersey, labor arbitration, Levinson and Communications Workers of America v, State of New Jersey (1984), in a New York City arbitration proceeding, Carmen Irons and Teamsters v. Pan American (1984), and in two private lawsuits, Gordon v. Raven Systems and Research Inc., 462 A.2d *10 1* 15 (D.C. 1983), and Smith v. A.T.& T. Technologies, 643 S.W.2d 10 (Mo. App. 1982), on remand, Cause NO. 44612, oiv. 13 (St. Louis Cty Cir. ct. 1985.

Mr. Repace's activities have involved close cooperation with antismoking organizations such as the Group Against Smoke Pollution (GASP), the Coalition on Smoking OR Health, and John Banzhaf's group, Action on Smoking and Health (ASH). ... It is clear, as his association with these organizations attests, that Mr. Repace is a fanatical antismoker. ... . Such a mindset necessarily affects Mr. Repace's judgment and taints his consideration of the issues with which he deals at EPA.

Nor have Mr. Repace's antismoking activities abated recently. Aside from his intense efforts within EPA and the New Zealand expedition discussed above (apparently funded in part by ASH of New Zealand), he has traveled far and wide – with funding from EPA and from antismoking groups – to present his message. Indeed, I am informed that just this past May Mr. Repace shared the podium with none other than Dr. Stanton Glantz at a session on antismoking strategy at the World Conference on Lung Health in Boston. At this late hour there may be little utility in exploring why Mr. Repace, with his demonstrated bias, has been allowed to carve out a fiefdom regarding ETS within the Office of Indoor Air and Radiation while, at the same time, he travels around the world at the invitation and expense of antismoking organizations to proclaim his extreme views on radio talk shows and in other non-scientific fora. I realize that this situation developed to a large extent before you took office, and I recognize that you cannot be expected to monitor personally all the extra-curricular activities of EPA's many employees. Nevertheless, I believe that the time has come to ensure that the agency's projects relating to ETS are handled in an appropriate manner.

It would be entirely reasonable, in my view, to conclude that the ETS compendium, policy guide and risk assessment are so flawed in conception and handling that they should be shelved pending a complete review by your office. If a decision is made ultimately to proceed with any or all of those projects, I would urge that entirely new documents be drafted within the agency or be commissioned, with safeguards being put in place to ensure that the documents are drafted and reviewed by persons having no prior ideological commitment to the outcome. Mr. Schlagenhauf will contact your Chief of Staff, Mr. Bender, in the near future to discuss these issues further. Again, I thank you for your attention to this important matter.

Enclosures

Sincerely,
Thomas J. Bliley, Jr.
Ranking Minority Member,
Subcommittee on Oversight
and Investigations

cc: The Honorable John D. Dingell,
Chairman, Subcommittee on Oversight and Investigations
Mr. William Rosenberg, Assistant Administrator for Air and Radiation"

I am unaware if this letter was ever sent, but I have no doubt whatsoever that the sentiments in it were conveyed verbally to EPA management from top to bottom, certainly by Rupp and by Schlagenhauf. In fact, industry documents show that John Rupp had met repeatedly with top EPA officials in 1989, including Deputy Administrator Jim Barnes, Assistant Administrator William Rosenberg, and Axelrad had been included in some of those meetings. However, at that time, I remained totally in the dark about any contacts between Schlagenhauf or Rupp and EPA management. In retrospect, it is clear that these behind-the-scenes maneuvers were designed to distance my management from me with the aim of separating me from all EPA work on ETS. In retrospect, there is little doubt that in large part, these protest meetings had further inclined Axelrad's malevolent attitude towards me. Moreover, the level of detail recounted in this draft indicates that the industry had been keeping extremely close tabs on my activities for years. In 1984 I was aware that EPA had been subject to a barrage FOIA requests for my leave and travel records masked by "document retrieval services" designed to hide the identity of the true requestor [TTID, T10411-2498]. In a little over a year's time, however, I would come into direct and open conflict with Schlagenhauf and his master, Bliley – an encounter that they would come to rue.

On June 25, 1990, EPA released a public review draft of the ETS policy guide (EPA, 1990). It was not a final document and had been sent to the Science Advisory Board (SAB) for review as well. Among the key points, it emphasized that, "According to the EPA classification of carcinogens, ETS is classified as a Group A Carcinogen. Group A Carcinogens are agents known to cause cancer in humans." In addition, it stated that, "The number of ETS-attributed lung cancer deaths in U.S. never-smoking adults is approximately 2,500 annually. The excess number of ETS-related deaths in former smokers is estimated at about 1,300 annually. The guide made four recommendations: 1. Based on the significant health risks associated with ETS, organizations should, wherever possible, eliminate involuntary exposure to ETS at work. 2. Involuntary exposure to ETS can be eliminated by creating enclosed, separately ventilated smoking rooms with direct external exhaust, or by prohibiting smoking indoors. 3. Whenever smoking restrictions are introduced, smoking cessation programs should be made available to employees. 4. Employees and labor unions should be involved in the development of smoking control policies in the workplace (EPA, 1990).

By June 1990, Philip Morris became concerned enough about the EPA Risk Assessment of Environmental Tobacco Smoke and the Policy Guide to issue a press release, co-authored by Steven C. Parrish, Senior Vice President of Philip Morris USA, and a former law partner in the industry's prime defense firm, Shook Hardy and Bacon, plus Thomas J. Borelli, who managed Philip Morris's Corporate Scientific Affairs Department. Borelli possessed a doctorate in biochemistry. According to a PM document written by Parrish in 1993, this department's mission was to "formulate policy recommendations for senior management; recommend specific strategies (scientific, technological, regulatory and political) for dealing with the problems posed to the company by secondhand smoke issues; to coordinate and supervise secondhand smoke-related scientific research and activities, and to coordinate the activities of PM's subsidiary companies with respect to secondhand smoke issues" (Source Watch, 2017).

The press release, dated June 22, began: "... The Indoor Air Division at the EPA plans to release soon a preliminary assessment of the effects of environmental tobacco smoke (ETS) on the lung, including an estimate of lung cancer deaths from ETS. The report was prepared by an outside consultant. ... It appears the EPA's consultant is putting a butcher's thumb on the scale of science. ... The EPA's Indoor Air Division is also releasing a proposed guide they suggest be used by state and local officials to minimize the supposed effects of ETS in the workplace. ... the issuing of workplace guidelines at this time is a clear indication of the social engineering goal of the Indoor Air Division. The EPA does not have the authority to regulate the workplace – that's OSHA's mission." Philip Morris's press release displayed the industry's deep fear of the workplace issue: they believed that OSHA would be far easier to manipulate than EPA due to the very nature of the OSH Act itself. Indeed, the industry had much to fear about smoking in the workplace: it was the number one issue leading to both voluntary smoking bans and legislated smoke-free indoor air laws. Within two years, Philip Morris would get its avowed wish: OSHA would take up the issue of smoking in the workplace, and this would lead me into a direct and open confrontation with the tobacco giants.

The EPA PTEAM Study

In a joint study with Harvard, the Research Triangle Institute and the California Air Resources Board, ORD carried out the " first large-scale probability-based study of personal exposure to particles." It was known by its acronym, as the PTEAM study. PTEAM's 178 randomly chosen volunteer participants wore personal monitors day and night during the fall of 1990 by representing 139,000 nonsmoking residents of Riverside, California. Led by Lance Wallace, fine particle monitors were deployed to collect concurrent indoor and outdoor samples. PTEAM found that "the two major sources of indoor fine particles were smoking (30%) and cooking (3%), while outdoor infiltration contributed 60%." Importantly, the Riverside field study found that "The cigarette source strength for $PM_{2.5}$ of 13.8 ± 3.6 milligrams per cigarette (µg/cig) is in excellent agreement with estimates from chamber studies." This was a vital number for mathematical modeling of secondhand smoke concentrations and lent credence to the cigarette emission data published by RJR scientists – although not to the misleading conclusions of their published papers.

Now consider this: During 1986, more than 50 million American smokers puffed 584 billion cigarettes every year (plus an additional 3.2 billion cigars, and 24.4 million pounds of tobacco for pipes and hand-rolled cigarettes), 90% of it consumed indoors. At secondhand smoke particulate emissions of 13.8 mg/cig, this suggested that about 8000 short (US) tons of toxic and carcinogenic fine particles would be liberated by unrestricted smoking in indoor environments – in homes and workplaces, restaurants and bars, from cigarette smokers alone, everywhere that smoking was permitted. In 1986 smoking indoors remained ubiquitous all over America. EPA's PTEAM study showed that in homes with smokers, each cigarette smoked was estimated to increase 12-hour average indoor $PM_{2.5}$ concentrations by 1.5 micrograms per cubic meter ($\mu g/m^3$). In a single smoker home, at a rate of 2 cigarettes per hour, assuming 8 hours of smoking, those 16 cigarettes would elevate the fine particle concentrations by 24 $\mu g/m^3$ over background. However, the PTEAM study results would not be published until 1996. By comparison, the Harvard Six City Study (1981) had similarly found a similar 24-hour average of 20 $\mu g/m^3$ above background in 22 single smoker homes (Spengler et al. 1981).

THE EPA SCIENCE ADVISORY BOARD BATTLE

In June 1990, Steven Bayard informed EPA management that ORD's draft ETS risk assessment was ready for initial peer review. A special independent scientific advisory board (SAB), constituted from its nine standing members plus an additional nine expert consultants, who reported directly to EPA Administrator William Reilly, were assembled to review the report and make recommendations for revision (Muggli et al., 2004).

There was a major battle over the composition of the SAB, in which I played a clandestine role in defeating the industry's nefarious plans. EPA's practice was to invite affected industries to nominate experts to serve on its SAB. It had done so in the case of the lead SAB in the early 1980's, when two lead industry purveyors of junk science faced off against Ellen Silbergeld of the Environmental Defense Fund, one of the world's experts on lead and mercury poisoning, in the most vituperative public hearing I have ever attended. The lead industry goons made the patently ludicrous argument that "feeding mice lead acetate caused them to gain weight, which showed that lead was an essential nutrient." It was blindingly obvious to anyone with half a brain that the wretched mice had gained weight from edema due to lead poisoning. The hearing devolved into a shouting match. In March of 1985, EPA began the second step in a long phase-out of lead in gasoline that began in 1973, ending in 1996 with a total ban.

In the present instance, not content with EPA adding one of the epidemiologists that the industry had recommended to its panel, Big Tobacco demanded that Dr. David Burns, who had been the editor of the 1986 Surgeon General's Report on Involuntary Smoking, be dumped from the panel. EPA had invited Burns to sit on the panel, and then after the industry's complaint, did an about face and gave him the bum's rush. I took great umbrage at this outrageous ploy. But two could play this game. I realized that several of the remaining panelists had either served as paid peer-reviewers for CIAR, solicited funding from CIAR, as two of them had, and one, Mort Lippman, the chairman of the ETS SAB, even served on CIAR'S science advisory board. I knew most of these scientists personally, and several, including Mort, were first-name friends. I had no reason whatsoever to believe that any of them were industry moles. The plain fact of the matter was that indoor air research funds were scarce, and it was easy to overlook the source.

Nevertheless, to counter the industry's propaganda offensive against Dave Burns, whom I knew well and respected, I leaked information about the prior CIAR funding of several SAB panelists to Paul Raeburn at the AP. The Associated Press ran a 669-word Raeburn story on November 8, 1990, titled *"EPA Smoking Panel Includes Scientists Linked to Tobacco Industry."* The lede read: "Six of the 16 members of a newly appointed Environmental Protection Agency panel considering the health risks of second-hand cigarette smoke have ties to a tobacco industry research organization, documents show. A seventh member of the panel was appointed upon the recommendation of the Philip Morris tobacco company, EPA officials said. 'They've stacked the deck with people who have close ties to the tobacco industry,' said Dr. Alan Blum, a founder of the anti-smoking group Doctors Ought to Care. 'It's pathetic.' ..." (Raeburn, AP, 1990). This effectively took the wind out of the sails of the industry's argument against Burns, and EPA was compelled to reinstate Burns to the panel. Mission Accomplished.

Philip Morris had proposed two nominees to the panel; they had recommended Dr. Ernst Wynder, whom I knew as a "safe-cigarette" proponent, as well as an epidemiologist, Geoffrey Kabat, on Wynder's staff. I didn't know Kabat. Steve Bayard asked my opinion on which of the two I would choose. I told him I would prefer Kabat over Wynder, whom I had met in the 1980's. I observed that Wynder was famous for experiments in the early 1950's that painted the backs of mice with tobacco tar, inducing tumors that demonstrated the carcinogenicity of tobacco smoke. However, he had made up his mind that passive smoking was not a risk factor for lung cancer. Moreover, a few years earlier, Dr. Ferdinand Schmidt, a German physician from Heidelberg, had written me an unsolicited letter warning that Wynder had been a long-time recipient of grant money from the German tobacco industry. [Schmidt was correct. Industry documents showed that in his budget projection for 1982-1985, Franz Adlkofer of the German cigarette industry (the Verband) had recommended "Cooperation with Professor Wynder. Adlkofer recommended continuous cooperation and stressed Wynder's pro-industry attitude vis-a-vis public smoking. Because of his expertise Wynder shall be paid US $100,000 for another year as VdC consultant" (Hirschhorn, 2000)].

A University of California San Francisco (UCSF) study of public comments on the Environmental Protection Agency's draft risk assessment of ETS showed that 72% of the comments received had criticized the draft 'as an incomplete and selective analysis of the scientific literature," and said that it "contained statistically flawed and inconclusive data." However, 84% of these negative comments were found to have been submitted by the tobacco industry or its paid consultants. By contrast, 64% of the remaining comments supporting the draft were submitted primarily by university faculty (34%) or by public health agencies (30%). The UCSF study concluded that the tobacco industry used the public comment period to create controversy by hiring consultants to criticize the draft, and that their criticism relied primarily on unrefereed sources not relevant to the health effects of ETS (Bero et al., 1993). The next task for ORD was to review the comments and revise the risk assessment accordingly for the final round of review.

In October 1990, EPA released a report, entitled *Current Federal Indoor Air Quality Activities* (EPA, 1990). It published a list of Federal indoor air activities each year since 1988. The Indoor Air Division's efforts had individual staff contact persons listed for the CIAQ, for policy development, for the research plan for MCS, for Training Needs, a manual for new home construction, for model schools IAQ, for IAQ/Radon in large buildings, private sector survey, Hazards in Schools, public information, national clearinghouse, and consumer information. For EPA's ETS activities, the Risk Assessment contact was Steven Bayard, The Guide to Workplace Smoking Policies contact was Bob Axelrad. There was no mention of the ETS Compendium, nor the Fact Sheet on ETS that were my responsibility. My name appeared nowhere.

THE INDUSTRY BATTLES THE VIKINGS

From 1980 to 1990, I had published 29 papers on secondhand smoke, and made more than 125 appearances, including conference presentations, invited talks before medical and scientific groups, television, radio, newspaper and magazine interviews, and testimony at the federal, state, and local level. My next international speaking engagement, in October of 1990, would place me into direct conflict with an industrial strength pack of tobacco moles. I was invited by NIVA, the Nordic Institute for the Study of Occupational Health, to lecture at a symposium on Environmental Tobacco Smoke and Health Effects of Passive Smoking in Oslo, Norway.

The conference was held in a delightful venue, a lodge high atop a hill overlooking the fiord of Oslo, with spectacular views. The conference organizers from Norway, Finland, and Sweden had invited knowledgeable researchers as speakers, but had also opened up registration to all comers. As a result, the tobacco industry took advantage by infiltrating the conference with a large pack of moles. I recognized many of them, including Gio Gori, the erudite former head of NCI's Safe Cigarette Program, who had gone over to the dark side and began consulting for Brown and Williamson Tobacco in 1980 after NCI came to its senses and abandoned that major-league folly. When Gori and I met at meetings, we would often trade jocular insults.

When I saw Gori among the band of industry moles clustered together at one end of the foyer, I shouted, "What is this? Some kind of Black Hat Convention?" It developed that they had come to sabotage the conference. The conference organizers, Tore Sanner of the Laboratory for Environmental and Occupational Cancer, Institute for Cancer Research, in Oslo and Maria Sorsa of the Institute for Occupational Health in Helsinki, had planned that the conference attendees would come to a firm consensus, after to a vote by all attendees. With this infestation by industry moles, achieving any kind of consensus except agreeing to disagree was of course impossible. Peter Lee, the statistician who formerly worked for British American Tobacco (BAT), who now earned his bread as a private consultant for BAT, reported back to his client with 21 pages of detailed notes on the conference. Lee wrote to his paymasters at BAT, pithily expressing the viewpoint of the industry consultants: "The speakers and attendees covered the spectrum from those who really felt smokers should be shot at dawn … to those who thought the whole evidence in relation to ETS inconclusive to say the least and who despised the 'religious' fanaticism of the former group. However, in general both sides were given the chance to put their views forward and discussion remained polite, though it was clear that some members of the anti-smoking brigade were somewhat put out by the strength of the opposing views, weakly trying to dismiss them as being only those of tobacco industry consultants and therefore valueless" [TTID 40097331].

In fact, nobody on the health side expressed the view that smokers should be shot, although I'm sure many privately felt tobacco industry executives were prime candidates for the firing squad. An Italian professor, Giuseppe Lojacono, introduced himself and tried to pump me for information. He had the tell-tale aura of a tobacco mole about him, and I was moved to ask, "How long have you been working for the tobacco companies?" He took umbrage at my question, and vehemently denied any industry connections. However, my suspicions proved to be correct: in a report dated Oct. 19, 1990, Lojacono reported in part to his industry paymasters just what they wanted to hear: "The Seminar's scientific conclusions were to have been the basis for the launch or re-launch of prevention strategies by WHO. Instead it was transformed into an open disagreement between some of the speakers and the majority of participants. The most heated discussion took place during what was probably the first public meeting between the EPA represented by J. Repace, and the critics of the Agency's recent report on ETS. Criticism of J. Repace was almost unanimous, because of the imprecision of his basic assumptions, all the more serious because they gave rise to 'terroristic' statements on the relationship between ETS/lung cancer, cardiovascular disease, and so on. … The Seminar was well attended by 'friendly' experts and consultants who will therefore be able to provide more exhaustive accounts of the proceedings" … Lojacono continued, describing his activities at the 53rd National Congress of the Italian Society of Work-Related Medicine and Industrial Hygiene. "I believe that the results of this Congress are most useful to pinpoint institutions and experts prepared to redimension the role and weight of ETS as a risk factor, in the larger area of IAQ [Indoor Air Quality]. This remains our prime objective in Italy" [TTID 2028350107]. The putative unanimity of criticism he described, however, was limited to the Black Hats of Big Tobacco.

But the most egregious event staged by the industry occurred on Wednesday noon on the closing day of the conference. On Tuesday, the Norwegian tobacco industry announced a press event to be convened at the Grand Hotel in downtown Oslo on Wednesday afternoon, for the express purpose of "summarizing the results of the Environmental Tobacco Smoke Conference" which they had just done their best to sabotage! A little after midday on Wednesday, a highly agitated Tore Sanner ran up to me, grabbed me tightly by the arm, pulled me towards a waiting car and shouted, "come – we are going to a press conference!" I protested, "But Tore, I don't speak Norwegian." "Come," he commanded with no further explanation. A half-dozen of us piled into cars, which drove very fast to the hotel. I trailed at the end of the group of furious Vikings, as they stormed into the press conference. The Tobacco apparatchik who organized the meeting attempted to deny us entrance, and a heated argument in Norwegian broke out between him and the bearded editor of the *Norwegian Medical Journal*. Tore informed me that the editor insisted that he had a right to be there as a member of the press.

We finally were allowed in, and I was astonished to see four Anglophone tobacco consultants sitting at the head table. My recollection is that they included Dr. Philip Witorsch of George Washington University, George Leslie, a consultant from the U.K., Peter Lee, and Gio Gori. The Vikings aggressively questioned them, soliciting their sources of funding, views on ETS, and their biases, and when it was my turn, I asked each one in turn only one question: "Do you believe that active smoking causes cancer, and if so, can you identify a threshold for effect." In an attempt to preserve their credibility, they all agreed that smoking did cause cancer, and none professed knowledge of a threshold dose. At that point, the red-faced tobacco flack threw up his hands and shouted in English, "I am cancelling this press conference!" It was great copy; the reporters diligently took photos and copious notes. However, the next day not a single word appeared in the Oslo press – the fix was in. Nor, I might add, did a word of this debacle appear in Lee's report to BAT. This confrontation set the stage for my heavy involvement in the successful battle for a smoke-free Norway several years later.

Back in Washington, in March 1991, The Tobacco Institute characterized the EPA in a press release as "a rogue regulatory elephant that must be stopped." And in an interview in August 1992, Thomas Lauria, a Tobacco Institute spokesman, boasted: "EPA is going to get the challenge of their lives on this report. I don't think they've ever dealt with the Tobacco Institute before. ... ." In the premier issue of the *American Smokers Journal,* issued at about the same time, the industry made good its threat, characterizing EPA as a "publicly financed advocacy group" bent on purveying "paranoia, hype and headlines ...whose positions were based not on science but on the personal convictions of some staff members and political pressure by outside groups." *American Smokers Journal* omitted mentioning the fact that the 16-member EPA ETS Science Advisory Board (SAB), *including the industry-recommended Geoff Kabat*, had unanimously endorsed EPA staff conclusions. [Virginian Pilot, 1991; Houston Post, 1992; American Smokers J., 1992; EPA SAB, 1992].

In the fall of 1991, I gave three more talks on secondhand smoke: one to the American College of Chest Physicians in Montreal; another at the University of California, San Francisco, Medical School, and the third continued a series of talks over a period of several years at Johns Hopkins University in Baltimore, beginning with the Department of Health Policy & Management. By this time, I had adopted a far more aggressive stance toward industry disinformation efforts. Recapitulating, in 1989 and 1990, in letters to the editor, in *JNCI*, Lowrey and I had attacked RJ Reynolds scientists who had made nicotine measurements in aircraft cabins, and rebutted two tobacco moles who had written critical letters to *Environment International* about Jud Wells' risk assessment paper, as well as the paper in *Risk Analysis*. However, I remained remote from EPA's effort to perform its risk assessment, which was now in the extremely capable hands of Steven Bayard and Jennifer Jinot. I contributed to Steven's requests for information, and he kept me informed on his progress towards the goal.

Ensconced in my new office in Crystal City, I began to focus on updating the ETS indoor air quality standard Lowrey and I had published in 1985 to reformulate it on nicotine, the premier atmospheric marker for ETS, and began my literature search using EPA's excellent technical library as well as the National Library of Medicine.

CHAPTER 12

EPA BRANDS ETS "GROUP A"

"In 1983, then Congressman Thomas Bliley Jr. (R-VA) wrote to the then Philip Morris Vice President of Research and Development Max Hauserman, asking for help to fight against the 'war on tobacco.' Bliley stated, 'You and 1 have a responsibility to all the working people affected by these tobacco wars. We have to keep up a solid front against the forces that are trying to destroy one of our most vital industries.' He went on to say, 'You can count on me to do all that I can.' ... Bliley kept his promise by lobbying and communicating the tobacco industry's concern to the EPA Administrator William Reilly. From the time of the release of the draft risk assessment in June 1990 to the release of the final report in December 1992, Bliley wrote at least 11 letters to Reilly touting industry messages of faulty science and flawed procedures. Many of the letters were highly detailed (the longest being 15 single-spaced pages) and some were edited by Covington & Burling lawyer Jim Goold and forwarded to Steve Parrish at Philip Morris."

[Muggli et al., The Tobacco Industry's Political Efforts to Derail the EPA Report on ETS. *Am J Prev Med* 2004;26(2).

In 1991 and 1992 Lowrey and I vigorously launched our next counterattacks on the industry and its moles. Our first salvo was a letter to the editor of *Environment International* rebutting BAT consultant Peter Lee's attack on Wells' 1988 paper which had estimated total adult mortality from passive smoking in the U.S. We first took apart Lee's suggestion that an "effect of ETS on lung cancer was not plausible on dosimetric considerations." We responded that, since smoking doses were carcinogenic, Lee's conclusion was the result of his assumption that the dose-response relationship between smoking and cancer risk was linear over several orders of magnitude of tobacco smoke dose from active smoking to passive smoking. There was no evidence for that. Further, we observed that a non-linear dose-response was both biologically plausible and fit the high-end and low-end data very well, whereas a linear dose-response plainly did not fit the data well at the low end. In fact, plotting the risk vs dose data points from the American Cancer Society's CPS-II study demonstrated that a linear extrapolation of the lung cancer risk in smokers as a function of dose, expressed in units of cigarettes per day, down to the dose of nonsmokers overestimated the observed lung cancer risk in nonsmokers, 12 lung cancer deaths per 100,000 person-years, by a factor of 3, whereas a non-linear extrapolation estimated it exactly (Repace and Lowrey, 1992).

Our second salvo involved a frontal attack on 23 of the tobacco industry's favorite bogus arguments aimed at perpetuating workplace smoking. In a paper published in *Tobacco Control* in 1992, provocatively titled "Issues and answers on passive smoking in the workplace: rebutting tobacco industry arguments," we contradicted industry propaganda by showing that ETS was significant relative to other indoor pollutants; that current atmospheric and biological markers were appropriate for ETS; that nonsmokers were exposed to amounts of ETS in the workplace sufficient to cause disease; that nonsmokers' exposures to ETS were properly assessed in epi studies; that there was a broad scientific consensus about the health effects of ETS; and that ventilation was an inadequate control for ETS, among other points (Repace and Lowrey, 1992).

British American Tobacco (BAT) was so galled by our critique that it responded with a letter to *Tobacco Control* attempting to rebut our attack while whitewashing the industry. It was authored by Sharon Boyse (aka Sharon Blackie), who was BAT's main scientific disinformation specialist for the UK, Europe, Asia and South America. She was one of the industry strategists (with Christopher J. Proctor and Clive Turner) most responsible for deflecting public and political attention away from the regulation of smoking in public places (Source Watch, 2016). Boyse said in part, that "Repace and Lowrey's article on passive smoking in the workplace claims to provide a rebuttal to arguments on the subject of environmental tobacco smoke (ETS) used by the tobacco industry. The authors imply or, in some cases, specifically state that the industry takes quotations, examples and studies totally out of context in formulating its arguments. I would argue that the industry does not do so, but that in fact it is Repace and Lowrey who could be accused of doing so in this article, in the enthusiasm of their attempt to discredit the scientific acumen of the tobacco industry. The paper is riddled with statements that simply cannot be justified by the current scientific data." She went on to attack the Fontham study of lung cancer and passive smoking that we cited, and which EPA had relied upon for making quantitative estimates, by deceptively citing a study by Wu-Williams, which reported a reduction in risk for women exposed to ETS, and another by Brownson who reported no statistically significant risk (Boyse, 1993; response by Repace and Lowrey, 1993).

With great relish, we fired back, arguing inter alia that, "In her letter to the editor protesting our indictment of the tobacco industry's highly deceptive practices, we are grateful to Dr. Sharon Boyse of the British-American Tobacco Company (BAT) for providing us with several textbook illustrations of how the tobacco industry quotes scientific studies and methods out of context and ignores contradictory studies in formulating its arguments on the subject of environmental tobacco smoke (ETS). ... Moreover, ... If only the highest ETS exposure categories are considered, for the 17 epidemiological studies of passive smoking and lung cancer (in Greece, Hong Kong, Japan, USA, Sweden, and China) where this information is reported, the odds ratio is 1.81 (90 % confidence interval = 1.60-2.05), ($p < 0.000001$), i.e., less than 1 chance in a million of a statistical error. Perhaps such a p-value is not considered significant enough by the tobacco industry?" (Boyse; Repace and Lowrey; 1993).

"IT WILL NEVER SEE THE LIGHT OF DAY"

After North Carolina Senator Jesse Helms (R) got the Office on Smoking and Health moved to Atlanta in an effort to hamstring its operations, Don Shopland transferred to the tobacco control program of the National Cancer Institute in Bethesda. NCI's tobacco program was overseen by the brilliant Joe Cullen, NCI's Deputy Director of Cancer Control. Cullen's COMMIT and ASSIST programs were state-of-the-art in nurturing nascent state tobacco control programs, and Joe had a big influence on Surgeon General Koop as well. After ETS Fact Sheet #5, the remaining major EPA ETS project I was working on was the ETS Technical Compendium. Don and I were the ETS Technical Compendium's co-editors. We divided up the individual chapters with each of us commissioning our own set of expert authors. The 280-page draft was completed in early 1991. The original draft contained ten chapters, covering the ETS waterfront using recognized experts on the subject matter, ranging from the effects of active smoking on smokers, to ETS concentrations, atmospheric and biomarkers for ETS, a review of the 1986 Reports of the Surgeon General and the NRC, modeling of exposure, effects of ventilation on odor and irritation, surveys of public attitudes toward smoking in public places, effects of smoking on children in day care settings, and the efficacy of smoking bans in the corporate world. Among those authors I had personally selected were Jack Spengler (Harvard), Brian Leaderer (Yale), Dietrich Hoffmann (AHF), Jonathan Samet (Johns Hopkins), and William Cain (Yale). All were nationally recognized experts on ETS.

Don and I sent the Compendium out for peer review to our respective communities of experts. One of those I sent it to was Stan Glantz at UCSF. Stan phoned me to complain, "Repace, it doesn't have a chapter on heart disease." I responded, "Glantz, you are a respected professor of cardiology in a respected department of cardiology in a respected medical school, why don't *you* write it?" Stan was uncharacteristically silent for about ten seconds, after which he responded, "OK, I'll do it." I ran it by Axelrad; he agreed, but said it was too late to issue a $500 contract to Glantz as we had the other authors. So Stan agreed to write it gratis. His co-author was Bill Parmley, the Cardiology Department chairman, and a nationally prominent cardiologist. Glantz and Parmley based their chapter on a peer-reviewed paper they had published in 1990 in *Circulation*, the prestigious journal of the National Heart Association (Glantz & Parmley, 1990).

The Glantz and Parmley compendium chapter discussed the evidence that implicated low dose exposure to tobacco smoke (passive smoking) as a causal agent that increased the risk diseases of the heart in nonsmokers, and reviewed the epidemiological, biochemical, and biological bases for this inference. They wrote, "the combined epidemiological and physiological evidence suggested that ETS exposure is a cause of heart disease in nonsmokers. This increase in risk translates into about 10 times as many deaths from ETS-induced heart disease as lung cancer and contributes 37,000 to the estimated 53,000 deaths annually from passive smoking (Wells, 1988). This toll makes passive smoking the third leading preventable cause of death in the United States today, behind active smoking and alcohol."

When Axelrad read this sentence, he became absolutely livid with rage. He erupted in a tirade, swearing that the *entire* Compendium, simply because it contained this heart disease estimate, "would never see the light of day." Where was this coming from? I completely failed to understand any rational justification for dumping the *entire* work because he disliked a chapter that simply quoted a published risk estimate from a peer-reviewed journal. Moreover, the compendium contained a plainly worded disclaimer on the cover page: *"The contents represent only those views of the individual chapter authors. It should not be construed as representing the views or policies of the participating organizations."* So it did not commit EPA to any specific risk estimate. And DHHS had given its imprimatur to the chapter as well. What was his problem? Was Axelrad taking his marching orders from malevolent voices outside the agency? Shopland and I had labored several years putting this 11-chapter document together. We had even invited the Tobacco Institute and Philip Morris to review it and reported this in the acknowledgements. After he stormed off, I built up a full head of steam. Axelrad was arbitrarily trashing several years of work by many people. I would not permit him to succeed.

I phoned Raeburn at the Associated Press, relating Axelrad's tirade and his "never-see-the-light-of-day" comment. He asked for a copy. I told him that I had no authority to release it, but that Stan Glantz, as a reviewer, had a complete copy of the draft document. After Glantz sent it to him, Raeburn read it and phoned me. "Jim, how do I get Axelrad on the record to admit that he's suppressing the Compendium?" I said, "Paul, he is such an [anatomical reference deleted], that all you have to do is ask him when the Compendium will be released; his unbridled temper will do the rest." Sure enough, when Raeburn called, his questioning predictably provoked yet another Axelrad rant. On May 29, 1991, Raeburn wrote an 865-word AP Wire Service piece titled,

"Unreleased Report Says Tobacco Smoke Kills 53,000 Non-Smokers Annually."

A draft report sponsored by the Environmental Protection Agency and other federal agencies concludes that second-hand cigarette smoke kills 53,000 non-smokers a year, including, 37,000 from heart disease. The EPA emphasized that the estimates do not represent official EPA determinations. Rather, the estimates are the views of scientific authorities the agencies commissioned to write the report, the EPA said. A final draft … was completed in April … but it has not been released. A copy was obtained by The Associated Press.

Public release of the document has been delayed indefinitely, said Robert Axelrad, director of the EPA's indoor air division. 'It has not been approved by the EPA. It may never be approved by EPA,' he said. …

In addition to making enemies in the national press and nonsmokers' rights organizations, Axelrad also burned his bridges with the National Cancer Institute. Asked for comment by Raeburn, Shopland opened fire on Axelrad with both barrels:

"Donald Shopland, coordinator of the smoking and tobacco control program at the National Cancer Institute and a contributor to the report, said that if Axelrad refused to release the report he would propose that the cancer institute release it. 'He is making a unilateral decision when this is a cross-agency document,' Shopland said. 'If it's really a multi-agency document, then he's not the one that makes that decision.' …

When Axelrad read the story, he went totally ballistic. He phoned Raeburn and began to hurl invective at him. Why Axelrad could possibly imagine that pissing on the shoes of a major national science reporter would not come back to blow up in his face is unfathomable.

The unkindest cut of all for Axelrad came when John Banzhaf, FOIAed EPA, forcing it to release the Compendium to ASH. Rubbing salt into Axelrad's wounds, Banzhaf then made copies available to the public on request. On June 13, 1991, ASH issued a press release,

"EPA DOCUMENT, PREVIOUSLY SECRET, BLASTS SECONDHAND SMOKE.

"A controversial Environmental Protection Agency (EPA) document, which the agency had so far refused to release, represents the strongest indictment of secondhand tobacco smoke since the 1986 Surgeon General's report, says Action on Smoking and Health (ASH), other conclusions; the document suggests that smoking by day care workers may be a major factor in the alarming incidence of respiratory diseases in infants and young children; that at a minimum it requires at least three times as much heating, cooling, and ventilation to keep air clean in rooms where people are allowed to smoke; and that tobacco smoke is the most important and most deadly contributor to Indoor air pollution.

As previously reported, one chapter of the draft document, entitled 'Tobacco Smoke: A Compendium of Technical Information,' concludes that Environmental Tobacco Smoke causes over 50,000 deaths among Americans each year, largely from heart disease brought on by exposure to smoke. Although EPA … says it doesn't endorse the figure at this time, the World Health Organization and the Surgeon General have both reported that an "estimated 53,000 Americans die each year as a result of secondhand tobacco smoke, a figure consistent with articles in major medical journals… ."

In this manner, this highly technical document, intended mainly for experts in the field, and therefore not of significant interest to the general public, got major publicity, burning not only Axelrad, but Big Tobacco to boot. I was elated.

Two weeks later, on June 15, Raeburn piled on again, exposing the black hand of Big Tobacco, as well as giving Axelrad another poke in the eye, in an article which read in part,

DRAFT EPA REPORT SAYS SECOND-HAND SMOKE KILLS 32,000 AMERICANS,
PAUL RAEBURN, Associated Press, Jun. 15, 1990, 5:58 PM ET, New York

"A finding that second-hand tobacco smoke causes 32,000 heart disease deaths in non-smokers has been incorporated into a draft Environmental Protection Agency report on passive smoking.

The report, a 'technical compendium' of the latest research on passive smoking, has not yet been released. Documents with information on its contents were obtained by The Associated Press from the Tobacco Institute and from the office of Rep. Thomas Bliley of Richmond, Va.

Bliley and the Tobacco Institute, an industry group, have pressed the EPA to revise or withdraw a chapter linking heart disease to passive smoking… ."

So Axelrad's antipathy to Glantz and Parmley's chapter could be traced directly back to marching orders he was taking from Congressman Bliley and Big Tobacco. Why on earth would he allow an affected industry to dictate changes in a government document? What the *hell* was wrong with this guy's ethics?

THE CONGRESSMAN FROM PHILIP MORRIS IS SMOKED OUT

By July 1991, Jeff Schlagenhauf, Congressman Tom Bliley's top tobacco troll, began maliciously plotting future areas that his malevolent master should pursue in support of Philip Morris's goals. Not only did Philip Morris bankroll Bliley for faithfully representing its interests, the industry drummed up a lot of extra customers for Bliley's private business, a chain of funeral parlors, one of which was fittingly located in Chesterfield County, Virginia, where the eponymously named Chesterfield Cigarettes were manufactured. The target areas that Schlagenhauf denominated were outlined in a four-page memorandum to the file:

PLAN OF ATTACK.
"There are several EPA items that need to be pursued: 1) Detailed analysis of where EPA failed to address its Guidelines for Carcinogenic Risk Assessment; 2) Inadequacy of EPA response to May 9 letter; 3) The bias of the panel reviewing the risk assessment; 4) The propriety of the fashion in which contractors were selected for the Policy Guide; 5) Relationship of EPA staff to anti-smoking activists; 6) Questioning of EPA staff; and 7) Question SAB [Science Advisory Board] Panel Members About Review."

- *"This is the time to pursue issues relating to Repace, et al. Need to use interviews, etc. to demonstrate the coordination and activity of EPA staff with these folks. Also demonstrate how relationships [of Repace] with Burns, Glantz, Samet, et al. were used to stack the [SAB] process."*
- *Interview EPA staff per Bender [Administrator Reilly's chief of staff] commitment. Pursue both scientific and procedural issues. Use this as forum to draw out anti-tobacco bias. Initial thoughts on interview list. ORD: Bayard, Farland, Wiltse. IAD: Claussen, Axelrad, Repace, SAB: Barnes, Flaak, Rodenberg, Osbourn. Additionally, should go for meetings*

with [EPA officials] Brettauer, Rosenberg, Habicht. Who else? Loehr, McClellan, ??? May need Bliley for meetings with [top OAR and ORD officials] Rosenberg and Brettauer. Need list of questions to ask each individual. Would seek to record/transcribe Q&A. Ask EPA Congressional Affairs to sit in and offer to provide transcript copy. Want to accomplish this during August recess." [TTID 87207987].

In addition, there were several other paragraphs showing how Bliley's ugly snout was intent on rooting into EPA's affairs. Schlagenhauf emphasized the need to FOIA documents by the Tobacco Institute, Philip Morris, RJ Reynolds and, in his words:

"find out what [EPA] have. At some point, need to do a staff memo to Bliley ... that sets out the case against EPA ... This would be released to the press at the same time it was sent to EPA for reaction. ... It would allow us to go on the offensive with the press. ... Full fledged assault on NIOSH CIB document* needed. This is the opening to go after all the Surgeon General's documents on passive smoking report. ... Need to use the Oversight Subcommittee's investigation into scientific fraud and NIH activities to raise scientific integrity issues on ETS research. Blot followup would be useful." [William Blot was an NCI cancer epidemiologist who also sat on EPA's ETS Science Advisory Board to peer-review the ETS risk assessment].

---

*[This referred to NIOSH CIB 54 on ETS in the Workplace (NIOSH, 1991)]

On May 29, 1991, a threatening letter from Bliley on the Subcommittee on Oversight and Investigations letterhead went out to Bill Blot, with the obvious intent of intimidating him. It questioned Blot's "failure to bring ... a study co-authored by you with Wu-Williams entitled, "Lung Cancer among Women in North-East China," ... one of the largest case-control studies to date on nonsmoker lung cancer. ... As you know, the Subcommittee has conducted extensive inquiries in the area of scientific integrity. Your failure to bring this significant research to the panel's attention during its deliberations raises serious concerns." This was followed by a series of fifteen questions that required a detailed response from Blot [TTID TI52200931].

Bliley's first question was *"Why did you not bring your research to the attention of other SAB panel members during your deliberations in December?"*

On NCI letterhead, Blot made a comprehensive 7-page reply to Bliley's inquiry. [W. Blot personal communication]. Among the issues that Bliley's letter raised was that of the Wu-Williams study of Lung Cancer among women in Northeast China, co-authored with Blot. Blot's reply was both predictable to anyone who understood the Wu-Williams paper and devastating to those who did not:

"The Wu-Williams study did not find an effect of passive smoking on lung cancer in women. However, the study also found that these homes in Northeast China were heated with unvented coal-burning devices called Kang and coal stoves, which released carcinogenic coal smoke which raised the lung cancer risk in these women by 20 to 50%, and obviously confounded an effect of passive smoking. The study in Shenyang and Harbin focused on other risk factors for lung cancer and was ill equipped to evaluate effects of ETS; thus, I had not thought of the study as a passive smoking study. In Shenyang and Harbin, located in Manchuria in northeastern China, air pollution levels are considered to be among the highest in the world.

Both are industrial cities, with China's largest copper smelter located in a central area of Shenyang. In addition to industrial air pollution, pollution from coal-burning 'Kang' and other heating devices is intense, so that indoor levels of various air pollutants can exceed those outdoors. Since some of the same constituents (e.g., polycyclic aromatic hydrocarbons) found in ETS are also found in pollution from burning fossil fuels, the possibly dominating effect of pollution from other sources made evaluation of ETS as an air pollutant and risk factor for lung cancer extremely difficult in this population" [Blot, 1991].

Bliley's 12th question asked, "In your opinion, based on EPA's Guidelines for Carcinogenic Risk Assessment, did the risk assessment you reviewed make the case for a class A designation? If so, please describe how you believe each of the seven hazard identification criteria set forth in EPA's Guidelines for Carcinogenic Risk Assessment were met in the draft risk assessment you reviewed."

Blot's reply was cogent:

"The draft EPA risk assessment document that I reviewed summarized evidence that indicates to me that prolonged exposure to ETS can increase the risk of cancer in humans (i.e., that ETS is a class A [human] carcinogen). As noted by the SAB panel, the case for a class A designation could have been made even stronger than presented in the draft document. This interpretation of the evidence derives from the biologic plausibility of the ETS-lung cancer association, its consistency and replicability across studies, the existence of dose response trends, the lack of evidence that the association is due mainly to bias or confounding by other risk factors for lung cancer, and the observation of increased risks at exposure levels found in typical environmental settings. Among the most important of these criteria is the biologic plausibility of the association. ETS arises from cigarette smoking.

Cigarette smoking is the dominant cause of lung cancer in this country and most others, with upwards of 20-fold excesses in risk in heavy smokers. Nonsmokers exposed to ETS inhale many of the same substances that smokers do, albeit in smaller amounts. Components of tobacco smoke have been detected in the blood and urine of nonsmokers, so there is no doubt that tobacco constituents are absorbed and metabolized by ETS-exposed nonsmokers. It is thus conceivable (plausible) that this lower level of exposure to tobacco smoke results in an increase in lung cancer risk. That we are dealing with a documented exposure to a known carcinogen provides the biologic basis for expecting that ETS may increase cancer risk.

I have already remarked upon the consistency and replicability of findings – increased risks among passive smokers were found in not just one or two studies, but many – and noted that there are dose-response trends, with risk tending to rise with increasing ETS exposures. The draft document also discusses bias and confounding, and finds (as did earlier National Academy of Sciences and Surgeon General's reports on ETS) no compelling argument that the ETS-lung cancer association is entirely due to either bias or uncontrolled confounding. Finally, a small increase in lung cancer risk–expected from knowledge that smoking causes large increases in risk–was actually observed among those exposed to ETS" [Blot, 1991].

THE SCHLAGENHAUF EPISODE

In late August 1991, a member of EPA's Congressional Liaison Staff appeared in my office one morning and informed me that my presence was required in the office of Congressman Thomas Bliley the following week, to undergo interrogation by a Bliley aide, Jeff Schlagenhauf. The interview would be confidential to the press and would be tape recorded. He said that several other EPA staff would also be summoned to appear. This rang alarm bells in my head. I knew that Bliley was a Republican congressman from a tobacco state who had barraged EPA with a series of abusive letters accusing EPA of being biased against the tobacco industry.

My health remained in a precarious state after my bout of sick building syndrome. I began to feel besieged by antagonists both inside and outside the agency. I was not being paranoid; in the wake of the earlier Sundquist attack in 1987, I had every reason to believe the tobacco industry was coming after me again. I told the Liaison (whose name I have forgotten) I didn't want to testify and explained why. He replied, "I understand your concerns, but you have to go." He then offered to provide an EPA lawyer to accompany me. I reluctantly agreed, and met with Don Nantkes, an EPA ethics lawyer whom I knew pretty well. When I spoke to Don about the meeting, he said, "Frankly Jim, I really don't know what my role would be here."

Okay… at this point, I realized that I badly needed the assistance of an outside attorney. I called the Advocacy Institute again. Mike Pertschuk's secretary said that Mike and all of his attorneys were on vacation, it being close to the Labor Day weekend. At that point I turned to John Banzhaf at ASH. I rang John up and asked if he might represent me. He invited me to ASH's office on H Street NW, a block from George Washington University, where he was a law professor. I explained what was happening, telling him that I intended to refuse to be interviewed under those circumstances. John agreed to assist, and together we hashed out the language I would use. Banzhaf also warned me that our interests might not overlap completely. I replied that it didn't matter.

But being forewarned, I decided to take out additional insurance. Mindful of the beneficial impact of the *Science* article by Eliot Marshall in 1987, I decided to call Paul Raeburn. I avoided using either my office or home phones. A Raeburn story in the AP would be my extra insurance policy for surviving the attack of these predators who prowled the jungle of Washington's savage tobacco politics. I told Raeburn that Bliley would be secretly taping EPA staff who were working on the EPA Risk Assessment, on the EPA Science Advisory Board Staff, or anyone else at EPA having anything to do with ETS. Raeburn asked me to let him know when my interview would happen. I also decided not to inform EPA that I would tell Schlagenhauf that I would refuse to be interviewed. In this manner, I could beard the lion in his own den.

The Tuesday after Labor Day, I appeared at Bliley's office in the Rayburn House Office Building at 10 AM, accompanied by the EPA Liaison, and Don Nantkes. We met John Banzhaf waiting for us in the hall. I introduced them to each other and said that Banzhaf was my attorney. As we entered Bliley's Congressional Office, we were greeted by a giant 3' x 3' collage of Philip Morris cigarette packs hanging on the wall behind his receptionist's head. Whoa! At that moment, I knew I had done the right thing (Figure 16). We were ushered into Schlagenhauf's large office, a mark of high status on Capitol Hill, and the Liaison introduced me, Nantkes, and Banzhaf. Schlagenhauf gaped at Banzhaf and exclaimed, "You're John Banzhaf?! The same guy who referred to Congressman Bliley as a 'water boy for the tobacco industry, and not a very bright one, at that'!" "Yes, yes, I believe I did say that," Banzhaf admitted with a faint smile. Nantkes, the Liaison and I looked at each other, astonished. Then we were off to the races. Schlagenhauf began by reciting his ground rules: the press was not to be informed, he would ask a series of questions which would be tape-recorded, and the proceedings were to be kept secret. I bluntly informed Schlagenhauf that, "I don't find those rules acceptable. I will not participate in some kind of star-chamber proceeding. If Congressman Bliley wants me to answer his questions, as is his right as a member of an investigative subcommittee, he can ask them in an open Congressional hearing, and I will be happy to respond. But I will **not** participate in any secret proceedings, which I regard as totally improper."

Schlagenhauf stared at me like a snake in the grass. He coldly replied, "Then we have nothing to discuss." My EPA minders looked stunned. Then we all trooped out of Bliley's office, and departed from Capitol Hill. I caught a cab back to EPA alone. I then immediately called Raeburn from a phone in a vacant office picked at random and told him what had transpired. Paul rang off and promptly phoned Schlagenhauf. He identified himself and announced, "I hear you're secretly taping EPA staff involved in the tobacco issue." Raeburn later told me that Schlagenhauf, caught with his pants down, made the egregious mistake of talking on the record for 45 minutes. Meanwhile, Banzhaf called a press conference to denounce Bliley for his underhanded tactics with the EPA. This is what he meant about our interests diverging. Actually, I thought they coincided completely.

The 505-word Raeburn story hit the newswires on the following day, August 29th, 1991. It read in part:

"BLILEY HAVING EPA STAFF QUIZZED ON SMOKING STUDIES
by Paul Raeburn, Science Editor, Associated Press, New York.

"A Virginia congressman is having individual, closed-door, taped interviews conducted by an aide with Environmental Protection Agency staff members who worked on studies on second-hand cigarette smoke. A spokesman for Rep. Thomas J. Bliley Jr., who has repeatedly attacked the studies, denied that the interviews in his office were an attempt to intimidate the EPA staff members. Several of those interviewed, however, said they were concerned that it is part of an effort to undermine their research on the health hazards of smoking. 'They're very nervous about going up there, and properly so.'"

Raeburn's AP story quoted Banzhaf as saying that "the questioning was improper, highly unusual in that such inquiries would be refused by most agencies who would assert executive privilege." Banzhaf continued, explaining that while it was not unusual for high ranking EPA officials to respond in person to official queries by congressmen, this "was the first to involve lower-ranking personnel." The AP story continued, describing the three EPA reports on secondhand smoke. The first mentioned was ORD's draft risk assessment, indicting ETS as a human carcinogen for nonsmokers. Raeburn then described the ETS compendium, citing the 53,000 estimated deaths from passive smoking, followed by the workplace smoking policy guide. Schlagenhauf was quoted, weakly bleating that it was simply a "private opportunity to gather information," … "and not an attempt to … pressure anybody." However, the article continued, one staffer "was just a secretary who signed a letter on behalf of her boss." One of the two EPA officials who accompanied me was anonymously quoted, saying that "Mr. Repace was exercising his legal rights [in refusing to answer any questions] and I can't tell you what's going to happen from here." The article reported that I could not be reached for comment. That was true. It was the safest way to distance myself from the fallout.

After the Raeburn story appeared, Axelrad went totally ballistic. He summoned me to his office, ordered me to close the door, and began bellowing spittle in a full blown out-of-control vulgar rant: "YOU STUPID FUCKING ASSHOLE, HOW COULD YOU INVITE JOHN BANZHAF INTO A PRIVATE EPA MEETING! HE'S MY ENEMY!!

I was stunned. He thinks Banzhaf is his enemy? I didn't recall Banzhaf ever interacting with Axelrad. Where on earth was this intemperate outburst coming from? Axelrad brayed on for twenty minutes, venting his spleen. I had nothing whatsoever to gain by responding to his vile tirade, so I tuned him out, and stared out the window. I became possessed by ambivalent feelings. On one hand, I was delighted that Banzhaf was taking the fall for the hard-hitting AP story. At the same time, I wondered how Axelrad could possibly be so moronic as to regard perhaps the most prominent spokesman for the nonsmokers' rights movement in the country, a public interest law professor and a natural ally for EPA's ETS work, as his personal enemy. *If Banzhaf is your enemy, who are your friends?* As Axelrad ranted on, I amused myself by paraphrasing Sam Rayburn's admonition to Lyndon Johnson: *"If you want a friend in Washington, Bob, get a dog."* Holding that thought, I nearly burst out laughing. Finally, he shouted "NOW GET THE HELL OUT OF MY OFFICE." Did he really imagine that making enemies with abandon was not going to come back to bite him in the ass? Did he sleep through his poly-sci program? Despite the abuse, I departed in an upbeat mood.

FIGURE 16. A SLIDE FROM MY SPRING 2006 DEAN'S LECTURE, THE SECONDHAND SMOKE WARS: BATTLES ON THE ROAD FROM SCIENCE TO POLICY, DELIVERED AT THE YALE UNIVERSITY SCHOOL OF PUBLIC HEALTH, 19 APRIL 2006.

Afterward, Raeburn told me that his exposé of Schlagenhauf and Bliley ran in over 400 newspapers around the country. Subsequently, every time Raeburn did another story on secondhand smoke – and he would do many more – he would mention the "53,000 secondhand smoke deaths in an EPA report." It was a perfect trifecta: I had gotten the Compendium released to the public with far more publicity than Shopland and I could ever have hoped for. I ended Bliley's industry-instigated inquisition of EPA Staff, nailed both Bliley and Schlagenhauf in the process, and screwed Axelrad to boot. I called Anne Donnelly, President of Virginia GASP, asking if she had a member from Richmond who could plausibly visit Bliley's office to photograph the cigarette collage. She did. However, when he went there the week following the Raeburn exposé, the incriminating collage had already been removed. It had now become a source of embarrassment for the Congressman From Philip Morris, who by the way, has me to thank for his sobriquet, which *Mother Jones Magazine* immortalized in an article entitled "Smoked Out" in its March/April issue in 1996.

One of Philip Morris's major strategic objectives was to block the EPA risk assessment from being issued. They intended to achieve this by getting the White House to transfer jurisdiction over ETS to OSHA, tacitly assuming that any potential OSHA regulation would focus on engineering controls such as ventilation and accommodation of workplace smoking in some benign fashion (Muggli, et al. 2004). As it turned out, they could not have been more wrong. In June 1991, the National Institute of Occupational Safety and Health (NIOSH) issued *NIOSH Current Intelligence Bulletin 54, Environmental Tobacco Smoke in the Workplace: Lung Cancer and Other Health Effects*. Its announced purpose was to disseminate information about the potential risk of cancer to workers exposed to ETS. *CIB 54* cited three papers by Repace and Lowrey, our 1980 *Science* and 1982 *ASHRAE Transactions* papers to support the notion that smoking in public access buildings polluted the air with fine particulate matter, and our 1990 *Risk Analysis* paper reviewing several risk assessments of ETS and lung cancer, suggesting a range of 3000 to 7000 nonsmokers' passive-smoking-caused deaths per year, placing our 5000 lung cancer death estimate right in the middle. CIB 54 cited our updated estimate that there was a nearly two-thirds probability of workplace exposure to ETS. NIOSH had flatly contradicted the industry's arguments that workplace exposures were much less important than home exposures.

NIOSH believed that although studies of ETS and lung cancer had not been gathered in an occupational setting, nevertheless ETS met the criteria of the Occupational Safety and Health Administration (OSHA) for legal classification as a workplace carcinogen. It concluded that, "NIOSH therefore considers ETS to be a potential occupational carcinogen and recommends that exposures be reduced to the lowest feasible concentration. All available preventive measures should be used to minimize occupational exposure to ETS." After all, if passive smoking caused lung cancer when nonsmokers were exposed in the home environment, exposure to ETS should be location independent, and therefore should also cause it in the workplace. With the 1986 Surgeon General's Report on Involuntary Smoking, and the 1986 NAS Report on ETS, NIOSH's *CIB 54* increased the number of authoritative U.S. reports to three, and backlit the stage on which the coming EPA-OSHA-Tobacco Industry drama would play out. NIOSH's conclusion had also neatly backstopped my firm belief that fundamentally, the ETS issue was primarily a workplace concern, although nearly all of the epi studies up to that time had been performed on the nonsmoking spouses of smokers.

In Schlagenhauf's July 30, 1991 Memo to the File, he had also outlined his grandiose General Plan of Attack on all federal agencies concerned with ETS, which included the White House Science Advisor, EPA, NCI, and NIOSH: … *"Full fledged assault on NIOSH CIB document needed. This is the opening to go after all the Surgeon General's documents on passive smoking report. In addition to seeking documents, letter similar to Reilly May 9 letter needs to be done. Needs to make distinction between NIOSH and OSHA. I think HHS fears OSHA will not go along with their program and is seeking to push them along. They are also trying to confuse the public/corporate America into believing OSHA has settled the question."* The industry clearly regarded OSHA as an easy mark.

HBI's PHONY STUDY OF ETS IN 585 OFFICE BUILDINGS

Meanwhile, frustrated by the failure of Sal DiNardi to produce bogus research discrediting Repace and Lowrey's ETS indoor air pollution papers in *Science* and *ASHRAE Transactions*, the industry began plotting its next major attack on our work. It decided to use the clandestine "Special Projects" of the CIAR as a vehicle for funding a very large study of fine particles in commercial buildings by Gray Robertson's newly enlarged company, renamed Healthy Buildings International (HBI). It was heavily supported by Big Tobacco. They had anticipated that HBI's exposure assessment effort would also be especially useful in the industry's assault on any future OSHA attempt to regulate workplace ETS and would neatly complement the dosimetric RJR/Oak Ridge 16 City Study. The HBI study, "**THE MEASUREMENT OF ENVIRONMENTAL TOBACCO SMOKE IN 585 OFFICE ENVIRONMENTS,**" was published in *Environment International* by Turner et al. (1992). It was a classic case of scientific fraud. And they nearly got away with this masterpiece of junk science. The HBI study concluded that, "a group of rooms used for light smoking (59.9% of total smoking rooms) was not significantly different from the nonsmoking rooms, in terms of the variables which contributed to the predictive ability of the model (RSP and nicotine). They concluded that, "with good ventilation, acceptable air quality can be maintained with moderate amounts of smoking." Turner et al. reported that HBI's "measurements showed ETS levels in smoking areas were considerably lower than the predictions of the Repace and Lowrey model." Further, they wrote, their results showed that there was a "threshold of 5 to 10 cigarettes /100 m²/hour below which office air quality would not be significantly affected. And finally, that the ventilation rate specified by ASHRAE Standard 62-1989 yielded acceptable indoor air quality "with moderate amounts of smoking." If true, such a threshold would justify smoking in a typical office setting. However, Lowrey and I had performed many controlled experiments in office settings and found HBI's conclusions to be highly suspect. My bullshit detector went off-scale.

HBI's pseudo-scientific assault on smoke-free indoor air had been previewed in layman's terms in HBI's slick bi-monthly publication, *Healthy Buildings International Magazine,* circulated world-wide. In an illustrated 7-page feature article in its Sept/Oct 1991 edition, entitled Tobacco Smoke Signals New Challenges for Managers, HBI reviewed the 1980 *Science* paper of Repace and Lowrey, observing that "Their model calculations and their measurement figures have been widely quoted in the scientific press, including draft EPA documents, and formal NIOSH position papers as recent as this year, thus showing that their data continues to have a great influence on public policy on indoor smoking. Unfortunately, Repace and Lowrey's data does not include much information from real-life smoking levels in typical offices…". This was true. However, two years later, it would turn out to be the only statement in the paper that was actually true. The sentence continued, "… and most up-to-date measurements by other researchers in typical offices have shown levels several-fold lower than their early models calculated." Then the article touted the great and wonderful advancement in measurements offered by HBI's 585 Office Environment Study, noting that "Complete smoking bans in a building – the ultimate "source control option – may not solve the fundamental cause of the problem and may backfire by transferring complaints from nonsmoking employees to disgruntled smokers." The article went on to promote designated smoking areas, smoking lounges, air cleaning equipment, 'common courtesy,' and the effectiveness of ventilation systems to remove internally generated pollution as preferred alternatives. We were unaware of this magazine article at that time. But the paper of Turner et al. did not escape our intense scrutiny.

In a four-page letter to the editor, Lowrey and I blasted Turner et al.'s paper. To begin with, our analysis indicated that Turner et al.'s conclusion that smoking under normal occupancy conditions in offices produced trivial indoor air pollution levels appeared to be an artifact deriving from volumetric smoker densities which were far lower than that for a typical office building with unrestricted smoking. Secondly, HBI's results were in conflict with the careful measurements of Turk et al. (1989) who had measured the impact of secondhand smoke on respirable particle (RSP) levels in 38 buildings in the Pacific Northwest. Turk et al. reported RSP levels from ETS averaging 51 $\mu g/m^3$ above background, double the RSP concentration from ETS that Turner et al. (1992) reported, despite air exchange rates that were nearly 70% higher than the ASHRAE Standard minimums in Turk's buildings. Moreover, 39% of Turk et al.'s measurements in smoking areas exceeded the 50 $\mu g/m^3$ level of EPA's PM_{10} standard (inhalable particulate matter 10 microns or less in diameter), while only 2.6% of the measurements taken in nonsmoking areas did. Turk et al. concluded that the pollutants in these buildings that "most frequently approached or exceeded recognized guidelines" were RSP concentrations, which were "usually associated with tobacco smoking."

Thirdly, we rebutted Turner et al.'s assertion that "the model of Repace and Lowrey over-predicted typical office concentrations of RSP from ETS was without foundation," because our model was based upon two parameters [smoker density and ventilation rate], neither of which had been measured by Turner et al. Finally, we concluded that "Turner et al.'s stated objective in their study was to provide information on levels of exposure to ETS which are alleged to be representative of conditions existing in modern office environments. Regrettably, the results they present are misleading, unscientific, and lacking in credibility." Our letter would provide the foundation leading to my fortuitous discovery two years later, that HBI's results in fact constituted a massive scientific fraud of the first water. A fraud that would first command the attention of a Congressional investigation by Henry Waxman (D) CA, and then become a count in a Racketeer Influenced Corrupt Organization (RICO) lawsuit against Big Tobacco by the Department of Justice a decade later. An interesting footnote: Simon Turner was reputedly the son of a BAT executive. This worm-eaten apple didn't fall very far from the termite-infested tree.

Not content with putting all their eggs in one basket, the industry proceeded with its plans to perform a second project using personal monitors for nicotine whose goal was to demonstrate that the home was the major source of ETS exposure of nonsmokers with the workplace a very distant second, which would feed into their arcane legal arguments against OSHA regulation of ETS in the workplace. This result was pre-determined. All they needed was to collect the right data to support the predetermined conclusion. This research had been pioneered by RJ Reynolds scientists and its survey design firm, Bellomy Research, unsurprisingly based in Winston-Salem, North Carolina. The RJR study was laundered through a research grant to Oak Ridge National Laboratory in Tennessee via Special Account 4 (Kessler, 2006). It would also set me on a collision course with the industry in its effort to derail the National Institute of Environmental Health Sciences' effort (NIEHS) to list ETS in its National Report on Human Carcinogens in 1998.

Philip Morris continued to be enormously concerned about the impact of smoke-free workplace laws on cigarette sales. An internal memorandum dated January 22, 1992, sent to Louis Suwarna, Director of New Products for Philip Morris USA, in its New York headquarters from John Heironimus, Divisional Vice President, is particularly illuminating:

TO: Louis Suwarna DATE: January 22, 1992
FROM: John Heironimus
SUBJECT: Impact of Workplace Restrictions on Consumption and Incidence, Summary of Major Findings

1. Total prohibition of smoking in the workplace strongly affects industry volume. Smokers facing these restrictions consume 11%-15% less than average and quit at a rate that is 84% higher than average. Only 6.4%-10.3% of smokers face total workplace prohibition but these restrictions are rapidly becoming more common.

2. Milder workplace restrictions, such as smoking only in designated areas, have much less impact on quitting rates and very little effect on consumption.

3. Smokers not in the labor force (retired, unemployed, housewives, etc.) quit at a rate 21% above average and have also reduced their consumption noticeably over the last few years. These smokers may be much more sensitive to price increases, economic volatility and health concerns.

4. From 1987 to 1991, the industry lost an estimated incremental 1.7% (9.5 billion units [cigarettes]) due to increasing workplace restrictions. If these trends continue, the industry will lose an additional 1.3% to 1.9% (8.4 to 11.4 billion units) from 1991 to 1996.

5. If smoking were banned in all workplaces, the industry's average consumption would decline 8.7%-10.1% from 1991 levels and the quitting rate would increase 74% (e.g., from 2.5% to 4.4%) [TTID 2023914280].

Thus, Philip Morris recognized that the EPA Risk Assessment and the potential OSHA imposition of smoking restrictions in the workplace each posed a major threat to industry profits. Although I was not privy to this memorandum in 1992, I had long realized that potential losses to industry profits must be the prime motivators of industry opposition to smoke-free workplaces. I was also firmly convinced that smoking had to be eliminated in the workplace as it was causing preventable morbidity and premature mortality in a captive audience of nonsmokers. No one in the environmental health community awaited the EPA ETS risk assessment more than I did. It was my brainchild; I had placed it on the initial agenda of the Indoor Air staff in 1987 and now it was finally coming to fruition. Aside from the obvious major public health value of the report, and the damage that it would inflict on Big Tobacco, I was fascinated to find out how close Lowrey and I had come to the Carcinogen Assessment Group's professional lung cancer mortality estimates.

In March of 1992, I was invited to speak on control of environmental tobacco smoke in the workplace at the Prevention '92 Conference, sponsored by the American College of Preventive Medicine, in Baltimore. As the secret documents of the industry show, this aroused the concern of Tom Humber, VP at Philip Morris's PR firm, Burson Marsteller. In a memo to Steve Parrish of Philip Morris, with a cc to Tom Borelli [director of science and environmental policy at PM], Humber wrote:

Burson - Marsteller

1850 M Street, N .W.   Thomas Humber
Suite 900   Senior Vice President
Washington, D .C. 20038.5890
202.833 .4483; FAX 202 .7753794

March 6, 1992
TO : Steve Parrish
FROM: Tom Humber
RE: Prevention '92' Meeting/Repace
COPY: Tom Borelli, Lisa Velenovsky

Situation:
Repace to speak on "Passive Smoking: Health Effects, Policy Development and Community Activism." Program lists him as PhD. with EPA, but we do not know if appearance has official sanction. He could use meeting to discuss Revised Risk Assessment. We would expect little press coverage unless set up with Paul Raeburn.

Options:
1. Pre-emptively challenge Repace's appearance to the EPA. If we've read signals right, he is something of an embarrassment, and there would be a fair chance of having him cancelled by EPA, having his remarks softened or having him speak as a private citizen. Successful or not, this option virtually guarantees a Raeburn story.
2. Let him go on, tape his presentation, hope he goes way overboard, plant some questions in the audience to help that along, tar him as EPA'S prime operative on ETS and use that, first politically and then publicly, to denounce the bias of the EPA.

This option has great appeal, few downsides and some interesting opportunities in the dynamics. If the EPA embraces him, we gain some credibility for bias. If the EPA tries to build distance from him, we then exploit his relationship to the SPI project [Bob Rosner's Smoking Policy Institute], questioning EPA honesty and calling further attention to the little tip-of-the iceberg scandal. This option is recommended.

3. News release/statement/backgrounder to be released at conference to deal with substance of Risk Assessment. Not. Don't create a story on his turf where it might not otherwise materialize.

4. News release/statement/backgrounder on substance of Risk Assessment for response if there is any coverage. This is necessary as a contingency, although little work is required since existing materials provide those talking points. Over the last few weeks, I have begun to think about the workplace studies excluded from consideration by EPA. Since that has some potency (albeit relative) and speaks directly to the OSHA phase of the battle, I'd like to develop the argument, and a meeting like this could provide some opportunity to test it, if there is to be any coverage. One last note. We and Lisa Barrera are checking new EPA ethics code to determine if possible ethics violations may enter into the picture. If so, this could add fuel to option #2 [TTID 2023583864].

Lisa Barrera had been the former Chief of Staff to John Hernandez, Acting EPA Administrator in 1983, who replaced the fired Anne Gorsuch for a time. Note that the coming battle with OSHA over ETS (which would not occur until 1994), was already well in the industry's contingency plans.

Philip Morris, following Burson Marsteller's playbook, conducted an "EPA-bashing" campaign resulting in a number of articles in major news publications which were consistent with the disinformation purveyed by its scientific moles. Journalists or columnists associated with right-wing think tanks such as the Competitive Enterprise Institute, the Heritage Foundation, the Cato Institute, and the Reason Foundation, all of which received five and six figure support from PM, were cultivated and obligingly wrote articles critical of EPA and tobacco control for their paymasters [Muggli, et al., 2004].

THE EPA REPORT ON ETS IS ISSUED DESPITE THE INDUSTRY'S BEST EFFORTS

Behind the scenes, in a presentation to Philip Morris's Board of Directors on June 24, 1992, Craig Fuller, Senior Vice President, Corporate Affairs, stated with respect to "the indoor air issue and PM's strategy:"

"I want to briefly discuss with you an issue which has been worked intensely in several areas of the company – environmental tobacco smoke. The work over the past few years and in the five months I have been here has involved our colleagues at PM USA the Legal Department, Scientific Affairs and others. Perhaps it is stating the obvious but let me just review what is at stake for Philip Morris, business in general and the EPA. For us, it is obvious. We are going to have another round of negative stories. But there is really more at stake than just bad press. This process will be drawn out over several months, and if at the conclusion of the process, the Administrator of the EPA who has no jurisdiction for regulating indoor air and has no real scientific foundation for approving restrictions on smoking. ... if he issues the Risk Assessment which asserts that secondary tobacco smoke is carcinogenic, we have a very difficult problem.

Our allies who have held the line in buildings, restaurants, shopping areas, sports complexes and other areas will almost certainly be forced to rethink their position. For the business community, the stakes are also high. From the outset, EPA has had as one of its highest objectives the capturing of the authority to regulate indoor air. To the extent that this Risk Assessment drives legislation to give EPA that authority ... and it will, the entire business community is threatened with yet another enormous cost. For, if the EPA is directed through legislation to regulate indoor air, they will regulate the sources of indoor air contaminants. ...

If we were fighting the conclusions of any other risk assessment than this one on tobacco, we could sink the thing at several different points along the way because the science is so bad – we call it junk science. But, EPA was clever. They picked the one area that intimidates most of their critics – tobacco smoke. If they can enter the world of indoor air regulation through this door they will. ... We are mounting a campaign to try and stop them. ... We have been referring to our initial approach as 'sand in the gears.' Our objective was to slow down the ETS risk assessment until we could get broader policy declarations out of the Administration. To be honest, we made every effort to prevent the Risk Assessment from going to the Science Advisory Board . . . unfortunately, EPA resisted at every stage, including a last ditch effort by some White House staff" [TTID 2047916010].

Well before becoming a Senior VP of Philip Morris, Craig Fuller was politically very well connected. In 1981, Fuller had been an apparatchik in the Reagan Administration, serving eight years in the White House, as Assistant to President Reagan for Cabinet Affairs. Then he became Chief of Staff to Vice President George H.W. Bush during the second term of the Reagan Administration. Why did Fuller fail to derail EPA's risk assessment despite all of his rock solid White House connections?

This is the inside story as related to me by Steven Bayard. In the spring or early summer of 1992, EPA Administrator Reilly and Louis Sullivan, Secretary of DHHS, had jointly decided they wanted the EPA Risk Assessment of ETS and Lung Cancer released before the end of the year. However, Eric Bretthauer, EPA's Assistant Administrator for Research and Development, had raised repeated obstacles the previous six months after the risk assessment had been completed, and had not signed off on it. According to Steven, the reason for this was that the White House, i.e., OMB, had not given him the green light. And this was "because D. Allan Bromley, the White House Science Advisor, was opposed to our attempts." OMB had a well-deserved reputation at EPA for being a black hole where proposed rules and regulations went to die.

However, said Steven, "things changed with two briefings I gave on the same day a few months later – a Wednesday, after Eric Bretthauer had informed me just that Monday - (probably Oct./Nov., '92) - that 'we', meaning I, needed to brief the DHHS Assistant Secretary of Health and the White House (i.e., D.R. Henderson, then head of Health for OMB)". At the meeting at OMB, attended by Henderson, Bretthauer, and one of Bretthauer's aides, Steven related that he briefed Henderson for about 5 minutes, and then Henderson stated, "I read the 1986 Reports of the Surgeon General and the NAS, and there wasn't enough there to convince me [of a lung cancer effect from passive smoking]." Steven said, "I agree, but there were only 14 studies at that time; but now there are 29 studies. I want to show you two tables from EPA's report: Table 5-10 shows the results of 19 studies giving statistical measures for the highest exposure categories only, and Table 5-11 gives the exposure response trends for females. [Table 5-10 showed that the probability that this increased risk of passive smoking was the result of a statistical error was less that one chance in a million (p<0.000001); while Table 5-11 analyzed the 14 studies with sufficient exposure-response data, with 10 of the 14 showing statistically significant trends for one or more exposure measures.] Henderson perused these two tables in silence for several minutes. Then he responded, "I'm convinced." In the limo on the way back, Steven said that "Bretthauer and his aide were giddy." Bretthauer turned to Steven, and said, "I'm going to sign off on the document's release today," and he did. Steven hand-carried the risk assessment over to DHHS and got a sign-off from Secretary Sullivan a few days later, and "releasing the Final [Risk Assessment of ETS] before the end of 1992, (i.e. before the change of Congressional Administration), became a top priority." The importance of Steven Bayard in successfully completing the ETS risk assessment cannot be overestimated. ORD's dioxin risk assessment had been worked on for over ten years and became a Sisyphean task that had never been brought to completion despite being a major ORD effort.

The EPA Report, *Respiratory Health Effects of Passive Smoking: Lung Cancer and Other Disorders*, was published in January 1993. It declared that "secondhand smoke causes lung cancer in adult nonsmokers and impairs the respiratory health of children." It classified secondhand smoke as a "Group A carcinogen," a designation signifying that there is sufficient evidence that the substance causes cancer in humans. The

Group A designation had been used by EPA for only 15 other pollutants, including asbestos, radon, and benzene. EPA emphasized that *alone among these Group A carcinogens, secondhand smoke was the only one that had actually been shown to cause cancer at typical environmental levels.* The report estimated that "approximately 3,000 American nonsmokers die each year from lung cancer caused by secondhand smoke; … with an estimated range of from 400 to 7,000 lung cancer deaths possible, but that in view of the generally conservative assumptions, EPA expects that the actual number may be greater than 3,000." EPA also estimated that "more lung cancer deaths are estimated to be attributable to ETS from combined non-spousal exposures – 2,200 of both sexes – than from spousal exposure – 800 of both sexes, a ratio of almost 3 to 1 for non-spousal to spousal smoking, based on both epidemiological and biomarker studies. [Repace and Lowrey's 1985 estimate was about 4 to 1.]

The EPA report continued (and this is where Steven showed his statistical chops): "The overall proportion (9/30) of individual studies found to show an association between lung cancer and spousal ETS exposure at all levels combined is unlikely to occur by chance (a statistical error less than 1 in 1000, ($p<10^{-3}$). When the analysis focuses on higher levels of spousal exposure, every one of the 17 studies with exposure-level data shows increased risk in the highest exposure group; 9 of these are significant at $p<0.05$ level [i.e. at the 95% confidence level], despite most having low power, another result highly unlikely to occur by chance [statistical error less than 1 in 10 million] ($p<10^{-7}$). Similarly, the proportion showing a statistically significant exposure-response trend is highly supportive of a causal association." [i.e., 10/14, yielding a statistical error less than 1 in a billion ($p<10^{-9}$)],

It added: "Every year, an estimated 150,000 to 300,000 children under 18 months of age get pneumonia or bronchitis from breathing secondhand tobacco smoke. Secondhand smoke is a risk factor for the development of asthma in children and worsens the condition of up to one million asthmatic children." For his effort, Steven received a richly-deserved gold medal plus a $5000 bonus from EPA for his herculean accomplishment.

In January 1993, at the time of the EPA report's release, Brennan Dawson, speaking directly for the Tobacco Institute, ignored the SAB's unanimous endorsement of the EPA Risk Assessment of ETS, and responded by blowing smoke. She insisted that "any number of world-renowned experts have looked at this report and said that the EPA has mischaracterized and manipulated the data" [Raeburn, 1993]. By contrast, the *New York Times* editorialized: "The continued effort of the Tobacco Institute to get Americans to ignore the best available science [on ETS] represents corporate irresponsibility of the rankest sort" [NY Times, 1993]. Meanwhile, Schlagenhauf, speaking for Congressman Bliley, declared that he hoped that "OSHA ... won't just take EPA's studies at face value," and warned that "any OSHA rule would have to be defended in court."

Indeed, the industry would not wait for the OSHA Rule to be proposed to attempt to discredit EPA's risk assessment. It took pre-emptive legal action five months later, on June 22, 1993, by filing suit against EPA in the U.S. District Court for the Middle District of North Carolina, in Winston-Salem, in the heart of cigarette manufacturing country. The Big Two tobacco companies, Philip Morris and RJ Reynolds, jointly filed suit, accompanied by a motley assortment of tobacco farmers, leaf processors, and distributors of tobacco. The suit charged inter alia, that "EPA's classification of ETS as a Group A carcinogen was capricious, violative of the procedures required by law, and unconstitutional." The industry sought a permanent injunction requiring EPA to withdraw its decision of January 7, 1993, and the accompanying risk assessment [U.S. District Court, 1993]. Leaving nothing to chance, the industry had shopped for a compliant federal judge, and found the perfect instrument in one William L. Osteen, in Winston-Salem, North Carolina, the home of R.J. Reynolds Tobacco. In 1974, Osteen, then a private attorney in Greensboro, N.C., had served as a paid lobbyist for tobacco farmers. In that capacity he had lobbied then Agriculture Secretary Earl Butz to drop a plan to end federal price supports for tobacco. Judge Osteen would not disappoint. The fix was in.

The Osteen Ploy was not the only arrow in the industry's quiver. Philip Morris also founded a front group called The Advancement of Sound Science Coalition (TASSC) to advocate "sound science in public policy decision making." To give TASSC a patina of legitimacy to cover the underlying dross of corruption, it recruited the Chemical Manufacturers Association, and organizations from the food, plastics, and chemical companies as allies. Philip Morris's actual intent was "to discredit the EPA Report, and to promote a risk assessment standard *that would ignore epidemiological studies whose relative risks were less than 2.0,* which would automatically discredit the vast majority of environmental risk assessment studies as "not worth worrying about" [Davis, 2002].

Then Philip Morris trotted out Tom Bliley, The Congressman From Philip Morris, the ranking minority member of the House Oversight and Investigations Subcommittee, their reliable water-boy. Bliley unleashed yet another vituperative blast at the EPA, based upon his "extensive investigation of the EPA's handling of the controversy surrounding environmental tobacco smoke or 'ETS'." Bliley asserted that, "in its consideration of ETS, the Agency has deliberately abused and manipulated the scientific data in order to reach a predetermined, politically motivated result. EPA's risk assessment on ETS released in January of this year claims that ETS exposure is responsible for approximately 3,000 lung cancer cases per year in the United States. Analysis of the risk assessment reveals, however, that EPA was able to reach that conclusion only by ignoring or discounting major studies, and by deviating from generally accepted scientific standards." Bliley had benefitted from $23,000 in tobacco PAC money during the previous election cycle, which made him the second highest receiver of tobacco money in the House of Representatives.

On July 21, 1993, Bliley testified before the House Committee on Energy and Commerce – Health and Environment Subcommittee. Bliley's vengeful statement is condensed in Appendix A. This 35-page diatribe, without a doubt ghost-written for Bliley by the Tobacco Institute and edited by his minion Schlagenhauf, was filled with venom and bile against EPA, and he singled out Yours Truly for especial mention (Steven Bayard and Stan Glantz were also disparaged). Bliley's assault was clearly designed with the intent to show that I, single-handedly, had manipulated the entire EPA, from the top down, to serve my "personal anti-smoking agenda." This gave no credit whatsoever to independent thinking by top EPA management and scientific professionals across the agency who had reviewed our ETS work product and signed off on it. Nor did he mention the numerous external reviewers. Insofar as the very real irregularities in contracting out the policy guide to the Smoking Policy Institute, this was Axelrad's blunder returning like a boomerang to whack him upside his head. In this he richly deserved every last bit of the slime that Bliley heaped on him. And it would not be soon forgotten by his embarrassed EPA bosses who got besmirched in the process. He had committed the unforgivable sin. Insofar as the Office of Technology Assessment's 1986 criticism of Repace and Lowrey's work, which Bliley cited in his diatribe, a review of what they actually did say is instructive:

"A number of researchers, including, notably, Repace and Lowrey and their colleagues, over the years, have documented the significant contribution of environmental tobacco smoke to indoor air pollution in studies in enclosed spaces (summarized in Repace and Lowrey, New York State Journal of Medicine paper,1985). Some of Repace and Lowrey's assumptions are inappropriate. In particular, in the method yielding the higher number, they assumed that the entire difference between the lung cancer death rate in a group of nonsmoking Seventh Day Adventists and in a group of nonsmoking (non-Seventh Day Adventist) Southern Californians was attributable to passive smoking At best, one can conclude that some part of the difference between the two populations may be due to differences in passive smoking rates, but the assumption that it is reasonable to attribute the entire difference to passive smoking is unjustified. The effect of these and other flaws on the final estimates calls into question the reliability of either of these numbers."

OTA's 1986 criticism was a little different from that of Herman Gibb's, who was supportive of the low-end estimate. The second problem with OTA's comment was that they apparently failed to understand that the low-end estimate was derived by a completely different method, and any error in the SDA method had no bearing at all on the one-hit model of extrapolation from the risks in smokers. Bliley's attack ignored our 1990 risk assessment paper in *Risk Analysis*, which summarized nine other risk assessments published in the peer-reviewed literature, and it also ignored the fact that EPA's 1992 risk assessment, done by professionals using very different methods, and at a time when there was far more data available, all of whom had reached nearly the same conclusions we had. Aside from that, the published criticism of our work that Bliley cited [his reference 15] as coming from "other scientific articles" was all from the industry's moles. Nevertheless, Bliley's rant in the Congressional Record surely did not escape EPA's notice. Without a doubt, it must have made Axelrad even more paranoid about my ETS activities than ever. On August 13, 1992, I received yet another memorandum on the subject of "Journal Articles," this time from my Section Chief, John Girman, reiterating Axelrad's fiat of March 1990. It read in part:

"I want to re-emphasize some points we discussed in our phone conversation on August 11. I was surprised to learn that you had submitted a paper on a public health standard for ETS to JAMA. Either Bob or I should have been informed well in advance of such a submission. Specifically, I remind you that the memo Bob A. wrote to you on May 18, 1990 directs you 'to ensure that your association with EPA does not appear and is not communicated in any way in any forum in which you speak or are published on the subject of environmental tobacco smoke unless you are specifically requested or authorized to speak or write on the subject by [Bob].' You have failed to do so in this instance. You should have informed Bob, in advance, that you planned to write a paper on ETS and submit it to a journal. Informing him of your actions after acceptance by the journal would not be acceptable."

To restate the directions provided in Bob's May 18, 1990 memo to you, at the time you begin planning to write a paper which would entail the use of government time, equipment or resources, or would list or imply any association with EPA, you are to provide Bob with a written notice about the paper. This written notice shall also include a brief description of the paper, where it would be submitted, and the anticipated date of submission. Prior to submission, a copy of the draft shall be given to Bob for review [Girman, 1992]."

The "public health standard for ETS" actually was submitted to *Risk Analysis,* not *JAMA*, and I had no intention whatsoever of allowing Axelrad to prevent it from being written or published, which was surely his intent. Moreover, I had become extremely suspicious of Axelrad's true motivation. I loathed and distrusted him. I took the path of least resistance by simply ignoring Girman's jab, just as I had ignored Axelrad's original blivet. If I had leaked either memo to the press, it would have blown up in Axelrad's face. But I just didn't need any distraction from my work, and I had no grudge against Girman. This turned out to be a fortuitous decision. As it turned out, our proposed indoor air quality standard for ETS would not be published until 1993, when I would no longer be serving in the Indoor Air Division.

When EPA's Risk Assessment of ETS was finally issued in late December 1992, Lowrey and I considered that we had hit a home run. EPA's professional risk assessors, using widely accepted professional methodology, came up with essentially the same results that we had arrived at using our quite different ad hoc methods in our 1985 ETS Risk Assessment paper. In an unanticipated bonus, EPA's ETS Risk Assessment gave our risk assessment quite a different reading than the OTA had: In Chapter 6, it stated:

"Repace and Lowrey (1985) suggest two methods to quantify lung cancer risk associated with ETS. One method is based on epidemiologic data, but, unlike the previous examples,

Repace and Lowrey use a study comparing Seventh-Day Adventists (SDAs) (Phillips et al., 1980a,b) with a demographically and educationally matched group of non-SDAs who are also never-smokers to obtain estimates of the relative risk of lung cancer mortality, in what they describe as a 'phenomenological' approach. The SDA/non-SDA comparison provides a basis for assessing lung cancer risk from ETS in a broader environment, particularly outside the home, than the other epidemiologic studies. It also serves as an independent source of data and an alternative approach for comparison.

Information regarding the number of age-specific LCDs [lung cancer deaths] and person-years at risk for the two cohorts is obtained from the study. The basis for comparison of the two groups is the premise that the non-SDA cohort is more likely to be exposed to ETS than the SDA group due to differences in lifestyle. Relatively few SDAs smoke, so an SDA never-smoker is probably less likely to be exposed at home by a smoking spouse, in the workplace, or elsewhere, if associations are predominantly with other SDAs. One of the virtues of this novel approach is that it contributes to the variety of evidence for evaluation and provides a new perspective on the topic."

I Escape The Indoor Air Division

Meanwhile, I had become fed up to my *schnozzole* with Axelrad's continual abuse. In early 1993, I managed a mutually agreeable temporary transfer, or "detail," in federal parlance, to the Exposure Assessment Branch of the Office of Research and Development, where I happily worked on exposure assessment of electromagnetic fields (EMF) and a person's internal radon dose from drinking radioactive well water from aquifers in radium-bearing soils. In approaching my study of EMF, I borrowed a portable data-logging electromagnetic field monitor, carrying it around with me for 24 hours, keeping a diary of my locations and time. Surprisingly, the digital electric clock next to my bed at night was the highest EMF exposure I received, *ten times* higher than the exposure directly beneath the 500 kilovolt power lines a half mile from my home. This called into question some of the epidemiological studies of cancers due to power line exposure. I contributed this data to an interagency guidance report on electromagnetic field exposures. I enjoyed the work, and best of all, I had supportive management, and didn't have to report to the odious Axelrad. I remained working in Crystal City in Arlington, Virginia, and the Indoor Air Division continued to pay my salary. It was a nice location, adjacent to a bike trail that ran from Roosevelt Island to Mount Vernon along the Potomac. I biked it daily during my lunch hour.

In 1988, I had given a paper at the Healthy Buildings '88 Conference in Stockholm arguing that indoor air quality standards were needed. This inspired me to begin work on developing an indoor air quality standard for ETS based on nicotine, the pre-eminent atmospheric marker for tobacco smoke. In order to accomplish this, I had to understand the pharmacokinetics of nicotine and its metabolite cotinine in the human body. I was initially helped by discussions with Jean Parker, a branch chief in EPA's Carcinogen Assessment Group, who was also a sick building refugee from Waterside Mall. Jean had been exiled to a private office on the 5th floor of our Crystal City building. I naively decided to go to the Georgetown University medical school bookstore to purchase some of the texts that Jean had suggested. When I arrived, I was completely overwhelmed with the vast number of medical books on display from wall-to-wall. I had absolutely no idea on where to find them. I realized that unless I had help I would leave empty-handed.

Suddenly I saw a young woman who looked like a medical student, and in a moment of inspiration, I said, "excuse me, but I'm a dumb physicist, and I would like to learn how to do pharmacokinetic modeling. However, I have no clue on what books I might need to buy. Can you possibly help me?" She said nothing, just grabbed me by the arm and led me around the enormous racks of books. One by one, she piled my arms high with a stack of books, including tomes on Clinical Pharmacokinetics, Respiration and Circulation, and the ABC's of Interpretive Laboratory Data. I profusely thanked her. They cost me a well-spent $300. Over the course of a year I pored over these textbooks and collected numerous research papers on nicotine and cotinine metabolism.

The EPA technical library, as usual, was a godsend in obtaining the reprints I needed to draft my new paper. The paper, titled "An Enforceable Indoor Air Quality Standard for Environmental Tobacco Smoke in the Workplace," co-authored with Al Lowrey, had 73 references, and was published in *Risk Analysis* (Repace and Lowrey, 1993). This paper did a number of things that had never been done before: it defined a dose-response relationship between atmospheric nicotine and cotinine in body fluids from secondhand smoke and lung cancer. I also developed a model to predict the range and average levels of the nicotine metabolite, cotinine, from passive smoking by nonsmokers in the U.S. population at large. This allowed us to conclude that for a substantial fraction of the 59 million nonsmoking workers in the U.S. workforce in 1993, current workplace exposure to ETS posed risks exceeding the *de manifestis* risk level above which carcinogens are strictly regulated by the federal government. And although we did not spell it out in this 1993 paper, it laid the groundwork for quantitatively relating levels of nicotine in air and cotinine in saliva, blood, and urine to OSHA's *significant risk* level. However, the implications for OSHA regulation of secondhand smoke would not be lost on Big Tobacco. And in fact, I was already thinking about how to do exactly that. It would culminate in a second paper in 1998.

The 1993 paper set the stage for a major public denunciation of me by Philip Morris that would be played out on the national stage at the U.S. Department of Labor, and involve numerous players from the passive smoking research community, plus Tom Bliley and Henry Waxman in Congress, the national press, several federal agencies, the White House, Philip Morris, R.J. Reynolds, a half-dozen RJR scientists, a pack of industry moles, and enough tobacco industry and trial lawyers at each other's throats to fill a crowded theatre. This would prove to be the most exciting time of my entire federal career.

Dr. Ron Davis, now editor of *Tobacco Control*, asked me to review a book, "*The Chemistry of Environmental Tobacco Smoke: Composition and Measurement*," authored by the Oak Ridge tobacco group, Guerin, Jenkins, and Thompson. It was funded by the CIAR as a "special project." My review concluded that the book was "a valuable compendium of useful information for ETS researchers. However, for those not intimately familiar with the ETS literature, particularly the reports of IARC, the National Research Council, the Surgeon General, and the EPA, the bias introduced by heavy reliance on tobacco industry research makes uncritical use of some of the conclusions in the book risky" (Repace, 1993). Nevertheless, in the following year, the Oak Ridge book would serve the disinformation needs of the tobacco industry very well indeed.

In 1992, industry consultant Larry Holcomb was still shamelessly beating Big Tobacco's drum on ETS in aircraft. He published a patently ridiculous review of the impact of ETS on indoor air quality in which he brazenly and moronically asserted that "ETS is a 'scapegoat for other pollutants on aircraft simply because of its high visibility,' a familiar and ludicrous industry theme that only a shameless bozo could argue with a straight face. In 1992, a week before the International Civil Aviation Organization was to meet in Montreal to consider, inter alia, a proposed ban on smoking on international flights, an editor for *Business Traveler,* a U.K. international travel magazine, authored an article which appeared in the *Globe and Mail,* Canada's national newspaper. It asserted that "the jury was still out on cabin smoke", and compared the harmful effects of tobacco smoke on aircraft to "excessive application of perfume or overindulgence in garlic." In the article, Holcomb was quoted and falsely described as "an adviser to the U.S. Government." The material upon which the article was based turned out to have been supplied by a U.K. tobacco industry consultant, and also contained disinformation from technical articles published by other tobacco industry moles in the U.S. and Australia. [Holcomb, 1988; Globe and Mail, 1992; G. Mahood, personal communication].

Naturally, no mention was made of the Dec. 1989 DOT report on the airliner cabin environment, that concluded that unrestricted smoking on aircraft "caused an estimated 14 premature lung cancer deaths per year in a flight attendant workforce of 85,000," and that "a total ban on smoking would provide the greatest benefit at the least cost."

THE WILEY CASE BEGINS

In 1993, while on still on detail to ORD's Exposure Assessment Branch, I received a call from a small law firm in Indianapolis concerning a nonsmoking nurse, Mildred Wiley, who had died from lung cancer. She had been exposed to ETS in the workplace over the course of her career at the Veteran's Administration (VA) hospital in Marion, Indiana, a facility for veterans with psychiatric disorders. Her husband, also a nonsmoker, had filed suit, *Dunn & Wiley vs. RJR et al.*, against the tobacco companies. I was contacted by Max Howard, the attorney for the plaintiff, and asked to provide expert advice on the case. In June, I took leave and flew out to Indianapolis, presented a slide lecture on passive smoking to educate the firm's attorneys, visited the hospital ward where Nurse Wiley had worked, took photos, and interviewed her former nursing colleagues. By 1993, the VA had banned smoking in its hospitals, and there was a large pile of discarded cigarette butts on the ground outside the main entrance to the building, a testament to the continuing pervasiveness of smoking.

Nurse Mildred Edna Wiley was born on September 26, 1934. She was diagnosed with terminal lung cancer on May 29, 1991, and died on June 24, 1991, at the age of 56. Considering that Ms. Wiley had never smoked and grew up in a smoke-free home, and that the fatal lung cancer probability for a 56-year old nonsmoking white woman was 7 in 100,000, her death should have been a very low probability event. This suggested that her workplace exposure must have been egregious. The Wiley case presented the following risk assessment problem: what was the probability that Nurse Wiley died from an ETS-induced lung cancer death due to workplace exposure at the VA hospital? My methodology posited that her risk was the product of three factors: the estimated lifetime average concentration of ETS to which she was exposed; the exposure-response relationship relating ETS exposure to the probability of lung cancer death that I had published; plus the duration of her exposure. The hospital staff estimated that a whopping 80% to 95% of the patients smoked and that 50% to 80% of the staff smoked. The 1992 US adult smoking prevalence was 25.6%, so the ward smoking prevalence was *triple* the national average. I measured the volume of each floor where she had worked and estimated the air exchange rate of the building in summer and winter. The building had operable windows, but no mechanical ventilation system.

From these parameters, I estimated that the smoke concentration in the ward of Building 16 ranged from 500 to 2500 $\mu g/m^3$, enormously high values. This calculation was consistent with testimony of a half-dozen of Nurse Wiley's co-workers whom I interviewed. For example: "it would take a long time to clear out all that smoke so you can see without a fog being above your head or down to your head." "Most of the time [the day room] was always smoke-filled ... a lot of times it was blue with smoke;" " No matter where you went in the hospital it was smoke, and more in the day rooms, ... It was bad; I mean it was bad in there." "Q. How would you describe the ... amount of smoke in the buildings of the VA Hospital?" A. "They were all bad, but [building] 16 was particularly bad ... ." To make matters worse, the nurses were required to hold cigarettes for disabled patients who couldn't hold them. This obscene practice was called "smoking the patients." So the nurses would be enveloped in a choking cloud of exhaled mainstream and sidestream tobacco smoke at ground zero. Nurse Wiley was exposed like this for 18 long years.

Using the exposure-response model derived in the 1985 risk assessment of Repace and Lowrey to calculate her risk, I estimated that the probability that Nurse Mildred Wiley died of lung cancer from her exposure to passive smoking on the job at the VA Hospital ranged from 70% to 94%. This case was a prime example of just how bad some workplace exposures could get. Furthermore, it was an illustration of how useful the models I had developed would be to justify workplace bans on secondhand smoke, as well as to achieve some measure of justice for workers injured or killed from tobacco smoke pollution of their workplaces. The Wiley case would not come to trial until 1998, when it would be taken over by trial lawyer Ron Motley's law firm, Ness Motley, in Louisiana.

CALIFORNIA, HERE I COME

In October of 1992, I was invited by the Office of Environmental Health Hazard Assessment (OEHHA) of the California Environmental Protection Agency to lecture on the Exposure and Dosimetry of Passive Smoking. I followed that up with invited testimony on risk assessment of passive smoking at the Public Hearing on Passive Smoking held by The California EPA. I lectured on the pharmacokinetics of nicotine and cotinine in passive smoking at the Dept. of Cardiology, University of California, San Francisco. Finally, I spoke on passive smoking and the nonsmoker at the Dept. of Civil & Environmental Engineering at Stanford University. The historian Robert Proctor was in the audience, and we chatted briefly afterward. In addition, I presented a chalk talk to Wayne Ott and Paul Switzer in Stanford's Department of Statistics discussing my measurements of secondhand smoke in the early 1980's. Wayne had retired from the Public Health Service and was now a Visiting Scholar in the Department of Statistics at Stanford. I had assisted Wayne in his successful quest for research funding from California's Tobacco-Related Disease Program, and he had developed a model that predicted RSP and carbon monoxide from ETS in real time. Switzer was Chair of the Statistics Department, but he also moonlighted as a statistical consultant for the tobacco industry. He had testified at the same OEHHA Public Hearing that I had, at the request of the tobacco industry, on risk assessment of passive smoking. After my Oakland testimony, Switzer had come up to me in the hall, and remarked that the tobacco people who had arranged for him to appear at the OEHHA Hearing and critique the epidemiology of passive smoking told him that I was a "flaming zealot." He said that he was surprised to see that my presentation was "so level headed and scientific." Switzer had a foot in both camps: he was doing admirable work with Wayne on measuring exposure to secondhand smoke and devising models to predict the levels, but at the same time, he also had been retained by the tobacco interests to critique the US EPA's Risk Assessment of passive smoking, and then OSHA's risk assessments in 1993, as well as the California EPA's ETS fact finding which would lead five years later to CalEPA's own risk assessment. On balance, I felt that Paul Switzer's ETS work with Wayne far outweighed his ETS efforts for the industry in importance.

CHAPTER 13
BIG TOBACCO SANDBAGS OSHA

"It is particularly ironic that Philip Morris, the largest domestic cigarette manufacturer, a billion dollar per year industrial giant who has until recently dominated the submissions to OSHA and the questioning of witnesses at the hearings, now feigns concern over the objectivity and fairness of the OSHA process. Philip Morris has spent millions in opposing this rule, both through an extensive advertising campaign, its massive written submissions and letter writing campaign which have flooded OSHA's docket office, and through the active and lengthy cross-examinations of those who spoke in favor of the proposed rule. Now, ostensibly because they want fairness and a full and complete record, they have chosen not to testify because they don't want to be submitted to the same rigors they inflicted on others."

[TTID 2046395331; Letter from Ronald L. Motley, Ness Motley, Loadholt, Richardson & Poole, to the Hon. John Vittone, Administrative Law Judge, U.S. Department of Labor, Dec. 12, 1994]

In late 1986, I had been contacted by Public Citizen, a Washington-based public interest organization. In the wake of the 1986 Reports of the Surgeon General and the NAS on secondhand smoke, they decided the time was ripe to petition OSHA to regulate smoking in the workplace and requested reprints of my scientific papers to support their efforts. Although skeptical that OSHA would be responsive to such a request, I gladly supplied copies. In May 1987, the Public Citizen Health Research Group and the American Public Health Association jointly filed the petition, asking OSHA to promulgate an Emergency Temporary Standard to prohibit smoking in indoor workplaces. In support of its petition, Public Citizen submitted four reports on passive smoking to OSHA: the 1986 Reports of the Surgeon General (SG), the National Academy of Sciences (NAS), the Office of Technology Assessment (OTA), and the Repace and Lowrey 1985 risk assessment. In response, OSHA contracted with Meridian Research, a private consulting firm, to provide a review of these reports.

The OTA report, *Passive Smoking in the Workplace: Selected Issues,* issued in May 1986, had not attempted to estimate risk. Rather, it focused on reviewing the existing epidemiological studies of health effects, describing the workplace smoking policies in effect in the government and private sectors, and discussing the factors that might govern the costs and benefits of developing workplace smoking policies. As discussed earlier, when Bliley had raised the issue, OTA also had commented favorably on our 1980 Science paper but with respect to our 1985 risk assessment paper, they had echoed the same criticism that Herman Gibb had voiced in 1984 on the latter. However, OTA did not mention Scott Weiss's favorable review of our risk assessment in the *American Review of Respiratory Diseases* published just three months earlier, in January 1986.

OTA observed that three agencies were responsible for 90% of all federal workplaces: the General Services Administration (GSA), the Department of Defense (DOD), and the Postal Service. While GSA had banned smoking in conference rooms, auditoriums, and elevators, it did not require open offices to be nonsmoking. DOD, which employed 1 million civilians and 2 million military, had prohibited smoking in conference rooms, classrooms, and auditoriums since 1977, and had permitted smoking in shared work areas "only if the ventilation is adequate," without defining what "adequate" meant. The Postal Service prohibited smoking in public areas and in the mail rooms but did not spell out policies for office areas. The Veteran's Administration (VA), which was responsible for 172 medical centers and 225 clinics had prohibited smoking in its medical centers in 1986, but still permitted smoking areas in waiting rooms and dining rooms and allowed patients whose doctors approved to be escorted to a designated smoking area.

OTA reported that since 1983, seven states and 70-plus communities regulated smoking in either public or private sectors. These were mere fractions of the total that did not. OTA noted that two recent surveys of private-sector workplace smoking policies had been conducted, one by the Office of Disease Prevention and Health Promotion in the U.S. Department of Health and Human Services (DHHS) and the other by a consulting firm hired by the Tobacco Institute. According to OTA, these surveys found that approximately 32 percent of workplaces with more than 750 employees and 36 percent of large corporations had smoking policies. The government survey also showed that "27 percent of all worksites with 50 or more employees have some form of smoking policy, and that the primary purpose of 40 percent of these policies was to 'protect nonsmokers'." OTA concluded that the majority of Americans supported the adoption of workplace smoking policies. And that protecting the 67 percent of the workforce who were nonsmokers had become a principal reason for the development of such workplace policies.

The Meridian Report described the SG's conclusions concerning the health effects of ETS exposure; the chemistry of ETS and the exposures of nonsmokers; the deposition and absorption of tobacco smoke constituents; plus the toxicity, acute irritant effects, and carcinogenicity of ETS as well as policies restricting smoking in public places and the workplace. It reported that the SG had stressed that, although the risks of passive smoking were "smaller than the risks of active smoking, the number of individuals injured by involuntary smoking is large both in absolute terms and in comparison with the number injured by some other agents in the general environment that are regulated to curtail their potential to cause human illness."

Further wrote Meridian, the SG had opined that "The extent of nonsmokers' exposure to ETS is highly variable among individuals at a given point in time, and little is known about the variation in exposure of the same individual at different points in time." It continued, reporting the SG report's three major findings: 1. Involuntary smoking is a cause of disease, including lung cancer, in healthy nonsmokers. 2. Compared with the children of nonsmoking parents, the children of parents who smoke have an increased frequency of respiratory infections, increased respiratory symptoms, and slightly smaller rates of increase in lung function as the lung matures. 3. The simple separation of smokers and nonsmokers within the same airspace may reduce, but does not eliminate, the exposure of nonsmokers to environmental tobacco smoke."

Meridian then compared the quantitative estimates of risk and exposure in the 1986 NRC/NAS report and by Repace and Lowrey (1985) reaching a conclusion rather different from OTA's: "Overall, the studies by Repace and Lowrey and the NRC are reasonable and thoughtful efforts that attempt to quantify the lung cancer risk of adult nonsmokers who are exposed to environmental tobacco smoke in the workplace and elsewhere. Although these two studies rely on very different approaches and data, they both estimate a similar magnitude of risk for this exposed population. Accordingly, the exposure and risk estimates presented in these studies cannot simply be dismissed." However, Meridian cautioned, there was "considerable uncertainty concerning the contribution of the workplace to nonsmokers' lung cancer risk, and that the NRC's risk estimate suggests that occupational exposure is not the primary source of exposure. This result does not agree with Repace and Lowrey's findings, which estimate that occupational exposure is the primary source of exposure to passive tobacco smoke." ... "What seems unequivocally clear at this time, however, is the need to resolve these issues by collecting data by means of personal sampling to ascertain the relative contribution of workplace exposure to a nonsmoker's overall exposure to environmental tobacco smoke from all sources." This was an excellent recommendation.

However, the anti-regulatory Reagan appointees at OSHA were cool to the notion of actually making any measurements, despite being a routine practice in OSHA's industrial hygiene investigations, and despite the fact that a template existed in the experimental work of Repace and Lowrey (1980; 1982). Justifying my initial skepticism, instead of mounting an effort to gather the missing workplace exposure data, OSHA denied both petitions, averring that "insufficient exposure information existed to demonstrate the existence of a grave danger," as the statute required. They could also have contracted it out to groups with proven expertise, such as Spengler's at Harvard. But no sale. In 1988, a new presidential election put the G.H.W. Bush administration in office, and in October 1989, ASH filed suit against OSHA requesting a review of its denial of ASH's previous petition. The Court denied ASH's petition, finding that OSHA had reasonably determined that it could not sufficiently quantify the risk to justify an emergency standard. In 1991 however, the new Bush appointees at OSHA issued a Request for Information (RFI) on workplace indoor air quality (IAQ) problems. They decided to combine tobacco smoke together with other indoor air issues, reportedly at the request of the AFL-CIO labor union. The purpose of the RFI was to obtain information necessary for a determination of whether regulatory action was required. Individuals, groups, unions, and industries submitted a total of 1200 comments. Many commenters felt that regulation was necessary to eliminate exposures to ETS in the workplace (OSHA, 1994). In March 1992, hard on the heels of the EPA Risk Assessment of Passive Smoking, the AFL-CIO petitioned OSHA to promulgate an overall IAQ Standard. Finally, following the election of Bill Clinton in November 1992, the new leadership U.S. Department of Labor made the decision to accelerate to a proposed rule.

Almost a year later, in the Fall of 1993, I received a call from Debra Janes, an epidemiologist in OSHA's Health Standards Promulgation Branch, inviting me to a meeting in which R.J. Reynolds scientists would make a presentation on ETS research to OSHA staff. Unlike Philip Morris, whose scientists were kept under lock-and-key, RJR scientists were encouraged to publish their ETS research in peer-reviewed journals. Actually, these publications contained useful data if read carefully by an expert, but it was obvious to me that their conclusions were carefully wordsmithed to be intentionally misleading. In fact, those conclusions generally were reliable guides as to what was NOT true.

I attended the meeting, at which two of RJR's scientists presented elaborate models involving partial differential equations that they used to predict nicotine and cotinine levels in every part of the human body, from head to toe. This was a red flag, suggesting that the industry had developed sophisticated PBPK (physiologically-based pharmacokinetic) models that could accurately predict the rapidity and amount of inhaled nicotine delivered to the brain, and hence titrate the desired nicotine "hit" in the desired time. This led me to another epiphany: *the tobacco industry was actually a rogue branch of the pharmaceutical industry.* David Kessler's Food and Drug Administration (FDA) would come to the same realization in 1994, based on its review of industry patents and a confidential industry informant aptly code-named "Deep Cough" (Kessler, 2001).

In their presentation, RJR scientists asserted that inhaled nicotine from secondhand smoke was not a reliable atmospheric marker for ETS; that there was no fixed relationship between RSP and nicotine as atmospheric markers for ETS, and that cotinine was not a reliable biomarker for ETS. My exposure models, together with experiments at Yale by Leaderer and Hammond on nicotine and RSP in the early 1980's, coupled with cotinine studies by Neal Benowitz at the University of California, as well as by Martin Jarvis at University College in London suggested otherwise. Reynolds' assertions pegged my bullshit detector at 100%. Their OSHA presentation was a case study in scientific disinformation. In support of their contention on the unreliability of atmospheric ETS markers, the Reynolds scientists showed a slide plotting RSP from

ETS against nicotine from ETS from a chamber study using smokers of the top 50 U.S. Brands of cigarettes; at first blush it looked like the side of a barn hit by buckshot from a distance of 30 feet and conveyed the instant impression that there was no RSP-nicotine correlation. At my request, they supplied copies of their presentation to OSHA. When I examined the hard copy of their slides, I noticed a peculiarity in the plot: *the RSP and nicotine were not plotted to the same scale, and the origin of the graph was suppressed.*

This made me curious as to what the data looked like when plotted to the same scale. The following weekend I digitized the data by hand using a neat graphic technique Joe Dresner had taught me at RCA. When plotted to the same scale, the RJR data displayed a very narrow range of nicotine emissions, averaging about 1.8 milligrams per cigarette and a broader range for RSP, averaging 13.8 milligrams per cigarette, similar to the results found earlier by Leaderer and Hammond (1991). My analysis of their data, which was not sales-weighted, showed a mean RSP/Nicotine ratio of about 8:1 averaged over the 50 brands. Sales-weighting emissions is important because in 1994, the big two tobacco companies accounted for 72% of cigarette sales: Philip Morris with 45%, and RJ Reynolds with 27% (Maxwell, 1996). By comparison, Leaderer and Hammond (1991) reported an RSP/Nicotine ratio of 9.8:1 for week-long measurements of 47 New York State residences occupied by smokers, with a high degree of statistical correlation (coefficient of determination, $r^2 = 0.64$).

I then recalled that the technique of creating a misleading impression by plotting the ordinate and the abscissa of a graph to two different scales and then suppressing the origin had been discussed extensively in Chapter 5 of Darrell Huff's wonderful little book, *How To Lie With Statistics.* After I showed my analysis of Reynold's misleading graph to Debra, she immediately asked me if I would consider coming over to OSHA on loan from EPA to help them with their rulemaking. I was over the moon. Because Axelrad was as anxious to be rid of me as I was of him, he readily agreed to pay my salary while I was detailed to OSHA. I showed up at the Labor Department building in early January 1994. My new boss was Sheldon Weiner, a gray-bearded physicist who was Chief of OSHA's Health Standards Promulgation Branch. The cerebral Sheldon was a welcome breath of fresh air, the exact opposite of Axelrad, whom I regarded as a pompous blowhard. He assigned me to the Indoor Air Team, led by epidemiologist Debra Janes.

In addition to Debra, OSHA's Team included Susan Sherman, the lead Labor Department lawyer, her associate, Susan Kaplan, Demetra Collia, a biostatistician, Lee Hathon, a ventilation engineer, Surender Ahir, a toxicologist, Saneya El-Mekawi and Edward Stern, both economists, Ken Stevanus, a mechanical engineer, and Long Loo, a safety engineer. Debra introduced me to this multidisciplinary group, who comprised a veritable league of nations. As an expat New Yorker, I felt very much at home with this multi-ethnic crew of colleagues. Introducing myself as a physicist who worked on indoor air pollution and secondhand smoke, I announced that I was on loan from Bob Axelrad's shop at EPA. Debra raised her eyebrows and carefully informed me that, "We know who he is, but we call him Bob *Axelhole.*" Smiling, I responded, "I see you're quite familiar with his outstanding personality." Axelrad's arrogance, braggadocio and hubris did not win him many admirers, at EPA or other federal agencies. Worse for him, his rabbi, Eileen Claussen, would depart later that year, leaving Axelrad's engine of political support at EPA running on fumes.

When I first met the gray-bearded physicist, Sheldon Weiner, PhD, Director of OSHA's Office of Standards Analysis and Promulgation, he complained that Labor Department Officials, from the Secretary of Labor on down, had given him a mere three months to draft a complex regulatory rule-making on both Indoor Air Quality (IAQ) and Environmental Tobacco Smoke (ETS) in the workplace, which he felt was impossible. He said, "OSHA has never before done a proposed rule in under a year, and I repeatedly and vigorously protested the lack of time, but was summarily overruled." I responded, "Sheldon, I've done a lot of work on both IAQ and ETS, and can help with the literature search and background write-up; I have a lot of material on floppy disk." He replied, "Fine, I'll give you two weeks to pull it together." That in turn was an outrageously short time; I said, "well, in that case, I'll need to work at home, and just come downtown for weekly staff meetings." And I did. For two solid weeks, I worked 14-hour days, pretty much seven days a week, and presented Sheldon with over 150 pages of background material on both IAQ and ETS on floppy disks. He was suitably impressed, and most of what I gave him actually wound up as content in the proposed rule in the Federal Register: The Federal Register published OSHA's proposal on April 4th, 1994; I have underlined the pertinent parts that would give Big Tobacco a terminal case of agita:

DEPARTMENT OF LABOR
Occupational Safety and Health Administration
29 CFR Parts 1910, 1915, 1926, 1928
[Docket No. H-122]
RIN 1218-AB37
Indoor Air Quality
AGENCY: Occupational Safety and Health Administration (OSHA), Labor.
ACTION: Notice of proposed rulemaking; notice of informal public hearing.

SUMMARY: By this notice, the Occupational Safety and Health Administration (OSHA) proposes to adopt standards addressing indoor air quality in indoor work environments. The basis for this proposed action is a preliminary determination that employees working in indoor work environments face a significant risk of material impairment to their health due to poor indoor air quality, and that compliance with the provisions proposed in this notice will substantially reduce that risk.

The provisions of the standard are proposed to apply to all indoor 'nonindustrial work environments.' In addition, all worksites, both industrial and nonindustrial within OSHA's jurisdiction are covered with respect to the proposed provisions addressing control of environmental tobacco smoke. The proposal would require affected employers to develop a written indoor air quality compliance plan and implement that plan through actions such as inspection and maintenance of building systems which influence indoor air quality.

Provisions under the standard also propose to require employers to implement controls for specific contaminants and their sources such as outdoor air contaminants, microbial contamination, maintenance and cleaning chemicals, pesticides, and other hazardous chemicals within indoor work environments. Designated smoking areas which are to be separate, enclosed rooms exhausted directly to the outside are proposed to be required in buildings where the smoking of tobacco products is not prohibited. Specific provisions are also proposed to limit the degradation of indoor air quality during the performance of renovation, remodeling and similar activities.

Provisions for information and training of building system maintenance and operation workers and other employees within the facility are also included in this notice. Finally, proposed provisions in this notice address the establishment, retention, availability, and transfer of records such as inspection and maintenance records, records of written compliance programs, and employee complaints of building-related illness.

The Agency invites the submission of written data, views and comments on all regulatory provisions proposed in this notice, and on all relevant issues pertinent to those provisions.

OSHA is also scheduling an informal public hearing where persons may orally submit their views. It is noted here that subsequent **Federal Register** notices may be published subsequent to this notice, if the public presents views leading to a substantial change in focus or it is otherwise determined to be appropriate.

OSHA's next step was to designate potential expert witnesses on secondhand smoke and indoor air quality to defend the proposed rule. As few members of our Indoor Air Quality (IAQ) Team passed on recommendations for suitable ETS witnesses, I nominated several experts by default, since I knew them by reputation as well as personally. These included Dr. Neal Benowitz, Stan Glantz, Kathie Hammond, Dr. Jonathan Samet, and Jud Wells. After the proposed IAQ Standard was publicized, and before the fall hearings, there was a "brown-bag" lunch with Joseph Dear, the Assistant Secretary of Labor for OSHA, to which the IAQ Team was invited, and Steven Bayard from EPA attended as well. Steven and I took the empty chairs flanking Dear at the conference table. Out of the blue, Steven asked Dear why the Department of Labor had not banned smoking in its buildings, as EPA had done several years earlier (at my instigation – I had drafted a memo for the Assistant Administrator, which was circulated among all EPA offices and approved, circa 1987). Dear replied that the unions had to approve, and they would likely object.

I chimed in that I had done several labor arbitrations where both government and private sector unions had protested similar restrictions, and I cited the case of AFGE/AFLCIO vs. U.S. Department of Health & Human Services (DHHS), in which the union had objected to DHHS's building-wide smoking ban, issued in May 1987, provoking a protest and an administrative hearing which the union had lost. This was the hearing before an Administrative Law Judge, on March 2, 1988, in Washington, DC, where Surgeon General Koop and I testified on behalf of DHHS. Dear was swayed by our arguments, and soon afterward the Department of Labor restricted smoking in its buildings. Later, our Indoor Air Team received two awards, for producing a viable proposed rule within the incredibly short time allotted: OSHA's Impact Award, and the Labor Secretary's Excellence Award from the U.S. Dept. of Labor, during a pizza party attended by Robert Reich and Joseph Dear in Secretary Reich's office. Figure 17 shows the official Labor Department photo of the IAQ team with Reich on the occasion of our Team's Award for producing the proposed rule. The short time period allotted for the proposal should have been taken as a warning sign of trouble ahead, but that was very far from our minds at this stage.

WHACKING MOLES IN THE MOSH PIT

In May 1994, I testified by invitation at the Maryland OSHA (MOSH) hearings on a proposal by the State Department of Licensing and Regulation to prohibit smoking in enclosed workplaces. It had been proposed under the MOSH Act by the Commissioner of the Division of Labor and Industry for the purpose of protecting Maryland workers from the hazards of ETS exposure. It relied on scientific studies that established ETS as a cause of lung cancer and coronary heart disease in non-smoking adults as well as those that cited the workplace as being a significant source of exposure to ETS. Significantly, The MOSH Act, enacted in 1973, was patterned after the federal OSH Act of 1970 and many of the provisions in the two acts were substantially the same.

Interestingly, in February 1994, The McDonald's hamburger chain had announced that all of its wholly owned fast food outlets would ban smoking immediately. Contemporaneously, the National Council of Chain Restaurants announced that 30,000 U.S. chain restaurants had already banned smoking and backed a bill to end smoking in all restaurants used by the public. As we shall see, these voluntary bans were a consequence of the quantification of risk by the EPA Report. The regulatory response by MOSH was another. In response, Brennan Dawson, a spokeswoman for the Tobacco Institute, denounced the restaurant group, saying "These people really have overstepped their bounds, and are trying to decide what is best for everybody, from the bingo halls to every workplace in the United States" (NY Times, 1994). So MOSH's proposal was not some wild-eyed scheme to deprive Maryland restaurant owners of their livelihood, except in the propaganda pronouncements of the industry.

The tobacco industry had major representation at the MOSH hearing. I recognized several industry consultants, including Roger Jenkins, Larry Holcomb, and Dr. Domingo Aviado among the 47 speakers. Representing the industry directly was the notorious tobacco lobbyist Bruce Bereano, a well-connected Maryland attorney who had once served in the State legislature. He was a fixture in testifying against restrictions on tobacco (he remains at it today). Bereano had been convicted that year of federal mail-fraud charges related to his private law practice, but that did not deter Big Tobacco one whit, and might have even made him more attractive to them. He was their kind of guy. I testified in support of the legislation in general but disparaged the provision for designated separately ventilated smoking areas on the grounds that testing by the State of California had shown that even well-designed rooms leaked smoke into nonsmoking areas.

I also denigrated the Tobacco Institute's submission criticizing the State's efforts to restrict smoking in the workplace as well as the industry's critique of my previous testimony in an earlier hearing. The attacks on my testimony were authored by both Larry Holcomb and Simon Turner of Healthy Buildings International (HBI). One of the pillars of the industry's argument was that in order to regulate ETS in the workplace, the State had to demonstrate that there was "significant risk of material impairment of health," i.e., a risk greater than 1 death per thousand workers per 45-year working lifetime. This was precisely the same argument that the industry intended to pursue in the upcoming federal OSHA hearings. I observed that by my calculations, the risk to the average restaurant worker was more than ten times OSHA's significant risk level.

I also gave Roger Jenkins' submitted testimony a knock, noting that his Oak Ridge/RJR study population was not representative of the workforce's ETS exposure, since it was weighted heavily with women of high socioeconomic status, who were more likely to have private offices with much decreased potential for workplace ETS exposure than the average female worker. I noted that Aviado didn't appear to understand that when calculating whether a mixture of toxic substances violated OSHA's significant risk level, a special weighting formula that incorporated the risks of each compound to calculate a combined risk of exposure had to be used. Aviado's methodology involved considering the toxic substances in a mixture one-by-one and disregarding a substance if its risk alone did not exceed OSHA's Permissible Exposure Limit (PEL). In this manner, a carcinogenic mixture like tobacco smoke which contained several dozen carcinogens, could be ruled an insignificant risk.

Along with the live testimony, the Board received a substantial amount of documentary evidence, including reports from state and federal agencies, scientific studies, and 33 volumes of material from Philip Morris. On March 2, 1994, the Board recommended that smoking be prohibited in most enclosed workplaces. In a 56-page report accompanying its recommendation, the Board had relied in part on the EPA Risk Assessment issued in December 1992. Further, the Board found that ETS contributed to heart disease and was responsible for 35,000 to 40,000 heart disease deaths annually. On March 8th, the Commissioner proposed a regulation prohibiting smoking in all enclosed Maryland workplaces.

Figure 17. Labor Secretary's Award Photo. OSHA's IAQ Team, from Left-to-Right: Front Row, Susan Kaplan, Labor Secretary Robert Reich, Debra Janes, Surender Ahir, Unknown. Second row, Michael Silverstein, James Repace, Lee Hathon, Long Loo, Unknown, Demetra Collia. Third Row, Unknown, Sheldon Weiner, Unknown, Ken Stevanus. Top row, All Unknown. Susan Sherman was absent. (U.S. Dept. of Labor Photo).

In a May 9th 1994 report, Anthony Andrade of Philip Morris, and J.T. Newsome of Shook Hardy and Bacon, reported on the hearing:

"On May 3, 1994, Maryland Commissioner of Labor, Henry Koellein, Jr., held a hearing in Catonsville, Maryland, on the proposed regulation prohibiting smoking in workplaces in Maryland. Elaine Patrick, an Assistant Attorney General who serves as counsel to the Department of Labor, also participated. Ms. Patrick also participated in the earlier hearings and is believed to be the principal author of the MOSH Board's report, or at least that portion of the report that deals with legal issues. … At the beginning of the hearing, there were approximately 150 people in the audience and a total of about 50 people addressed the Commissioner; most also provided written submissions. The number of the people in the audience dwindled throughout the day. At the beginning, there were also four television crews, a radio station and some print reporters present. There was also a reporter for BNA [Bureau of National Affairs]. However, most of the reporters left before the lunch break. Commissioner Koellein did not ask any witness questions, but Elaine Patrick questioned several of the witnesses. Her questioning was fairly even-handed which is in contrast to her questioning of tobacco industry witnesses at the earlier hearings which was fairly aggressive. No questions were asked of any witness by members of the audience. …

1. **scientific:** In favor of proposal: - (1) Dr. Walter Stewart - Johns Hopkins Hospital. Dr. Stewart testified principally based on the Helsing heart disease study on the question of

whether there was a 'significant risk' from ETS in the workplace as defined by OSHA as one death in 1,000 workers. He calculated that the overall lifetime heart disease risk from ETS (men and women combined) was 21 in 1,000 workers and, therefore, even if the workplace exposure was only 1/20th of that at home it would still be one in 1,000 or a "significant risk." He also briefly indicated that the lung cancer risk is somewhat smaller. (2) Dr. Frances Stillman - Johns Hopkins University School of Medicine. Dr. Stillman testified concerning the experience they had had in banning smoking at Johns Hopkins Hospital. (3) Dr. Elizabeth Fontham - Dr. Fontham gave a fairly long and detailed presentation concerning her studies of ETS. She focused on their efforts to adjust for age, race, geographic region, occupation, etc. She concluded that the lung cancer risk ratio for non-smoking women was 1.30. Her study may have some workplace data. She said her study provided strong support for causation of lung cancer in the home and some suggestion for the workplace.

(4) James Repace. Repace responded to some earlier tobacco industry criticisms of his presentations and provided a written response to the Tobacco Institute's submission to the MOSH Board. Repace also testified that the risk from lung cancer is 3 in 1,000 workers and is 30 in 1,000 workers for heart disease so that either with respect to lung cancer or heart disease ETS poses a 'significant risk.' He mostly uses RSP and concluded that the risk was significant for lung cancer at 92 $\mu g/m^3$ and for heart disease at 9 $\mu g/m^3$. As discussed below, he also commented on the presentations of Jenkins and Aviado. During the testimony of other witnesses, Repace frequently 'smirked' at comments he disagreed with. (5) Dr. Daniel Ford - Johns Hopkins. Dr. Ford is a medical doctor and also a clinical epidemiologist. He gave nearly an hour's presentation beginning with the discussion of the science of epidemiology and continuing through to his conclusion that the risk from heart disease is sufficient that ETS should be banned." … [TTID 2023893525].

I will admit that I do have a tendency to smirk when my bullshit detector goes off. Ironically, I had assisted Fran Stillman in planning the Johns Hopkins Hospital smoking ban, and I also had recommended that NCI fund the Correa Proposal that was the genesis of the Fontham et al. study of passive smoking and lung cancer.

The MOSH regulation obviously came as a shock to Philip Morris. On July 22, 1994, several area businesses in Talbot County, along with several trade associations, and several tobacco companies filed a complaint for declaratory and injunctive relief and a motion for an interlocutory injunction in the Circuit Court for Talbot County. They sought to have the regulation, COMAR 09.12.23, declared "void, invalid, and unenforceable" and to have the court enjoin its implementation on August 1, 1994. On August 11 and 12, 1994, Judge J. Horne conducted a two-day evidentiary hearing on the Appellees' motion for an interlocutory injunction. Seventeen witnesses testified, including many local businesses and two economists who testified as expert witnesses for the Appellees. The State called no witnesses. A substantial amount of documentary evidence was submitted to the court by both sides. The trial judge granted the injunction. The State appealed to the Court of Special Appeals. The case, Fogle v. H & G Restaurant, Inc. et al., No. 69, September Term, 1994, was decided in favor of the State.

However, in 1995, the industry made an end run around MOSH. Tobacco and business interests heavily lobbied the Maryland State Legislature and then Governor Paris Glendening, who then exempted the hospitality industry from the workplace ban. This allowed large restaurants and bars to establish separately ventilated enclosed areas for smoking (Washington Post, 1995). Very small taverns and restaurants were exempted completely. These exemptions would persist for more than a decade.

A LIGHTNING ROD FOR INDUSTRY ATTACKS

On May 26th 1994, The Los Angeles Times had published a front-page article by Medical Editor Sheryl Gay Stolberg:

"**COLUMN ONE; SCIENCE STOKES THE TOBACCO DEBATE**; RESEARCH ON RISKS OF SECONDHAND EXPOSURE HAS FUELED AN ANTISMOKING REVOLUTION. CIGARETTE MAKERS ARE FIGHTING FIRE WITH FIRE, PRODUCING REPORTS THAT DISCOUNT THE DANGERS." It noted in part, that due to the EPA report declaring secondhand smoke to be 'Group A' human carcinogen, "secondhand smoke is now one of the nation's most pressing and divisive public health issues." It noted that the industry was "fighting back hard," by filing a lawsuit attempting to invalidate the EPA's findings. The article described the press campaign against EPA, "In full-page newspaper ads, R.J. Reynolds says its research shows that nonsmokers are exposed to 'very little' secondhand smoke, even when they live or work with smokers. [Reynolds said that] 'In one month, … a nonsmoker living with a smoker would breathe the equivalent of smoking 1½ cigarettes." The article continued, describing the results of a new Gallup Poll indicating that "38% of Americans support a ban on smoking in restaurants – up 10% from three years ago. Support for workplace smoking bans is at 32%, up eight points from 1991." … [However] it observed that researchers on secondhand smoke "had little funding and even less support from mainstream health groups, such as the American Cancer Society and the American Heart Association."

"Perhaps no researcher has struggled longer or harder than James Repace. [a physicist who] in the late 1970s, stumbled upon the idea that secondhand smoke could be measured as air pollution. [Repace] took measurements at bars, bowling alleys and office buildings. … [His findings were published] in the prestigious journal *Science* … in 1980." … the *Science* article helped make Repace one of the nation's leading authorities on secondhand smoke; the media often quote him and the government often uses him as an expert witness." The article went on to discuss the fallout from the Sundquist Affair and noted that it had had an adverse impact on my EPA career, despite being cleared of all charges. … "… he has been forced to leave the EPA. [He was told that] he is a lightning rod for complaints from the tobacco industry." [He is now] 'on loan' to OSHA" [TTID RJR 533002521 70090 0558].

Interestingly, Philip Morris, in its 540-page submission to national OSHA in August 1994, zealously attacked the work of Repace and Lowrey 52 times, especially our 1980 paper, which continued to gall them 14 years later. PM quoted letters by its moles trashing our work, referencing in particular, the Turner/HBI and RJR/Oak Ridge studies. It even devoted an entire 31-page appendix to attacking our 1993 *Risk Analysis* paper, "An Enforceable Indoor Air Quality Standard for Environmental Tobacco Smoke in the Workplace." In that work we had combined atmospheric and pharmacokinetic modeling and measurement with a dose-response relationship to estimate the risk to nonsmoking workers from smoking in the workplace [TTID 2025468841].

The appendix summarized Philip Morris's arguments succinctly:

"In their paper, Repace and Lowrey claim to have developed a model which permits using atmospheric nicotine measurements to estimate nonsmokers' ETS lung cancer risks in individual workplaces for the first time. The model is a modification and extension of previous exposure and risk models developed by the authors. Both models were heavily criticized in the scientific literature. The report presents no new data on workplace exposures to ETS, and the model that is developed to assess exposure and risk does not utilize available epidemiologic data or actual exposure data from the published literature.

The available epidemiologic data on the workplace provide virtually no support to the claim that ETS exposures are associated with an increased risk of lung cancer for nonsmokers. Moreover, actual measurements of constituents of ETS in the air of offices, restaurants and public places are five to ten times lower than the exposure estimates generated by Repace and Lowrey's theoretical model.

The estimates for 'acceptable' and 'obvious' risks proposed by the authors are based upon erroneous exposure estimates for ETS-related respirable suspended particulate (RSP) (smoke particles), nicotine and cotinine, a substance converted from nicotine by the body. The calculated "acceptable risk" for airborne RSP attributable to ETS is 1,000 times lower than the permissible exposure levels set by the World Health Organization, the U.S. EPA and Health and Welfare Canada; the calculated 'acceptable risk' level is also well below background levels reported for RSP in smoke-free environments. The suggested permissible airborne exposure level for nicotine is so minuscule that it is below detection limits for sophisticated air monitoring devices, and the level of 'obvious risk' calculated for cotinine levels in the body fluids of nonsmokers is attainable by the ingestion of common foods – potatoes, tomatoes, eggplant and fruits – in the absence of any exposure to ETS" [TTID 2025468841].

And they continued to argue, based on a 1992 book co-authored by CIAR "special project" grantee Roger Jenkins, that the RSP measurements we had made in our 1980 paper were mostly "dust," not ETS, and that typically, "only 25% to 35% of the RSP present in an environment where smoking takes place is due to ETS." This assertion ignored four large scale studies in the pre-1994 literature showing that weekly-average RSP in naturally ventilated smoking homes increased by 25 $\mu g/m^3$ to 47 $\mu g/m^3$ above background (Dockery and Spengler, 1981; Lebret et al., 1987; Leaderer and Hammond, 1991; Wallace, 1996). And as for the bogus "potatoes, tomatoes, and eggplant" argument, stay tuned. The references Philip Morris used to attempt to discredit the work of Repace and Lowrey, which remained its greatest threat in the context of the OSHA hearings read like a Who's Who of 28 assorted industry scientists, consultants, fellow travelers, rogues and moles: Adlkofer, Burch, Carson, Davis, Eatough, Erikson, First, Gori, Gross, Hedge, Holcomb, Idle, Jenkins, Johnson, Kabat, Kilpatrick, Kirk, Koo, Lebowitz, Lee, Letzel, LeVois, Mantel, Oldaker, Turner, Proctor, Schwartz, and of course, good old Ted Sterling.

Since 1981, I had been involved as an expert witness in 20 workplace cases, including 9 labor arbitrations (five on behalf of the Federal Government), and 11 legal cases. I had been on the prevailing side in all but the four private ones done before the major health reports of the Surgeon General and the NAS in 1986. By the end of 1994 I had published 40 papers on ETS. These papers explored the air pollution and health impacts of secondhand smoke, the dimensions of the social issue, developed models to predict workplace exposure and risk, and demonstrated that ventilation could not control secondhand smoke. Further, I had developed pharmacokinetic models to predict risk and air pollution exposure due to secondhand smoke from the nicotine metabolite, cotinine in blood, saliva, and urine. I had demonstrated that ETS in the workplace was a major health and welfare threat to nonsmoking workers. I had also learned a great deal about exposure and the diseases of secondhand smoke incurred by workers in both white and blue-collar workplaces. Philip Morris obviously took our work as a grave threat in the context of workplace regulation.

It had become crystal clear that secondhand smoke was a major health problem for workers often resulting in bitter labor disputes and litigation. Philip Morris was well aware of these problems from Shook Hardy and Bacon's bi-annual summaries of "Reports on Recent ETS and IAQ Developments." In Germany, Shook Hardy reported, ETS in the workplace had actually had resulted in "Clashes between smokers and nonsmokers," due to the lack of workplace smoking restrictions. Why does this sound familiar? In fact,

223

a survey of German workplaces had reported "severe" problems in 66% of companies it surveyed, and "dramatic" conflicts in another 22% [TTID 2029056697]. This was similar to reports in the late 1970's in the U.S. [Repace, JNYAM, 1981].

The balance of Philip Morris's telephone-book-thick submission argued the following points:

> • "The proposed [OSHA] standard fails to demonstrate that exposure to ETS in the workplace is associated with any significant material impairment of health. • The analysis of risk is not scientifically sound. • Significantly, OSHA fails to include measured ambient exposure data for ETS in its estimate of the risk allegedly posed by ETS in the workplace, despite the fact that such studies were available to OSHA. • Contrary to scientific data and the legal mandate [i.e., the Supreme Court's Benzene Decision], OSHA's proposed rule assumes, without support, that there is no safe threshold for ETS exposure in the workplace. • The proposed standard is overly broad and unduly burdensome, legally unsupported, and impractical. • The proposed standard fails to consider alternative approaches to overall indoor air quality, which would include and address ETS, such as the 'building systems approach'. "

In particular, Philip Morris argued that "OSHA failed to establish that existing exposures to ETS in the workplace pose a significant risk of material impairment to the health of nonsmokers." In other words, Philip Morris was contending that any possible risks were less than the "significant risk" level that the Supreme Court set as a test to justify OSHA regulation, and therefore were legally insufficient to allow OSHA to act. The 1993 *Risk Analysis* paper of Repace and Lowrey directly contradicted this premise. Further, it was the only published work at that time to estimate risk on the basis of air nicotine, and to show that a substantial number of studies of nicotine in workplaces showed that workers' exposures exceeded OSHA's significant risk level for lung cancer.

In June 1994, in response to unrelenting industry attacks on its 1993 risk assessment, EPA issued a report co-authored by Steven Bayard and Jennifer Jinot, *Setting the Record Straight: Secondhand Smoke is a Preventable Health Risk*. Summarizing the arguments made at length in the 1992 EPA Risk Assessment of ETS, EPA struck back:

> "A recent high-profile advertising and public relations campaign by the tobacco industry may confuse the American public about the risks of secondhand smoke. EPA believes it's time to set the record straight about an indisputable fact: secondhand smoke is a real and preventable health risk. EPA absolutely stands by its scientific and well documented report. The report was the subject of an extensive open review both by the public and by EPA's Science Advisory Board (SAB), a panel of independent scientific experts. Virtually every one of the arguments about lung cancer advanced by the tobacco industry and its consultants was addressed by the SAB. The panel concurred in the methodology and unanimously endorsed the conclusions of the final report. The report has also been endorsed by the U.S. Department of Health and Human Services, the National Cancer Institute, the Surgeon General, and many major health organizations.

> **Classification of Secondhand Smoke as a Known Human (Group A) Carcinogen:** The finding that secondhand smoke causes lung cancer in nonsmoking adults is based on the total weight of the available evidence and is not dependent on any single analysis. This evidence includes several important facts. First, it is indisputable that smoking tobacco causes lung cancer in humans, and there is no evidence that there is a threshold below which smoking will not cause cancer. Second, although secondhand smoke is a dilute mixture of mainstream

smoke exhaled by smokers and sidestream smoke from the burning end of a cigarette or other tobacco product, it is chemically similar to the smoke inhaled by smokers, and contains a number of carcinogenic compounds.

Third, there is considerable evidence that large numbers of people who do not smoke are exposed to, absorb, and metabolize significant amounts of secondhand smoke. Fourth, there is supporting evidence from laboratory studies of the ability of secondhand smoke both to cause cancer in animals and to damage DNA, which is recognized by scientists as being an instrumental mechanism in cancer development. Finally, EPA conducted multiple analyses on the then-available 30 epidemiology studies from eight different countries which examined the association between secondhand smoke and lung cancer in women who never smoked themselves but were exposed to their husband's smoke. Since the epidemiology studies are the major thrust of the tobacco industry arguments against the EPA report, these studies are examined in more detail below.

The Epidemiology Studies: The most important aspect of the review of the epidemiology studies is the remarkable consistency of results across studies that support a causal association between secondhand smoke and lung cancer. In assessing the studies several different ways, it becomes clear that the extent of the consistency defies attribution to chance. When looking only at the simple measure of exposure of whether the husband ever smoked, 24 of 30 studies reported an increase in risk for nonsmoking women with smoking husbands. Since many of these studies were small, the chance of declaring these increases statistically significant was small.

Still, nine of these were statistically significant, and the probability that this many of the studies would be statistically significant merely by chance is less than 1 in 10 thousand. The simple overall comparison of risks in ever vs. never exposed to spousal smoking tends to hide true increases in risk in two ways. First, it categorizes many women as never exposed who actually received exposure from sources other than spousal smoking. It also includes some women as exposed who actually received little exposure from their husband's smoking. One way to correct for this latter case is to look at the women whose husbands smoked the most.

When one looks at the 17 studies that examined cancer effects based on the level of exposure of the subjects, every study found an increased lung cancer risk among those subjects who were most exposed. Nine were statistically significant. The probability of 9 out of 17 studies showing statistically significant results occurring by chance is less than 1 in ten million. Probably the most important finding for a causal relationship is one of increasing response with increasing exposure, since such associations cannot usually be explained by other factors. Such exposure-response trends were seen in all 14 studies that examined the relationship between level of exposure and effect. In 10 of the studies the trends were statistically significant. The probability of this happening by chance is less than 1 in a billion.

It is unprecedented for such a consistency of results to be seen in epidemiology studies of cancer from environmental levels of a pollutant. One reason is that it is extremely difficult to detect an effect when virtually everyone is exposed, as is the case with secondhand smoke. However, consistent increased risks for those most exposed and consistent trends of increasing exposure showing an increasing effect provide strong evidence that secondhand smoke increases the risk of lung cancer in nonsmokers. EPA estimates that secondhand smoke is responsible for about 3,000 lung cancer deaths each year among nonsmokers in the U.S.; of these, the estimate is 800 from exposure to secondhand smoke at home and 2,200 from exposure in work or social situations."

Philip Morris U.S.A. responded with a public-relations counter-attack intended to imply that the government had decided years before that secondhand smoke was harmful, and then cooked the science to justify the policy conclusion. In a full-page ad in the New York Times on June 27, 1994, readers were queried: "WERE YOU MISLED?"

EPA's conclusion that the workplace and social exposures were nearly 3 times as great a risk than domestic exposures not only supported OSHA's proposed rule, it directly contradicted the industry's assertion to the contrary in its comments to OSHA based on Jenkins' RJR/Oak Ridge Study. Moreover, to our great delight, EPA's reiteration that the workplace risk was greater than that in the home not only supported the model-based conclusions of Repace and Lowrey (1985) nine years earlier, that the workplace was four times as important than exposures at home, but reinforced OSHA's legal basis for regulating ETS in the workplace. (In a larger sense, the workplace vs. home argument was a total red herring, as nonsmoking workers exposed only at work obviously had zero home exposure).

On August 13, 1994, RJR trotted out one of its big guns: The Principal Scientist at RJR, Toxicologist Chris Coggins, who weighed in with his own attack on Repace and Lowrey (1993), submitted to OSHA's Docket (Proposed Rule on Indoor Air Quality 59 Fed Reg. 15968, April 5, 1994), [TTID 2046369181]. He asserted that "The Repace and Lowrey (1993) model outlined in 'An Enforceable Indoor Air Quality Standard for Environmental Tobacco Smoke in the Workplace' suffers from serious factual flaws that render it useless as a basis for establishing acceptable ETS exposure levels. RL's model does not rely upon any actual measurements: their approach is entirely theoretical and contains large numbers of illogical assumptions. RL's conclusions are completely hypothetical and are contraindicated by scientific facts."

Coggins proceeded to attack our estimate of daily exposure of the typical nonsmoker, claiming it that it was a gross overestimation, citing in support of this contention data reviewed by industry mole Holcomb and by RJR's Oak Ridge consultants, Jenkins and Guerin, to suggest that our estimates – grounded on our published field measurements as well as the Harvard Six-Cities study – were an order of magnitude too high. He obfuscated the difference between exposure and dose, asserted that our 10:1 ratio of ETS-RSP to Nicotine was wrong, again referring to Holcomb's review and the HBI 585 building study by Turner (although our ratio was based on chamber data measured by Leaderer and Hammond).

He claimed that there was no fixed relationship between airborne nicotine and body fluid cotinine because it was not a reliable quantititative marker for ETS due to individual variability (our Monte Carlo Analysis, Repace et al. (1998), unpublished at this juncture, would show that all relevant biological variables combined added 40% to the variance), that contributions of nicotine-containing vegetables added a significant source of nicotine to body fluids (which Martin Jarvis and I had demolished in companion BMJ articles in 1994).

Next, he claimed that the SDA-nonSDA lung cancer difference was actually due to major lifestyle differences other than exposure to ETS. He attacked our de minimis risk level as well below the limit of detection of "most" air-monitoring devices (it wasn't below the limit of detection of the Hammond monitor). Finally, Coggins asserted most workplace studies were not statistically significant, dismissing the statistical significance generated by meta analysis.

In August of 1994, Jud Wells published a review paper, Passive Smoking as a Cause of Heart Disease, in *the Journal of the American College of Cardiology* (*JACC*). He estimated that in 1985, 62,000 Americans had died from ischemic heart disease associated with exposure to environmental tobacco smoke. Later that month, the tobacco industry's propaganda machine launched a massive pre-emptive attack on OSHA. Firing salvo after salvo savaging OSHA, the industry churned out full-page ads in the national and local newspapers fomenting smokers' fears that their right to smoke in their own homes and even their cars would be taken away by over-reaching government bureaucrats. A classic example of the genre appeared in *The Washington Post* on Tuesday, August 16, 1994, in a full-page ad on page A16. Sponsored by the R.J. Reynolds Tobacco Company, a blurry photo designed to suggest violent action portrayed a private home surrounded by police with guns drawn. The caption, displayed in a large bold-faced font, read: "**Come out slowly sir, with your cigarette above your head.**" It accused the government of attempting tobacco prohibition and suggested the homes of "known smokers" could be raided, and that neighbor would be encouraged to inform upon neighbor. Lest smokers miss the point, the OSHA docket number H-122 was listed in a footnote as being part of this attempt.

In anticipation of the OSHA hearings, Philip Morris retained attorney Pat Tyson, who had formerly worked in the Solicitor's Office at the Department of Labor. Tyson had deep familiarity with the internal workings of OSHA, its personnel, its strengths, and its weaknesses. For example, in a typical OSHA hearing in the past, a thousand or so comments on a rule had been received, with just a few dozen or so actually being substantive. By the time the comment period on the proposal had closed, the tobacco industry's massive advertising campaign had generated the most comments that OSHA had ever received on a rulemaking: a staggering *one hundred ten thousand* comments in the required quadruplicate, a hundred-fold more than OSHA had ever received before. One of the industry commenters was none other than the arch villain, Theodor Sterling. Sterling submitted voluminous testimony to the OSHA docket (Docket # 71, Sterling et al.). Sterling's comments were acknowledged to be "supported by Philip Morris U.S.A." However, a disclaimer stated disingenuously that the conclusions "do not necessarily reflect the views of Philip Morris U.S.A." Sterling concluded that, "In their estimate of ETS effects, OSHA has violated just about every rule of good applied science. ... One is tempted to speak of junk science in relation to OSHA's procedures. ... Given the present ... data, no increase in lifetime lung cancer risk associated with workplace exposure to ETS has been demonstrated. The data required for a valid assessment of ... heart disease risk [from] workplace exposure does not yet exist."

Taking leave on the 13th of September, I flew up to Halifax, Nova Scotia, where I had been invited to address the Health Control Subcommittee of the Nova Scotia Parliament on the Risks and Control of Passive Smoking. My local guide was an attractive young woman who worked for a local affiliate of the Canadian Lung Association. As we chatted, I asked her how she came to work for the Lung Association. She said, "I used to tend bar in a very smoky local pub. Despite being just a high-school graduate, I earned $40,000 a year, with tips. One night, I collapsed behind the bar with a severe asthmatic attack, and by the time they got me to the emergency room, which fortunately was across the street from the bar, I had stopped breathing. I nearly died. The doctors told me that if I wanted to avoid a fatal attack, I should quit my job and get one that was smoke-free. The only smoke-free job available was working for the Lung Association. It doesn't pay well, but I'm still alive."

As an asthmatic, I could readily empathize with her. However, she would have a dozen years to wait before the provincial legislature acted to make their bars smoke-free. Nova Scotia's workplaces and public places, including restaurants, bars, and casinos, failed to go 100% smoke free until December 1, 2006. Her poignant tale underscored the widespread failure of occupational health and safety agencies all over North America to protect workers in non-industrial settings. I had her sad story on my mind a week later when the OSHA hearings began in Washington. The OSH Act of 1970, 29 USC 654, specifies that "Each employer shall furnish to each of his employees, employment and a place of employment which are free from recognized hazards that are causing or are likely to cause death or serious physical harm to his employees." Given the 1986 reports of the Surgeon General, the National Academy of Sciences, together with the 1992 report of Environmental Protection Agency, this was prima facie evidence that ETS was a "recognized hazard likely to cause death to workers."

On the 24th of September, Clare Purcell at the Philip Morris Research Center in Richmond, VA, raised the alarm over Repace and Lowrey's 1993 paper in *Risk Analysis*. In a memo to other PM staff and management, she noted:

From: Purcell, Clare on Fri, Sep 24,1993 2:25 PM
Subject: Repace-Lowrey article
To: Keane, Denise; Lattanzio, Ted; Pages, Robert; Parrish, Steve

The Repace-Lowrey article in Risk Analysis appears to be specifically aimed at OSHA – it proposes theoretical ETS exposures to non-smokers in the workplace (based on modeling) that exceed a de minimus [sic] level. Denise and I spoke with Leo Dreyer and Pat Tyson and agreed that: – it will certainly make its way into the OSHA docket; -PM and others should counter it in the docket; • In the absence of actual workplace exposure studies theoretical exposures will carry some weight with OSHA. Accordingly, Shook Hardy is preparing a critique of the article with the assistance of R&D-Richmond. They will also identify any third party scientists who may be interested in responding to the article via a letter to the editor, or otherwise. We will factor this information into our ongoing evaluation of a PM building study. I recommend that we seek approval to go forward with a pilot study in 1993 [TTID 2028361848].

Although the OSHA rulemaking was not on the horizon when our 1993 *Risk Analysis* paper had been published, Purcell was right on the mark that it would carry some weight in that context. Our abstract read in part:
"…We develop a model which permits using atmospheric nicotine measurements to estimate nonsmokers' ETS lung cancer risks in individual workplaces for the first time. … Modeling of the lung cancer mortality risk from passive smoking suggests that *de minimis* [i.e., "acceptable" (10^{-6})] *risk* occurs at an 8-hr time-weighted-average exposure concentration of 7.5 nanograms of ETS nicotine per cubic meter of workplace air for a working lifetime of 40 years. This model is based upon a linear exposure-response relationship validated by physical, clinical, and epidemiological data. From available data, it appears that workplaces without effective smoking policies considerably exceed this *de minimis* risk standard. For a substantial fraction of the 59 million nonsmoking workers in the U.S., current workplace exposure to ETS also appears to pose risks exceeding the *de manifestis* risk level above which carcinogens are strictly regulated by the federal government" (Repace and Lowrey, 1993).

In fact, assuming a standard workweek, OSHA's standard working lifetime was 45 years, and we had assumed a 40-year working lifetime, so the daily average de minimis exposure would be even lower, at 6.7 nanograms of ETS nicotine per cubic meter of air (ng/m^3) for the probability of a fatal lung cancer to be 1 in a million (10^{-6}). Thus, significant risk would occur at 6700 ng/m^3. Expressed in the context of OSHA's Significant Risk level at 1 in 1000 (10^{-3}), the Oak Ridge/RJR measurements of workplace secondhand smoke nicotine levels, adjusted to a daily 8-hour exposure, ranged from about 6500 to a little over 14000 ng/m^3, with an arithmetic mean of about 4800 ng/m^3 (Jenkins et al. 1996). And HBI had reported measurements of workplace secondhand smoke nicotine levels in its 585 Building study ranging from <2.5 to about 12500 ng/m^3, with an arithmetic mean of 6700 ng/m^3 (Turner et al. 1991). In other words, by their own measurements taken at face value, and using the exposure-response relationship from our paper, workers in most office workplaces would exceed Significant Risk. Therefore, our paper loomed as an ominous threat to the industry's argument that nonsmokers in workplaces that allowed smoking were "at low risk of lung cancer from secondhand smoke." And this was without even considering the risk of fatal heart disease from passive smoking, which was already on OSHA's horizon.

THE OSHA HEARING MARATHON BEGINS

The hearing on OSHA's proposal convened on Tuesday morning, September 20, 1994. OSHA had estimated that 74 million U.S. workers were nonsmokers, and that less than 29% of them worked in smoke-free workplaces. Moreover, smaller companies were half as likely to be smoke-free than were large ones. The basis for the rule was OSHA's preliminary finding that "employees working in indoor work environments faced a significant risk of material impairment to their health due to poor indoor air quality, and that compliance with the provisions proposed in this notice will substantially reduce that risk." The proposed rule would allow designated smoking areas if they were practicable *but would allow no work to take place in these areas.* This was a non-starter for the industry.

Under the OSH Act, as modified by the Supreme Court's Benzene Case (AFL-CIO v. American Petroleum Institute, 1980), before OSHA can promulgate any permanent health or safety standard, it "must find that a significant risk of harm is present in the workplace and that the new standard is reasonably necessary to reduce or eliminate that risk." In that decision, OSHA noted, the "Benzene Court clearly indicated that a risk of one death per thousand [workers] would be considered significant, and that the Agency would be justified in prescribing reasonable efforts to reduce such a risk." OSHA estimated that ETS exposure at work caused between "144 and 722 deaths from lung cancer per year," and between "2094 and 13,000 deaths from heart disease per year, among nonsmoking American workers," and that the heart disease risk over a working lifetime of 45 years amounted to "between 7 and 16 cases per thousand," which when combined with lung cancer, the significance of the risk "is very great."

To accomplish its quantitative risk assessment, OSHA had relied on two main epi studies: The Fontham Study (1991) [Lung cancer risk from ETS] and the Helsing Study (1988) [Heart disease risk from ETS] for its quantitative estimates of effect. EPA had also used the Fontham study in its risk assessment. The Fontham study had concluded that, over all, "a 30% increased risk of lung cancer was associated with exposure to environmental tobacco smoke from a smoking spouse, and a 50% increase was observed for adenocarcinoma of the lung. A statistically significant positive trend in risk was observed as pack-years of exposure from a spouse increased, reaching a relative risk of 1.7 for pulmonary adenocarcinoma with exposures of 80 or more pack years. [A pack-year is a unit of secondhand smoke exposure for one year from a spouse who smokes one pack of cigarettes per day.] Other adult-life exposures in household, occupational, and social settings were each associated with a 40-60% increased risk of adenocarcinoma of the lung." The Helsing study found in part, that "among the white population aged 25 and over [in Washington County, MD], 4,162 men and 14,873 women had never smoked, death rates from arteriosclerotic heart disease were significantly higher among men (relative risk (RR) = 1.31, 95% confidence interval (CI) 1.1-1.6) and women (RR = 1.24, 95% CI 1.1-1.4) who lived with smokers, after adjustment for age, marital status, years of schooling, and quality of housing."

The tobacco industry's strategy to combat the proposed rule centered around demonstrating that U.S. workplaces failed to meet OSHA's "significant risk" guideline. Using R.J. Reynolds/Oak Ridge 16-City study, the industry intended to argue that the bulk of ETS exposure – and by implication, the bulk of the risk – was from spousal smoking in the home, and therefore beyond OSHA's legal jurisdiction. As icing on the cake, Gray Robertson's Healthy Buildings International 585 Building ETS study would be used to supply independent confirmation using its field measurements in office workplaces. By combining the two complementary studies, this would show that workplace exposures were far less than domestic exposures and well below significant risk as well and would thus provide clear evidence that ventilation was controlling ETS in the office workplace. Since my own work suggested that typical workplace exposures would exceed the significant risk level, and that ventilation could not possibly yield acceptable risk, as a member of the panel receiving testimony, I expected to have a field day in questioning the industry's witnesses.

A major logistical impediment for OSHA was that so many written comments had been received during the request for comment period that a separate file room had to be allocated to hold them and temporary hired help had to be hired to hand-stamp their submissions to the IAQ docket. Debra Janes complained that previously OSHA had never received more than a thousand written submissions. Approximately 800 persons and organizations filed Notices of Intent to Appear to testify, also a record. These entities included labor unions, restaurant associations, health organizations, as well as Philip Morris, RJ Reynolds, and The Tobacco Institute. The industry submitted boxes and boxes and boxes of voluminous technical comments in quadruplicate, with the clear intent of burdening OSHA staff with tons of paper. This was a standard dirty trick by lawyers representing guilty companies in toxic tort litigation. In addition, the industry had solicited comments on postcards from tens of thousands of smokers using national advertising, requesting that they delegate their comment time in the hearing to the industry's lawyers. By this clever legal stratagem, permitted under OSHA's arcane hearing rules, the tobacco attorneys were able to pool together hundreds of hours of hearing time that they could then use to exhaustively cross-examine OSHA's designated expert witnesses, as well as representatives of any other organizations or individuals who independently supported the rule. This dirty pooling strategy allowed the industry to virtually take control of the hearing. OSHA would twice extend the public hearing, until it became a grueling daily marathon, dragging on until May 1995.

OSHA opened with its presentation, presided over by Administrative Law Judge John Vittone. Dr. Michael Silverstein gave the opening statement, which read, in part:

"My name is Michael Silverstein. I'm a physician and occupational health specialist, and Director of Policy for the Occupational Safety and Health Administration. I'd like to thank you all for your presence here today. Accompanying me are John Martonik, Acting Director of Health Standards for OSHA; Ms. Debra Janes, Epidemiologist and Project Officer for this standard; Ms. Demetra Collia, Biostatistician in the Office of Risk Assessment; Dr. Surender Ahir, Toxicologist in the Office of Risk Assessment; Mr. Lee Hathon, Ventilation Engineer of OSHA's Health Response Team; Mr. Ken Stevanus, a Mechanical Engineer in the Office of Risk Reduction Technology; Ms. Saneya El-Mekawi and Mr. Edward Stern, Economists in OSHA's Office of Regulatory Analysis; Mr. Hank Woodcock, Industrial Hygienist and Engineer of OSHA's Directorate of Technical Support; Mr. Long Loo, a Safety Engineer of OSHA's Directorate of Technical Support; and Mr. James Repace, Physicist on detail to OSHA from the Environmental Protection Agency.

According to reports published by the Environmental Protection Agency, the National Research Council, the Department of Health and Human Services, many of the damaging elements in tobacco smoke, in fact, are more concentrated in so-called sidestream smoke than in that which smokers take into their own lungs. There is a growing body of evidence showing that exposure to environmental smoke on the job causes disease, including lung cancer, in healthy non-smokers. Restaurant workers, for example, may take in substantially more smoke than someone living with a smoker, and as much or more benzo(a)pyrene, a known carcinogen, as active smokers. In California, waitresses have the highest death rate of any group of female workers. Waitresses die of lung cancer at four times the average rate for women who work, and they die of heart disease at two and a half times the average rate.

…

OSHA has conducted a thorough review of this and other scientific data to support its preliminary conclusion that there is significant risk from contaminated indoor air at the work place. Much of that evidence will be presented and discussed in the course of this hearing. The accumulating evidence has had a major impact on public opinion. Most Americans now believe that second-hand smoke is dangerous, and favor measures to protect them from this risk. An ABC News/Washington Post poll found that 78 percent of the public believes second-hand smoke to be a health risk. A separate Gallup poll found that by the same margin, 78 percent, respondents viewed environmental smoke as very or somewhat harmful. In a CBS News/New York Times poll, 67 percent supported an outright ban on smoking in all public places – a tougher measure than OSHA envisages here. While we do not make rules on the basis of opinion polls, it's noteworthy that our proposal is, if anything, less aggressive than mainstream opinion would warrant."

After a second statement by Martonik, Judge Vittone opened the panelists up for questions, which were answered in the main by Martonik, Silverstein, or Janes, sometimes in consultation with the remaining panelists. After about an hour, Big Tobacco's attorneys began their onslaught. The tobacco team included Ted Grossman (RJ Reynolds), John Rupp (Tobacco Institute), Pat Tyson, Brennan Dawson, and Richard Carchman (Phillip Morris). Figure 18 shows one of the early days of the hearing before it adjourned to the larger Labor Department Auditorium due to overcrowding.

The industry's lawyers, paralegals, and other support staff formed at least half of the audience of more than 100 persons plus the press and numerous television cameras. An internal backgrounder prepared by a Philip Morris staffer summarized OSHA's proposal and the industry's response strategy and tactics [TTID 2501341198]. It read in part:

"The proposed OSHA (Occupational Health & Safety Administration) workplace rule consisted of two main sets of provisions – those dealing with general indoor air quality issues and those dealing with environmental tobacco smoke. If smoking is to be permitted, the proposed rule would require designated smoking areas which are to be separate, enclosed rooms, exhausted directly to the outside. The ultimate goal of the hearing is to gather information to enable OSHA to formulate a final version of the rule if they deem that to be appropriate in light of the evidence and comments received at the hearing. OSHA is expected to issue a revised rule in 1995 based on the information produced during the hearing process. The publishing of the revised rule begins anew the comment/hearing process described above. When and if a final rule is adopted by OSHA (experts predict it could take as long as eight to ten years), a challenge to the rule in federal court is likely by one or more parties who are dissatisfied with the rule. Every rule proposed and adopted by OSHA has been challenged in court."

Brennan Dawson of the Tobacco Institute; Dr. Richard Carchman of Philip Morris; and Patrick Tyson, an attorney and former Acting Administrator of OSHA, represent Philip Morris. Tyson explained that in his opinion OSHA has exceeded its authority because the US Supreme Court has determined that OSHA can only regulate a significant risk – not ban a product to prevent any exposure. He explained that in the past OSHA has determined 'permissible exposure limits' for various toxic substances but the current proposal would violate OSHA's authority by establishing a 'zero exposure level' for environmental tobacco smoke. Dr. Carchman pointed out the numerous weaknesses in the scientific basis for OSHA's proposed rule, while Ms. Dawson emphasized the ability of employers to resolve any workplace ETS problems without resorting to additional federal regulation" [TTID 2501341198].

In addition, the backgrounder indicated that PM's major tactical goal was to discredit OSHA's reliance on the two key passive smoking epidemiological studies in its risk assessment, the Fontham (1991) study for lung cancer, and the Helsing (1988) study for heart disease [TTID 2501341198].

RJR Attorney Ted Grossman led off the questioning by attacking OSHA's reliance on "weak epidemiology and old data on workplace smoking policies." In the afternoon, Myron Weinberg, funded through CIAR "Special Projects," attacked OSHA's "reliance on the Fontham epidemiological study in its quantitative risk assessment," and the lack of a dose-response relationship in that study. (Actually, a fair reading of Fontham's Figure 1 in her study showed a clear dose-response relationship). Lowrey and I had published an estimated dose-response relationship between secondhand smoke particles and lung cancer in 1985, followed by an indoor air quality standard as well in a separate paper, and one on nicotine in 1993 (Repace and Lowrey, 1985a, 1985b, Repace et al., 1993). Both OSHA and the industry were well aware of this. In fact, before the hearing I had explicitly suggested to Martonik that OSHA set a PEL for ETS. However, he made a cogent argument for not going down that road: "If we set a non-zero acceptable risk level, workplaces would be subject to inspection for violations, and OSHA has only 500 inspectors for the whole country. If we set an IAQ standard for ETS, we might get tens of thousands of complaints, and we simply wouldn't have the capacity to handle them." Good point.

Later that afternoon, John Rupp weighed in, representing the Tobacco Institute. Rupp questioned why OSHA had not mentioned the industry's views in its proposed rule. Laying it on thick, he attacking OSHA for relying on spousal studies to quantify risk, and OSHA's reliance on source control rather than ventilation. Martonik responded by rejecting that approach as unable to reduce ETS satisfactorily. Repace and Lowrey's demonstration of this fact years ago was now an arrow in OSHA's quiver. Moreover, the 1986 NAS report observed that, "ventilation engineers have viewed ETS as the most problematic common indoor pollutant." The NAS also had noted that if just 10% of the persons in a space were actively smoking, a realistic data-based assumption (Repace and Lowrey, 1980), that the ventilation rate per person requirement would need to be 53 cubic feet per minute per occupant (cfm/occ), where occupants were a mixed group of smokers and nonsmokers, and pointed out that the highest ventilation rate that ASHRAE was recommending was 35 cfm/occ. (For offices, it was 20 cfm/occ). Similarly, the 1986 Surgeon General's Report had stated that, "separation of smokers and nonsmokers in the same room or in different rooms that share the same ventilation system may reduce ETS exposure but will not eliminate exposure."

After Rupp was done, the rest of Big Tobacco's tag-team piled on. Pat Sirridge of Shook Hardy & Bacon, Philip Morris's attorney, began attacking OSHA's reliance on the Helsing study of heart disease despite the absence of workplace exposure data in that study. [This was a hand-waving argument. If secondhand smoke exposure caused heart disease in the home, why should it suddenly become innocuous in the workplace?] Then turncoat Pat Tyson debated Silverstein over whether OSHA had ever regulated a workplace contaminant down to zero risk (as if that were a bad thing), or whether there were not insuperable enforcement problems with OSHA's proposed no-work-in-smoking areas rule.

Later that day, Grossman announced that RJ Reynolds had submitted an alternative risk assessment to the docket which argued that the workplace risk ratio was "1.0" (i.e., no increased risk from ETS at all). Then he threw down the gauntlet after a comment by Silverstein that "there was no evidence of a threshold level of ETS that was acceptable. Grossman begged to differ, asserting that, "Dr. Repace on your panel has published such a threshold." Silverstein parried that "OSHA did not think there was available evidence to justify a threshold for ETS." The following day Grossman again raised the issue with Silverstein, who then responded that in any case "dilution ventilation could not achieve the 'acceptable risk' level that Repace had established [TTID, 51268 23339 et seq.] I was amazed by the blatant duplicity of Grossman's remark. In 1985, Lowrey and I in our *New York State Journal of Medicine* paper, had estimated for a typical office it would require a totally impractical 270-fold increase in ventilation rate to reduce the lung cancer risk to attain a maximum acceptable level of one lung cancer death per 100,000 workers at risk per working lifetime. Moreover, our calculation did not even consider the additional risk of heart disease from ETS, which had not been published until late 1980's and become widely accepted in the early 1990's.

FIGURE 18. JUDGE VITTONE, STANDING, FACING LABOR DEPARTMENT ATTORNEY SUSAN SHERMAN WHO WAS FLANKED BY TOBACCO LAWYERS. OSHA STAFF AND TOBACCO INDUSTRY STAFF SAT RESPECTIVELY ON THE LEFT-HAND AND RIGHT-HAND SIDES OF THE HEARING ROOM (AUTHOR'S PHOTO).

OSHA's witnesses then began their presentations, starting with Stan Glantz. Stan began his testimony with an assault on the tobacco industry's lawyers who were "nitpicking various studies that OSHA had relied upon." Then Glantz switched to his work on the risks of passive smoking to the heart. He followed up with his analysis of tax data from 15 cities that had enacted smoking bans, showing that they had "absolutely no effect on restaurant sales." When he finished, it was the industry's turn to cross-examine Glantz. Pat Sirridge criticized Glantz for his "close relationships" with several other OSHA witnesses or panelists, including Repace, Wells, Benowitz, and Hammond [TTID 51268 2357]. Sirridge was followed by Rupp, who castigated Glantz as a "long-standing anti-tobacco activist, who had led Californians for Nonsmokers' Rights, in the early 1980's." Then Rupp attacked Glantz's restaurant study for well over an hour with well-prepared criticism, followed by Grossman who tried to get Glantz to define the "minimum level of harm."

By this time the Shook Hardy reporter described Glantz as "weary," after so many hours being battered by industry goons. But Stan's ordeal did not end there. Next up was an industry toxicology consultant, Michael Lowe, who challenged Glantz's interpretation of several studies, to which he responded by accusing Lowe of taking "quotes out of context." Taking quotes out of context was a standard industry dirty trick. If a witness didn't know the literature well, it would trip him up. However, Glantz knew it cold, demanding that Lowe read the omitted qualifying quotations from the cited manuscripts into the record. Despite his punishing cross-examination, Stan acquitted himself well, and in the words of the Shook Hardy reporter, "Tobacco industry observers were uniformly impressed with Glantz's delivery of his direct testimony, (which had estimated that

ETS kills between 30,000 and 60,000 nonsmokers from heart disease, far greater than the 3000 to 5000 deaths from lung cancer) and found it to be 'impressive.' He is obviously knowledgeable, well-read in his particular field, and does not exhibit a superficial animosity toward the tobacco industry." [TTID 51268 2363].

It was an enervating day, setting the tone for the tobacco lawyers' persistent badgering cross examination of OSHA's witnesses, which would be repeated again and again and again during the following weeks and months. On September 26, OSHA witness Dr. Neal Benowitz, one of the world's experts on ETS biomarkers, testified that the nicotine metabolite, cotinine, in blood, saliva, or urine was the most specific available marker of exposure to ETS, and that it was a valid quantitative marker of the level of ETS exposure. Further, he testified, although certain foods contained small amounts of nicotine, a nonsmoker would have to eat "massive quantities" in order to develop cotinine levels comparable to passive smoking. In fact, in the companion articles that Martin Jarvis and I had published in the *British Medical Journal* in January 1994, we had made precisely that point, respectively quantifying the bushels of raw vegetables of nicotine containing *Solanecae* (tomatoes and eggplants) one would have to gorge daily. Figure 19 illustrates the point. I used this photo in my slideshows to debunk bogus industry claims about dietary sources of nicotine.

Benowitz was followed by Wayne Ott, who was now a visiting scholar at Stanford University. Wayne, who had written a book on *Environmental Statistics and Data Analysis*, and had published many important scientific papers, discussed the modeling of secondhand smoke at length. He was then cross-examined by John Rupp. Wayne proved to be a very tough and unshakable witness. Rupp concluded his cross-examination with questions about Repace and Lowrey's now 14-year-old field study. Wayne vigorously defended our work, refusing to concede to Rupp's insinuations that both the equipment we used and the data we collected were obsolete. Since May of 1992, Wayne had been making measurements on secondhand smoke himself using a Piezobalance and was collecting similar data in the Oasis Grill in Redwood City, California, in a marathon 3-year-long longitudinal study that he would publish in 1996. Afterward, I overheard Rupp complaining to fellow tobacco lawyers about what a difficult time that he had in cross-examining Wayne. [Lance Wallace recalled that industry lawyers later attempted to have Judge Vittone declare Wayne a "hostile witness."]

Taking leave, I flew to Paris to present an invited speech discussing the EPA Report on Environmental Tobacco Smoke at a Symposium on Passive Smoking at the 9th World Conference on Smoking and Health during the week of Oct 10-14, 1994. At the Conference, Matt Myers, who was then an attorney for the Heart, Lung, and Cancer Societies' Coalition on Smoking or Health, convened a rump discussion session for the American attendees. At that meeting, I raised the issue of tobacco industry lawyers' abusive treatment of OSHA's witnesses, who, I said, were "being killed with lengthy cross examination." I pleaded with Matt for legal help. He promised to see what he could do.

While I was in Paris, Gray Robertson of Healthy Buildings International (HBI) testified at the OSHA hearing on October 14th. Robertson stated that he was "testifying at the request of the Tobacco Institute." He opined that, "OSHA was overstating the ETS problem because no federal building allows smoking and fewer than 20% of commercial buildings allow discretionary smoking today." He implied that ventilation was able to handle ETS because "ventilation rates are far higher today than they were back in the '70s and '80s when the studies relied upon by OSHA in its rule-making were conducted" [TTID 51268 2410]. This of course was a bald-faced lie, delivered with a posh British accent. Robertson blamed "poor ventilation and microbial contamination" for indoor air quality problems. He urged OSHA to adopt ASHRAE standard 62-1989, and frequently stated that the increased ventilation flows provided by this standard would allow for moderate smoking when coupled with dilution infiltration. Citing a 1989 study he had conducted of 95 buildings in New York City at the request of R.J. Reynolds, Robertson said he found "extremely low levels of nicotine in offices and restaurants allowing smoking." He contrasted this with OSHA's nicotine permissible exposure limit (PEL) which was 500 micrograms per cubic meter, whereas his average measured range was "4.3 to 6.3 micrograms per cubic meter ($\mu g/m^3$)" [TTID 21268 2411]. [Even if true, these levels still corresponded to 6 to 9 times OSHA's Significant Risk level using Repace and Lowrey's (1993) exposure-response relationship.]

However, Robertson's arguments were specious for two reasons. First, the plain language of OSHA's PEL for nicotine vapor showed that it strictly applied to nicotine vaporized from raw or cured tobacco leaves in the air of tobacco barns or cigarette factories, and not nicotine from tobacco combustion as an atmospheric marker for ETS. Second, because as the 1992 EPA report showed, the average measured nicotine levels in homes and offices were about the same. And on that simple basis, the ETS concentrations would be about the same. (The actual risks of course, would be dependent on the inhaled doses, which in turn were dependent upon exposure duration and proximity, which were not reflected by a simple concentration measurement. This was a depth of understanding either far beyond Robertson's ken – or beyond his willingness to accept a fact when his income depended on ignoring it.)

Susan Sherman cross-examined Robertson on just how OSHA might develop a PEL for ETS. Robertson replied that it should be based on nicotine as well as RSP but (naturally) could not actually say where those levels should be set [TTID 51268 2417]. In Rupp's follow-up attempting to rehabilitate Robertson, he elicited the following nonsense: Robertson said that OSHA's statement in its preamble that "natural ventilation systems were not designed to control the by-products of smoking and may have been based on ancient data, because modern ventilation systems are designed to handle some moderate amount of smoking."

FIGURE 19. THE AUTHOR ILLUSTRATING THE AMOUNT OF RAW EGGPLANT (AUBERGINE) THAT A PERSON WOULD HAVE TO CONSUME *DAILY* TO EQUAL JUST 15% OF THE DOSE OF NICOTINE PASSIVELY INHALED BY THE TYPICAL NONSMOKER. THAT'S A BOATLOAD OF EGGPLANT PARMIGIANA. EGGPLANT HAS THE GREATEST CONCENTRATION OF NICOTINE OF ANY EDIBLE PLANT, BUT FORMS A MERE 0.05% OF THE AVERAGE AMERICAN'S DIET. (REPACE, 1994) [AUTHOR'S PHOTO].

ASHRAE Standard 62-1989, Ventilation For Acceptable Indoor Air Quality written under the dark influence of Big Tobacco, had the following vague disclaimer: "Therefore, with respect to tobacco smoke and other contaminants, this Standard does not, and cannot, ensurethe avoidance of all possible adverse health effects, but it reflects recognized consensus criteria and guidance." While the standard did state that it assumed a moderate amount of smoking, the disclaimer essentially conceded that it had not been designed to prevent health effects from ETS. [TTID 51268 2418]. In fact, the prescriptive Standard 62-1989, far from being an improvement over the ventilation rates in 1973, had about the same recommended ventilation rates for offices and restaurants as the "ancient" descriptive Standard 62-1973 had, while for bars and cocktail lounges (30 cfm/occupant), the current recommendation was considerably *lower* than in 1973 (35 to 50 cfm/occupant). So, Robertson was dissembling. Moreover, he conveniently failed to mention that the ventilation rates recommended by ASHRAE were mandated only for odor control. And that the odor test panel was biased because only half of it consisted of nonsmokers, while the other half were smokers whose tolerance for tobacco smoke odor was far greater. Robertson was a ubiquitous presence on TV with his "building doctor" persona, promoting his message about the wages of poor indoor air quality in which he downplayed the role of tobacco smoke. He had gotten off very lightly that day. But this would turn out to be an ephemeral reprieve. Our friend Gray would get what was coming to him – in spades.

My impassioned plea to Matt Meyers in Paris paid off with big dividends. Matt recruited several lawyers from a group of 60 law firms that had launched the Castano product liability litigation in Louisiana against several tobacco companies. An old acquaintance, Ron Motley, was among them. I had first encountered Motley at one of Dick Daynard's symposia on tobacco litigation at Northeastern University School of Law in Boston, at which I had made several presentations. (At the outset of my first presentation, the law school's antique 35 mm slide projector jammed and incinerated my slide. I had to ad lib the remainder of my talk without slides. On the upside, this impressed the audience, who were mostly trial lawyers. An able Toastmaster improvises.)

Two weeks later, a Shook Hardy rapporteur recognized the sea change:

"The tone of the hearings took a dramatic turn today with the unexpected appearance of Ronald Motley, a plaintiff's attorney active in smoking and health litigation, including ETS cases. Until today, the testimony this week had been dominated by the views of tobacco growers and associations and small businesses, which opposed OSHA's proposed rule. The strong focus on individual rights, freedom, and social accommodation had sometimes given the proceedings a personal, and occasionally even a warm quality. That all changed today when Ron Motley got up, identified his appearance on behalf of the American Medical Association and numerous others and began his cross-examination of a 'smokers' rights' group [The National Smokers' Alliance (N.S.A.)]."

Motley got the Smokers' Alliance goons to admit it was a creature of Burson Marsteller, the public relations firm employed by Philip Morris. The Shook Hardy rapporteur continued,

"Motley was seated with a group that included Matthew Meyers (Coalition on Smoking or Health) and a team of at least a dozen presumed attorneys and others, including Richard Daynard (TPLP) [Tobacco Products Liability Project], who observed or assisted him in his cross-examination. Matthew Meyers also cross-examined the N.S.A. panel. Attempting to undermine the witnesses' testimony concerning weaknesses in ETS science, he directed similar questions, in turn, to the panel, obtaining acknowledgements that the witnesses had not read the EPA report, nor the studies on which the EPA report was based, nor other studies [TTID 51268 2441]. Matt Meyers also scored a direct hit on Mark Holan, of the Oregon Smokers' Rights group, whom Motley had forced Holan to admit was a creation of RJ Reynolds. He obtained 'numerous acknowledgements' in a highly confrontational cross-examination that Holan 'had not presented the full conclusions of the publications he cited'" [TTID 21268 2442].

The battle over the OSHA rule was finally on a level playing field, to the great consternation of Philip Morris. At an awards ceremony feting its OSHA Team in September 1995, the Chairman of Philip Morris would complain that "The Castano Consortium saw the OSHA hearings as a wide open opportunity to cross examine those who testified, in order to create a public record that they could draw upon to bolster their liability suits" [TTID, 2045865349]. Now ain't that a shame. They were just doing to Big Tobacco exactly what it had done to OSHA's witnesses. Turnabout is fair play.

LOWREY AND I EXPOSE HBI'S SCIENTIFIC FRAUD

Soon after returning from the Paris Conference in October, I received a curious call from Phil Barnett, one of Congressman Henry Waxman's two tobacco aides; the other one was Rip Forbes. At that time Waxman (D) CA was chair of the House Subcommittee on Health and Environment, a post he would lose in January 1995, in the wake of the House takeover by Republicans. Phil told me that Waxman had subpoenaed two boxes of records from HBI in the course of his investigation of CIAR-funded research, and that they appeared to be quite technical. He asked me if I would come down to Waxman's office, look them over, and advise if they had any value. During the long lunch break in the hearings, I eagerly rushed over to the House Office Building. Phil thanked me as he ushered me into a back office filled with boxes of paper. I sat down to go through the contents, and soon discovered that they contained the raw data sheets from HBI's 585 Office Building ETS investigations as well as HBI's summary reports to the CIAR on those measurements. I realized that it would take some time to go through the material, and asked Phil if I could take them home, as I was tied up during the day with the OSHA hearings. He agreed, and I spent about a week during the evening hours going through the piles of paper. I came to the stunning conclusion that I was seeing evidence of a massive scientific fraud. I drafted an 18-page analysis for Waxman. It showed that HBI's conclusions were not supported by its own data, even if one took it at face value. However, the data itself was highly suspect as it was so marred by unsubstantiated entries, discrepancies, and misclassification that it obviously constituted a major scientific fraud.

But I had an overriding political problem. My active participation in Waxman's investigation could well compromise the OSHA IAQ Hearings. I phoned Lowrey, asking him if he would read, edit, and present the work as the sole author, making any changes he felt comfortable with, and then testify before the committee. As an accomplished Toastmaster, he enthusiastically agreed. On December 18, 1994, Al presented his report to the Waxman Committee. He had coordinated closely with Barnett and with a scientifically-trained FBI agent in preparation. The Lowrey Report was a blockbuster. It concluded in part that, HBI's data contained many unexplained anomalies, including (a) reported data for which there were no measurements; (b) discrepancies between numbers on data sheets and the summaries of that data that HBI reported to CIAR; (c) misclassification of areas contaminated with ETS nicotine as nonsmoking rooms; (d) large numbers of highly unusual zero readings for particle measurements in rooms where smoking was observed, (e) significant under-reporting of room area in many situations, creating the misleading impression that large numbers of cigarettes smoked in small areas nevertheless led to low particle concentrations and (f) cleaning of the Piezobalance so that it would create anomalous zero particle concentrations. Scientific analysis of the HBI data showed that, under conditions of so-called "moderate smoking," the effect of ETS on indoor air quality was actually 40-fold greater than HBI had asserted both publicly and in its published scientific papers.

Lowrey's report complemented the devastating independent supporting testimony offered by two HBI former technicians, Reginald B. Simmons and Gregory Wulchin, before Waxman's subcommittee. On January

14, 1995, the *National Journal* reported on the hearing in an article titled, "Is it Science – or Smoke and Mirrors?" It reported that HBI's technicians testified that "field data were often altered by the top executives (HBI Vice President Peter Binney or Robertson) at the firm," and that Waxman's investigation had concluded that their affidavits had raised serious questions about possible 'scientific fraud.' " The article continued, that "Alfred H. Lowrey, a research chemist at the Naval Research Laboratory, ... told the panel that HBI's 'conclusions are not supported by their own data,' and that according to an internal company memorandum quoted in the subcommittee report, HBI officials boasted that the firm has "brought balance to the [indoor air quality] debate by promoting acceptance that [environmental tobacco smoke] is in fact a minor contributor." Another former HBI employee, Jeffrey R. Seckler, was quoted as saying, "that he testified at public hearings for HBI more than 20 times from February 1989 to September 1991" ... and that "Robertson had instructed him that he should 'never disclose' that he was appearing on behalf of tobacco interests 'unless I was asked that question directly.' "

But then Robertson and his minion Simon Turner, received an enormously lucky break. Henry Waxman's tenure as Subcommittee Chair expired with the House takeover by Republicans in January 1995. Chairmanship of the larger Committee on Energy and Commerce fell into the hands of none other than the arch industry water boy, Thomas Bliley, who immediately shelved the Waxman report, terminating the investigation. Bliley stated that he "opposes further regulation of the [tobacco] industry." Although the Waxman investigation was buried, I remained determined to expose HBI's scientific fraud. In 1995, Lowrey and I penned a Letter to the Editor of *Environment International*, in which we summarized the Waxman subcommittee's investigation, now issued as a Staff Report, and flatly stated: "Based on this new information, we believe the paper of Turner et al. (1992) has insufficient scientific credibility and should be retracted from publication." We quoted the National Academy of Sciences definition of scientific misconduct: 'Beyond honest errors and errors caused through negligence are a third category of errors: those that involve deception. Making up data or results (fabrication), changing or misreporting data or results (falsification), ... strike at the heart of the values on which science is based. Anyone who engages in any of these practices is putting his or her scientific career at risk.' Turner et al.'s (1992) paper has no scientific value. It should be retracted" (Repace and Lowrey, 1996).

Alan Moghissi (1996), in an editorial, wrote that he had offered Turner three options: (1) make the raw data available to an individual chosen by the editor; (2) the authors could write a letter to the editor stating their case; (3) the authors would do nothing. Turner et al. picked option (2). Moghissi published Turner's rebuttal and our letter together and in an accompanying editorial stated that: "No scientific publication appreciates allegations of misconduct directed at its authors. We would have preferred if Turner et al. would have chosen to make their data available to an independent scientist for reassessment. The resulting paper would have gone a long way in resolving the problem. However, based on the legal advice the authors believe that such an approach may have adverse implications. Once more it appears that the interest of science and the legal system have collided and science has lost." Privately, Moghissi called and apologetically told me that he was afraid of a lawsuit by HBI. However, this was not to be the end of the HBI story for Big Tobacco. A decade later, the HBI fraud would re-emerge as a separate count in the Justice Department's RICO prosecution of the corrupt practices of the tobacco industry.

The Brain of Dr. Idle

On November 3rd, Dr. Jeffrey Idle, a professor of pharmacogenetics at the University of New Castle (UK), testified at the behest of Philip Morris. Idle stated that his dosimetric model demonstrated that "ETS could not reach a level of concern in the workplace," based on OSHA's Permissible Exposure Limits (PELs) for the ETS constituents, hydrazine and benzene. These are just two of the 250 toxic constituents of ETS, but what about the remaining 248? In fact, for another two of those substances, 4 amino biphenyl and beta napthylamine which were potent bladder carcinogens, there were *no* permissible exposures at any level. These conveniently escaped Dr. Idle's notice. OSHA had just estimated that the entire ETS mixture of toxic and carcinogenic substances exceeded the Significant Risk Level. And EPA had indicted the ETS *mixture* as a Group A carcinogen, also contradicting Idle's assertion. Finally, secondhand smoke was produced by human smokers, and was not generated by any industrial process in the work environment. Therefore, banning ETS from the workplace would not violate the OSH Act, which contained language preventing OSHA from establishing a level for a toxic substance that would put an industry out of business.

Then Idle blithely asserted that "intersubject variability prohibited reliance on cotinine as a surrogate for all ETS smoke constituents." This was, of course, patent nonsense when applied even to groups as small as several hundred persons. In 1993 Lowrey and I had published a pharmacokinetic model for nicotine and cotinine, showing that it predicted median urinary cotinine levels of 6.2 nanograms per milliliter for U.S. nonsmokers. By comparison, the median urinary cotinine levels reported in the Fontham study that OSHA was relying on were 5.6 ng/ml for 728 persons in 5 U.S. metropolitan areas, an 11% difference. And with respect to plasma (serum) cotinine, we predicted a level of 1.1 ng/ml for U.S. smokers, compared to an observed level of 1.1 ng/ml in 232 nonsmokers in Portland Maine, a 0% difference (Repace and Lowrey, 1993). Poor Dr. Idle had dug himself such a big hole by failing to do his homework, that I was motivated to pull a chestnut out of my pocket that I'd picked up on my way to work. I rolled it on the table as he droned on, whispering to my fellow panelists, "this is the brain of Dr. Idle." We all tried hard to suppress the urge to break out laughing. It provided a welcome note of levity in the interminable hearings. I still have that chestnut as a keepsake.

On November 15, industry consultant Maurice Levois attacked the Helsing Study. He argued that "OSHA's calculations of heart disease deaths associated with ETS exposure relied on … The Helsing study [which] suffers from serious methodological problems." One of LeVois' central points was that research on ETS and heart disease risk 'probably shows a publication bias,' meaning that there is a tendency only for studies demonstrating an association to be reported in the literature. He even made the ludicrous suggestion that, "the worse the study was, the more likely it was to show an association with ETS and heart disease." He added that "if many of these studies were on any topic other than ETS, they would not be published" [TTID 2501341203].

That same day, Stan Glantz returned to the fray, and began sitting with the OSHA panel, feeding questions to Susan Sherman, and later cross-examining industry witnesses on ETS and heart disease issues himself. Philip Witorsch later testified on behalf of the Tobacco Institute, arguing, inter alia, that there was a "threshold for most carcinogens." This was an amazing whopper; I was tempted to pull out my chestnut again. On November 16, Kathie Hammond of UC Berkeley testified for OSHA, emphasizing that nicotine was an appropriate atmospheric marker for ETS, and that the concept of "cigarette equivalence" was being misused by the tobacco industry. The industry had been expressing both exposure and risk in terms of cigarette equivalents of nicotine inhaled out of the air. This misuse had been explicitly discredited in the 1986 Surgeon General's Report, which cited a calculation that Lowrey and I had performed in our *Science* article. One of the ways we tried to interpret nonsmokers' exposure in those very early days, was to express the inhaled quantity of secondhand smoke as low tar cigarette equivalents. This was to counter the industry's arbitrary use of high tar cigarette equivalents on the sensible notion that "sauce for the goose is sauce for the gander." The Surgeon General (1986) contrasted the two methods of calculation to demonstrate the futility of this approach to assess either exposure or risk. A serendipitous benefit.

PHILIP MORRIS ABANDONS THE OSHA HEARING

On November 22, Philip Morris withdrew from the OSHA Hearings without testifying. They had been scheduled to appear on December 1st. Instead, in a 17-page letter to Judge Vittone, Philip Morris complained:

"Our two primary concerns are as follows: (1) the participation of plaintiffs' product liability counsel to further their personal and financial interests has distorted a legitimate administrative hearing (Section I infra): and (2) the inclusion of two well-known anti-tobacco activists who are not OSHA employees but serve in an 'official' capacity on the OSHA panel (Section II infra) makes it clear that the proceedings are anything but objective and fair – despite the Secretary of Labor's and OSHA officials' pledges at the outset of the hearing.

Philip Morris' reasons cited the oh-so-unfair cross-examination by the five plaintiff's attorneys, especially by Ron Motley, detailing its complaints for the ensuing 8 pages, then turned to Yours Truly for another remarkable 7 pages, venting their spleen about the damage I had done to their interests, replete with voluminous footnotes that I have omitted for brevity:

"For reasons that are not disclosed by OSHA on the record, OSHA obtained the services of Mr. James Repace on detail* from the U.S. Environmental Protection Agency. OSHA is well aware that Mr. Repace has been one of the most strident, outspoken anti-tobacco activists in the United States. Mr. Repace's 'loan' from the EPA, and Mr. Repace's ongoing involvement in OSHA's rulemaking process, call into question the Department's precepts of a fair and impartial hearing.

Mr. Repace, who is now actively serving as a member of the OSHA panel present at these hearings, has an anti-tobacco involvement that is long-standing and well-documented* However, it is Mr. Repace's involvement on the OSHA panel, not his views as an individual, that is of great concern. Consider the following summary of some of Mr. Repace's activities in light of the Assistant Secretary of Labor's admonition on Monday, September 19, 1994, that 'we enter these hearings with no rigid preconceptions.' (OSHA Press Release, September 19, 1994).' In 1980, even before the first major ETS health claims appeared in the scientific literature, Repace co-authored an article with A.H. Lowrey reporting on particulate matter in the air of various indoor environments such as bars, ... restaurants, and bingo parlors, without distinguishing whether those particulates were from ETS or some other substance or activity. On the basis of these observations, the article claimed that "indoor air pollution from tobacco smoke presents a serious risk to the health of nonsmokers . . . [that] deserves as much attention as outdoor air pollution.'

In 1985, Repace co-authored (again with A.H. Lowrey) an article purporting to show that ETS was riskier than 'all regulated industrial emissions combined.' This second article by Repace and Lowrey, which represented an attempt at quantitative risk assessment, has been severely criticized by both government and private sector scientists. Well before he was 'loaned' to OSHA to work on the Proposed Rule, Mr. Repace worked with advocacy organizations such as the Group Against Smokers' Pollution ('GASP') and Action on Smoking and Health ('ASH'). As a member of the OSHA panel, he now sits in judgment of their testimony. Since the 1970s, Mr. Repace has also appeared as a witness in grievance proceedings regarding smoking in the workplace and testified before various legislative bodies to support governmental restrictions on smoking. Consider in this regard Mr. Repace's statements to the press in reaction to the defeat of an anti-smoking legislative proposal in Maryland in 1980: 'People aren't going to stand for this. Now that the facts are clear, you're going to start seeing nonsmokers becoming a lot more violent. You're going to see fights breaking out all over. Washington Star. April 5, 1980.'

During the late 1980's Mr., Repace became involved with EPA'S determination to classify ETS as a Group A carcinogen. - He outlined plans for a handbook designed to promote the elimination of ETS. Mr. Repace was in part responsible for two long-term projects – an 'ETS literature compendium' and an 'ETS workplace smoking policy guide,' – as well as a smaller project, An 'ETS fact sheet.' These projects were clearly reflective of the agenda first pursued in Mr. Repace's 1980 article.

Mr. Repace has even traveled internationally to appear at various conferences and media events to promote smoking restrictions. For example, in 1990 Mr. Repace went to New Zealand to support anti-smoking legislation in that country. Perhaps even more problematic, however, is that while Mr. Repace was actively involved as an OSHA panel member in this rulemaking, he journeyed to Paris, France, to make a presentation on environmental tobacco smoke. The abstract submitted by Mr. Repace for the October 1994 - 9th World Conference on Tobacco & Health states: 'Passive smoking continues to be a central focus of attention for researchers, public health authorities and the general public. A very wide scientific consensus has been developing on the existence of long-term adverse effects 'on health' (notably lung cancer) from exposure to environmental tobacco smoke (ETS); estimates of the [magnitude] of these effects vary, as does the weight that different authors give to the findings from available epidemiological studies. This consensus translates into measures, educational and regulatory, to protect people from involuntary exposure to ETS. These measures are discussed in respect to the occupational and general environment and in relation to their rationale (technical and economic), effectiveness and actual implementation, particularly within Europe and in the United States, with a view to their application in other areas of the world.'

Thus, before the majority of the scheduled testimony had been received on the OSHA Proposed Rule, Mr. Repace claimed a consensus on one of the very issues he is charged with reviewing objectively and fairly on behalf of an agency of the U.S. government. He also provided technical assistance to Dr. Stanton Glantz, another self-described 'anti-smoking activist' (who, significantly, is now also appearing as an active member of the OSHA panel), in the preparation of two anti-smoking films on ETS.[19] In a 1991 letter to an EPA official from Thomas S. McFee of the Department of Health and Human Services, a request was made for Mr. Repace to continue testifying on behalf of smoking restrictions 'as part of his official duties.' The letter acknowledges such assistance by Mr. Repace – all of which occurred several years prior to OSHA's promulgation of the Proposed Rule. Long before his involvement at OSHA, and well before any testimony was tendered at OSHA, Mr. Repace had publicly stated that as many as 5,000 people in the U.S. die each year from exposure to ETS.

Mr. Repace's long-standing, firmly-held and publicly disclosed positions on the subject of ETS demonstrate a serious conflict-of-interest in the context of his role as a member of the OSHA panel in these proceedings. Simple fairness dictates that Mr. Repace should never have been included as an official member of the OSHA panel. Subsequent to the commencement of Mr. Repace's 'on loan' involvement at OSHA, OSHA selected 'a number of experts' to offer testimony at the OSHA hearings in support of OSHA's rule. Not surprisingly; these witnesses included long-standing and well-documented anti-tobacco advocates such as Drs. Glantz and Judson Wells. A consideration of Dr. Glantz's anti-smoking activities is also appropriate in light of the Assistant Secretary of Labor's admonition that 'we enter these hearings with no rigid preconceptions'" (N.B., there were very lengthy footnotes to each of the paragraphs) [TTID 93141031].

Philip Morris went on to pillory Stan Glantz in a similar vein for another four pages, castigating him for his seminal work on the mechanisms of passive smoking-induced heart disease, and for off-hand comments from his colorful and entertaining lectures, dutifully recorded by industry flacks, as a self-described "lunatic" on the issue of passive smoking, that ETS helped pay his mortgage, and – I love this one – "Glantz concluded by stating that 'we are all on a roll and the bastards are on the run and I urge you to keep chasing them.'" They cited his participation on the OSHA panel representing OSHA as an "impropriety."

Philip Morris concluded its diatribe with an attack on OSHA, complaining that "our oral testimony would neither be received nor examined by OSHA with the requisite impartiality, and as such will not be given." The letter was co-signed by Anthony J. Andrade, a PM attorney, and Patrick Tyson, external counsel from the law firm of Costangy, Brooks, and Smith [TTID 93141031].

In the wake of this virulent personal attack by Philip Morris, Susan Sherman suggested it might be prudent if I sat in the audience, rather than on the stage. I didn't mind this at all: there was an annoying bright light shining directly into the panel's faces from a TV camera in the back of the auditorium. It had been present since the first day of the hearing and was the only one remaining. Liberated from the limelight, I went up to the cameraman and asked who he was and who was getting his feed; he replied that he was from Reuters but wasn't told who had commissioned the expensive taping; I felt certain that it was the industry.

To my delight, R.J. Reynolds scientists remained in the fray, which vitiated the impact of Philip Morris's withdrawal. They testified over 3 days from January 17 – 19, 1995. On the 17th, they attacked our 1980 *Science* paper, which they obviously felt was still hurting them 15 years later. They attacked the Piezobalance that we had used, questioned our measurement of short-term averages, and emphasized that it measured only area concentrations, not workers' personal exposures. They implied that people smoked differently in 1990 than in 1980, and while the "extreme" levels we measured in 1980 were possible, they were unrealistic in 1990. They touted the RJR/Oak Ridge study measurements, which they said showed RSP levels at 0.5% of OSHA's estimates. Then they disparaged OSHA's equivalence of domestic and workplace ETS exposures, arguing that domestic doses were far higher than those in the workplace. They did not address the obvious problem that for nonsmokers exposed at work only, this had no relevance whatsoever.

Next, the Reynolds scientists dismissed the use of nicotine and cotinine as quantitative markers for ETS. As evidence, they cited variability in cotinine among different individuals, the same hoary chestnut advanced by RJR's consultant, the hapless Dr. Idle. They argued that RSP and nicotine in ETS were poorly correlated and therefore nicotine could not be used to quantitatively predict RSP levels from ETS. On the 19th, they were questioned by Stan Glantz and others. Following them, I had my turn to question RJR. I had copied a couple of their graphs onto overhead slides, and superimposed one on top of the other, pointing out that by their own data, secondhand smoke RSP and nicotine decayed at the same rate, which clearly failed to support their conclusions. They continued to insist that it did. After the RJR testimony concluded, Don deBethizy, a toxicologist who at that time was Director of Product Evaluation, Research and Development for R.J. Reynolds, and the boss of the scientists who testified, came up to me at day's end and introduced himself. We shook hands, and he queried, "How did my boys do?" I smiled and replied, "I'm very pleased." And I was, although not for the reasons that deBethizy might have opined. Unlike Philip Morris, RJR had stuck it out, and in the course of trying to discredit my work, they had presented me with a bounty of intentionally misleading data and criticism of my work that was immensely valuable. Their data would soon provide grist for further work, and a serendipitous opportunity to kick Joe Camel in the caboose.

Sam Chilcote of the Tobacco Institute reported to the Executive Committee on January 10, 1995, relating how CIAR "special project" grantee Roger Jenkins had performed in the OSHA Hearings on January 4th [TTID TI41041303]

"On January 4th, Roger Jenkins testified about his 1994 Oak Ridge study, … 'the largest study of its kind,' according to Jenkins. He explained that the study involved about 1600 nonsmoking subjects from 16 cities around the country. Participants were asked to wear sampling pumps at their workplace and away from their work locations, including shopping, dining, sleeping, etc. Jenkins said the ORNL study results contradicted the findings of a 1993 study by EPA's James Repace that indicated a typical nonsmoker is exposed to about 143 micrograms of nicotine per day. Jenkins explained that the ORNL study, which even used a higher breathing rate, found an exposure of about two micrograms of nicotine per day in more than half of the study's participants. Jenkins added, 'It's clearly difficult to conclude from this data set that the typical exposures are more than 100 micrograms per cubic meter [sic] a day. About 80 percent of our study subjects received exposure to less than 20 micrograms of nicotine per day.' … 'Jenkins also said that while the participants perceived their greatest exposure to ETS to be in the workplace, the study found that absolute exposures in terms of micrograms of material are larger in the home than in the workplace by a factor of at least four to six, depending on the individual components.' "

In his cross-examination of Jenkins, trial lawyer Randy Hopper asked: "I have just one question for you: Did it ever occur to you at any point that it might possibly affect the outcome of this study when it has that much involvement by the tobacco industry, who has a financial stake in the outcome of these proceedings? And that you are claiming to provide the best and the largest and the most important study? Did it ever occur to you? That someone might question the integrity of that? Dr. Jenkins replied: "Oh. Absolutely. Absolutely, we thought that people would question the integrity of it. But if you're implying that I would alter my testimony or alter my..." Mr. Hopper: "I'm not implying anything." Dr. Jenkins: "If you're... Well, but your question. It's very easy for anybody to infer that from that kind of a question. And I think my record speaks for itself." Roger and I were in complete agreement on that score.

The Oak Ridge Study was intended to serve two basic goals for the industry: first, to cast doubt on Repace and Lowrey's estimate of nonsmokers' ETS exposure, and second, to portray the workplace as a minor source of exposure compared to the home. In 1994, despite the fact that tens of millions of workers were exposed to secondhand smoke in the workplace, the *only* estimates of workplace exposure extant were those provided by Repace and Lowrey and the RJR/Oak Ridge study. This would not change until 1996, when the CDC weighed in with its marvelous NHANES study of cotinine in the blood of nonsmoking workers who were exposed to ETS at work only, at home only, and both and neither.

When the marathon seven-month hearing ended in March 1995, it then became post-hearing comment time. This gave the industry – and Philip Morris – another bite at the apple. This one tobacco company alone had submitted "in excess of a quarter million pages of scientific, legal, and economic testimony and submissions refuting the proposed workplace smoking ban" [TTID 2045865349]. Philip Morris's chairman would boast at PM's October 1995 Awards Ceremony for its OSHA Team, that, "Our PM team helped 150 business people attend the hearings in Washington, D.C. and testify against the proposed workplace smoking ban. The team also recruited more than 30 internationally prominent experts who testified against the ban and submitted additional material to the record in support of their testimony. A PM crew of 20 or more individuals was present at the hearings – or providing back-room support nearby – for the entire run of the hearings" [TTID 2046044560].

I SKEWER JOE CAMEL AND THE MARLBORO MAN

Both Philip Morris and RJ Reynolds submitted Post-Hearing Briefs. Despite their refusal to testify, Philip Morris entered Post-Hearing Comments arguing in part that:
- OSHA has not shown that ETS at exposure levels found in the workplace poses a significant risk of material health impairment to employees.
- OSHA cannot demonstrate that its proposed zero tolerance of nonsmoker exposure to ETS in indoor workplaces is reasonably necessary or appropriate to reduce a significant risk of material health impairment to employees.
- OSHA's proposal to ban workplace smoking except in specially designed smoking rooms

is not justified because other, less drastic alternatives, which OSHA did not adequately consider, can address any workplace smoking issues.

- OSHA's attempt to single out ETS, when almost all ETS constituents are found in indoor air from other sources, is unjustified.
- OSHA significantly underestimated the burden and costs that U.S. businesses and federal, state and local governments would incur if the Proposed Rule is implemented. It seems clear that OSHA cannot justify or support its current Proposed Rule on indoor air quality and indoor smoking. …"

R.J. Reynolds, in their February 9th 1995 post-hearing brief, argued in part:

"There is no rational basis for OSHA to ban workplace smoking and single out environmental tobacco smoke from other indoor air constituents for regulation. On every critical issue, the best available evidence is clear:

• There is no substantial evidence that current workplace ETS exposures present a significant risk of material impairment to health. • • Current workplace ETS exposure does not present a significant risk of lung cancer. • • Current workplace ETS exposure does not present a significant risk of cardiovascular disease.

• Workplace smoking issues can be addressed by controls other than workplace smoking bans. • • Workplace smoking issues can be addressed by simple accommodation. • • Compliance with ASHRAE Standard 62-1989 substantially reduces workplace ETS exposures. • • Reasonable increases in ventilation substantially reduce workplace ETS exposures. • • Separating smokers from nonsmokers substantially reduces workplace ETS exposures. • • An appropriate combination of accommodation, ventilation, separation, and air-cleaning controls substantially reduces workplace ETS exposures. • A workplace smoking ban places enormous and unwarranted burdens and costs upon U.S. businesses, and federal, state and local governments. • • Separately ventilated and negatively pressurized smoking rooms are enormously expensive. • • Separately ventilated and negatively pressurized smoking rooms are not the most cost-effective approach to workplace smoking issues. • • The record contains substantial evidence that private markets and public institutions have sufficiently addressed workplace smoking issues. • • The record contains substantial evidence that a workplace smoking ban will have a devastating economic impact on small businesses. • • There is no substantial evidence that a workplace smoking ban is economically feasible.

OSHA's proposed workplace smoking ban violates every Executive, Judicial, and Legislative limitation on OSHA's authority to promulgate occupational safety and health standards. The deficiencies in OSHA's Proposed Rule are so obvious that the proposal cannot be viewed as a legitimate exercise in standard setting." [TTID 515736365]

In their Post-Hearing Brief, RJR took my name in vain more than 250 times in their 464-page brief, taking considerable pains to attempt to discredit any reliance by OSHA on my corpus of work. They left no stone unthrown, attacking my measurements, models, and calculations showing that ventilation could not control ETS. Frustratingly, I had no obvious way of rebutting their post-hearing comments, as I was a member of the OSHA panel, not a witness with legal standing to comment. Suddenly, in early May 1995, Sheldon Weiner informed me that I must now return to EPA, but for my yeoman service to OSHA, I would receive an Outstanding Performance Rating. This would soon prove highly advantageous in my defense against Axelrad's renewed efforts to heap slime on me.

My sudden return to EPA afforded me a stellar opportunity to make a post-hearing brief myself, by inserting a rebuttal to the assaults on my work by RJR and Jenkins into the OSHA Docket. This masterstroke was accomplished as follows. I wrote a 29-page memorandum to Steven Bayard on EPA letterhead, "in response to your request for comment on EPA's official submission to the OSHA docket." By mutual agreement, Steven promptly inserted my memorandum into the Docket late on a Friday afternoon, on the last day and the last hour that post-hearing comments could be submitted, as an addendum to his own officially-cleared EPA post-hearing comment – without informing EPA. On the following Monday, Steven then informed his management at EPA that "he might have made a mistake" in including my memo without official clearance, and Bill Farland, Steven's office director, wrote a letter to OSHA, withdrawing my memo from EPA's official comment on the grounds that there had been "insufficient time for EPA clearance for its scientific and policy content." Nevertheless, my memorandum – as intended – remained physically in the OSHA docket, where it then became part of the official record.

I had written a brief abstract to my submission: "Comments submitted by MW Ogden of RJ Reynolds, academic consultant Prof. Jeffrey Idle, Dr. Stanley Greenfield of ICF-Kaiser, consultant Dr. Robert Nilsson, Gradient Corporation, and Dr. Roger Jenkins of Oak Ridge National Laboratory, the CIAR "special project" researcher, are reviewed. It was obvious that many of their comments were in conflict with theory or experiment or were based upon workplace measurements which were atypical." My analysis was highly technical, and used Ogden's own measurements, which I thought were excellent, to refute his misleading conclusions. In brief, Ogden argued that gas-phase nicotine was a poor marker for particulate-phase RSP from ETS, because nicotine had "unusual decay characteristics." Lowrey and I had argued that for ETS, a 10:1 RSP/nicotine ratio should be used to predict ETS RSP from ETS nicotine in spaces based on three independent studies by researchers I trusted. [This ratio would become widely adopted in 5 years, after Joan Daisey, director of Lawrence Berkeley Laboratory's Indoor Air Program, published a seminal paper in *Environmental Health Perspectives* which showed that a 10:1 ratio could be derived directly from Roger Jenkins own 16 Cities' raw data, which would not be made available until 1998]. Joan would make it clear that this ratio would obtain in rooms where smoking occurred regularly, such that the nicotine outgassing from room surfaces created an equilibrium where surface deposition and re-emission balanced.]

In any case, my analysis of Ogden's chamber data showed that the RSP/nicotine ratio was linear with the number of cigarettes smoked with a ratio of about 8:1, close to that found by Leaderer and Hammond in their 1981 chamber study. Secondly, I calculated that their measurements of RSP and nicotine from the top 50 US cigarette brands showed an emission of about 14 milligrams (mg) of RSP per cigarette with a 23% standard deviation, and a corresponding emission of 1.8 mg of nicotine with a 16% standard deviation [about two thirds of normally distributed data fall within one standard deviation of the mean]. In other words, the tremendous variability that Odgen's experiment allegedly showed was actually bogus. Moreover, since the cigarette market was dominated by the top 5 brands, with Marlboro capturing about 40% of the sales, it was apparent that in practice, the variance in emissions in real-world settings would be much smaller. This was important for modeling workplace concentrations. And happily at this point, my model was no longer the only one.

My suggestion that Wayne Ott apply for research funding from California's Tobacco-Related Disease Research Program (TRDRP) had born fruit, and Wayne and colleagues at Stanford developed a real-time model, confirmed by measurements, that was far more sophisticated than our steady-state model. Ott et al. (1992) concluded that, "When the parameter values used by Repace (1987) in his habitual smoker model (to predict RSP concentrations) are substituted in our general model, the two models agree." Finally, we had independent confirmation that our steady-state mass balance model for the prediction of secondhand smoke in buildings was structurally correct. I stated that my model indicated that data reported for field measurements by RJR, Oak Ridge, and HBI all corresponded to ratios of smoker density to air exchange rate that were "abnormally low" for workplaces, and therefore yielded commensurately low concentrations of RSP from ETS.

Then I turned to Oak Ridge's measured salivary cotinine data. I pointed out that based on Jenkins's data (which in fact had been measured by RJR scientists, on subjects selected by RJR's survey firm, Bellomy Research, Inc., rather than by Jenkins) (Barnes et al., 2006), OSHA's Significant Risk level would be exceeded. Moreover, by using a pharmacokinetic model I developed in 1995 and later published (Repace, et al., 1998), the ETS RSP levels had to be fully two orders of magnitude (a hundred fold) higher than Jenkins/ RJR reported. I made a detailed graphical analysis of Jenkins' data, showing that contrary to established science, which indicated that nicotine intake and cotinine excretion were linearly related, i.e., proportional, his nicotine and cotinine data showed a quadratic (non-linear) relationship that was un-physical. In fact, it contradicted the law of conservation of mass, indicating that the 16 Cities data was erroneous in some fashion. However, I noted, his salivary cotinine values *were* reasonable. This suggested that Jenkins' reported nicotine numbers "differed significantly from that anticipated from either theory or experiment." I concluded that the RJR/Oak Ridge data set showed "nicotine values much lower than predicted ... or reported for typical offices," and that it would be "imprudent for OSHA or EPA to rely on data from [that] study."

In Idle's OSHA testimony, he had made the ludicrous assertion that dietary nicotine "from French fried potatoes" in the American diet would yield the same nicotine exposure as did passive smoking. I observed that to the contrary, citing my peer-reviewed commentary in the *British Medical Journal* in 1994 using US Department of Agriculture data on American consumers' consumption of nicotine-containing vegetables (Solanaceae), that dietary nicotine from all sources would "contribute at most 1% of salivary cotinine" found in passive smokers. Moreover, it was the potato *skins* that contained nicotine, and these of course, were removed before frying (Repace, 1994). Did Brits eat their fish and chips with the skins on?

Martin Jarvis, in a companion letter, had calculated that a nonsmoker would have to gorge "90 kg (198 lbs) of tomatoes per day" to result in cotinine levels comparable to those in passive smokers (Jarvis, 1994). Idle had further asserted that "exposure to ETS components in the workplace is so low that it cannot plausibly be associated with increased risk of lung cancer or heart disease." However, our (completed but as yet unpublished) Monte Carlo model estimated that only 1% of workplaces with unrestricted smoking would have risk levels from lung cancer and heart disease combined that were below the 1 death per 1000 workers per 45-year working lifetime associated with OSHA's Significant Risk level. So Idle was batting 1000 on the bozo scale.

Finally, I turned to the comments of Dr. Greenfield from the consulting firm, ICF-Kaiser. In brief, he argued without supplying any supporting data, "that it is quite possible that an adult could be exposed to ETS RSP and ETS nicotine at different times." Since both ETS constituents were emitted at the same time from the same cigarette, I observed that this was "bizarre and physically impossible, and an incredible theory." Then he argued that the fraction of time that smoking could occur would be a "maximum of 1/3 regardless of the number of smokers." Greenfield also presented no data to support this contention, whereas in our 1980 *Science* paper, in visiting 19 premises at random we found an average of 11% of the occupants smoking. At a population average smoking prevalence of 33%, this indicated that the average smoker would spend 1/3 of each smoking hour actively smoking at an average rate of 2 cigarettes per hour, and if three or more smokers were present and smoking at random, there would be one or more cigarettes being smoked at any instant in time. [In 1996, in a brilliant data-based confirmation of our hypothesis, Wayne Ott would time eight smokers in Harry's Hofbrau, a restaurant/bar in Redwood City, California, with a stopwatch over the course of 50 minutes; he observed an average of 2.2 cigarettes per smoker, or about 2.6 cigarettes per smoker per hour, with a range of 1 to 5 cigarettes being smoked during any minute (Fig. 9.7, Repace, 2007)]. Greenfield's other criticisms amounted to little more than nit-picking and hand-waving, and don't bear repeating. I wondered *what was this guy smoking?*

Philip Morris (PM), in its post-hearing comments devoted six pages to "Analysis of a model for the prediction of ETS Nicotine Exposure and Cotinine Dose in Nonsmokers Developed by Repace, et al." PM asserted that "the model employs numerous assumptions, many of which are contrary to fact and clearly not 'the best available evidence' for estimating ETS exposures." ... "Criticisms of Repace's earlier model demonstrated that it greatly overestimated nonsmoker exposure to ETS (nicotine and respirable suspended particulate) when compared to actual measured exposures." And what were those "actual measured exposures?" None other than measurements reported by RJR scientists Oldaker and Bohanon in five office buildings in two separate papers, and industry mole Ted Sterling in another.

PM then asserted that despite the fact that our model predicted levels of air nicotine in offices and saliva cotinine in office workers consistent with observations in papers by academics Hammond and Emmons, respectively, with a high degree of accuracy, "whether or not the selected data truly "verify" the Repace, et al. model is an open question. "Indeed, ... the nicotine exposure levels reported by Hammond are ... several times higher than measurements reported in virtually every other recent study in the literature." And what were those 'recent studies?' One was by the long-time CIAR-funded tobacco mole Phillips from Corning Hazelton (which later morphed into Covance Labs) in the UK (TTID 2505443955; TTID PM3006639539; Phillips et al., 1996] and the other two were by Jenkins at Oak Ridge and Ogden at RJR. Philip Morris went on to raise a number of other criticisms of the comparison of our model to the limited field data available. While it was true that the cotinine study of Emmons in 90 Massachusetts office workers and the nicotine measurements in a dozen Massachusetts offices by Hammond were limited, they were the only available data not measured by a tobacco company or its "special project" consultants, which were, of course, intended to deceive.

In 1996, in a national survey of US adult non-tobacco users, the U.S. Centers for Disease Control (CDC) would report that nonsmokers with work-only ETS exposure had geometric mean ETS serum cotinine doses about 2½ times those nonsmoking workers who had no work or home ETS exposure (Pirkle et al., 1996). And, that "both the home and workplace environments significantly contribute to environmental tobacco smoke exposure in the United States." This supported the conclusions of Repace and Lowrey in 1985. CDC found that nonsmokers reporting both home and work exposure had mean levels of 0.926 ng/mL, nearly 7½ times higher than those with no work or home exposure, at 0.124 ng/mL (Pirkle et al., 1996). My rebuttal to the industry and its moles and consultants in the OSHA hearing provoked a new round of post-post-hearing comments by the tobacco industry. It was more of the same tedious bloviation and does not bear repetition. I did not bother to comment on them.

The OSHA hearing raised enormous alarm in Philip Morris corporate circles. In an 11-page August 3, 1995 memorandum, entitled "OSHA SETS THE STAGE FOR A SEPARATE, FINAL ETS RULE," it laid out an impending disaster scenario:

"American business is one signature away from a final OSHA rule which would eliminate smoking in all domestic workplaces. ... there is nothing legally, procedurally, substantively or scientifically that can be done to block OSHA from publishing a final rule on ETS after November 13, 1995. ... the facts indicate that OSHA is systematically and strategically working toward a final rule on indoor smoking. ... OSHA has assembled a core group of anti-tobacco advocates to develop the standard that bans ETS and indoor smoking in the workplace [including] Stanton Glantz, James Repace, Judson Wells, Jonathan Samet, Michael Hodgson, Katherine Hammond, Neil Benowitz, Steve Bayard. ... The OSHA panel and their experts will never voluntarily accept a position other than one that states that ETS causes disease in nonsmokers including lung cancer, heart disease, respiratory deficiencies, irritation and asthma."

"... In fact, OSHA's statements [citing those by Secretary Robert Reich and Assistant Secretary Joseph Dear, as well as John Martonik, and appearance of a new risk assessment expert, Adam Finkel] over the last fifteen months indicate an anti-tobacco view … in all of the foregoing, the active role of the EPA in orchestrating the OSHA rulemaking should not be overlooked. … The EPA has working contractual relations in over two dozen countries involving indoor air quality. The EPA would vigorously market a final rule banning smoking in the workplace through its international network. James Repace, Steven Bayard and Jennifer Jinot of EPA (who have been involved at OSHA) have already taken that message internationally. … In this regard, note the FOIA generated talking points prepared at EPA for an EPA meeting with [Assistant Secretary] Joe Dear. Among other things, they indicate an involvement at OSHA not only of the EPA, but of Congressman Waxman as well."

Bryan-Jones and Bero (2003) in an analysis of tobacco industry documents, public commentary and media coverage, found that the tobacco industry implemented five strategies to attempt to defeat the OSHA Indoor Air Quality Rule: maintain scientific debate about the basis of the rule, delay deliberation on the rule, redefine the scope of the rule, recruit and assist labor and business organizations in opposing the rule, and finally, increase media coverage of the tobacco industry position. When all these had failed they played their trump card. The industry resorted to the last refuge of scoundrels: the new Republican Congress, elected in 1994, led by the notorious Newt Gingrich (R) GA. It was the Very Best Congress That Tobacco Money Could Buy.

Steven Bayard had gone over to OSHA in 1995, where, he said, as a condition of his new job, which involved a promotion, *he was forbidden from working on ETS*. Think about that. Steven related that the Gingrich-led Congress had cut NIOSH's budget by 25%, and then covertly threatened OSHA with similar treatment if it did not deep-six its indoor air proposal. OSHA soon capitulated. In 1995, OSHA immediately disbanded the indoor air team as soon as the hearings ended, leaving the hapless project officer Debra Janes high and dry to handle 110,000 comments all by her lonesome self. She soon departed OSHA for a new job at the Mine Safety and Health Administration. And despite all the *Sturm und Drang* generated by OSHA's Hearings, despite their importance for occupational health, what did the Clinton-appointed Department of Labor and OSHA officials, from Robert Reich and Joseph Dear on down have to say publicly? Not one word.

The ill-fated OSHA rulemaking, despite all of our hard staff work and all of the hard work of the expert witnesses and trial attorneys, died a slow death, languishing until December 17, 2001 when OSHA withdrew its Indoor Air Quality proposal and terminated the rulemaking proceedings. John L. Henshaw, the Assistant Secretary of Labor explained that:

"OSHA is withdrawing its Indoor Air Quality proposal and terminating the rulemaking proceeding. In the years since the proposal was issued, a great many state and local governments and private employers have taken action to curtail smoking in public areas and in workplaces. In addition, the portion of the proposal not related to environmental tobacco smoke (ETS) received little attention during the rulemaking proceedings, and much of that consisted of commenters calling into question significant portions of the proposal. As a result, record evidence supporting the non-ETS portion of the proposal is sparse." (Federal Register 66:64946).

Prior to that point, ASH had sued OSHA to force it to issue the rule. However, ASH in a press release on December 14, 2001, stated in part that,

"Action on Smoking and Health (ASH) has agreed to dismiss its law suit against the Occupational Safety and Health Administration [OSHA] to avoid serious harm to the nonsmokers' rights movement from an adverse action OSHA had threatened to take if forced by the law suit to do so. In its court filing, OSHA had argued that it might not be feasible to ban smoking in restaurants, and that developing some hypothetical measurement of tobacco smoke pollution might be a better remedy than prohibiting smoking. Because this also had the virtue of avoiding federal pre-emption, it earned the blessing of the grassroots anti-smoking organizations, who pragmatically decided to work for smoke-free workplace laws from the bottom up, town by town, city by city, and state by state. ...

However, in its court response, ASH noted that smoking bans in California, Maryland, and many other jurisdictions clearly prove that smoking bans are feasible, and that there is no evidence that any level of tobacco smoke however measured would ever meet OSHA's regulatory mandate to prevent worker deaths. Nevertheless, it became clear that OSHA would use this (and perhaps even stronger) language in a formal OSHA decision if ASH continued to press its law suit, and that such language could seriously hurt efforts to pass nonsmokers' rights legislation at the state and local level, and to get relief for nonsmokers in court suits and administrative proceedings.

Another major threat was that, if the agency were forced by ASH's law suit to promulgate a rule regulating smoking in the workplace, OSHA – at least under this administration – would be likely to pass a very weak one. This weak rule in turn could pre-empt future and possibly even existing nonsmokers' rights law – a risk no one is willing to take. ASH therefore reluctantly agreed to dismiss the law suit after consultation with other leaders in the nonsmokers' rights movement. As a result of ASH's dismissal of its law suit, OSHA will now withdraw its rulemaking proceeding related to workplace smoking but will do so without using any of the damaging language which they had threatened to include."

But make no mistake, it was another big scalp in the industry's belt. During the year, I managed interviews on PBS's NOVA ['Can Buildings Make You Sick'], *Consumers Reports* ['The Truth About Secondhand Smoke'], *Physics Today (1995)* ['Exposing the Dangers of Tobacco Smoke'] and gave another in my series of lectures at Johns Hopkins School of Public Health. I also published a paper on Risk Management of Passive Smoking at Work and at Home in a legal journal (Repace, 1994).

In July 1995, Stan Glantz and colleagues issued a remarkable and heroic series of publications concerning the secret papers of tobacco giants Brown and Williamson (B&W) and its parent company British American Tobacco (BAT). They had been leaked to Glantz by a disgruntled paralegal, whistleblower Merrell Williams. These became known as the *Brown and Williamson Documents*. Glantz et al. (1995) reported that the documents showed that the involvement of tobacco industry lawyers in the selection of scientific projects to be funded was in sharp contrast to the industry's public statements about its review process for its external research program. Moreover, the documents demonstrated that scientific merit was in no way a consideration in the selection of external research projects. And that the research projects were actually intended to generate good publicity for the industry, to cover up the fact that tobacco use and secondhand smoke were harmful and to influence policy makers not to enact smoking restrictions.

Barnes et al. (1995) reported that Brown & Williamson (B&W) and BAT began conducting ETS research in the mid 1970s, about when I began my own studies. BAT researchers found that sidestream smoke produced irritation in nonsmokers, that it contained toxic substances, and that it was carcinogenic in laboratory tests. Nevertheless, throughout the 1980s, BAT and B&W repeatedly denied that exposure to ETS was proven dangerous to health, quietly burying their own research that showed a clear and present danger. Further, the documents showed that the industry funded scientific research whose stated internal purpose was to anticipate and refute the damning evidence against ETS. The whole wretched tale is told at length in Glantz et al.'s book, *The Cigarette Papers* (1998).

Big Tobacco Renews its Attacks on Ashrae and EPA

In early 1995, the industry remained concerned about ASHRAE as well as the fallout from OSHA's proposed ETS rule. In an unidentified PowerPoint presentation (bearing the hallmarks of Philip Morris) titled "Support to Legal and Corporate Affairs, OSHA dated January 11th 1995, the briefing noted that "OSHA's Proposed Rule forces zero exposure of nonsmokers to ETS in the workplace by banning smoking or constructing separate smoking lounges and emphasized that "ETS is the only substance targeted (by OSHA) for source control – even known human carcinogens." It noted that OSHA's proposed rule would require that ventilation systems (HVAC) to be operated in compliance with building codes in force at the time of construction. It then explained that ASHRAE developed professional consensus standards for HVAC design, and that ASHRAE Standards have been widely adopted into ventilation codes by regulatory authorities around the world [TTID 2050994075].

The briefing then got to the heart of the problem: "ASHRAE Standards Committee 62 has become an anti-smoking battleground. Its membership includes: Gene Tucker, EPA – Chairman, William Cain, Prof. Surgery USC [Univ. of Southern Ca], Andrew Persily, NIST, Jonathan Samet, Johns Hopkins U, Richard Daynard, Attorney, Northeastern U, Ole Fanger, EC, and Michael Hodgson, MD, U of Conn." It noted that "while the current [1989] standard calls for a ventilation rate of 20 cfm/person with moderate smoking, the proposed revision deletes the moderate smoking provision and will require significantly higher ventilation rates if smoking is permitted." It called for action: "if we do nothing, we will have a very unfavorable standard making it easier for OSHA to adopt and give building owners and employers more impetus to ban smoking. We will be funding a study to determine the comfort acceptability at moderate smoking levels as a function of ventilation rate by Jim Woods at Va Tech. Why Woods? – Respected and influential member of ASHRAE – We have a relationship from previous work - An OSHA witness and has been retained by OSHA to draft the final rule - Recognized around the world as an IAQ authority – Believes in source control, but he is objective 'the data's the data' – We need an ongoing relationship with Woods. ... We don't know what OSHA's final rule will be but there will be one ... PEL based? Spatial separation? Isolation of smokers?" [TTID 2050994075].

As for Gene Tucker, the industry disposed of this troublesome EPA scientist by administering the usual Congressional waterboarding, based on the usual trumped-up "conflict of interest" charges. Tucker's sad story was reported in the *Indoor Air Review* of August 1995, quoted in part [TTID TI3621-2576]:

"Accusations by a Republican congressman that federal official Gene Tucker became an ASHRAE committee chairman after he helped give the trade association a $200,000 federal grant dominated the news coming out of the ASHRAE Summer Meeting held in San Diego, June 24-28. Conflict of interest charges from Rep. Joseph Barton of Texas surfaced just before Tucker's scheduled departure from the ASHRAE Standard 62-1989 committee. At the meeting, the news even overshadowed the continued development of revising 62-1989, the most controversial indoor air quality and ventilation standard to date. His term was up this summer as part of a normal four-year rotation; however, some committee members said Tucker was not asked to return. Tucker is also special assistant to the director of the Pollution Prevention and Control Division of the Environmental Protection Agency (EPA) in Research Triangle Park, N.C. That's why Barton said the situation could be a conflict of interest and is calling for an independent investigation into the grant signed over to ASHRAE by several officials, including Tucker. Tucker told the *Wall Street Journal* that in 1991, he was not an ASHRAE member when ASHRAE recruited him to head the 62-1989 committee, where he served voluntarily and without pay."

The industry's concerns about one Gene Tucker were made clear in 1999 in a 35-page Appeal to ASHRAE's inclusion of what they regarded as a damaging Addendum to ASHRAE Standard 62 1989 [TTID 2083488598]:

> "In 1992 Dr. W. Gene Tucker, Chief of EPA's Indoor Air Branch nominated individuals to form a new Standing Standards Project Committee (SSPC 62) to consider revisions to Standard 62-1989. EPA's policy recommendation and publications at that time stated that smoking should be restricted to separately ventilated areas or banned from buildings. A number of the committee members nominated by Dr. Tucker shared EPA's position concerning the issue of severely restricting or banning smoking indoors. This issue is addressed in more detail infra at ~ 59-63. In addition, Dr. Tucker nominated a committee predisposed towards the interests of 'academia and government.' See comments of ASHRAE Standards Project Liaison Subcommittee Member Waller Clements who indicated that Dr. Tucker kept him off of SSPC 62, instead preferring 'academia and government people.'"

In 2002, Andrew Persily, a Division Chief at the National Institute of Standards and Technology (NIST), an internationally recognized expert on ventilation and indoor air quality, and a long-time member of the ASHRAE 62 committee, would describe ASHRAE's efforts to revise this standard in a paper delivered at the International Conference on Indoor Air Quality and Indoor Climate in 2002, in Monterey, California (Persily, 2002). I was in attendance. His presentation described the malign influence of the tobacco industry, delivered with great restraint. He began by discussing the history of ASHRAE Standard 62 as it evolved from a purely ventilation standard in 1973 to limit the buildup of carbon dioxide and odors indoors through its transition into ventilation for acceptable indoor air quality in 1981, through its long struggle with the tobacco industry during the 1980's and its capitulation to the tobacco industry in 1989, to the adoption of a revision (Addendum 62e) in 1999 that removed a note to the table of minimum outdoor air requirements stating that these rates accommodated "a moderate amount of smoking."

This was done, Persily said, because since the 1989 publication of the standard, "numerous public health and governmental authorities declared environmental tobacco smoke (ETS) to be a significant health risk. The committee removed this note based on the inconsistency between the stated purpose of the standard to 'minimize the potential for adverse health effects' and the presence of ETS." Persily complained, without naming the source, of "a layer of controversy, procedural changes and politics that has distracted the committee and ASHRAE during the revision process." In fact, the source of this controversy was the tobacco industry, which appealed the publication of Addendum 62e, to ASHRAE's Board of Directors and ultimately to ANSI (The American National Standards Institute). These appeals were denied, and the elimination of the smoking accommodation language became part of the standard when it was republished as ASHRAE Standard 62-1999. This was a major defeat for Big Tobacco.

The "controversy" Andy Persily described was manufactured out of whole cloth by the tobacco industry, which treated ASHRAE with much the same contempt that it had for the Surgeon General, OSHA, NIOSH, and the EPA. In 1981, the American Society of Heating, Refrigeration, and Air Conditioning Engineers (ASHRAE) had adopted a ventilation standard (62-1981) which called for considerably higher ventilation rates for smoking buildings than for nonsmoking buildings, imposing an extra cost penalty on smoking buildings. At that time, Standard 62 was being revised on a 5-year cycle, using a committee process that invited the membership of affected industries. Taking full advantage of this inclusive process, the tobacco industry stacked the committee with its representatives, including an industry lawyer, and one committee member who was secretly retained as a consultant, as later reluctantly disclosed in a legal deposition (Hal Levin, personal communication). Using disruptive parliamentary maneuvers that wore the committee down

(Gene Tucker, personal communication), and by threatening litigation, the tobacco industry had persuaded ASHRAE to abandon higher ventilation rates for smoking buildings (Repace, 1991). In 1989, as previously noted, the revised ASHRAE standard 62 wound up being issued three years late, with a single ventilation rate for both smoking and nonsmoking buildings, enabling tobacco industry propagandists to claim that ASHRAE ventilation standards adequately controlled tobacco smoke. Tobacco industry representatives, both overt and covert, remained a permanent fixture on key ASHRAE and ASTM committees.

More Hirayama Bashing

Despite the 1992 EPA report incorporating more than 30 studies of passive smoking and lung cancer, the industry never gave up trying to discredit Hirayama's never-to-be-sufficiently-damned seminal paper associating passive smoking with lung cancer. In 1995, long-time industry consultant Peter Lee published a paper in the *International Archives of Occupational and Environmental Health*, entitled "Marriage to a smoker may not be a valid marker of exposure in studies relating environmental tobacco smoke to risk of lung cancer in Japanese non-smoking women." It was simply an attempt to refute Hirayama's 1981 study by attempting to show that Hirayama's results were confounded by massive misclassification of Japanese smoking women as nonsmokers. The work was originally conceived as a CIAR grant proposal by Japanese investigators, but after processing by the Tobacco Institute's law firm, Covington and Burling in 1991, it had been reworked by Peter Lee and Chris Proctor, and the Japanese names were removed. Predictably, the new lawyer-laundered paper concluded that cotinine measurements indicated that 22 out of 106 women who claimed nonsmoking status were actually smokers. The Lee-Proctor paper asserted that because spousal smoking studies had a *potential* for misclassification bias, they therefore had "little scientific basis." However, internal tobacco industry documents showed that the industry tried to hide its massive involvement in drafting Lee's paper, only acknowledging its "financial support" (Hong & Bero, 2002).

On July 25, 1995, *The New York Times* reported that in 1972, Claude Teague Jr., a Reynolds R&D executive wrote in a confidential memo that, "In a sense, the tobacco industry may be thought of as being a specialized, highly ritualized segment of the pharmaceutical industry. Tobacco products uniquely contain and deliver nicotine, a potent drug with a variety of physiological effects." So this confirmed my epiphany about Big Tobacco being a rogue branch of Big Pharma when I saw the Reynolds presentation at OSHA in 1993.

CHAPTER 14

SPARRING WITH THE CONGRESSIONAL RESEARCH SERVICE

"Dr. Repace says he was subsequently warned by his supervisor, Robert Axelrad, director of the indoor air division, to halt his work on passive smoke. 'I was told very specifically that if I wanted to write any more scientific papers on ETS. I would have to get them approved by the division head, and he made it pretty clear they wouldn't be.' Dr. Repace recalls. The EPA denies suppressing Dr. Repace's work on secondhand smoke. 'The EPA's work on secondhand smoke speaks for itself,' says Dr. Axelrad. 'It changed the landscape of tobacco control in the U.S.'"

[The Wall Street Journal, April 28, 1998].

When I returned to EPA from OSHA in May of 1995, Axelrad was not thrilled. I was still working in Crystal City in Arlington Virginia, and the Indoor Air Division was in Washington. There was nobody looking over my shoulder. At that time, the Indoor Air Division had expanded. My new first line supervisor was John Girman, a scientist hired from the Indoor Air Group at Lawrence Berkeley Lab in California. Although John dutifully followed Axelrad's commands, I liked and respected him for his competence and his candor. In a telling phone conversation, John asked me to inform him once a week, in writing, what I was working on, *"So we can assure Bliley that you're not a loose cannon."* I was stunned by Girman's candid admission that Axelrad's attempts to suppress my work dating back five years to March 1990 were being done on marching orders handed down from The Congressman From Philip Morris! This was prima facie evidence of grossly unethical behavior by Axelrad. I agreed to keep John informed. I imagined that as long as I kept any mention of secondhand smoke out of those weekly reports, I would remain out of Axelrad's crosshairs. I was wrong.

Axelrad remained implacably determined to get rid of me, one way or another. In my October performance review, he attempted to give me a "minimally satisfactory" performance rating. I outright refused to accept it. I finally had my fill of his sociopathic behavior. Axelrad's rabbi, Eileen Claussen, had departed EPA in 1993, taking away his political protection, and I saw my opening. Claussen's successor as Office Director was the newly-appointed Ramona Trovato. This afforded me a long-awaited opportunity for payback. I wrote a lengthy letter to Ms. Trovato, detailing Axelrad's abusive language and his arbitrary rejection of my work. I appended copies of my three accolades from OSHA, my Outstanding Performance Rating and the two IAQ Team awards, from OSHA and the Secretary of Labor. I heard through the grapevine that Trovato brought this up in her review of Axelrad's performance, adding to his more serious problems.

AXELRAD'S BLUNDER BITES HIM ON THE ASS

Apparently, my missive arrived in Ms. Trovato's inbox at a particularly inopportune time for Axelrad, who was already experiencing some immensely well-deserved political travail. This was due to a major avoidable folly. I had originally proposed that we should put out a contract for bids tailored such that a respected and experienced national figure, such as Dr. David Burns, who had edited several Surgeon General's Reports, would emerge as the preferred candidate to develop the Policy Guide, but Axelrad wanted his own man. So, he hired his own man. The problem was that he arrogantly broke federal contracting rules to do this. This did not escape the industry's notice. And it had incurred the ire of Congressman John Dingell (D) Michigan, the powerful Chairman of the House Subcommittee on Oversight and Investigations of the Committee on Energy and Commerce. And the Ranking Minority Member of that committee was none other than Tom Bliley.

Seizing a larger opportunity to discredit EPA, Bliley provoked an investigation by the EPA's Inspector General of Axelrad's botched handling of the contract for the Smoking Policy Guide. So, despite Axelrad's help in trying to suppress my work at his behest, the ingrate Bliley threw Axelrad under the bus. In 1993, both Congressmen Dingell and Bliley had criticized EPA's contracting procedures, and Dingell had denounced "EPA's pattern of contract mismanagement as a cesspool." *Inside EPA,* a private newsletter, had reported in July 1992 that:

"Referring to documents obtained by the subcommittee, Chairman Dingell alleges that Robert Axelrad, head of the EPA's Indoor Air Division, contacted SPI [the Smoking Policy Institute] through its Executive Director, Robert A. Rosner, in July 1988 for the purpose of urging SPI to submit a contract proposal, and then steered this subcontract to SPI. The project in question concerned a workplace smoking policy guide to be completed by SPI as part of the EPA's effort to monitor the health effects of environmental tobacco smoke (ETS). Subcommittee records show that in a letter dated July 11, 1988, Mr. Axelrad outlined the goals of the proposed ETS policy guide to Mr. Rosner, even mentioning that the EPA had approximately $30,000 available for work on the handbook. 'I believe this is clear evidence that EPA … solicited SPI's proposal to do this work,' Congressman Dingell wrote EPA Administrator William K. Reilly on April 15, 1992. 'EPA even told SPI the amount of funds available for this work. … .'"

So in return for slavishly following Bliley's lead to neutralize me as a threat to the industry, Axelrad was repaid with a Bliley-instigated IG investigation. Naturally, the naïf Axelrad did not fare well in the Inspector General's investigation since every charge laid against him was true. In a letter to Bliley, EPA's Inspector General, Joseph Martin, completely agreed that there had been contracting abuses by Axelrad. In a meeting with EPA's Administrator attended by several staff members, in his defense, Axelrad complained that 'sole-sourcing' was widely practiced at EPA. Steven Bayard, who attended that meeting, said that he had piped up to general amusement, "Yeah, but you were the only one stupid enough to put it writing."

In fact, sole-sourcing, i.e., hiring a contractor preferentially, was easily and legally accomplished by writing requirements into a request for bids such that only highly qualified bidders could match. This technique weeded out incompetent low bidders and saved the government money. We did this all the time at NRL. At Sarnoff, in the private sector, this was not an issue. Of course, this required the contract writer to be technically sophisticated in the field. If Axelrad had developed any technical competence in the field of indoor air, he was very good at concealing it.

After an incident at EPA's Crystal City building in which wax was stripped off all of the floors using some kind of volatile solvent, I found that I could no longer breathe the building air without suffering lung inflammation. My lungs had been severely injured in the 1989 sick building episode. At that time, the Indoor Air Division was being relocated to a brand-new building across the street from the Department of Labor, but characteristically, Axelrad demonstrated that he had learned nothing about the prevention of indoor air pollution problems during his tenure as head of the Indoor Air Division. He ordered the Indoor Air Division staff to move into the new quarters before construction had ceased. This was another greenhorn blunder.

When I arrived, the air in the building was filled with choking plaster dust that burned my eyes and lungs. I informed him that I could not tolerate the building. At that point, I peremptorily moved home, joining the vast majority of EPA's sick building victims. All I needed was a physician's note, which I obtained from Dr. Mark Bradley, who had treated many EPA staff who suffered from sick building syndrome. A key provision in EPA's agreement with its union was that the Health and Safety Division would make the sole determination as to who could work at home, *not* an individual's supervisor. I was well aware of this. Subsequently, an infuriated Axelrad made repeated demands that I move back into a building that was making me sick. I ignored them. Determined to get his way, over a period of months he wrote probably a dozen memos to the Health and Safety Division arguing that my work-at-home tenure should be terminated. Each time, I would counter with a longer memo accompanied by a note from my doctor, warning that working in a dusty building would be harmful to my health. I was well acquainted with the Health and Safety people who knew this was a hot potato. So, EPA's Health and Safety officers collectively sat on their hands and ignored his demands. Axelrad finally realized that Resistance Was Futile. He had been assimilated by the Borg.

Suddenly in November of 1995, the Radon and Indoor Air Divisions were combined into the newly-created Office of Radiation and Indoor Air. Axelrad was soon given the "lateral arabesque" made famous in the 1969 book, *The Peter Principle*, and eliminated as Division Chief, a long overdue action. The new Chief at the helm of the Indoor Air Division was Ms. Mary Smith, an affable woman who brought in cakes and doughnuts to share with the staff. In her first staff meeting, she asked for suggestions about new directions for the Indoor Air Division. I immediately responded that we might proceed with commissioning a heart disease and passive smoking risk assessment. She smiled, replying that, "Unfortunately, that's not politically acceptable. Any subsequent ETS effort by the indoor air division will be restricted solely to its effects on children." This signal came through loud and clear – EPA's future ETS efforts would be safely channeled into an area that did not threaten the tobacco industry's profits. The fix was in.

I was far more interested in the risks of ETS exposure in the workplace, which had the potential to change public policy. Assessing the risks to children exposed mainly at home did not. Accordingly, my focus remained on publishing our Monte Carlo (probabilistic) model that related atmospheric nicotine and body fluid cotinine from secondhand smoke to workplace risks of lung cancer and heart disease. Seeing which way the wind was blowing, I avoided mentioning this effort to Ms. Smith. This was a major piece of modeling work and represented several years of collaborative effort with Jennifer Jinot and Steven Bayard, incorporating vital data from the work of academics Katherine Hammond and Karen Emmons, who had respectively measured nicotine in office workplace air and cotinine in office workers in separate studies that we used to calibrate our model.

Our paper had six goals. The primary goal involved estimating the levels and significance of workplace ETS exposure and dose on nonsmokers. This had first required developing a physical model to predict nicotine concentrations in the office workplace. Then we developed a pharmacokinetic model to predict body fluid cotinine levels in nonsmoking office workers due to passive smoking. Using Monte Carlo methods, we calculated frequency distributions for workers' exposure and dose. To validate our models, we compared their predictions to existing field observations of nicotine in office workplace air and salivary cotinine of workers exposed to ETS only at work. To estimate risk, we developed exposure- and dose-response relationships between airborne nicotine and salivary cotinine and the risk of ETS-induced lung cancer and heart disease. Finally, we estimated the magnitude of mortality from ETS exposure for workers in office workplaces with unrestricted smoking.

The Monte Carlo models we developed allowed predictions of the range of nicotine expected to be encountered in office air, as well as the range of cotinine in the body fluids of office workers. The essence of our Monte Carlo technique was to replace each individual parameter in the point-estimate atmospheric and pharmacokinetic equations I had developed with the expected range for each of the parameters. The results were gratifying. In probabilistic form, the models were able to estimate with a substantial degree of accuracy, both the mean and median concentrations as well as the range of exposure of nicotine measured in the air of nine Massachusetts workplaces with unrestricted smoking measured in a study by Kathie Hammond at Berkeley. This same was true for salivary cotinine dose measured in 89 nonsmoking Rhode Island white-collar workers who reported being exposed to ETS only at work, measured by Karen Emmons at Harvard. We concluded that the good agreement between model predictions and field observations over most of their ranges "suggests that the models we have developed for nicotine and cotinine incorporate the parameters necessary and sufficient for their prediction." Mated with the risk model developed by Repace and Lowrey (1993), this permitted an estimate of the mortality from passive smoking in U.S. office workers: 4000 heart disease deaths and 400 lung cancer deaths annually. Our peer-reviewed paper would be published in the journal *Risk Analysis* (Repace et al., 1998). It would be my 55th scientific paper.

I discovered much later that our study had been secretly replicated in 1999 by Donald Leyden, Worldwide Scientific Affairs, Philip Morris International in Neuchatel, Switzerland. Using the same software and the same assumptions, he got essentially the same results. In spite of this, he concluded, "The validation of the model proposed by Repace et al. by using area nicotine measurements rather than personal monitoring, and by using data from subjects not related to those measurements is seriously flawed" (TTID 2074405512). Although to the best of my knowledge the work of Leyden was never published, I was also concerned about this issue. At the time, this first approximation was the best we could do with the extremely limited available data. While other data measured by the industry existed, particularly RJR's 16 Cities Study, I didn't trust it as far as I could throw Roger Jenkins. In any case, this was the first time a Monte Carlo model of secondhand smoke exposure and dose had ever been published, and the results were reasonable. I would revisit this problem in a paper with Tom Bernert at CDC and Wael Al Delaimy of UCSD in 2006 in a controlled chamber study of exposure and dose in human subjects at CDC in Atlanta. To be continued.

In addition to my clandestine effort on Repace et al. (1998), I worked on several official EPA assignments during these years: I reviewed reports on the Health Effects of Low Level Ozone; the PM10 Draft Criteria Document; EPA's Indoor Air Quality Diagnostic Manual; the ASHRAE Handbook; and the EPA Carpet Brochure. I wrote a report on Indoor Air Pollution and the Asthma Epidemic. Kim (I no longer recall her last name), my new immediate supervisor, who replaced the now-retired John Girman, was a pleasant young woman engineer who expressed surprise at my 43-page Asthma Report, into which I had put significant effort. She exclaimed, "*This is good!*" I wondered what she had been told about me. I suspected that Axelrad had poisoned the well by defaming me to the new division management. EPA's Indoor Air Division began a robust and gratifying effort to combat the asthma epidemic, an effort that endures to this day.

Meanwhile, I coauthored a publication with Don Shopland in the *Maryland Medical Journal* on smoking restrictions in Maryland, a book chapter with Al Lowrey on secondhand smoke in Budapest, Hungary, a letter to the editor of *Risk Analysis* defending the 1993 paper of Repace and Lowrey on an Enforceable Indoor Air Quality Standard for ETS, and a letter to the editor of *Lancet* on the AMA and tobacco history (Shopland et al., 1995; Lowrey et al., 1995; Repace and Lowrey, 1995; Repace, 1995) . Letting sleeping dogs lie, I avoided reporting any of these publications to my new management.

The Industry Manipulates The CRS Against The EPA

During this period, I was invited to attend a workshop on Capitol Hill to review a draft report, *Environmental Tobacco Smoke and Lung Cancer Risk,* prepared by the Congressional Research Service (CRS) at the behest of unspecified members of Congress. EPA was represented by Steven Bayard, Jennifer Jinot and Yours Truly. There were a number of other legitimate researchers and academics, including Michael Alevanja of NCI, Terry

Fontham of LSU, Kathie Hammond from Berkeley, and Dr. Al Munzer of the Washington Adventist Hospital and past president of the American Lung Association, plus several representatives of the CRS. Representing the tobacco industry were RJR scientist Chris Coggins, CIAR "special project" grantee Roger Jenkins of Oak Ridge, Gary Huber of the U. of Texas, two familiar industry consultants, Max Layard and Maurice Levois, plus Paul Switzer from Stanford. Switzer was still publishing first class work on ETS modeling and measurement with Wayne Ott but remained a critic of EPA's Risk Assessment on behalf of the industry. Kentucky Senator Wendell Ford (D), a well-known tobacco industry supporter and unapologetic smoker, wandered in and out of the room like Darth Vader as we deliberated. Disappointingly, but not surprisingly, given the strong presence of the industry on this panel, the draft CRS Report was heavily biased toward tobacco industry sponsored research, and leaned heavily on the RJR/Oak Ridge workplace smoking study.

My written review of the CRS draft concluded,

"In sum, the CRS draft *ETS and Lung Cancer Risk* agrees that a consensus has been reached that ETS is carcinogenic. The CRS draft arrives at two main conclusions: (1) The risk from ETS appears to be concentrated in that portion of the population at risk which has extensive ETS exposure, which the report asserts is essentially concentrated in a minority of those nonsmokers exposed in the home. (2) Workplace exposures are significantly less than home exposures, and therefore OSHA's assessment of ETS risk in the workplace may be significantly overestimated. ... The draft CRS report, *ETS and Lung Cancer,* fails to provide a comprehensive review and analysis of the scientific literature on ETS. Further, its two main conclusions are wrong because they are based upon an exposure assessment which is not scientifically supportable. ...

• "The report's general conclusion that any risk from ETS is concentrated in only a small portion of the population is based ... on values of nicotine concentration measured in the RJR-Oak Ridge study. However, this conclusion is not supportable because calculations show that, assuming a single smoker home, the median value of residence size in the RJR-Oak Ridge study is 6200 square feet, which is four times greater than that of the typical single family U.S. home.

• The report's general conclusion that any risk from ETS is negligible for nearly all nonsmokers who are exposed in the workplace, is based on ... values of nicotine concentration measured in the RJR-Oak Ridge study. However this conclusion is not supportable because calculations show that the mean and median values of workplace smoker density in the RJR-Oak Ridge study are respectively 14% and 1.7% of those for a typical U.S. office with 2 smokers per thousand square feet.

• This report needs a complete rewrite followed by another round of external peer review from researchers who have published in the field, and who do not have industry ties. The revised report should be reorganized along the standard lines of hazard assessment, exposure assessment, dose-response, and risk characterization. A comprehensive literature search should be performed, and the viewpoints of the major reports which have been published on ETS since 1986 should be summarized on each of the topics considered. ...

• The report's reliance on unpublished, un-peer-reviewed, and unrepresentative ETS exposure data should be dismissed, and reliable published data and model results substituted. ... Perhaps my most serious criticism is CRS's flawed attempt at ETS exposure assessment. The CRS-ETS draft report unaccountably relies heavily upon unpublished, un-peer-reviewed and admittedly unrepresentative data on ETS nicotine concentrations generated by R.J. Reynolds, Bellomy Research, and Oak Ridge workers. ... CRS assumes, without foundation, that these data are typical of U.S. workplaces, when one of the authors of the study (Roger Jenkins) testified, as shown by the transcript of the OSHA Indoor Air Hearings, that the study was not representative of U.S. population exposure. The RJR-Oak Ridge data cannot be used for this purpose. …

In other words, the values for both the mean and median smoker density in the RJR-Oak Ridge workplaces are highly atypical and far below normal."

The CRS did not afford me the opportunity to comment on its revised report. However, Mike Callahan, Director of EPA's National Center for Environmental Assessment in Washington, was. Callahan wrote a pointed letter to Dan Mulhollan, Director of CRS. Callahan began by damning the final revision with faint praise, and then concluded by giving it the Full Monty:

"It appears that some of the comments provided by us and other reviewers were incorporated into the final report of November 14, 1995. … We were also pleased to note that, using the non-threshold model, CRS's best estimate of approximately 2,800 lung cancer deaths annually in U.S. nonsmokers from ETS exposure was similar to the estimates of the EPA (1992) and the National Research Council (1986). Moreover, CRS's acknowledgement of the potentially large public health impact of ETS on heart disease in calling for additional research and assessment was a welcome addition. However, the final report does not redress some of our major concerns, and there are also new sections with which we do not concur. …

As a general comment, while the EPA risk assessment was a comprehensive analysis of the total weight of evidence, the CRS report selectively focuses on a few recent U.S. studies. We also believe that the CRS report repeatedly exaggerates uncertainties and is far too equivocal in drawing conclusions. …

In addition to the inability of the epidemiology studies to establish a threshold due to their lack of sensitivity, there is no demonstrated mechanistic basis for drawing such a conclusion. It is indefensible to presume a nontrivial threshold for a genotoxic carcinogen (i.e., a carcinogen that can irreversibly damage DNA, at conceivably minute exposures) that has been shown, despite the difficulties of exposure misclassification and low study power, to cause lung cancer at typical environmental exposure levels. …

In summary, while the final report is an improvement over the draft, the overemphasis on uncertainties and the proposal of an unsupportable threshold model for environmental tobacco smoke risk severely limit its credibility."

This scathing critique by an EPA Office Director was devastating. The assumption of a "threshold" for a known genotoxic carcinogen [able to break DNA bonds and initiate cancer] was patently ludicrous. This was an argument pulled out of Big Tobacco's playbook of pseudoscience. The final CRS report downplayed the Oak Ridge study while still attempting to preserve its credibility, indicating that my comment had struck home. It stated in part:

"Noting the tobacco industry's involvement in the [Oak Ridge] study, critics claim that it underrepresented the amount of ETS exposure among nonsmokers. The study sampled a disproportionately low number of smoker-occupied workplaces. Out of 1,356 workplaces sampled, only 168 (12.4 percent) allowed smoking without restriction. National estimates of workplace smoking prevalence suggest that a significantly higher percentage of workplaces allow smoking (see later section on occupational ETS exposure). However, it is not possible to determine whether the recruitment procedures used in the study led to the selection of participants whose ETS exposure in smoker-occupied indoor environments was significantly below average exposure levels for nonsmokers nationwide." [CRS, 1995]

The RJR/Oak Ridge Study's recruitment process, of course, was determined by Bellomy Research, an RJR-hired survey firm, not by Roger Jenkins, who was mostly a figurehead in this RJR-orchestrated research. The final CRS report was issued on November 14, 1995 (Redhead and Rowberg, 1995).

Tobacco State Senators Mitch McConnell (R) Kentucky, Jesse Helms (R) North Carolina), Fritz Hollings (R) South Carolina, and John Warner (R) Virginia, took a more sanguine view of the CRS Report. In a joint letter to Assistant Secretary for OSHA Joe Dear, dated November 17, 1995, they wrote:

"Dear Mr. Dear:

The Congressional Research Service (CRS) has just completed a report entitled "Environmental Tobacco Smoke and Lung Cancer Risk". The report concentrates on possible health effects of environmental tobacco smoke (ETS).

The report represents a detailed examination of the ETS issue, raising serious issues about reports by the Environmental Protection Agency (EPA) and Occupational Safety and Health Administration (OSHA) which have advocated strong antismoking measures, CRS research specialists conclude: there is no scientific justification for smoking bans, de facto bans, or regulatory action such as the proposed rule issued (April 5, 1994) by your agency.

The study challenges critical assumptions made by your agency to support your proposed smoking ban in all U.S. workplaces. CRS also notes that if OSHA had conducted an analysis of all of the available studies on smoking in the workplace, it would likely have found no increased cancer risk due to ETS. The report states, 'Had OSHA performed a meta-analysis, it seems likely that it would have found no increased lung cancer risk from occupational ETS exposure.'

As you know, CRS provides objective and impartial research and analysis for Members of Congress. We are interested in your views on this important research study and its implications for all forced smoking bans by the Federal government."

MULTIPLE CHEMICAL SENSITIVITY

In October 1995, I presented a paper, *Indoor air pollution and multiple chemical sensitivity* (MCS) at the Occupational Safety & Health '95 Conference in Toronto. This was at my own expense and done on leave. In September of 1996, now that Axelrad was no longer an obstacle, I decided to expand it and write it up as a white paper for the new management of the Indoor Air Division. I laid out the dimensions of the MCS problem and pointed out that although there was a lack of research on the topic, it needed to be addressed by occupational and environmental health authorities. My abstract read:

"Indoor air pollutant concentrations in non-industrial buildings are determined essentially by the ratio of the source strength to the air exchange rate. However, society requires virtually no controls over the quantity and toxicity of volatile chemicals used in non-industrial buildings, whereas non-industrial ventilation rates are often limited by the desire for energy conservation, resulting in the accumulation of xenobiotic chemicals in indoor atmospheres. As a result, the occurrence of indoor air pollution in indoor environments has become pandemic,

259

often producing morbidity. Sick building syndrome has become a phenomenon of the late 20th Century, and multiple chemical sensitivity (MCS), a poorly understood and highly controversial phenomenon bearing features evocative of solvent-induced neuropathy, appears to be one of the its extreme forms. There is a lack of scientific research concerning MCS, and yet governmental bodies, confronted with a growing and vocal population of persons claiming this affliction, have recognized the phenomenon and are making pragmatic risk management decisions. A possible etiology for MCS is suggested by recent research. This paper discusses factors affecting exposure and response to indoor air pollution, as well as options for risk management.

The relationship of MCS to indoor air pollution is discussed in connection with two prominent sick-building incidents which resulted in large clusters of MCS patients, the EPA Building in Washington, DC, and the Camp Hill Hospital in Halifax. It is proposed that the severest consequences of indoor air pollution, such as MCS, can be prevented by limiting total volatile organic compounds (TVOCs). Many VOCs are neurotoxic. A simple indoor air quality model shows that realistic emissions in office buildings can cause very high VOC exposures. When breathed by sensitive individuals, this creates a plausible scenario for the occurrence of sick building syndrome. Combinations of appropriate ventilation rates, avoidance of human exposure, or substitution of materials and products which have lower emission potential can be employed to prevent human contact with potentially sensitizing concentrations. Overall the IAQ procedure of ASHRAE 62-1989 would be used, with the biggest sources driving ventilation rates. This discussion paper is intended to provide a basis for development of public policy and a public information document on how the most serious consequences of indoor air pollution can be managed or prevented."

To illustrate the concept, I described the results of two case studies, one of which was the EPA building. The other was the Camp Hill Hospital in Halifax, Nova Scotia. It illuminated the institutional denial of MCS, while still adopting a pragmatic approach:

"**The Camp Hill Medical Center.** Located in Halifax, NS, Camp Hill consists of three interconnected buildings employing 1100 staff who operated an acute medical care facility, a chronic health care facility for war veterans, and a psychiatric hospital. Built in late 1987, by 1989, approximately 600 of 1100 staff were reported down with sick building syndrome, and a number of these developed MCS-like symptoms. Many of the latter subsequently joined together in a 100-member support group known as the Camp Hill Environmental Victims Society. Camp Hill acknowledges that many staff on sick leave and perhaps some still at work have developed chemical sensitivities. In October 1990, indoor air quality investigators found a number of problems, including unacceptable levels of phenol from disinfectants, elevated formaldehyde from a detergent, a defective ventilation system, and reported that many workers had breathing problems, difficulty focusing, fatigue, headaches, chest pains, menstrual abnormalities, memory loss, and eye irritation. Several patients reported rashes. Up to 100% of staff in some areas were off work at times during the fall of 1991. At the end of January 1992, 92 people were on sick leave, and as many as 150 personnel have been on sick leave due to these problems.

An investigative report published in 1992 suggested that many victims had symptoms of solvent exposure, but measurements could not confirm this suspicion. Today, the hospital believes that certain 'culminating incidents' occurred, one in 1989, when ventilation systems in one building were lubricated without being shut off. Another culminating incident was believed to have occurred as a result of discovery of a white powder on building surfaces which was traced to four different amines used as corrosion inhibitors in boiler-water additives which had leaked into the building humidification system. After five years of problems, the cost of reducing hospital services, environmental studies, lost time by hospital staff, building renovations, compensation, employee counseling and sick pay had exceeded $1.5 million, and the total bill has been estimated as $5 million by 1993. For the injured workers, the Workers Compensation Board has refused to accept a diagnosis of MCS or to pay for treatments not recognized by insurance or medical authorities. An environmental medicine clinic funded by the government has been established to study the MCS phenomenon in Halifax. Headquartered at the Victoria General Hospital, there are 100 clinic patients, and more than 450 on the waiting list, including 79 Camp Hill staff."

Despite the new Indoor Air Division management, my effort to get EPA involved in the MCS issue remained futile. Although my white paper was a serious, non-polemical, scientific and lengthy (41 page) discussion document written by an expert, I failed to interest the new management in this issue. They were conflict-shy and disinterested in doing anything serious to make a difference in an important but clearly controversial area of their responsibility. I heard nothing back from IAD management. I became disgusted and decided to concentrate on what I did best. Then I learned of an effort led by the Agency for Toxic Substances and Disease Registry (ATSDR) to study the issue. In 1995, The Environmental Health Policy Committee, Department of Health and Human Services, formed an Interagency Working Group on Multiple Chemical Sensitivity. They defined MCS as a "health outcome, with a debatable validity, that poses policy and medical challenges to federal agencies and health practitioners. From the interagency collaboration, a draft report entitled *A Report on Multiple Chemical Sensitivity (MCS)* was developed, and considered relevant scientific literature, previous recommendations of various experts and current as well as past federal actions. After assessment by a panel of experts, the report was made available to the public for review and comment." I submitted my paper to ATSDR as a private citizen.

Ultimately, three years later, in August of 1998, the Interagency Workgroup on MCS would issue a milquetoast whitewash that concluded in part:

"The workgroup reviewed the scientific literature pertinent to multiple chemical sensitivity (MCS), considered recommendations from various expert panels on MCS, reviewed past and current federal actions, and developed technical and policy recommendations. The workgroup considers policy makers and researchers at agencies concerned with MCS issues to be the primary audience for this report. It is currently unknown whether MCS is a distinct disease entity and what role, if any, the biochemical mechanisms of specific chemicals have in the onset of this condition. The workgroup finds that MCS is currently a symptom-based diagnosis without supportive laboratory tests or agreed-upon signs of clinical manifestation. The workgroup knows of no reports in the literature of definite end-organ damage attributable to MCS.

However, scientific knowledge changes over time as additional findings are reported. It is therefore important not to lose sight of lessons from the past in which suspected health effects of environmental exposures were verified at a later date through scientific research." In September of 2000, the Workgroup added a summary of public comments that concluded: "In response to the Interagency draft report on MCS, 460 comments were received. Comments were received from health care professionals, individuals, individuals with MCS, and organizations. Government agencies were the most supportive and individuals were the least supportive. Many of the comments citing limitations of the report can be generalized as follows: Frank Mitchell's involvement in the writing of the report is a conflict of interest, and ultimately biases the report; the report should include information from other government agencies as well as findings of MCS doctors who study/treat those with MCS; the bibliography is incomplete and more literature needs to be reviewed and included in the report; the report should recommend avoidance measures; and the report should be used as a tool for health care professionals, government agencies, employers, and the general public, and as such, it should be free of any and all biases.

Public comments citing the strengths of the report can be generalized as follows: the report is a good start to recognizing MCS, the report is a comprehensive review of the issues encompassing MCS, and the document is a useful tool for those who deal with MCS. When including form letters, approximately 70% (n=282) of the responses were not supportive of the report and recommended substantive changes, or that no final report be produced. The other 30% (n=110) included those who were supportive of the report as written or with editorial changes. ... The degree of support varied among groups submitting comments. Government agencies were the most supportive in which 4/4 (100%) comments expressed some degree of support ... , and individuals, as a category, were the least supportive because 183/208 (88%) comments expressed a lack of support."

What exactly did this whitewash accomplish? Where were the recommendations for research by federal agencies?

Although marginalized by the Indoor Air Division management, outside of EPA I continued to play a role in the politics, policy, and science of secondhand smoke. I gave an interview, mostly on deep background, to the *Washington Post Magazine*, in an article by Morton Mintz, with the inflammatory title, "Second-hand Money," whose article described "how the tobacco institute, its PR agents at Fleishman Hillard and its lawyers at Covington & Burling helped turn a smalltime Fairfax businessman into an international authority on indoor air quality and cigarette smoke." Published on March 24th, it was a major exposé of HBI and in particular, Gray Robertson. It quoted the accusations of fraud by several former HBI employees, the Waxman investigation, and Al Lowrey's report accusing HBI of massive scientific fraud. Mintz described Robertson's relationship with the Tobacco Institute's attorneys at Covington as an expert witness in secondhand smoke injury cases, Robertson's $20,000 per month retainer, and how "Robertson became one of America's leading spokesmen on indoor air quality and tobacco smoke." "Robertson or his HBI colleagues testified 129 times before federal, state and local government bodies that were considering restrictions on indoor smoking; their expenses were paid by the Tobacco Institute, which kicked in an extra $8000 monthly subsidy to pay for expenses. Some former HBI employees say that in public, HBI speakers were under strict instructions not to reveal their connections to the tobacco industry unless asked directly." Mintz noted that "With Fleishman-Hillard's help – the PR firm's fees and expenses were ultimately paid by the Tobacco Institute – Robertson and his HBI colleagues toured American cities, promoting their theories of ventilation and decrying indoor smoking restrictions on television, radio and in print. *People Magazine* published a puffy profile of Robertson, the 'building doctor,' and included a charming picture of Robertson leaning against an office building with a stethoscope. Neither in that story nor in many other media appearances were HBI's (or Fleishman-Hillard's) financial ties to tobacco revealed."

I had given an extensive interview, recounted in his 800-page tome, *Ashes to Ashes*, to Richard Kluger, published by Knopf in April 1996. He sent me an autographed copy "with thanks and admiration." Kluger's book described "America's Hundred-Year Cigarette War, the Public Health, and the Unabashed Triumph of Philip Morris." Kluger had written a letter to me in January 1989 concerning Ted Sterling: "Before I forget, let me confirm my comment to you about Sterling and his professions of not working for the industry. In the years shortly before his assault on you at *Science* and the ASHRAE meeting, according to documents that surfaced in the Cipollone trial, Sterling received a grant of $610,000 running from mid-'77 to mid-'80 for continuing critical review of the major factors in the etiology of diseases emerging from statistical studies (that's the language in the document) plus a second grant in that period of $127,932 for 'Retrospective Analysis of Environmental Contacts of Patients with Respiratory Cancer' and other diseases. These grants were funneled through the industry's Ad Hoc Committee of lawyers that superintended grant applications on matters of particular pertinence to potential litigation and ongoing p.r. concerns. He may not have sold them his soul, but they were certainly helping him keep it well upholstered." He added: " Because your work has been so influential, I'm going to give it some considerable space in the book... ." [TTID 2075274696].

On the policy front, the Centers for Disease Control invited me to present on the Health Risks of Environmental Tobacco Smoke - Policy Issues, at an International Workshop for Strengthening Collaboration on Tobacco Or Health Issues Among WHO Collaborating Centers, in Atlanta, GA, Co-sponsored by World Health Organization Substance Abuse Programme. In October, I was invited by the National Cancer Institute to present two talks locally, *Where There's Smoke – Cigars, The Latest Trend*, and *Maintaining a Comprehensive Approach to Tobacco Control - The Continuing Need for Clean Indoor Air Laws,* at its ASSIST Information Exchange Training Conference - Building Momentum for Tobacco Prevention: Planning for the Future, co-sponsored by the American Cancer Society.

In late November 1996, I took leave and made my second foray into Norway, invited by Dr. Tore Sanner to lecture on Environmental Tobacco Smoke Exposure, Dose, and Risk at The Institute for Cancer Research, at the University of Oslo. I stayed in the guest suite on the top floor of the Norwegian Radium Hospital. While wandering around the building, I discovered an enormous swimming-pool-sized hot tub on the ground floor in which a number of men and women were bathing, balded as a result of cancer therapy. I wondered how many had been smokers. They were mixed in with a group of extremely well-mannered healthy high school students, both male and female. I asked the facility's director about this; she responded, "we do this to cheer up these cancer victims, many of whom are very depressed." Outside a large window wall, an ice-and-snow covered flowing fountain provided a visually soothing backdrop. I was invited to dinner at the home of Jacqueline Eckgren, active in Norway's non-smokers' rights movement.

I had met Jackie in Stockholm in 1984 at an international conference on indoor air. Mike Lebowitz had given a symposium speech in which he downplayed the health effects of secondhand smoke. Speaking from the audience, I strongly attacked his argument. Mike defended his stand, with the reply, "the whole issue can be handled by 'common courtesy.' " This was a response right out of the industry's playbook. During the intermission, Lebowitz lit up one of his trademark roll-your-own cigarettes in the lobby, puffing away furiously. Jacqueline, dressed in a bright pink dress, came up to him, saying she was allergic to tobacco smoke, and asking "could you please smoke outside? Lebowitz snapped, "If you don't like it, you can go outside yourself." So much for common courtesy.

During my stay in Oslo, Jackie, who gave vocal lessons, invited me to listen to rehearsals by a chorus of young blonde women who sang gloriously. The only dining place in Oslo that was smoke-free was a vegetarian restaurant not far from the docks. I ate there three times during my stay; the cuisine was excellent. Tore invited me to tour the former villa of Vidkun Quisling, the fascist politician who seized power when the Germans invaded Norway during World War II, in a Nazi-backed coup d'etat. He also took me on a tour of a five-story building in downtown Oslo that had served as Gestapo headquarters during that era.

Lowrey Fades Away

A sad postscript. During the year, my long-time close friend, colleague, jogging partner, and fellow gourmet club member, Alfred Holland Lowrey, whose company I had enjoyed for 25 fun-filled years, was asked to retire from the only job he had ever held. NRL, like most high quality research laboratories, had an unwritten but widely practiced rule: on average, older scientists were less productive than younger ones, and were paid more. So, when they were eligible for retirement, unless they were in management, they were encouraged to leave, often by transfer to non-research positions. Faced with this unpleasant alternative, Al became very depressed. I advised him that with his excellent computational skills, he could write his ticket as a consultant and double dip with his government pension. Although he concealed it well, Al had become inconsolable, and one day he ended his life. Al's memorial service was held at the Paint Branch Unitarian Church. I spoke about the early years of our collaboration, and related that one day, Al and I were sitting on a park bench overlooking the Potomac near the Titanic Memorial in Washington DC's Southwest. We were laughing uproariously, taking great delight in the impact of our work, and a woman passerby came up to us and remarked, "I've never seen two grown men have so much fun."

Stanford Research Confirms Our Early Work

Sixteen years after the appearance of Repace and Lowrey's 1980 Science paper, Wayne Ott, Paul Switzer, and John Robinson (1996) collaborated on a brilliant longitudinal study of fine particles in the Oasis Tavern in Redwood City, California, measuring RSP with a Piezobalance on 26 dates prior to California's restaurant smoking ban, and on 50 dates subsequent to the ban, 24 of which were made in the two months immediately after smoking was prohibited. It was the very first pre-and post-ban study ever conducted. During 26 visits over a two-year period during which smoking was allowed, the average indoor RSP concentration was ~57 $\mu g/m^3$ higher than the outdoor concentrations. RSP average concentrations measured on 24 visits immediately after smoking ended dropped to only ~6 $\mu g/m^3$ above the outdoor levels, a decrease of 90%. Moreover, although limited to a single tavern, the number of measurements was very large, which made it an enormously important result. These measurements were made possible by California's 1994 restaurant smoking ban. The California Tobacco Related Disease Research Program funded their study; it was one of the very few funding sources for ETS exposure research outside of the tobacco industry's CIAR.

Further, Ott et al. (1996) noted, "based on smoking habits, Repace (1980) hypothesized that about one-ninth (11.1%) of the persons in public places were actively smoking at any instant of time, and Repace and Lowrey (1980) reported an average of 8.8% based on counts of smokers in a great variety of locations in 1979 in Washington, D.C. Table 4 [in Ott et al., 1996] shows 20 separate visits between September 29, 1979, and February 20, 1980, to this same California tavern to test Repace's hypothesis by counting active smokers but not making any measurements. … The proportion of the customers who were actively smoking in 1979-1980 ranged from 6.3% to 14%, with an average of 8.8% – identical to the value reported by Repace and Lowrey (1980)." Wayne's study provided firm independent confirmation both for our model and our conclusion that tobacco smoke accounted for most of the fine particle pollution in indoor spaces. Wayne's paper showed clearly that the RSP pollution came primarily from smoking, and not from "dust caused by people," as the tobacco industry had bloviated.

The Wiley Case Goes Bust

The Wiley Case finally went to trial in 1998, but the judge ruled that I was barred from testifying because I had been proffered as an expert witness in an untimely manner. *The Wall Street Journal's* coverage of the trial stated in part, "Internal documents and testimony by former industry insiders have taken a toll on the industry's defenses, observers say. In cross-examination of Roger Jenkins, an expert called by the industry, a Ness Motley lawyer offered so much evidence of the witness's financial ties to the cigarette makers that one juror started laughing. Jeffrey L. Furr, an attorney representing RJR Nabisco Holdings Corp's Reynolds tobacco unit, said the plaintiffs were asking industry witnesses about documents unrelated to their professional responsibilities. But skeptics say the plaintiffs might not be able to convince the jury that Ms. Wiley's cancer was really caused by secondhand smoke. The tobacco companies, as they invariably do in individual lawsuits, also pointed to other possible reasons why Ms. Wiley was diagnosed with lung cancer" [TTID 2077315797].

Despite his best efforts, Ron Motley lost the Wiley case in March after a six-week trial. Big Tobacco's expert witnesses successfully confused the jury by arguing that "Wiley died from pancreatic cancer that had spread to her lungs and was unrelated to secondhand smoke." [They glossed over the fact that pancreatic cancer is also caused by tobacco smoke or that the metastasis could have been the opposite way, from lung to pancreas.] They even outrageously contended that her "anti-smoking" physician "purposely misdiagnosed Wiley with lung cancer." In 1993, Mildred Wiley's treating physician, Dr. Nikki Turner, had written to the Department of Labor in support of Ms. Wiley's disability claim: "The issue at present is whether this death is related to environmental tobacco smoke, and during her employment at the VA Hospital in Marion, Indiana, was this patient exposed to this environmental toxin. It is documented by my initial history and physical examination as well as subsequent discussions with the patient's husband during her time in the hospital that she was indeed heavily exposed to tobacco smoke. This patient did not smoke nor did her husband nor did the rest of her family. Her parents did not smoke." … Dr. Turner reviewed the literature linking secondhand smoke to lung cancer, citing opinions of the Surgeon General, NIOSH CIB 54, the Fontham study, the EPA report, and the 1993 paper of Repace and Lowrey on passive smoking and the workplace, rebutting tobacco industry arguments. Dr. Turner concluded: "Therefore, based on an objectively obtained history and physical examination, hospital clinical course, autopsy studies obtained at the time of-death, occupational exposure history, and extensive scientific data - part of which have been cited in the above paragraphs - I feel that there is indeed a direct relationship between Mildred Wiley's lung cancer and her exposure to environmental tobacco smoke for the previous 18 years. It is my firm opinion that her illness, disability, and subsequent death were directly related to and caused by working in environmental tobacco smoke."

Mildred's husband Philip had won a survivors' pension in an earlier disability claim based on Dr. Turner's affidavit [TTID 2078023836]. The AP reported that, "On December 8, 1995, the Department of Labor ruled that the widower of a former Veterans Administration hospital nurse should receive compensation due to her secondhand smoke-related cancer death. The Labor Department ordered the Department of Veterans Affairs to pay Philip E. Wiley of Charlotte, NC $21,500 every year (half of his wife Mildred's yearly salary) until his death. Although there have been damage awards in the past for respiratory problems associated with secondhand smoke, this was the first case involving death related to secondhand smoke" [AP, 1995].

As 1997 rolled around, the cigar issue began to heat up; the only published data on air pollution from cigars heretofore was the 1982 ASHRAE paper by Repace and Lowrey. The National Cancer Institute (NCI) invited me to participate in a workshop on cigar smoking in February; in July I gave an interview on cigar smoke pollution to *Newsweek*; in September, I lectured on cigar smoke pollution at the National Conference on Tobacco and Health in Houston, co-sponsored by NCI and the American Cancer Society.

In October, Dr. Cecilia Sepulveda of the Cancer Unit of the Chilean Ministry of Health in Santiago, via the Pan American Health Organization (PAHO), invited me to conduct a two-day seminar on Environmental Tobacco Smoke in Chile as part of the 3rd Chilean Congress on Epidemiology. My first thought was "Chile – isn't that where they have all the earthquakes?" I put together a program, inviting a several colleagues from EPA and CDC to participate. I gave several lectures, respectively on the Hazard, Exposure and Dose, Dose-Response, and Control of ETS, as well as on Tobacco Industry Disinformation. The conference venue was in the delightful seacoast town of Viña Del Mar, adjacent to the port city of Valparaiso. I was also asked to participate in a Multi-media Press Conference in Santiago on the Contribution of ETS to Air Pollution Exposure in the Chilean Population.

During the press conference, Cecilia got into hot water by truthfully answering a press question about the embarrassing smoking habits of her boss, Chile's Health Minister. A reporter asked, "Isn't he part of the problem?" "Yes, I suppose he is," she responded. Her comments made headlines in the local media, and she was abruptly fired. Fortunately, she subsequently managed to be hired into an equivalent position with the Cancer Unit of the City of Santiago. I found Santiago to be a beautiful city, with broad tree-lined boulevards and pleasant residential neighborhoods that I could imagine living in. However, I soon learned that Santiago had a significant outdoor air pollution problem as well as an indoor air one. We had been there 3 days when the winds suddenly shifted, revealing the spectacular snow-capped Andes Mountains. They had been obscured by Los Angeles style smog that covered the city like a blanket.

Hilarine and I experienced our first earthquake in Viña del Mar. We had just finished a delightful meal with about a dozen epidemiologists from the conference when the waterfront restaurant began swaying. I had thought that the restaurant was on land – perhaps it was on a barge? I noticed a group of waiters standing transfixed at the bar, and suddenly Cecilia shouted, "We're having an earthquake." She courageously ran upstairs to the ladies' room to retrieve Hilarine; when they returned, we all fled out onto the street. It turned out that we were about 100 kilometers from the epicenter where a house had collapsed, killing six people. Viña survived with only a few broken windows. The next morning we were told that there had been mild aftershocks all night, but we slept through them peacefully in our solidly built hotel.

In our hotel there were notices to put our waste toilet paper in a covered crock instead of flushing it down; the wastewater was piped untreated directly into the sea and the city authorities didn't want the paper washed up on the beaches. Several years later, I would discover that Portugal's seacoast city of Oporto had a similar problem. Half of EPA's budget is devoted to building wastewater treatment plants in lakefront, riverside, and seacoast cities throughout the U.S., courtesy of the federal Clean Water Act, brought to Americans from Washington, DC, by "Big Government" using taxpayers' dollars. Contemplate the alternative.

In September of 1997, the California EPA issued its final report on the Health Effects of Exposure to ETS, which had its origins in the 1992 workshop at which Paul Switzer and I had testified on opposite sides of the issue. Cal EPA came to very strong conclusions: that ETS caused ischemic heart disease as well as lung, breast, and nasal sinus cancer in adults, and nationally, caused between 35,000 and 62,000 heart disease deaths annually from passive smoking as well as 3000 lung cancer deaths, plus a plethora of respiratory effects in hundreds of thousands of children each year. These estimates confirmed and extended the 1992 US EPA Risk Assessment, and further supported the heart disease risk assessment of Jud Wells.

At EPA, the Indoor Air Division's management remained disinterested in pursuing a risk assessment of passive smoking and heart disease, as well as with the issue of MCS. So, as I became eligible to retire after 30 years with the federal government in February 1998, I announced to my new management that I intended to depart at that time. Meanwhile, my published papers remained an obsession with the industry. At Philip Morris's quarterly Science and Policy Strategy meeting in New York on December 12, 1998, they listed "The Repace Model," as one of the three items on their agenda, along with the IARC ETS lung cancer study and OSHA [TTID PM3006807327].

In 1997, Roger Jenkins appeared as a witness for the tobacco industry in a suit by flight attendants against the tobacco industry for injuries sustained from passive smoking on aircraft. According to *The Los Angeles Times*, "During testimony Tuesday [Judge] Kaye barred industry witness Roger Jenkins, a chemist at Oak Ridge National Laboratory and co-author of a study on secondhand smoke, from discussing the research on grounds that R.J. Reynolds Tobacco Co.'s assistance with field work and lab analysis made it suspect." "This trial reminds me of Alice in Wonderland," Kaye remarked with jurors out of the courtroom. "Every day it gets curiouser and curiouser." (Levin, 1997).

In January 1998, just before I retired from EPA, I exhausted another chunk of annual leave by giving an invited talk: *Environmental Tobacco Smoke: the Hospitality Industry Workplace*, at the "Smokeless in Hawaii Conference," sponsored by the Hawaii Dept. of Health in Honolulu. Don Shopland was also one of the invited speakers. I gave an interview on KHON TV on indoor air pollution from cigars, and discovered that the tropical shirts I sported in summer were known as "Aloha Shirts" in Hawaii. At dinner, I was delighted to discover edible orchid blossoms on my seafood platter. On the South Shore beach at Waikiki, the Pacific surf was really rough, but not as insanely rough as the monstrous 30-foot-plus waves on Oahu's North Shore, mounted by certifiably demented surfers who rode them in after being towed out by jet-skis, competing for that year's Darwin Award to see who would be the first to subtract himself from the Gene Pool. The beach was plastered with Big-Wave Warning signs. Hilarine and I prolonged our heavenly stay at a bed-and-breakfast on the Big Island, one of whose volcanoes, Mauna Loa, belched smoke constantly. When the smoke fumigated neighboring islands, it was called "vog," short for volcanic fog. So even Hawaii didn't escape air pollution.

In an augury of my future consulting career in secondhand smoke, Mr. Michael Sternberg, representing the National Restaurant Association, testified on April 1st 1998 in U.S. Senate Hearing 105-678, on Environmental Tobacco Smoke, before the Committee on Environment and Public Works. Sternberg summarized the Restaurant Association's position on ETS: "… many members of the National Restaurant Association have elected to ban smoking from their establishments, while most others have provided a separate section for smokers and nonsmokers. It's a choice and it's one that should be left to the individual restaurateur. … We believe, Mr. Chairman, that the market is working as it should to determine individual restaurant smoking policies. No blanket Government directive is needed. This is particularly true, since it is individual citizens who decide which restaurants to frequent. They are free to choose restaurants that reflect their own taste with regard to food, ambience, convenience, as well as smoking policy." This callous policy trampled on the right of restaurant staff to a safe and healthy workplace.

A few months later, the suit that Big Tobacco brought against EPA in 1993 was finally decided by Judge Osteen. His decision, issued in July 1998, concluded:

"IN THE UNITED STATES DISTRICT COURT
FOR THE MIDDLE DISTRICT OF NORTH CAROLINA
WINSTON-SALEM DIVISION
… The court will direct the entry of judgment in favor of Plaintiffs' motion for summary judgment and vacate Chapters 1 thru 6 of and the Appendices to EPA's Respiratory Health Effects of Passive Smoking: Lung Cancer and Other Disorders, EPA/600/6-90/006F (December 1992). To ripen its judgment for purposes of appellate review pursuant to Fed. R. Civ. P. 54(b), the court will make an express determination that there is no just reason for delay. … An order and judgment in accordance with this memorandum opinion will be filed contemporaneously herewith will direct the entry of judgment in favor of Plaintiffs' motion for summary judgment This the 17th day July 1998.

*[Signed] William L. Osteen
United States District Judge"*

EPA promptly appealed the Osteen ruling. However, the appeal would not be decided until 2002. Chapters 1 thru 6 of the EPA report included respectively the Summary and Conclusions, the Introduction, the estimation of ETS exposure, Hazard Identification I, Hazard Identification II, and the Population risk of Lung Cancer from Passive Smoking. The remaining two chapters dealt respectively with Respiratory Disorders other than cancer and Risk Assessment of Respiratory Illness in Children from ETS. On July 21, 1998, Jim Lehrer reported the ruling on *The PBS Newshour* in a piece entitled:

Second-Hand Smoke: Smoke Screen?
"In 1993, the federal environmental protection agency said second-hand smoke is harmful. The EPA report stated second-hand smoke 'is responsible for approximately 3,000 lung cancer deaths each year in non-smoking adults and impairs the respiratory health of hundreds and thousands of children.' Six months later, the tobacco industry filed a lawsuit that challenged the EPA's findings.

Last week, in North Carolina, the federal judge in the case sided with the industry, saying the EPA made serious mistakes five years ago in evaluating the risk of second-hand smoke. In his ruling, Federal District Judge William Osteen said the 'EPA publicly committed to a conclusion before research had begun' and the 'EPA disregarded information and made findings on selective information.' That, the judge said, put into question the agency's 1993 decision to designate secondhand smoke a Class A carcinogen or a proven cause of cancer in humans. Only 15 other highly reactive substances, including asbestos and radon, are ranked Class A carcinogens.

The EPA report on second-hand smoke was the impetus for hundreds of jurisdictions around the United States to ban smoking in public places, including restaurants, office buildings, and airports. The report also has been used as evidence in lawsuits against the tobacco companies. In a video news release a tobacco executive said the new ruling attacking the EPA report is likely to undercut the basis for future suits claiming injury from second-hand smoke.
ELLEN MERLO, Senior Vice President Corporate Affairs, Philip Morris: 'I think this ruling gives us is an opportunity for reasonable dialogue, for developing reasonable options and solution to deal with the whole issue of secondhand smoke, like ventilation technology, working together to ensure that we're upholding the rights and the preference of both smokers and nonsmokers alike.'
JIM LEHRER: And the judge's decision last week doesn't change anything from your point of view?
CAROL BROWNER, 'Administrator of EPA: We stand by our science. I think the judge made a procedural ruling. What he essentially said is that industry, that R.J. Reynolds should have sat at the table to review the science. And we don't agree with that. We think independent scientists — as we did — are the appropriate people to review a body of scientific evidence.'
CHARLES BLIXT, R.J. Reynolds executive vice president and general counsel: 'This opinion wasn't about any abuse of procedure, Jim. This opinion was about abuse of power by the EPA. What the EPA essentially did was deliberately mislead about the American people what about what science has proven about second-hand smoke. The judge's opinion cut right to the heart of that science. ... the judge specifically found that the EPA came to a pre-determined conclusion then cherry picked data, excluded any data which didn't support their pre-determined conclusion, changed the rules of science, didn't follow the law, and didn't follow its own internal regulatory procedures. ...'

JIM LEHRER: So is it your position, the industry's position, that second-hand smoke is not harmful to health?

CHARLES BLIXT: 'It's not our position that second-hand smoke is not harmful to health. It's our position that the science doesn't support any finding or any conclusion that second-hand smoke causes cancer or heart disease or any of these other diseases that were listed. ...'

CAROL BROWNER: 'More importantly, what you have here is a judge. A judge in Winston-Salem, North Carolina essentially trumping the scientific opinion of 18 independent scientists. Trumping the opinion of the Surgeon General, the National Academy of Sciences. ...We looked at all of the science, we reached conclusions, we presented those to independent scientists, we asked the tobacco industry what they thought about those in a draft form. They gave us thousands of pages. They appeared for hours before the scientists reviewing these findings and at the end of the day, the conclusion was unanimous. Secondhand smoke is bad.' "

So, although the industry had suffered reverses, it had succeeded in neutralizing OSHA and hamstringing EPA, and turning me into a pariah with the Indoor Air Division. However, all was not quiet on the Western Front. The Cigarette Papers and the Minnesota Litigation had given us access to the secret internal files of Big Tobacco. As for me, with my retirement imminent, I felt liberated for the first time in 10 years. And, I had developed all of the tools I needed to tell a compelling story about secondhand smoke: I had established that it was a major source of indoor air pollution. That work had been confirmed by researchers at Harvard, Yale, and Stanford. I had developed mathematical models that enabled me to calculate the levels of fine particles and nicotine in indoor spaces, past, present, and future. I had developed models that enabled the estimation of the risk of fatal lung cancer and heart disease from secondhand smoke exposure and dose. I had demonstrated that ventilation and air cleaning could not possibly control ETS to de minimis risk levels. And I had developed pharmacokinetic models that enabled me to map nicotine from secondhand smoke exposure into the dose of its metabolite cotinine in blood, urine, and saliva. These were powerful weapons with which I could continue to fight against secondhand smoke in the workplace. It only remained to be seen if I could manage to establish myself in a new career.

PART THREE
THE END GAME

CHAPTER 15

HAVE SLIDES, WILL TRAVEL

"Giving credence to a researcher with a political agenda during your December meeting, James Repace, a known anti-smoking advocate, appears to have been instrumental in getting your NTP panel members to approve your recommendation that environmental tobacco smoke be listed as a human carcinogen. For example, panelist Michele Medinsky, who was troubled by the weak relative risks reported in the studies in humans (as well she should be), said she was 'comforted quite a bit' by Mr. Repace's comments… Dr. Medinsky: 'I guess the relative risks in this for environmental tobacco smoke are from my perspective quite low. And that was – that was troubling me this entire time. And I think James Repace's comments … if we could actually get a control group that was truly unexposed that the relative risk would go up comforted me quite a bit.'"

Letter from Martha Perske, 159 Hollow Tree Ridge Road, Darien, CT 06820 to Dr. C.W. Jameson, Chairman, Review Committee for the 9th *Report on Carcinogens,* National Toxicology Program EC-14, P.O. Box 12233 Research Triangle Park, NC 27709.

The Smoke Industry finally got its wish to get rid of the "thorn in its side" at the EPA. Let's see how well that worked out for them. I submitted my retirement papers, and left federal employ with great relief in February 1998, with a Civil Service Pension of less than half-salary. Inspired by the legion of industry moles who consulted for the tobacco industry, I decided that I, too, would become a secondhand smoke consultant, except for two things: I would work for the good guys, and I actually knew what I was talking about. I informed my family of my intentions. Much to my delight, my highly computer literate and talented children built a website for me, obtained the domain name, did the computer programming to post the details, and paid for it! I hired an accountant to incorporate my business, Repace Associates, Inc.

By the end of 1997, I had published 55 papers, of which 46 dealt with secondhand smoke, and at least two of these were arguably widely known and respected. I had published in a wide variety of journals: scientific, engineering, environmental, medical, public health, legal and even law. I had given talks to medical, engineering, public health, and environmental groups, and at major universities. I had been noticed by the international tobacco control community. According to a Canadian friend, John Garcia, who had worked in tobacco control for both Health Canada and NCI, I was "a brand name in secondhand smoke, like Coca Cola." Being the "Coke of Smoke" augured well for future consulting. My website announced international consulting services, lectures, instructional courses on secondhand smoke, public testimony on legislation, legislator education, decision-maker briefings, secondhand smoke measurements and analysis, analysis of industry documents, assessment of engineering controls, and litigation support. I loved being an expert witness in legal cases involving secondhand smoke injury to plaintiffs, or in labor arbitrations. There were virtually no industry arguments that I hadn't heard and hadn't developed counter-arguments to. Further, along with Stan Glantz (who didn't do consulting), I was one of the few go-to-guys for the national and international media on the issue of secondhand smoke at that time. In 1997, I had been listed in Who's Who in the East. As it turned out, I had to do very little marketing; my reputation was sufficient.

And I soon discovered that if you Build A Website, They Will Come. I posted my curriculum vitae on my website, along with a series of reports with hard content. I imagined that I would do the lion's share of my consulting work for the U.S. Government. Except for a couple of major jobs for the National Cancer Institute in 1998, I was mistaken. The industry had done their best to make my life as a civil servant miserable, and now it was Payback Time. I was not the "anti-smoker" that they loved to defame me with. But I was virulently anti-tobacco industry and armed with scientific weapons and the knowledge and skills to deploy them in public settings in ways that laymen could grasp. I was ready to rock and roll. Coincidentally, during 1998, word of my retirement from EPA spread throughout the nonsmokers' rights and public health community. To my surprise and delight, I was honored by four awards recognizing my efforts to eliminate smoking in public places: a Lifetime Achievement Award from the American Public Health Association, a certificate of appreciation from Julia Carroll at Americans For Nonsmoker's Rights, another from John Banzhaf at ASH, and one from the Prince George's County Civic Federation.

During 1998-1999, I coauthored two more papers with Neil Klepeis and Wayne Ott on indoor air pollution from cigars [Figure 20]. We reported that cigars produced 30 times as much carbon monoxide and five times as much fine particulate air pollution as cigarettes, and the air at cigar social events had a higher concentration of those two pollutants than encountered in the bumper-to-bumper rush-hour traffic in the San Francisco Bay Area. Cigar aficionados, take note. (Repace et al., 1998; Klepeis et al., 1999). Finally, our Monte Carlo modeling paper of atmospheric and biomarkers of secondhand smoke, coauthored with Jennifer Jinot, Steven Bayard, Kathie Hammond and Karen Emmons, was published (Repace et al., *Risk Analysis (1998)*. It allowed the prediction of nonsmokers' lung cancer and heart disease risk from nicotine in air and cotinine in saliva, blood, or urine. Figure 21 illustrates our results. Our paper came to the attention of Edward (Ted) Sanders,

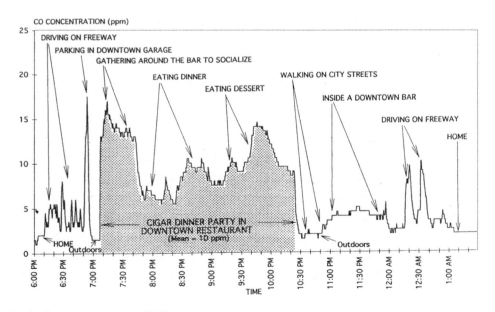

FIGURE 20A. CARBON MONOXIDE (CO) CONCENTRATIONS, INCLUDING BACKGROUND, MEASURED WITH A CONCEALED PERSONAL MONITOR BEFORE, DURING, AND AFTER A CIGAR BANQUET AT A DOWNTOWN SAN FRANCISCO RESTAURANT IN **1998** (KLEPEIS ET AL., 1999; REPACE ET AL., 1998). THE **EPA CO** STANDARD IS 9 PPM, 8 HR TIME-WEIGHTED AVERAGE.

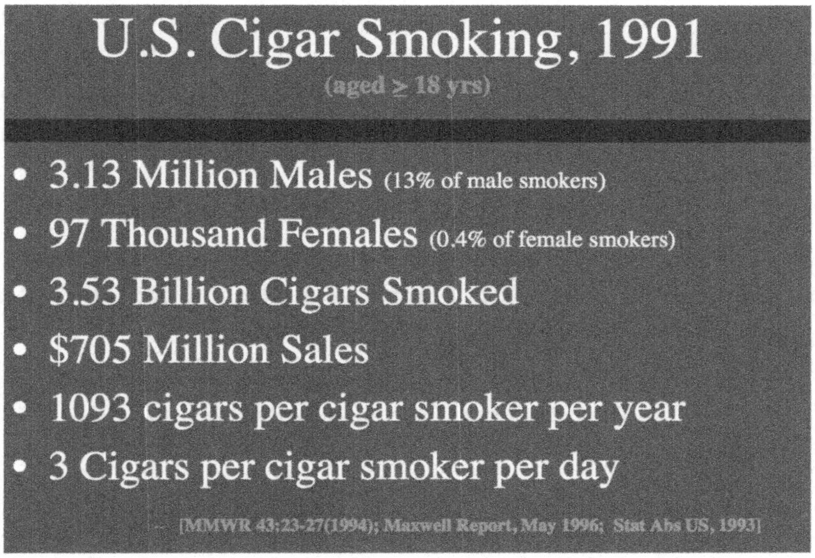

U.S. Cigar Smoking, 1991
(aged ≥ 18 yrs)

- 3.13 Million Males (13% of male smokers)
- 97 Thousand Females (0.4% of female smokers)
- 3.53 Billion Cigars Smoked
- $705 Million Sales
- 1093 cigars per cigar smoker per year
- 3 Cigars per cigar smoker per day

[MMWR 43:23-27(1994); Maxwell Report, May 1996; Stat Abs US, 1993]

FIGURE 20B. CIGAR STATISTICS, UNITED STATES, 1993 [AUTHOR'S SLIDE].

Vice Director of Research for Fabrique Tabac Reunies (FTR) Neuchatel, Philip Morris's Scientific Affairs Division (SAD), and apparently gave him a bilious case of agita. SAD was designed to "address all issues facing the Industry, embracing knowledge in the biological sciences, chemistry, physics, psychology, mathematics & statistics, engineering & patent matter" [TTID 2501254601]. Sanders' primary responsibility was ETS. He reported to Richard Carchman, Vice President for Scientific Affairs, Research & Development, Philip Morris, USA [TTID 3990113120; 2505430210]. On the 29th of April 1998, Sanders wrote to Carchman, saying in part,

> "After several further hours of wading through the Repace & Lowrey 1993 paper, I can conclusively state that there is no —— way that we can do justice to this whole issue in less than one month, and I don't guarantee the month. This is anything but a simple issue. … It is obvious that this will be time consuming. Secondly, I should point out that there is really nothing new in the 1998 paper, with the exception of the Monte Carlo simulation. Everything else rests on the same old arguments. For almost three years I have been trying to get someone to carry out a thorough analysis of the Repace, Lowrey risk assessment. The best effort that resulted was the Sterling analysis, which falls far short of the mark. It should be noted that it took them more than one year (and who knows how much money) to come up with a piece of junk. … I will firm this up in the next couple of days. Ted" [TTID 2505776951]

In fact, Ted, there *was* something new that you missed on first reading (Figure 21 A,B). It showed that our models for both atmospheric concentrations of nicotine and our pharmacokinetic models of body fluid cotinine were capable of accurately predicting the data observed by other researchers in real-world studies of secondhand smoke concentrations in offices and secondhand smoke doses in office workers. This was the essence of the scientific method. Moreover, this paper, published in a peer-reviewed journal, also included a risk model that we had previously published that was used to estimate the lung cancer mortality risks for workers, extended to predict heart disease mortality as well.

The abstract to our paper (Repace et al. 1998) read:

> "We model nicotine from environmental tobacco smoke (ETS) in office air and salivary cotinine in nonsmoking U.S. workers. We estimate that: an average salivary cotinine level of 0.4 ng/ml corresponds to an increased lifetime mortality risk of 1/1000 for lung cancer, and

1/100 for heart disease; >95% of ETS-exposed office workers exceed OSHA's significant risk level for heart disease mortality, and 60% exceed significant risk for lung cancer mortality; 4000 heart disease deaths and 400 lung cancer deaths occur annually among office workers from passive smoking in the workplace, at the current 28% prevalence of unrestricted smoking in the office workplace."

On May 4th 1998, Sanders had second thoughts, and followed up his April 29th memo with a second one to the four-person team he'd assembled, with cc's to Carchman and Helmut Reif, PM's Director of science and technology and Carchman's boss at FTR SAD, Neuchatel.

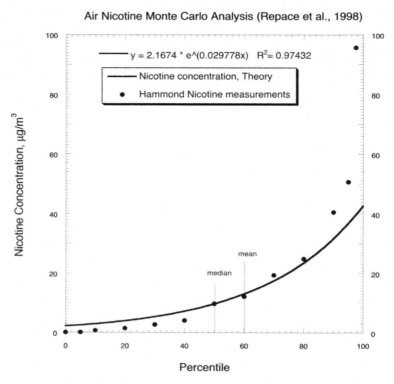

TOP: FIGURE 21A, MONTE CARLO ANALYSIS OF NICOTINE IN THE AIR OF 12 MASSACHUSETTS OFFICES; THEORY VS EXPERIMENT.

"Subject: Repace Article - Recently, Repace, Jinot, Bayard, Emmons, and Hammond published an article dealing with air nicotine and saliva cotinine as indicators of workplace ETS exposure and risk (Risk Analysis, 18: 71-83, 1998). At first reading it would appear that there is nothing new in this article, with the exception of two Monte Carlo simulations dealing with levels of nicotine in air and saliva cotinine. However, the situation is more complex than it might appear, since Repace, et al., change some of the assumptions made in earlier papers without addressing the changes these assumptions will have on the application of the total model. In addition, the model developed over the years by Repace, et al., is extremely complex, rests on numerous assumptions, and often ignores data which would tend to invalidate the model."

Sanders then outlined six assignments for his team, due by May 29th 1999. [TTID 2505776947].

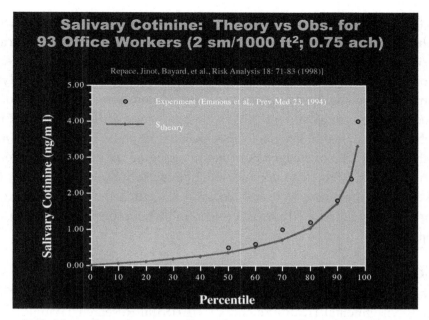

BOTTOM: FIGURE 20B, MONTE CARLO ANALYSIS OF SALIVA COTININE IN 93 RHODE ISLAND OFFICE WORKERS. THEORY VS. EXPERIMENT, FIGURES FROM REPACE ET AL, 1998 (AUTHOR'S SLIDES). THE MODEL ASSUMES ASHRAE STANDARD 62-1989 OCCUPANCY AND VENTILATION FOR EACH VENUE, PLUS 1991 US SMOKING PREVALENCE (29%).

This attempt to discredit our model also failed to be completed on schedule. On December 2nd 1999, a draft proposal allocating $100,000 to Sanders' team to "Manage external studies to investigate the scientific validity of the parameters and distributions used in Repace's Monte Carlo method, the model used for RSP and nicotine as a function of ventilation and smoker density, and Repace's subsequent risk assessment by August 31, 2000 Deliverable – Several manuscripts" [TTID 2073188473]. As far as I am aware, this effort never came to fruition. Perhaps it was because our paper was well received by the legitimate academic research community in 1999. The Monte Carlo model of Repace et al. (1998) for predicting ETS-nicotine exposures was favorably reviewed by Jaakkola and Samet (1999) and by Spengler (1999). Further, Samet and Wang (2000) delivered another blow to the industry, observing that "the calculations made possible by the exposure, dose, and risk models of Repace et al. (1998) for estimating risk of lung cancer illustrate that passive smoking must be considered as an important cause of lung cancer death from a public health perspective." Poor Ted Sanders must have been chewing his liver.

Soon after I retired, *The Wall Street Journal* article describing me as "Enemy No. 1" of the tobacco industry gave me marketing publicity that I couldn't have bought for a megabuck. I was on a roll, and got invited to give 22 talks that year, in Honolulu, Washington DC, Baltimore, North Carolina, San Francisco, Detroit, Montreal, North Dakota, Boston, New York State, Houston, Indianapolis, Toronto, and Ottawa, plus Chile, Portugal, and Greece. And I gave interviews on secondhand smoke to KHON TV, *USA Today, The New Scientist*, as well as *The Wall Street Journal*. I served as an expert witness in four legal cases: a child custody proceeding in Syracuse, NY, an office worker in North Dakota, a lung cancer case in Atlanta, and a putative class action case by Atlantic City and Las Vegas Casino Workers against the Big Tobacco (Badillo & Avallone v. American Tobacco et al.) In the first three, the plaintiffs prevailed.

The fourth one was successfully sandbagged by Big Tobacco's lawyers. This case was also was my first battle with tobacco lawyers as an expert witness. As such, I approached it with some trepidation. When I arrived at the law firm where the deposition was held, I encountered a half-dozen of these legal beasts. A deposition is a legal procedure involving interrogation by the opposition's lawyers. Both parties to the litigation are entitled to depose the other's witnesses. It is designed so that both sides understand the arguments of the other side's experts before trial, so as to expedite the proceedings. In practice, attorneys use depositions to gain information so they can impeach the opposing expert's testimony during cross-examination at trial. My prime interrogator among the gang of six was the bearded Jeff Furr of Womble Carlyle, external counsel to RJ Reynolds. I immediately recognized him as one of OSHA's antagonists at the Indoor Air Rule Hearings. At first, I was nervous, fearing a tough struggle but as the hours-long grilling went on, I realized that I knew far more about the subject than they did. I began to anticipate my response to each question like a spear-hunter stalking his prey in the jungle. The overeager Furr and his gang of six blew their opportunity, and I began to gain confidence. Afterwards, I felt I had done a creditable performance. Regretfully, the casino workers' attorneys, who worked on contingency, were unsuccessful in getting the judge to certify the workers as a class. To try each worker's case individually was a cost-prohibitive proposition for these small law firms, and so the effort was dropped.

THE NTP HEARING ON LISTING ETS IN THE 9TH REPORT ON CARCINOGENS

Don Shopland at NCI asked me to testify at a public hearing on December 2nd 1998, organized by the National Institute for Environmental Health Sciences (NIEHS) in Research Triangle Park, North Carolina. NIEHS was considering whether it should list ETS as a human carcinogen in *The National Toxicology Program's (NTP) 9th Report on Carcinogens*. Don said that the tobacco industry had signed up many witnesses to oppose the listing, and that much of their presentation would be technical. He insisted it was necessary for me to be there as a counter-weight to the industry's massive disinformation effort. I salivated at the opportunity. The *NTP Report on Carcinogens* Program conducts hazard identification activities for various substances to which Americans may be exposed. The NTP Report is important for federal agencies, such as EPA and OSHA, that regulate human exposures to environmental and occupational agents. In other words, the NTP reports are of considerable national and international import. Shopland gave me a list of those who would testify for the industry in the hearing. I flew down to Raleigh and stayed nearby with old friends, Al and Rita Basilico. Al, a retired IBM electrical engineer, was one of Bob's fraternity brothers at NYU who had also contracted Hodgkin's Disease. He now ran a small software firm. NCI paid the freight plus a consulting fee, but I represented myself.

My testimony, which used overhead slides, made extensive use of the Monte Carlo paper of Repace et al. (1998) to specifically rebut the testimony of Jenkins and his British counterpart, Keith Philips, whose ETS measurements in several European countries for Covance Labs (formerly Corning-Hazelton) were redolent of HBI's. Both of these "Special Projects" were funded by CIAR, and were described in 1993 by John Rupp, general counsel to CIAR, as among those that had "contributed significantly to the industry's ongoing efforts to oppose unwarranted smoking restrictions" (Kessler, 2006). [Other CIAR-funded mole studies included the Malmfors/SAS study of smoking on aircraft, and the "Asia Project" of Sara Liao in Hong Kong (Kessler, 2006; Repace, 2004 ; TTID 2023053717]. Conveniently, both Philips and Jenkins had given their presentations immediately before mine, allowing me to rebut them point by point while their testimony was fresh in the panel's minds. Forewarned by Don Shopland, I had already come prepared with slides to do exactly that.

My testimony argued that:
- "There is no question that ETS is a human carcinogen. Cigarettes & cigars are big emitters of carcinogenic polycyclic aromatic hydrocarbons.
- If the summary lung cancer risk estimate of approximately 1.2 were corrected for background exposure, it would double to 2.5. Two-thirds of the lung cancer risk in cigarette smokers who do not inhale is attributable to ETS. This was reported in the 1979 Surgeon General's report.

- Epidemiologists' ETS exposure assessment methods yield 'depressed' odds ratios. However, modeling can be used to predict ETS exposures and risk.
- The model of Repace et al. (1998) accurately predicts the nicotine levels in offices measured by Hammond. This model also accurately predicts salivary, urinary and serum cotinine levels from air nicotine, including the observations reported by the CDC's NHANES survey of the national population dose of serum cotinine.
- The nicotine/cotinine studies by RJR/Oak Ridge and CIAR-funded Covance labs in Europe were unphysical and the RJR/Oak Ridge study was inconsistent with the findings of CDC's NHANES study. I concluded that these industry-funded studies were unreliable."

In the questioning that followed my presentation, NIEHS Subcommittee member, toxicologist Dr. Michelle Medinsky, expressed concern over the low relative risks reported in the ETS epidemiological studies. I replied that the true risk attributable to ETS was actually not as small as reported by most epidemiological studies, because of the difficulty in finding truly unexposed controls. And exposed controls, "tainted" by their exposure to ETS, depressed lung cancer odds ratios. I raised the difficulty in finding a truly unexposed control group by questionnaire, emphasizing that low risk estimates are an artifact of the flawed way that many epidemiological studies had estimated subjects' exposures. I emphasized that CDC's NHANES Study (Pirkle et al., 1996), in analyzing national blood serum cotinine data, had found that while only 39% of adult nonsmokers had reported ETS exposure, 88% had detectable blood levels. Furthermore, those reporting no exposure at work or at home had cotinine levels 20% of those exposed at home only and 40% of those exposed at work only. In the early U.S. passive smoking and lung cancer epidemiological studies, subjects exposed at work only were counted as "unexposed," and only women whose husbands smoked were counted as "exposed." This resulted in "confounding." Confounding can obscure a real effect of passive smoking on lung cancer mortality.

I argued that to make the best estimate of the true ETS risk to the general nonsmoking population, one should compare their lung cancer mortality rates to those of controls such as California Seventh-Day Adventists (SDAs), whose religious practices proscribed smoking, whereas the case-control studies that formed the preponderance of epidemiological studies of passive smoking and lung cancer compared lung cancer incidence among subgroups of the general population based on self-reports of exposure to ETS. Moreover, SDAs tended to socialize mainly with co-religionists, and many also worked for SDA-run organizations. Consequently, the nonsmoking SDAs had little domestic, social, or workplace exposure to ETS. If this were done properly, the actual average general population lung cancer risk from ETS would be increased 2.5-fold compared to the 1.3-fold commonly reported in most epi studies. I noted that Lowrey and I had discussed this in our 1985 paper in *Environment International*.

In addition, CDC reported that they found no evidence of an effect of dietary nicotine on population serum cotinine levels. This indicated that our inferences on the negative effect of tainted controls in epi studies, and on the lack of influence of dietary nicotine on cotinine levels had been right on target. I emphasized that the CDC's study directly contradicted assertions to the contrary that the industry had argued to OSHA and was now making again to the NIEHS panel [TTID 2078129783]. Figure 22 shows the overlap slide clearly illustrating the problem of tainted controls in a statistical survey of serum cotinine in the general population studied by CDC (Pirkle, et al., 1996). Even most of the later epidemiological case-control studies traditionally had placed lung cancer victims in the "self-reported exposure at home or at work or both" category and compared those patients with controls from the "self-reported no ETS exposure either at home or at work" category. But – as the histogram in Figure 22 shows, in 1988-1991, more than half of nonsmokers who reported "no ETS exposure" (yellow bars) actually had finite cotinine values, indicating exposure to ETS, and a substantial number had cotinine doses sufficiently large (orange bars) that they overlapped with those who did report exposure at home or at work (red bars). This of course, confounded the epidemiological studies of ETS and lung cancer. [I note here that CDC reported that 12% of nonsmokers had no ETS exposure in 1989-1990. By comparison, Repace and Lowrey (1985) had estimated in the mid-1980's that 14% had none.]

As Figure 22 makes clear, some of the group of nonsmokers who reported being exposed to ETS actually had doses as low as some of those who reported no exposure, and some of the group who reported no exposure had doses as high as the group who reported ETS exposure. In other words, assessing ETS exposure from self-reports without clinical verification introduced a bias in the risk ratio. This effect could only work in one direction: to depress the odds ratios, making the effect on lung cancer appear smaller than it actually was, and washing out statistical significance. This is why clinical epidemiology, based as it is on repeated cotinine measurements to confirm exposure over time, works best. However, such studies are very expensive when done on large populations, reserving these longitudinal clinical studies to well-funded government agencies, like the CDC. It surprised me that so few epidemiologists and risk assessors had grasped this fact; although Steven Bayard was not one of them. He had adjusted for cotinine in the EPA risk assessment.

Tobacco industry lawyers, consultants, and scientists infested the audience like roaches. Among the parade of those testifying on behalf of the industry before the panel were many of the Usual Suspects plus a few stringers. Roger Jenkins (Oak Ridge/RJR) argued that his 16-city study results showed that EPA's assessment of background exposure was wrong, washing out its reported statistical significance. Keith Philips (Covance Labs), promoted the absurd notion that his industry-funded 12 European City data showed that when expressed in terms of "cigarette equivalents" of nicotine, nonsmokers exposed at home or at work would be exposed to less than half a cigarette per year. Evidently, he hadn't read the 1986 Surgeon General's report, which rejected cigarette equivalents as measures of either exposure or dose. Chris Coggins (Lorillard Tobacco), attempted to cast doubt on mouse studies of carcinogenesis and their use as animal models for classification of carcinogens.

THE INDUSTRY CONSULTANTS' TESTIMONY

Paul Levy (U. of Chicago), led off, attacking Jud Wells' 1998 meta-analysis paper on workplace lung cancer. Richard Carchman (Philip Morris USA) attempted to argue that a large IARC study of passive smoking and lung cancer in Europe showed "no statistically significant overall increases in risk ... in the study," and that if it had properly accounted for confounding and smoker misclassification, the risk would have been reduced by 50% or more. Industry consultant William J. Butler, of Environmental Risk Analysis, Inc., cast doubt on the reliability of the large Brownson and Fontham epidemiological studies of passive smoking and lung cancer. Next up was Gerhard Scherer (Verband der Cigarettenindustrie, i.e., the Association of German Cigarette Manufacturers, whose membership included the German and Austrian tobacco companies, Reemstma, Brinkmann, H van Landwyck, Austria Tabak, and three smaller companies), as well as the German branches of three transnational cigarette companies, PM, RJR, and BAT) [Hirschhorn, 2000]. Scherer presented data on his biomonitoring of ETS exposure in nonsmokers purporting to show that cotinine levels in nonsmokers reporting no ETS exposure were only 10% of those reporting ETS exposure.

Gio Batta Gori (Health Policy Center) asserted that ETS and mainstream smoke were quite different, that meta-analysis of workplace exposures showed essentially no elevation in risk, and that although the spousal studies did, 90% were not statistically significant [Gori avoided mentioning that ETS was more toxic per gram than mainstream smoke, and ignored EPA's contrary analysis of statistical significance]. Finally, Gori asserted that ETS could be considered to be an irritant, but not a carcinogen [despite the presence of a raft of carcinogens in the smoke]. Ronald G. Marks (U. of Florida) argued that his analysis of the data sets of four large epi studies of passive smoking and lung cancer showed that dietary factors were more important, that ETS "cancelled out" of his statistical model, and finally that his analysis of the literature showed that no dose-response has been established. However, in response to a panelist's inquiry, he admitted that he had not submitted his work for publication.

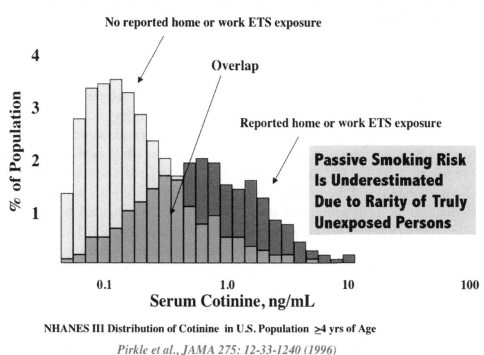

88% of U.S. Population is Exposed to ETS; but only ~40% Report Exposure

NHANES III Distribution of Cotinine in U.S. Population ≥4 yrs of Age

Pirkle et al., JAMA 275: 12-33-1240 (1996)

FIGURE 22. HISTOGRAM ILLUSTRATING THAT MORE THAN HALF OF NONSMOKERS REPORTING "NO EXPOSURE TO ETS" IN 1988-1991 (YELLOW BARS ON LEFT) IN FACT ACTUALLY WERE EXPOSED TO ETS (ORANGE BARS IN CENTER), AND SOME HAD COTININE DOSES COMPARABLE TO THOSE EXPOSED AT HOME OR AT WORK (RED BARS ON RIGHT). THE ORANGE OVERLAP AREA DEMONSTRATES THE CONFOUNDING OF ETS EXPOSURE AS DISCUSSED IN THE TEXT (AUTHOR'S SLIDE).

Finally, Maurice LeVois (LeVois Associates) argued that "recall bias" (poor memory of exposure) in epi studies was significant [neglecting to mention that this would depress odds ratios], and that publication bias [failure to submit negative results for publication] was even more insidious [and highly speculative], that there was weak consistency in studies across countries [an argument specifically refuted by EPA's analysis], and finally that 17 constituents of ETS were "ubiquitous in the environment, suggesting that "a maximum of 8%" of exposure to these compounds came from ETS [this was patent nonsense, as there was little or no clinical or experimental data to support this, and there were hundreds of toxins in ETS]. His arguments, like those of the other consultants, were recycled tobacco industry talking points that had gone stale after having been argued to and rejected by both EPA and OSHA.

THE NTP PANEL'S DEBATE

Then the subcommittee began to debate the issues. Bingham endorsed my argument on Seventh Day Adventists. Hecht agreed that ETS exposure was hard to measure using epidemiological studies and noted that Scherer's and Hecht's own work both showed that ETS-exposed persons had higher levels of a potent tobacco-specific lung carcinogen, NNK. Frederick suggested that the conclusion that ETS was a human carcinogen was "inescapable." Mirer dismissed the notion that unpublished data presented to the subcommittee as additional evidence that supported an ETS effect should be rejected, because the epi data were persuasive, and that ETS and mainstream smoke were respectively low dose and high dose of a carcinogen. Henry said she was troubled by the industry's claim that following cessation of exposure, risks became minimal. Zahm echoed my argument regarding the scarcity of truly unexposed persons with respect to the IARC study, concluding that this would "dilute" the risk estimates in the IARC study and that she found the "known human carcinogen" classification persuasive. Medinsky then dropped the other shoe, asserting that although the low risk ratios had been troubling her, my comments and those of Steve Hecht that they would increase with the appropriate comparison group "comforted me quite a bit." Finally, Frederick said that the "impressive" written submission by Spears of RJ Reynolds had convinced him of the *exact opposite* of Spears' conclusion, and that he felt that ETS was a "major problem." The subcommittee then voted unanimously to recommend that ETS be listed as "known to be a human carcinogen" in NIEHS's 9th Report on Carcinogens.

One of the tobacco minions sitting right behind me shouted in dismay, *"Shit – we lost!"* So, despite all of this heavyweight firepower the industry unleashed on the NTP panel, as one industry-funded observer, Multinational Business Services, put it in his report: "Mr. Repace's public comment presentation seemed to carry considerable weight with the RC Subcommittee and influenced its decision" [TTID 2063890444]. It was a very satisfying moment, and the breathing public has Don Shopland's perspicacity to thank for that. NIEHS solicited final public comments, and then forwarded the nomination to the National Toxicology Program executive committee, comprised of representatives from EPA, OSHA, FDA, NIOSH, and NCI. The Executive Committee was then chaired by Linda Rosenstock, the Director of NIOSH. In 1989, NIOSH had declared ETS to be a "potential occupational carcinogen," recommending that workers' ETS exposure be reduced to the "lowest feasible concentration." The National Toxicology Program's *9th Report on Carcinogens* was issued on May 15, 2000; Environmental Tobacco Smoke was posted in a list with only 46 other substances, including radon, benzene, and asbestos, designated as substances "Known to be Human Carcinogens." The tobacco industry was batting 1 hit for 7 at-bats – they had knocked OSHA out of the park, but the NAS, the Surgeon General, NIOSH, the EPA, the California EPA, and now NIEHS, had all affirmed that ETS caused lung cancer in nonsmokers. I had input into every single one, either through public testimony (Cal EPA and NIEHS) or via my published work. At the end of my first year of retirement, the gross income from my business plus my pension now exceeded my former federal salary by $10,000, and I was having a hell of lot more fun.

As for pesky Martha Perske, she apparently had a very big axe to grind. In 1993, she had confessed, "I am a smoker. I'm also a professional illustrator. I have spent long hours at a drawing board with a cup of tea and a pack of cigarettes next to me" [TTID T12567-0436]. However, Martha was a bit more than just another smoker. She was a representative of the American Smokers' Alliance [TTID 204655720; TTID T12567-0436; TTID TI 22567-0429]. As Landman and Glantz (2009) wrote: "Nominally an independent smokers' rights advocate, Perske completed media training at RJ Reynolds and was in direct contact with RJ Reynolds employees and representatives. Perske wrote letters to academic journals, newspapers, and legislators to advance industry views on SHS and forwarded any replies she received to RJ Reynolds" [TTID TI 22567-0428].

AND IN OTHER NEWS...

Nineteen Ninety-Nine started off with a bang. President Clinton announced in his State of the Union Address that the Justice Department would sue the tobacco industry to hold them accountable for the "hundreds of billions of dollars" that consumption of cigarettes imposed on the taxpayers. This in turn led to heightened press interest in secondhand smoke as well. During the year, I gave seven TV interviews, five radio interviews, and 34 presentations, talks, and newspaper interviews. The Union for International Cancer Control (UICC) invited me to a week-long conference on sunny Gran Canaria in the Canary Islands in late February, a delightful time to be away from DC's frigid winter weather. Our hotel had a large outdoor pool populated by numerous Europeans who fled the long icy winter darkness of their Northern climes. Hilarine and I dined al fresco on the hotel veranda every morning, sharing our breakfast table with chirpy little canaries who brazenly looted morsels from our plates. The UICC had asked me to put together a Fact Sheet on Secondhand Smoke with a couple of other experts. I enlisted Ichiro Kawachi at Harvard and Stan Glantz at UCSF as co-authors (Repace et al., 1999). Our work product burgeoned to 28 pages, far in excess of the one or two pages the UICC expected. It summarized the state of the art in secondhand smoke, in the areas of heart disease and lung cancer hazard, exposure concentrations, dosimetry, dose-response relationships, risk estimates, and ventilation debunking, as well as the economics of smoking bans.

Our Fact Sheet displayed a plot of taxable sales for California restaurants and bars from 1991 through 2002 demonstrating that California's bans on smoking in restaurants in 1995 and bars in 1998 had yielded no loss of income to the hospitality industry, refuting long-standing tobacco industry propaganda and real or imagined hospitality industry fears [Figure 23]. We graphed the seminal results of the 1994 British Doctors Study [Figure 24]. In their famous 40-year prospective epidemiological study of 34,439 male British doctors from 1951 to 1991, Doll and Peto et al., (1994; 2004) had studied the mortality of British physicians by smoking status. In a striking testament to the killing power of inhaled tobacco smoke, by age 70, fully half of the doctors who smoked had already died, compared to just a fifth of nonsmoking doctors. By age 85, there were four times as many nonsmoking doctors alive than smoking doctors.

To put the Doll and Peto study into plain language, smokers make a Faustian Bargain with tobacco: in return for the dubious pleasure of nicotine addiction, which most fall prey to as vulnerable teens, they will pay with years of poor health and a greatly shortened lifespan. The more they smoke, the sooner they die. Note that the curve for nonsmokers would have been higher but for the widespread exposure to secondhand smoke. In 1994 and 1996, Martin Jarvis surveyed plasma cotinine in 15,312 self-reported English non-smokers. Detectable concentrations of cotinine were found in 90% (Jarvis et al., 2001). This was quite similar to the 88% found in the CDC's NHANES III study (Pirkle, et al., 1996).

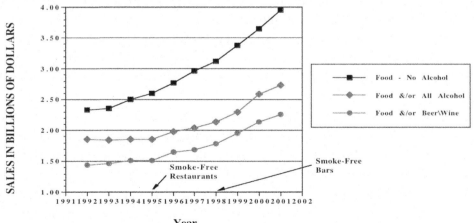

FIGURE 23. CALIFORNIA RESTAURANT AND BAR SALES FROM 1991-2002 SHOWING THAT THE RESTAURANT AND BAR SMOKING BANS IN 1995 AND 1998 RESPECTIVELY HAD NO EFFECT ON SALES (REPACE ET AL., 1999).

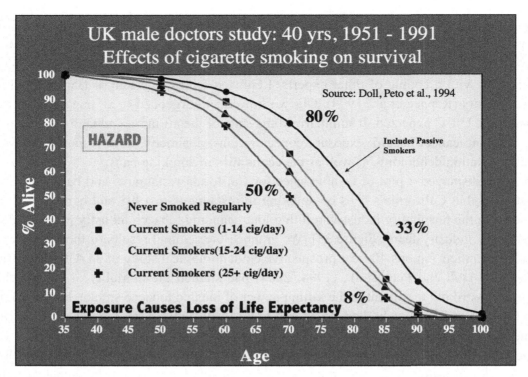

FIGURE 24. RELATIVE LIFESPANS OF MALE SMOKERS AND LIFELONG NONSMOKERS. THE HALF-LIFE FOR REGULAR PACK OR MORE PER DAY SMOKERS IN THE STUDY IS 69 YEARS, WHILE IT IS 82 YEARS FOR NEVER SMOKERS. A PACK-A-DAY SMOKER HAS 25 TIMES THE LUNG CANCER RISK OF A LIFELONG NONSMOKER AND 24 TIMES THE RISK OF COPD. (REPACE ET AL. FACT SHEET ON SECONDHAND SMOKE, 1999)

Meanwhile, the industry's disinformation campaign on secondhand smoke continued unabated. Exploiting the 1998 Osteen decision, Gio Gori and John Luik coauthored a book, *Passive Smoke: The EPA's Betrayal of Science and Policy,* published by the Fraser Institute in Vancouver. Like Gori, Luik had long been a tobacco industry industry consultant. However, the biographical abstract for each author made no mention of this. In 1993, Luik had drafted a paper for The Confederation Of European Community Cigarette Manufacturers Limited, according to a memorandum dated 19 March 1993 from John Lepere, its chairman, to colleagues on the Confederation. Lepere noted that Luik had submitted the draft and requested the Confederation's comments and suggestions before finalizing it. Lepere noted that Luik's paper "will be on the agenda for discussion during the next meeting of our Working Group on Smoking at the Workplace and in Public Places in Brussels on Wednesday, 31 March 1993 [TTID 2501139683]. The Gori-Luik book concealed its tobacco industry funding. The industry had laundered the funds by funneling them through the right-wing Fraser Institute which had solicited grants from BAT to establish a "Centre on Risk and Regulation" [rabble.ca, 2009; TTID 32510139].

In June 2001, a CBC Television report investigated Luik's academic credentials. It reported that during Luik's professorship at Brock University, its Dean of Humanities, Cecil Abrahams, had discovered that Luik had made misleading statements about visiting professorships at other academic institutions and had added books and articles that did not exist to his list of publications. Abrahams told reporters: "I certainly would not trust anything John Luik says because he must be the worst case of fraud that I have come across and I've been an administrator at universities for a long period of time, both in North America and in Africa, and I think he's by far the worst case of fraudulent behaviour" [Public Interest, 2015]. Of course, this would have made him very attractive to the industry.

The Gori-Luik book did not disappoint its paymasters: The preface asked: "Does second-hand smoke result in thousands of deaths every year in the U.S. and Canada? If you have been listening to health advocates in the media, the answer is an emphatic yes. This premature conclusion is largely based on a 1993 report by the U.S. Environmental Protection Agency which concluded that second-hand cigarette smoke caused around 3000 deaths per year among nonsmokers. This report was used by anti-tobacco activists to secure bans (full or partial) on indoor smoking in the U.S. and Canada." The preface went on to note that "In a recent ruling, Judge William Osteen of the Middle District of North Carolina, invalidated the EPA study … [concluding] that the researchers at EPA … cherry-picked data in order to reach a preconceived conclusion." In 2006, federal judge Gladys Kessler, would cite the Gori Luik tome in one of the fraud counts in the trial of the tobacco industry under the RICO statute, noting that "the authors did not disclose tobacco industry funding" [Kessler, 2006].

Among my international trips in 1999, I flew to Greece, Portugal, Australia and New Zealand. In late November, The Heart Foundation of Australia had invited me to lecture, give interviews, and lobby legislators in Sydney, Melbourne, Adelaide, and Hobart. The "Ozzies" were extremely hospitable; Hilarine and I were invited out to dinner by Prof. Simon Chapman and his wife, and into the homes of Ms. Anne Jones (the very same Ms. Jones who had entertained me in London) and Dr. Arthur Chesterfield-Evans, all prominent anti-smoking activists. The seafood was exquisite in Sydney, especially the Tasmanian oysters, which tasted of the sea and practically melted in your mouth. The first night we were there, we were on our own, and Hilarine and I ordered Peking Duck in a downtown Chinese restaurant. The chef came out and proudly displayed a wonderfully browned whole duck for us. However, when our dinner was served, we each got just three small strips of skin off of its back on large plates for $30. After Hilarine vehemently objected, they grudgingly brought out a bit more. We obviously had wandered into a tourist trap.

In early December, we flew across the Tasman Sea to New Zealand at the behest of Smoke-free New Zealand. As we flew over Auckland, the city below was a spectacular carpet of lavender Jacaranda tree blossoms. I lectured in Auckland and Wellington, and did radio and newspaper interviews. Dr. Murray Laugesen and his wife invited us to spend a weekend at his retreat on the razorback Island of Waiheki, a fast-ferry ride away from Auckland, with its hillside villas and spectacular views of the Cerulean Blue Gulf of Hauraki. We jogged on the beach, and gazed at the splendiferous cloud of red blossoms on the Puhutukawa Tree, also known as the New Zealand Christmas Tree. Life Was Good.

In 2000, my consulting continued unabated with 27 events, including testimony before the New York City Council, the New Jersey Regional Health Commission, the Philadelphia City Council, the New Bedford Massachusetts Health Board, and in four legal cases. Internationally, I made my second foray into Portugal, giving a one-week course on Involuntary Smoking to the Masters in Public Health program at the University of Porto. I lectured again at Johns Hopkins, this time at the Department of Environmental Health Sciences, gave talks at the University of North Carolina, the Nebraska Health Department, at Rutgers University for the New Jersey Health Officers annual meeting, and to the tobacco control program in Attleboro, Vermont. I remained popular with the press. The Lincoln Nebraska Health Department arranged three newspaper interviews, plus several TV and radio interviews. In another expedition to Winnipeg, Canada I participated in a live public radio broadcast debate with a woefully ill-prepared nightclub owner. I also did a telephone interview with an Australian radio station in Tasmania.

I made my first foray into the world of outdoor pollution from secondhand smoke, in a debate with my friend Simon Chapman, then the editor of the journal *Tobacco Control*, with whom I differed on the subject of outdoor smoking bans. Based on my experience with smoke-stack pollution, I believed they were justified and Simon didn't. Several years remained before I would be able to support that statement with my own experimental data.

To keep the pot boiling, I gave three conference presentations on secondhand smoke, one at the World Conference on Tobacco or Health in Chicago, another at the annual meeting of the International Society of Environmental Epidemiology in Buffalo, New York, and a third at the annual meeting of the International Society of Exposure Analysis in Monterey, California. To top it off, I coauthored a paper with 14 other researchers in *JAMA* on the state of the science on cigar smoking [Baker et al., 2000].

DUNCAN V. NORTHWEST AIRLINES

To its credit, Northwest Airlines had prohibited smoking on all its domestic flights in 1988, a year before the ban was mandated under federal law. It was the first carrier to do so. However, like the remainder of U.S. carriers, Northwest continued to allow smoking on flights to and from Japan for another decade. Northwest asserted that it "was responding to customer preferences and competition from Japan Air Lines," which then also allowed smoking. Hagens Berman, a Phoenix, Arizona law firm, had first represented Northwest's flight attendants in a contingency suit against the airline in 1998. The Associated Press reported that the lead plaintiff, Julie Duncan of Seattle, a Northwest flight attendant for 27 years, blamed secondhand smoke for her breathing impairment and other ailments. Duncan sought to represent an entire class of 4,000 past and present Northwest employees who were affected by the airline's previously permissive smoking policy. *Duncan v. Northwest*, first filed in January 1998, had been dismissed later that year by a federal judge who ruled that such claims were barred by federal law. In April of 2000, an appellate court overturned the lower court ruling in a 3-0 decision [Associated Press, 2000].

In the fall of 2000, an attorney for Hagens Berman retained me to serve as an expert witness for the plaintiffs. I performed a risk assessment, *In the Matter of Duncan v. Northwest Airlines, Inc.* in November 2000. The firm provided me with numerous documents from the airline that reported such details as load factors (percent of seats occupied), cabin ventilation, percent smoking occupancy, and various depositions. I estimated the secondhand smoke atmospheric exposures and biomarker doses for Northwest Airlines' flight attendants on Northwest's 747s and DC10s plying the Asia route. I then applied my risk models to estimate ETS atmospheric markers such as respirable particles (RSP) and nicotine in the aircraft cabins, as well as pharmacokinetic models for the nicotine metabolite, cotinine in the blood, urine, and saliva of flight attendants. The models predicted atmospheric and biomarker levels for Northwest's aircraft and flight attendants within the range of measurements reported for aircraft with smoking in the scientific literature. I concluded that the average concentration of ETS-RSP on board these large aircraft at a smoking prevalence of 33% was approximately 327 $\mu g/m^3$. This corresponded to cabin air pollution de facto violating the daily National Ambient Air Quality Standard for fine particulate pollution ($PM_{2.5}$) by 70% on average. Violations of this standard are associated with increased risk of hospital admissions, emergency room visits, respiratory symptoms and disease, decreased lung function, alterations in lung tissue and structure and in respiratory tract defense mechanisms, placing the afflicted at increased risk of infectious diseases such as pneumonia.

Further, assuming an 8-hour-long exposure, a flight attendant would develop a serum cotinine dose of about 1.9 nanograms per milliliter (ng/ml). This was a bit above the 30th percentile that Mattson et al. (1989) had measured for Air Canada flight attendants flying four-hour transcontinental flights. I associated this dose with a 70% increased risk of being diagnosed with coronary heart disease. I estimated that average ETS exposure on board would produce an annual excess mortality risk in a cohort of 4000 flight attendants of about 2 deaths per year, which was 22 times OSHA's Significant Risk Level. In addition, I estimated that asthmatic flight attendants risk of respiratory death, emergency room visit, hospital admission, asthmatic attack, bronchodilator use) would be increased by 45% to 78%. I asserted that ETS would have caused nonsmoking flight attendants to suffer severe symptomatic effects, including eye, nose, and throat irritation, persistent headaches, dizziness and nausea, coughing, and shortness of breath due to exposure to secondhand smoke. I concluded that "to within a reasonable degree of scientific certainty, plaintiffs' increased risk of lung cancer, heart disease, respiratory impairment, and other diseases from exposure to secondhand smoke on board Northwest's Asia-route aircraft portended future injury and violated contemporary standards for acceptable environmental or occupational exposure to carcinogens, toxins, and air pollution."

Eleven years later, Beatty, et al. (2011), would report on a medical study of three hundred sixty-two flight attendants, collecting data on their experiences as flight attendants, their medical histories, smoking histories, and SHS exposures. They compared this to a matched control group of national population sample of similar age and smoking history from the CDC's NHANES 2005-2006 national cohort. The University of California San Francisco researchers found that this cohort of flight attendants had a 63% increased prevalence of chronic bronchitis, a 256% increased prevalence of emphysema, and a 50% increased prevalence of sinus problems, despite a lower prevalence of other medical illnesses including high blood pressure, diabetes, high cholesterol, heart failure, cancer, and thyroid disease. Amongst never-smoking flight attendants, there was a doubled risk of daily symptoms (relative to controls) of nasal congestion, throat, or eye irritation per 10-year increase of years of service as a flight attendant prior to the smoking ban.

Unfortunately, in 2001, the trial court granted the defendant's motion for summary judgment on the medical monitoring cause of action, on the basis of its "reluctance to allow damages for enhanced risk without an accompanying present injury" and holding that Washington State does not recognize an independent tort for medical monitoring, although the plaintiff could have pursued medical monitoring as a remedy if there had been another existing cause of action. In other words, flight attendants had to wait until they actually got sick or died from secondhand smoke exposure before they could pursue such a claim in Washington State. Pooh!

In 2000, I also did my first legal case involving secondhand smoke infiltration in multi-unit housing, *Sagatelian v. South Lake Apartments*, in Pasadena, California. Ms. Sagatelian's leafy garden apartment complex was right around the corner from CalTech. Her lawyer refused to allow me to measure nicotine in her condo on the grounds that her neighbor might be refraining from smoking inside for the duration of the litigation. Instead he hired Rick Diamond from Lawrence Berkeley Laboratory to measure infiltration between the units using carbon dioxide from dry ice. Under the rules of litigation, the defendant had to allow access to her apartment. Rick's test demonstrated that infiltration was occurring. So far, so good.

In court, to illustrate the principle of smoke infiltration to the jury, I used a couple of two-liter plastic bottles filled with water and connected by a plastic tube to simulate a conduit for inter-unit infiltration. I injected red vegetable dye into one bottle and gently heated it on a hotplate to illustrate the process. As the red dye migrated between the bottles, it provided a great show-and-tell. I was confident that we would prevail. But we lost. I was shocked. Ms. Sagatelian's lawyer did an exit interview with the jury. In essence, the jury felt that the "little old lady smoker defendant" was an object of sympathy and the "preachy non-smoking plaintiff" was not. Ms. Sagatelian, a paralegal who had borrowed against her retirement to fund her case, was bankrupted. She was forced to sell her unit to pay her legal fees, and she drove off into the Central Valley with her two little dogs, in a vintage red BMW sporting the license plates "K9Passion." This was another sad but important lesson: lawsuits are a crapshoot. Being in the right is no guarantee of winning. *Sagatelian* was the first of four legal cases I did in 2000.

The second involved Ms. Becky Leonard, a real-estate agent who frequently visited the smoky Rollette County Records Building in North Dakota daily to pull records. During her visits, she would develop acute symptoms from secondhand smoke. Fortunately, *Leonard v. Rollette County* was tried before a sympathetic judge, who ordered the building to become smoke-free.

The third case was a re-match with Big Tobacco: The Los Angeles City Attorney filed a multi-billion dollar lawsuit against 16 tobacco companies (cigarette, cigar and pipe tobacco), in the *People of the State of California v. Philip Morris et al.* The suit accused the defendants of violating Proposition 65 — California's Safe Drinking Water and Toxic Enforcement Act — by not warning the public about the health risks of secondhand tobacco smoke. The city sought $2.5 billion and an injunction against the sale of tobacco products in California until the companies give "clear and reasonable warning" about the toxic dangers of breathing secondhand tobacco smoke.

I was one of eight expert witnesses in this case. My proposed testimony centered on four issues: ETS risk assessment and analysis; selecting an appropriate mathematical model for evaluating human health risks; the role of experimental data and models for evaluating risk; and information concerning ETS exposure and risk for various health end-points. I was deposed by another tag-team of a half-dozen tobacco lawyers in August of 2000. One of these legal barbarians appeared to have no other purpose than to glare at me for hours. My deposition lasted two days, and I hammered home the points that the risks of active smoking had no known threshold of effect and that the issue was not whether doses that nonsmokers encountered could cause the known diseases of smoking, but rather how big the risk was. Back in January 2000, the judge had dismissed the Prop 65 claims brought by plaintiffs Los Angeles and San Jose, ruling that "[as] the evidence proffered is undisputed and established Defendants' wholesale lack of control over the exposure of 'secondhand smoke' to non-consumers, as a matter of law it must be said that Defendants herein owed Plaintiffs no duty to warn non-consumers of secondhand smoke that may have been emitted by the ordinary use by consumers of the tobacco products manufactured and distributed by Defendants."

However, a third plaintiff, the American Environmental Safety Institute, was allowed to proceed with its claim that the tobacco companies violated California Business and Professions Code section 17200 by committing unfair business practices by denying that secondhand smoke causes cancer, reproductive toxicity, sudden infant death syndrome, asthma, heart disease, alterations in lung development, lower respiratory tract diseases and emphysema. To the best of my knowledge, this case was settled out of court. The fourth legal case involved three prisoners with secondhand smoke irritation complaints in New York State; it is tough to win prisoner cases unless they become seriously ill; they did not prevail. I recall that the judge's ruling, which regarded these complaints as frivolous, dripped with scorn. Off the record, he described the plaintiffs as "a pack of rotten inmates." Aside from that, it was a very good year. In May of 2000, I made a third trip to Portugal as an ad hoc advisor to the World Health Organization for a multi-national workshop on Policies to Reduce Exposure to ETS. We dined out one evening in a steakhouse restaurant that had great food but was super-smoky. Our host, Dr. José Calheiros, complained to the manager, who replied that the smoke bothered him too, but what could he do? One of the major obstacles to obtaining smoking restrictions in Portugal was the high smoking prevalence, especially among physicians and other medical personnel. To give you a sense for how high this was, several years later, a Portuguese teaching-hospital surveyed medical workers' smoking behavior and tobacco control attitudes just before the national ban came into force in January 2008. Smoking prevalence was 40.5% in males, 23.5% in females 43.2% in auxiliaries, 26.1% in nurses, 18.9% among physicians, and 34.7% among other non-health professionals. During my first visit to Portugal in 1998, when I lectured at the Instituto do Ciencias Biomedicas de Abel Salazar, Universidade do Porto, I had been denounced by a pediatrician who asserted that I was "bringing in dangerous ideas from the United States that could only serve to demonize Portuguese physicians who smoked." My hosts were shocked. Particularly so, because this guy was the Portuguese Delegate to the EU on smoking and health. In my experience, a high smoking prevalence persisted among physicians in several Mediterranean countries during the late 20th Century, especially in Greece.

That year I also did several consults in Canada, for the Ontario Tobacco Research Unit in Toronto, the Ottawa Council on Smoking and Health, and the Regional Health Authorities in British Columbia, Saskatchewan, and Manitoba. The latter one was in December, and giant snowflakes were descending upon Winnipeg. I went for a stroll around the block, and noticed that there were electrical outlets on the parking meters outside my hotel. I queried my host, who informed me that their purpose was to plug in "block heaters." "What's a block heater?" I asked. "It's an electric blanket to keep the anti-freeze in your engine block from freezing solid from the cold." He then related that a few years earlier, he had moved to Winnipeg from a less frigid part of Canada, and noticed his next-door neighbor putting up his Christmas lights in October. He asked, "Why are you putting up your Christmas lights so early?" The neighbor replied, "You're new here, aren't you?"

In 2000 and on into 2001, I continued to traverse the country spreading the gospel of the severe health effects of passive smoking, the futility of ventilation as a control measure, and the consequent necessity for smoking bans. I did presentations for health groups and legislators in Vancouver, Ottawa, New York City, Indiana, Minnesota, Oklahoma, North Dakota, Louisiana, Kentucky, and Colorado, as well as for the CDC in Georgia, Louisiana, and Oregon. In April 2001, I lectured in Oklahoma, giving talks in Tulsa, Oklahoma City, Enid, McAlister, and Lawton, plus numerous radio, TV, and print interviews. I visited the poignant memorial to the 168 victims of the Oklahoma City bombing by an anti-government fanatic; there were pictures of the victims and stuffed animals posted by relatives of the survivors on a fence overlooking the grounds, which were populated by 168 empty chairs in neat rows. During 2001, I co-authored three papers, two with Dr. David Mannino at the CDC in Atlanta analyzing the health effects of ETS on children based on NHANES cotinine data, and one with Monique Muggli in Dr. Richard Hurt's group at the Mayo Clinic on the tobacco industry's scientific strategies aimed against ETS (Mannino et al. 2001a, 2001b; Muggli et al. 2001).

MAKING TROUBLE IN HONG KONG

In May of 2001, the Hong Kong Council on Smoking and Health flew me in on a Boeing 777 in business class. The unaccustomed luxury of seats that reclined flat for sleep, the great food and drink on the plane, the business class lounges with free food, booze, relaxed atmosphere, and comfortable seating in the airports at either end would forever spoil me for international travel.

I spent a week in Hong Kong consulting for the Hong Kong Council on Smoking and Health, where I did a World Tobacco Day presentation for government officials and the public on *Tobacco Industry Disinformation*, and lectured at the Hospital Authority in Kowloon. I presented at a press conference on the *Hong Kong Catering Workers' Cotinine Study* of 104 nonsmoking hospitality industry workers who had been exposed to secondhand smoke at work only. I co-authored a report, Hong Kong Council on Smoking and Health No. 8, *Second-hand smoke exposures and passive smoking in non-smoking catering workers in Hong Kong: the combined risks for heart disease and cancer,* with members of the Department of Community Medicine at the University of Hong Kong, showing that catering workers were at high risk of heart disease and lung cancer from passive smoking. Our press conference included a lecture, *Passive smoking: The big picture: monitoring and risk assessment: what should we be doing next?* sponsored by the Hong Kong Council on Smoking & Health - A multidisciplinary seminar with HKCOSH Research Committee, the HK Environmental Protection Department, the University of Hong Kong Department of Community Medicine and Medical and Health Research Network. Figure 25 shows a slide from this lecture from my analysis of the cotinine data. Our paper would be published five years later (Hedley, et al. 2006).

Three articles on our study appeared in the South China Morning Post. The first one reported in part:

South China Morning Post, Wednesday, May 16, 2001
Revealed : restaurant workers' level of risk
MARY ANN BENITEZ and FELIX CHAN

"Non-smoking restaurant workers have 5-1/2 times more nicotine in their bloodstream than non-smokers in smoke-free workplaces, increasing their risk of dying from lung cancer and heart disease, according to a ground-breaking study. Based on the results, researchers estimated one in 33 catering workers - about 150 a year - would die from heart disease and lung cancer because of passive smoking in Hong Kong. The findings prompted calls yesterday for the Government to protect workers' health by immediately banning smoking in the workplace."

Dr. Anthony Hedley, chair of the Council on Smoking and Health, was quoted: "The principle must be that no worker should have to work in air contaminated by tobacco smoke in order to hold a job." And I emphasized that the average catering worker exposed to second-hand smoke only at work "has a three-per cent combined excess risk for heart disease and lung cancer due to passive smoking over a 40-year working lifetime… ." [in perspective, this was 30 times the U.S. OSHA's Significant Risk level.] A second article, **Territory trails the field over restrictions on lighting up,** by MARY ANN BENITEZ, noted that Hong Kong lagged behind most developed countries and some Asian neighbours in restricting workplace smoking. Again quoting Dr. Hedley: "These proposals are entirely consistent with the need to intervene and the policy stand taken by many other governments," and Dr. Judith Mackay, who was a WHO consultant on tobacco control and director of the Asian Consultancy on Tobacco Control, said "the proposals were nowhere near as stringent as the rules in Singapore," as well as yours truly: "Progress in banning smoking at work has been made in the past two years in Australia and New Zealand… ."

A third *South China Morning Post* article gave voice to the opposition:

Health chief stands by smoking ban. by PATSY MOY.
"The top health official said yesterday the Government was determined to ban smoking in indoor public areas despite strong criticism from legislators who say the proposal is too radical and difficult to enforce. … At a Legco [HK Government] panel meeting on Monday, lawmakers attacked the Government's plan to turn Hong Kong into a no-smoking city, saying the ban was too radical. … Long-time smoker and non-affiliated legislator Andrew Wong Wang-fat accused the Government of smearing smokers and reducing them to the same level as drug-takers. … ."

Except for one rushed working dinner in an Italian restaurant whose pizza was not up to snuff, I had several outstanding dinners during my stay, The most memorable was on the first day of my arrival. Dr. Tony Hedley, Chair of the Department of Community Medicine, treated me to a sumptuous repast at the very British Aberdeen Boat Club. Late into the mild Hong Kong evening, the two of us dined al fresco on a terrace overlooking the Harbor and killed off two bottles of excellent wine. When our desserts arrived, I loosened my belt to make room, and later as we were leaving, in my inebriated state, I forgot to tighten it again. I got up and walked back into the restaurant. Suddenly I felt a draft on my legs as my pants slid down to my ankles. I said, "Tony, I'm afraid we're having an 'Ugly American' episode." Our waiters and the bartender roared with laughter as I hoisted my pants back up. The day before I left HK COSH gave me a farewell banquet at the Jockey Club. I sat at a 25 foot round table, surrounded by public health officials and other Hong Kong notables, including Dr. Judith MacKay. We were served by liveried waiters who served gourmet Chinese cuisine, including such delicacies as Bird's Nest Soup.

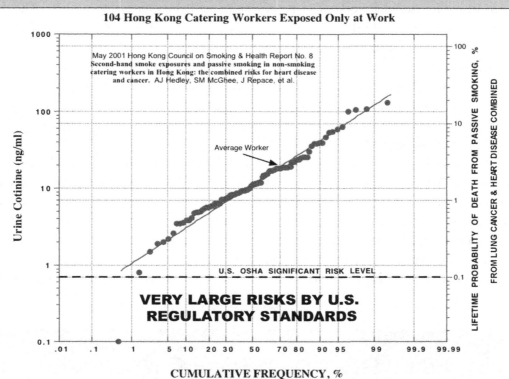

FIGURE 25. URINE COTININE AND WORKING LIFETIME CHANCE OF DEATH FROM PASSIVE SMOKING IN HONG KONG CATERING WORKERS (AUTHOR'S SLIDE PRESENTATION). BY U.S. STANDARDS, EVERY SINGLE WORKER'S DOSE EXCEEDED OSHA'S SIGNIFICANT RISK. [*NOTE THAT THE LOG-PROBABILITY PLOT DISPLAYS EVERY DATA POINT AND IS SUPERIOR TO THE USUAL BOX PLOTS FAVORED BY CLASSICAL EPIDEMIOLOGISTS.*]

In October, I journeyed out to Colorado, sponsored by the American Lung Association. I spoke in Denver, Colorado Springs, Pueblo, Grand Junction, and Fort Collins, giving a dozen radio, two TV, and three press interviews. That Fall, I served as an expert witness in three legal cases: another prisoner case in New York State (lost), a second prisoner case in Michigan (won), and a casino workers' case in New Orleans, *Mullen et al. v. Treasure Chest* (won).

MULLEN ET AL. V. TREASURE CHEST

The Treasure Chest case is illustrative of the problems casino workers face and the utility of the exposure and risk assessment methods I had developed to prove harm to the workers and the culpability of management in such cases. Mr. Dennis Mullen, Ms. Sheila Bachemin, and Ms. Margaret Phipps, all employees on board the Treasure Chest Riverboat Casino (TCC) on Lake Pontchartrain, suffered from aggravated asthmatic attacks from secondhand smoke on the job. Mr. Mullen and Ms. Bachemin collapsed on the job from acute exposure and were hospitalized, Ms. Phipps had to undergo emergency inhalant therapy. They were all warned not to return to work on the smoking decks. Although the casino had a nonsmoking deck, the owner, *bastardo* that he was, denied them reassignment and peremptorily fired all three. All three suffered from chronic occupational asthma that was not present prior to their employment at the Treasure Chest. Dr. Kathleen McNamara, the GP in the HMO who treated many TCC workers, stated that of the 300 TCC workers who had chosen her for their primary care doctor, 30% to 50% suffered respiratory illnesses similar to that incurred by the three original plaintiffs. Dr. McNamara opined that ETS aboard the TCC was the origin of their medical problems.

Using mathematical modeling, I estimated levels of secondhand smoke particles on the ship that proved to be accurate to within 1% of subsequent measurements. The levels indicated that their secondhand smoke exposure significantly elevated the workers' risks of asthma and emergency room visits. The defense moved a Daubert Motion, a legal principle designed to exclude testimony not generally accepted by the scientific community (i.e., junk science), but the defense motion failed in the face of a robust defense by Yours Truly, and the case settled for an estimated $2 million. This casino owner could be successfully sued for on-the-job injuries because the Jones Act, the law governing riverboat casino workers treated them for legal purposes as "seamen," who could sue ship owners pursuant to the Act. Land-based casino workers, with very few exceptions, only have recourse to workers' compensation, a very poor substitute. Figure 26 shows a view of the Treasure Chest Riverboat Casino.

Martzell and Bickford, attorneys for the plaintiff, had the cheek to stiff me out of part of my fee after I had won their case for them. I promptly filed a complaint with the Grievance Committee of the Louisiana Bar Association. After a full year of trading rebuttals, the Committee agreed that M&B had stiffed me indeed, but – in the best Louisiana tradition of dealing with Damn Yankees – bizarrely asserted that "it had not risen to the level of an unethical act." However, the exchange may have provoked some embarrassment. A week later, Scott Bickford faxed me a release to sign, offering to settle for half of the $7000 he owed me. I signed it. Half a loaf is better than none. New Orleans would not pass smoke-free workplace legislation that included casinos until January 2015.

FIGURE 26. THE TREASURE CHEST RIVERBOAT CASINO ON LAKE PONTCHARTRAIN IN NEW ORLEANS (AUTHOR'S PHOTO).

CHAPTER 16

'TWAS LIKE A NOBEL FOR SMOKE

---

*The Flight Attendant Medical Research Institute Dr. William Cahan Distinguished Professor Award. This board-designated award is named for the late Dr. William Cahan, a surgeon at Memorial Sloan-Kettering Cancer Center for over 50 years, who was a pioneer in the national movement to fight the health hazards of tobacco and second hand smoke. The award is for three-years at $200,000 per year and is made in recognition of the recipients' ongoing work in combating the diseases caused by exposure to second hand tobacco smoke. **Innovators Combating Substance Abuse** is a national program of The Robert Wood Johnson Foundation that recognizes and rewards those who have made substantial, innovative contributions of national significance in the field of substance abuse. Each award includes a grant of $300,000, which is used to conduct a project over a period of up to three years that advances the field.*

---

http://famri.org/researchers/awards_history.html; http://www.rwjf.org/en/library/research/2009/07/innovators-combating-substance-abuse.html.

From 1975 to 2002, I funded my research on secondhand smoke out of pocket, using borrowed equipment and volunteer assistants from state and local health departments as well as non-smokers' rights groups. So, when I became aware of two big competitive monetary awards suddenly available from NGO's in the field of tobacco-related research, I applied for both. I hoped I might grasp the brass ring in at least one.

THE FAMRI AWARD PROPOSAL

The first application on the horizon was FAMRI's Distinguished Professor Award. The FAMRI award had its origins in flight attendant litigation. In October 1991, Stanley Rosenblatt, a Miami, Florida trial attorney, and his wife, Susan, an appellate lawyer, filed a class action lawsuit, *Broin v. Philip Morris et al.*, on behalf of non-smoking flight attendants against several cigarette manufacturers. The David and Goliath suit demanded damages for diseases and deaths suffered by plaintiff flight attendants from exposure to secondhand tobacco smoke in airliner cabins. In 1997, after a prolonged battle against all odds, The Rosenblatts prevailed, and the case settled for $300 million. The settlement provided for medical monitoring for the early detection of secondhand smoke diseases in flight attendants. It also funded the establishment of a medical and scientific research organization, the Flight Attendant Medical Research Institute (FAMRI). FAMRI was formed in 2000 as a non-profit foundation located in downtown Miami, by Biscayne Bay.

I proposed to FAMRI that I would mount a frontal attack on the tobacco industry's obstruction to smoke-free laws in the hospitality industry, emphasizing that,

"The Big Four tobacco companies have drawn a line in the sand and are fighting with all their resources to preserve smoky restaurants and bars. In many states, they have pre-empted local control over smoke-free premises by weak state laws. They do this for two basic reasons: first because they know once they lose the hospitality industry, smoking will be completely marginalized. Secondly, it is an important marketing venue for their products. They continue to deny the health consequences of passive smoking while admitting it is a 'nuisance' issue for nonsmokers. They have funded fraudulent research purporting to show that secondhand smoke exposures in hospitality venues is 'low.'

Third, to control this 'low nuisance' ETS concentration, ventilation strategies are proposed. Behind the scenes, the tobacco industry has pressured ASHRAE, the American Society of Heating, Refrigerating, and Ventilation Engineers, to recommend ventilation rates 'for the control of tobacco smoke.' Having first succeeded (with ASHRAE Standard 62-1989) and then failed (with ASHRAE Standard 62-1999) the tobacco industry using both direct and covert measures is now trying to establish special ventilation rates for the hospitality industry. …

"In order to combat these problems, over a period of 25 years, I have developed the tools of ETS exposure assessment, which use ETS atmospheric markers such as respirable particles (RSP) and nicotine, and ETS dosimetry, which uses ETS biomarkers in blood, urine, and saliva. I have employed these tools to educate nonsmokers to the risks of passive smoking, to promote and defend the right to a smoke-free workplace, and in secondhand smoke litigation to redress injuries to flight attendants, nurses, office workers, casino workers, railroad workers, and other workers, as well as adults and children exposed at home, and even asthmatic prisoners, all of whom have suffered injury from secondhand smoke, and some of whom have lost their lives.

These tools can be used at the local level and are invaluable in pre-emption states as well as in areas which can implement smoke-free legislation. … In alliance with public health boards, as well as two universities, I have conducted three pilot projects to measure cotinine in hospitality workers. In the two that have been made public so far, the major publicity surrounding their release has given major impetus to smoke-free restaurant legislation. However, some important projects remain unfinished."

My proposed focus would be on research, education, and policy efforts. Chief among the ten ETS projects I proposed to pursue under the Award, was a "Rosetta Stone" paper laying out the theory relating atmospheric markers for ETS to each other, and to body fluid biomarkers for ETS especially targeted on the hospitality industry, an ETS exposure assessment paper, and outreach via lectures, rebuttals to tobacco industry disinformation on secondhand smoke, and purchase of state of the art office equipment, especially a new desktop computer and a 35 mm slide digitizer to enable PowerPoint slide presentations. So, I was proposing to fight junk science with real science and public outreach.

My FAMRI Award nomination was initiated by an old friend, Dr. Alan Blum, a major antagonist of the tobacco industry. who was a charter member of FAMRI's medical advisory board. Alan was and still is the director of The University of Alabama Center for the Study of Tobacco and Society in Tuscaloosa, which he established in 1999. From 1977 to 2002, he directed DOC (Doctors Ought to Care), a national nonprofit organization dedicated to counteract tobacco use and promotion. As editor of the *New York State Journal of Medicine* and the *Medical Journal of Australia* in the 1980s, he published the first-ever theme issues of any medical journal devoted entirely to a consideration for ending the world tobacco pandemic. He is a gifted and charismatic speaker, especially eloquent on debunking the tobacco industry's deceptive advertising and promotion. For his outstanding work, Alan also received the Surgeon General's Medallion from Dr. C. Everett Koop. I spent two weeks on this application and regarded getting it as a long shot. My nomination was also supported by Stan Glantz, my long-time friend, confidant, supporter, and publicist.

THE INNOVATOR AWARD PROPOSAL

In the case of RWJF, my application was supported by another friend, Dr. Jack Henningfield, a luminary in the field of nicotine addiction who had been a previous recipient of an Innovator award, as well as the ever-reliable Stan Glantz. Jack was an adjunct professor at Hopkins and Vice President of Pinney Associates, which did consulting on tobacco issues. The RWJF monetary awards were modeled in part after the MacArthur Foundation Awards, and designed to bring a comparable level of prestige to the field of substance abuse. They were highly competitive. My 6-page proposal attacked the keystones of Big Tobacco's Accommodation program. These lay in the health effects denial implicit in the Big Tobacco lawsuit resulting in the notorious federal court decision of North Carolina Judge Wm. L. Osteen that "nullified" the 1992 EPA report on Passive Smoking and Lung Cancer (Osteen, 1998), and the Oak Ridge National Laboratory's touted *Black Dog Pub* study (Jenkins, et al., 2001) that purported to show that ventilation controls ETS. I wrote that neither Osteen's (1998) industry-biased pseudo-scientific arguments nor Jenkins' deceptive RJR-funded and conducted 16-Cities research had been subjected to a scientific dissection in the peer-reviewed literature. Furthermore, "annoyance" from tobacco smoke air pollution had never kept pace with the ever more stringent air quality standards. I proposed to develop, publish, and publicize credible scientific research to deal with these three major ETS issues; in order equip advocates with new strategic weaponry in the up-hill battles for a smoke-free hospitality industry. At the top of my agenda was a repeat of the Black Dog Pub study. A précis of my six-page application read:

> "Mr. Repace will conduct on-site physical measurements of certain bars and restaurants in order to quantify the influence of secondhand smoke on the indoor air quality in the most-polluted and least-regulated type of indoor environments. This work will be submitted to peer-reviewed scientific journals for publication to contribute to the body of knowledge about the range of exposure to air which has been contaminated with secondhand smoke. He will use 21st Century state-of-the-art technology to make real-time measurements of exposures to airborne carcinogens and other fine particles from tobacco smoke, and to assess the risk of such exposures to both hospitality industry workers and patrons. He will collaborate in this field-work with state and local public health and clean air officials as well as other tobacco-smoke researchers. This work will assist advocates in the movement to provoke awareness of the health consequences of indoor air pollution and policies promoting clean indoor air, much as has been achieved with outdoor air pollution control."

I flew out to Chicago at RWJF's invitation to present my proposal orally to the RWJF advisory committee, which I discovered was chaired by another old friend, Dr. Ron Davis, the former director of DHHS's Office on Smoking and Health. Ron later became President of the American Medical Association.

I HIT THE JACKPOT

I was shocked and shocked again, when I received *both* prizes back-to-back, one in April 2002 and the other in June of that year. This meant receiving a mind-boggling *Nine Hundred Thousand Dollars* over a three-year period to support my research. In amazement, I remarked to Hilarine, "It's like winning the Nobel Prize For Smoke, if there were such a thing." I was finally able to afford as much professional equipment as I needed.

When the FAMRI grant began, in April of 2002, my first purchases were a MacPro computer with a 30-inch cinema display, two Xerox high-speed office printers, one black and white, and one color, plus a high-end Canon fax machine. Soon after receiving the Distinguished Professor Award, FAMRI asked me to prepare a scholarly paper on flight attendants' secondhand smoke exposure on aircraft. Long concerned with this problem, I was well positioned to write this. I had submitted testimony to the Civil Aeronautics Board in 1979 suggesting that smoking be banned on aircraft due to the inadequacy of aircraft ventilation systems in controlling secondhand smoke. I had modeled flight attendants' exposures in the 1980 paper of Repace and Lowrey. I had worked on a research plan for the World Health Organization dealing with smoking on aircraft in 1984. I had testified on modeling of secondhand smoke on aircraft before the National Academy of Sciences Committee on Airliner Cabin Air Quality in 1985. I had served on the Department of Transportation's Cabin Environmental Effects Review Committee in 1989. My risk model was one of the two used to estimate risk to flight attendants in the 1989 DOT Report, *Airliner Cabin Environment: Contaminant Measurements, Health Risks, and Mitigation Options*. I had testified before the House Aviation Subcommittee, on the Airline Smoking Ban in 1989. I had given expert testimony in the *Duncan v. Northwest Airlines* class action in 2001. And I was familiar with the slew of deceptive and outright junk science papers authored by industry scientists and tobacco moles, respectively, aimed at convincing regulators that aircraft ventilation systems were perfectly capable of controlling tobacco smoke. My "Smoky Skies" paper would come to fruition in 2004. Between 2004 and 2010, the FAMRI award would support the publication of no less than 14 research papers, in *Tobacco Control*, *MMWR*, *Archives of Environmental Health*, two papers in *ASHRAE IAQ Applications*, *Nicotine and Tobacco Research*, *JOEM*, *Toxicological Sciences*, *BMC Public Health*, *The American Journal of Public Health*, and *Environmental Research*, plus two book chapters, as well as nine conference presentations. FAMRI got a good bang for its buck, and I had a hell of a good time to boot.

LIKE 'CANARIES IN THE COAL MINES'

What was it like to breathe smoke while working in an aircraft cabin for years on end? Patty Young began her flying career at American Airlines in 1966 and flew for 37 years. Soon after starting her new job, Patty began a decades-long struggle to have smoking banned on all flights. She related, "Because of what I was seeing and hearing from the non-smoking flight attendants. From the start they told me how wonderful the job was because I would be meeting intelligent, interesting people and going to exciting destinations. Some of them also told me that they had the lungs of smokers ... and they had never smoked. Some ended up with lung cancer and died. When I repeatedly asked the medical professionals how a non-smoker could have smokers' lungs and the diseases of smokers, they had no answers. ... Flight Attendants are the canaries in the coal mines... ."

Lani Blissard flew for American Airlines for 36 years. She stated, "For those non-smoking Flight Attendants who flew before the smoking ban, the cabin conditions were horrific. Indelibly stamped in our minds are images of this intolerable situation...smoke so thick after the no-smoking sign went off that you could not see from the aft jump seat to the front of the cabin, fires started by dropped cigarettes, teeth and light hair discolored by the smoke—and the pungent smell of your uniform after every flight. Beyond the images, there were burning eyes, bloody noses and frequent respiratory infections ... ."

Leisa Sudderth, a mother of twins, flew for American Airlines for more than 27 years. She said, "I remember the complete dread of waiting for the 'No Smoking' sign to go off after takeoff. It was extremely difficult to get a 200-pound beverage cart ready for service with stinging eyes as the entire cabin quickly filled with toxic cigarette smoke." Kathleen Cheney began flying for Eastern Airlines in 1968. She recalled, "In 1987 I was diagnosed with a smoker's throat cancer—having avoided cigarettes all my life. Such avoidance wasn't enough protection from the damage done by other people's tobacco smoke. I never got to work in a smoke-free airplane. … I now fight degenerative chronic obstructive pulmonary disease (COPD)." Bland Lane retired from Pan American World Airways and United Airlines after 48 years of service. Smoking was not banned from international flights until 2000. Bland developed COPD due to her smoke-filled years in airline cabins and died from it in 2007. I met and befriended these courageous flight attendants and was saddened by their tales of suffering at my first FAMRI conference. Their stories are illustrative of the wages of unrestricted smoking in the workplace, and how difficult was their struggle for smoke-free air on aircraft against the combined opposition of both airline management and Big Tobacco.

INNOVATORS COMBATTING SUBSTANCE ABUSE

When the Innovator Award kicked in later that year, I decided that before I bought any monitoring equipment, I should query some experts in environmental monitoring concerning the latest advances in real-time 21st Century equipment. I queried Matti Jantunen, Lance Wallace, and Wayne Ott for advice on state-of-the-art monitors at the International Society of Exposure Science (ISES) meeting in Vancouver in August 2002. Based on their expert advice, on Lance's experience with field studies, on Matti's practical experience monitoring air pollution in Finland, I decided to buy two MIE portable real-time fine particle monitors, and on Wayne's advice with carcinogen monitors and on data-logging instruments, I purchased two EcoChem real-time airborne carcinogen monitors for particle-bound polycyclic aromatic hydrocarbons (PPAH), a Langan real-time carbon monoxide/carbon dioxide/temperature monitor and two Kanomax Piezobalances for calibration purposes. I also obtained an ultrasonic ruler for measuring ceiling heights, a laser rangefinder for measuring room area, plus a Dell PC laptop (clunky compared to my Mac), for synchronizing the Windows-based monitors and downloading their data, two radio-controlled "atomic" clocks to provide monitor synchrony, and a MacPro laptop to perform the analysis, graphing, and to make slides for my presentations. I also bought several sophisticated computer programs and other software with which to run the computers and analyze my data. I spent well over $40,000 for these professional tools of the trade. I was now loaded for bear.

THE FINNISH EVALUATION OF THE HEALTH RISKS OF ETS

In 2002, The Finnish Ministry of Social Affairs and Health requested the Scientific Committee on Health Effects of Chemicals to evaluate the existing scientific data on the health risks of environmental tobacco smoke, with special emphasis on current ETS exposures in Finland. In an editorial published in a supplement to the *Scandinavian Journal of Work, Environment, and Health*, which contained eight articles on ETS by European experts from the Finnish Institute for Occupational Health, Zitting et al. (2002) summarized the results of that evaluation, giving important weight to the 1992 EPA Report, the 1994 OSHA Proposal on ETS in the Workplace, and to eight of the papers of Repace et al. from 1980 through 1998:

> "Environmental tobacco smoke is one of the most widespread occupational health hazards of today. … around 300,000 workers are exposed to tobacco smoke at their workplaces in Finland. Among these people, about 10% are exposed for almost their entire worktime; this group includes mainly those who work in restaurants, bars, hotels, and similar places. …
>
> The amendment of the Finnish Tobacco Control Act (1995) restricted indoor smoking at work to rooms isolated from other premises and equipped with proper ventilation. … Because smoking in restaurants was not entirely prohibited by this amendment, questions rose about the possible need for a health-based exposure limit for tobacco smoke, and the criteria to be applied for smoke-free premises. …

The assessments and estimations of Repace et al (20–27) were based mainly on studies from the 1980s, which estimate that a citizen of the United States who is involuntarily exposed to tobacco smoke will get a daily dose of 0 – 14 mg of [ETS-RSP] with an average value of 1.4 mg. ... Using this data, Repace & Lowrey estimated that exposure to environmental tobacco smoke would cause 7.4 lung cancer deaths per 100,000 person-years [per µg/day lifetime exposure]...

Later Repace & Lowrey (25) ... concluded that a nicotine concentration of ... 6.7 ng/m^3 in indoor air (8-hour time-weighted average) would cause a risk of 1×10^{-6} during 45 work years. In Finland, the average exposure at work is estimated to be 10 µg/m^3 in restaurants and 2 µg/m^3 in other occupational sectors (16). The presumption from the Repace model that a daily exposure to a nicotine concentration of 6.7 µg/m^3 from environmental tobacco smoke for 45 years causes 1 case of lung cancer per 1000 exposed workers annually leads to the conclusion that current exposure to environmental tobacco smoke in Finland would cause some 50 lung cancers during 45 years of exposure — approximately 1 case/year. Similar assumptions for domestic exposure would result in approximately 8 cases annually. In Norway, the exposure standard of 10 µg/m^3 for facilities where smoking is allowed is based on the estimations of Repace and his co-workers." ... (Zitting et al. 2002).

It was clear that our work was taken seriously abroad, despite the best disinformation efforts of the multi-national tobacco cartel and its industrial-strength moles.

THE WILMINGTON PUB CRAWL

Because of the Robert Wood Johnson Foundation's emphasis on publicizing important research results, my Innovator Award Grant would enable me to inflict major damage on the tobacco industry's secondhand smoke propaganda campaign and even greater benefit to public health than I had ever imagined. It all began serendipitously in September 2002, when I received a call from the Chief Health Officer of the State of Delaware. He related that the Delaware Legislature had passed a statewide smoke-free workplace law that amended the Delaware Clean Indoor Air Act of 1994. The amended Act banned smoking in restaurants, bars, and casinos that previously had been excluded. The new law would take effect on November 27, 2002, but opponents had threatened repeal when the new legislature convened in 2003. The Health official asked if I could monitor air pollution in these hospitality venues before and after the new statute took effect. I replied, that yes, I could do that with one important proviso: it had to be done clandestinely to avoid changing the establishments' behavior either by increasing ventilation rates or by discouraging smoking during the monitoring. He responded that this was not possible; the Health Department, as a state agency, would have an obligation to disclose the monitoring in advance. But after some cogitation, he opined that there might be a way to circumvent this problem, and told me he'd get back to me. A few days later, Deborah Brown, CEO of the American Lung Association of The Mid Atlantic, phoned me. She informed me that the Delaware Lung Association would be pleased to sponsor my monitoring studies and provide the necessary volunteers to assist with the measurements as well.

I bought two wheeled airline carry-on sized cloth suitcases to conceal the two-foot long MIE fine particle monitors with their tandem battery packs and pumps, plus two camera bags for the remainder of the equipment. As the MIE pumps were noisy, I packed them in acoustic insulation. I used Tygon tubes connected to grommets to vent the air intakes and exhausts of the monitors to the exteriors of the suitcases (Figures 27A and 27B). In this manner, my research assistants and I could trail our equipment clandestinely into any restaurant, bar, or casino, record the date and time of entry and egress from the establishment for later data analysis, without disturbing what we were trying to measure – or being given the boot by wary management. With these new research tools to collect real-world data, I was now equipped to combat the tobacco army's junk science arguments with 21st Century weaponry.

On Friday, November 15, 2002, I took the AmTrak to Wilmington, Delaware, and set up my equipment in a hotel room. Deb Brown had denominated eight smoky venues for sampling. Shortly before 6 PM, Deb and her crew of two arrived, I gave them instructions as to their roles, and we embarked upon our odyssey. It lasted until midnight. That evening, we visited eight smoking locations: a casino, 6 bars of various types, finishing at a super-smoky pool hall. We counted the active smokers and total persons present every ten minutes and measured the space volumes of all venues using electronic rulers (partly by pacing in the complex geometry of the Delaware Park Casino). We recorded each event on 3"x5" file cards to enable correlating the time-stamped monitor readings with our activity pattern diaries and stopwatch readings. The real-time measurements went off without a hitch. The monitors recorded indoor and outdoor fine particles, carcinogens, carbon dioxide, carbon monoxide, relative humidity, temperature, and time. We planned to perform the follow-up measurements in early 2003, after Deb was satisfied that compliance with the State smoking ban in these same venues was 100%.

Not long afterward, I received a call from the Health Department of the City of Toronto, Canada, alerting me to a study touted by the Ontario and Toronto Restaurant Associations which purported to show that a so-called high-tech ventilation system controlled secondhand smoke in contiguous nonsmoking sections upstream of smoking sections despite large open connecting passageways. Both restaurant associations vehemently opposed the smoke-free workplace proposals newly announced by the City of Toronto. They insisted that their demonstration study in a local pub had actually achieved nonsmoking area secondhand smoke concentrations comparable to venues with total smoking bans. Toronto City staff sent me a copy of the study, whose senior author was none other than CIAR "special project" grantee Roger Jenkins of Oak Ridge (Drope et al., 2003). Jenkins study, sponsored by the Hotel Association of Canada, concluded,

> "This small study provides important evidence to the regulator, the hospitality industry and the nonsmoking public that there are cost-effective alternatives to a prohibition of smoking in hospitality establishments, alternatives that can satisfy the concerns and interests of both nonsmoking and smoking customers. … this study clearly shows that a suitably designed ventilation system installed in a restaurant/bar with both smoking and nonsmoking sections can produce ETS levels in the nonsmoking section that are not statistically different from those found in venues where smoking is prohibited" (Jenkins et al., 2001).

The Jenkins et al. study had been conducted in the Black Dog Pub in Greater Toronto, which had a highly uncommon 'displacement' ventilation system. It employed an unusual single-pass outdoor air supply stream flowing from the nonsmoking section into the smoking section and then vented outdoors through a heat-recovery unit. For such a system to work properly, it should have air supply grilles set in or near the floor. This one had them in the ceiling. Nearly all buildings in North America had ventilation systems that recirculated most of their air to conserve heating and cooling. Moreover, the "nonsmoking" control venues strangely had measurable nicotine contamination, indicative of the presence of tobacco smoke. Further, employee exposure in the smoking bar area was ignored. These anomalies sent up red flags. The study's conclusions did not appear remotely plausible.

THE BLACK DOG PUB STUDY

I decided that ETS measurements in the Black Dog Pub would be a perfect segue from the Delaware study. I phoned several Canadian friends, including Ken Johnson, an epidemiologist with Health Canada in

Ottawa, Gar Mahood, Director of the Nonsmokers' Rights Association in Toronto, and Prof. Roberta Ferrence, Director of the Ontario Tobacco Control Research Unit (OTRU) at the University of Toronto, to request their assistance with the study. Jacqui Drope, a Research Associate at OTRU, and Gar's wife, Helen, a nurse, opted to assist as well, volunteering to occupy a table in the smoking section. [Jacqui is presently Managing Director of the Global Cancer Prevention for the American Cancer Society in Washington DC.] Since Ottawa's smoke-free bar law offered the perfect opportunity to measure air quality in non-smoking control bars, I determined that I would first measure fine particles ($PM_{2.5}$) and particulate polycyclic aromatic hydrocarbon carcinogens (PPAH), temperature (T°C), relative humidity (RH), carbon monoxide (CO) and carbon dioxide (CO_2) (as an index of ventilation rate) in preliminary pub crawl with Ken in a half-dozen smoke-free bars in Ottawa on Thursday evening, December 12th 2002, over a six-hour period (Figures 26 & 27). Being just a month after the 9/11 attack in New York, I requested a private screening of my several bags full of arcane scientific equipment and bundles of cables at National airport.

FIGURE 27A. THE AUTHOR WITH CARCINOGEN AND FINE PARTICLE MONITORS CONCEALED IN CAMERA BAGS AND ROLL-ON LUGGAGE DURING THE OTTAWA PUB CRAWL (PHOTO BY KEN JOHNSON).

At 7 PM on Friday, December 13th, 2002, our intrepid Canadian-American team descended upon the Black Dog Pub in Greater Toronto. Ken and I deployed the monitors beneath the tables concealed in the wheeled suitcases, simultaneously in the nonsmoking restaurant section and the smoking bar section, and our Toronto-based volunteers assisted by rotating at the same table in the smoking section in scheduled half-hour shifts for the four hour duration of the monitoring period almost until midnight. This ensured continuous occupancy of the same tables under which our monitors were concealed. In this way, our volunteer nonsmokers could avoid suffering for four hours breathing smoky air in the bar area, which was jam-packed with smokers (Figure 28).

As our confederates occupied their assigned tables, Ken and I counted the active smokers and all persons present every ten minutes using clicker-counters and measured the space volume with infrared laser and ultrasonic rulers. There were an average of 32 persons in the bar area and 51 in the restaurant area. The monitor results for fine particles and carcinogens from the smoke-free Ottawa pubs showed levels little different from outdoors (except for one venue with oil candles causing high carcinogen levels). By contrast, the levels in the smoking section of the Black Dog were quite high, and typical for a smoky bar. The nonsmoking section did have considerably lower levels than the smoking section, as expected. However, the pollution levels in the nonsmoking section were twice as high as outdoors (40 µg/m^3 vs. 21 µg/m^3) for fine particles (RSP), and three times as high for PPAH carcinogens (16 ng/m^3 vs 4.4 ng/m^3). The food and drink in the Black Dog Pub were of excellent quality; the air quality – contrary to the Restaurant Associations' claims – was poor. I felt pity for the actual large black shaggy dog who wandered about the premises wagging his bushy tail and begging for table scraps. Figures 28 and 29 show the smoking and nonsmoking sections in the Black Dog respectively.

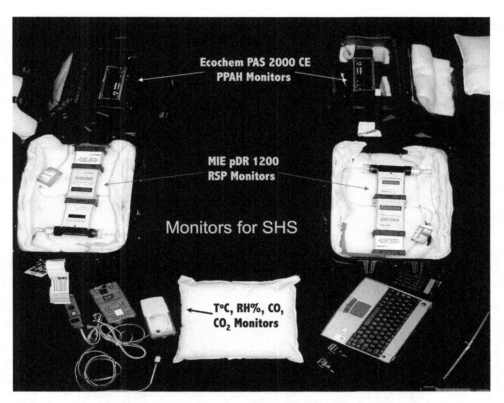

FIGURE 27B. CONCEALED MONITORS FOR SECONDHAND SMOKE (SHS) & VENTILATION (PHOTO BY KEN JOHNSON). THE PILL-CONTAINERS WERE USED AS NOISE MUFFLERS AND THE AIRLINE LUGGAGE TAGS FOR VERISIMILITUDE.

On the 20th of January 2004, at the request of Cancer Care Ontario and the Ontario Campaign Against Tobacco, I presented a press conference in Toronto on our December 2002 study of the Black Dog Pub and the Ottawa Pub Crawl, which was billed as "Failure of Displacement Ventilation to Control Secondhand Smoke." This received widespread publicity in the City of Toronto and embarrassed the owner of the Black Dog. Genuinely interested in clean air in his pub, he decided to make his pub nonsmoking. I received an alert from Gar Mahood, Executive Director of the Non-smokers' Rights Association. I decided on the spot to fly to Toronto to do follow-up measurements. I asked Gar if he could arrange for volunteer table sitters again and called up Ken Johnson at Health Canada. I put together my monitoring packages, and almost two years to the day after our first visit, our entourage again descended upon the now smoke-free Black Dog Pub, on Friday, Dec. 10, 2004 at 7 PM.

As in 2002, one set was deployed in the bar area, and the other in the restaurant area. we made real-time measurements of fine particles (RSP), carcinogens (PPAH), temperature, relative humidity and carbon dioxide (CO_2) simultaneously indoors for nearly 5 hours, as well as outdoors before and after the indoor measurements, for about an hour. We again counted the number of persons present every ten minutes. And of course, we managed to eat, drink, and schmooze for five hours. We even got to pet the large black dog that still roamed the eponymously named premises. Figure 30 shows the layout. The area of the bar was 101 m², and that of the restaurant 64 m², with a 3 m ceiling height (in Canada, they sensibly use the metric system like the rest of the modern world, rather than the clunky English system used only by the retrograde U.S.A.). There were 34 persons in the bar area and 37 persons in the restaurant area, averaged over the 5-hour period, in 2004. This compared to 50 persons in the bar area (an average of 7 active smokers) and an average of about 51 persons in the restaurant area in 2002 (zero active smokers).

As it turned out, the RSP level in the nonsmoking area pre-ban was 40 µg/m³, while post ban it had declined to 16 µg/m³, a 60% decrease, while the PPAH level declined from 16 µg/m³ pre-ban, to 3.1 ng/m³ post-ban, an 81% reduction (Repace and Johnson, 2006). So, when compared to this highly-touted "high-tech" ventilation, a smoking ban provided a 60% to 80% improvement in air quality in the non-smoking section contrary to the Jenkins paper. Figure 30 shows the floor plan and ventilation flow plus the comparison of pre-and-post-ban results. In 2002, the average RSP level in the smoking section was 199 µg/m³, compared to 33 µg/m³ when the bar went smoke-free in 2004, an 83% drop. The average carcinogen (PPAH) level in the bar during smoking was 152 ng/m³ compared to 5.7 ng/m³, a 96% decline under smoke-free conditions. These results contradicted the Jenkins study's claims. I performed a follow-up study in two Mesa, Arizona restaurants in 2003 that also did not support the claims that displacement ventilation controlled secondhand smoke in the nonsmoking sections of either restaurant, reinforcing the earlier Black Dog pre-ban results. (Repace and Johnson, 2006).

FIGURE 28. THE BLACK DOG PUB SMOKING BAR VIEWED FROM THE NONSMOKING SECTION IN THE 2002 STUDY (AUTHOR'S PHOTO).

FIGURE 29. THE BLACK DOG PUB NONSMOKING RESTAURANT AREA IN 2002. REAR, FROM LEFT TO RIGHT, KEN JOHNSON, GAR MAHOOD, & JIM REPACE. FRONT, TWO NSRA VOLUNTEERS (AUTHOR'S PHOTO).

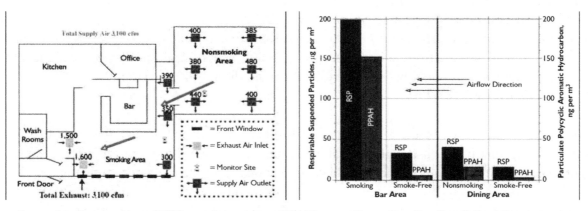

FIGURE 30. FINE PARTICLES (RSP) AND CARCINOGENS (PPAH) IN THE BLACK DOG PUB PRE & POST SMOKING BAN. THE LEFT PICTURE SHOWS THE LAYOUT OF THE PUB; THE NUMBERS ON THE INLETS & OUTLETS REFER TO THE AIRFLOW RATES. THE RIGHT BAR GRAPH SHOWS THE RESULTS. "SMOKING" AND "NONSMOKING" DATA WAS COLLECTED IN 2002. THE "SMOKE-FREE" DATA WAS COLLECTED IN 2004 [REPACE & JOHNSON, 2006].

Two years earlier, I had given an interview to *Engineered Systems Magazine*, disparaging the ability of ventilation and filtration systems to control secondhand smoke. My reservations were echoed by David Bearg, a ventilation engineer from Concord Massachusetts. However, the article also interviewed representatives of equipment manufacturers in Florida and Montreal who had touted the merits of displacement ventilation, a hitherto untested technology for ETS control. The article reported that two Mesa Arizona restaurants that had installed two such displacement systems that had made similar claims of efficacy in hopes of circumventing Mesa's restaurant smoking ban. This magazine also quoted Elia Sterling, the elder son of Ted Sterling, who had taken over the reins of Theodor Sterling and Associates after the old man passed away from Parkinson's Disease. Like the father, the son had embraced the Dark Side: he was a dyed-in-the-wool consultant to the Tobacco Industry, and represented their interests with ASHRAE, BOMA, and ASTM, among others.

Engineered Systems quoted Elia Sterling boasting that, "several studies he's conducted showed establishments helped eliminate their ETS issues by simply operating and maintaining their mechanical systems as they should be — not by putting in any significant investments into their systems" [TTID 2080409207].

Two years earlier, in a submission to the Workers' Compensation Board of British Columbia, Physicians for a Smoke-free Canada had denounced the Sterlings, père et fils, asserting that "The Sterling family dynasty, statistician father Theodore and ventilation 'expert' son Elia have been shilling for the tobacco industry around the world for decades. Earlier reference was made to money paid up to 1990. The payouts continue. As recently as 1997, Philip Morris paid Elia Sterling US $87,000 for work to be performed by Theodore Sterling. No one should doubt that the tobacco industry is intimately involved with current so-called 'ventilation solutions' being authored by Elia Sterling" (Physicians, 2000).

During 2002, I gave 16 domestic and 2 international presentations, plus testimony in two secondhand smoke legal cases, one of which was on behalf of flight attendants against the tobacco industry filed in Miami, Jett et al., v. Philip Morris, et al.

DRIVING THE SMOKERS OUT OF IRELAND'S PUBS

In February 2002, I flew to Dublin to do a major consultation for the Office of Tobacco Control of The Republic of Ireland. I gave several radio and TV interviews, as well as academic seminars at Dublin Castle, and more importantly, did a briefing for the Environmental Matters Committee of The Dail (The Irish Parliament). An internal Philip Morris memorandum [TTID 2067453623] reported a news account from the *Irish Times*:

> **"U.S. expert claims 150 Irish bar workers per year will die from ETS, the Irish press reports.** The Irish Office of Tobacco Control organized a seminar on ETS featuring former US Environmental Protection Agency scientist and ETS expert Mr. James Repace, the Irish press reports. According to the *Irish Times*, Mr. Repace said that in Ireland 'about 150 bar workers a year in Ireland will die from ill health caused by ETS.' Reportedly, Repace estimated that 800 to 900 deaths a year could be caused by ETS among the wider population (*Irish Times, The Irish Independent,* 12/02/02)."

Figure 31 shows a plot of Maurice Mulcahy's real-time carbon monoxide data that I used to estimate the bartenders' risk. In this figure, using pharmacokinetic modeling, 8 ppm of CO from ETS is equivalent to a serum cotinine level of 9.9 ng/mL, which would be at the upper extreme of passive smoking (Jarvis, 2001). It had been sent to me on request by Tom Power, Director of Ireland's Office of Tobacco Control.

The Tobacco Manufacturer's Association reported the alarming news in greater depth:

> "Date : 13-Feb-2002; Source : *Irish Examiner*; Title : **Refusing To Butt Out, Minister Vows To Stub Out Smoking** HEALTH Minister Michael Martin has vowed to press ahead with further restrictions on smoking in pubs, despite opposition from publicans. Mr. Martin said he was determined to introduce stricter smoking controls on pubs because of the clear evidence that passive smoking causes serious illness. The Tobacco Bill being debated by the Dail this week will give the minister powers to introduce smoking bans by regulation on public places not specified by existing legislation. Speaking at an Office of Tobacco Control conference in Dublin yesterday, Mr. Martin promised to implement extra controls on 'a whole range of places' following the anticipated enactment of the legislation by Easter …

Mr. Martin said he was heartened by positive public reaction to his proposals. He pointed out that there was clear evidence about the dangers of environmental tobacco smoke, ETS, or passive smoking, as highlighted by one study at the conference that estimated that around 150 Irish bar workers will die from an ETS-related illness each year. The Minister said people had to recognise that pubs were workplaces for thousands. He said: 'The health threat from ETS cannot be linked with legal or ethical arguments used by the tobacco industry about the 'right to smoke'. Meanwhile, the trade union which represents bar staff in Ireland called for a total ban on smoking in the workplace. Mandate spokesperson John Douglas said such a measure was necessary as experience had shown that voluntary codes to reduce smoking in the workplace did not work. International smoking expert and physicist James Repace told the conference that the risk of ETS for non-smokers was 'grossly underestimated' " [TTID 526303357].

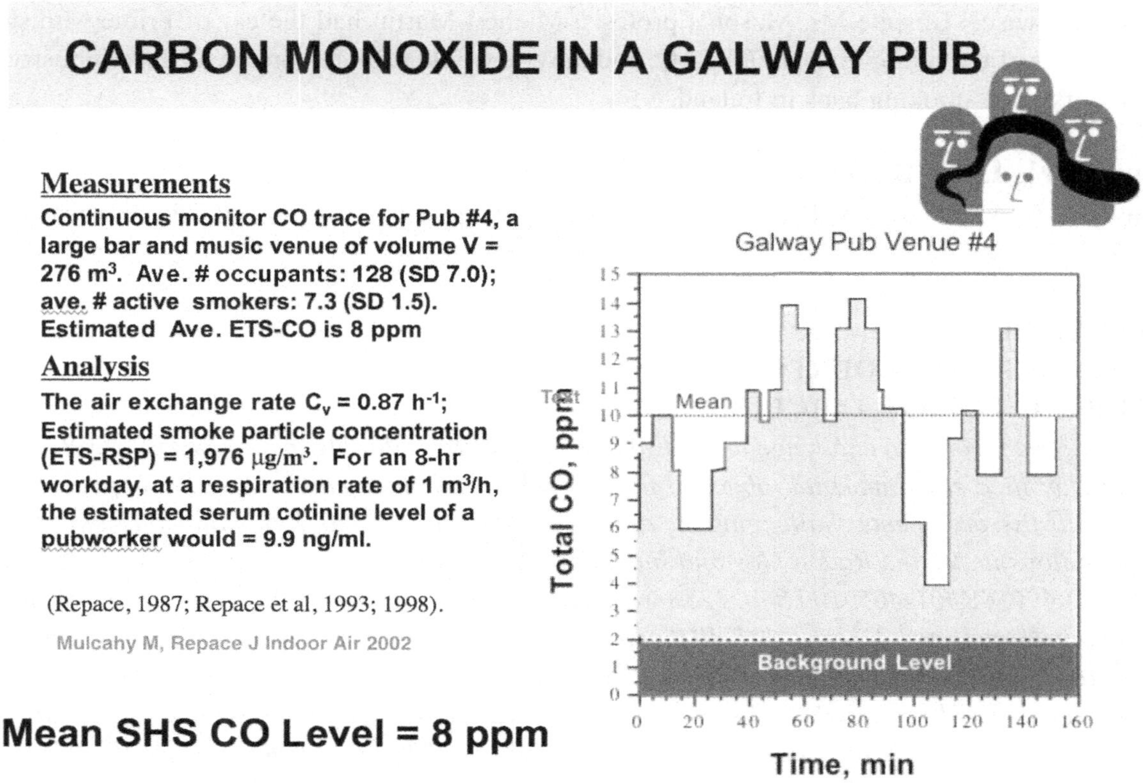
CARBON MONOXIDE IN A GALWAY PUB
Measurements
Continuous monitor CO trace for Pub #4, a large bar and music venue of volume V = 276 m³. Ave. # occupants: 128 (SD 7.0); ave. # active smokers: 7.3 (SD 1.5). Estimated Ave. ETS-CO is 8 ppm
Analysis
The air exchange rate Cv = 0.87 h⁻¹; Estimated smoke particle concentration (ETS-RSP) = 1,976 µg/m³. For an 8-hr workday, at a respiration rate of 1 m³/h, the estimated serum cotinine level of a pubworker would = 9.9 ng/ml.
(Repace, 1987; Repace et al, 1993; 1998).
Mulcahy M, Repace J Indoor Air 2002
Mean SHS CO Level = 8 ppm
Galway Pub Venue #4
Total CO, ppm
Mean
Background Level
Time, min
0
20
40
60
80
100
120
140
160

Figure 31. Carbon Monoxide levels from Secondhand Smoke (Yellow Area) and Background (Green rectangle) in a Galway, Ireland Pub (Mulcahy & Repace Presentation at Indoor Air 2002). The ETS-RSP levels estimated from ETS-CO are extreme: Double the US EPA's Air Pollution Emergency Level for $PM_{2.5}$. An estimated 17% of the Pub's Occupants were Smokers, with an Average of 7.3 Smoking over the 2 hour and 40 minute Sampling Time. The Equations Converting ETS-CO into ETS-RSP and Serum Cotinine were Derived in Repace (1987) and Repace et al. (1998)

Tom Power, Director of the Office of Tobacco Control, who ran a first class operation, booked us into an elegant hotel in downtown Dublin. Tom was a witty and urbane man, technically competent and very PR savvy, as well as a true trencherman. He royally entertained Hilarine and me with gourmet dinners. At the Dail, I was treated to a seven course luncheon banquet replete with excellent wine. Afterward I regaled the dozen and a half or so members of the environmental committee with an impromptu if not totally sober lecture on secondhand smoke. It was well received. Outside, I was surprised to see pickets marching with signs protesting abuses by the Catholic Church.

My activities on behalf of Irish tobacco control did not go undenounced by the Irish tobacco industry. Phil Mason, the managing director of P.J. Carroll & Co Ltd of Dublin, wrote the *Irish Times* on February 21, 2002 in response to an article I had authored in that publication on February 11th, entitled, "Right to live overrides right to smoke." Founded in 1824, Carroll's was Ireland's oldest tobacco manufacturer and had become a subsidiary of British American Tobacco. Mason complained in a long letter, that "before your readers can begin to take a view on whether it is sensible to ban smoking in public places," they needed "a little more clarity, both in respect to the author and the science he used to support his views." Mason averred, on the basis of the U.S. Osteen Decision on the US EPA ETS Report and the failed attempt by OSHA to regulate secondhand smoke in the workplace, that "In short the assertions by Mr. Repace – particularly his scaremongering 'estimate' that approximately 150 bar staff lose their lives each year due to ETS – such claims have not been backed up by any independent objective scientific research and it is misleading for Mr. Repace to contend otherwise." Despite Mr. Mason's protests, Micheál Martin had the ear of Prime Minister Bertie Ahern, the leader of the ruling Fianna Fáil party, and the axe would soon fall on the tobacco industry's efforts to prevent workplace smoking bans in Ireland.

THE INDUSTRY'S LUCK BEGINS TO RUN OUT

Meanwhile, back in the USA, The United States Court of Appeals for the Fourth Circuit vacated Osteen's ruling [Case # 98-2407]:

> **PUBLISHED**
> **UNITED STATES COURT OF APPEALS**
> **FOR THE FOURTH CIRCUIT**
> *"This case involves a challenge to the Environmental Protection Agency's (EPA) 1993 Report that classified environmental tobacco smoke as a known human carcinogen. On appeal, EPA presents five arguments challenging the district court's decision that EPA violated its statutory obligations under the Radon Gas and Indoor Air Quality Research Act (Radon Act), Pub. L. No. 99-499, §§ 401-405, 100 Stat. 1758 (reprinted in 42 U.S.C. § 7401 note). First, EPA argues that the district court incorrectly held that the Report was reviewable final agency action under the Administrative Procedure Act (APA), U.S.C. §§ 702, 704. Second, EPA contends the district court erroneously concluded that plaintiffs—Flue-Cured Tobacco Cooperative Stabilization Corporation, Council for Burley Tobacco, Universal Leaf Tobacco Company, Phillip Morris Incorporated, R.J. Reynolds Tobacco Company, and Gallins Vending Company (collectively plaintiffs)—had proper standing to challenge EPA's Report.*
> *Third, EPA contends that it complied with section 403(c) of the Radon Act which required, among other things, that EPA appoint an industry representative to serve on an advisory group during EPA's research program regarding secondhand smoke. Fourth, EPA argues that even if it violated the Radon Act's mandate to establish properly an advisory committee for consultation, that error was nonetheless harmless and not grounds for vacating EPA's Report. Finally, EPA contends that the district court improperly exceeded the scope of judicial review of agency action by engaging in an intrusive review of the scientific and methodological judgments underlying EPA's conclusions in the Report.* **Because the Report is not reviewable agency action under the APA, we vacate the judgment of _the district court and remand for dismissal._**
> *Vacated and remanded by published opinion. Judge Widener wrote the opinion, in which Judge Motz and Judge Howard concurred"* (2002).

BIG TOBACCO DEPOSES AXELRAD IN THE **RICO** CASE

On September 22, 1999, the United States had brought a massive lawsuit against nine cigarette manufacturers and two tobacco-related trade organizations. The Government alleged that "Defendants have violated, and continued to violate, the Racketeer Influenced and Corrupt Organizations Act (RICO), 18 U.S.C. §§ 1961-1968, by engaging in a lengthy, unlawful conspiracy to deceive the American public about the health effects of smoking and environmental tobacco smoke, the addictiveness of nicotine, the health benefits from low tar, "light" cigarettes, and their manipulation of the design and composition of cigarettes in order to sustain nicotine addiction." By 2002, depositions of industry personnel and lawyers were being taken by the Justice Department. Likewise, tobacco industry attorneys were taking depositions of federal workers and others who might testify in the litigation. Among those being deposed was none other than Bob Axelrad, who had been acknowledged in the EPA report as "providing the foresight, funding, and perseverance" that made the report possible. As far as the funding and perseverance, this was true. Foresight? Not so much. The government's attorney was Ms. Sharon Eubanks. His interrogator was Thomas A. Duncan, of Shook Hardy & Bacon on behalf of Big Tobacco. My name came up 58 times in Duncan's questions, and the Q and A's focusing on my role in EPA's ETS work products filled 58% of the 179 pages of transcript. The industry's fixation on me had not abated one whit. Axelrad's responses were quite guarded after being thrown under the bus by Bliley. Although he engaged in a wee bit of revisionist history concerning the ETS compendium. His Q&A's are reported in part:

Q. [Duncan] "How was it that [Repace] was working on [EPA's ETS issues] primarily?" A. [Axelrad] "… I don't know how and when he came to work on them, but my understanding was that he was a fairly well-known and published researcher on the topic… ." Q. "You supervised him, right?" A. "For a period of time." Q. "Was it the case that Mr. Repace pretty much did what he wanted to do within general guidelines?" A. "Mr. Repace was a GS-14 at the time. … But as the position is defined there is a high degree of latitude in independence and judgment expected." Q. "Was it your opinion that Mr. Repace had his own ETS agenda?" A. "I knew he had a very strong interest in the topic." Q. "Did he have his own vision in the ETS area?" A. "… I was not aware of his having a specific agenda … I would say he's got a perspective of his own with respect to secondhand smoke. … That it poses a very significant health risk to nonsmokers."

Q. "While you were supervising Mr. Repace, … did his public activities ever cause you to have to discuss [them] with him?" A. "Yes. … He had the right at all times to speak … and work in areas … related to secondhand smoke. And his opinions were not always identical with the position as it stood at that time of EPA." Q. "Did you ever have any concern that Mr. Repace might take information that he had access to by virtue of his official government position and disseminate that as a private citizen in the public?" A. "No, not really." Q. "Did that ever occur?" A. "Not that I know of." Q. "Did you ever have cause to formally discipline him, Mr. Repace?" A. "… I recall … a reprimand letter … that I was obligated under the rules to issue. … It was based on a report provided to me by the Inspector General's Office. … It had to do with allegations that Mr. Repace had conducted personal business on government time and used government equipment for personal business."

Q. "What personal business was that?" A. "My recollection was that the allegations dealt with him having letterhead for a consulting business that he ran on the side." Q. "… Other than the time you issued the letter of reprimand … did you ever have informal sessions with him where you had to tell him to adjust his behavior, for instance?" A. "Yes." Q. "How long have you been a government supervisor?" A. "I am currently not a supervisor. But I was … for approximately nine years." Q. "Based on your experience would you characterize Mr. Repace as a supervisory challenge for you?" A. … "There was a substantial issue surrounding the draft chapter of a document." … "It was a collection of individually authored papers [i.e., the

Compendium] that had been initiated by several government agencies in addition to EPA… ."

Q. "Who were the authors of some of these documents?" … "Glantz?" A. "In a subsequent chapter that was added later, yes." Q. "What was the specific issue that, not to be cute, that you took issue with Mr. Repace on?" A. It had to do with the paper drafted by Mr. Glantz … and … William Parmley. … And it had to do with the characterization of risk associated with secondhand smoke." Q. "And cardiovascular disease?" A. "And cardiovascular disease."

Q. "What had Mr. Repace done that you took issue with?" A. It was not something that he did as much as what he did not do, which was to give me good input and sufficient information during the development of that chapter. … He should have alerted me to the presence of certain risk estimates that were inserted into the chapter." Q. "What was wrong with the risk estimate?" … A. "The problem … was that these numbers had become associated inappropriately with EPA as the source of those numbers, which was simply not the case." Q. "How did that happen?" A. "… the chapter was released to the media without any approval from anyone at EPA." Q. "How was it released? Wouldn't that be your job to release it?" A. "It would be under normal circumstances my responsibility, along with other co-sponsors of this document, … other agencies from NIH." …

Q. "Who released it to whom?" A. "What I suspect and what I know are somewhat different things. I believe that the author of the chapter released it to a reporter for the Associated Press." Q. "Is that Mr. Glantz?" A. "Yes. … I believe that this had been acknowledged by Mr. Glantz." Q. "What did that have to do with Mr. Repace?" A. "I don't know … But Mr. Repace was managing this project and, as such, should have been sensitive to those issues and brought them to my attention in advance and ensured there was no premature release of any of the information contained in that document."

Q. "Was Mr. Repace's failure to advise you of the risk estimates inserted in these comments willful or inadvertent?" A. "I don't know." Q. "Did you ask him?" A. "Yes. … he did not consider [the insertion of the numbers] a major change in the document." … But when I expressed great concern about the presence of the number and its release, he felt that given the nature of the chapters and the nature of this report and the draft nature of the chapter, that it was not necessarily that big a deal."

Q. "During at least part of your management supervisory career you have supervised scientists, right?" A. "Yes." … Q. "What kinds of things do you look for in a good public service scientist…?" A. "I want them to be technically competent. I want them to exercise good judgment in terms of the information they communicate. I want them to be able to communicate technical information in a manner that is understandable to me and other policymakers. I want them to be willing to take direction." Q. You say that with a smile. I take it that Mr. Repace was not entirely willing to take direction?" A. "Many of the people that I have worked for have been a challenge – or that have worked for me." … "Looking back today, it would be hard for me to say that he was as objective as I ideally would like."

Q. "Did he have any connection with Stanton Glantz?" A. "Other than knowing him and recommending to me that we incorporate a chapter … to be drafted by Mr. Glantz, I wasn't privy to any other relationship with him." … Q. "Do you know if Mr. Repace was involved with ASH?" A. "I seem to recall telling Mr. Repace that he better correct something with [ASH Director] Mr. Banzhaf." Q. "And the fact that you told someone who reported to you that he better fix something with a leader in that organization [Action on Smoking and Health] tipped you off that he has some relationship with that organization, right?" A. "Some relationship.

But the nature of it I don't know. Q. The risk numbers that were inserted into this [Glantz] chapter by the authors … Did Mr. Repace agree with those numbers?" A. To the best of my recollection, he thought that they were credible numbers." Q. Did the EPA officially think that those were credible numbers?" A. … "We had no opinion."

Q. "You say you looked at a few letters from Mr. Bliley, is that correct? A. "Yes." Q. "Do you remember which specific letters they were, by the way?" A. "There were an awful lot of letters from Mr. Bliley … ." Q. Well, what was the gist of those letters?" A. "The gist of the letters had to do with the process for review of several activities related to secondhand smoke that the EPA was involved in." Q. "So you told me that you were involved in arranging for funding for the ETS risk assessment, correct?" A. "Yes." Q. "Whose idea was it to do an ETS risk assessment, to perform one? A. "I am not certain who specifically raised the idea. But I would imagine that it came out of discussions that I had with Dr. Bayard while he was in my office."

Q. "Well, let's talk about the ETS risk assessment. What was the purpose for doing an ETS risk assessment?" A. "… There were multiple purposes. But the first of those was an attempt to update the science of the respiratory health effects of secondhand smoke since the issuance in 1986 Surgeon General's report and the 1986 report of the National Academy of Sciences, National Research Council, both of which address secondhand smoke. … The second purpose was to attempt to classify environmental tobacco smoke within the carcinogen assessment guidelines that EPA was using at that time. And third was to attempt, if possible, to quantify the extent of the risk associated with respiratory health effects of secondhand smoke."

Q. "Whose idea was it to do an ETS risk assessment, to perform one?" A. "I am not certain who specifically raised the idea. … I am the one who requested it I think it would be safe to say." Q. "Did you consult with any of your supervisors as to whether the risk assessment should be done?" A. "Eileen Claussen." Q. "It turned out, I guess that environmental tobacco smoke became a hot button topic, didn't it?" A. "Yes." Q. "Would you say that it became politically charged?" A. "Yes." Q. "The tobacco industry was interested, correct?" A. "Yes." Q. "Public health officials were interested?" "A. "Yes." Q. "Anti-smoking groups were interested?" A. "Yes." Q. "Would it be fair to say that some of the political aspects and advocate aspects of this issue spilled over into your very office?" A. "We certainly were involved in many facets of the issue, including responding to a variety of inquiries from Congress."

Q. "Correct. And in fact you had one of your employees or someone who reported to you in the federal government actually blurring the lines between his official job and his private activities in that arena, correct?" A. "I would say that he had activities outside the federal government. But I don't know that he intentionally was blurring the lines. I have … spoken to him about assuring that he … did disclaim very faithfully, that role. But it was primarily precautionary."

Q. "Look at that, please. … Have you seen that letter before? … Exhibit 2 is a letter on US EPA letterhead dated 16 September '91, signed by James L. Repace, addressed to Professor Banzhaf. Do you recall that letter?" A. "Yes." Q. "Would it be fair to say that that letter was drafted by Mr. Repace at your insistence, if not direction?" A. "To the best of my recollection, that would be correct." Q. "I want you to look at the last page, please. … Did you, in fact, tell Mr. Repace that his actions may have seriously compromised his credibility with the Agency?" … Did you intend to convey that message when you found out what had happened? [refers to Banzhaf's role in the Schlagenhauf affair].

A. "Yes." Q. "My question really is the entire issue of ETS, whether or not we are talking about the Compendium, whether or not we are talking about the Fact Sheet, and the Risk Assessment, was a charged, politically hot issue, some of which spilled into your office with your own employee; correct?" A. " Correct." …

Q. "In all of the comments that you saw, both in your official capacity at EPA and as private citizen, Robert Axelrad, did you ever see any comments that you deemed to be outright falsehoods?" … A. "The reporter that I recall writing the most on the issue was an Associated Press reporter by the name of Paul Raeburn." Q. "And you thought that some of the substance of those reported stories was false?" A. "Yes. … my concerns were with attributions made in stories he wrote, specifically connecting heart disease risk estimates we spoke about earlier and the document known as the Technical Compendium and representing those and allowing them to be represented as somehow reflective of EPA positions or characterizing them as an EPA report despite many attempts to make clear that those individually authored papers were simply and strictly representing the views of those individual authors alone."

Q. "That part of getting it to the press, however it got there, matters, though?" A. " The fact that it got to the press without the approval of EPA matters." … Q. "Do you know where [Raeburn] was getting his information?" A. " I imagine he got it from a great many sources, including without much success, from me in terms of clarifications. But I say quotes from I believe Mr. Glantz and probably Mr. Banzhaf in articles that he wrote, among others." Q. "Any from Mr. Repace?" A. " I don't remember specifically if he was quoted in any Raeburn articles." Q. "So you don't know if he was involved in any of that reporting?" A. " I don't, no."
…

Q. "Whose idea was it to publish "Indoor Air Facts, No. 5?" A. " I actually don't recall whose idea it was." Q. "On the first paragraph of Exhibit 3 [Fact Sheet #5] starting with "It is a known cause" … is there a reason you didn't use exposures to environmental tobacco smoke increases your risk of lung cancer?" A. " This is not precisely worded as I would like it to be." Q. "Where did you get the facts or at least the numbers portrayed, such as 50 million smokers, 600 billion cigarettes, 4 billion cigars and 11 billion pipes full of tobacco?" A. " I believe these were provided by Jim Repace." Q. "Does it follow that because people spend 90% of their time indoors that 90% of smoking occurs indoors?" A. " I really don't know. I really don't know." Q. "Is there another way to interpret that?" A. " I don't recall what the calculation underlying that "467,000 tons of tobacco are burned indoors" – it would appear to suggest that that is what it means." Q. "But in any event, it is not supported by attribution, right?" A. " No." [*In fact, as the industry had been well aware for a dozen years (TTID 2021180527), these numbers came out of Repace and Lowrey (1990), but the reference had been deleted by EPA in its internal review of the draft Fact Sheet*].

Q. "Did you intend this to be a factual recitation about ETS, Or was it also meant to scare people as a shock document?" A. " … So our goal was to disseminate that information which was previously developed by government entities and which we considered to be very credible information." Q. "On the right side 'There are 43 carcinogenic compounds in tobacco smoke.' Is that meant to be environmental tobacco smoke, mainstream, or sidestream, do you know? A. " I don't know." Q. "Can I assume based on this, at least this first part, that Mr. Repace wrote most of this?" A. "He wrote some significant portion of it. But I wouldn't say that he wrote all of it."

Q. "Do you know which EPA research it was that showed that ETS is the major source of mutagens indoors when smoking occurs?" A. "… Joellen Lewtas, I believe was heading that program." Q. "Where it says 'impact on children' and says 'passive smoking induces serious respiratory symptoms in children … does it go on to name what those serious symptoms are?" A. " It names three of them, yes." Q. "Is sputum production, in your view, a serious respiratory symptom?" A. "… No I would not say that sputum is what I would call a serious respiratory symptom … Again it is not as precise as I would like it to be." Q. "Look at 'ETS and Cancer.' It says … 'In 1986, an estimated 23,000 US nonsmokers died from lung cancer and the Surgeon General attributes a substantial number of those deaths to passive smoking. Is that accurate?" A. " … I certainly hope they are."

Q. " 'ETS and Heart Disease,' the next paragraph … reads 'The Interagency Task Force on Environmental Cancer, Heart, and Lung Disease Workshop on ETS concluded that the effects of ETS on the heart may be of even greater concern than cancer-causing effects on the lungs. ETS aggravates the condition of people with heart disease, and several studies have linked involuntary smoking with heart disease. Do you know what studies he is referring to? A. " No, I do not." … Q. "Let's go on to 'Removal of ETS from Indoor Air.' … Would I be wrong in interpreting this section of the fact sheet to be that, in fact nothing except restrictions on smoking to certain areas that are separately ventilated and directly exhausted to the outside or eliminating smoking entirely are the only two that even come close to working?" A. "I think what we are basically saying … is that the most effective way to minimize exposure is to either restrict smoking entirely or to limit it to properly designed, properly ventilated smoking rooms."

Q. "Would it be safe to say that Mr. Repace was a big influence on you starting the EPA risk assessment?" A. " I think he was a partial influence. I don't know that I would characterize it as big." Q. "The next section, 'The Public Reaction to ETS.' … Especially the … sentence … 'In a 1987 Gallup National Opinion Survey, 55% of all persons interviewed, including smokers and nonsmokers, were in favor of a total ban on all smoking in public places.' Could a reader of your fact sheet conclude that the EPA is urging a total ban on all smoking in public places?" A. " I won't claim authorship of that sentence. … This is another circumstance where I would prefer that it had been worded differently."

Q. "Would it be unreasonable for persons outside the EPA to look at your fact sheet and determine that … the EPA, that environmental tobacco smoke was a known human carcinogen?" A. " I think it would be reasonable for them to conclude that we concurred with the findings of two reports put out by other agencies, the Surgeon General and the National Research Council, in terms of their conclusions." … "I think the fact that this document came out of our office and the risk assessment was done independently by the Office of Research and Development provides some separation between this document which was intended to simply reflect already published information."

Q. "Is it your testimony that you did not tell Dr. Bayard that he needed to get a risk assessment done and get it done within three months? A. " I don't recall saying that to him." Q. "I am showing you what is marked as Exhibit 4, which is a memo re Maryland OSHA testimony [1994]. Have you seen that document before?" A. "No." Q. "Do you know what Bayard is cited here as saying in reference to you, "He still doesn't know what he is doing?" "Q. Do you know what he is talking about?" A. " I have no idea. … This also to me does not in any way shape or form suggest that he is saying I don't know what I am doing about my job. It could mean any number of things."

BUSTED BY THE BOUNCER

On Friday, January 24th, 2003, I returned to Wilmington to make the follow-up measurements in the eight now smoke-free Delaware venues: The Delaware Park Casino, Timothy's Bar, Logan House Bar, Kid Shelleen's Bar, Washington Street Ale House, the Backstage Café, Kahunaville Games, and Bankshots Pool Parlor, making the same air quality measurements as before, and doing the person-counts. In one venue, Logan House, a very crowded college bar with 188 persons jammed in wall-to-wall, cheek-by-jowl, I was counting persons with my mechanical clicker-counter when after about 25 minutes, I got busted. I was confronted by the bouncer, a great hulking grubby beast who sported a two-day growth of stubble. He demanded to know, "Are you counting heads? Are you counting heads? You're coming with me." He escorted me to the club owner who asked what the hell I was doing. I admitted that I was working for the Lung Association, which was interested in whether patronage had changed in the wake of Delaware's smoke-free law. He said it was none of their business, and unceremoniously gave me the boot. On the way out, I grabbed my roll-on bag and happily departed with 25 minutes of solid data.

THE MESA ARIZONA CAPER

Next on the agenda was a follow-up study to the Black Dog Pub, done in two Mesa, Arizona pubs. I knew about these venues from my friend, Dr. Leland (Lee) Fairbanks, a resident of nearby Tempe, and President of Arizonans Concerned About Smoking, with whom I had served on Dr. Koop's National Advisory Committee. Lee said that TGI Fridays and the Macaroni Grill persuaded the Mesa City Council to exempt them from Mesa's restaurant smoking ban. Both had made the same claims of SHS control by high-tech displacement ventilation similar to those that the Restaurant Associations in Canada had made about the Black Dog Pub. Through Lee's good offices, I managed to obtain the assistance of a large number of volunteers from the Coalition for a Tobacco Free Arizona, Arizona Clearing the Air, the Arizona Department of Health Services, Smoke-Free Chandler, and Arizonans Concerned About Smoking.

In March, I flew out to Phoenix. We booked dinner for a dozen volunteers, during which we planned to monitor the air quality, measure the space volume, and counted smokers and persons present in the smoking and nonsmoking sections of the TGI Fridays (TGIF) and the Macaroni Grill in Mesa. When we walked into the TGIF, we were confronted by an unpleasant smell of disinfectant from the restroom, a sure tipoff that its exhaust fan was broken. This malfunction resulted in an unbalanced ventilation system that pulled air from the smoking section into the nonsmoking section. Unsurprisingly, the fine particle levels were 50% higher in the nonsmoking section than in the smoking section, and 41 times higher than outdoors. Moreover, cooking smoke was being exhausted from the kitchen into the dining area, another clear sign of a seriously out-of-balance ventilation system. As for the Macaroni Grill, fine particle levels were three times higher in nonsmoking area than in the smoking area and 33 times higher than outdoors. In this case, both the kitchen and the smoking section were positively pressurized with respect to the nonsmoking dining room instead of being negatively pressurized, as sound ventilation design would require. Clearly, both of these pubs had ventilation systems that were improperly designed, installed, operated, or maintained and were significantly out of balance. In 1999, I had appeared before the Mesa City Council and predicted that displacement ventilation would not control secondhand smoke. These measurements, especially taken together with the Black Dog Pub data, which had been performed with a properly balanced air handling system, provided substantial evidence that my surmise had been correct. Furthermore, it demonstrated that the pub owners paid scant attention to the operation of their ventilation systems.

There was one more essential experiment I wanted to conduct to further insulate my measurements from industry criticism. I flew out to Silicon Valley and Wayne Ott, a Stanford graduate student, and I calibrated all of the particle monitors gravimetrically against cigarette smoke in a series of controlled experiments in

Wayne's guest bedroom Figure 32. Wayne modified my Piezobalances so he could tap into their real-time signals via a Fluke multimeter interfaced with his computer and wrote a program to analyze and plot the real-time data. He provided access to Stanford's pump-and-filter gravimetric sampler equipped with a particle size discriminator to separate out the fine particles from the coarse. We were able to conclude that my MIE fine particle optical monitors registered particle levels within the experimental error of the calibration methods, and that there was no meaningful difference among the MIE (when used with the appropriate calibration factor), the Piezobalance, and the Stanford "Gold Standard" gravimetric method. Equipped with this calibration factor, I could now write up the results of my Black Dog and Mesa experiments for publication.

Most researchers used University of Kentucky (UKY) Research Cigarettes for controlled experiments. Instead, as Repace and Lowrey and done in 1980, Wayne and I used commercial Marlboro cigarettes that were smoked by 40% of U.S. smokers, not a pack of lab rats. Marlboros differed in their secondhand smoke emissions from UKY cigarettes, and thus were far more representative of the secondhand smoke encountered by nonsmokers in buildings.

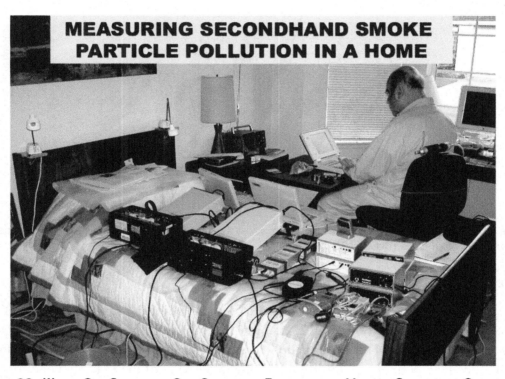

FIGURE 32. WAYNE OTT SETTING UP OUR CALIBRATION EXPERIMENT TO MEASURE SECONDHAND SMOKE USING PIEZOBALANCES, AN MIE PARTICLE MONITOR, FOUR ECOCHEM PARTICULATE CARCINOGEN MONITORS, AND THE STANFORD CYCLONE FOR GRAVIMETRIC MEASUREMENT OF FINE PARTICLES (AUTHOR'S PHOTO).

Our experiment was later discussed in a Stanford textbook (Ott, Steinemann, and Wallace, 2007). Figure 33 shows that the Marlboro cigarette RSP measured by the MIE (x) tracked the carcinogens measured by the EcoChem (♦) as well as the RSP measured by the Piezobalance (o). Further, that the average value measured by the Stanford gravimetric "gold standard" cyclones (—) agreed well with the averages of both particle monitors, and, finally, that Wayne's mathematical model for real-time RSP from ETS tracked the RSP vs. time curve from these cigarettes extremely well (solid blue line). We ran a small fan to ensure uniform mixing. In other words, this experiment demonstrated the accuracy of the real-time monitors in measuring secondhand smoke and the validity of the mass-balance model for predicting secondhand smoke concentrations in real-world settings (Repace, 2007). Figure 32 shows Wayne operating the experimental setup. Figure 33 plots the results, demonstrating that even smoking one cigarette per hour over a period of 8 hours in a 13' x 13' room with an air exchange rate comparable to what would expect in an office setting, can raise the RSP concentration from a background of less than 10 $\mu g/m^3$ to peak levels of nearly 600 $\mu g/m^3$, and average 250 $\mu g/m^3$, with similar results for particle-bound carcinogens (PPAH) in units of ng/m^3.

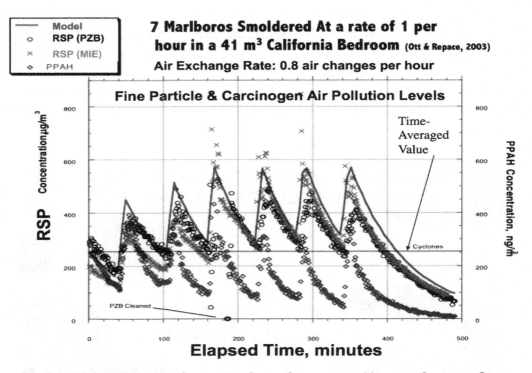

FIGURE 33. EIGHT HOUR STUDY OF THE SECONDHAND SMOKE GENERATION OF MARLBORO CIGARETTES SMOLDERED AT A RATE OF 1 PER HOUR (REPACE, 2007).

"A KILLER ON THE LOOSE"

In 2003, I gave 28 talks, interviews, and presentations, including lectures at the Center for Tobacco Control and Policy at the University of California, San Francisco, and the Johns Hopkins Department of Environmental Health Sciences. Foremost among these was a major bashing of the British American Tobacco's (BAT) secondhand smoke disinformation campaign. ASH of the U.K. had commissioned me to write a report to support ASH's push for workplace smoking bans in the face of the BAT's aggressively promoted propaganda that ventilation could control secondhand smoke. Like BAT, ASH's primary target was the British hospitality industry. In December of 1998, the British Government, supported by the UK Department of Health, published a White Paper - *Smoking Kills*. Inter alia, the document proposed a so-called "voluntary charter" mutually agreed with representatives of the UK hospitality industry. Naïve in the extreme, the White Paper proposed an "Approved Code of Practice" (ACoP) to Supplement the Health and Safety and Work Act of the UK. Fourteen industry associations, representing sectors such as pubs, restaurants and casinos endorsed and promoted it. Hospitality Venues were expected to have a written smoking policy and to display signs showing which of the five optional levels of policy they adhered to:
- no smoking;
- separate smoking and non-smoking areas;
- ventilated premises with separate areas;

- ventilated premises with smoking allowed throughout;
- smoking allowed throughout.

Except for the no smoking option, not a thought or care was given to the hapless nonsmoking waitstaff's health.

The UK Dept. of Health [DH] "hoped that this partnership with industry would lead to increased provision for non-smoking customers in pubs and restaurants. Voluntary targets were agreed such that 50% of all such premises should have a formal smoking policy and carry an external sign and that 35% of these should restrict smoking to designated and enforced areas and/or have adequate ventilation." The wishy-washy White Paper noted that "43% have met the first standard (below target) and 53% the second (above target). DH notes that few pubs are entirely smoke-free and that around half of those complying with the Charter do so by allowing smoking throughout." An obvious flaw was that in the main, few workers would be able to enjoy smoke-free premises, and "adequate ventilation" essentially meant compliance with totally inadequate building-code specified ventilation.

The Public Places Charter on Smoking was an even weaker hospitality-industry-sponsored self-regulatory alternative specifying a voluntary opt-out from the Government-sponsored ACoP of the White Paper. *The Public Places Charter* promoted "practical techniques to resolve the public smoking issue through ventilation and/or non-smoking areas." This was essentially BAT's position. Internal BAT documents showed that it clearly knew that ventilation and air filtration were ineffective at cleansing the air of environmental tobacco smoke. Nevertheless, the company had extensively promoted both ventilation and smoking sections to the hospitality industry since the mid-1990s. BAT's strategies to promote these ineffective initiatives worldwide were seen internally as "viable solutions to circumvent smoking restrictions and to gain global marketing opportunities" (Leavell et al. 2006).

My report, which ASH had titled "*A Killer on the Loose, An Action on Smoking and Health special investigation into the threat of passive smoking to the U.K. workforce,* was published as an attractive 2-color 24-page booklet in 2003. *Killer* criticized both the ACoP and BAT's reliance on ventilation. Drawing upon my research, *Killer* made the following points:

- "An estimated 12,000 U.K. nonsmokers die annually from secondhand smoke (SHS) exposure at home, at work, and in social venues. In fact, SHS pollution now causes as many deaths annually as did the great London Smog 50 years ago and triple the annual number of road deaths from traffic accidents.
- Within the at-work category, data is sufficient to calculate risks for three subgroups: about 900 office workers, 165 bar workers, and 145 manufacturing workers are estimated to die from passive smoking each year in the U.K. That's more than three deaths a day in these three categories alone.
- For manufacturing workers, three-fold as many are estimated to die from passive smoking than work-related deaths from all other causes. 17% of bar workers are estimated to die from passive smoking at current exposure levels. The SHS-caused deaths among office workers adds an estimated 9% to the total occupational mortality from all causes in all occupations.
- Recent U.S. and Canadian measurements show that during smoking, secondhand smoke accounts for about 90% of the fine-particle air pollution levels and 95% of the airborne carcinogens in hospitality venues.

- Under the hospitality-industry-sponsored *Public Places Charter on Smoking*, which promotes ventilation as a control for secondhand smoke, it is estimated that five of every 100 bar workers would die from workplace passive smoking, yielding 66 deaths per year.

- Engineering half-measures, proposed in BAT's *Charter*, were evaluated by modeling and compared with air quality measurements in Canadian and U.S. venues. These methods clearly show that the Charter-specified air exchange rate would create an air pollution hazard, violating the daily U.K. air quality standard for particulate air pollution by three-fold.

- Attempts to control the toxic and carcinogenic properties of secondhand smoke by ventilation are futile, requiring tornado-strength rates of air flow.

- The intent of the Health and Safety at Work Act 1974, which places a general duty of care for employers to provide a safe working environment, is not being satisfied for passive smoking. Without an Approved Code of Practice or legislation to **ensure** smoke-free workplaces, nonsmoking workers will continue to die needlessly" (Repace, 2003).

ASH invited me to London to promote these ideas. Over a three-day period, from April 8-10, 2003, I gave multiple media interviews on BBC Radio 5 Live, BBC Wales, BBC Northampton, BBC Scotland, and Viking FM. I spoke at the "Don't Choke on the Smoke' Conference in London, sponsored by the Trades Union Congress and the Chartered Institute of Environmental Health. Several hundred environmental health specialists and health and safety union representatives attended. When I presented slides of the data I had collected but not yet published from my Delaware pre-and-post smoking ban study, there was a collective gasp from the audience. The results were electrifying, foreshadowing the international firestorm to come in 2004 when my Delaware paper would be published in *JOEM*.

Deaths from Air Pollution in the U.K.

- **Great London Smog, 1952: 12,000 deaths**

- **Great Secondhand Smoke, 2003: 12,000 - 14,000 deaths**

Air Pollution Kills

FIGURE 34. SLIDE FROM MY UK PARLIAMENT PRESENTATION, APRIL 10, 2003.

Next, I testified before the All Party Parliamentary Group on Smoking and Health, in the UK House of Commons. An impressive painting of Winston Churchill hung outside the meeting room. It was my very first Power Point presentation using my new Mac laptop with a remote controller. No longer limited to 35 mm slides or overheads, my presentations henceforth utilized 21st Century technology (Figures 34 & 35). Maurice Mulcahy, whose carbon monoxide measurements in Galway Pubs proved crucial to estimating the risk to Irish bartenders, also testified. Afterward Maurice and I took in the sights together. Later, I had lunch in an Indian restaurant with Martin Jarvis, one of the world's leading experts on cotinine studies, and dined that evening as a guest in the home of Anne Jones, who was active in UK tobacco control. The British smoke-free regulations, *The Smoke-free (Premises and Enforcement) Regulations 2006, No. 3368,* would be enacted on the 13th of December 2006, and finally put into place on the 1st of July 2007.

FIGURE 35. SLIDE FROM MY UK PARLIAMENT PRESENTATION, APRIL 10, 2003.

In perspective, the methods and tools that my colleagues and I had developed and deployed over the preceding 22 years now enabled the estimation of nonsmokers' mortality from secondhand smoke in the general nonsmoking population and in groups of workers using several methods: dose-response models using cotinine in the body fluids of nonsmokers, epidemiological inference, and indoor air pollution exposure-response models for SHS. Further, I could evaluate putative secondhand smoke control methods such as ventilation, air cleaning, and spatial separation and compare them in efficacy to smoking bans. In this way, I was able to discredit the bogus argument that measures short of smoking bans could yield acceptable risk to nonsmoking workers. These methods could also be employed to estimate risk for workers injured from secondhand smoke inhalation in their workplace.

Sir Richard Buys The Beer

In August 2003, Dr. Kari Reijula, of the Finnish Institute of Occupational Health, invited me to present two talks at the 12th World Conference on Tobacco or Health in Helsinki, Finland: the first was a 20-minute presentation, "Secondhand Smoke: Exposure, Dose, Risk, and Control," in the Main Session on *Passive Smoking*, plus a half-hour seminar, "Global overview on exposure to secondhand smoke," in a Workshop on *Passive Smoking at Work*. In the latter presentation, I compared urine cotinine levels in bartenders and waiters with the average population doses from six countries. The measurements in Boston were from my collaboration with Jim Hyde and Doug Brugge at Tufts (unpublished), the Hong Kong data from collaboration with Dr. Tony Hedley at U. of Hong Kong, the Montreal cotinines from collaboration with Dr. Louis Lavergne at U. of Montreal (unpublished), and the remainder from published data in Ireland, England, and New Zealand. I added in the published general nonsmoking population cotinine distributions from England and the U.S.A. to show how far above the population norm these hospitality workplace doses were.

Using the pharmacokinetic models colleagues and I had developed in 1993 and 1998, I estimated the fine particle exposure (SHS-RSP) corresponding to the measured doses (Repace and Lowrey, 1993; Repace et al., 1998). Where cotinine was measured in blood instead of urine, I converted the data into urine cotinine equivalents. Among all bar staff, Galway Ireland topped out, followed closely by Boston, Montreal and London. Wait staff generally had lower levels than bartenders. All nonsmoking hospitality workers' cotinine doses vastly exceeded the general population distributions measured in both the U.K. and the U.S. A log-probability plot of the data is shown in Figure 36.

During the conference, Hilarine and I attended a sumptuous banquet for a dozen or so invited speakers at a yacht club on an island in the harbor to which we were ferried. Just before sunset, we started off our seven-course dinner with a schnapps toast. *Skol!* Later that week, Kari Reijula took us on a tour of *Ainola*, the country home where the Finnish composer, Jan Sibelius, had lived. His choral works are among my favorites. It was located at Järvenpää, an art colony on a lake, and was now a museum. Sibelius had the rare gift of color synesthesia, a neurological condition in which musical sounds evoke colors in the mind. Carousing with his artist friends, he would go on two-week benders, often spent in the Koppeli pub in Helsinki, leaving his wife at home to care for their seven children. While I attended the meeting, Hilarine and Lani Blissard, one of the flight attendants from FAMRI, engaged in a bit of sightseeing. All of Europe was enveloped in a massive heat wave at the time, a harbinger of climate change. We had flown in from a blisteringly hot weekend in Paris that was nearly unbearable except for our hotel and the Bateau Mouches, which thankfully were air conditioned, and our Helsinki hotel was a sweltering hotbox. The windows in our room were narrow slits covered with a perforated grille that allowed little outdoor air to enter. We requested a fan from the flabbergasted concierge who sputtered, "We don't have such things here."

During the meeting, Stan Glantz arranged for the two of us to sit down and chat with Sir Richard Doll, the world-famous British epidemiologist and one of his aides over beer. Sir Richard sprang for the drinks. We later met his collaborator, Richard Peto, a skeptic concerning lung cancer and passive smoking, like Ernst Wynder. Tony Hedley and his group from Hong Kong were there, as were Dr. Greg Connolly from Boston and Maurice Mulcahy from Galway. I also met two new friends, Dr. Giovanni Invernizzi and Ario Rupprecht of the tobacco control program of The National Cancer Institute of Milan, who came to the meeting to make contact. Ario had brought a MetOne particle monitor with him, and as kindred spirits, we roamed around Helsinki making measurements of secondhand smoke in outdoor cafés, including the Koppeli, which still survives, and on the sidewalks of busy city streets in downtown Helsinki. Due to the heat wave, the Koppeli's outdoor patio was mobbed. We got excellent data and managed to make the first measurements of outdoor secondhand smoke on restaurant and pub patios. The outdoor air pollution levels in several outdoor cafés with many smokers were 5 to 20 times higher than on the sidewalks of busy downtown streets polluted by bus, truck, and auto traffic, as shown in Figures 37 & 38.

SANDBAGGED AT STRESA

Later that year, while Hilarine and I were attending the 13th Annual Conference of the International Society for Exposure Science at scenic Lago Maggiore in Stresa, Italy, Giovanni invited me to speak to the Tobacco Control Group at the National Cancer Institute of Milan. We travelled by train from Stresa. After my talk, they awarded me a "Certificate of Excellence in Smoke Studies." Later, we dined with the entire tobacco control group at a local pizzeria, and I measured carcinogen levels inside and outside with an EcoChem PAH monitor that I had brought along. The level of carcinogens was quite as high outdoors as it was in the smoking section, which Ario attributed to the effect of pervasive oily smog from smoky diesel exhaust visible in the streetlights.

At the Stresa meeting, our conference seminar, *Secondhand Smoke in the Hospitality Industry*, at which Wayne Ott also presented, was co-chaired by Marco Maroni of Italy and Bernd Seifert of Germany. Maroni charged the seminar speakers to limit their presentations just to "the flaws in your studies." This was totally bizarre, as we only had a scant five minutes each to discuss the actual content of our papers. I immediately suspected that Maroni was a tobacco mole who had been ordered to sandbag our seminar. I ignored his instructions, as did Wayne, who gave one of his usual sterling presentations. The other presenters did not. Later, Giovanni Invernizzi informed me that Signore Maroni had testified for the defendants in Italian secondhand smoke litigation, and he also felt strongly that Maroni was an industry mole. Interestingly, Maroni was an associate of Bob Axelrad. That had attracted the notice of Big Tobacco.

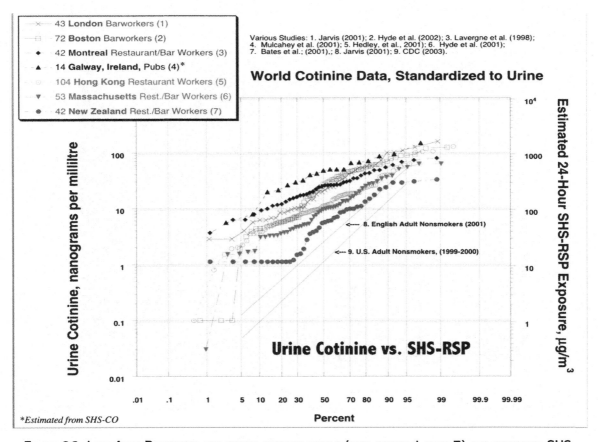

FIGURE 36. LEFT AXIS: BARTENDER AND WAITER COTININE LEVELS (DATA POINTS 1 THRU 7) AND ESTIMATED SHS-RSP INHALED DOSES (RIGHT AXIS) IN SIX COUNTRIES COMPARED TO GENERAL POPULATION LEVELS IN THE US AND THE UK (STRAIGHT LINES 8 & 9) (AUTHOR'S SLIDE, WORLD CONFERENCE ON TOBACCO OR HEALTH PRESENTATION, HELSINKI, FINLAND, REPACE, JL (2003).

OUTDOOR FINE PARTICLE AIR POLLUTION: SHS vs. TRAFFIC

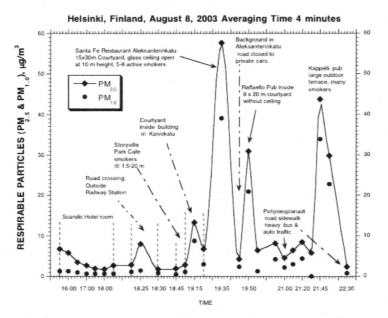

FIGURE 37. OUTDOOR PARTICLE MEASUREMENTS OF SECONDHAND SMOKE AND AUTO EXHAUST AT THE 12TH WORLD CONFERENCE ON TOBACCO OR HEALTH, HELSINKI, FINLAND, AUGUST 2003 (RUPPRECHT AND REPACE, 2003).

FIGURE 38. OUTDOOR PARTICLE MEASUREMENTS AT THE 12TH WORLD CONFERENCE ON TOBACCO OR HEALTH, HELSINKI, FINLAND, AUGUST 2003. FACING THE CAMERA: ARIO RUPPRECHT, HOLDING THE METONE, HILARINE REPACE, AND MAURICE MULCAHY (AUTHOR'S PHOTO).

Eight years earlier, Charles Lister and Jennifer Green of Covington & Burling had taken special notice of the Maroni-Axelrad association. In a revealing 1995 memorandum to their tobacco industry clients, they wrote in part:

Overview of Principal Europe-wide Threats to Public Smoking
Involving Air Quality Standards

"An overview of six principal threats to public and workplace smoking which have emerged on a Europe-wide level in connection with proposed or existing air quality standards or guidelines. … These were

(1) a Europe-wide air quality standard mandating increased ventilation for smoking areas … if adopted, the proposed new standard would be very prejudicial to public and workplace smoking.

(2) A European database identifying sources of indoor air quality problems and suggesting rules and solutions; (preliminary results already identified ETS as an 'important' problem … Those results emphasize the importance of source controls, rather than the airflow approach preferred in (for example) the current ASHRAE standard. Source controls invite restrictions upon smoking.

(3) a proposed new outdoor air quality standard likely to prove a model for similar legislation regarding indoor air … Among the air pollutants … to be placed under new limit values would be carbon monoxide and benzene. Both are associated with smoking, as are particulates.

(4) Revised WHO guidelines for air quality likely to make ETS a major issue … we also learned that a preliminary paper [reported] that ETS represents a major air quality problem. In effect, it urges that the revised WHO guidelines should identify ETS as such a problem and should recommend stringent steps to curtail public and workplace smoking.

(5) A NATO program related to indoor air that 'undoubtedly has smoking as a major target' expected to be an important vehicle for extending EPA's ideas into Europe … it involves a program principally driven by Robert Axelrad of U.S. EPA's indoor air group to encourage improvements in indoor air, particularly in Central and Eastern Europe. *Axelrad works closely with Professor Marco Maroni, a senior researcher in the pesticides and occupational health institutes in Milan* [Italics mine].

(6) Energy saving programs, because improved indoor air quality and energy savings would both be arguably served by additional smoking restrictions. A seventh issue, reorganization of the European Occupational Health and Hygiene Unit, which would give workplace issues a higher visibility, which is expected to result in a higher regulatory priority for indoor air issues" [TTID 2048785823].

On my way back to Washington, I stopped off in Dublin to speak at an Irish seminar on the economics of tobacco control and gave another interview with the *Irish Times*. With my trusty EcoChem, I made airborne carcinogen measurements inside and outside a local smoky pub whose doors were open to the outdoors where diesel buses plied their routes, and found as I had in Milan, high indoor levels due to smoking but also high outdoor air carcinogen levels due to diesel exhaust pollution. Later that year, I gave a plenary talk at the National Conference on Tobacco or Health in Boston; I also lectured at Valparaiso University in Indiana in December.

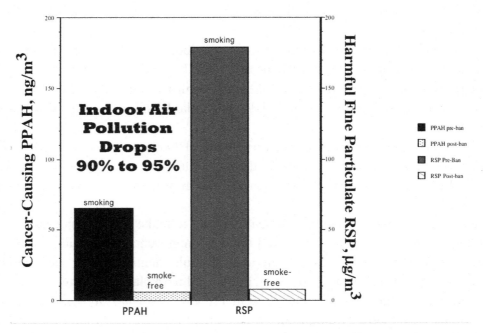

FIGURE 39. COMPARISON OF CARCINOGENIC PPAH AND FINE PARTICLE RSP PRE-AND-POST BOSTON SMOKING BAN IN 6 BOSTON PUBS (REPACE ET AL., 2006).

BANNED IN BOSTON

Meanwhile, prompted by Dr. Greg Connolly, then Director of the Tobacco Control Program of Massachusetts, Prof. Jim Hyde at the Tufts University School of Medicine in Boston contacted me with an offer to join with him and Prof. Doug Brugge to collaborate on a study of secondhand smoke exposure and dose in Massachusetts bartenders and waiters. As our research proceeded, Jim asked me to become a visiting assistant clinical professor in the Tufts Department of Public Health and Community Medicine, an unexpected honor. My appointment would last until 2011. Our collaboration would lead to three published research papers. The most important one (Figure 39) involved replicating the Delaware Study with a pre-and-post smoking ban study of air quality in 7 Boston Pubs (Repace et al., 2006).

Excluding one of the pubs that had a serious air pollution problem due to a defective deep-fat fryer in its kitchen that spilled smoke and carbon monoxide into the restaurant, we found that Pre-smoking-ban RSP levels in the remaining 6 pubs averaged 179 μg/m³, 23 times higher than the post-ban levels, which averaged 7.7 μg/m³, indicating that 96% of the RSP was due to ETS. Pre-smoking ban levels of fine particle air pollution in all 7 of the pubs were in the *Unhealthy* to *Hazardous* range of EPA's Air Quality Index, exceeding the National Ambient Air Quality Standard for fine particle pollution ($PM_{2.5}$) by nearly 4-fold. In 6 of the pubs with valid ETS data, pre-ban indoor carcinogenic particulate polycyclic aromatic hydrocarbons (PPAH) averaged 61.7 ng/m³, nearly 10 times higher than post-ban levels of 6.32 ng/m³, indicating that 90%

of the PPAH was due to ETS. Post-ban particulate air pollution levels were in the Good AQI range (Figure 39). These results replicated the 2003 Wilmington measurements in a big-city setting (Repace, et al., 2006).

NORWAY REDUX

In October 2003, Erik Nord, a Senior Researcher at the Norwegian Institute of Public Health, wrote a letter to the Editor of *BMJ*, titled *Passive smoking: Non-smoking researchers' personal values cause conflict of interest*. Nord took umbrage at the Norwegian Government's justification for its smoking ban, complaining in part,

> "Editor – In Norway, Parliament passed legislation in the spring of 2003 that bans smoking in all pubs, cafes and restaurants from June 2004 [3]. Not even separate smoking rooms will be allowed, on the grounds (a) that waiters will have to enter such rooms from time to time and (b) that even very limited exposures to environmental smoke is 'documented' to be a significant health hazard. … "The Minister of Health ordered a report on passive smoking that would give the necessary scientific basis for proposing a total smoking ban in pubs and restaurants. The assignment was given exclusively to two scientists [Tore Sanner and Erik Dybing] who, for all their expertise, are known as having strong feelings against smoking and for many years have been heavily engaged in anti-smoking campaigns. … As noted above, the end point of this chain of information is an allegation by the Minister of Health that significant risk of heart disease from passive smoking is 'documented' even at low levels of exposure. It turns out that the initial information is in fact (a) not evidence in the ordinary sense of the word and (b) not about heart disease" … [*BMJ*, 2003].

The Health Ministry's Report had cited three papers of mine in quantitative support of its heart disease contention: Repace et al. *Risk Analysis* 1998; Repace and Lowrey, *Risk Analysis* 1993, and Repace and Lowrey *Environment International* 1985. Nord's complaint was redolent of ad hominem industry arguments. I responded with a rebuttal letter of my own, stating in part:

> "Editor – In a misguided attempt to clarify the issue of the influence of conflict of interest on passive smoking studies raised by Richard Horton, Nord wrongly asserts that the scientific basis for Norway's workplace smoking ban is unsound. Nord believes that the basis report prepared by the Health Ministry is rife with "conflict of interest" and does not support a risk of passive smoking at what he asserts are "low levels." Nord's criticism focuses on three of my papers, referenced in the report. Nord asserts that the Health Ministry report's heart disease dose-response relationship is 'undocumented' and that assumptions concerning linearity of cancer risk at what he calls 'low levels of exposure' are 'unjustified'. Our meta-analysis-based passive smoking heart disease risk model predicts occupational passive-smoking heart disease mortality in the middle of the range estimated by U.S. OSHA for U.S. workers.
>
> In our cancer risk exposure-response model, the response is derived from the lung cancer mortality rates in 2 large cohort studies of passive smoking in the U.S. and Japan, while population-average exposure is based upon modeling, and is consistent with exposure and dose measurements for nonsmokers from tobacco smoke air pollution [5,6,7]. In validation, our model was able to quantitatively predict, within 5%, both the risk ratio and risk rate observed in the American Cancer Society's CPS I passive smoking study (ACS-CPS I). Our model of passive smoking induced lung cancer risk has been widely accepted, e.g. [8-10]. Thus, the Norwegian report's assumptions based in part on my work are both well documented and properly justified (references omitted) [Repace, *BMJ* 2003].

In 2004, Nord would denounce my work again in a letter to the editor of *Dagbladet,* an Oslo newspaper, when I returned for another lecture. His strident criticism failed to convince the Norwegian Government to rescind its ban. Norway would be the second European country to implement a smoke-free workplace law, following Ireland.

In October of 2003, I was contacted by an attorney in Farmington Hills, Michigan in the case of a short-order cook who worked in a bowling alley in the town of Madison Heights to serve as an expert witness in his secondhand smoke injury case. This cook, a lifelong nonsmoker, had developed cancer of the larynx that he attributed to secondhand smoke at work. I flew out and descended upon the bowling alley with all of my new real-time monitoring equipment.

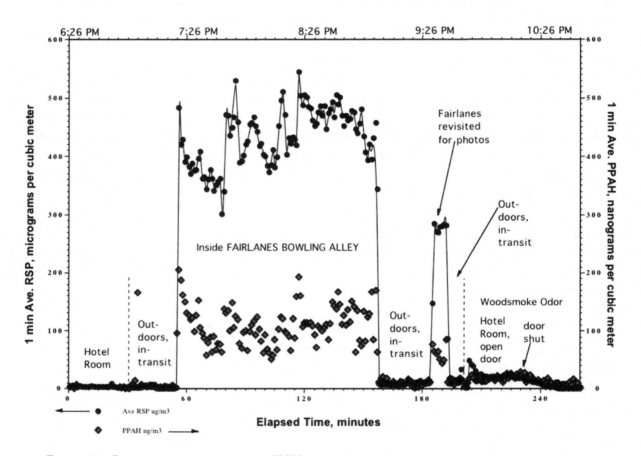

Elapsed Time, minutes

FIGURE 40. REAL-TIME RESPIRABLE PARTICLE (RSP) AND CARCINOGENIC POLYCYCLIC AROMATIC HYDROCARBON AIR POLLUTION (PPAH), INDOORS IN A HOTEL ROOM, OUTDOORS IN PARKING LOTS, IN TRANSIT IN AN AUTO, AND INSIDE THE 259,000 FT³ (7334 M³) MADISON HEIGHTS, MICHIGAN BOWLING ALLEY, AN AVERAGE OF 9.5 CIGARETTES WERE BEING SMOKED AMONG 206 PERSONS DURING THE FIRST 1 HOUR AND 40 MINUTE VISIT. THE TOURNAMENT ENDED AT 9:00 PM. MOST BOWLERS HAD DEPARTED BY THE TIME OF THE SECOND VISIT AT 9:30 PM (REPACE JL, UNPUBLISHED). THE FIGURE ILLUSTRATES THE POWER OF REAL-TIME MEASUREMENTS AFFORDED BY 21ST CENTURY TECHNOLOGY.

On Friday, December 4th, I conducted clandestine measurements in real time, inside and outside the 22,000 square foot bowling alley for four hours, from 6:30 PM to 10:30 PM. There were 206 bowlers, of whom an estimated 14% were smokers (an average of 4.6% actively smoking). As graphed in Figure 40, the average fine particle levels inside and outside were 432 µg/m³ and 5 µg/m³, respectively, indicating that fully 99% of the RSP was due to ETS. For carcinogens, those levels were 109 ng/m³ and 8 ng/m³, respectively, indicating that 93% of the PPAH was due to ETS. While the smoker density was quite low, at 0.13 active smokers per hundred cubic meters, so was the air exchange rate, at a stifling 0.2 air changes per hour, corresponding to carbon dioxide levels of 1406 ppm and 416 ppm indoors and outdoors respectively.

The fine particle levels in the Fairlanes averaged 50 to 100 times outdoors, and the carcinogen levels averaged about 100 ng/m^3, also about 50 to 100 times the outdoor levels. Over the course of an evening, at an estimated respiration rate of 1 m^3/hour, for 2 hours, the nonsmoking cook would have inhaled 200 ng of tobacco tar. Assuming he had been exposed like this for 200 days per year, for ten years, he would have inhaled 400,000 nanograms of particle-bound polycyclic hydrocarbons, in addition to the other several dozen carcinogens in tobacco smoke tar and gases, which certainly would have increased this short-order cook's risk of laryngeal cancer. It seemed to me to be an easily prosecuted case against the bowling alley management, but before I could finish my report, the cook got cold feet and abandoned his suit. Another unfortunate victim of secondhand smoke. And yet another indication of how secondhand smoke continued to pollute public venues even in the early years of the 21st century.

We had measured secondhand smoke in a bowling alley in Bowie, MD in 1978 (Repace and Lowrey, 1980); the level had averaged 202 µg/m^3, about half of the level I measured in Madison Heights in 2003. The outdoor level in Bowie had been 49 µg/m^3, (rather high by 21st Century standards) indicating that 76% of the indoor pollution was due to ETS. As a young man, I had enjoyed bowling, but soon gave it up due to the aggravation of my asthma by secondhand smoke pollution.

CHAPTER 17

THE INDUSTRY FALLS UNDER THE HAMMER

"TRENTON, N.J. (AP) Which is more harmful to your health, a smoky bar or a city street filled with diesel truck fumes? Well, you might want to skip your next happy hour. Smoky bars and casinos have up to 50 times more cancer-causing particles in the air than highways and city streets clogged with diesel trucks at rush hour, according to a study that also shows indoor air pollution virtually disappears once smoking is banned. Conducted by the researcher who first showed secondhand smoke causes thousands of U.S. lung cancer deaths each year, the study found casino and bar workers are exposed to particulate pollution at far greater levels than the government allows outdoors. ..."

Study: Air Worse in Smoky Bars than on Truck-choked Roads, *by Linda Johnson,*
The Associated Press, 2004-09-19 [1000 words]

Two thousand and four turned out to be inauspicious for the tobacco industry and totally excellent for me. The Justice Department had indicted the industry for a criminal conspiracy under the federal RICO statute on September 22, 1999. It finally came to trial in September 2004. In February of that year, I coauthored an article in the *American Journal of Preventive Medicine* titled The Tobacco Industry's Political Efforts to Derail the EPA Report of ETS (Muggli et al., 2004). Our paper discussed previously secret tobacco industry documents that detailed its nefarious political strategies aimed at derailing the 1993 EPA risk assessment on ETS.

We reported that the industry had lobbied the GHW Bush Administration to approve an executive order that would have: imposed new risk assessment standards for federal agencies, thus delaying the release of the EPA report; transferred ETS jurisdiction from the EPA to OSHA, thus obviating the need for the release of the EPA report; and had used the malevolent Congressman from Philip Morris to apply enormous political pressure on EPA by alleging improper procedure and policy at EPA. We documented how a single member of Congress in conjunction with his staff, tobacco industry attorneys, and industry executives plus a cherry-picked former North Carolina tobacco lobbyist and tobacco farmer, who as a federal judge, had successfully delayed legal implementation of the EPA risk assessment, placing a propaganda cloud over its validity. This lobbyist turned federal judge accomplished this simply by ruling in the industry's favor in its junk lawsuit against the risk assessment. EPA was not vindicated until December 2002, when the U.S. 4th Circuit Court of Appeals overturned Judge Osteen's ruling. The documents showed that the industry expended whatever effort was necessary to protect itself from public health policies that would adversely affect consumption of cigarettes and diminish its profits.

The Delaware Study Goes Viral

Before submitting the Delaware pre-and-post smoking ban study for publication, I had researched several journals. I settled on *The Journal of Occupational and Environmental Medicine (JOEM)*. *JOEM* published in-depth, peer-reviewed research articles to keep occupational and environmental medicine specialists up-to-date on new developments in the prevention, diagnosis, and rehabilitation of environmentally induced conditions and work-related injuries and illnesses. Since so much of my work had been of great interest to preventive medicine physicians and the public health community, I felt it was an appropriate venue. The editor decided to make it a Fast Track article. Papers selected for the Fast Track by *JOEM* were deemed "cutting-edge, groundbreaking, and high-impact papers of highest importance to the field." At 18 journal pages, it was a comprehensive experimental and theoretical study of air quality and ventilation pre-and-post smoking ban in the hospitality industry. The Delaware paper was published in the September 2004 issue. It delivered a catastrophic hit to the tobacco industry's global efforts to prevent smoking bans from taking hold. It drove a stake right through the heart of the tobacco industry's persistent propaganda about "people dust" and its bogus claim that "ventilation could control tobacco smoke pollution in workplaces." I endeavored to anticipate every scientific criticism that could be thrown at it by the industry and its moles (Repace, 2004).

Respirable Particles and Carcinogens in the Air of Delaware Hospitality Venues Before and After a Smoking Ban, began by reviewing the state of play with respect to hospitality industry smoking bans, as well as the industry's tiresome claims about ventilation and tobacco smoke. I then segued into a discussion of the theoretical determinants of secondhand smoke in the air, smoker density and air exchange rate. I presented a model that predicted the expected concentration of fine particles from secondhand smoke in Delaware bars and casinos given the state-wide smoking prevalence coupled with the code-specified ventilation rates. Next I presented experimental measurements demonstrating that fine particles and carcinogens were copiously emitted by tobacco products, and discussed the operation and experimental calibration of the data-logging monitors used in the study. I summarized the results of controlled experiments with these monitors that Wayne Ott and I had done at Stanford. They showed that secondhand smoke fine particle and carcinogen emissions tracked each other but that the carcinogens had higher decay rates. The pièce de résistance was the comparative field measurements made in the eight Delaware venues before and after the smoking ban. The results showed a strong statistical correlation between the airborne fine particle and carcinogen concentrations and the observed smoker density in those venues. They showed that variation in the measured concentration among the various venues could be explained by variations in smoker density and air exchange rates. And when the measured levels were compared to those on the nearby Interstate 95 during the peak 5 to 6 PM evening rush hour, they demonstrated that outdoor air was not a significant contributor to the indoor levels prior to the smoking ban.

The abstract posed a provocative question followed by the answer:

> *How do the concentrations of indoor air pollutants known to increase risk of respiratory disease, cancer, heart disease, and stroke change after a smoke-free workplace law? Real-time measurements were made of respirable particle (RSP) air pollution and particulate polycyclic aromatic hydrocarbons (PPAH), in a casino, six bars, and a pool hall before and after a smoking ban. Secondhand smoke contributed 90% to 95% of the RSP air pollution during smoking, and 85% to 95% of the carcinogenic PPAH, greatly exceeding levels of these contaminants encountered on major truck highways and polluted city streets. This air-quality survey demonstrates conclusively that the health of hospitality workers and patrons is endangered by tobacco smoke pollution. Smoke-free workplace laws eliminate that hazard and provide health protection impossible to achieve through ventilation or air cleaning* (Repace, 2004).

The model utilized the prevailing ASHRAE Ventilation Standard, the engineering design ventilation rates that were prescribed for well-ventilated premises based on their maximum occupancy per unit floor area. The model assumed default ceiling heights (they dropped out of the calculation). For smoking prevalence, I assumed that venue occupants had the Delaware statewide smoking prevalence of 23%. From this, the average smoker density that one would expect in each venue class (casino, bar, or pool hall) can be estimated. Plugging these values into the Habitual Smoker model allowed prediction of the fine particle air pollution level due to secondhand smoke, assuming that the average smoker smoked 2 cigarettes per hour and emitted 14 milligrams of tobacco tar per cigarette. The resultant modeled values, with outdoor RSP levels added from the Delaware State air monitoring network, would serve as ballpark numbers to expect in a field survey *and as a basis for generalizing the results to hospitality venues as a class, as well as to assess how well the ventilation system was actually controlling secondhand smoke pollution.* The US National Ambient Air Quality Standards (NAAQS) for fine particles ($PM_{2.5}$) were used evaluate the health effects of short-term (24-hour) exposure as well as the annual exposure of the workers. Violation of these health-based standards places the exposed population at increased risk of premature death, hospitalization, emergency room visits, and adverse respiratory effects from occupational exposure.

The amount of ventilation that would be required to meet the federal air quality standard in typical hospitality workplaces in Delaware could then be readily estimated. I concluded that at average smoking prevalence and full occupancy, at ASHRAE–prescribed ventilation rates, a restaurant, bar, or casino worker would breathe unclean air, i.e., secondhand smoke fine particle air pollution levels would violate the health-based NAAQS. This then formulated the hypothesis to be tested against the field measurements. In detail, I deployed carbon dioxide monitors to assess the ventilation. And by measuring the venues' space volumes, counting persons and smokers, and comparing the results pre- and post-smoking ban, plus measuring the outdoor levels, the contribution of smoking to indoor air pollution levels could then be assessed for each venue visited. From the controlled experiments, I could interpret the particle levels as a function of smoker density.

Pre-ban data (Figure 41) showed that the measured average of the fine particle air pollution levels for the eight venues, when expressed as an annual average exposure, violated EPA's annual NAAQS health-based outdoor air quality standard by a factor of 4.6, significantly increasing the hospitality workers' risk of respiratory disease. Moreover, the measured carcinogen levels due to smoking were 2½ times higher than on city streets and highways heavily polluted with outdoor air pollution from diesel trucks during rush hour. By contrast, the post-ban fine-particle levels (Figure 42) for every venue except the pool-hall did not differ from outdoor levels. However, the pool hall's carcinogen concentration had declined nearly 99% post-ban, indicating that the post-ban particle levels were not due to secondhand smoke. Put another way, the comparison of pre-ban and post-ban indoor air concentrations in Delaware's hospitality industry showed that 90% of the fine particle pollution and 95% of the airborne carcinogens were attributable to tobacco smoke. The results of my research, nearly 25 years after the *Science* paper of Repace and Lowrey (1980), stood the test of time. As discussed earlier, Wayne Ott had published similar results for fine particles in the *Journal of the Air and Waste Management Association* in 1996 in a two-year longitudinal study of fine particle levels in a single Redwood City Tavern before and after California's smoking ban. Figures 41 and 42 are the very same ones that induced gasps from the London audience in 2003. They would now provoke a firestorm all over America and beyond.

When I received the Robert Wood Johnson Foundation Grant, I was told that if my research turned out to be of general interest, I should alert M. Booth & Associates, RWJF's public relations firm in New York. Its VP, Dennis Tartaglia, worked with me on a press release. He managed to interest Linda Johnson, an Associated Press health and science reporter based in New Jersey, into doing a story. I gave Ms. Johnson a lengthy interview, walking her through the paper section by section; she was a quick study. Her subsequent

Associated Press story went viral. M. Booth's Preliminary Report to RWJF in September 2004 summarized the blockbuster coverage as follows:

"M Booth & Associates' communications program on James Repace's September 2004 *Journal of Occupational and Environmental Medicine* paper achieved outstanding results by many measures:

- Volume of coverage was extraordinary:
  - ○ More than 530,000,000 media impressions
  - ○ More than 500 stories ... and still counting
  - ○ National/international reach
- All Top 50 markets in U.S. - in print, online and broadcast media
- CNNInternational.com, *International Herald Tribune*
- Heavy representation in influential, top-tier media with broad reach
- AP (3 stories), UPI, *New York Times, Washington Post, Osgood File* (CBS), USA Today. com, CNN.fn, MSNBC.com, *Discovery Health Channel*
- Quality of coverage was 'exceptional:
  - ○ Most stories were in-depth (initial AP story was 1,000 words)
  - ○ Key messages highlighted in nearly all stories:
- 'Smoky bars are far worse than polluted highways.'
- 'Ventilation doesn't alleviate the problem.'
- 'Carcinogens virtually disappear after a smoking ban.'
  - ○ Mr. Repace's science supported in stories by key independent scientists
- Left little opportunity for industry 'junk science' charges
- Extensive initial media coverage created 'buzz' and stimulated additional coverage, including editorials in key newspapers that cited study results in calling for smoking bans
  - ○ Editorials in *Atlanta Journal-Constitution, Baltimore Sun, Cincinnati Enquirer, Milwaukee Journal Sentinel*
  - ○ Study cited in two additional Associated Press stories
- Local advocates, public health officials and hospitality workers capitalized on this media interest and used the paper to enhance their efforts to protect the public from secondhand smoke and generate additional news stories
  - ○ Advocates featured prominently in many stories
- Robert Wood Johnson Foundation's public health leadership spotlighted
- Innovation - and the work of a leading Innovator - showcased
- Coordination with RWJF and grantees enabled them to get information out to the community early - before the industry could respond.

Mr. Repace's study design – comparing air pollutants in smoky bars and casinos to those on busy interstates, tunnel toll booths and truck-choked city streets – provided a ready-made consumer story approach that we emphasized in our news release and media outreach. This comparison, the ineffectiveness of ventilation and the need to protect hospitality workers became the headlines for most stories written on the study: 'Air worse in smoky bars than on truck-choked streets.' – Chicago Tribune, 9/20/04; 'Smoking area filtration fails the sniff test.' Atlanta Journal-Constitution, 9/15/04; 'Secondhand smoke worse than firsthand exhaust.' Minneapolis Star Tribune, 9/20/04; 'Air Worse in bars than on street.' – Miami Herald, 9/21/04; 'Smoke bans a big help for casino workers.' San Francisco Chronicle, 9/21/04."

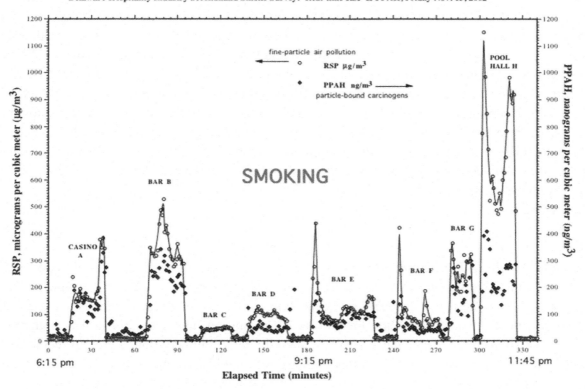

FIGURE 41. REAL-TIME RESPIRABLE-PARTICLE (RSP) AIR POLLUTION AND AIRBORNE CARCINOGENS (PPAH) IN A CASINO, 6 BARS, AND A POOL HALL BEFORE THE SMOKING BAN, NOVEMBER 15, 2002 (REPACE, 2004).

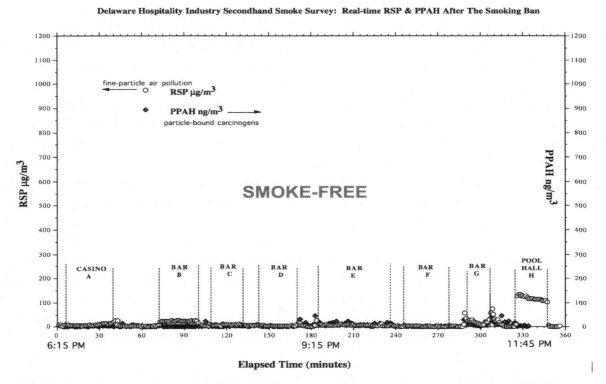

FIGURE 42. REAL-TIME RESPIRABLE-PARTICLE (RSP) AIR POLLUTION AND AIRBORNE CARCINOGENS (PPAH) IN A CASINO, 6 BARS, AND A POOL HALL AFTER THE SMOKING BAN, JANUARY 24, 2003 (REPACE, 2004).

In his cover letter to Prof. Jack Henningfield, who managed the Innovator Program at Johns Hopkins, Tartaglia reported: "In looking at the impact of this communications effort, I would say it is extremely significant, not just in terms of volume of coverage and numbers of people reached [media impressions] but in influence. The study had been cited repeatedly – in additional news stories and op-eds – and I suspect it will continue to be for quite some time. This means to me that the study has become one that people will talk about, that there is 'buzz,' and this is an indication that its influence will continue to spread." A year later, in December 2005, Henningfield's Johns Hopkins Medicine *Innovations* quarterly newsletter summed up the impact: "The effort resulted in international media coverage, reaching more than half a billion people through 530+ stories worldwide. Bolstered by the study, major newspapers issued editorials calling for clean indoor air policies. Local tobacco control advocates used the study to leverage their media efforts. The study was cited in newly introduced legislation across the U.S."

Major damage.

BAD ACTS

Meanwhile, fulfilling John Rupp's prophesy, the tobacco industry was indeed wallowing in the very deepest of shit. The Government's RICO case had been filed on September 22, 1999. In June of 2000, over the half-dead bodies of the House Republican Leadership, the House of Representatives had authorized the Justice Department to spend $12 million to fund its RICO lawsuit, under an amendment authored by the heroic Henry Waxman with the strong support of the Clinton Administration. It finally came to trial on September 13, 2004, coincidentally in the midst of the storm of publicity engendered by the AP article on the Delaware Study. The lead RICO prosecutor was Ms. Sharon Eubanks. (Sharon and I would do a YouTube Video, *Bad Acts*, together in 2014). Eubanks and her team of crack paralegals recognized early on that "the continuing bad acts that we needed to focus on for RICO purposes were to be found in the industry's conduct and behavior in the realm of secondhand smoke. The industry fought hard to keep secondhand smoke out of the case. They knew the facts surrounding secondhand smoke were detrimental to them, and that those facts had not yet been fully developed by any plaintiff in any litigation thus far" (Eubanks & Glantz, 2013).

Eubanks and her astute ETS paralegal, Betty DiRisio, discovered that British American Tobacco had acknowledged as long ago as 1986 that secondhand smoke issues were the most serious threat to their business. Betty had discovered Philip Morris's 'Operation Downunder,' formed in June 1987 at a meeting in Hilton Head, North Carolina, the very same one in which John Rupp had told the group that the industry was in 'deep shit' as a result of the 1986 Surgeon General's Report linking secondhand smoke with lung cancer, and that the industry had a 'serious credibility problem.' Eubanks said, "Stated simply, the secondhand smoke story was that, like the story on active smoking, the industry's conduct regarding passive smoking was equally full of fraud … The aims of the many different industry secondhand smoke organizations were to coordinate an official industry position on passive smoking and to fund projects supporting the industry's position that tobacco smoke was not a proven health risk to nonsmokers."

This trail of deceit led straight back to tobacco lawyer John Rupp. Eubanks continued, "When I examined John Rupp, I noticeably lost my cool: it was clear that I despised the man. I wasn't alone in that. John Rupp is the partner at … Covington and Burling who ruthlessly masterminded the industry's scientific and regulatory responses to secondhand smoke issues. He also worked extensively with the industry on lobbying efforts and prepared witnesses to testify at regulatory hearings. Gene Borio in his daily blog from the courtroom, *Tobacco on Trial*, observed 'The distaste for this witness in the visitor's gallery seemed palpable.' Borio's Blog for October 31, 2004, titled "The Repace Purge," related:

> "One of the oddest events of Mr. Rupp's 2nd day of testimony Thursday occurred during his
> cross …, when Mr. Rupp described an incident in which the industry had tried to get a scientist

(unnamed) removed from EPA's Risk Assessment study. Ms. Eubanks began her redirect by asking Mr. Rupp, 'That scientist was James Repace, wasn't it?' and then began a ringing defense of Repace, asserting that the TI had wanted Repace fired from the EPA. Some sample dialog (paraphrased): Ms. Eubanks: 'You took actions to get him in trouble, Yes or No.'"

"Mr. Rupp: 'No. ... We were not trying to cause him problems with his job, we were asking the EPA to eliminate what we saw as a conflict of interest. There were lots of other activities he could have done. Ms. Eubanks: You are not an official to make such a judgment. ... Ms. Eubanks' knowledge of this event and spirited defense of Mr. Repace startled me because: 1) Repace is mentioned only twice, and minimally, in the 1500 pages or so of the government 'Proposed Findings of Fact and Factual Memo, and 2) The dialog with Webb came late in the day – so her defense of Mr. Repace [bespoke] an extensive depth of knowledge of the issue that goes beyond even the government's case'" (Eubanks & Glantz, 2013).

The detailed transcript of Prosecutor Eubanks's re-direct examination of John Rupp's anti-Repace activities in the RICO Trial reads as follows [Pages 04337-04339]:
"THE COURT: All right. Ms. Eubanks?
REDIRECT EXAMINATION OF JOHN P. RUPP BY MS. EUBANKS:
Q. Mr. Rupp, we might as well get it out in the open, because it's in your written direct. This employee that you're talking about is Mr. Repace, isn't it?
A. Yes.
Q. And you did take actions, didn't you, to try to get Mr. Repace in trouble with the EPA while he was employed there, didn't you'?
A. No, you asked me that during my deposition.
Q. I'm asking you again, and I would like you to answer the questions 'yes' or 'no' without reference to your deposition, if you're in a position to do that, please.
A. The answer is no.
Q. You did not take any action at all that might have led to a disciplinary action against Mr. Repace, is that your testimony?
A. That is correct. We asked – we did not ask for disciplinary action.
Q. You asked that he be removed, did you not?
A. From the particular function with respect to ETS. We did not ask him to be fired or disciplined or otherwise disadvantaged in any way.
Q. Wait a minute, let's deal with that for a moment.
Mr. Repace was working on the EPA ETS Risk Assessment project?
A. Yes.
Q. That was a major part of his activity at the time, and you knew that, isn't that so'?
A. That is correct.
Q. And so –
A. That was the cause of our concern.
Q. And so, it's your testimony that you didn't undertake any action that would cause him problems with his job simply by suggesting that he be removed and work on some other project; is that correct?
A. The – may I answer?
Q. It's a 'yes' or 'no' question. Is that your testimony?
A. We were not trying to cause him any problems in his job. We were trying to ask the agency

– we were asking the agency to eliminate what we perceived to be a conflict of interest. There were lots of other activities that the EPA was involved in at that time.

Q. Mr. Rupp –

A. And a number of other activities that the EPA was involved in at that time, many of the things that Mr. Repace could have done –

Q. You were not an official at the EPA at the time to be in a position to make such a judgment about an employee and what it is that that employee could do. And isn't it true, that you never once suggested to the EPA particular other projects that would be appropriate for Mr. Repace because you saw that as not an appropriate role for you; isn't that correct?

MR. WEBB: Objection, that's a compound question. There were two different – I believe two different parts to that question.

THE COURT: I believe so, but I think you're focusing on the latter part.

MS. EUBANKS: That's correct, Your Honor.

THE WITNESS: We regarded it as inappropriate for us to tell the agency what things Mr. Repace ought to be assigned to do, that's true. But we certainly were not asking for any disciplinary proceeding. We were not asking for him to be removed from his job. We were simply pointing out what we believed to be a conflict of interest that had developed and urging the agency to deal with the conflict of interest before the project reached its conclusion."

So. From the mouth of one of its most faithful servants, Big Tobacco had kept close tabs on my activities at EPA, becoming well-informed of my doings by its spies and moles, coupled with its flagrant abuse of the Freedom of Information Act (FOIA). Like a striking cobra, The Tobacco Institute had unleashed their malicious minion Sundquist against me to thwart my ETS efforts, and by extension to disrupt EPA's efforts on secondhand smoke. No one else at EPA was driving this issue at this time. But when the Sundquist effort failed, the industry kept up its pressure by lobbying to have me forbidden to work on ETS, which would have had the same result. And much later, Rupp's description of the lobbying effort to quash my involvement in ETS raises the question – did Rupp's pressure result in Axelrad's edict essentially forbidding me from publishing papers on ETS as well as killing off the ETS Compendium? Was he the weakest link in the EPA chain of command, a useful idiot for the tobacco industry?

Gene Borio's Blog described the Sundquist-provoked Inspector General's investigation of me as "a rather ugly incident," quoting the infamous May 1987 Tobacco Institute memorandum that that orchestrated the investigation. Eubanks said that the government attorneys regularly read Borio's blog "for both comic relief and insight, as he was a daily observer in the courtroom and knowledgeable about the subject." Later in the trial, Eubanks wrote: "When one of the defendant's attorneys was arguing and using statements from Rupp to support his argument, Judge Kessler remarked, 'Do you expect me to believe anything that Mr. Rupp said?'"

Another shocking episode involved attorney Don Hoel, Shook Hardy and Bacon's long-time main ETS hatchet man. He had done his dirty work at the law firm for 30 years. Eubanks wrote, "Shook Hardy and Bacon, with Hoel's assistance, was instrumental in organizing the tobacco industry's response to the secondhand smoke issue on which he was particularly active and served on the Committee of Counsel." To appreciate what happened next, you would have to have experienced a withering cross-examination on the witness stand by a sharp lawyer. I have been through this dozens of times, and no matter how well-prepared you might be, it is never without apprehension and anxiety. It raises your blood pressure and heart rate. You have to have a thick skin to do it.

While Hoel surely must have been a very clever lawyer to become a major player in the tobacco wars, he had always been working in the shadows. Now he was in the full glare of a public trial, being forced to disclose the dark schemes that he had successfully kept closeted for decades. As Eubanks related, "Hoel had been on the stand for about an hour, and Gregg (a government prosecutor) was just getting warmed up." Hoel had been forced to concede points that would demonstrate the existence of a criminal (RICO) enterprise connecting the various defendant tobacco companies, which he surely realized. "Suddenly, Hoel collapsed on the stand and fell over on his face. Although paramedics soon arrived, he died a few hours later." *Sic transit gloria mundi.*

THE SAD CASE OF LARRY RAY THAXTON

Many of the victims of Hoel's efforts on behalf of the industry to deny the health risks of passive smoking did not live nearly as long, nor die such a quick and painless death. One of these was Mr. Larry Ray Thaxton, of Chattanooga, Tennessee. I watched his videotaped death-bed deposition: balded by radiation, face bloated with edema, weeping and wiping his eyes as he gasped out his agonized testimony. I had been retained as an expert witness in the case by attorney John Moss of the Atlanta law firm of Jones & Granger in 1998. After years of legal delays, the case was in the final stage before trial, with the deposition of expert witnesses. The lawsuit, *Thaxton vs. Norfolk Southern Railway et al.*, involved a railway workers' lung cancer from passive smoking, and on the 30th of December, I was deposed by the railroad's attorneys in Atlanta. The Thaxton Case is a classic illustration of the application of forensic science to estimate a worker's risk from toxic air pollutants on the job.

Larry Ray Thaxton was born on Feb. 13, 1956. He went to work as an outdoor laborer for the Norfolk Southern Railway at the age of 26 in 1982, laying track for a decade of his 14-year employment by the railroad. During this period, he often slept in company-owned bunk-trailers in the railroad's work-camps scattered throughout the South. Over these years, despite his repeated complaints, Larry Ray, a lifelong nonsmoker, was forced to share his cramped quarters with as many as five to ten smokers, who often stayed up playing cards through most of the night, exposing him to week-long overnight exposure to secondhand smoke. In depositions by John Moss, Thaxton's former co-workers described the conditions in the trailer: "A whitish gray cloud of smoke hung two feet off the ceiling; 70% to 80% of the gang were smokers" (JW); "At times the smoke was like a pool hall – it would be floating in the air, all the way to 1994" (EHL); "About 95% of the T&S 15 Gang smoked – they'd play cards in there every night, it got pretty thick in there, real foggy … they'd have windows open, doors, seven or eight people smoked" (SR); "I was an ex-smoker, but I couldn't stay in the smoke to talk or breathe, your nose would stop up, sometimes you couldn't see from one end to the other. After smoking was banned in 1994, guys continued to smoke" (EEP).

Larry Ray himself described the smoke as so thick that "you can see the smoke. You can wave it around, you could move it around." In October of 1995, Larry Ray was diagnosed with lung cancer at the age of 39. He filed suit against the Norfolk Southern Railway under the Federal Employers' Liability Act [45 USC, §51 et seq.], claiming that his lung cancer was caused by the environmental tobacco smoke from his co-workers during his overnight stays in the Railroad's sleeping trailers. Thaxton alleged that the Railroad had failed to provide him with a reasonably safe place to work in that he was repeatedly exposed to secondhand cigarette smoke. He also claimed that the defendants' medical agents failed to inform him in a timely fashion about a spot on his lung that they found during a chest X-ray and that because of this delay, the cancer grew and spread undetected in his body. In May of 1996, just eight months after his ominous diagnosis, Mr. Larry Ray Thaxton died from lung cancer at 40 years of age.

As an expert witness, I had to surmount two basic forensic challenges: First, I had to make a defensible estimate of Larry Ray's ETS exposure over a period of 14 years. Second, I had to estimate his baseline risk of lung cancer as a 39-year old nonsmoker, separately from the additional risk that his secondhand smoke bunk trailer exposure imposed, while taking into account any potential non-workplace exposure he might have gotten. At first blush, this appeared to be a formidable task. So I decided to attack this problem by reenacting the crime. One of the great advantages of being an expert witness in litigation is the ability to gain co-operation from one's opponents through the legal discovery process. I asked John Moss to request access to one of Norfolk Southern's bunk trailers. The railroad permitted us to use one the railroad's in its Sevier Trailer Camp in Knoxville, Tennessee. I then requested that he hire four smokers, so that I could conduct a controlled experiment to measure ETS fine particle concentrations and assess the trailer's air exchange rates from the decay curves with the doors open and closed.

On June 23 and 24, 1998, I re-enacted Larry Ray's exposure in a controlled experiment, using the four smokers recruited by John Moss, two women and their two adult daughters. Both Moss and the Railroad's attorney were present as observers the whole time. I wore a gas mask; neither lawyer was similarly equipped. During the experiments, the women smoked and played cards. I measured the trailer volume and deployed my Piezobalance at the opposite end of the trailer, to get a well-mixed measurement. On the first day, I measured fine particles with the trailers' two doors closed and the air conditioning on. The air exchange rate with the AC on and the doors closed was 1.7 air changes per hour (ach), determined from the slope of the $PM_{2.5}$ decay curve. The steady state $PM_{2.5}$ concentration from cigarette smoke rose from a nonsmoking background of 6 $\mu g/m^3$ to a whopping 2000 $\mu g/m^3$, double the "significant harm" level for outdoor air pollution episodes. With the doors at both ends open, the air exchange rate was 9.1 ach. Because of the high humidity penetrating in through the open doors, the Piezobalance began to malfunction, and I had to terminate the measurement. So, the steady-state ETS concentration in this case had to be estimated using mathematical modeling. It was 400 $\mu g/m^3$, comparable to a smoky bar.

Once the smoking had stopped, with the doors closed, the 95% removal time for the smoke was 6 hours, with the doors open, it took a little under 1 hour to clear. Figure 43 shows the experimental bunk trailer. The windows were at the upper and lower bunk levels. Our four Knoxville smokers had smoked up a storm, averaging 2.9 cigarettes per hour per smoker over the two days' experiments, about 50% higher than the U.S. average smoking rate Repace and Lowrey (1980) had estimated. As our smokers were packing up to leave, one of the older women asked, "What shall we do with our butts?" With a set-up like that I couldn't resist. I cracked deadpan, "You can haul your ashes on out of here." She remarked, smiling, "I see scientists do have a sense of humor."

FIGURE 43. THE BUNK TRAILER IN NORFOLK SOUTHERN'S SEVIER TRAILER CAMP, KNOXVILLE, TENNESSEE, IN WHICH I REENACTED LARRY RAY THAXTON'S SECONDHAND SMOKE EXPOSURE IN 1998 (AUTHOR'S PHOTO).

The smoke level with the trailer doors closed was identical to the level we had measured in the conference room experiment in 1978 with seven chain smokers, and the level with the trailer doors open was similar to the levels we had measured at a firehouse bingo game and a pizzeria in that paper. Using the habitual smoker model, I was able to generalize those measurements using the depositions of the T&S 15 Gang's description of the duration of the smoking and the open/closed status of windows and doors. I had bounded the range of exposure with my measurements and modeling, and from Larry Ray's deposition, determined the duration of his exposure. So, based on these, I could estimate his average exposure over the course of his employment. This neatly solved my first forensic problem.

The second one was to perform the complex risk assessment. Here, the first hurdle to surmount was how to estimate the cumulative lung cancer mortality rate for male nonsmokers in the 26 to 40-year age bracket. Searching through National Cancer Institute Monograph 8, I discovered the needed data from a table reporting the lung cancer death (LCD) rate in the American Cancer Society's (ACS) CPS II study of U.S. male nonsmokers by age group. Using curve fitting, I estimated a mathematical function from which I could calculate the cumulative LCD probability for a white male nonsmoker from ages 26 to 40. This would be my baseline.

I asked Steven Bayard to critically review my calculations. He observed that I had arrived at the correct answer, but that my method was not mathematically defensible. He pointed out the error, and I corrected it. Now that I was on solid ground, I posited that Mr. Thaxton's total lung cancer risk was composed of three parts: first, his background risk assuming zero secondhand smoke exposure, second, his added risk from social exposures to smoke outside of work, and third, his added risk from exposure in the railroad bunk trailers. His ETS lung cancer risk from his work (bunk trailer) and social passive smoking was proportional to the average exposure concentration in each setting, his average respiration rate during the exposure, and the duration of his exposure in each social or work setting, e.g., restaurants and bars, or the bunk trailers. (He had no home exposure as man or boy).

From our risk assessment paper, Repace and Lowrey (1985), I had previously estimated the ETS particulate exposure of a typical nonsmoker at 1430 micrograms per day. Using time-activity patterns for adult males, I estimated that the fraction of that exposure due to social exposures was 125 micrograms per day. Using data from the depositions, it appeared that Mr. Thaxton was exposed to the equivalent of nearly 8 smokers for 4 hours nightly for 182 days per year, over a period of ten years, assuming generously that the doors were open for half of the time. I added in a proximity factor to account for the very cramped quarters and short distance between him and his smoking bunkies, based on ETS research by my Stanford colleagues. I estimated his bunk trailer dose at about 3200 micrograms of tobacco tar per day over a ten-year period. That would be the rough equivalent of smoking nearly a thousand cigarettes, or 100 cigarettes per year. The second hurdle to jump was to determine "hazard functions" from which I could estimate the cumulative LCD mortality probability from background, plus the two sources of Larry Ray's ETS exposure: social, and bunk trailer.

I began with the American Cancer Society's (ACS) CPS II male curve of lung cancer mortality rates for a given five-year age group. CPS II was a study of 516,000 men ranging in age from 30 to 111 years, of whom ~413,000 were nonsmokers. In this manner, I was able to conclude from a comparison of the areas under the curves, that Larry Ray Thaxton's cumulative lung cancer death (LCD) risk was *doubled* relative to that observed in male nonsmokers in the ACS study, due to his secondhand smoke exposure in Norfolk Southern's Trailer Camps, as shown in Figure 44. The open circles are smokers' rates (for comparison) and the open squares are nonsmokers' rates in the ACS cohort, while the black diamonds are my estimates of Larry Ray's lung cancer risk rate as a function of age and exposure to ETS in the bunk trailer only. The ACS data are from the National Cancer Institute's *Smoking and Tobacco Control Monograph No. 8, 1996*, which is deservedly dedicated to Larry Garfinkel.

CPS II MALE NONSMOKERS, MR. THAXTON, & CPS II MALE SMOKERS

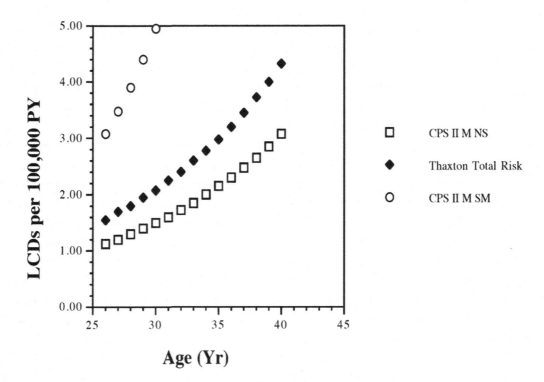

FIGURE 44. COMPARISONS OF THE OBSERVED LUNG CANCER RATES, AGES 25 TO 40, FOR THE AMERICAN CANCER SOCIETY'S ACS CPS II MALE NONSMOKERS (OPEN SQUARES) AND THE ACS CPS II MALE SMOKERS (OPEN CIRCLES), WITH MY ESTIMATED RATE FOR LARRY RAY THAXTON DUE TO HIS ETS EXPOSURE IN THE BUNK TRAILER (BLACK DIAMONDS). THE CUMULATIVE RISK FOR EACH SEGMENT IS ESTIMATED BY INTEGRATING THE AREA UNDER THE CURVES (REPACE JL, IN THAXTON V. NORFOLK SOUTHERN RAILWAY).

Before trial, my methodology had to survive the inevitable *Daubert* challenge. In previous litigation, I had been confronted many times with the following dilemma: how to combat a *Daubert* Motion to exclude my testimony either as beyond my demonstrated expertise, or as junk science invented out of whole cloth. As cheap fodder for mounting such challenges, there were bogus arguments compiled from a long history of tobacco industry attempts to discredit my work, using expensive PR campaigns, letters to the editor and papers published by its scientific, engineering, and medical moles over a 25-year period, plus attacks by congressmen designed to impugn my reputation. In response to such anticipated *Daubert* challenges, I had compiled lists of my peer-reviewed publications, papers written by experts in the field that used or commented on my measurements and risk models, references to my work in authoritative government reports, and speaking invitations at major universities, congress, and before government agencies. A highly condensed version as of 1998 gives the reader a sense of the arguments incorporated in my reports to successfully defend against the *Daubert* challenges that were brought in virtually every toxic tort lawsuit in which I had served as an expert witness (I updated it with each subsequent trial):

"I have authored or co-authored a total of 60 scientific publications in the scientific, medical, and engineering literature, 2/3 of them in peer-reviewed archival journals, of which 52 concern the hazard, exposure, dose, risk, and control of ETS. Since 1979 I have made approximately 250 presentations on ETS, including national and international scientific and medical meetings, lectures at U.S. and foreign universities, and testimony in both legislative and legal forums. I have served as a peer-reviewer for California's Tobacco Related Disease Program, on its Epidemiology and General Biomedical Peer Review Panels. Similarly, I served as a peer-reviewer on the National Cancer Institute's Special Study Section to award grants for epidemiological research on passive smoking.

The ETS measurements and the ETS exposure, dose, and risk models that I have published have achieved widespread scientific acceptance, sustained over a period of two decades. My exposure models have been cited in all the major reports on ETS in the U.S. (SG, 1986; NRC, 1986; NIOSH, 1991; EPA, 1992; CalEPA, 1997; and NTP, 2000). My exposure and risk models had been used by researchers in New Zealand, Canada, Scandinavia, and the U.S. to estimate the risk for lung cancer death from exposure to passive smoking and had been cited by numerous researchers, including Weiss (1985), Surgeon General (1986), NAS (1986), IARC, 1987; Kawachi et al. (1989), Wigle et al. (1987), Tancrede et al. (1987), Ott et al. (1992), EPA (1993), Jaakkola and Samet (1999), Spengler (1999) Samet and Wang (2000), Zitting et al. (2002) and Siegel and Skeer (2003)."

Following the railroad attorney's failure to mount a successful *Daubert* challenge to my report, coupled with compelling medical testimony from Thaxton's physicians, Thaxton v. Norfolk Southern settled out of court on January 19, 2006, for an estimated $2 million, on behalf of his widow, Jackie, and their now fatherless child.

THE ROSWELL PARK OUTREACH

Meanwhile, the damage to the tobacco industry from the Delaware study continued to mount. The world-wide publicity surrounding the research and the calls for smoking bans in the press fired up many researchers internationally who would replicate it in their own countries. One of the earliest efforts had its genesis when a young researcher, Mark Travers, a staffer at The Roswell Park Cancer Institute in Buffalo, NY, phoned me one day and asked if I could assist him with calibration of a compact new aerosol monitor, the TSI SidePak. He flew down, and we performed a calibration experiment together, using both my Piezobalance as well as the calibrated MIE monitors. We went to The Glory Days, a local pub, and ran them side-by-side in the smoky bar. We also measured the outdoor aerosol.

I was astonished to see the monitor reading over 100 μg/m^3 outdoors, instead of the expected 5 μg/m^3 to 10 μg/m^3. I thought my equipment was malfunctioning. Then I decided to check EPA's AirNow website. I found we were having a Code Orange Day for fine particle air pollution. I was measuring outdoor air pollution transported by the wind from poorly controlled mid-West coal-fired power plants, an unwelcome testament to interstate transport of pollutants. However, it served a very useful purpose of enabling a joint calibration of the SidePak on both secondhand smoke and the outdoor aerosol. We co-authored a paper on pre-ban and post-ban fine particle levels in 14 Western New York bars and restaurant/bars, just two months after the Delaware study appeared in print (Travers, et al., 2004). By June 2018, according to Google Scholar, my Delaware study would be cited 284 times in papers by other researchers, many of whom replicated the study using SidePak monitors loaned to them by the Roswell Park Cancer Institute's tobacco control program.

Mark's measurements replicated my Delaware findings: average fine particulate levels declined by 90%, from 412 μg/m^3 down to 27 μg/m^3, after implementation of New York State's Clean Indoor Air Law. The genie was now out of the bottle. Mark Travers would go on to become a prominent figure in secondhand smoke exposure research. And largely thanks to Mark, the TSI SidePak monitor, because of its small size and its user-friendly software, became the real-time particle monitor of choice for most secondhand smoke field studies. I bought two for future studies, retiring my two-foot-long hard-to-conceal MIE monitors with tandem monitor, pump, and battery, after several years of yeoman service.

Later, Roswell Park researchers, led by Andy Hyland, in a brilliant stroke, obtained grants from FAMRI and NCI to buy several dozen SidePak monitors, and established an international program in which they trained researchers in their use via a web-based training course, and loaned out the monitors gratis. Ultimately, Roswell Park' collaborators collected data in an astounding 32 countries: Argentina, Brazil, Canada, Mexico, United States, Uruguay, Venezuela, Armenia, Belgium, Faroe Islands, France, Germany, Greece, Ireland, Poland, Portugal, Romania, Spain, United Kingdom, Ghana, Lebanon, Pakistan, Syria, Tunisia, China, Laos, Malaysia, New Caledonia, New Zealand, Singapore, Thailand, Vietnam, and Ireland. In a paper published in *Tobacco Control* in 2008, Hyland et al., (2008) would report that "Levels of indoor fine particle air pollution in places with observed smoking are typically greater than what the World Health Organization and US Environmental Protection Agency have concluded is harmful to human health". The innovative Roswell Park program was an exemplary example of synergy in research. The momentum began to build internationally for smoke-free laws.

FLYING THE SMOKY SKIES

My FAMRI-commissioned paper, "Flying the smoky skies: secondhand smoke exposure of flight attendants", was published in *Tobacco Control* (Repace, 2004). Its objective was to assess the contribution of secondhand smoke (SHS) to aircraft cabin air pollution and flight attendants' secondhand smoke exposure relative to the general population. I analyzed all of the published air quality measurements on aircraft, and dosimetry studies performed on flight attendants, which I then generalized by modeling. Flight attendants reported suffering greatly from secondhand smoke pollution on aircraft. Both government and airline-sponsored studies had concluded that secondhand smoke created an air pollution problem in aircraft cabins. On the other hand, tobacco industry-sponsored studies yielding similar data concluded quite the opposite: that ventilation controlled secondhand smoke and that secondhand smoke pollution levels were low (Figure 45). Further, between the time that non-smoking sections were established on US carriers in 1973, and the two-hour US smoking ban in 1988, commercial aircraft ventilation rates had declined three times as fast as smoking prevalence. This led to the inescapable conclusion that "the aircraft cabin provided the least volume and lowest ventilation rate per smoker of any social venue, including stand up bars and smoking lounges, and afforded an abnormal respiratory environment."

Measurements of cabin pollution using personal monitors showed little difference in secondhand smoke exposures between flight attendants assigned to smoking sections and those assigned to non-smoking sections of aircraft cabins. I concluded that based on in-flight air quality measurements in 250 aircraft, generalized by modeling, when smoking was permitted aloft, 95% of the harmful respirable suspended particle (RSP) air pollution in the smoking sections and 85% of that in the non-smoking sections of aircraft cabins was caused by secondhand smoke. Typical levels of SHS-RSP on aircraft violated the then current fine particle federal air quality standard by an average of threefold for flight attendants and exceeded secondhand smoke irritation thresholds by 10 to 100 times. From cotinine dosimetry, I estimated that secondhand smoke exposure of typical flight attendants in aircraft cabins was 6-fold that of the average US worker, and 14-fold that of the average person. Thus, ventilation systems massively failed to control secondhand smoke air pollution in aircraft cabins. These results had adverse implications for the past and future health of flight attendants. In fact, three years later a survey of 1007 nonsmoking flight attendants who were exposed to secondhand smoke on aircraft found a significant association between hours of smoky cabin exposure and self-reported sinusitis, middle ear infections, and adult-onset asthma (Ebbert et al., 2007).

In a recent update on the sequellae of flight attendant's exposure to secondhand smoke on aircraft, Jacob et al. presented a poster, billed as a FAMRI Clinical Practice Health Report, at FAMRI's 15th Annual Scientific Symposium in Miami in 2016. Their study reported on health conditions suffered by 58-year old U.S. flight attendants who had experienced an average of 17 pre-ban years of in-flight exposure to

ETS, compared to controls who were selected from a statistical sampling of the US general nonsmoking population by CDC's NHANES National Cotinine Study. Jacobs et al (2016) reported that flight attendants had increased risk of thyroid disease, stroke and breast cancer relative to the general population controls aged 58 years. In addition, they had higher rates of sinus conditions, asthma, chronic bronchitis, shortness of breath, cough, and nasal congestion.

SECONDHAND SMOKE ON CRUISE SHIPS

In October 2004, I presented a paper on outdoor air pollution from secondhand smoke on cruise ships at the 14th Annual Conference of the International Society of Exposure Analysis, in Philadelphia. My field study was conducted on two cruise ships underway at 20 knots at sea in the Caribbean. It showed that secondhand smoke in various smoking-permitted outdoor areas of the ship tripled the level of carcinogens to which nonsmokers were exposed relative to indoor and outdoor areas in which smoking did not occur, despite the strong breezes and unlimited dispersion volume (Figures 46 & 47).

Moreover, outdoor smoking areas were contaminated with carcinogens to nearly the same extent as a popular casino on board in which smoking was permitted. These were, as far as I know, the first and only indoor/outdoor measurements of secondhand smoke on cruise ships ever made. I took data during two otherwise delightful ten-day cruises to the Caribbean.

According to Cruise Fever (2018) "many changes have been made in the cruise industry in the last 10 years in regards to smoking. The trend has been for tighter restrictions on cruise ships just like we have seen in public areas and restaurants on land. Even if a large number of cruisers on ships want to smoke, the cruise lines have been listening to complaints aboard their ships and with smoke being so hard to contain, more restrictions have been the result." Most of a dozen cruise lines reviewed now ban smoking in cabins and on balconies, and most permit smoking only in limited outdoor areas or in certain lounges and casinos.

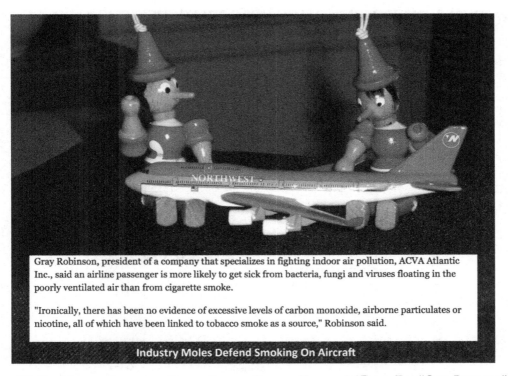

Gray Robinson, president of a company that specializes in fighting indoor air pollution, ACVA Atlantic Inc., said an airline passenger is more likely to get sick from bacteria, fungi and viruses floating in the poorly ventilated air than from cigarette smoke.

"Ironically, there has been no evidence of excessive levels of carbon monoxide, airborne particulates or nicotine, all of which have been linked to tobacco smoke as a source," Robinson said.

Industry Moles Defend Smoking On Aircraft

FIGURE 45. TEXT SOURCE: PERMANENT BAN ON AIRLINER SMOKING URGED – LATIMES. THE "GRAY ROBINSON" WAS A MISIDENTIFIED REFERENCE TO GRAY ROBERTSON, LATER OF HBI, INC. (AUTHOR'S PHOTO ART).

HTTP://ARTICLES.LATIMES.COM/1989-06-22/BUSINESS/FI-3269_1_CIGARETTE-SMOKE-FLIGHTS-AIRLINE.

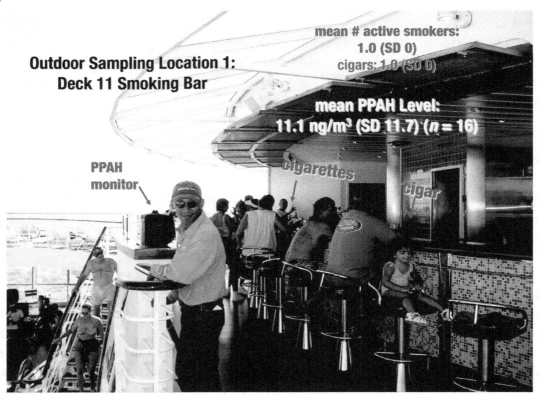

FIGURE 46. MEASURING OUTDOOR AIR POLLUTION ON A CRUISE SHIP (REPACE, 2004).

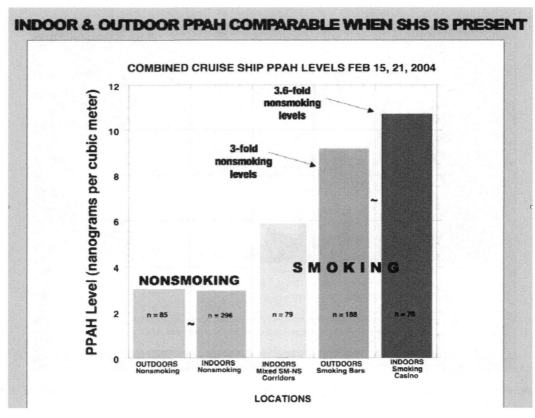

FIGURE 47. INDOOR & OUTDOOR AIR POLLUTION ON A CRUISE SHIP (REPACE, 2004).

THE DIKE BREAKS

On the 29th of March 2004, Ireland became the first country in the world to introduce a smoking ban in indoor workplaces. Smoking was banned in all bars, restaurants, cafes, and hotels (excluding bedrooms, outdoor areas, and properly designed smoking shelters). The ban aimed to protect workers, particularly those in the hospitality industry, from the adverse health consequences of secondhand smoke exposure, including lung cancer, coronary heart disease, and asthma (Mulcahy et al., 2005). A decade later, the ban was celebrated in an article in the *Irish Independent,* by Anita Guidera – 20 JANUARY 2014:

> *"No Smoking! Ireland makes history with cigarette ban. HISTORY was made in March 2004 when Ireland became the first country in the world to introduce comprehensive legislation banning smoking in workplaces. Months beforehand, fuming publicans claimed the ban would sound the death knell for the Irish pub, and threatened legal challenge to the impending legislation being spearheaded by Health and Children Minister Micheal Martin. In Cork, they called for the minister to be sacked for "being a zealot." But on March 29, the ban went ahead, and overnight, ashtrays vanished from over 10,000 pubs, as well as clubs and restaurants. Those caught smoking faced a hefty €3,000 fine."*

It preceded the June 2004 Norwegian ban, which had been voted in earlier, but delayed in its implementation. I had lectured in Norway in 1990, 1996, and again in April 2004, at the behest of the Norwegian Office of Tobacco Control. The Norwegian ban was reported by BBC News, on Tuesday, 1 June 2004:

> *"Norwegians ban smoking in bars - Norway has introduced a nationwide ban on smoking in restaurants and bars - following a similar move in Ireland. The Norwegian government says the ban is needed to protect people who work in the catering industry from the effects of second-hand smoke. Opinion polls suggest a majority of Norwegians support the change, which permits smoking outdoors. Ireland introduced its ban in March, and has hailed the move as a success. Other countries including Tanzania, South Africa and the Netherlands, as well as parts of the US, have also introduced bans or restrictions."*

Similarly, I had lectured in New Zealand in 1990, and again in 1999, firing up efforts to ban smoking in public places. In 1985, New Zealand had launched its first comprehensive tobacco control program. At that time, "smoking was common in offices, even in the Department of Health." A 1990 law, the Smoke-free Environments Act, made offices smoke-free. Finally on 3 December 2003, the Parliament amended the 1990 law, and on December 10, 2004, New Zealand became the world's third country with a national smoke-free law. The law covered all indoor public workplaces and hospitality venues, passenger aircraft, pubs, bars, nightclubs, charter club bars, restaurants and casinos. Subsequent studies have shown very high levels of compliance. (Laugeson, 2004; Wikipedia, 2017). National smoke-free workplace laws enacted by the Irish, Norwegian, and New Zealand governments launched international shock waves that would sweep around the globe like a tsunami, greatly damaging tobacco industry efforts to oppose smoking bans throughout Europe and beyond.

JOUSTING WITH BAT IN HONG KONG

On the 24th of October 2005, sponsored by the Hong Kong Council on Smoking and Health (HKCOSH) I made a return visit to Hong Kong, where I would engaged in scientific combat with a professional bloviator for British American Tobacco. I was housed in a university-owned pagoda high up in the hills of Hong Kong, with a panoramic view of the city. They served breakfast, lunch, and dinner to guests. Tony picked me up the day of my testimony before the Hong Kong Legislative Council (locally known as "LegCo" – pronounced ledge-co). On the way, he pointed out a large skyscraper with numerous portholes for windows. He said, "we call it the house of a thousand assholes." (I am not making this up, you can Google it). It would be a good site for BAT's Hong Kong office.

The issue in front of LegCo was Bill 2005, which proposed to ban smoking in all workplaces, including the hospitality industry. The LegCo proposal stated that:

"Following a consultation exercise conducted in mid 2001, anti-smoking advocates, the healthcare sector and the majority of the public have been urging the Administration to implement a smoking ban in indoor workplaces and public places. At the sitting of the Legislative Council on 20 October 2004, the motion calling for expeditious implementation of a total smoking ban in workplaces, restaurants and indoor public areas was carried by a large margin. Internationally, the adoption of the Framework Convention on Tobacco Control (FCTC) by the World Health Organization (WHO) in May 2003 has heightened momentum for tightening tobacco control laws worldwide."

On my way to the witness table, a Chinese gentleman sitting in an empty row quietly slipped a thin folder under my arm as I passed him. An usher then directed me to sit at the witness table alongside an Englishman, who I was astonished to learn, was none other than the Dark Prince of BAT himself: Chris Proctor, Head of Science & Regulatory Affairs for British American Tobacco. Proctor testified first, spouting the usual industry drivel that "the health effects of passive smoking were unproven," and that "although ETS might be irritating or offensive to some, it could be controlled by a combination of ventilation and designated smoking rooms." He reprised the arguments made earlier by Philip Ho Wing-Hong, corporate and regulatory affairs manager of British American Tobacco Hong Kong, who said the tobacco industry was willing to introduce overseas ventilation technology to the city. Ho had asserted that, "At some places like bars on higher floors, mahjong parlours and saunas, a total smoking ban is difficult. In Malaysia a very strict air quality standard was being set," he said. "Operators could decide which method to use to improve air quality, whether by strengthening the ventilation system or banning smoking." As Proctor blathered on, I perused the folder I had been surreptitiously given – it turned out to be a copy of his slides. How very convenient. I had not anticipated a debate, but as I went through my own presentation, a computer slide presentation with 45 slides, this copy of Proctor's slides enabled me to rebut his testimony point by point by point (Figure 48). My prepared testimony had anticipated BAT's arguments, and emphasized the inability of ventilation to control secondhand smoke and the hazards of smoking rooms to nonsmokers who had to work in them:

CONTROLLING TOBACCO SMOKE POLLUTION:
VENTILATION, SMOKING ROOMS, SMOKING BANS –
WHAT WORKS AND WHAT DOESN'T?

1. Secondhand Smoke kills: cancer, heart disease, respiratory disease – all caused by exposure.
2. Risks from Secondhand Smoke are very high particularly in the HK entertainment and hospitality industries: 150 estimated deaths per year among 200,000 catering workers.
3. Engineering controls such as ventilation or air cleaning are condemned as unacceptable by engineering and occupational health authorities because they fail to eliminate Secondhand Smoke.
4. To produce acceptable risk using ventilation or air cleaning requires tornado-like ventilation rates.
5. Air quality studies in casinos, pubs, and restaurants show that Secondhand Smoke contributes 90-95% of harmful respirable particulate and carcinogen pollution.

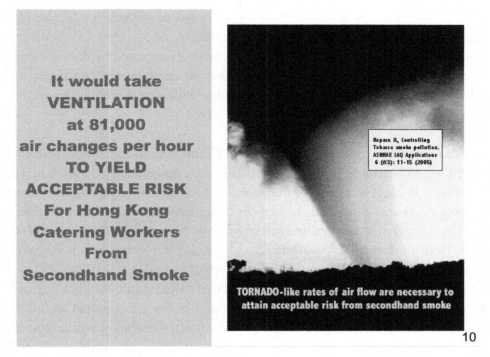

Figure 48. Slide from my presentation to Hong Kong's LegCo hitting BAT where it hurts.

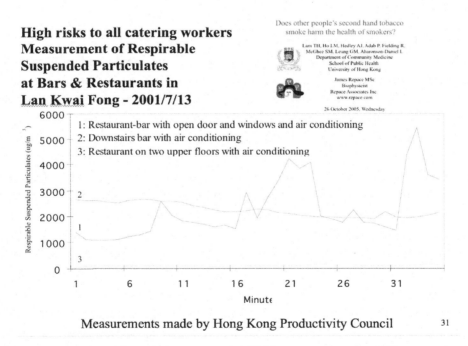

Figure 49. Slide from Tony Hedley's presentation at HKU showing enormous RSP levels in restaurants and bars in the Lan Kwai Fong district of Hong Kong.

6. Air quality studies demonstrate that Secondhand Smoke creates far worse pollution than heavy automobile and truck traffic.

7. Designated smoking rooms, even when well-designed, will leak toxic smoke into nonsmoking areas.

8. Designated smoking rooms significantly increase the risk to smokers from each other's Secondhand Smoke.

9. Smoking bans reduce pollution in hospitality venues to outdoor air levels. Workplace smoking bans reduce smoking prevalence.

10. Rumored economic losses from smoking bans are not supported by data in New York City, which experienced a surge in hospitality cash receipts and employment, in the year following the ban. New York's 2003 smoking ban continues to enjoy widespread public support. New York smoking prevalence is 21.6% compared to Hong Kong's 16%."

Tony Hedley, Sarah McGhee, and another member of their department sat high in the visitors' gallery watching the proceedings. Afterwards, Tony told me that Proctor had made "ugly faces and ape-like gestures" during my presentation. I thought this echo of Perfidious Albion was not helpful to his cause. The following day, I participated in a press conference on *Hazards of Designated Smoking Rooms to Smokers* given at the Hong Kong University School of Medicine, and in a seminar on *Secondhand Smoking and Health* (Figure 49).

Two years later, BAT's effort to defeat Hong Kong's smoke-free workplace law would finally go up in smoke. On January 1st 2007, Hong Kong would revise its Smoking Ordinance (Cap. 371) to include all indoor workplaces. Most public places, including restaurants, internet cafés, public lavatories, as well as beaches and most public parks were included in the law. Some bars, karaoke parlors, saunas and nightclubs were exempted until July 1, 2009. (Smoking in unventilated saunas? Really?). Previous smoke-free regulations that covered elevators, public transport, cinemas, concert halls, airport terminals and escalators dated back to between 1982 and 1997. Smoke-free requirements in shopping centers, department stores, supermarkets, banks, game arcades had previously been enacted in July 1998.

A Pyrrhic Victory For The Government

In February 2005, the U.S. Government's RICO suit rested, and the defendant tobacco companies put on their defense. Lorillard's attorneys attacked the government's witnesses and attempted to repair the damage the government's cross-examination did to its witnesses. BAT had engaged in such lies, misrepresentations, and blatant non-compliance with court orders in its defense that Judge Kessler slapped it with a $250,000 fine. Philip Morris laughably asserted that it had "turned around and was now a socially responsible company," but its failure to comply with court orders by destroying documents, plus objecting to every question when it was cross-examined resulted in a $2.75 million fine, and the exclusion of the testimony of eleven of its perfidious witnesses. Reynolds defended itself with a "take-no-prisoners tobacco lawyer with dirty hands" who had engaged in the cover-up himself but proved to be an inept defense counsel. Only Liggett, to its credit, would admit that nicotine was addictive and that smoking caused diseases. Prosecutor Eubanks affirmed that "we had little trust for anything defense counsel said that could not be independently verified." While the government won its case, it was a Pyrrhic Victory: Eubanks had asked for a $280 billion disgorgement penalty, which had been endorsed by Judge Kessler, but the DC Court of Appeals overturned it. So the industry did not have to pay through its snotty nose. This was a "body blow" to the government's case. (Eubanks & Glantz, 2013). The case went to Judge Gladys Kessler for a final decision, which would be issued in 2006. And I would be astonished by her verdict on the secondhand smoke count.

ASHRAE ISSUES A POSITION DOCUMENT ON ETS

In another major blow to Big Tobacco, on June 30th 2005, The ASHRAE Board of Directors issued a *Position Document on Environmental Tobacco Smoke*. This was an unequivocal statement that supported Repace and Lowrey's long-standing contention that secondhand smoke could not be controlled by ventilation. It pulled no punches.

"ASHRAE concludes that:

- "It is the consensus of the medical community and its cognizant authorities that ETS is a health risk, causing lung cancer and heart disease in adults, and exacerbation of asthma, lower respiratory illnesses and other adverse health effects on the respiratory health of children.

- At present, the only means of effectively eliminating health risk associated with indoor exposure is to ban smoking activity.

- Although complete physical separation and isolation of smoking rooms can control ETS exposure in nonsmoking spaces in the same building, adverse health effects for the occupants of the smoking room cannot be controlled by ventilation.

- No other engineering approaches, including current and advanced dilution ventilation or air cleaning technologies, have been demonstrated or should be relied upon to control health risks from ETS exposure in spaces where smoking occurs. Some engineering measures may reduce exposure to some degree while also addressing to some extent the comfort issues of odor and some forms of irritation.

- An increasing number of local and national governments, as well as many private building owners, are adopting and implementing bans on indoor smoking.

- At a minimum, ASHRAE members must abide by local regulations and building codes and stay aware of changes in areas where they practice, and should educate and inform their clients of the substantial limitations and the available benefits of engineering controls.

- Because of ASHRAE's mission to act for the benefit of the public, it encourages elimination of smoking in the indoor environment as the optimal way to minimize ETS exposure."

OUTDOOR SECONDHAND SMOKE ON THE UMBC CAMPUS

Over the course of 2005, I gave 17 talks. One of these summarized a report of my study of outdoor air pollution from secondhand smoke on the campus of the University of Maryland at Baltimore (UMBC). It was commissioned by the University's Health Unit to overcome the skeptical faculty senate's reluctance to support an outdoor smoking ban within any number of feet from building doorways, unless there was hard data to support it. Complaints from nonsmoking students and faculty apparently did not count. I seized the opportunity to ask the Health Unit to recruit ten student smokers; they were induced to cooperate by $10 gift certificates to the student bookstore. I made controlled measurements with the smokers arrayed in a ring of chairs centered around my real-time particle and carcinogen monitors and kept expanding the circle to see how the outdoor smoke levels declined with distance from a point source. I found that the smoke level did not approach background until about 7 meters, or 23 feet, from the source. The experiment was designed with smokers arrayed on chairs in a ring around the monitor such that the smoke impacting the monitors was due to a single smoker (since the wind blew from only one direction at a time). To the best of my knowledge, these were the first controlled experiments ever made of outdoor secondhand smoke. Figure 50 shows the monitors and the smoker array, and Figure 51 shows the results. The faculty senate passed the ban the following year, and the Staff Handbook was revised to state:

"It is the policy of UMBC to regulate smoking on University properties since tobacco smoke has been found to be a Class A human carcinogen. This policy is designed to protect and enhance outdoor and indoor air quality in the University's buildings and to contribute to the health and well-being of the UMBC community, in general. Smoking is prohibited within 20 feet of all building openings including doorways, air or ventilation intake systems, entryways, and windows. Smoking is also prohibited on UMBC's main street area (from the entrance to the Kuhn Library to the street adjacent to the Administration and Recreational Activity Center), and the patio area outside the Commons."

I would make good use of this data a decade later. In September of 2015, among several other witnesses, I was invited to testify on a bill to ban smoking on outdoor terraces of bars and restaurants in Quebec by the Coalition québécoise pour le contrôle du tabac. I flew to Quebec City and testified on Bill 44, *An Act To Bolster Tobacco Control,* before a committee of the National Assembly. A study commissioned by The Union of Bar Owners of Quebec had asserted that "Air quality on open-air terraces would not be significantly affected by smokers," if separated by just 1.5 meters (a bit less than five feet). I observed that their claim was contradicted by three different U.S. studies, two of which were mine, which showed that harmful levels of secondhand smoke fine particles and carcinogens from a single cigarette smoked on outdoor terraces occurred at downwind distances measurable out to 7 meters, and that nonsmoking wait staff serving the smoking sections would be surrounded by a sea of smoke. I further pointed out that since the UMBC study showed that secondhand smoke pollutants decline inversely with distance, smoke from multiple smokers would reach out proportionally to greater distances, and thus the smoking sections proposed by The Union of Bar Owners of Quebec must be rejected [Repace, 2015].

And so it was: on 26 November 2015 the Quebec National Assembly passed Bill 44. It mandated the following:

"This Act ... prohibits smoking in motor vehicles in which a minor under 16 years of age is present, in outdoor play areas intended for children, on the grounds of vacation camps and at skating rinks that are used by minors, and on terraces. It also prohibits smoking within a nine-metre radius from any door, air vent or window communicating with enclosed spaces to which the public has admittance."

FIGURE 50. VOLUNTEER STUDENT SMOKERS AT THE UMBC CAMPUS SURROUNDING THE RSP AND CARCINOGEN MONITORS IN THE ROLL-ON BAGS (CENTER) (AUTHOR'S PHOTO).

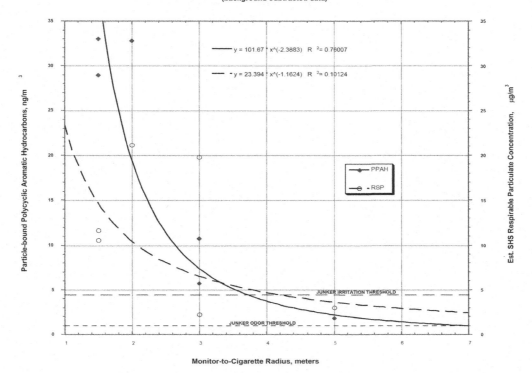

FIGURE 51. A PLOT OF THE FINE PARTICLES AND CARCINOGENS VS. DISTANCE FROM THE SMOKERS TO THE MONITORS (AUTHOR'S SLIDE).

CHAPTER 18

NOBODY FOOLS WITH RICO

"Internally, Defendants Recognized That ETS is Hazardous to Nonsmokers.
Defendants recognized that secondhand smoke contained high concentrations of
carcinogens and other harmful agents. Defendants also recognized that the research
from the public health community showing that ETS caused disease was persuasive
evidence of the harmful effects of secondhand smoke and could be adverse to their
position. Most importantly, research funded by Defendants themselves provided
evidence confirming the public health authorities' warnings that nonsmokers exposure
to cigarette smoke was a health hazard. ... Internally, Defendants expressed concern
that the mounting evidence on ETS posed a grave threat to their industry. ... Defendants
undertook joint efforts to undermine and discredit the scientific consensus that ETS
causes disease. ... Defendants acted through a web of coordinated and interrelated
international and domestic organizations."

United States of America et al. v. Philip Morris USA, et al., Civil Action No. 99-2496 (GK)

On August 15, 2006, the federal government dealt the industry a massive blow. Judge Gladys Kessler ruled in the federal RICO case, finding that the defendant tobacco companies had violated the Racketeer Influenced and Corrupt Organizations Act (RICO), liberally tarring the industry's lawyers with a large brush and bushels of feathers: "At every stage lawyers played an absolutely central role in the creating and perpetuating of the Enterprise and the implementation of fraudulent schemes. They devised and coordinated both national and international strategy; they directed scientists as to what research they should and should not undertake; they vetted scientific research papers and reports as well as public relations materials to ensure that the interests of the Enterprise would be protected; they identified 'friendly' scientific witnesses, subsidized them with grants from the Center for Tobacco Research and the Center for Indoor Air Research, paid them enormous fees, and often hid the relationship between those witnesses and the industry; and they devised and carried out document destruction policies and took shelter behind baseless assertions of the attorney-client privilege." The judge imposed injunctive remedies against Philip Morris, Altria, R.J. Reynolds, Brown and Williamson, Lorillard, American Tobacco, and BATCo. Among these were the abolition of the Council for Tobacco Research, The Tobacco Institute, and the Center for Indoor Air Research, plus making corrective disclosures about addiction, the adverse health consequences of smoking and secondhand smoke, and the manipulation of cigarette design. In addition, the verdict imposed the obligation on those companies to create document repositories providing government and public access to all industry documents disclosed in litigation (Eubanks & Glantz, 2013).

Stan Glantz took full advantage of this, incorporating all those documents into the UCSF's Legacy Tobacco Documents Library (LTDL) database [later renamed Truth Tobacco Industry Documents (TTID)]. As of May 31, 2018, TTID contained 89,863,283 OCR-searchable pages in 14,793,283 formerly secret internal industry documents. Stan created it in 2002 through a multi-million dollar grant from the American Legacy Foundation, placing it in the UCSF Library and Center for Knowledge Management. Nearly two-thirds of the documents were from the decades 1980 to 2000. Less than 0.2% are post-2000's. About 10% were undated. TTID was built to house and maintain tobacco industry internal corporate documents produced during litigation between 46 U.S. States and the seven major tobacco industry organizations. These internal documents allowed access to the clandestine history of the workings of this vast racketeering enterprise run by corporate criminals in business suits and their shyster lawyers. Stan himself was one of the two major scientist enemies of the industry; typing "Glantz" in the search field yielded 22,300 documents as of August 8, 2017. The other one was yours truly: typing in "Repace" yielded 22,659 documents. The industry hated me about as much as they hated Stan, a legend in tobacco control. By comparison, "Koop" (Surgeon General C. Everett Koop) was the king of search hits, with 41,536 documents found. "Shopland" generated 9,030 hits, and Don was mentioned in a Philip Morris document thusly: "Shopland is the former Director of the Office of Smoking and Health. He remarked in 1986 that 'of all the issues, this [ETS] is the one that will propel the United States toward a smoke-free society'" [TTID 2023988627].

The part of Judge Kessler's Final Amended Opinion in the Tobacco Industry's RICO conviction that dealt with ETS fraud by the industry covered 196 pages, nearly 12% of her 1682 page opinion, indicating its widespread scope. The United States established by a preponderance of the evidence that Defendants and others comprised an association-in-fact enterprise ("Enterprise") and that each Defendant participated in the conduct, management, and operation of the Enterprise through a pattern of racketeering activity in violation of 18 U.S.C. § 1962(c). The racketeers included Philip Morris, R.J. Reynolds, Brown & Williamson, a subsidiary of British American Tobacco, American Tobacco, Lorillard, and Liggett. One of the major counts in the Racketeering conviction was the '**Defendants Have Publicly Denied What They Internally Acknowledged: that ETS Is Hazardous to Nonsmokers**' [Boldface mine].

Judge Kessler (2006) concluded in part:

"Defendants' collective effort to maintain an open question as to the health effects of cigarette smoking was not limited to whether cigarettes caused disease in smokers themselves. During the 1970s, scientific evidence suggesting that exposure to cigarette smoke was hazardous to nonsmokers began to grow, and public health authorities began to warn of a potential health risk to both adults and children. Fearing government regulation to restrict smoking in public places and sensing a decrease in the social acceptability of smoking, Defendants were faced with a major threat to their profits. In 1974, Tobacco Institute chairman Horace Kornegay warned that smoking restrictions not only impacted sales but also 'could lead to the virtual elimination of cigarette smoking.' … Reynolds CEO Ed Horrigan wrote Lorillard executives in 1982: 'We all know that probably the biggest threat to our industry is the issue of passive smoking.' ... A 1986 BATCo document stated: 'The world tobacco industry sees the ETS issue as the most serious threat to our whole business.' …

Philip Morris Companies Vice Chairman Bill Murray was advised at a presentation by Project Downunder Conference attendees, in 1987: 'The situation can't get any worse. Sales are down, can't be attributed to taxes or price increases. ETS is the link between smokers and non-smokers and is, thus, the anti's [anti-smoking activists] silver bullet.' … In response, Defendants crafted and implemented a broad strategy to undermine and distort the evidence indicting passive smoke as a health hazard. Defendants' initiatives and public statements with respect to passive smoking attempted to deceive the public, distort the scientific record, avoid adverse findings by government agencies, and forestall indoor air restrictions. Defendants' conduct with respect to passive smoking continues to this day, when currently no Defendant publicly admits that passive exposure to cigarette smoke causes disease or other adverse health effects. ...

The first industry committee dedicated specifically to addressing ETS concerns was formed as early as 1975. The committee, chaired by Shook, Hardy & Bacon counsel Don Hoel, met under the direction of the Research Liaison Committee to address ETS-specific projects which, at the time, were funded via Special Account 4. Regular members of this committee, sometimes referred to as the Public Smoking Committee or Advisory Group, included company scientists from Reynolds, Philip Morris, B&W, and Lorillard. Defendants reestablished this committee in 1984 under the name of the Tobacco Institute ETS Advisory Group, or TI-ETSAG. ETSAG met almost monthly to propose, review, and manage scientific projects that the Committee of Counsel approved for funding. Regular members of ETSAG also included company scientists from Reynolds, Philip Morris, B&W, and Lorillard, in addition to Tobacco Institute representatives, Don Hoel, and Covington & Burling attorney John Rupp. While neither Liggett nor American directly participated in ETSAG, both participated with the funding of approved projects (Kessler, 2006).

The Center for Indoor Air Research ('CIAR') was formally established in 1988 to carry out industry-funded research related to passive smoking; the original charter members were Defendants Philip Morris, Reynolds, and Lorillard. Moreover, a large number of industry-favorable CIAR projects were approved directly by the CIAR Board of Directors without any review by its SAB [Science Advisory Board]. These committees and organizations furthered Defendants' collective goals by: (1) coordinating and funding Defendants' efforts to generate evidence to support its position that there remained an 'open controversy' as to the health implications of exposure to ETS; (2) leading the attack on the Government's efforts to act on evidence linking ETS to disease; and, (3) in the case of CIAR, appearing to be an independent research funding organization when it was really a facade for concealing industry participation in certain studies.

There is overwhelming evidence demonstrating Defendants' recognition that their economic interests would best be served by pursuing a united front on smoking and health issues and by a global coordination of their activities to protect and enhance their market positions in their respective countries. To further their shared objectives, the Defendants, over an extended period of time, created, controlled, used, or participated in an astonishing array of international entities, including, among many others (all of which will be discussed infra), the Tobacco Manufacturers' Standing Committee ('TMSC'), which became the Tobacco Research Council ('TRC') and then the Tobacco Advisory Council ('TAC'); the International Committee on Smoking Issues ('ICOSI'), which became the International Tobacco Information Center, Inc. ('INFOTAB') and then the International Tobacco Documentation Center ('TDC'); and the Center for Cooperation in Scientific Research Relative to Tobacco/Centre de Coopération pour les Recherches Scientifiques Relatives au Tabac ('CORESTA').

It is clear ... that the following individuals ... each played a central role in coordinating Defendants' efforts and ensuring that a united front was developed and followed on smoking and health issues: Sharon [Boyse] Blackie, a BAT scientist; John Rupp, Covington & Burling attorney; Charles Green, RJR Principal Scientist; Helmut Reif, Principal Scientist at a Philip

Morris subsidiary and member of CIAR Board of Directors; Richard Carchman, Philip Morris Director of Scientific Affairs; J. Kendrick Wells III, B&W General Counsel; and Christopher Proctor, BATCo Head of Scientific & Regulatory Affairs at Chadbourne & Parke in United States between 1989 and 1993. …Through the consultancy program, the tobacco industry was successful in reaching 'public, scientific and governmental audiences.' In the words of B&W counsel Kendrick Wells: 'The consultants groups' operation is essentially a public relations program, not a scientific operation.' … in a Philip Morris January 31, 1989 report titled 'Boca Raton Action Plan,' the company details its worldwide ETS initiatives, including placing consultants in scientific seminars, using consultants to resist aircraft smoking bans, using consultants to oppose restaurant smoking restrictions, the creation of Burson-Marsteller 'News Bureau' programs in Europe for media distribution, and the coordination with other industry groups, such as INFOTAB and CORESTA.

Defendants sponsored and planned various ETS symposia or conferences throughout the world to generate data which supported the industry's ETS position. These conferences included a 1974 Bermuda conference, a 1983 Geneva workshop, a 1984 Vienna conference, a 1987 Tokyo conference, the 1989 McGill 'symposium,' and others. The presentations made at these conferences were thereafter publicized in the United States by Defendants as examples of independent scientific statements in support of the industry's position that ETS was not a proven health hazard. In a June 28, 1998 memorandum from Hoel to Philip Morris's Todd Sollis describing Shook, Hardy & Bacon's ETS efforts for the industry, Hoel bragged: Since 1974, SHB has been actively engaged in the organization and development of ETS conferences and symposia. … Once the proceedings from these conferences are published, they provide information that is useful in dealing with the attacks of anti-smoking activities" [Kessler, 2006].

I was well aware of these workshops. I avidly collected the proceedings, which I used to guide my research. I had a useful rule of thumb: if the industry or its moles asserted the truth of statement, it was almost invariably false. For example, "ETS is only a minor source of indoor air pollution;" "ETS can be controlled by ventilation;" "You would have to spend 1000 hours in a smoky room to inhale the equivalent of a single cigarette;" "Odds ratios less than 2 are unreliable;" "Hirayama's study is not valid;" "the Garfinkel study contradicts the Hirayama study;" "misclassification of smokers as nonsmokers is responsible for spurious results in epi studies of passive smoking and lung cancer;" "nicotine and RSP are unreliable markers for ETS;" "cotinine in nonsmokers is mainly due to dietary intake, not ETS;" "body cotinine cannot be used to predict atmospheric exposure to nicotine;" "there are very few if any deaths attributable to ETS exposure;" "the exposure-response curve from active smoking to passive smoking is linear." And on, and on. To paraphrase Aleksandr Solzhenitsyn, Such arguments were little more than quasi-sophisticated disinformation, dressed up like an aging prostitute with the cosmetics of science.

Deliberate inhalation of tobacco smoke caused premature mortality at the levels to which smokers were exposed. The more they smoked, the quicker they died. There was a known exposure-response relationship. Common sense dictated that since there was no known threshold for effect, there must be a risk at low doses. Moreover, despite the crude methods that epidemiologists had to assess ETS exposure, i.e., spousal smoking status, lung cancer and heart disease mortality were actually being observed at environmental levels of exposure to secondhand smoke. And this occurred despite the "low doses" being two orders of magnitude lower than the doses of smoke inhaled by active smoking. This implied to me that this relationship was non-linear and likely increased steeply from low levels of exposure to high, saturating at the high exposures experienced by active smokers. Lowrey and I, in rebutting linearity arguments by industry consultant Peter Lee in a letter to *Environment International* in 1992, demonstrated this for lung cancer (Repace and Lowrey, 1992) [In fact Pope et al. (2011) would show a similar non-linear effect for heart disease mortality as well]. As physical scientists, Lowrey and I were familiar with non-linearity in physical and chemical processes, and of course biological processes are based on physics and chemistry.

To recapitulate why our work posed such a threat to the industry: there was reliable concentration data coming from the Leaderer-Hammond chamber experiments at Yale in the early 1980's showing a stable relationship between nicotine and RSP, and our ETS concentration model applied to their data was able to predict the levels of RSP as a function of ventilation rate over a broad range of rates comparable to those found in mechanically ventilated buildings (Repace and Lowrey, 1982). By the early 1990's, I discovered that a simple mass-balance model could be used to predict the levels of body fluid cotinine from atmospheric nicotine, and that atmospheric nicotine could be used to estimate atmospheric fine particle air pollution concentrations. Further, by applying the methods of industrial hygiene to measuring environmental concentrations of ETS, we had been able to compare our measurements to EPA's health-based outdoor air standards to show that indoor fine particle air pollution from ETS was usually much worse than outdoors, which was already being subject to control via the Clean Air Act. As physical scientists, we used a standard scientific paradigm: develop a theoretical framework, called a "model" which incorporated all of the basic physical and biological parameters in an Occam's Razor approach, also known as the KISS Principle (*Keep It Simple, Stupid.*) Then compare the predictions of the model to observations. And finally, publish the results in peer-reviewed journals, and present them to scientific and medical audiences to get experts in the field to critique the results. Our research had survived these tests. This gave us a significant advantage over the vast majority of industry moles.

By sheer serendipity, I found myself in a position where I had a national platform and a certain amount of political protection, although at the time I never gave it a conscious thought. My conviction that secondhand smoke contaminated buildings, that it could sicken and kill, and that the only reliable method of protection against this toxic substance was to make workplaces smoke-free, began to permeate the body politic. And so, conflict with this powerful and ruthless industry was inevitable.

I was surprised to learn that Lowrey and I were mentioned in Judge Kessler's RICO decision, and formed a significant part of both the government's ETS case and her decision (Kessler, 2006):

> **"a. The Development of the Consensus**
>
> ¶3326. In 1980, following the lead of earlier researchers, James Repace of the United States Environmental Protection Agency and Alfred Lowrey of the United States Naval Research Laboratory conducted measurements of respirable particulates (hazardous particles less than 4 microns in size in the air) in cocktail lounges, restaurants, and public halls in both the presence and absence of smoking. Repace and Lowrey found that short-term measurements in rooms with smokers yielded high respirable particulate concentrations, varying from 100 to 1000 micrograms per cubic meter. …
>
> ETSAG [the ETS Advisory Group] funded projects as CTR Special Projects, with no SAB review, because the ETSAG 'was more litigation oriented.' Another purpose of the ETSAG was to fund projects in order to 'get scientific publications that would be of use in litigation.' … The Hoel Committee reported to and provided updates to the Committee of Counsel, which was authorized to approve ETS projects for funding. … From 1984 to 1988, the ETSAG was responsible for developing and managing the following passive smoking projects, all funded through CTR as Special Projects, without the approval of its Scientific Advisory Board:
>
> **ORNL Personal Nicotine Monitor**, developed by Roger Jenkins and Michael Guerin at the Oak Ridge National Laboratory (ORNL) and Reynolds. The project involved the

development and field testing of the personal nicotine monitor originally designed and developed by Dr. Muramatsu of the Japan Tobacco and Salt Public Corporation [JTI]. The method of measurement was intended to reveal that nicotine levels in ambient air were very low. Approved funding via ETSAG: $855,000.

Indoor air particulate sampling, by Salvatore DiNardi. The purpose of this project was to 'refute [the] oft-cited paper of Repace and Lowrey (1980),' concluding that nonsmokers were exposed to high levels of airborne particulate due to ETS. Approved funding via ETSAG: $688,878.

Indoor air testing/surveys, by ACVA. The purpose of the project was to show that the 'vast majority of [indoor air] complaints are directly caused by airborne dust, bacteria, and/ or fungi' as well as poor ventilation, 'and not to the presence of ETS.' Approved funding via ETSAG: $13,800.

Portable air sampler, developed by Reynolds. The purpose of the sampler was to take 'measurements' of air in aircraft, restaurants, homes, and workplaces, to show that everyday indoor air contains very small amounts of ETS. While the sampler was created by Reynolds, 'scientists from PM, B&W, Lorillard and Reynolds will participate.' Testing was carried out in numerous cities – including New York, Ottawa, Dallas, and others – using the Reynolds apparatus. The results were then used to resist smoking restrictions in those cities.

Epidemiological and other scientific critiques, by industry consultants Lee Husting, Theodor Sterling, David Sterling, Demetrios Moschandreas, Marvin Kastenbaum, and James Kilpatrick. The purpose of these critiques was to cast doubt on the epidemiological studies showing an association between passive smoking and lung cancer. Known approved funding via ETSAG: $198,034 (Husting); $70,000 (D. Sterling).

ETS allergy testing, by Tulane University researchers John Salvaggio and Samuel Lehrer. In Hoel's words, 'it is expected that even the extreme case of the allergic asthmatic will not show physiological responses to ETS.' Approved funding via ETSAG: $263,117.

Aircraft cabin air quality measurements, by R.J. Reynolds using the R.J. Reynolds sampler apparatus described above. Lawyers reviewed all project proposals prior to funding and papers prior to publication. For example, a November 21, 1986 legal bill from Shook, Hardy & Bacon to Philip Morris, Reynolds, Lorillard, and B&W listed the following work under the heading of 'Science and Research: [R]eview Sterling memorandum re Vancouver ETS seminar; attorneys and analysts conference re Dr. First and ETS Advisory Group projects . . . review Koo manuscript . . . review DiNardi proposal . . . review ORNL paper submission on ETS; review IITRI project proposals and abstract . . . telephone conference with Dr. Sterling regarding clearance of manuscript . . . review and analyze ETS Advisory Group agenda . . . review research project and send to general counsel . . . correspondence and telex to Dr. Rylander . . . telephone conference with Dr. Sterling regarding clearance of paper on smoking by occupation.' . . .

Numerous meeting minutes and summaries illustrate the extent to which ETSAG group members, particularly attorneys from Shook, Hardy & Bacon and Covington & Burling, designed, monitored, and carefully controlled projects initiated by the group. ... The ETSAG reviewed and edited papers written by researchers it had not funded, but were funded by other industry organizations. For example, a record of the May 22, 1986 ETSAG meeting recorded the following with respect to a paper by long-time industry consultant Theodor Sterling critiquing the model used by Repace in estimating annual deaths attributable to ETS: 'Sterling on Repace – Kastenbaum (TI) has had a conversation with Sterling suggesting he rewrite his papers before submitting for publication. The consensus is that Sterling has a good series of papers on Repace but needs to rewrite. Especially noted is the need not to appear to support the Repace model. . . . Hoel will follow up.' ...

Defendants coordinated the actions of the ETSAG with those of other international industry bodies. For example, on April 8, 1986, a joint meeting of the ETS Advisory Groups from the United States, the United Kingdom, Germany, and INFOTAB took place in London 'to discuss scientific and public relations problems relating to environmental tobacco smoke' and to 'avoid duplication of the various efforts.' Osdene and Green presented a summary of ETSAG projects to the assembled group. ... For two days in March 1987, the entire ETSAG met with representatives of the U.K. Tobacco Advisory Council (TAC), the German Verband der Cigarettenindustrie (VdC), and Japan Tobacco (JTI) at the L'Enfant Plaza Hotel in Washington, D.C. Each group presented its projects for discussion at this meeting. A public affairs presentation at this joint meeting stated that the industry needed to have a 'systematic programme of research designed to refute the major allegations made against us.' In addition, 'Successful PA work on ETS will depend on the case remaining 'not proven,' and the need to ask you to keep producing work that challenges the anti-smokers' argument.' Participants also agreed that the ETS research needed to utilize 'neutral scientists' and the ETS issue needed to be expanded into overall 'ambient air quality.'

In 1991, the book '*Other People's Tobacco Smoke*,' a compilation of articles, all written by tobacco industry consultants, was published. The book was edited by A.K. Armitage, industry consultant and member of ARIA. However, the only mention of industry involvement was one half of a sentence by the editors at the end of a brief 'Acknowledgments' paragraph thanking both their wives and Philip Morris International for their 'cooperation and assistance.' The Tobacco Institute also tried to create the illusion of independence in its press releases and other publications attacking research implicating ETS as a cause of disease.

These press releases cited industry consultants and conferences without reference to their tobacco industry source, instead describing them as: • 'independent scientific teams' (referring to IT Corporation, a Special Account 4 recipient) • 'an expert on substances in indoor air' (referring to David Weeks, a paid industry ETS consultant) • 'a prestigious panel of scientists at an international symposium' (referring to the industry's ETS consultants at the McGill Symposium) • 'a US lawyer specializing in antitrust and trade regulation law' (referring to John Rupp). • 'Maurice LeVois, Peter Lee, and Joseph Fleiss' (long-time paid industry consultants) who all provided an 'objective review'. • 'independent scientists' Flamm and LeVois (noting ties to Federal Government including FDA, CDC, VA, but failing to disclose ties to tobacco industry). • '[a]n independent analysis of more than 300 major private and public buildings by ACVA Atlantic, Inc., an indoor air quality analysis firm, identified tobacco smoke as a major contributing factor to air quality complaints in only four percent – twelve buildings.'

The articles, letters, and submissions of the industry consultants to regulatory bodies were sometimes reviewed and edited by lawyers prior to publication. *For example, written responses by industry ETS Consultant Peter Lee to James Repace and Judson Wells were revised by both Shook, Hardy & Bacon and Covington & Burling prior to submission to a journal* [italics mine]. Similarly, Covington & Burling made revisions prior to submission to an article criticizing the EPA risk assessment by industry ETS consultants Flamm and Todhunter, and a letter to the editor by ETS Consultant Gio Gori criticizing an adverse study by Brownson.

(3) The 1992 HBI 585 Building Study. In 1989, CIAR funded a project by industry consultant 'Gray' Robertson and HBI … to assess indoor air quality and ETS in offices. The project cost $138,387 and resulted in the 1992 published paper 'The Measurement of Environmental Tobacco Smoke in 585 Office Environments' (the '585 Building Study'). The paper concluded that ETS components in 'typical office workspaces' were lower than had been previously reported. In conducting the study, HBI falsified and manipulated the data. HBI field technician Gregory Wulchin testified at trial that he conducted a number of the ETS inspections underlying HBI's published 585 building study.

Wulchin examined eight of his ETS field reports that were included in the data underlying the published paper and found that false data entries had been made. Wulchin testified that at least one of his data sheets had been altered by Robertson. Wulchin identified similar errors transposing several other data recordings that had been made by other HBI technicians. In addition, Wulchin testified that the readings in two of his field reports demonstrated unacceptably high levels of particulate from cigarette smoking in rooms where there was good ventilation.

As a result of these irregularities and others, Wulchin testified, 'My experience with HBI data as well as [my] review of HBI reports, leads me to conclude that HBI's data contained unexplained entries that raise serious questions about the integrity of its studies.' The Court credits his testimony for the following reasons: Wulchin was a former employee who harbored no animus against HBI; he had nothing to gain from testimony that was adverse to HBI; his testimony was specific and internally consistent; under cross-examination, he was neither evasive nor hostile.

After the 585 Building Study was published, the results and data were the subject of a 1994 Congressional examination. The Subcommittee on Health and the Environment obtained HBI's then-existing ETS data forms and compared them to the data that was submitted in an interim report to CIAR. Discrepancies were identified that would have affected the levels of ETS reported by HBI's study. Wulchin confirmed that HBI's data collection forms were often changed to minimize measurements of ETS: 'It is my belief that there were other instances in which HBI reduced field measurements of high levels of particulates in rooms where smoking occurred. . . I conducted a number of tests summarized in the CIAR report. My review of the report indicates that HBI mischaracterized and made numerous alternations in the data I collected.'

Some of the criticisms made by HBI employees and tobacco industry scientists about HBI methodology were also made by James Repace, EPA, and Alfred Lowrey, Naval Research Laboratory, widely published authors on ETS and indoor air quality, in a 1992 letter to the editor shortly after the 585 Building Study was published. For example, from the data provided in the paper, Repace and Lowrey were able to determine that HBI took measurements of smoking areas within larger rooms, and HBI did not report the volume of any rooms in which readings were taken.

In addition, Repace and Lowrey criticized the lack of science underlying the study: air exchange rates were not reported; the number of buildings was not reported; the locale of the buildings was not reported; the types of buildings were not reported; the ages of the buildings were not reported; the types of air handling systems were not reported; the time of year recordings were made was not reported; the proximity of the detector to smokers was not reported; and there was no discussion of or comparison with earlier findings, as would normally be the case in scientific studies. (See also [1986] Surgeon General's Report, stating number of cigarettes burned, the size of the room, the effective ventilation rate, and smoke residence time are all important variables in determining levels of secondhand smoke exposure).

Defendants themselves recognized the flaws in Robertson's scientific methodology. In April 1991, even before the allegations of scientific fraud publicly surfaced the following year CIAR Board members Spears (Lorillard), Green (Reynolds), and Pages (Philip Morris), discussed a proposal by HBI to gather additional data related to ETS and indoor air quality. CIAR rejected funding the proposal because it lacked scientific merit. Despite the evidence of scientific fraud, in March 1992 the Tobacco Institute cited the 585 Building Study as scientific authority in its comments opposing adoption of OSHA's IAQ Rule. (Reynolds' 1992 OSHA submission).

As recently as 2000, the HBI paper was cited by industry consultant Roger Jenkins in a journal article. The published paper on the 585 Building Study acknowledged, 'Funding for this work was made available in part by the Center for Indoor Air Research, Linthicum, Maryland.' As detailed above … this statement does not provide the reader an accurate picture of Robertson/HBI's long-standing, lucrative financial relationship with the tobacco industry.

…

Conclusions: Scientists have been concerned about the health effects of environmental tobacco smoke since at least the late 1960s, after the issuance of the Surgeon General's Report on Smoking and Health. However, no scientific consensus about the hazards of ETS to non-smokers (particularly to babies and young children), as well as to smokers who also inhale the sidestream smoke which is a component of ETS, was reached until 1986. That year the Surgeon General issued his Report concluding that ETS is a cause of disease and that children of smoking parents have a higher frequency of respiratory infections and symptoms; the National Research Council of the National Academy of Sciences issued its report on '*Environmental Tobacco Smoke, Measuring Exposures and Assessing Health Effects*,' concluding that ETS increases the incidence of lung cancer in nonsmokers and that children of smoking parents suffer greater respiratory problems; and the World Health Organization's International Agency for Research on Cancer (IARC) issued its Monograph concluding that tobacco smoke is carcinogenic to humans.

Significantly, Defendants were well aware of, and worried about, this issue as early as 1961 when a Philip Morris scientist presented a paper showing that 84% of cigarette smoke was composed of sidestream smoke, and that sidestream smoke contained carcinogens. In addition to understanding, early on, that there was a strong possibility that ETS posed a serious health danger to smokers, Defendants also understood the financial ramifications of such a conclusion. In 1974, the Tobacco Institute's president Horace Kornegay acknowledged that indoor air restrictions designed to defuse the passive smoking issue 'could lead to the virtual elimination of cigarette smoking.' In 1980, the CEO of R.J. Reynolds, Ed Horrigan, stated that 'We all know that probably the biggest threat to our industry is the issue of passive smoking.' In the 1990s, a Philip Morris report identified 'the social acceptability of smoking practices [as] the most critical issue that our industry is facing today. … Attacks on acceptability are almost exclusively based on claims that ETS can cause diseases in the exposed population.' Despite the fact that Defendants' own scientists were increasingly persuaded of the strength of the research showing the dangers of ETS to nonsmokers, Defendants mounted a comprehensive, coordinated, international effort to undermine and discredit this research. Defendants poured money and resources into establishing a network of interlocking organizations.

They identified, trained, and subsidized 'friendly' scientists through their Global Consultancy Program, and sponsored symposia all over the world from Vienna to Tokyo to Bermuda to Canada featuring those 'friendly' scientists, without revealing their substantial financial ties to Defendants. They conducted a mammoth national and international public relations campaign to criticize and trivialize scientific reports demonstrating the health hazards of ETS to nonsmokers and smokers. Defendants still continue to deny the full extent to which ETS can harm nonsmokers and smokers. Some Defendants, such as BATCo, R.J. Reynolds, and Lorillard, flatly deny that secondhand smoke causes disease and other adverse health effects; some, such as Brown & Williamson, claim it's still 'an open question'; and others, such as Philip Morris, say that they don't take a position and that the public should follow the recommendations of the public health authorities. To this day, no Defendant fully acknowledges that the danger exists" [Kessler, 2006].

In the 1930 film, *Little Caesar*, Edward G. Robinson, playing the gangster Rico Bandello, a scion of organized crime, drawls: "Nobody fools with Rico, see, nobody!" At the bitter end, he is gunned down by the law.

THE BLACK DOG BITES

In June of 2006, the second Surgeon General's Report dealing with secondhand smoke in ten years was published. It was titled, *The Health Consequences of Involuntary Exposure to Tobacco Smoke*. The Surgeon General declared that secondhand smoke killed an estimated 3,000 plus adult nonsmokers from lung cancer, approximately 46,000 from coronary heart disease, and 430 newborns from sudden infant death syndrome. annually. In addition, secondhand smoke caused other respiratory problems in nonsmokers such as coughing, phlegm, and reduced lung function. The Report endorsed the notion that the estimated number of deaths from coronary heart disease was 15 times as great as those from lung cancer. This was a tremendous vindication of Jud Wells' seminal work.

The 2006 Report quoted my papers 19 times, including those in *Science, Risk Analysis, the British Medical Journal, the Maryland Medical Journal, Tobacco Control, the Journal of Occupational and Environmental Medicine, The American Journal of Public Health, Chest, Archives of Pediatric & Adolescent Medicine,* and even a lengthy report on ETS and Ventilation that I did for the California EPA in 2000. My 2006 paper in *JOEM*, Correlating Atmospheric and Biological Markers in Studies of Secondhand Tobacco Smoke and Dose in Children and Adults, on pharmacokinetic modeling of nicotine and cotinine was described as a "major addition to the literature." This was a significant endorsement of the quality and importance of our publications, in sharp contradistinction to the attacks by the tobacco industry and its moles.

In November of 2006, our Black Dog Pub Study, embellished by data from two restaurant bars in Mesa Arizona and six nonsmoking Ottawa bars, took a healthy bite out of the industry's high-tech ventilation arguments. It was a fantastic present for my 68th birthday. Another 700-word AP Wire Service story appeared, this time touting our Black Dog/Mesa paper, Can Displacement Ventilation Control Secondhand ETS? co-authored with Ken Johnson, which had appeared in *ASHRAE IAQ Applications* in its Fall 2006 issue. The AP article was published on November 1, 2006, By LINDA A. JOHNSON (no relation to Ken), Associated Press Writer, Trenton, N.J.

"Study: New ventilation systems don't clear smoke as touted
By LINDA A. JOHNSON, Associated Press Writer, Nov. 1st 2006, Trenton, N.J.

State-of-the-art ventilation systems used to clear cigarette smoke from bars and restaurants don't eliminate dangerous soot and carcinogens and can push their levels higher in non-smoking sections than in smoking areas, researchers concluded. ... Two Mesa, AZ restaurants that had claimed their ventilation systems would comply with that city's smoke-free restaurant law were included in the study, published Tuesday by an engineering journal... . But contaminants monitored in the restaurants' nonsmoking sections were higher than in their bars and many times worse than outdoor air, said lead researcher James Repace, a second-hand smoke expert and visiting professor at Tufts University School of Medicine."

I stated that the study demonstrated that the high-tech displacement systems promoted by the tobacco and casino industries to control tobacco smoke failed to do their job. Hammering the point home, I noted that, "You'd need tornado-like ventilation." The AP article observed that the following week, three states: Ohio, Arizona, and Nevada had ballot initiatives to ban smoking in public places, along with alternatives supported by the R.J. Reynolds Tobacco Co. to exempt bars, casinos or other adult venues. ... It reported that in one Mesa venue, I had measured the average levels of inhalable particles that raise risk of heart and lung disease at three times the level in the nonsmoking section than in the smoking area. And that carcinogenic polycyclic aromatic hydrocarbons, were 50 percent higher in the nonsmoking restaurant area than in the contiguous smoking bar. ... Then it mentioned the Black Dog study in Toronto that had "soot and carcinogen" levels in its nonsmoking section much higher than in six Canadian smoking bars with normal ventilation systems measured in Ottawa, and that the post-ban carcinogen measurements had dropped to the outdoor level while the "soot levels fell sharply."

The article quoted Patrick Breysse, then an environmental health sciences professor at Johns Hopkins Bloomberg School of Public Health (and since 2014, Director of CDC's National Center for Environmental Health and the Agency for Toxic Substances and Disease Registry, ATSDR), Gil Cormier, chairman of American Industrial Hygiene Association's indoor air quality committee, and Terry Pechacek, a CDC scientist who worked on the Surgeon General's report, all of whom supported our study's conclusions. The AP reported that the 2006 U.S. Surgeon General report on secondhand smoke as well as "the top U.S. standard setters on ventilation," ASHRAE, which published the study, both concluded ventilation technology could not control secondhand smoke" (Johnson, AP, 2006). As late as 2006, as Judge Kessler concluded, the industry was still actively resisting workplace smoking bans. On December 11th, Dennis Tartaglia sent me another telephone-book thick compilation of media coverage, relating the delicious fact that three more states passed state-wide smoke-free workplace bans. Arizona's ban was sweeping; New Jersey's law covered all workplaces, including restaurants and bars, but exempted casinos, while Nevada's statute covered workplaces, including restaurants, although it also exempted its massive casino industry, home to 54% of the nation's commercial casinos.

The publicity had generated over 60 million media impressions the previous month. In addition to the *AP* story, it was carried by two other news syndicators, *Health Day* and *Scripps-Howard*. Among many newspapers, *The New York Times* carried it both in print and on-line, while the *Washington Post* carried it online. *The Christian Broadcast News* network, heard in over 200 countries, also carried it. I discussed it live on the Tavis Smiley Show for 7½ minutes, broadcast by Public Radio International over 727 affiliated stations and XM Satellite radio. Maximum damage. When added to the publicity over the Delaware paper in 2004, the total media hits for my two papers combined reached 700 million. I think RWJF got their PR money's worth.

However, Rush Limbaugh, the wingnut talk-show host, vehemently disagreed. Surfing the waves of bloviation in a November 2nd 2006 broadcast, he quoted from the AP article, playing the Smoke Nazi Joker right out of the Tobacco Institute's well-worn rigged deck of cards:

"Smoking Ventilation Systems DO Work

BEGIN TRANSCRIPT (in part). RUSH: this is an AP story – 'Study: New air systems don't clear smoke – State-of-the-art ventilation systems used to clear cigarette smoke from bars and restaurants don't eliminate dangerous soot and carcinogens and can even push their levels higher in nonsmoking sections than in smoking areas, researchers concluded. Their findings from three restaurants in a little studied field come just a week before voters in Arizona, Nevada and Ohio consider dueling smoking-related initiatives.' " … Now, the … ventilation system is called thermal displacement. … Thermal displacement is entirely different. … How do I know this? Because I have it. … I am a regular cigar smoker. … 'They've been heavily promoted by the tobacco industry and the casino industry as a way to accommodate both smokers and nonsmokers, Repace said.' … But the idea that it doesn't work is bogus, and I wanted to get my two cents in on this simply because … I don't like the anti-smoking Nazis … these people have … a political agenda … ."

Limbaugh wasn't the only windbag to attack my research on secondhand smoke. When I Googled my name, there were several so-called smoker's rights websites that catered to tobacco trolls who slandered me with various degrees of vulgar and inflammatory denialism on secondhand smoke, such as Velvet Glove Iron Fist, Smokers Club, and NYClash. They merit no further mention.

During 2006 I gave 13 presentations and published 6 papers in peer-reviewed journals in addition to the ASHRAE paper. One was published in the *British Medical Journal*, "Blowing Smoke – British American Tobacco's Air Filtration Scheme and the UK Public Places Charter on Smoking," that demolished BATs ventilation arguments (Leavell et al, 2006). It made four basic points: Ventilation and air filtration are ineffective at removing environmental tobacco smoke. •Despite this knowledge, BAT extensively promoted these technologies to the hospitality industry. •Internal documents show such strategies were viewed as viable solutions to circumvent smoking restrictions and gain global marketing opportunities. •A total ban on smoking in public places is the only way to protect all employees from environmental tobacco smoke.

Another paper, "Risks for heart disease and lung cancer by workers in the catering industry" co-authored with Tony Hedley and his group at the University of Hong Kong, in *Toxicological Sciences*, showed major morbidity and mortality risks to Hong Kong restaurant workers from secondhand smoke. This was the first paper to assess the risk of lung cancer and heart disease from urine cotinine in a group of hospitality workers. We estimated that deaths in the Hong Kong catering workforce of 200,000 occurred at the rate of 150 per year for a 40-year working-lifetime exposure to SHS. We also used cotinine levels to show that 30% of workers exceeded its 24-hour Hong Kong particulate air quality standard and that 98% exceeded the annual air quality objectives due to workplace passive smoking (Hedley et al., 2006).

A third paper, in *BMC Public Health,* was the before-and-after a smoking study of secondhand smoke in seven Boston Bars, with Jim Hyde and Doug Brugge at Tufts. It replicated my Delaware study, finding that with respect to pre-ban levels, post-ban air pollution measurements showed 90% to 95% reductions in carcinogens and fine particles respectively, with post-ban levels differing little from outdoor concentrations. Ventilation failed to control secondhand smoke, while Boston's smoking ban eliminated this risk. A fourth paper, appearing in 2008, was coauthored with Kiyoung Lee and Ellen Hahn's group at the University of Kentucky at Lexington (where I had carpetbagged with a presentation on ETS and Ventilation to a very large and very sympathetic group of academics, public health workers and clean indoor air activists, in 2001). Lee et al. (2008) showed that the 2003 smoking ban in Lexington reduced fine particle air pollution in ten hospitality venues from an average of 199 $\mu g/m^3$ to 18 $\mu g/m^3$, or by 91%, in another replication of my Delaware study, while in the control city of Louisville with no smoking ban, levels in 9 comparable venues remained well above 300 μg/m³ at comparable times.

Lexington's smoking ban was like a dagger to the heart of Kentucky tobacco culture, striking its second largest city, located in the heart of the state's Bluegrass Region. Kentucky's heritage was so steeped in tobacco growing – the state's agriculture commissioner still kept a "Thank You For Smoking" sign on his desk – that the legislature had never bothered to pass a local pre-emption ban, as had been done in many other states. (Such bans pre-empt localities from passing stricter smoke-free laws than the in-thrall-to-Big-Tobacco state legislatures allowed). The total number of North American venues where published peer-reviewed secondhand smoke measurements had shown 90% or better declines in air pollution as a result of the new smoking bans in Wilmington DE, Boston MA, Toronto ON, and Lexington KY, had now increased to two dozen.

I co-authored a fifth paper in *JOEM* with Wael Al-Delaimy of UC San Diego and John Bernert of CDC that set out a group of "Rosetta Stone Equations." These equations enabled correlating clinical and atmospheric measurements of dose and exposure much broader than previously possible. They permitted the calculation of atmospheric nicotine and fine particles from secondhand smoke from measurements of cotinine in blood, urine, and saliva. We validated this using controlled chamber experiments in 40 adults at CDC. We also correlated hair nicotine and urine cotinine for 127 infants exposed to parental smoking. The sixth was a book chapter, co-authored with Jim Hyde and Doug Brugge at Tufts, showing how to use urine cotinine levels to evaluate the efficacy of workplace smoking policies (Repace et al., 2006). It was a very good year.

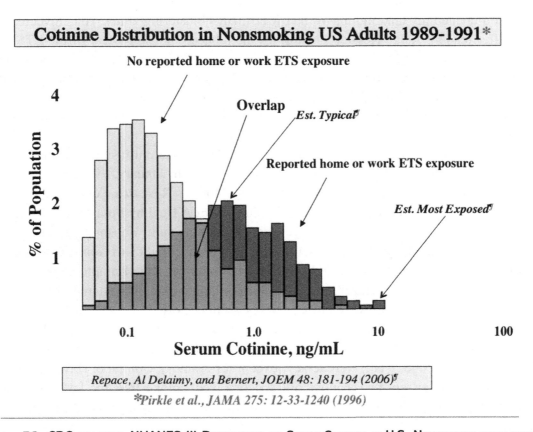

FIGURE 52. CDC-MEASURED NHANES III DISTRIBUTION OF SERUM COTININE IN U.S. NONSMOKING POPULATION (1988–1991), VERSUS ROSETTA MODEL PREDICTIONS FOR TYPICAL AND MOST-EXPOSED PERSONS IN U.S. POPULATION EXPOSED AT HOME OR AT WORK (RED & ORANGE BARS) ADULT NONSMOKERS REPORTING NO WORK OR HOME EXPOSURE ARE REPRESENTED BY THE YELLOW BARS. (AUTHOR'S SLIDE). THIS HISTOGRAM VALIDATES THE EXPOSURE ASSESSMENT MODELING OF REPACE AND LOWREY (1985).

Figure 52 repeats Figure 22 with the result of Rosetta Stone modeling of the U.S. nonsmoking adult population's serum cotinine in 1990 added in. The Rosetta Stone paper (Repace et al., 2006), predicted doses for the typical and most-exposed adult nonsmokers that agreed very well with the measurements of the CDC in the NHANES study of serum cotinine in nonsmoking adults in the U.S. population at the end of the 1980's (Pirkle et al., 1996). In other words, the values of nicotine (and by extension, RSP) that Repace and Lowrey (1985; 1993; 1998) predicted for the typical and most-exposed nonsmokers, and from which we had derived our exposure- and dose-response relationships, were accurate for that era. Or as we had liked to joke at NRL, "not bad for government work."

By the end of 2006, I had published fifteen papers using my grant funds, thirteen funded by FAMRI, and two funded by RWJF, with more to come. During the year I gave several presentations on the Boston Bar Study to international audiences of researchers, notably at a joint meeting of the International Society of Exposure Science and the International Society of Environmental Epidemiology in Paris in September and presented a paper on outdoor air pollution from secondhand smoke at the 13th International Conference on Tobacco or Health in Washington, DC, in July.

In April, Brian Leaderer, whose chamber studies in the early 1980's were so important for validation of our habitual smoker model, was now Deputy Dean of the Yale University School of Public Health. Brian invited me to present the Spring 2006 Dean's Lecture, and to my delight, requested a presentation on the politics of secondhand smoke and public health. The title of my talk was "The Secondhand Smoke Wars: Battles on the Road From Science to Policy." The large audience of students and professors paid rapt attention, perhaps because I opened my talk quoting Walker Merriman's blustering "Fuck You" invective back in 1980. In retrospect, after reading Judge Kessler's history of the tobacco industry's fear of the ETS issue, I am not surprised at the industry's vitriolic response to our *Science* and *Environment International* papers. Figure 53 shows one of the slides from my Yale presentation, lampooning the Congressman From Philip Morris. His photo looks like it came from an advertisement for his chain of Bliley Funeral Homes in Richmond VA. No doubt Marlboro smokers drummed up a lot of customers for Bliley's business, which had a symbiotic relationship with Philip Morris. One skeletal hand washes the other.

Up until 2002, I had funded my research out of pocket. The massive infusion of grant money in that year was now paying off, and it would keep paying off in future years. In January, I visited Congressman Bliley's home base of Richmond Virginia, and the home of Philip Morris's Research Center and one of its cigarette factories. I gave a press conference sponsored by Virginians For A Healthy Future describing the monitoring study I had organized in 12 Virginia hospitality venues, 11 smoking and 1 nonsmoking, in 19 outdoor locales, and 5 highway locations in four diverse areas of the state. Indoor air quality was Good in the single nonsmoking venue, as well as in all outdoor and transit-related locales, Moderate in the Hampton Roads Tunnel, while air quality in the smoking venues was Hazardous, and 18 times higher than in the tunnel. The Virginia study and the report I did for the California EPA are posted on ResearchGate.org.

I also made a presentation to the state health department in West Virginia, and did an analysis for the Netherlands Government of a bogus study of Dutch Bars claiming that ventilation controlled secondhand smoke (it didn't). During 2006, Utah, New Jersey (except for casinos), Colorado, Hawaii, Louisiana (casinos excepted), Ohio, Nevada (except for casinos), and Arizona went smoke-free, the latter three states after my ventilation study appeared. I was on a roll, the bastards were on the run, and payback was sweet; it was a Very Very Good Year.

And so, Fuck YOU, Walker Merriman, and The Horse and Camel You Rode In On.

Tom Bliley -- The Congressman From Philip Morris

Bliley, who served 20 years in the U.S. House of Representatives before retiring in 2000, wrote at least 11 letters to EPA Administrator William Reilly touting industry messages of faulty science and flawed procedures.
The letters included attacks on James Repace, who was then an EPA air policy analyst and staff scientist.

[Muggli ME, Hurt RD, and Repace JL. The Tobacco Industry's Political Efforts to Derail the EPA Report on ETS. Am J Prev Med 2004;26(2):167–177.]

Rep. Tom Bliley
(R-Virginia): Chairman of the
House Commerce Committee

FIGURE 53. LAMPOONING THE CONGRESSMAN FROM PHILIP MORRIS, WATER BOY FOR BIG TOBACCO (AUTHOR'S SLIDE).

CHAPTER 19

YOU BET YOUR LIFE

According to the second amended complaint, Januszewski et al. vs. Horseshoe Hammond ... USDC, NDIN, Hammond Div., 2:00CV352JM, 22 June 2004, twenty three current and former employees, 17 women and 6 men, allege that the Empress Casino III, now known as Horseshoe Casino Hammond, a shipboard gambling casino sailing out of Hammond Indiana on Lake Michigan, has exposed its workers to dangerous levels of secondhand smoke due to a failure to provide adequate ventilation. Plaintiffs Januszewski, et al. allege that the air aboard the EHC was filled with smoke at unsafe and unhealthy levels, such that they have suffered numerous illnesses, injuries, and disabilities. Plaintiffs also allege that the Defendants knew or should have known that the ventilation and air scrubbing facilities were inadequate. Plaintiffs further allege that the air aboard the EHC [Empress Horseshoe Casino] was unsafe and likely to lead to harm to the crew, and that despite repeated complaints about the deleterious effects of being required to work in such conditions, and advice from its own experts, that EHC's heating, ventilating, and air conditioning (HVAC) system was not adequate to provide a safe working environment, defendants failed and refused to correct the situation. This failure is alleged to be the proximate cause of various occupationally-related injuries and illnesses that Plaintiffs have suffered and will suffer in the future as a result of prolonged exposure to the smoke on the ship.

Expert Report of James Repace, re: Januszewski et al. vs. Horseshoe Hammond, March 2006.

Casino gambling is a popular American pastime. In 2007, 25% of the adult U.S. population, 54 million persons (aged ≥ 21 years) visited casinos an average of ~7 times per gambler. Nationally, 467 commercial casinos generated gross gaming revenues totaling $34.13 billion, paid $5.79 billion in state and local taxes, and employed 360,818 workers who earned $13.8 billion. In addition, 29 states had 456 tribal casinos, employing 204,000 persons. The gaming and tobacco industries have adamantly opposed smoke-free casinos, promoting ventilation alternatives instead. As a result, secondhand smoke has been epidemic in casinos. In 2007, only 8 of 23 states plus Puerto Rico had 100% smoke free commercial casinos or racinos (casinos at race tracks), while smoke-free casinos on Indian reservations were unheard of (Repace, 2009, 2011).

As a consequence, there were many casino workers who suffered from workplace secondhand smoke poisoning. Normally, a worker suffering a work-related injury can only file for workers' compensation. In such cases, the employer's liability would be strictly limited by law to fixed amounts set by the States. However, for certain classes of workers in industries in interstate commerce regulated by the federal government, such as railways (Federal Employers Liability Act or FELA), used in *Thaxton v. Norfolk Southern,* and ships (Jones Act), employed in *Mullen et al. v. Treasure Chest*, as well as for federal employees, the applicable laws differ. Such was the case for workers on the Empress Horseshoe riverboat casino (EHC), who for legal purposes, are covered by the Jones Act. Thus for legal purposes, it is as if they were in the merchant marine. In other words, they can sue the riverboat's owner for negligence.

FELA and Jones Act cases attract the interest of trial lawyers, who front the costs of litigation, profiting only if they prevail. If they win, the cash recovery is limited only by the provable damages, and is usually many times greater than that provided by State Worker's Compensation, often extending well into seven figures. I had, as was my custom in these complicated "toxic tort" cases, prepared a lengthy report on which to base my courtroom testimony, utilizing documents produced by the plaintiff and the defense in the discovery phase of the case, laying out the problem as I understood it, with my analysis highlighting the probable causes, and the expected health effects for persons in the affected group. These reports served to educate the plaintiff's attorneys and medical experts on the scientific issues, and to guide their questions in my direct testimony and in cross-examination of the defense. The way trials are conducted under U.S. law, an expert witness must respond to direct questions by an attorney and cannot simply treat the courtroom as a lecture hall. However, an experienced expert witness can manage to pack a lot of information into a reply to an expertly worded question by one's lawyer, or an inexpertly worded one by the opponent's lawyer.

Testimony of an expert medical witness is legally required to personalize the alleged adverse health effects to a particular individual plaintiff. As a non-physician scientist, I would not be permitted to do this by the judge. The next step would be a deposition, which is an interrogation by the defendant's attorney with the aim of discovering weaknesses in the plaintiff's case and flaws in the expert's testimony that could be used to discredit the expert in trial. The trial lawyer in this case, David Schachtman, a Chicago attorney, asked me to find other experts in both medicine and risk assessment, and I recommended Dr. David Mannino, a physician formerly with the CDC's tobacco program with whom I had co-authored three secondhand smoke papers. Dave was now chair of Pulmonology at the University of Kentucky School of Medicine. I also recommended Steven Bayard, who was now retired from EPA and doing consulting in biostatistics.

In many cases, the trial judge will try to get the parties to arbitrate the case in lieu of a trial, which saves both sides a great deal of effort and money if mutual agreement can be reached. On Halloween eve, 2007, I flew to Chicago to testify in the arbitration of this case, captioned *Januszewski et al. vs. Horseshoe Hammond*. My report laid out the problem, which echoed the *Mullen vs. Treasure Chest* Case.

The Empress Casino III riverboat casino was designed and built for cruising out of the Lake Michigan Port of Hammond Indiana. Until December 1, 1999, when it was acquired through a merger by Horseshoe Gaming and renamed the Horseshoe, the Empress/Horseshoe Casino (EHC) underwent a series of modifications, including the addition of a 4th deck, that increased the passenger capacity to 34% beyond the original design. So far so good. However, the redesign did not include a commensurate increase in the ship's ventilation capacity. This was a major folly, identical to that committed by the penurious ship owner in the *Treasure Chest* case. My damning conclusions followed from a cotinine test of five workers, plus an examination of 192 separate carbon dioxide (CO_2) measurements conducted by the EHC's own consultants on fourteen separate occasions from 1997 to 2002. Exhaled carbon dioxide from human occupancy can be related to ventilation rate using an equation in ASHRAE Standard 62.

On at least eight occasions over a period of several years, EHC's naval architects, its insurance company's industrial hygiene consultants, and its own engineering and gaming personnel repeatedly expressed concern about the gross inadequacy of the ship's ventilation system due to its failure to remove tobacco smoke adequately. As the Habitual Smoker model shows, failure to increase the already inadequate ventilation capacity commensurately when the passenger capacity, i.e. the smokers per unit volume, was increased (among many other reasons) this would invariably result in a massive increase in secondhand smoke pollution on the boat.

As Figure 54 shows, the CO_2 monitors located in the ventilation ducts, logged by computer daily, indicated that ventilation capacity was inadequate on all four decks of the ship, according to ASHRAE Standard 62-1989, which recommended design rates of outdoor supply air for casino ventilation systems. CO_2 measurements differed by time of day, deck, and location on a deck. Based on documents obtained during the legal discovery phase of the litigation and made available to me on request, I compared the CO_2 levels from September 1997 through April 2002, which averaged 903 ppm above background, with those made at year's end in 2004 and in early 2005, subsequent to a major ventilation system renovation, which averaged 217 ppm above background. With background subtracted, this clearly indicated that ventilation rates in the post-renovation period were more than 4 times as great as in the pre-renovation period when the workers' injuries occurred. Any CO_2 value exceeding the ASHRAE Standard guideline of 800 ppm indicates substandard ventilation rates. Figure 54 shows the overall daily average for New Years' Eve, Dec. 31, 2004 is 689 ppm, while on Thursday, Jan 6, 2005 it is 546 ppm, a difference of 143 ppm, showing that the differences between day and evening on a single day can be larger than the differences between days, and that the differences between monitors at various positions on deck varies from day-to-day, large on some days, small on others, justifying averaging over all monitors, times of day, and days in a given time period. The table insert gives the statistics for the combined means and medians of the CO_2 data for the 5 sensors.

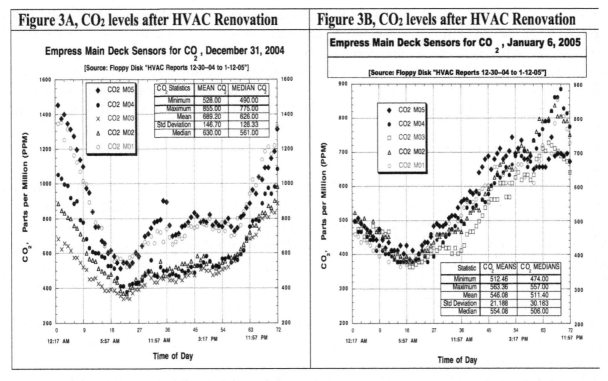

FIGURE 54. GRAPHS OF THE CARBON DIOXIDE (CO_2) LEVELS IN THE EHC FROM THE SHIP'S IN-DUCT MONITORS, REFLECTING HUMAN OCCUPANCY POST RENOVATION BY TIME OF DAY AND BY DECK (MO1 TO MO5) FOR TWO DIFFERENT DAYS IN 2004-2005. EACH HORIZONTAL TICK REPRESENTS 1 HOUR OVER A 24-HOUR PERIOD (REPACE EXPERT REPORT, *JANUSZEWSKI ET AL. VS. HORSESHOE HAMMOND*, 2006). HIGH CO_2 LEVELS EXCEEDING 800 PPM REFLECT INADEQUATE VENTILATION. CO_2 LEVELS ABOVE BACKGROUND RESULT FROM EXHALED BREATH AND REFLECT HUMAN OCCUPANCY. THUS, THE LOWEST LEVELS OCCUR AROUND 6 TO 7 AM, WHEN OCCUPANCY IS AT A MINIMUM, AND THE HIGHEST LEVELS OCCUR AROUND MIDNIGHT. THESE MINIMUM/MAXIMUM CO_2 LEVELS ALSO COINCIDE WITH THE LOWEST AND HIGHEST LEVELS OF SECONDHAND SMOKE RESPECTIVELY. CASINOS ARE TYPICALLY OPEN 24/7. THE MEASURED LEVELS INCLUDE THE OUTDOOR BACKGROUND.

Although the ventilation upgrade in 2002 yielded compliance with ASHRAE Standard 62-1989, two subsequent Standards, 62-1999 and 62-2001, changed the rules, stating that ASHRAE ventilation rates no longer applied to casinos with smoking. Moreover by 2004, *ASHRAE standard 62, Ventilation for Acceptable Indoor Air Quality*, stated that ventilation rate requirements for smoking venues could not be determined until "cognizant authorities determined a secondhand smoke concentration yielding an acceptable level of risk." This, of course, has never happened.

So, in a predictable series of personal disasters prior to the renovation, twenty-three EHC casino workers, ranging in age from 26 to 61 years, developed serious respiratory illnesses; one developed heart disease, another developed cancer, and one suffered incapacitating migraines. Two of the workers were pit bosses, and the remaining twenty were blackjack, roulette, or craps dealers, and one was the ship's captain. At the time that the suit was filed, in 2004, seven of these workers had quit due to illness, four had been fired because they could no longer work (as in the Treasure Chest case), eleven remained working but were all sick, and the captain had died. Twenty-two of the plaintiffs had severe respiratory disease, and eleven of them were suffering from adult-onset asthma. All twenty three workers attributed their symptoms to being gassed by heavy secondhand smoke exposure on the riverboat. The suit alleged that the casino's owners had exposed these workers to dangerous levels of secondhand smoke due to a failure to provide adequate ventilation.

In 2005, after the ventilation had been vastly increased by renovations that had occurred in late 2002, I entered the arena. I immediately requested that the plaintiffs' attorneys obtain urine cotinine measurements from those plaintiffs still working, to quantify their current dose of secondhand smoke, and to provide a basis for estimating their risk of acute and chronic secondhand smoke diseases before and after the renovation. Among the eleven dealers still actively working, five women agreed to supply urine samples for cotinine determination. Note that body fluid cotinine reflects personal exposure to SHS and incorporates duration and proximity effects as well. This makes such measurements invaluable for forensic purposes. I estimated that these five workers had *post renovation* geometric mean serum cotinine equivalents, that were 13 times higher than a national probability sample of all U.S. women in 2001-2002 from CDC's NHANES study. Using this as a representative sample of all the sickened workers, by scaling back to pre-renovation CO_2 levels, I estimated that their mean pre-renovation secondhand smoke dose was an enormous 52 times that of the typical U.S. nonsmoking adult female in 2002.

Moreover, even *after* the renovation, workers' air pollution exposure (estimated from their cotinine levels) to secondhand smoke fine particle air pollution (267 $\mu g/m^3$) exceeded the level of the U.S. National Ambient Air Quality Standard for $PM_{2.5}$ by nearly four-fold. This was in the "Very Unhealthy Range." Prior to the renovation, the NAAQS had been exceeded by an estimated ten-fold (1070 $\mu g/m^3$), corresponding to the "Significant Harm" level of air pollution.

Next, assuming conservatively that SHS was no more toxic than fine particulate matter in the outdoor air, I calculated that prior to the June 2002 renovation, the absolute risk of an acute attack due to workplace secondhand smoke for those workers suffering from asthma had been increased by 142%. But the smoke levels even after the HVAC system was renovated still corresponded to an increased risk of occupational asthma of 42% relative to the average Hammond Indiana resident. As for non-asthmatic plaintiffs' risk of serious respiratory illness from SHS, that had increased by an estimated five to seven-fold, depending upon their duration of workplace SHS exposure, while for asthmatic plaintiffs, the increase was 15 to 21-fold above baseline.

Getting into deeper waters, for workers at the median cotinine level who were employed *before* the HVAC upgrade in June 2002 (all the listed plaintiffs) the estimated combined working lifetime mortality risk was 36 deaths per thousand. This was 36 times OSHA's Significant Risk level. For ischemic heart disease alone, Significant Risk was exceeded after only a single year of exposure, and for lung cancer, after just 5 years of exposure. To put this into a graphical perspective, Figure 55 shows the Plaintiffs' estimated risk from exposure to SHS was 300 to 400 times *de manifestis* risk (i.e., the level above which toxic hazards in air, water, or food are invariably federally regulated). This enabled me to conclude that, "to a reasonable degree of scientific certainty," that EHC Casino management had exposed its workers to dangerous levels of secondhand smoke.

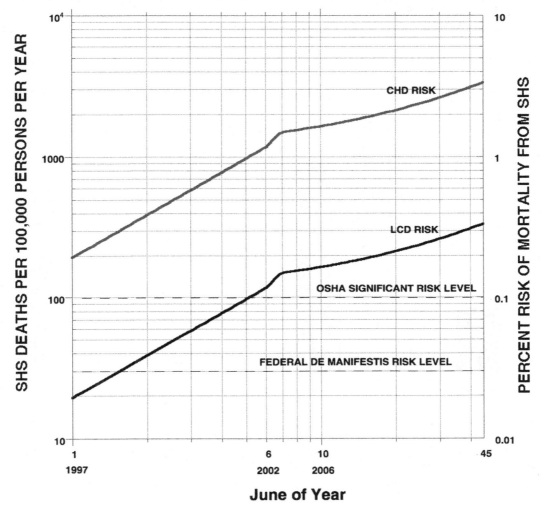

Empress/Horseshoe Median Worker LCD & CHD Risk vs Duration of Employment for Workers Employed from June 1996 and after June 2002

FIGURE 55. A PLOT OF EHC WORKERS' ESTIMATED RISK OF CORONARY HEART DISEASE (CHD) AND LUNG CANCER DEATH (LCD) RISK AS A FUNCTION OF DURATION OF EMPLOYMENT IN THE CASINO, EXTRAPOLATED TO A 45-YR WORKING LIFETIME ACCORDING TO STANDARD OSHA METHODOLOGY, AS ESTIMATED FROM WORKERS' URINE COTININE. THE CASINO VENTILATION WAS UPGRADED IN JUNE 2002. (REPACE EXPERT REPORT (2006) IN THE MATTER OF, *JANUSZEWSKI ET AL. VS. HORSESHOE HAMMOND*).

Then the fireworks began. The Defendants hired two of their own experts to attack my report, one of whom was none other than our old friend Roger Jenkins, and the other, one R.C. James, an industrial hygiene consultant. James criticized my calculation of fine particulate matter from cotinine to assess exposure, asserting that I had used worst-case assumptions, that I failed to discuss uncertainty, and that the Rosetta stone equations had "high error rates." In rebuttal, I fired back, noting that my published papers had included lengthy discussions of all of these issues, and furthermore had been widely accepted by the academic scientific community.

Jenkins trotted out his long-time insistence that atmospheric nicotine and body fluid cotinine were not quantitatively related, nor was there such a relationship between air nicotine and fine particles in secondhand smoke. I observed that this was contradicted by the law of conservation of mass, and that a number of workers had shown that there was a 10:1 ratio between nicotine in air and fine particles from secondhand smoke, including a published analysis of Jenkin's *own* raw data by Joan Daisey of Lawrence Berkeley Lab (Daisey, 1999). This demonstrated that Jenkins' arguments not only were contradicted by his own data, but for legal purposes, could be labelled as far out of the scientific mainstream (to say the least). The arbitrator pondered both sides' arguments and decided in favor of plaintiffs *Januzsewski et al.* for a rumored ten to twenty million dollars. This case whetted my appetite for making more measurements of air quality in casinos.

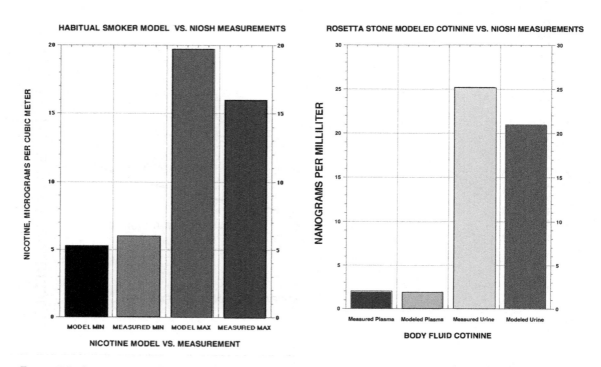

FIGURE 56. APPLICATION OF THE ROSETTA STONE EQUATIONS (REPACE ET AL., 2006) TO PREDICTED VS. MEASURED NICOTINE EXPOSURE (56A) AND COTININE DOSE (56B) FOR BALLY'S CASINO WORKERS FROM SECONDHAND SMOKE. FROM AN ANALYSIS OF A NIOSH HEALTH HAZARD EVALUATION IN BALLY'S CASINO IN ATLANTIC CITY, NEW JERSEY (REPACE, 2015). [N.B., THE TERMS 'PLASMA' AND 'SERUM' COTININE ARE USED INTERCHANGEABLY IN THE LITERATURE].

After the case settled, a nettled R.C. James pressed his attack on the accuracy of the Rosetta Stone model by applying it (incorrectly) to an analysis of data collected by NIOSH in Bally's Casino in Atlantic City, New Jersey in 1995 (James et al., 2008). I ran across it as I was writing this chapter seven years later. In response to a complaint by workers in Bally's Casino in Atlantic City, New Jersey, Trout and Decker (1995) had conducted a NIOSH Health Hazard Evaluation (HHE), measuring workers' plasma and urine cotinine and both area and personal breathing zone nicotine as well as area RSP. Trout et al. (1998) subsequently published a summary of their data in *JOEM*, notably *omitting* the RSP measurements that they reported in their HHE. In rebuttal, I was inspired to post my own analysis of the NIOSH data on ResearchGate.org, as shown in Figure 56 (Repace, 2015). Using the Rosetta Stone Model, I estimated mean and median plasma and urine cotinine values for 14 of 29 Bally's Casino workers for which adequate data was reported. The model estimates differ from the NIOSH- measured values by 10% to 15% for the medians, and by 7% to 17% for the means. This reasonable agreement between theory and experiment suggests that the Rosetta Stone Model is useful for estimating the secondhand smoke doses that nonsmoking workers get from workplace secondhand smoke to a reasonable degree of scientific certainty. In addition, the Habitual Smoker model (Repace, 2007), using NIOSH-measured CO_2 levels to calculate the range in air exchange rates, and using ASHRAE default occupancy plus U.S. smoking prevalence predicts area air nicotine concentrations for Bally's casino ranging from 5 to 20 $\mu g/m^3$. By comparison, NIOSH measured area nicotine concentrations in Bally's casino ranged from 6 to 16 $\mu g/m^3$. This is one of the things I love about science. Criticism of one's work can lead to advances in understanding. So many thanks for the brass-knuckled assist, R.C.

In July 2007, I co-authored a paper in *Morbidity and Mortality Weekly Report* with Ursula Bauer and colleagues of the New York State Department of Health, designed to assess changes in indoor SHS exposure in respondents to the New York Adult Tobacco Survey. This was accomplished by comparing saliva cotinine among nonsmoking respondents in June and July 2003, before New York's statewide ban on smoking in indoor workplaces and public places, including restaurants and bars to the lower post-ban levels. Post-ban cotinine levels decreased by 47.4%, indicating that comprehensive smoking bans reduce SHS exposure of nonsmokers (Bauer et al., 2007). The use of cotinine as a quantitative biomarker to assess workplace secondhand smoke exposure was now widely accepted.

A couple of years earlier, Wayne Ott, Anne Steinemann, and Lance Wallace had collaborated as editors to publish the first textbook on exposure science. The book, titled *Exposure Analysis,* was published in 2007. The flyleaf described the text in part as follows: "Written by experts, **Exposure Analysis** is the first complete resource in the emerging scientific discipline of exposure analysis. A comprehensive source on the environmental pollutants that affect human health, the book discusses human exposure through pathways including air, food, water, dermal absorption, and, for children, non-food ingestion. …The book summarizes existing definitions of exposure, dose, and related concepts and provides the mathematical framework at the heart of these conceptual definitions. Using secondhand smoke as an example, the book illustrates how exposure analysis studies can change human behavior and improve public health." It is now used as a textbook at Stanford.

I authored the chapter on secondhand smoke, which both Lance and Wayne peer-reviewed. After several rounds of some more brass-knuckled brawling with my good buddies, which significantly improved my draft chapter, it was ready for prime time. My 39-page chapter, titled *Exposure to Secondhand Smoke*, incorporated a lengthy table listing 172 toxic substances contained in secondhand smoke, which included a detailed list of its 33 hazardous air pollutants, 47 hazardous wastes, 67 known carcinogens, and 3 regulated outdoor air pollutants, with references to the authorities that had made those determinations. To the best of my knowledge, this table is unique in the literature. The chapter noted that "SHS appears to contribute the overwhelming majority of carcinogenic particle-bound polycyclic aromatic hydrocarbons in the air of most buildings where smoking occurs. SHS-carbon monoxide levels measured in pubs are in the range that produces acute cardiovascular effects. This chapter discusses the toxic constituents of SHS, and the prevalence of nonsmokers' exposure, as well as factors determining exposure and dose."

My introduction noted that "the microenvironments of greatest importance are those where the population spends the most time: at home and in the workplace. In-vehicle exposure is also of concern due to the high concentrations observed. Use of a personal exposure monitor to estimate relative contributions of smoking, cooking, and diesel exhaust to a person's RSP exposure is illustrated. How such personal exposures combine into a population distribution is illuminated, and the major U.S. field study of SHS dose in the population is deconstructed. Field studies and controlled measurements of SHS concentrations in homes and workplaces are reviewed. SHS emission and removal rates are discussed in the context of the time-averaged mass-balance model for estimating concentrations in naturally and mechanically ventilated buildings, and examples for homes and bars are given."

The chapter gave an updated derivation of the habitual smoker model that incorporated improvements to the model derived by Wayne Ott in the 1990's that corrected for non-equilibrium portions of the growth, equilibrium, and decay curve, something that the earlier adjustments given in my 1987 IARC modeling chapter did imperfectly. However, the steady state model remained unchanged, and proved to be fairly accurate in its predictions. The chapter graphically displayed CDC data showing that a substantial number of American nonsmokers who claimed that they were "unexposed" to secondhand smoke in national surveys had levels of cotinine in their blood that overlapped considerably with nonsmokers who admitted exposure (Figure 21 in this book). This explained to a larger audience that prospective epidemiological studies could underestimate the magnitude of lung cancer from passive smoking if they did not periodically measure cotinine, which most of them failed to do, resulting in misclassification of a substantial fraction of exposed nonsmokers (Repace, 2007).

The tobacco industry's moles had long asserted that any misclassification that occurred was due to smokers who deceived, either pretending to be nonsmokers in such surveys, or who were too stupid to know the difference, and thus any reported effect of passive smoking was simply due to misclassified active smokers. I never bought into that patently bogus argument, which had been effectively discredited by Jud Wells in the late 1980's. The chapter summed up the authoritative consensus on passive smoking-induced disease in 2006: "The Surgeon General, the National Academy of Sciences, the International Agency for Research on Cancer, the National Institute for Occupational Safety and Health, the U.S. Environmental Protection Agency, the Occupational Safety & Health Administration, the National Cancer Institute, the California EPA, and the National Toxicology Program variously concluded that nonsmokers' exposure to secondhand smoke (SHS) causes fatal heart disease; lung, breast, and nasal sinus cancer; asthma induction and aggravation; middle ear infection; sudden infant death syndrome; and respiratory impairment; as well as irritation of the mucous membranes of the eyes, nose, and throat. ... SHS is now widely accepted as the third leading preventable health hazard after active smoking and alcohol; nevertheless, it continues to be a widespread indoor pollutant in many homes, workplaces, and public access buildings in the United States and abroad. SHS has been estimated to cause as much as 2.7% of all deaths in the United States annually. ... Despite growing trends toward indoor public and workplace smoking bans, SHS exposure continues for half of all children at home in the United States, and for most bar and casino workers. And a depressing statistic: despite that decline in smoking prevalence from about 43% in 1965 to about 23% in 2001, the absolute number of smokers in 1965 in the U.S.A. was 50 million, but in 2001 had declined by only 6% to about 47 million" (Repace, 2007).

By 2017, the number of states that had 100% smoke-free gambling (excluding bingo) had increased to 18 plus Puerto Rico, while casinos in 23 states remained polluted with secondhand smoke. Five states plus Guam did not permit state-regulated gambling, and one state (Maine) banned smoking in casinos opened on or after July 2003 (Americans For Nonsmokers' Rights, April 3, 2017).

MULTI-UNIT HOUSING BECOMES THE NEW FRONTIER

I began to think of the last frontier of unresearched major secondhand smoke problems: multi-unit housing. I contacted my old friend, Katherine Hammond, who was now a professor at Berkeley. Kathie kindly arranged for me to obtain, through her lab chief, Charles Perrino, a number of her passive nicotine monitors, and I began a new service, advertised on my website, that offered measurement of nicotine levels to nonsmoking apartment dwellers suffering from secondhand smoke infiltration problems. In the coming years this extremely frustrating and socially contentious issue would assume vastly increased importance.

On November 7th, I gave an interview to *the New York Times* on secondhand smoke infiltration into nonsmokers' units in multi-unit housing. In addition to collecting data on nicotine in nonsmokers' apartments around the country, I studied the physics of infiltration. When coupled with self-reports of symptoms, I began to realize that this was a major public health problem that had gone unaddressed by legislation. I was hearing from clients who reported their apartments to be uninhabitable due to smoke pouring through cracks and holes in building structures or in the HVAC system. But smoking apartment inhabitants felt strongly that their home was their castle. Although it was certainly not true that your home was your castle when your neighbors blasted loud music at all hours of the night, interfering with your quiet enjoyment. Smoke infiltration in multi-unit housing was a new and unresearched area of indoor air pollution. In an article titled, "A New Arena in the Fight Over Smoking: The Home," *The Times* reporter wrote that:

> "Growing movement to restrict smoking in apartments and condominiums is having some success. … Researchers have analyzed whether smoke can be contained in various kinds of apartment buildings and found that the percentage of shared air generally ranges from 10 percent to 50 percent, with upper floors most at risk, said James Repace, a biophysicist who performs research on secondhand smoke in collaboration with the Tufts University School of Medicine. 'There is a tremendous unmet demand for smoke-free housing in America,' Mr. Repace said, 'and it boggles my mind that the real estate industry has not recognized that and tried to profit from it.'" (Semrad S, *NY Times*, Nov. 5, 2007)

More about this in Chapter 22.

I'VE BEEN SMOKING ON THE RAILROAD

My second railroad passive smoking case involved a nonsmoking conductor on the Long Island Railroad: *U.S. District Court, Eastern District of New York, Civil Action No. CV 04-4194, Hepburn v. Long Island Railroad.* From 1973 to 1988, David Hepburn had been a conductor on the Long Island Railroad's (LIRR) diesel and electric trains, traveling from Montauk on the eastern tip of Long Island to Manhattan on its western border. Hepburn routinely worked in the smoking cars, where 100% of the passengers were smokers. I had commuted myself on the New Haven, New York Central, and Pennsylvania Railroads from 1956 to 1965 in the metropolitan New York area, and recalled very well that the smoking cars were like gas chambers. You could scarcely see from one end to another through the choking clouds of smoke. In the 1970's, David Hepburn, at the age of 23, began working for the LIRR, conducting on four to six trains daily on trips of 1 hour or more duration, where half of the train consisted of smoking cars. For fully half of his workday, Conductor Hepburn was breathing secondhand smoke at smoking car levels. By the 1980's, only two or three rail cars per train still remained smoking, but the levels of smoke in these cars was higher, and his work hours were longer. Often, he had to manually open balky doors in those cars because they had been gummed up by tobacco tar. Hepburn's exposure decreased when smoking cars on trains were banned by the railroad in January 1988, but smoking still persisted in the railroad's bar cars, because the smokers paid only lip service to the LIRR's poorly enforced smoking policy.

In November 2001, Hepburn developed a pronounced swelling in his neck, and was diagnosed with Stage IV metastatic oral, head and neck squamous cell carcinoma as well as aortic insufficiency and suffered from migraines as well. He was first treated with surgery, which removed his saliva glands causing him great and permanent discomfort. This was followed up by radiotherapy. He was forced to retire on medical disability in May of 2002, at the age of 51. David Hepburn had inhaled secondhand smoke on the LIRR for 28 years. He had been unable to work since and continued to suffer from the traumatic effects of his radical surgery. Hepburn filed suit against the LIRR, alleging that his cancer was due to secondhand smoke exposure on the job. In 2006 Mr. Hepburn's attorney, Ms. Diane Paolicelli, asked me to serve as an expert witness in his case.

Again, taking advantage of the legal discovery process, I was able to obtain access the LIRR's records and obtain sufficient information to estimate the smoker density and ventilation rate of the various railcars and break rooms he worked in, and to determine the duration of his SHS exposure. I estimated, to a "reasonable degree of scientific certainty," that David Hepburn, a life-long nonsmoker, was exposed to extremely high levels of air pollution from secondhand smoke, far in excess of those encountered in smoky bars, nightclubs, and gambling venues, as a result of his on-the-job exposure to secondhand smoke. Laying out my calculations in a 40-page report, I demonstrated that the ventilation rates on LIRR's smoking cars were grossly inadequate, because while they had smoking occupancies even higher than encountered in a stand-up bar, they had ventilation rates only 1/6th as high.

Mr. Hepburn's estimated work-related SHS exposure was 10 to 20 times as great as the average U.S. adult male nonsmoker, so high that his intake of tobacco tar was comparable to smoking one-half to one pack of low-tar cigarettes daily, well into the range of an active smoker. He would have inhaled an estimated dose of potent upper respiratory carcinogens ranging from about 2 to 4 micrograms daily from working in the railroad's smoky trains and break rooms. By this time, the Surgeon General had long declared active smoking to be a known cause of head and neck cancer. Moreover, the LIRR had repeatedly ignored the Surgeon General's increasingly alarming pronouncements of the potential harm from secondhand smoke in 1972, 1975, 1979, 1981, 1984, and 1986. Hepburn testified that there was a "culture of smoking among employees and passengers." It would appear that this was an open and shut case of employer negligence resulting in a workers' injury. Or so one would have thought.

On July 24th 2007, the Long Island newspaper, *Newsday*, reported in an article by Steve Ritea:

"Testimony began yesterday in a case brought by a former Long Island Rail Road conductor who claims he developed cancer after years of walking through smoke-filled cars to collect commuters' tickets before smoking was banned on the railroad in 1988. [Hepburn testified that] 'It was so smoky you could hardly see through the car.' ... Hepburn's lawyer vowed ... to establish a clear link between secondhand smoke and the head and neck cancer her client developed, [but the] attorney for the railroad said there is no solid proof of a connection. ... U.S. District Court Judge Leonard D. Wexler told the eight-member jury yesterday he expects the case to last nearly two weeks."

However, it proved to be a lost cause. The irascible geriatric Judge Wexler proved to be an insuperable obstacle. He repeatedly castigated both attorneys, and reserved especially venomous comments for the able Ms. Paolicelli, and even interrupted my direct testimony to brag about his "credentials" in risk assessment, apparently having attended a course given by some right-wing think tank designed to poison the minds of judges. His patently undeserved ridicule of Ms. Paolicelli in front of the jury was so blistering that she requested a mistrial. Judge Wexler granted it, but sneered, "You might get another jury, but don't think you're going to get another judge next time." She didn't. The second time around I testified via videotaped deposition. We lost the case. It was a bitter loss for David Hepburn, who has to live with his disability for the rest of his life without compensation, as a result of this callous judge whose remarks undoubtedly biased the jury. And it infuriated me.

CHAPTER 20

YOU CAN'T FIGHT CITY HALL

"The long-time boss of the Harlem numbers racket is ready to take his latest gamble. The legendary underworld figure Ray (Spanish Raymond) Marquez is betting he can beat the city with a $15 million lawsuit – one that blames his bladder cancer on the secondhand cigarette smoke he inhaled at Rikers Island and the Tombs [New York City Jails]. The civil suit, which Marquez filed in 2001 after a 29-month stint behind bars, is set to go to trial next month in Manhattan Supreme Court following years of bitter legal battles with the city.

"Harlem numbers king taking on city with $15 M secondhand smoke suit,
By JOSE MARTINEZ, DAILY NEWS STAFF WRITER, New York, Monday, *March 10th* 2008.

In April of 2008, I served as an expert witness in a prisoner case where the plaintiff had been denied bail, and jailed for two years in New York City's infamous Rikers Island prison. The plaintiff, Raymond Marquez, was a notorious figure in the annals of New York City's numbers racket. On May 27, 2008, *The New York Times* published a story recounting some of Marquez's history:

> **"Convicted Gambler Whose Lawyer Is His Son, By JOHN ELIGON** ... "From the 1950s into the 1990s, the elder Marquez, now 78, was spending most of his time at his gambling parlors in Harlem, building a reputation as Spanish Raymond — the notorious kingpin of the illicit numbers racket. ... He served eight years in a federal prison ... Marquez says that the numbers business is as extensive as it has ever been in the city. At least 5,000 betting parlors ... are operating with little interference from the police... .

THE STRANGE CASE OF SPANISH RAYMOND

Raymond Marquez was arrested on New York State gambling charges in 1994. The prosecutors alleged that he had a "small fortune that was ripe for confiscation through fines and tax liens. ... Under the nickname Spanish Raymond, he became a legendary figure in Harlem and East Harlem with a penchant for stylish clothes, glittering jewelry, luxury cars and yachting. ... Up here the name Spanish Raymond and the way he operated is sort of a legend," said Lieut. Gregory J. Levine of the Manhattan North Public Morals District. We concentrated on him for almost two years and this time we got him good." Marquez pleaded guilty to the state gambling charges and paid a $1 million fine. However, in a subsequent dispute over an error by the City in a signed plea bargain, Marquez demanded that his guilty plea be withdrawn and his fine returned. The City upped him one by declaring Spanish Raymond's former numbers operation "an unincorporated business," suing both him and his wife Alice for $6.5 million in unpaid back taxes. These taxes, they claimed, were due from crimes he committed from 1990 to 1993. Spanish Raymond fired back in an interview with the *Times*, "They don't tax burglars or bank robbers for their illegal activities, why should they tax anybody else for their illegal activities?" (Raab, 1994, 1997).

Vast numbers of New Yorkers played the numbers, and most juries regarded bookies as quasi-legitimate businessmen. They often refused to convict defendants like Raymond Marquez. His activities had seriously pissed off the gimlet-eyed prosecutors of the City of New York, and they determined to hang him out to dry. Increasing the stakes, Manhattan District Attorney Robert Morgenthau obtained a court order to attach in excess of $35 million in assets owned by Marquez and his wife (Raab, 1994, 1997).

They followed this with the crowning blow: Marquez had been granted bail in the federal case brought on gambling charges in the 1970's for which he had served time in prison. Rubbing salt into Spanish Raymond's wounds, the City shopped for a compliant judge who deemed Spanish Raymond a "flight risk," and denied him bail. He was kept in the City's Rikers Island Jail without trial for 29 months to pressure him into paying up. While in jail, Marquez developed bladder cancer. The City afforded him minimal treatment at Belleview Hospital. Unsurprisingly, a few months later he had a recurrence, and he was finally allowed bail. Subsequently, he was successfully treated at Sloan Kettering during February and March of 2001 and had remained in remission since.

Then it was Spanish Raymond's turn at bat. With his son David, a Long Island trial lawyer, serving as his attorney, Raymond went to trial, and was acquitted on the gambling charges filed by the Manhattan district attorney. Then he defeated the City's charges in his tax case, and on a roll, he then sued the City for damages related to his bladder cancer. In the fall of 2006, I received a call from David Marquez, who asked if I would serve as an expert witness in his father's case. He flew down from New York to discuss the case. Hilarine and I entertained him for dinner. We found him to be an engaging, intelligent and flamboyant person, and liked him instantly. Afterwards, David related the particulars of the case. After hearing him out, I said that this case has a major obstacle: the fact that Raymond had smoked ½ to 1 pack of cigarettes daily for 30 years. This would certainly be raised by the City as a plausible defense. However, I observed, the smoking had ended when he was about 46 years old. This meant that by the time he was jailed by the City, Raymond had quit smoking for 24 years. When exposure ceases, risk declines with time. Moreover, two of his treating physicians had informed him that his bladder cancer was caused by exposure to secondhand smoke, and his oncologist had agreed to testify as an expert medical witness in the case. So, I could see a plausible line of attack for the plaintiff's experts. I was excited by the scientific challenge and agreed to take on Spanish Raymond's case.

However, there were a number of forensic issues for me to solve for this case to succeed. First, I needed to estimate Raymond's secondhand smoke exposure in jail. This was a problem because he had been held for varying lengths of time in five different buildings at Rikers, as well as The Tombs jail in Manhattan, during his court appearances. Thus, Raymond Marquez would have been exposed to a spectrum of smoker densities and air exchange rates during his stay in each of the jail buildings in which he had been imprisoned. Based on prison records obtained in discovery, I painstakingly compiled a list of occupancies for each of the six jails, and the number of days he had spent in each one.

Next, I used a survey that the city had done in 2002 to determine the smoking prevalence among its inmates. It turned out to be an amazing 61%, nearly triple the smoking prevalence of the typical New York City resident population. The inmates' average smoking rate was easy to calculate from the detailed cigarette sales records each of the NYC jails kept. It appeared that each smoking inmate smoked an astronomically high daily average of 72 cigarettes, or better than 3½ packs per day, more than double the average rate for the general non-institutionalized population. This already signaled to me loud and clear that the prison was a gas chamber filled with secondhand smoke.

Step by step, I had to discover the code-prescribed ventilation rates for each jail building. Complicating this was the fact that each of the jail's ten buildings had been built in a different era, ranging from 1933 to 1991, and the applicable ventilation codes had changed over the years. I Googled each successive ventilation code and downloaded it. Finally, I needed the volume of each cellblock. This was necessary to calculate their air exchange rates, as well as their smoker density. It proved to be aggravatingly difficult, because the Department of Corrections stonewalled, refusing to provide this information, which should have been readily available from the building blueprints. So, David was forced to visit every single one of the 21 different locations in the six jail buildings where Raymond had been housed to measure the space volumes himself. In my experience as an expert witness in several other prisoner cases in New York State, contempt for the inmates, and the stonewalling of their attorneys by arrogant prison authorities was just business as usual. In cases I did in other states, I had no problem in getting copies of building schematics, and even obtained a walk-through video tape for one of them.

In a previous case in 2002 [Alamin v. Coefield 96 Civ. 1630], where due to blatant stonewalling by the authorities at Green Haven Prison in Stormville, NY, I had to go to the maximum security prison myself, get my hand stamped with indelible ink, get buzzed through five electronic doors, and spend two hours pacing off the cell block volume myself. As we were leaving and I walked through the grim corridors with the prison official and Alamin's lawyer, I was stunned by the fact that every prisoner I passed in the long lines waiting to enter the mess hall was black. There was just one anomaly, a pale, chubby, middle-aged balding white man standing out like a bleached raisin in a bushel of brown ones. We gazed at each other in mutual astonishment. I recalled this incident to David Marquez over dinner. He remarked, "I know that guy, he was a client of mine. He had an affair with a married woman, and the two of them decided to bump off her husband and collect his life insurance. So, he hires a hit man to do the job. The husband got killed, but the hit man bungled it, got himself arrested and ratted out his solicitor to get a lighter sentence. The victim's wife successfully managed to avoid complicity, and my client was convicted of murder. He's now serving a life sentence, and the widow moved to Miami with the proceeds."

Ultimately, I managed to calculate the ventilation rate per occupant, the number of occupants and the space volumes for all 21 areas in the six jails in which Raymond Marqez had been sequestered during his imprisonment. I obtained data sufficient to estimate the number of smokers and their average smoking rates as well. Using the Rosetta Stone Equations, this enabled me to calculate the smoker density and air exchange rate to plug into the habitual smoker model. Then I could estimate the average and range of Raymond's fine particle and carcinogen exposure from secondhand smoke and translate that into an estimated serum cotinine level for comparison to the national NHANES database. In this manner, it appeared that Mr. Marquez's weekly exposure to secondhand smoke particles and carcinogens was nearly triple that of a Western New York State bartender. Furthermore, his estimated mean cotinine level exceeded the mean for all U.S. males by a factor of 40. For good measure, I compared his estimated cotinine level to the actual cotinine levels that I had been able to obtain in three other prisoner cases: it differed by just 11%.

The next hurdle to surmount was the issue of *General Causation*: what was the relationship between tobacco smoke and bladder cancer? There was no question whether smoking caused bladder cancer or not. It did. There were two potent bladder carcinogens in tobacco smoke: 4-aminobiphenyl (4APB) and 2-napthylamine (2NPA) that were also listed by OSHA as industrial carcinogens *with short latency periods between onset of exposure and appearance of disease in workers*. The epidemiological evidence concerning the magnitude of the risk at the lower levels of exposure involved in passive smoking in the very few studies published was positive, but unfortunately none were statistically significant, a common problem usually resulting from poor exposure assessment and small numbers of cases. So, in the absence of the necessary study of passive smoking and bladder cancer, the obvious alternative was to extrapolate his increase in risk from active smoking data.

This I could readily accomplish using a prospective epidemiological study of 58,279 Dutch smokers aged 55 to 69 by Zeegers et al. (2002) (Figure 57B).

The third hurdle to jump was the nettlesome fact that Raymond had been an active smoker for 30 years. The Zeegers study also allowed me to estimate the decline in risk of bladder cancer for ex-smokers as a function of elapsed time since the last cigarette. After 30 years of smoking, Raymond's risk of bladder cancer from smoking was about twice that of a nonsmoker at the time that he quit smoking in 1976. Beginning with his quitting date, I plotted his decline in risk as a function of time for 22 years until he was jailed at Rikers (Figure 57 A). This enabled me to conclude that by 1998, his residual risk was essentially the same as a never smoker, i.e., at background levels.

Then the issue of *Specific Causation* arose. Was Raymond Marquez exposed to enough smoke for a long enough time to cause bladder cancer in a nonsmoker? If so, his medical experts would be able to testify that Marquez's bladder cancer, to a medical certainty, was caused by tobacco smoke. Because bladder carcinogens in tobacco smoke had demonstrated short latency, and since Mr. Marquez had previously smoked, this ipso facto increased his susceptibility to future exposure, and arguably shortened the remaining latency period. Next, I had to calculate whether his jailhouse secondhand smoke exposure had significantly increased his risk of cancer. I estimated that Mr. Marquez' risk of bladder cancer as an ethnic white Hispanic was increased over baseline by an average of 76% with a range of 37% to 152%. This was more than sufficient. And since the 5-year survival rate for bladder cancer was about 77%, he would have had a roughly 23% risk of dying from bladder cancer within 5 years. This translated into a risk of 6 bladder cancers per thousand persons exposed at that level. To put this into a different perspective, recall that OSHA defines a working lifetime risk of 1 death per thousand workers as a "significant risk of material impairment of health." EPA decision rules for hazardous pollutants defined a full lifetime risk of 3 deaths per 10,000 persons as a de manifestis risk, invariably worthy of regulation. Raymond's exposure was 20 times higher. Next, I compared his estimated exposure to the U.S. Air Quality Index and found that it corresponded to the "Significant Harm" level for fine particle air pollution. This comported with Raymond Marquez's deposition on the smokiness of jail air variously describing it as "outrageous", "palls of smoke", "a lot of smoke, a lot of discomfort in breathing" and "visible to the eye". This was clearly consistent with levels of smoke near the upper part of the range of concentrations I had measured in smoky bars, bingo games, and pool halls. And it also satisfied the requirement of specific causation.

Finally, I turned to the issue of just how well the jail had been run. I observed that, "It is abundantly clear that the New York City Department of Correction did not manage the risk of secondhand smoke in its jails according to sound public health principles. As long ago as 1990, the New York State Clean Indoor Air Act required that all State-owned and run facilities adopt smoking policies that reduced involuntary exposure to secondhand smoke. In 1995, the New York City Clean Indoor Air Act applied similar requirements to municipal-owned and run facilities within the City limits. The provisions of the Act include smoking restrictions in workplaces, where all public and common areas were required to be smoke-free. Smoking was restricted, but not prohibited, in other enclosed work areas. In 1998, the New York City Department of Correction was notified that it was in violation of this Act. In short, to within a reasonable degree of scientific certainty, Mr. Marquez's risk of bladder cancer has been significantly increased by his exposure to SHS in New York City's jails. Finally, this increase in risk sustained by Mr. Marquez could have been totally prevented if New York's Department of Correction (NYDOC) obeyed the law and protected the inmates in its care from SHS, and heeded the advice of numerous public health, environmental health, and occupational health authorities that secondhand smoke was a cause of human morbidity and mortality. Instead, NYDOC smoking policy actively encouraged smoking by both inmates and guards in its prisons, and abetted inmates' smoking by retailing nearly 5 million packs of cigarettes to these inmates in just one of its six jails alone during Mr. Marquez's tenure."

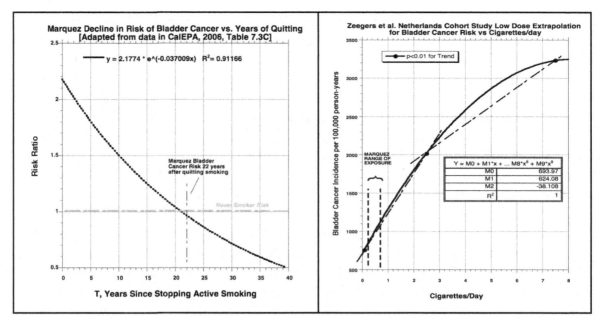

FIGURE 57A, LEFT, DECLINE IN BLADDER CANCER RISK IN EX-SMOKERS; THE BACKGROUND RISK FOR NEVER SMOKERS IS THE HORIZONTAL GREEN LINE AT A RISK RATIO OF ONE FIGURE 57B, RIGHT, EXPOSURE-RESPONSE FOR INCREASED RISK OF BLADDER CANCER VS. CIGARETTES SMOKED PER DAY (CPD). AT THE LOW-DOSE END, THE RISK APPROXIMATES A LINEAR RELATIONSHIP: BLADDER CANCER RISK = 694 + (624 CASES PER 100,000 PY)(CPD), REPRESENTED BY THE RED DOTTED-AND-DASHED LINE FROM ZERO TO 2½ CPD. THE CURVES WERE PLOTTED BASED ON CAL EPA DATA PLUS THE DATA GIVEN IN THE ZEEGERS STUDY. THE PARAMETERS OF THE CURVE FIT IN FIGURE 57B ARE INSET IN THE BOX (REPACE JL, MARQUEZ EXPERT REPORT, 2007).

Then it was the defense's turn. The City hired two expert witnesses to attack my 107-page report. The first was their medical expert, one Dr. Wishnuff, who asserted that there was no evidence that passive smoking increased the risk of bladder cancer, so the general causation argument was not met, and that even if it had been met, the latency period was too short. This prompted the City's defense lawyer, Scot Gleason, who was their top toxic tort specialist, to immediately file a *Frye Motion*, which is New York State's version of the federal *Daubert Motion*, designed to exclude expert testimony that was not generally accepted science. The City made a motion for Summary Judgment to exclude my testimony. As part of the City's brief, the following issues were raised: **"Major Defense Issue #1: How can the plaintiff argue that he contracted bladder cancer from secondhand smoke exposure when there is not a general consensus in the medical community that exposure to secondhand smoke is a cause of bladder cancer?"**

I made an 8-point rebuttal to Issue #1, saying in part: That the Surgeon General (2006) has stated "there is no safe level of exposure to SHS; that dose-response relationships for active smoking can provide insights into the expected magnitude of disease resulting from the exposure of nonsmokers to ETS;" … "Although the mathematical forms of these models vary, none have included a threshold level of active smoking that must be passed for lung cancer to develop." Well, then how does this apply to bladder cancer? I argued that EPA emphasized the use of models in dose-response assessment for environmental carcinogenesis, noting: "Dose-response assessment for each tumor type is performed in 2 steps: "assessment of *observed* [epidemiological] data to derive a point of departure" from which "extrapolation to lower doses to the extent that is necessary" is made. That two studies identified higher levels of hemoglobin adducts of the bladder carcinogen 4-aminobiphenyl in nonsmokers exposed to SHS, "providing supporting evidence that nonsmokers exposed to ETS may be at increased risk of bladder cancer." That risk factors identifying susceptible individuals include "disease, altered organ function, lifestyle, and lifestage, that can augment key events in carcinogenesis." That

"When cancer effects in exposed humans are attributed to exposure to an agent, the default option is that the resulting data are predictive of cancer in any other exposed human population." And finally that, *"The default procedure for the observed range of data [e.g. in smokers] when a biologically based model is not used is to use a curve-fitting model for incidence data."* Plaintiff was clearly an elderly man in ill health, and subject to an unusual lifestyle involving the stress of prison life and very heavy exposure to SHS. So far, so good.

The next problem was to rebut Gleason's **"Major Defense Issue #2: "**Was the plaintiff, while in defendants' custody, able to establish that he was exposed to enough cigarette smoke during his twenty-nine (29) month pretrial detention in various DOC jail facilities to have developed bladder cancer while in custody?" My rejoinder to this argued that I had showed that the Plaintiff was exposed to levels of tobacco smoke at such high doses that they were closer to active smoking than to the average nonsmokers' exposures to SHS, and therefore the active smoking data was pertinent. Also, using established EPA methodology, I was also able to show that this shortened the plaintiff's latency for onset of disease within his period of incarceration.

Dr. Wishnuff raised the issue of the lack of "statistically significant" epi studies of passive smoking and bladder cancer. While this was true, he ignored the elephant in the room: secondhand smoke contained the potent bladder carcinogens, 4 ABP and 2 NAP, and was a known cause of bladder cancer in smokers. Further, the California EPA had noted that there were "serious limitations in the passive smoking and epi studies, and that hemoglobin adducts of bladder carcinogens had been detected at higher levels in passively exposed nonsmokers than in unexposed nonsmokers." Finally, Wishnuff asserted that the issue of appropriate disease latency had remained unaddressed, ignoring my extensive appendix dealing specifically with this issue. Not to be outdone in raising specious arguments, Scot Gleason weighed in, asserting that "in estimating the SHS exposure of Mr. Marquez, Repace used a "model that required so many assumptions that it has never been subjected to peer review and that does not generate result that scientists would view as accurate or reliable." This hand-waving argument failed because I had cited a number of authorities that had deemed my model reliable. Then I sparred a couple of rounds with Gleason's second defense expert. The City brought in a Mr. Springston, a so-called ventilation engineer who attacked my ventilation calculations. His arguments were ineffectual, easily dispatched, and don't bear repetition.

So, the City's *Frye Motion* failed, and I was admitted as an expert witness. Then the City played the trump card from its rigged deck. A week before trial, the original trial judge mysteriously disappeared and was replaced by a *new* judge. In the next surprise from Gleason's grab bag of nefarious legal trickery, he persuaded the new judge to *again* review my credentials as an expert, forcing me to preview my courtroom presentation in a videoconference before the new judge and the opposing attorney. So, the defense got a sneak preview of their main antagonist's courtroom testimony. I suspect they were not at all pleased. While the new trial judge admitted my testimony, the damage was done. But the worst was yet to come.

The day before trial, I flew up to New York, and checked into a downtown Manhattan hotel near the courthouse. On the morning of the trial, David picked me up and drove us to the courthouse at 60 Centre Street. He was quite upbeat, but looked a bit peaked; he confessed to having slept just 3 hours the night before. He said that in addition to his father's case, he had to keep current with his other cases. We walked into the empty courtroom in Manhattan Superior Court about a half-hour before trial. David strolled over to the jury box, and pulled a flask out of his pocket. Sprinkling its contents on the floor of the jury box, he intoned, "With this Holy Water, I bless this jury, that it may reach a just verdict." In retrospect, he should have drenched the judge's bench with it.

The City's next ploy was really dirty pool, the dirtiest I have ever seen in the sixty legal cases I had been involved in. I had just been sworn in and was sitting in the witness box ready to testify. David was all set to hand out copies of my slides to the jury. Suddenly the new judge holds up his hand and summons the two opposing counsel to a bench conference. Addressing both attorneys, he says, "Let's step out into the hall."

He then waves off the court stenographer, commanding, "You – stay here!" I wonder, *What the hell is going on?* When they return from the hallway conference, it gets even weirder. David, who is about to elicit my direct testimony suddenly says, ***"The Judge ruled that you can't show your slides to the jury."*** What? I am totally stunned; this has never happened to me before in the dozens of trials I was involved in. Presenting complex testimony without benefit of pictorial slides will make my presentation incomprehensible to this jury of laypersons. David and I do our best to repair the damage, but I know this trial is going south.

At noon, I went to lunch with David and his parents, and I found Raymond to be a pleasant and urbane man. The afternoon was devoted to Scot Gleason's cross-examination of my testimony, and again without slides, my counter arguments went over the heads of the jury. My daughter, Justine, who lives in Manhattan, attended part of the trial that day. Over dinner with her in a great Brazilian restaurant that evening, she said, "It was like an episode of *The Sopranos.*"

The next day, David bitterly complained to the judge that his ruling barring my slides was patently unfair to his client. The judge replied disingenuously, "*I never said he couldn't show his slides to the jury, I said they couldn't be entered into evidence.*" Afterward, David said "We were sandbagged." Raymond got so pissed off that he told David, "You can pay your experts' fees out of your own pocket." But it wasn't David's fault. The City was never going to let the notorious Spanish Raymond, who had vexed them for 30 years, get a fair trial. My best guess is that the first judge wouldn't go along with this farce so they replaced him with a ringer. The City's Law Department was quick to rub salt into our wounds. In a gloating press release on May 13, 2008, it bloviated:

"New York, May 13, 2008 – New York City has prevailed in a case that attracted attention from *The New York Times, the Daily News,* the *New York Post* and other media venues, with several citing it as an example of the ridiculous lawsuits that are brought against the City – and which taxpayer dollars unfortunately must be spent defending. The matter involved Raymond Marquez, commonly known to authorities as 'Spanish Raymond' and believed to be the longtime chief of a notorious Spanish Harlem numbers betting racket that ran from the 1940s to 1990s. In 2001, Marquez filed a $15 million civil lawsuit against New York City's Department of Correction.

Marquez claimed that his bladder cancer, diagnosed in September 2000, was caused by secondhand cigarette smoke he inhaled at the Tombs and Riker's Island during 29 months behind bars while awaiting trial. The only problem? Marquez also claimed that his *30-year smoking history* had nothing to do with his getting bladder cancer, although active smoking is the No. 1 cause of bladder cancer. Marquez admitted in his court testimony that he smoked a half-pack to a pack a day from age 15 to age 45. Incredulously, though, he also claimed that he never inhaled. After a two-week trial, a Manhattan jury unanimously (6-to-0) rejected Marquez's arguments late Friday and found that the City was not negligent in the way it ran Riker's Island.

After asking one question regarding verdict form technicalities – and after only an hour and 15 minutes of deliberations – the 5-woman, 1-man jury found for the City. One juror told the City after the verdict that 'it was very easy to come to a decision in the City's favor on the question of negligence.' There has been no recurrence of Marquez's bladder tumor since early 2001, when he had surgery. 'We are very pleased that the jury unanimously agreed that the City did nothing wrong in the way it ran Riker's,' said Scot Gleason, lead trial counsel for the City. 'This is a perfect example of some of the ridiculous cases that the City must defend against – and on which we waste incredible amounts of taxpayer dollars.' … Opposing counsel David Marquez, the plaintiff's son, jokingly complained to the judicial hearing officer during jury selection about how aggressively the City and attorney Scot Gleason had pursued this matter. 'I feel like I'm competing against Gregory Peck in *To Kill a Mockingbird,* so how can I win?' … ."

On May 14, 2008, John Eligon of *The New York Times* reported:

"A man who was notorious among the city's law enforcement officials for being a leader in the illegal numbers business has lost a lawsuit against the Department of Correction that blamed the Rikers Island smoking policy for his bladder cancer. … Scot Gleason, the lead lawyer for the city in the case, said he believed he sold the jury on two major points. "We never violated any laws," he said. He said he also persuaded the jury to consider society's attitudes toward smoking at the time Mr. Marquez was in Rikers, 1998-2001, not what they are now."

What a load of legal bullshit, Mr. Gleason. The Eighth Amendment of the United States Constitution prohibits the federal government from imposing excessive bail, excessive fines, or cruel and unusual punishments. The U.S. Supreme Court has ruled that this amendment's Cruel and Unusual Punishment Clause also applies to the states. This was the most egregious case of cruel and unusual punishment – without even being convicted of a crime – that I ever saw. Raymond Marquez had been denied bail in 1998, during the second term of New York City's over-the-top mayor, Rudy Guiliani, a former U.S. prosecutor who had presided over the era of "broken windows policing" of his police commissioner, William Bratton, which held that minor disorders and violations created a permissive atmosphere leading to more serious crimes (Wikipedia, 2017). Rudy even praised an off-duty detective who shot an unarmed squeegee man. Bottom Line? *You can't fight City Hall.*

In Other Developments

Earlier that year, Dr. José Calheiros from Portugal had invited me to lecture in Spain and Portugal. I flew business class to Spain to give a presentation at the invitation of Dr. Manel Nebot to the Barcelona Health Department's secondhand smoke research group, after which we dined in a very nice tapas restaurant, and Manel showed José and me the city. I visited the bizarre and wonderful Casa Museu Gaudi, the surreal house of the architect, Antoni Gaudi, which has hardly a straight line in it. Then José and I flew to Lisbon where I briefed the Portuguese Surgeon General on secondhand smoke, followed by a public lecture that evening at the Gulbenkian Museum. Situated on several acres in the heart of the City, the Calouste Gulbenkian Foundation is located in a serene green oasis beautifully landscaped with huge trees, flowering shrubs, and large ponds. The museum has a substantial collection of Middle Eastern, Asian, and European Art. At the time of his death in 1955, Gulbenkian, a British oilman and philanthropist, was said to have been worth between $300 and $900 million.

I wrapped up my trip to Lisbon with a sumptuous dinner in a fine waterfront restaurant, entertained by my gracious hosts, Dr. José and Mr. Charles Buchanan, an official with the Luso-American Friendship Association, which had generously funded my trip. I devoured a couple of the most delicious calamari, 18 inch octopus tentacles that tasted like they had just come from the sea, accompanied by a bottle of excellent wine. The following evening, José and his girlfriend, Dr. Sofia Ravara, entertained me in their Lisbon apartment with another fine dinner. One of the wonderful things about my trips around the world was the great friends I made in the public health community.

Returning home, I lectured at Johns Hopkins, Stanford, and the University of Nevada Reno, giving presentations on forensic applications of exposure science at Hopkins and secondhand smoke in casinos at the latter two. During the year I published two more papers, one on secondhand smoke pollution in Kentucky's hospitality industry in the *Journal of Environmental Health* (Lee et al., 2008), and the other in the *William Mitchell College Law Review* on benefits of outdoor smoking restrictions (Repace, 2008). The high point of the year was finally achieving our long-time goal of a smoke-free Maryland: All enclosed workplaces, including restaurants, bars, and private clubs, had become 100% smoke free on February 1, 2008. A bulletin issued by Americans for Nonsmokers' Rights announced that, "Maryland's statewide smoke free victory followed years of hard work to enact strong smoke free laws at the local level, which covered 50% of Maryland's population, including laws in Montgomery County, Howard County, Prince George's County, Takoma Park, Kensington, Baltimore and Rockville." It only took 28 years of struggle...

In June of 2008, ASHRAE reissued its *Position Document on Environmental Tobacco Smoke,* reaffirming that ventilation was not a valid control for secondhand smoke [ASHRAE, 2008]. During the year, I had given 11 talks, interviews, and presentations, and measured secondhand smoke outdoors on a college campus and two cruise ships. It was a very good year. Aside from the Spanish Raymond debacle.

CHAPTER 21

BEATING THE HOUSE AT ITS OWN GAME

"The ... 2008 Pennsylvania Clean Air Act lets casinos devote half the gaming floor to smoking. ... Harrah's, in Chester, features huge rotating neon signs to guide players. ... At Parx, the popular and profitable slots box in Bensalem, overhead arrows offer nonsmokers no relief. ... Biophysicist and former EPA official James Repace has spent 30 years ... in the study of secondhand smoke. He secretly tested air quality at Harrah's and Parx in 2007 - one-word review: toxic - and suspects it's worse under the bogus partial smoking ban. ... Repace asks, 'how does the smoke know where to stop?'"

M. Yant Kinney: Casinos and regulators blind to smoking rules. The Philadelphia Inquirer, May, 12, 2010.

It began February of 2008, when I was asked by the United Autoworkers, Region 9A, to testify before the Connecticut Legislature on air quality in Connecticut Indian Casinos. My testimony began as follows:

"The Bill before you, *An Act Prohibiting Smoking in Regulated Areas of Casinos*, is important because Secondhand Smoke (SHS) is a significant threat to the health of casino workers and casino patrons. Although modern casinos may have large space volumes and state-of-the-art ventilation systems, these cannot eliminate SHS. Similarly, although some casinos maintain nonsmoking areas, these areas are not smoke free. This has been demonstrated in Connecticut Casinos. On February 23, 2008, (last Saturday night), scientists from the Roswell Park Cancer Institute in Buffalo, NY measured respirable particles (RSP), a federally regulated outdoor air pollutant, using a real-time portable air pollution monitor in both the Foxwoods and Mohegan Sun Casinos here in Connecticut (Skeps et al., 2008). They have shared their data with me for this hearing. Figure A shows RSP pollution in the smoking areas of both Foxwoods and Mohegan Sun are similar and about 7 times outdoors.

Figure A also shows that while the nonsmoking areas in both casinos are lower than in the smoking areas, they remain heavily polluted with RSP at levels 4 to 5 times outdoors. Figure 2 shows that whether it's nonsmoking Bingo, Poker, or Slots, RSP remains 3 to 5 times outdoors, and in all cases 2 to 4 times the level of the Federal Clean Air Standard. This is not surprising and agrees well with measurements I have made in the Delaware Park Casino in Wilmington, DE in 2004 (Repace, 2004), and Harrahs, Philadelphia Park, and the Mohegan Sun Casinos in Pennsylvania (Repace, unpublished). In the Delaware Park Casino, air quality measurements I made demonstrated a 90 to 95% drop in fine particle and carcinogen air pollution in this casino after a state-wide workplace smoking ban."

However, the Mohegans had drunk the Kool Aid sold by Big Casino and Big Tobacco: the Associated Press in an article captioned, **"Tribes upset over bill to ban smoking at casinos,"** reported that:

"The chairman of the Mohegan Tribe said on March 25th, he'll take the state of Connecticut to federal court if a bill to limit smoking in the state's two tribal casinos becomes law. Bruce 'Two Dogs' Bozsum said he'll also withhold the state's 25 percent share of the Mohegan Sun casino's slot machine revenues. … Both the Mohegans and the Mashantucket Pequots, owners and operators of Foxwoods Resort Casino, provide the state with about $400 million annually. …. He said 90 percent of the tribe's property… is already smoke-free. 'We've been doing a great job of doing it already,' he said." (AP, 2008).

My second casino encounter, referenced in my Connecticut testimony, had begun in the summer of 2007 with a phone call from Ms. Joy Blankley Meyer, with the American Lung Association (ALA) of Pennsylvania. Joy was also the Executive Director of the Pennsylvania Alliance to Control Tobacco (PACT). Joy commissioned me to design and conduct a study of secondhand smoke in Pennsylvania casinos. Although Pennsylvania's Clean Indoor Air Act made smoking illegal in restaurants, office buildings, schools, sports arenas, theaters, bus and train stations, as well as most bars, an exemption permitted smoking in up to 50% of casino gaming floors. I designed a study to monitor atmospheric fine particles ($PM_{2.5}$), carcinogenic particle-bound polycyclic aromatic compounds (PPAH), and ventilation (using CO_2) and for good measure, added a component of urine cotinine measurements using Lung Association volunteers as human monitors in the guise of gambling patrons.

As I knew from my previous experiences in the Treasure Chest and Empress/Horseshoe cases, callous casino management stubbornly clung to the preservation of smoking on their gaming floors despite the health hazard to their workers. In this caper, I used a large array of high-tech monitors, including two Sidepaks, one borrowed from Wayne Ott, and I bought another, using Wayne's instrument to calibrate the new one. I also had monitors for carbon monoxide (CO), carbon dioxide (CO_2), temperature and relative humidity, plus two Ecochem carcinogen monitors, all with real-time data logging capability. I used a Piezobalance to verify the calibration of the particle monitors. All the miniaturized instruments were easily concealed in two shoulder-carried camera bags that could be deployed almost anywhere without arousing undue suspicion. So, in August 2007, Joy, her assistant, Jennifer Kulaga, and I descended upon three Pennsylvania casinos with our two monitoring packages. We visited the Mohegan Sun (in Wilkes-Barre), the Philadelphia Park, aka Parx (in Bensalem), and Harrah's (in Chester). We counted the total number of persons, the number of active smokers, and measured the space volume using a combination of ultrasonic and infrared laser distance monitors plus pacing.

Meanwhile, our eight ALA volunteers gambled and inhaled secondhand smoke in the Philadelphia Park, The Meadows (in Meadowlands) and at Presque Isle Downs (in Erie). They submitted urine samples for cotinine testing before and after their hours' long visits to the casinos. All of these casinos were modern structures, built between 2006 and 2007. My study addressed the following research questions: "(1) What were the levels of air pollution from respirable particles (RSPs) and carcinogenic PPAHs inside and outside these casinos? (2) What was the change in urine cotinine experienced by a casino patron and the equivalent personal breathing zone exposure to RSPs and PPAHs from secondhand smoke (SHS)? (3) Could the average level of RSP air pollution from SHS in the casinos be predicted and generalized by a model? (4) Based on extrapolation from the measured SHS exposure and dose data, how big were the risks of lung cancer and heart disease mortality from SHS for casino workers, what was the air pollution hazard to patrons and workers, and how great were the odor and irritation levels for nonsmokers from SHS in these modern casinos?"

Secondhand smoke exposure is defined as the atmospheric concentration that contacts a person's boundary. SHS dose is defined as the inhaled, absorbed, and metabolized body fluid concentration of cotinine, the major metabolite of nicotine, incorporating exposure duration. I related exposure and dose using the Rosetta Stone Equations.

On average, these casinos had a relatively low average of 6% of the patrons smoking at any one time, and ventilation rates per occupant 50% higher on average than those formerly recommended (30 cfm/occ) under ASHRAE Standard 62-1999 for casinos with smoking. Despite these favorable factors, the RSP concentration measured inside the three Pennsylvania casinos in which smoking was permitted averaged 6 times that of outdoor levels and the PPAH concentrations averaged 4 times outdoors. This clearly exposed nonsmoking workers and patrons to harmful levels of air pollution. Moreover, in the Mohegan Sun, the sole casino with a separate nonsmoking floor, RSPs were almost 3½ times outdoors and PPAHs were 37% higher than outdoors, as a result of SHS infiltration from the smoking salon. Based on measured RSP levels, nonsmokers' SHS odor and irritation thresholds were massively exceeded in smoking areas and considerably exceeded in the nonsmoking area. Satisfyingly, the Active Smoker Model predicted the combined RSP observations to within 14%.

Based upon the cotinine-derived RSP levels, I estimated that secondhand smoke in Pennsylvania casinos produced an excess mortality of approximately 6 deaths per year per 10,000 workers at risk (10,000 was also approximately the total number of Pennsylvania casino workers in 2007). In perspective, this was 5 times the rate at which Pennsylvania coal miners have died in mining disasters and 26 times OSHA's significant risk level for exposure at that level for a 45-year working lifetime. Nonsmoking workers or patrons exposed to casino smoking at the observed level of occupancy for 8 hours would experience 'unhealthy air' according to the US Air Quality Index. And at maximum occupancy, this would become 'very unhealthy' air. I applied the cotinine-derived PPAH exposures from SHS from the volunteers to calculate the casino workers estimated 24-hour PPAH carcinogen exposure. It was more than 5 times the average outdoor background from our baseline measurements in the monitored casinos. In October of 2008 I presented our measurements of secondhand smoke in Pennsylvania Casinos at the ISES meeting in Pasadena, CA. The atmospheric and biomonitoring methods I had developed to assess the risks of secondhand smoke over the years had been brought to full fruition in this study (Repace, 2009).

In 1998, the German Research Council had classified ETS as a human carcinogen. A decade later, my SHS exposure and risk assessment models were being employed to assess lung cancer risks in the German hospitality industry. In order to assess retrospective exposure and cumulative workplace risk from ETS in German hospitality workers, Kolb et al. (2010) of the Institute for Occupational, Social and Environmental Medicine, University Hospital of Ludwig-Maximilians University in Munich, had performed an extensive literature search, reviewing 575 publications. Of these 46 made the final cut. Kolb found that mathematical models for retrospective exposure assessment were "predominantly based upon a model by Repace and Lowrey (1980, 1985, 2000)." Other models … found results consistent with Repace and Lowrey … ." "Taking uncertainties for assessing diseases such as lung cancer into account," … "having adapted it to the German hospitality sector, [the model of Repace and Lowrey] appears to be capable of approximating the cumulative exposure."

MEASURING SECONDHAND SMOKE IN "THE BIGGEST LITTLE CITY IN THE WORLD"

Encouraged by the results of the Pennsylvania casino study, and aided by the good offices of Wayne Ott, who was now a visiting scholar at Stanford University in the Department of Civil & Environmental Engineering, I suggested to Prof. Lynn Hildemann that she might profitably apply for a 3-year grant from the Flight Attendant Medical Research Institute (FAMRI) to study secondhand smoke in casinos. Lynn won the grant, and she assembled a team consisting her three PhD environmental engineering students, Ruoting Jiang, Viviana Acevedo-Bolton, and Kai-Chung Cheng, plus Wayne, Neil Klepeis, and me. We began our casino odyssey on September 1st 2007. We considered making measurements in Atlantic City, Las Vegas, or Reno. Reno won out, as I had a knowledgeable friend there, Prof. Chris Pritsos, chair of the Department of Nutrition at the University of Nevada, Reno, who was already studying cotinine in casino workers, and was actively advocating for casino workers' health. Chris offered his assistance. Our plan was to design and carry out measurements of secondhand smoke in 44 casinos. Our first team effort was carried out on 8 casinos in Reno, Nevada, which has a neon sign arching over its main thoroughfare advertising itself as the "Biggest Little City In The World." Chris enabled us to get university rates at the Siena Casino/Hotel in downtown Reno, and generously loaned us two of his staff to assist with measurements in the CalNeva and provide information on the others. Ruoting, Viviana, and Kai spent two successive weekends there; on the first they measured fine particles inside and outside the Atlantis, Silver Legacy, and Grand Sierra casinos. On the second weekend, I joined them and we measured the space volume, counted the active smokers and total persons, and measured fine particles, carcinogens, and carbon dioxide inside and outside the Cal Neva, Harrah's, the Siena, the Tamarack, including their nonsmoking restaurants, and for comparison, in the Fernley Nugget, the only smoke-free casino in the state, located 35 miles outside of town. As usual, our monitoring equipment was concealed in camera bags.

While I analyzed our Reno results, the rest of the team flew back to California to measure fine particles in a statewide survey of California Indian Casinos. Although California prohibited smoking in commercial casinos in 1994, the ban did not extend to California's Tribal casinos, because they were on Indian lands regulated by the tribes, subject to treaty agreements that had been negotiated with the Federal Government in the 19th Century. These treaties did not mention gambling casinos.

In the California phase of the study, the rest of the team measured fine particles ($PM_{2.5}$) as well as casino volume, effectiveness of separation of smoking and non-smoking areas, and area person and smoker density. They visited 37 of the 58 Indian casinos for one to three hours on weekend or holiday evenings, using two or more concealed monitors. Their measurements showed that the average $PM_{2.5}$ concentration for the smoking slot machine areas was fully nine times as high as outdoors, whereas contiguous casino non-smoking restaurants were four times as high from infiltrating smoke. Levels in non-smoking slot machine areas varied: complete physical separation from smoking yielded $PM_{2.5}$ concentrations essentially the same as outdoor levels, but the other two separation types failed, with mean levels ranging from two to four times as high as outdoors. Secondhand smoke contributed 89% of the elevated $PM_{2.5}$ concentrations in smoking casino slot areas. Average $PM_{2.5}$ concentrations in smoking areas exceeded the level of EPA's 24-hour clean air standard during 90% of the casino visits, indicating how polluted the air was [Jiang, et al., 2010].

As I wrote up the Reno results which involved the 8 casinos, I was inspired: why stop at 8? Why not use this paper as a vehicle for comparing the results of every single casino study ever published? I performed a literature search for published papers, and contacted a number of colleagues in government and academia, all of whom were willing to share their raw data. The combined data allowed us to arrive at some general conclusions concerning the impact of secondhand smoke over the entire casino industry and on the health of casino workers. Our data compilation encompassed casinos in California, Delaware, Nevada, New Jersey, and Pennsylvania, allowing us to develop a frequency distribution for fine particulate pollution for 66 casinos with smoking, with 3 nonsmoking casinos for comparison, as shown in Figure 58. Geometric means for fine particles inside the smoking casinos averaged 13 times outdoors, while the levels in the three nonsmoking casinos were slightly less than outdoors, indicating that 92% of the air pollution in smoking casinos was coming from secondhand smoke.

In a subset of 21 Reno and Las Vegas smoking casinos, 86% of the fine particle air pollution in adjacent nonsmoking casino restaurants was due to secondhand smoke. For the subset of 10 Nevada and Pennsylvania smoking casinos where carcinogens had been measured as well as particles, when respective background concentrations were subtracted, fine particle air pollution was strongly correlated with both airborne PAH carcinogens and with smoker density, but interestingly, *not* with ventilation rates. Carcinogen levels in 8 smoking casinos in 3 states averaged 4 times outdoors. The nonsmoking casinos' fine particle and carcinogen air pollution did not differ from outdoor levels. We concluded that casino ventilation and air cleaning practices failed to control secondhand smoke, that drifting secondhand smoke contaminated unseparated nonsmoking areas, and that smoke-free casinos reduced indoor air pollution to the same low levels found outdoors. And most importantly for human health, we concluded that fine particle air pollution from secondhand smoke in approximately half of all the smoking casinos measured exceeded a level known to produce cardiovascular morbidity in nonsmokers after less than two hours of exposure, posing acute health risks to patrons and workers (Repace et al. 2011).

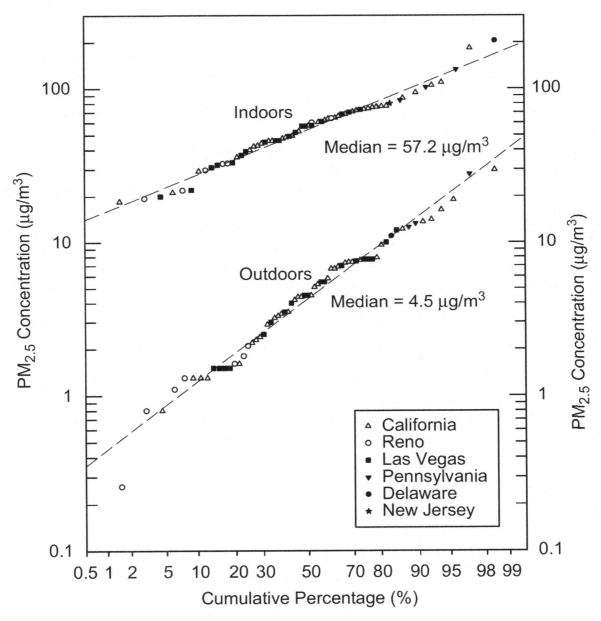

FIGURE 58. A LOGARITHMIC PROBABILITY PLOT SHOWING THE CUMULATIVE PERCENTAGE OF US CASINOS EXCEEDING A GIVEN PM$_{2.5}$ LEVEL. INDOOR (N=66) AND OUTDOOR (N=65) PM$_{2.5}$ CONCENTRATIONS FOR 66 VISITS TO 66 SMOKING CASINOS IN 5 STATES: 26 IN NEVADA (RENO AND LAS VEGAS), 35 IN CALIFORNIA, 3 IN PENNSYLVANIA, AND ONE EACH IN DELAWARE AND NEW JERSEY (REPACE ET AL., 2011).

Our inferences concerning heart disease risk for SHS were supported by the 2010 expert committee report of the National Academy of Sciences Institute of Medicine, *Secondhand Smoke Exposure and Cardiovascular Effects: Making Sense of the Evidence,* which stated: "On the basis of its review of the available experimental and epidemiologic literature, including relevant literature on air pollution and PM [airborne particulate matter], the committee concludes that there is a causal relationship between smoking bans and decreases in acute coronary events." The NAS estimated that decreases in acute myocardial infarction (AMI) in the 11 studies ranged from about 6% to 47%, depending on characteristics of the study, including the method of statistical analysis. So the clear inference is that failure to enact general smoking bans increases cardiac risk by 6% to 47%.

However, perennial tobacco industry consultant Peter Lee (2011), popped up with a contrarian view, asserting that due to "major weaknesses in many studies and meta-analyses, the impact of secondhand smoke on heart disease effect was at most 2.7% (2.1–3.4%)." Later, in 2014, Lee would publish a follow-up asserting that, "Though the findings suggest a true effect of smoking bans, uncertainties remain, due to the weakness of much of the evidence, the small estimated effect, and various possibilities of bias." Lee's article, published in one of the industry's favorite laundries for its mole papers, *Regulatory Toxicology and Pharmacology,* unsurprisingly made no mention of his funding source.

In 2012, Stan Glantz and Erin Gibbs began to retroactively study the frequency of monthly ambulance calls in rural Gilpin County, Colorado, 6 years before and 6 years after Colorado's 2006 smoke-free workplace law, which had excluded casinos. They found a statistically significant 23% county-wide drop ($P<0.001$), in general ambulance calls, but no significant change, ($P>0.9$), in calls that originated from the exempted smoky casinos. After the smoking was banned in Colorado casinos in 2008, they repeated the comparison. Post-ban calls originating from the now smoke-free casinos dropped by a statistically significant 19%, ($P<0.001$), while ambulance calls from elsewhere in Gilpin County remained static. This suggested that the health effects of secondhand smoke exposure occurred acutely. The authors note that Gilpin County is a major gambling destination. The 2009 Census showed a resident population of 5604, but the visitor population can exceed 40,000 at any given time as a result of people working at, staying at, or visiting local casinos and hotels in Black Hawk and Central City. They concluded, "exempting casinos from smoke-free laws results in more people suffering medical emergencies" (Glantz and Gibbs, 2013). This of course, is what had happened in the Treasure Chest and Empress Horseshoe casinos. Their study contributed further empirical evidence supporting our conclusion that casino workers and patrons really were at elevated risk of heart attacks from secondhand smoke at the levels found in casinos. Although the Glantz and Gibbs paper did not classify the reasons for the ambulance calls, what else but a heart attack (or severe asthmatic attack induced by secondhand smoke) would constitute a medical emergency?

The long-term consequences of chronic SHS exposure for casino workers were grim. In February of 2008, a New Jersey Judge issued a workers' compensation ruling on behalf of a casino worker injured by secondhand smoke. It was reported in part as follows:

Judge says secondhand smoke contributed to Claridge dealer's lung cancer
By Regina Schaffer, Press of Atlantic City, Wednesday, February 13, 2008.

"Kam Wong never smoked. Her husband didn't smoke. As a dealer at the Baccarat and poker tables at Claridge Casino Hotel, however, Wong breathed in cigarette smoke throughout her late-night shifts. That, according to a state workers' compensation judge, was the cause behind her lung cancer. In a preliminary ruling issued Monday, Judge Cosmo Giovinazzi found that 10 years of secondhand smoke exposure materially contributed to Wong's lung cancer, according to her attorney, Lawrence Mintz. … Giovinazzi awarded Wong 60 percent partial disability, plus lost wages for the six-month period between her first and second lung surgeries, totaling about $150,000, Mintz said."

And Ms. Wong had company: In 2005, Vincent Rennich, a 52 year-old casino pit boss in the Tropicana Casino in Atlantic City was in a car accident. His car was totaled, and he was rushed to the hospital. His X-rays and CAT scans picked up an anomaly in his right lung resulting in removal of a third of the organ. It proved to be lung cancer. Vince had never smoked and had worked in casinos for 25 years. He blamed the second-hand smoke he inhaled at the casino and filed a civil suit against the Tropicana seeking damages and demanding that smoking be banned on casino floors in New Jersey, the only venues exempted from the state's smoking ban. The following weekend, Rennich was fired. "How can they fire a guy with lung cancer?" Mr. Rennich asked. "What, I'm suddenly no good after 25 years?" (*New York Times*, 2007). I was an expert witness in Vince's case. In 2010, his lawsuit against his ex-employer was settled out of court for $4.5 million. He now works in Delaware's smoke-free Dover Downs casino, where he reported, "A lot of the guys from Atlantic City came down there to work because they couldn't stand the smoke." "His lawsuit became a rallying cry for the ultimately unsuccessful effort to ban smoking in the nation's second largest casino market" (*The Glouster County Times*, 2010).

THE COMMERCE CASINO CAPER

In 2013, at the request of the Los Angeles law firm Cummings and Franck, I made real-time measurements of fine particles inside and outside of the Commerce Casino, a poker casino in East LA. The dealers objected to being forced to work in the smoking room. The smoking cardroom was located in a tent-shaped building that the casino ludicrously claimed was an "outdoor patio," and therefore exempt from California's ban on smoking in commercial casinos. Sounded to me like somebody was paid off. Anyhow, my objective was to assess the risk to the dealers, bankers, and other casino workers from the diseases of secondhand smoke exposure at work. With the assistance of a confederate hired by the firm, I deployed two concealed SidePak AM510 real-time particle monitoring packages on Friday evening, February 8th, 2013. We sampled the smoking and non-smoking poker rooms inside, and the parking lot outside. I circulated one monitor outdoors and in both card rooms, which were packed with patrons, while my associate confined himself to two card tables in the smoking room and the outdoor parking lot. The monitors showed that the air quality in the Commerce Casino's smoking room was *Unhealthy,* according to the California quality index for $PM_{2.5}$. The air quality in the separate nonsmoking card room and outdoors was *Good*. At this writing, the case remains in litigation, with a trial anticipated for late 2018.

I estimated that the casino dealers working the smoking room had a 36% increased risk of asthma induction, plus a combined excess lung cancer and heart disease mortality risk of 32 deaths per 1000 workers for a 45-year working lifetime. Figure 59 shows the air quality data from outdoors, and in the smoking and nonsmoking rooms. Figure 60 shows the interior view of the smoking card room, illuminated by lights hung from the ceiling of this so-called "outdoor patio." While the hallway outside the sliding glass doors was vented to the outdoors, these doors were kept locked, and the building had a mechanical ventilation system. My nonsmoking confederate, Adam Vignola, played blackjack at two card tables while monitoring the secondhand smoke for 74 minutes, and measured the outdoor $PM_{2.5}$ for 27 additional minutes. The mean $PM_{2.5}$ level at the blackjack tables, which averaged 2 to 3 smokers, and 4 players plus the dealer, was 196 $\mu g/m^3$, (which worked out to the 98th percentile when compared to the 66 casinos in Repace et al., 2013). By comparison, the $PM_{2.5}$ level was 12 $\mu g/m^3$ outside in the parking lot, indicating that 94% of the pollution was from SHS.

THE DR. RON DAVIS SMOKE-FREE LAW.

In 2011, I was asked by Janet Kiley, of the Tobacco Section of The Michigan Department of Health, to evaluate the effectiveness of Michigan's Dr. Ron Davis statewide smoke-free law. The law was named after my old friend, Ron Davis, who had sadly passed away in 2008, at the age of 52, from pancreatic cancer. Following his service at DHHS's Office on Smoking & Health, Ron had been Chief Medical Officer of the Michigan Department of Health from 1991 to 1995, and had served as President of the American Medical Association from 2007 to 2008. Following the pre-ban/post-ban protocol from my Delaware study (Repace, 2004), Janet's health department team provided before-and-after SidePak measurements of fine particle air pollution in 78 restaurants in 13 cities in Michigan, plus three Detroit casinos that had been exempted from the law by the state legislature. It is one of the largest studies ever done.

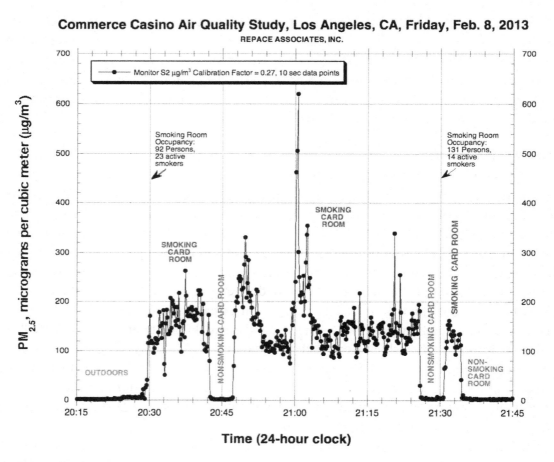

FIGURE 59. FINE PARTICLE AIR POLLUTION (PM$_{2.5}$) INSIDE THE COMMERCE CASINO'S SEPARATE SMOKING AND NONSMOKING CARD ROOMS, AND OUTDOORS (REPACE, 2013, UNPUBLISHED).

The Michigan Health Department team measured fine particles in six geographic regions of the State: Southeast, West, Upper Peninsula, Northern Lower Peninsula, Thumb, and Central. Included were the cities of Ann Arbor, Detroit, Flint, Grand Rapids, Kalamazoo, Lansing/E. Lansing, Marquette, Midland, Novi, Saginaw, Sault Ste. Marie, Traverse City, and West Branch. The 78 restaurants combined had a total observed patronage of 2964 persons, and 201 active smokers, for an active smoking prevalence of 6.8%. Multiplying 6.8% by 3 yielded an estimated restaurant smoking prevalence of 20.4%, using the rule-of-thumb devised by Repace and Lowrey (1980). By comparison, Michigan's statewide prevalence in 2009 was 19%. *Not bad for government work, Eh?*

FIGURE 60. VIEW OF THE COMMERCE CASINO'S SMOKING CARD ROOM (REPACE, 2013).

Before the smoking ban, 85% of the restaurants studied had Poor to Dangerous air quality, averaging *Unhealthy*, prior to the smoke-free law's enactment. After the ban, 93% of these restaurants had *Good* to *Very Good* $PM_{2.5}$ air quality. The smoke-free law had reduced mean fine particle air pollution levels by 92%. However, the three Detroit casinos, which had *Unhealthy* air quality when we measured it, remained in the *Unhealthy* range as a result of their exemption from the Dr. Ron Davis Law, a big loss for their workers.

This was a grand opportunity to see how well the Habitual Smoker Model predicted $PM_{2.5}$ concentrations in restaurant venues 31 years later. The model, with outdoor background added, predicted 93 $\mu g/m^3$ for the typical Michigan Restaurant, compared to an observed median of 91 $\mu g/m^3$, a difference of 2.2% (Shamo et al., 2015). Adjusting the predicted value by the range in observed active smoker density yielded, again with background added, a range of 28 $\mu g/m^3$ to 216 $\mu g/m^3$, which corresponded to the 10th and 80th percentiles of the measurements. Was this good or what? Figure 61 shows the results.

The take-home message is this: if modeling can predict the median level and range of fine particle air pollution in 78 restaurants in the State of Michigan with such a high degree of accuracy based on ASHRAE Standards for ventilation rate and occupancy plus state-wide smoking prevalence, unless there is a need to assess compliance, or for public relations purposes, there is actually no real policy need for regulatory agencies to conduct measurements to determine the air quality impact of smoking on indoor air in offices, factories, retail stores, etc., unless it's done for enforcement purposes.

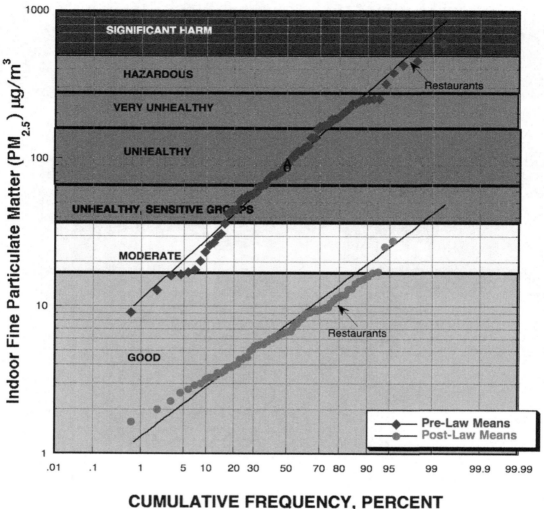

FIGURE 61. LOG-PROBABILITY PLOT OF PRE- AND POST-SMOKING BAN DATA OF THE 78 RESTAURANTS IN THE MICHIGAN 13-CITY STUDY. EACH DATUM REPRESENTS ONE RESTAURANT'S AIR QUALITY MEASUREMENT. THE FEDERAL 24-HOUR AIR QUALITY STANDARDS ARE SHOWN FOR COMPARISON. (REPACE REPORT, 2013; SHAMO ET AL., 2015).

HOW ABOUT THE SHS RISK TO BARTENDERS?

Tending bar involves the greatest exposure to toxic indoor air pollution from tobacco smoke of any occupational group. Following the 1986 US Surgeon General's Report declaring secondhand smoke to be a cause of lung cancer, the number of municipal laws restricting smoking in public places began to increase in North America. However, as discussed previously, during the 1980's and 1990's, such laws were vigorously resisted by both the hospitality and tobacco industries, who predicted future economic losses to bar and restaurant owners, denied the health risks of secondhand smoke, and promoted ventilation alternatives to smoke-free laws. In the U.S. in 2012, according to the Bureau of Labor Statistics, there were approximately 550,000 bartenders. Up until the early years of the 21st Century, few bar workers had the privilege of working in smoke-free bars.

According to Americans for Nonsmoker's Rights (2018), 25 states plus Puerto Rico and the U.S. Virgin Islands, with a total population of 200 million, have 100% smoke-free laws covering bars of all sizes and without separately ventilated smoking rooms, leaving 13 rogue states with no protection for bar staff (or patrons) from secondhand smoke exposure. Bitler et al. (2011) surveyed a random sample of about 1400 US bartenders in eating and drinking places from 1992 to 2007, finding that just about half of those staff were self-reported current nonsmokers, while two-thirds of all workers in eating and drinking places were nonsmokers. I was very interested in measuring how much workplace secondhand smoke exposure bartenders actually got on the job, since they routinely worked at arms-length from a battery of inebriate smokers whose smoking rates were enhanced by booze. I had previously collected cotinine data measured in Montreal and Boston bar and restaurant workers from which I could estimate air pollution doses using the Rosetta Stone equations, but for one reason or another, those colleagues who had collected the data failed to produce a completed manuscript.

However, in 2011, in a Phase II continuation of a previous study of Toronto bartenders' urine cotinine data (Bondy, et al. 2009), that the Ontario Tobacco Research Unit (OTRU) of the University of Toronto had collected in 2004 before and after Ontario's Smoke-free Workplace law, Prof. Roberta Ferrence of the OTRU asked me to estimate the secondhand smoke exposure and risk for that cohort of bar staff based on their data. I had published a study in 2006 of 8 volunteer patrons in 3 Bismarck, North Dakota bars that used urine cotinine to estimate personal exposure to secondhand smoke fine particle and particle-bound carcinogens during 6-hour visits using the Rosetta Stone equations (Repace, Hughes, and Benowitz, 2006). The Bismarck study (Figure 62) found that the air pollution in those smoky college bars was "Code Red" or *Unhealthy* for $PM_{2.5}$ (compare to Figure 61). These results were consistent with our actual measurements of air pollution in 6 Wilmington Delaware bars and 14 Western New York bars (Repace, 2004; Travers et al. 2004). I proposed using the same methodology on the Toronto bartenders' data and to extend the analysis to estimate the risk of premature mortality.

As discussed earlier, in Toronto, Canada's largest city, the Ontario Restaurant Association had aggressively and successfully lobbied the city council against passing smoke-free workplace laws for years prior to 2004. Instead they promoted a deceptive secondhand smoke "ventilation solution" demonstration project, which was later totally discredited by the early publicity of our Black Dog Pub study results (Repace and Johnson, 2006). After a failed attempt in 1997, Toronto and its surrounding municipalities finally succeeded in implementing a ban on indoor smoking on June 1, 2004 that included bars, bingos, and casinos. The Province of Ontario implemented the similar *Smoke-Free Ontario Act* on May 31st, 2006, embracing the remainder of the province.

We employed the full armamentarium of tools that my colleagues and I had developed since 1980 and pushed the envelope by estimating heart disease risk using widely accepted $PM_{2.5}$ models derived by C. Arden Pope and colleagues (2009) from $PM_{2.5}$ outdoor air pollution studies, for comparison with my alternative methods derived for SHS-$PM_{2.5}$. Our methodology went as follows: using the approximately 10 nanogram per milliliter difference between the bartenders' pre-ban and post-ban median urine cotinine levels as input into the Rosetta Stone equation, incorporating the reported 8-hour average workday, we estimated that the average inhaled secondhand smoke fine particle personal exposure at work for our 91 Toronto bartenders was about 420 $\mu g/m^3$; with a 7 $\mu g/m^3$ outdoor background added, this was comparable to the measured area-monitored level of 412 $\mu g/m^3$, with a 27 $\mu g/m^3$ background, measured in 14 bars and restaurant bars in Western New York State in 2003 (Travers et al., 2004). Similar results for 15 bars were obtained by Charoenca et al., in Thailand in 2013, who measured an average of 488 $\mu g/m^3$, also with a 27 $\mu g/m^3$ background. The Toronto bartenders' average air pollution dose corresponded to "*Very Poor Air Quality*," as judged by 3-hour Canadian Air Quality Standards.

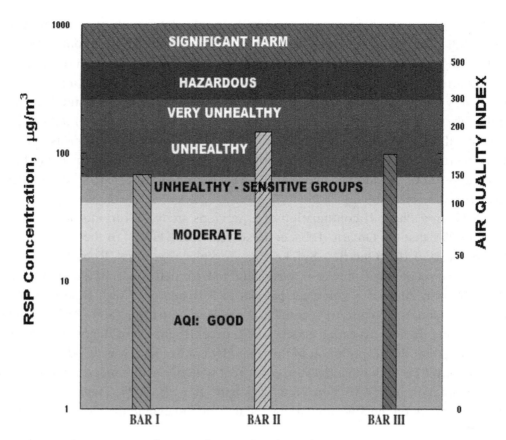

FIGURE 62. THE BISMARCK COTININE BAR STUDY (REPACE, ET AL., 2006).

Pre-law, 97% of the Toronto bar workers' doses had exceeded the 90th percentile for Canadians of working age. (Compared to their UK counterparts, the Toronto bartenders' doses averaged about 30% less than measured in English and Scottish bartenders studied by Jarvis.) Using the dosimetric risk model of Repace et al. (1998), we estimated an annual mortality rate of about 6 deaths per year among the Toronto bartender population, amounting annually to 102 deaths per 100,000 workers from secondhand smoke-induced heart disease and lung cancer combined. (By US OSHA standards, this would amount to 46 times Significant Risk.) In perspective, this was nearly 2½ times the annual occupational disease fatality rate for the entire provincial workforce in Ontario. Our combined premature mortality estimate for the bartenders from secondhand smoke was comprised of 5 deaths per year from heart disease, plus one from lung cancer.

By comparison, applying the estimated 140 µg/m³ daily average excess fine particle exposure for the bartenders to the alternative $PM_{2.5}$ and chronic ischemic heart disease exposure-response model of Pope et al. (2009), we estimated the risk of inhaling the same amount of fine particulate matter daily was about 4 deaths per year. This similarity of risk estimates using these alternative approaches lent credence to our heart disease risk model. Finally, we estimated the annual social cost of those 6 workers' lives lost from secondhand smoke at work at about $60 million Canadian dollars (US $50 million) using the US EPA figure for the value of a statistical life lost to pollution (Repace, et al., 2013). Tending a smoky bar is hazardous to one's health and incurs large health costs for the affected individuals.

SECONDHAND SMOKE AND BREAST CANCER

Meta-analyses conducted by both California Environmental Protection Agency (CalEPA) (in 2005) and the U.S. Surgeon General (in 2006) suggested a 60-70% increase in breast cancer risk confined to younger, primarily premenopausal women who had never smoked, associated with chronic exposure to SHS. Their findings were based on toxicologic and epidemiological weighing of evidence for both active and passive smoking as well as biology. The CalEPA concluded that the relationship was causal, while the Surgeon General concluded only that the evidence was only suggestive, based in particular on the lack of an established causal relationship between active smoking and breast cancer.

In April 2009, a Canadian Expert Panel on Tobacco Smoke and Breast Cancer Risk was assembled by OTRU at the University of Toronto. This panel, which included both Canadian and American experts, reviewed the latest evidence. They conducted a meta-analysis of five studies with good measurement of lifetime exposure to active and passive smoking and found that each about doubled the risk of premenopausal breast cancer. The panel concluded that earlier studies with either poor or no assessment of lifetime secondhand smoke exposure had underestimated the true risk of both active and passive smoking breast cancer as a result. The cohort studies reviewed suggested that higher pack-years and longer duration of active smoking appeared to increase breast cancer risk 10% to 30%. Further, the panel found that those long-term smokers with N-acetyltransferase 2 (NAT2) slow acetylation genotypes (half of North American women, depending on ethnicity) had a 45% to 50% increased breast cancer risk for 20 or more pack-years of smoking.

The Canadian panel concluded that based on the weight of evidence from epidemiologic and toxicological studies and understanding of biological mechanisms, the associations between active smoking and both pre- and postmenopausal breast cancer were also consistent with causality. For secondhand smoke, they concluded that the association between SHS and breast cancer in younger, primarily premenopausal women who have never smoked is consistent with causality. However, the evidence was considered insufficient to pass judgment on SHS and postmenopausal breast cancer (Collishaw, et al., 2009). The essentially identical breast cancer risk the panel reported for both active and passive smoking suggests to me that the exposure-response relationship between tobacco smoke exposure and breast cancer rises very steeply from the levels at which nonsmokers are exposed and flattens out at the far greater levels to which smokers are exposed, similar to the non-linear exposure-response relationship for heart disease reported by Pope et al. (2009).

CHAPTER 22

BREATHING YOUR NEIGHBOR'S SMOKE

A Greenbelt man's secondhand smoke lawsuit against his neighbors and housing cooperative ... has gone up in smoke, but experts say this may not be the last such case. The two residences had a common wall. ... Kathleen Hoke, director of the University of Maryland Legal Resource Center for Tobacco Regulation, Litigation and Advocacy said that, "As we went smoke-free in our workplaces and in public places, ironically, the place where people felt they were less safe was in their home. On the other hand, many people feel it's their right to smoke in the privacy of their own homes..."

Gazette.net, Maryland Community News Online, Friday, July 25, 2013.

Secondhand smoke infiltration in multiunit housing is a widespread problem in North America today. Due to the permeability of attached structures, the high emission rates of toxic air pollutants from tobacco combustion, and inter-unit pressure differences, secondhand smoke can readily migrate from one apartment unit to another. In 2011, there were an estimated 34 million occupied multi-unit buildings, ranging from 2 to more than 50 units; of these, 77% were rented, the remainder were owned, and the median year of construction was 1974 (US Census, 2011a).

Using national and state representative data from 2009, King et al. (2012) estimated that 25.8% of U.S. residents, or 79.2 million persons, live in multi-unit housing (ranging from 10.1% in West Virginia to 51.7% in New York). Of these, an estimated 79% have smoke-free home rules. Among U.S. residents with smoke-free home rules, about 45%, or 28 million multi-unit housing inhabitants report secondhand smoke infiltration in their apartments each year, ranging from 26,000 in Wyoming to 4.9 million in California (King et al., 2012). In a national random survey of 418 U.S. multi-unit housing residents, Licht et al. (2012) reported that, among all respondents, 56% supported smoke-free building rules. Of the 36,011 municipalities in the US (US Census, 2007), as of October 2014, 171 of 236 in 28 states banned smoking in public or subsidized multi-unit housing (although the degree of enforcement appears to be poor). However, by 2014, just 15 municipalities had prohibited smoking in private market-rate multi-unit housing, and 14 of the 15 ban smoking on balconies or patios as well, all in the San Francisco Bay Area (ANRF, 2014).

The 2006 Report of the U.S. Surgeon General, *The Health Consequences of Involuntary Exposure to Tobacco Smoke*, cautioned that there is "no risk-free level of exposure to secondhand smoke" and that "even small amounts of secondhand smoke exposure can be harmful." The Surgeon General warned that there has been growing concern about the impact of secondhand smoke exposure in multi-unit housing, including commercially owned apartments and apartments, as well as public housing, and recommended the adoption of smoke-free policies.

In most jurisdictions, getting smokers to voluntarily stop smoking in their own homes has been generally futile. Further, it has been very difficult for affected nonsmokers to convince skeptical or somnolent condominium or co-op associations to change their policies. Not to mention the additional costs involved in selling a condo that's full of smoke plus the cost of moving. For renters, it has been nearly impossible to persuade landlords to allow a lease to be broken due to smoke infiltration without heavy penalties, unless one is willing to break it through expensive legal action.

In 2006, I saw an opportunity for research in this area, and began advertising nicotine monitoring services on my website, www.Repace.com. Through the good graces of my friend and colleague, Prof. Katherine Hammond at Berkeley, I was able to obtain passive nicotine monitors on consignment, and I charged a fee of $500 for producing a defensible legal report to demonstrate infiltration (usually about 50 pages in length). Clients fronted an additional $100 for monitor analysis, payable to the University of California at Berkeley. I required each client to provide photos of the interior and exterior of their building, a narrative describing any symptomatic effects they perceived from secondhand smoke infiltration, and whether they had sought medical attention as a result. This information was incorporated in the report (Figure 63).

By June 2018, I had collected monthly-average nicotine concentration data on 73 complaint residences in California, Colorado, Florida, Maryland, Massachusetts, Minnesota, New York, New Jersey, Minnesota, North Dakota, Pennsylvania, Tennessee, Utah, Virginia, and Washington, DC, as well as the Canadian Province of Quebec. And, I had testified in about a dozen legal cases for J.P. Szymkowycz in Maryland, DC, and Northern Virginia. J.P. filed suit solely against the smoker in all but two of the cases, avoiding the deep-pockets insurance companies who defended landlords and homeowners' associations. He managed to prevail in every single one except the first, which became a teaching experience.

Nonsmoking residents with secondhand smoke infiltration complaints typically report a mixed bag of one or more associated health and symptomatic effects such as sinusitis, bronchitis, chronic fatigue, cough, bronchospasm, eye and throat irritation, breathing difficulties, asthma aggravation, offensive or intolerable odor, health risk concerns, inflamed lungs, hypotension, atrial fibrillation, choking, nausea, vomiting, chronic cough, shortness of breath, emotional distress, and mucus hypersecretion. Some have been hospitalized, and many have sought medical treatment. All who tried sealing or caulking leaks or using air cleaners reported failure to eliminate or even control exposure acceptably. Some even used so called "air fresheners," which act as odor masking agents. Such devices only add additional VOCs to the air and often create additional symptoms (Steinemann, 2017). Several reported that their homes were uninhabitable and had to move out temporarily or permanently. Some moved in with friends or relatives or into hotels and motels and one poor woman was forced to sleep in her car. One hapless Maryland couple sold their smoky condo, bought another, and wound up with the identical problem in their new apartment. In addition, three business clients not included in the above statistics were severely impacted. One, a spa located next to a cigar bar, was smoked right out of business when its clients were gassed.

SHS occurs in multi-unit housing at every income level, from public housing to luxury condos – I've had wealthy clients who lived in penthouse apartments in Manhattan and poverty-stricken pro-bono clients residing in subsidized housing in rural Massachusetts and everything in between. All had similar complaints of health symptoms and lack of habitability of their apartments due to secondhand smoke infiltration from neighbors' smoking. These words, taken verbatim from the self-reports of a representative sample of a baker's dozen of my clients illustrate their anguish:

"Secondhand smoke infiltration is intolerable. affects my health and my ability to function. I can't bear to be in my own home, I developed a cough I couldn't get rid of smoke causes headaches, difficulty in breathing and malaise. I collapsed twice from secondhand smoke exposure. I'm unable to use my space normally for any purpose. My worst symptoms are

16 HOMES AND 2 COMMERCIAL PREMISES WITH SECONDHAND SMOKE INFILTRATION COMPLAINTS

FIGURE 63. SECONDHAND SMOKE INFILTRATION OCCURS IN MANY BUILDINGS, CAUSING MISERY FOR AFFLICTED NONSMOKERS. THESE REPRESENT JUST A FEW OF MY 73 CLIENTS.

headaches lasting for hours. my home has become uninhabitable. I have to wear a face mask the entire time 1'm in my apartment. I have itchy, watery eyes, throat constriction, cough and bronchospasm. I developed reactive airway disease, vocal cord closure, use emergency inhalers. I experience choking, nausea, sore throat and airway irritation. I take cough medicine constantly. At times the smoke is so bad that I can't stay in my own home, and have to [leave]. When I walk in the door from work, the smoke burns my eyes and throat. At times I eat dinner out, because I can't bear to be in my own home. Several of my friends refuse to come over, as they don't want to be around the smoke. I had to take my husband to the hospital because of an acute asthma attack due to the smoke, and we have both been getting headaches."

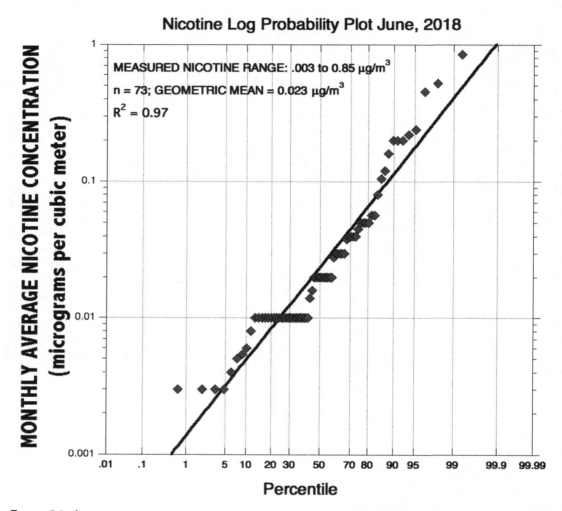

FIGURE 64. A LOG-PROBABILITY PLOT OF NICOTINE VALUES MEASURED BY THE AUTHOR IN NONSMOKERS' APARTMENTS IN MULTI-UNIT HOUSING. OCCUPANTS OF ALL 73 UNITS COMPLAINED OF SECONDHAND SMOKE INFILTRATION AND WERE PROVIDED WITH PASSIVE NICOTINE MONITORS (J.L. REPACE, UNPUBLISHED DATA).

In one case, an upscale Georgetown condo in DC, the enraged homeowner successfully sued his neighboring smoker, then prevailed in his suit against his condo association for failure to comply with the nuisance clause in its bylaws. In the Washington, DC metropolitan area, I participated as an expert in over twenty cases before homeowner's associations or courts of law involving intrusions of secondhand smoke where the complainants received decisions or settlements that protected their right to smoke-free environments. The nicotine values associated with these 73 complaint apartments shown in Figure 64 range from 0.003 µg/m³ to 0.85 µg/m³.

Note that a microgram is a very small amount, a millionth of a gram, in one cubic meter of air, an amount of air that most adults at rest would take more than an hour to inhale. Yet, these individuals had one or more of the adverse symptoms in reaction to these low nicotine levels, as shown in Figure 64. This suggests that nicotine is a surrogate for components of secondhand smoke that are far more potent acute irritants, and are present in amounts sufficient to provoke such debilitating symptoms. Nicotine by itself has cardiovascular effects such as vasoconstriction. Figure 63 shows 16 residences and 2 commercial premises, a small but illustrative sample of the types of buildings where secondhand smoke infiltration caused misery, and worse, for my affected 73 residential and 3 commercial nonsmoking clients.

To study this issue in more detail, after our casino research ended in 2011, Lynn Hildemann at Stanford applied for a grant from California's Tobacco Related Disease Research Program (TRDRP). Her application was successful, and Lynn's two postdocs, Viviana, and Kai-chung, plus Wayne, Neil, and I became consultants on her new three-year TRDRP grant, which became a vehicle for the PhD thesis of Phil Dacunto, a Lieutenant Colonel in the Army Rangers. Phil spent the first two years of his research conducting controlled experiments. He studied the nicotine, fine particle, and VOC emissions of cigarettes and from various foods being cooked and calibrated the monitors. Phil developed a sophisticated computer model to differentiate fine particles from cooking and incense from those in secondhand smoke based on simultaneous measurements with several different types of monitor.

In the third year of the study, we measured secondhand smoke infiltration and pressure differences between adjacent smoking and nonsmoking motel rooms in Redwood City, California. This controlled experiment utilized monitoring equipment worth hundreds of thousands of dollars. It included fine particle monitors, carcinogen monitors, active nicotine monitors, detectors for carbon dioxide, carbon monoxide, relative humidity, temperature, inter-unit pressure differences, and ultrafine particles. Lance Wallace drove down from Santa Rosa to assist with the latter. The primary object of these experiments was to test Phil's models for source apportionment, i.e., to figure out what fractions of the aerosol in the receptor unit were due to smoking, cooking, or incense when one or more were being used in the source unit. A secondary goal, which was of primary interest to me, was to research the relative decay rates of fine particles and nicotine from secondhand smoke as they penetrated through the common wall from the smoking unit to the nonsmoking unit, as this had never been done, and all I had to work with previously in my research was the monthly-average nicotine level.

For the field study portion of his research, Phil recruited five San Francisco Bay Area nonsmoking multi-unit households whose occupants had complained to the health department about secondhand smoke infiltration in their homes. Phil authored three papers with Kai Chung, Viviana, Neil, Wayne, Lynn, and me as co-authors. The first of these described the results of sixty-six experiments with a SidePak and a gravimetric sampler to quantify the monitor calibration factors and to estimate emission factors for common indoor sources including cigarettes, incense, cooking, candles, and fireplaces. The second one detailed Phil's logistic regression models that correctly predicted the presence of cigarette smoke more than 80% of the time in both source and receptor rooms, with one model correct in 100% of applicable cases. Chemical mass balance (CMB) analysis of the source room provided significant $PM_{2.5}$ concentration estimates of all true sources in 9 of 13 experiments.

The third paper described Phil's field studies of gases and particles over 6 to 9-day periods in five nonsmoking multi-unit homes with reported secondhand smoke intrusion complaints in 2012. Nicotine tracer sampling verified intrusion in all five homes. Modeling and CMB analysis enabled identification and quantification of some of the precise periods of intrusion. Phil's computer models identified SHS in eight periods corresponding to when residents' diaries logged secondhand smoke odor episodes, and CMB provided estimates of SHS magnitude in six of these eight periods. Both approaches properly identified or apportioned all six cooking periods used as no-SHS controls (Dacunto et al., 2013a, 2013b,2013c).

Both approaches enabled identification of suspected SHS in five additional periods when residents did not report smelling smoke. The time resolution of this methodology went beyond sampling methods involving single tracers (such as nicotine), enabling the precise identification of the magnitude and duration of secondhand smoke intrusion, which is essential for accurate assessment of human exposure. In all five units – three in San Jose, one in Palo Alto, and one in San Francisco – active nicotine monitors demonstrated clearly that secondhand smoke intrusion did in fact occur in all of the complaint homes, ranging from 0.004 $\mu g/m^3$ to 0.014 $\mu g/m^3$. Identified smoking sources included downstairs neighbors, a next-door neighbor, and a neighbor across the hall. In those cases, secondhand smoke variously entered neighboring nonsmokers' units through bathroom exhausts, under-sink pipe gaps, a front door, and a heating duct.

While one resident (the man in San Francisco) had moved away, I was able to contact the remaining four of the five residents, including three men and five women, and one couple with children, to inquire as to their symptoms. The complaints and weekly average nicotine concentrations of these eight persons included nausea, headache, difficulty breathing, sore throat, cough (0.008 $\mu g/m^3$); headache, dizziness, difficulty breathing, malodor (0.014 $\mu g/m^3$); fatigue, eye and throat irritation, nausea, difficulty breathing, congestion (0.004 $\mu g/m^3$); and chest pain, difficulty breathing, headaches, nausea, eye, nose & throat irritation, fatigue, loss of sleep, bad odor, consulted physician and symptoms resolved after moving out (0.006 $\mu g/m^3$). Referring to Figure 64, this range embraces the 5th to the 40th percentile among my 73 complaint residences with positive nicotine results.

To put SHS particulate levels into perspective, Junker et al. (2001), in a seminal chamber study of 28 healthy normal young women, reported a median level for sensory (eye, nose, and throat) irritation of 4.4 $\mu g/m^3$ for secondhand smoke particles. (SHS-PM$_{2.5}$). In other words, half of an exposed healthy normal nonsmoking population will be irritated at exposure levels less than 4.4 $\mu g/m^3$. At this low 4.4 $\mu g/m^3$ level of SHS-PM$_{2.5}$, 67% of the nonsmokers in the Junker et al. (2001) study judged the air quality to be unacceptable. Further, Junker et al. found that the median odor-detection level for healthy normal adults in this study was ~1 $\mu g/m^3$. Thus, half of an exposed nonsmoking population will find SHS-PM$_{2.5}$ to be detectable and offensive at levels less than 1 $\mu g/m^3$. In Phil's Bay Area study, the peak secondhand smoke particulate levels in these homes sometimes spiked as high as 20 $\mu g/m^3$ to 70 $\mu g/m^3$. These values respectively are about 4.5 and 16 times the median irritation level found in the Junker et al. (2001) study, and 20 to 70 times the median malodor level. No wonder these nonsmokers complained.

A Note on the Physics of Secondhand Smoke Infiltration

The physics of air movement in buildings dictates that smoke from burning tobacco, marijuana, cooking, or incense will travel from unit to unit driven by pressure differences between apartments, from spaces of higher pressure to spaces of lower pressure, through holes in walls, ceilings, floors, ventilation systems, electrical outlets, plumbing openings, and cracks around doors into corridors, or even from adjacent balconies and patios through open windows in summertime. These inter-unit pressure differences are driven by a combination of wind pressure, cool air entering a building at lower levels and rising as it warms (stack effect), the operation of exhaust fans, or simply opening windows. Due to the atmospheric pressure gradient, the pressure difference between indoors and outdoors is directed inwards at the bottom of the building, and outward at the top of the building, with the plane of neutral pressure lying somewhere between the two. In a high-rise building, due to operation of HVAC systems, elevators, wind pressures, exhaust fans and opening of windows, airflows can be very complex, time dependent, and multidirectional, with air flows (and secondhand smoke) from apartments penetrating to apartments below and above as well as laterally (Lstibruk, 2006; 2014).

An engineering study of air infiltration of 35 apartments in four Minnesota Buildings in 2011 found that 8% of these units had 25% to 70% of their air infiltrating from neighboring apartments, and that sealing of cracks and holes plus increased ventilation reduced infiltration only by 25%. Despite these professional remediation efforts, 75% of the secondhand smoke infiltration remained (Bohac and Hewett, 2010).

The results of one of our controlled experiments is shown in Figure 65. Our Gang of Six conducted this study in the Pacific Inn Motel in Redwood City, California. It consisted of measurements in two adjacent motel rooms, one in which smoking was permitted, and the other in which it was not. Kai-chung served as our volunteer smoker (the data from this series of experiments persuaded him to quit). Both rooms were instrumented with particle and nicotine monitors, and the pressure difference (in units of Pascals) was measured during the experiment. We used an exhaust fan to create a controlled negative pressure in the nonsmoking (receptor) room with respect to the smoking (source) room. As Figure 65 shows, in this experiment, the ratio of background-subtracted $PM_{2.5}$ to Nicotine from secondhand smoke in the source room is 50:1, but after it has migrated through the walls under negative pressure into the receptor room, the ratio has increased to 148:1. This suggests that the sorption rate of nicotine as it migrates through small cracks and openings between units may be much greater than for particles; i.e., a small amount of nicotine indicates a much larger concentration of fine particles and other SHS pollutants, particularly gaseous volatile organic compounds, where the bulk of the irritation and risk obtains. Occupancy of a motel room is generally not continuous, and these rooms are cleaned post-occupancy, so that nicotine sorbed on and outgassing from surfaces might be less than in an apartment occupied full-time by smokers. In the latter case, the $PM_{2.5}$ to Nicotine ratio will be of the order of 10:1 due to the out-gassing of nicotine coating room surfaces, or so-called "third-hand smoke" (Repace and Lowrey, 1993; Matt et al, 2013).

SECONDHAND SMOKE INFILTRATION LITIGATION: A CASE STUDY

Schuman v. Greenbelt Homes, Inc., and Popovic, a civil action in which I was one of the expert witnesses for the plaintiff, perfectly illustrates the sociological problem from the widely different perspectives of the afflicted nonsmokers, the outraged smoking neighbors, the reluctant building management, the antagonistic attorneys, the out-of-their-depth judges attempting to be fair, and the sparring expert witnesses.

In February of 2009, I received a call from Max, my #1 son, concerning a problem which David Schuman, his friend and former neighbor, was experiencing. David, a NASA procurement attorney in his 40's, had complained about secondhand smoke infiltrating his cooperative row house, Unit Q, in the Washington DC suburb of Greenbelt, Maryland. One frosty evening, I sat down with Max and Dave over pizza and beer in a local pizzeria. Dave explained that for many years, his next-door neighbors in Unit R, Darko and Svetlana Popovic, had smoked inside and outside their unit, creating a health hazard and a nuisance for him from their intruding secondhand smoke. In recent months, particularly over the winter, conditions had deteriorated and become intolerable. Schuman complained of a heavy smoke smell on most nights. He stated that he had difficulty breathing, rapid heart rate, watery eyes, congestion, headaches and trouble sleeping. His doctor treated him for bronchitis-like symptoms for several months.

Schuman was often forced to open his windows during frigid weather to dissipate accumulating secondhand smoke (SHS) infiltrating from Unit R. He related that the smoke was particularly bad between 6 and 11 p.m. weekdays, even later on weekends, and was the worst during the winter months when all the windows in his apartment were closed. He asserted that he could not continue to live with smoke entering his apartment. To make matters worse, he had previously invested $65,000 in renovating his two-bedroom row house. In an attempt to stop the smoke, Schuman had sealed the area around the electrical junction box where infiltration seemed the heaviest. He repeatedly entreated the Popovics, and Greenbelt Homes, Inc., the cooperative association, to resolve the issue amicably. None of his efforts succeeded, and Schuman remained very concerned about the effects of the smoke on his health. However, the Popovics insisted that it was their absolute right to smoke as they wished in their home.

Accordingly, I provided Schuman with a passive nicotine monitor to assess the level of secondhand smoke infiltration into his home. He deployed it for 33 days, during the month of March and on into early April, and then mailed it to the Hammond laboratory for analysis. The monitor tested positive for nicotine, at 0.050 $\mu g/m^3$.

Schuman's home is the on the right side of the fence in third row and first column of the photos in Figure 63, and the Popovics' is on the left side of the fence. The view shown is the rear side of these row houses. Compared to the 72 other apartment homes with secondhand smoke infiltration complaints in thirteen states and the District of Columbia that I had tested as of June 2018, it was at the 80th percentile of complaint homes (Figure 64).

To put this into perspective, if the ratio of 148:1 for secondhand smoke particles to nicotine from the Pacific Inn experiment was applied here, this would suggest a level of particulate matter from secondhand smoke of $(148)(0.05\ \mu g/m^3) = 7.4\ \mu g/m^3$, exceeding the median level for secondhand smoke irritation in the Junker study by 68%. I drafted a report for Schuman that concluded, "to within a reasonable degree of scientific certainty, that Mr. Schuman is exposed to unhealthy levels of secondhand smoke from a cigarette smoker in his neighboring townhouse, that poses both acute and chronic hazards, and that is irritating and malodorous as well. Attempts to remedy the situation by sealing openings between the premises have been unsuccessful. This unhealthy SHS infiltration condition can only be remedied by elimination of smoking in the interior of the neighboring townhouse."

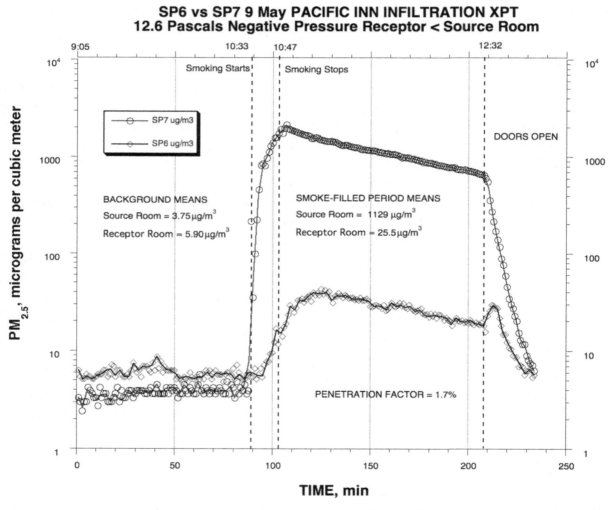

FIGURE 65. PENETRATION OF FINE PARTICLES AND NICOTINE THROUGH A MOTEL WALL FROM A SMOKING ROOM INTO AN ADJACENT NON-SMOKING ROOM IN THE STANFORD EXPERIMENTS. 1.7% OF SECONDHAND SMOKE PM$_{2.5}$ PENETRATED THE WALLS (19 μg/m³), WHILE ONLY 0.58% OF NICOTINE (0.13 μg/m³) DID. AS A RESULT, THE RATIO OF SHS-PM$_{2.5}$ TO NICOTINE INCREASED FROM 50:1 IN THE SOURCE ROOM TO 148:1 IN THE RECEPTOR ROOM. SP6 AND SP7 ARE THE FINE PARTICLE MONITOR DESIGNATIONS RESPECTIVELY FOR THE RECEPTOR AND SOURCE ROOMS. THE PASCAL IS A UNIT OF PRESSURE. 12.5 PASCALS = 0.00181 POUNDS PER SQUARE INCH (PSI). (REPACE ET AL., UNPUBLISHED).

Dave Schuman and I then met with the elected officials of the Cooperative association, and we each made presentations. The association's representatives met separately that same evening with Darko and Svetlana Popovic. Darko was employed as a Serbian-language broadcaster for the Voice of America in Washington DC. According to WHO, as of 2009, smoking was widely permitted in indoor offices or bars and restaurants in Serbia, male smoking prevalence was 38%, and female smoking prevalence was 30%, nearly double the smoking prevalence in Maryland for both genders respectively. Both Popovics were well-educated, articulate, and adamant in their belief that they had a perfect right to smoke in their own home, and that any smoke infiltration between units was the responsibility of the Association and Schuman, not theirs. This set the stage for a major confrontation between an unstoppable force (Schuman) and immovable objects (the Popovics), with the Greenbelt Homes Association as an extremely reluctant arbiter.

Schuman further complained that during mild and hot weather, he could not keep his window open when the Popovics smoked outside on their patio, as the smoke would penetrate through his open windows, and he was effectively denied the use of his own patio when Popovic smoked, as the two yards adjoined each other. This became a separate bone of contention. Accordingly, in a subsequent experiment I measured the 20 minute average PPAH carcinogen levels averaging 2 nanograms per cubic meter (ng/m^3) <u>above background</u> in Schuman's living room and kitchen with the windows open while Mr. Popovic was smoking on the patio, and both David and I experienced significant eye and throat irritation due to the secondhand smoke. To anyone technically trained, this clearly demonstrated that secondhand smoke had infiltrated Schuman's home from outdoors. Unfortunately, this was not in the judge's skill set.

Judge Albert W. Northrup convened the trial in the County Seat of Upper Marlboro, on August 17th 2011. There had been an earlier hearing in which Judge Northrup denied plaintiff's petition for a preliminary injunction.

Schuman's attorney, J.P. Szymkowicz, outlined his case, in part:

> "... In this case, there's a contract, Member's Handbook and the bylaws [that specify] ... that anything that's a nuisance, annoyance, inconvenience or causes damage to the members of the cooperative violates the nuisance clause. ... with Mr. Schuman and Ms. Ipolito's [Popvic's neighbor on the other side] comments that secondhand smoke from the Popovic house is causing them annoyance and inconvenience. It smells bad; kind of drives them crazy; makes them sick. ... It's a nuisance case.
>
> If this were Metallica [a raucous heavy metal band] being played at very high volume at midnight, we wouldn't need to have an audiologist come in and measure the sound. We wouldn't need to have somebody testify as to the medical impact because there may not be a medical impact on somebody that listens to Metallica unwillingly at midnight if it annoys or inconveniences them, which loud music undoubtedly would do. There would be no need for expert testimony. ...

Then GHI's defense attorneys presented their opening statement, in part:

> "Michael Goecke with my colleague, Jason Fisher, on behalf of Greenbelt Homes, Inc. ... Your Honor, there are two claims, only two claims, pending against Greenbelt Homes, Count Two, common-law action, breach of the implied covenant of quiet enjoyment; Count Five is a claim for negligence. ... Those are the only two claims pending against Greenbelt. Your Honor, ultimately, this case is about what is reasonable. What is it reasonable for someone to do in their home? What is it reasonable for someone to do in their yard?

In this context, in a cooperative, this is a community in garden style homes. They are tied together. They share walls with their neighbors. What is reasonable in that context? Has there been an unreasonable interference with Mr. Schuman's use and enjoyment of his property? Has Greenbelt Homes done anything unreasonable? Was there a duty that they breached? Did they not act like a reasonable cooperative should have? Did they not act like a reasonable landlord should have? … The evidence will not support his case." …

On November 3rd, 2011, after a five-day trial, that included impassioned testimony by the plaintiffs, defendants, and sparring by the opposing expert witnesses, Judge Northrup issued his ruling, stating in part:

… "We're going to start with Greenbelt Homes, Inc. [GHI]. I didn't find any bad faith on their part. We previously disposed of the punitive damages claim. They helped to negotiate this. They originally did the sealing some years ago. They assisted with the member complaint process. They certainly didn't [suggest] that Mr. Schuman move. That … certainly would have been outrageous. On the other hand, GHI is [not] a smoke-free community. There's a membership. There's a – we'll call it a majority rule type situation. You go to the membership panel. They make a decision. There was a point in this case where Mr. Schuman said he didn't realize he could take it further to the membership. There is a handbook. The procedure is there. If he chose not to take advantage of that, that's his decision. And I'll note that there were no other complaints. I do feel the business judgment rule applies in this case, and I think that they have complied with that.

But let's turn to some of these other efforts. The first effort at sealing. Mr. Schuman says that it didn't fix it. He says, instead, that the Popovics changed their smoking habits and, therefore, it was not a problem from 1998 to 2008. On the other hand, Ms. Ipolito, who is on the other side of a firewall instead of just a hollow wall, says that she continued to smell smoke during that period of time. …

I want to turn to some of the expert testimony. Mr. Repace did not calculate the risk from outside smoke coming in. His study didn't measure secondhand smoke from outside, with the windows closed. [In a demonstration of his monitor in the courthouse] He [testified that] it showed two nanograms, I believe it was. This was similar to the measurements in Mr. Schuman's house and that question came up. … And the answer was because the courthouse gets its air from the outside. Well, Mr. Schuman's house gets its air from the outside as well. So, in this, we're still learning. … [*N.B. Here, Judge Northrup confuses Schuman's 2 ng/m^3 <u>above</u> background with the Courtroom's 2 ng/m^3 background level as a result of clever lawyering by GHI's attorneys*].

This is the last, great unresolved area. He said at the first hearing, for example, secondhand smoke dissipates in 25 feet. In the next hearing he changed his view based on new data. So one must ask what will tomorrow's new data be? It's, as he said, an evolving area. Dr. Gots [GHI's defense expert] testified. But both these people may have some bias. Mr. Repace clearly has – this is a significant and admirable effort on his part, the secondhand smoke issue. … on balance, I would lean toward Mr. Repace's testimony in that, in my mind, secondhand smoke is not good. It's harmful. It presents a risk.

Dr. Munzer [Shuman's medical expert] mentioned that the surgeon general's report is, quote, the gold standard. Dr. Munzer didn't examine Mr. Schuman. He reviewed the records. [Schuman's] reaction to secondhand smoke may be transient and is, quote, minor. There are, he says, he admits, other possibilities. Finally, he says there is no specific likelihood that Mr.

Schuman will develop a disease due to secondhand smoke in this case. Dr. Granite [Shuman's treating physician] says smoke contributes to Mr. Shuman's symptoms. … The report of Dr. Granite was not admitted. However, ... He was able to provide no direct or specific link to any medical problem by Mr. Schuman related to secondhand smoke.

These discomforts must not be more than those ordinarily to be expected in the community and incident to the lawful use of the offending property or business. If they exceed what might be reasonably expected and caused unnecessary damage or annoyance, then the Court, in an appropriate case, will ask. I can't find, in this case, that it is unreasonable, and I will quote from Mr. Schuman, and you can find this on his supplemental brief at page 25. He's talking about the symptoms and respiratory issues. 'I experienced them when I experienced the smoke. I didn't experience them when there wasn't smoking, and I didn't experience them when the Popovics stopped smoking inside.' That's his testimony.

Having said all of that, … I am not going to issue a declaratory judgment that all secondhand smoke is bad or a nuisance per se or must be banned. The preliminary injunction is moot. I will find for the plaintiff … to the extent that I will grant, by consent, a permanent injunction with regard to inside smoking by Mr. and Mrs. Popovic. Beyond that, I will find for the defendant [with respect to outdoor smoking]. It's been a long case. I hope I've given sufficient record for everybody to go wherever they go from here. Do I find irreparable injury in this case? No, I can't: Let me make sure I haven't missed anything else. I can also quote Mr. Popovic. Earlier on he said, "this is the wrong example, the wrong case and the wrong time" or something to that nature, and I think that's, perhaps, a good summation of the case."

Following the trial, Schuman appealed twice, to the Special Court of Appeals, and then to the Maryland Supreme Court. Both Appeals were denied, which set a problematic precedent. It was a bitter defeat for Dave Schuman. As for his smoking neighbor, after the cancer death of his wife, Mr. Popovic sold his co-op unit to nonsmokers and moved back to Serbia, where he could smoke to his heart's content.

In the wake of the Schuman case, legislation to ban smoking in multi-unit housing in Maryland was introduced in the House of Delegates by Montgomery County Delegate Ben Kramer. David and I and John O'Hara, as well as many members of Maryland GASP, all testified before the State legislature in favor of Kramer's bill. However, it failed in the face of heavy opposition from the potent apartment house and tobacco lobbies. Following that defeat, Kramer reintroduced his bill so that it pertained solely to Montgomery County, but even that was defeated. As a last resort, Kramer attempted to persuade the liberal Montgomery County Council to enact a local multi-unit housing ban. However, it crashed and burned there too.

Despite the unfavorable precedent in the appellate court, in 2013, 5½ years later, a new case in New York City shocked the real estate world; on March 2, 2016, *Habitat Magazine* reported:

— "In a decision that's sure to fuel the smoking debate in every co-op in the city, a state Supreme Court judge has awarded more than $120,000 in back maintenance, interest and attorney fees to a co-op shareholder who claimed that smoke from other apartments had permeated her unit and rendered it uninhabitable.

The judge wrote: "… if you want to … rent out residences, you [must] insure that your tenants are not forced to … breathe carcinogenic toxins." The lawsuit was filed by Susan Reinhard, who bought [her] Connaught Tower co-op … in 2006 but never occupied [it] … ."

Another shoe dropped on February 3, 2017, when the U.S. Department of Housing and Urban Development (HUD) rule to ban smoking in public housing throughout the nation came into effect. According to HUD,

"This rule requires each public housing agency (PHA) administering public housing to implement a smoke-free policy. Specifically, no later than 18 months from the effective date of the rule, each PHA must implement a "smoke-free" policy banning the use of prohibited tobacco products in all public housing living units, indoor common areas in public housing, and in PHA administrative office buildings. The smoke-free policy must also extend to all outdoor areas up to 25 feet from the housing and administrative office buildings. This rule improves indoor air quality in the housing; benefits the health of public housing residents and PHA staff; reduces the risk of catastrophic fires, and lowers overall maintenance costs" (HUD, 2017). However, HUD's rule does not apply legally to privately-owned housing. Moreover, from my experience, it appears that while PHA's comply de jure with the HUD rule, de facto enforcement of their smoke-free policies appears to be minimal to non-existent.

A perception exists in some quarters that banning smoking in the privately-owned individual units of multi-unit housing is illegal. The Tobacco Control Legal Consortium (TCLC) has stated that landlords and apartment associations may prohibit smoking or refuse to allow smoking for new, and in many cases existing, occupants. According to the TCLC, there is no judicially recognized "right to smoke" in a multi-unit dwelling, whether the dwelling is privately owned or is public housing. Residents of multi-unit dwellings have a variety of common law remedies for stopping secondhand smoke infiltration. A resident of a multi-unit dwelling who can show that secondhand smoke exposure limits a major life activity can use the federal Fair Housing Act to seek to end the secondhand smoke infiltration. Landlords and apartment associations can prohibit smoking in their leases and governing documents, although they may be able to take action even without such language (Shoenmarklin, 2009). Smoking in multi-unit housing apparently will remain a contentious issue for some time to come.

Active smoking at any level of consumption is well-known to be the single biggest cause of COPD. Chronic irritation of the mucus membranes of the lung can cause COPD. Several recent studies have implicated secondhand smoke as a cause of COPD in nonsmokers. There are nearly 5 million California nonsmokers with smoke-free home rules who have suffered from secondhand smoke infiltration in their apartments. A UCLA study estimated that there are 61,000 cases of COPD associated with household smoking in neighboring Los Angeles County alone, and nearly a quarter of a million cases in all of Southern California, including Orange County.

At this writing, I am serving as an expert witness in *Sorenson v. Overlook at Anaheim Hills, et al. OCSC Case No. 30-2016-00869276,* in the City of Anaheim in Orange County, California, in the Los Angeles metropolitan area. This is without a doubt one of the worst cases of injury from secondhand smoke infiltration I have ever seen. The plaintiff, a lifelong nonsmoker, was exposed to secondhand smoke infiltrating into her Orange County apartment from one to two chain smokers in the apartment below for five years, from April 2011 through September 2016. Cooking smoke added to this pollution. The smoke infiltrated through ten points of entry into her bedroom, living room, bathroom, and laundry closet. In June 2011, she began to have acute breathing difficulties, suffered from eye, nose, and throat irritation, coughing, shortness of breath, and on occasion, headaches and lightheadedness. She attributed these symptoms to secondhand smoke infiltrating from the apartment below.

By August 2015, she had developed reactive airways disease, accompanied by a lingering cough, and in December 2015, she was medically diagnosed with chronic obstructive pulmonary disease (COPD). By November 7, 2017, she was diagnosed as suffering from "shortness of breath on exertion." Since 2006, multiple agencies of the State of California have warned that air leakage between apartments could expose nonsmokers to secondhand smoke from neighboring smokers, placing those nonsmokers at risk of irritation and allergic reactions, as well as acute and chronic cardiopulmonary and carcinogenic adverse health effects.

Using a mathematical model, I estimated a range of respirable particulate secondhand smoke concentrations generated by the plaintiff's chain-smoking neighbors in the unit below as high as the levels found in the smokiest restaurants, bars, and casinos ever reported. A portion of this secondhand smoke generated in the unit below infiltrated into Ms. Sorensen's unit, at levels I estimated to range into the *unhealthy* to *hazardous* zone when compared to the health-based federal air quality index for outdoor air. Even at the lowest end of the estimated range, those levels of secondhand smoke exceed the median level of irritation caused by secondhand smoke reported in the Junker et al. (2001) study of female nonsmokers.

CHAPTER 23

THE FAROE ISLANDS FARRAGO

The Faroe Islands are an autonomous province of Denmark in the North Sea situated between Scotland and Iceland and over 1000 km from the mainland. The Faroes are a rugged archipelago with an oceanic climate, windy, wet, and cloudy. Despite their 62° northerly latitude, temperatures average above freezing throughout the year because of the Gulf Stream. The name translates as "the islands of sheep." Tórshavn is the largest town in the Faroe Islands and its capital; it is the administrative, economic, and cultural centre of the Faroes. Tórshavn is located in the southern part on the east coast of the island of Streymoy. To the northwest of the city lies the 347-meter (1,138 ft) high mountain Húsareyn, and to the southwest, the 350-meter (1,150 ft) high Kirkjubøreyn. The town proper has a population of 13,000 (2008), and the greater urban area a population of 19,000. The Vikings founded the first parliament here around year 900. In the area around the harbor is the seat of government, the Faeroese parliament. Nearby are shops, restaurants, hotels and a cinema." The island is noted for its pristine air and water quality, and is a refuge for children with cystic fibrosis, a severe respiratory condition that seriously shortens lifespan, and is greatly aggravated by air pollution exposure.

Wikipedia; Reveal L, personal communication.

In late 2009, I received an email from Ms. Lynn Reveal evocative of the 1970's Piscataway incinerator follies. Lynn had worked in public health in the San Francisco Bay Area where she became aware of my work on indoor and outdoor air pollution from secondhand smoke. Lynn and her attorney husband, Michael, now lived in the Faroe Islands where they ran a small business consulting firm located on the main island of Streymoy. Lynn and Michael dwelt in a hilltop community of homes known as *Inni á Gota,* in the town of *Hoyvík* on the outskirts of Tórshavn. These homes *were* heated by piped-in hot water brought to temperature from waste heat in a remote trash incinerator and in an electric power plant. Such "distant heating plants," as they are called, burn everything from heavy oil to wood pellets to trash, and are quite common in Denmark.

The local heating company had announced plans to build a new plant with very short smoke stacks located on the seacoast just below the community. The company building the plant commissioned *Averhoff Energi Anlæg A/S,* a Danish consulting firm, to prepare an environmental impact statement (EIS). The local environmental health department, called the Umhvørvisstovan in Danish, provided the EIS to reassure the community of the proposed plant's safety. However, after perusing it, the board of the *Inni á Gota Homeowners' Association* became deeply concerned about the possible air pollution impact of smoke from the proposed new plant, for several reasons. First, the proposed smokestacks and the nearest homes were little more than 87 yards (~80 meters) apart, and the neighborhood kindergarten lay only 109 yards (~100 meters) away. Second, the smokestacks were very short, with their tops barely rising to the ground level of the hilltop on which the homes lay. Third, the plant would burn high sulfur fuel oil. Three strikes and you're out.

Despite these grievous flaws, The Averhoff Report benignly concluded that the proposed plant would have little air pollution impact on the community. The Tórshavn Umhvørvisstovan, possessing no particular air pollution expertise, failed to raise any objections to the plant siting. Lynn sent me a Google Earth photo of her community, with her overlay of the topography surrounding the community, as shown in Figure 66. The seacoast lies to the east on the right side of the figure. The proposed heating plant is the blue rectangle in the Figure showing that the ground level of the proposed plant site lies at 90 meters above sea level. The white rectangles in Figure 66 show the elevation of the topography above sea level. The tops of its three 20 meter-high smokestacks would reach to a height of 110 meters. By comparison, the ground level of the Inni á Gota Community to the Northwest, lay at 100 to 113 meters, with the rooftops of its homes rising to about 107 to 121 meters above sea level. So clearly many of the roofs of the homes rose as much as six meters (~20 feet) *above* the tops of the proposed stacks. The Faroese Telecom HQ sat on ground 90 meters above sea level, with its rooftop air intakes rising to 106 meters, i.e., only 4 meters (13 feet) below the tops of the stacks, allowing for no margin of safety (L. Reveal, 2012).

CHALLENGING THE AVERHOFF REPORT

The community decided that The Averhoff Report was a whitewash. And they were right. The site of the proposed plant was located on the coast between the sea and the community and would obviously be subject to strong sea breezes that could blow its stack gases into the hilltop community's homes and the elementary school. It was clear that they did need my assistance. Although I had not performed smokestack air pollution

FIGURE 66. TOPOGRAPHICAL VIEW OVERLAID ON A GOOGLE EARTH VIEW OF THE INNI Á GOTA COMMUNITY (TOP CENTER), SHOWING THE LOCATION (BLUE RECTANGLE) OF THE PROPOSED DISTANT HEATING PLANT AND THE FAROESE TELECOM BUILDING (L. REVEAL, PERSONAL COMMUNICATION).

calculations since the Blue Plains days of the early 1970's, I had reviewed stationary source (smokestack) regulations for EPA for a half dozen years in the 1980's. I was sympathetic to the community's plight and intrigued by the scientific challenge. I agreed to consult for the Homeowners' association. Because the Averhoff Report was written in Danish, Lynn provided an English translation, and performed valuable background research on Danish and European stationary source air quality regulations for me as well. My bible for air pollution dispersion calculations was a thin tome called *Turner's Workbook of Atmospheric Dispersion Estimates* (Turner, 1970; 1994). I had relied on the 1970 version in my successful attacks on the proposed sludge incinerators at Blue Plains and Piscataway, more than 30 years earlier. Turner's workbook, originally an EPA document, is a wonderful primer on how to estimate the air pollution impact of various stationary sources of air pollution such as smokestacks. It is chock full of tables and equations which show how to calculate such things as the effects of wind and turbulence on the plume, the height to which the plume is expected to rise, explains how to estimate the downwind atmospheric dispersion of smokestack emissions, and discusses the limitations and sources of uncertainty in modeling plume behavior. It is based on the Gaussian plume model.

A BRIEF DISCUSSION OF PLUME BEHAVIOR

To gain a proper appreciation of what the arcane atmospheric physics of plume behavior involve, here is a plain English explanation: When fuel or other combustibles are burned, they emit the toxic acid gases sulfur dioxide and nitrogen dioxide plus harmful soot, which is fine particulate matter containing heavy metals and carcinogens. All these pollutants are combined in an aerosol that is heavier than air. As a result of the thermal energy released per unit time during combustion, this very hot aerosol, called a *plume* in environmental fluid dynamics, expands energetically upward through the stack and is emitted into the atmosphere with a certain upward momentum, due to inertia, depending upon the combustion temperature of the fuel and the stack diameter.

Because these pollutants are initially much hotter than the ambient air, they are less dense than the surrounding atmosphere when they leave the stack. So each bolus of pollutant in the stack gases behaves like an ascending hot air balloon. The combination of upward momentum and higher temperature, which gives the plume buoyancy, causes it to rise. As the plume collides with the molecules of the cooler surrounding air, it transfers energy, gradually losing its buoyancy and momentum, and eventually stops rising. The peak altitude to which the stack gases rise and the direction in which the plume is blown are affected by the speed and direction of the prevailing winds and the vertical temperature profile of the atmosphere. Normally, but not always, atmospheric temperatures decrease with altitude. The exception is when there is an atmospheric temperature inversion.

The smoke plume will spread out differentially in both the vertical and horizontal directions as it travels downwind. Thus, the plume expands as it travels and the pollutant concentration will decrease accordingly as it travels away from the stack. The *dispersion*, or degree of plume spread in the horizontal and vertical directions, is governed by the amount of turbulence, i.e., the degree of stability of the atmosphere. A turbulent atmosphere leads to greater plume spread and therefore produces a less dense downwind pollutant concentration. On the other hand, a stable atmosphere induces lesser plume spread and thus yields a denser downwind concentration.

Meteorologists define the change in atmospheric temperature as a function of altitude by a technical term called the *lapse rate*. The lapse rate is highly variable, as it is affected by radiation, convection, and condensation, and this affects the shape of the smokestack plume. The lapse rate typically averages about −0.65°C per hundred meters of altitude. A strong decrease in the vertical temperature profile will cause the plume to "loop" up and down roughly like a sine wave as it travels downwind. A weak decrease in vertical

417

temperature will cause the plume envelope to resemble a tilted ice cream cone and is called "coning." A plume emitted into very stable air will develop "fanning," a plume much flatter vertically than it is wide, like a squashed horizontal ice cream cone. Strong sunlight leads to unstable air, while nighttime conditions are conducive to stable air. Cloudy conditions lead to neutral stability, and are common in the Faroes.

Because the density of the atmosphere decreases vertically but not laterally, the plume spread differs in the vertical (z) and horizontal (y) directions perpendicular to the (x) direction of smoke travel downwind (Figure 67). As the plume is blown downwind and spreads out, it becomes less and less concentrated the further it travels. If there is no wind (calm conditions) the plume rises until it is as cool as the surrounding air, and then subsides because the combustion gases and particles are denser than air. However, if there is a temperature inversion (i.e., a layer of air aloft in which the temperature *increases* with altitude instead of decreasing), the cooling plume can become trapped beneath the inversion layer, i.e., a layer of warm air lying atop a layer of cool air. The purpose of the smokestack is to ensure that the smoke plume containing these toxic gases is emitted well above the height of the downwind communities, until the combination of plume rise, distance, and atmospheric turbulence disperse and dilute the toxic pollutants so that they don't pose a threat to public health. In some cases, a very tall stack is required to accomplish this. The tallest smokestack in the world is that of the GRES 2 Power Station in Kazakhstan, which is 420 meters (1377 feet) tall. (Wikipedia, 2017; Structurae, 2017).

MODELING PLUME BEHAVIOR

Because the plume concentration cannot be measured prior to construction of the emitting facility, obviously it would be folly to build it and find out afterward that its design was inadequate to disperse the plume safely. Instead, atmospheric dispersion models of varying degrees of sophistication are employed. Air pollution specialists use such models to estimate the concentration of the various pollutants at the ground level, comparing those levels to air quality standards set by environmental health authorities. Because of the mathematical complexity involved, these models typically require complex computer programs to arrive at their predictions. The air quality standards incorporate both pollutant concentration and duration of exposure, and if complied with, they should limit the amount of pollution inhaled by the population at risk at ground level to safe levels. Needless to say, even quite sophisticated plume dispersion models are not perfect, their uncertainties are not always apparent, and the users of the models are not always diligent in their applications or are totally cognizant of their limitations. Wayne Ott said that in the 1970's, he compared the predictions of some of EPA's early microscale air quality models to actual data from EPA's network of local monitoring stations, and found relatively poor agreement, to the modelers' consternation. It is a complex, time-consuming, and expensive undertaking to attempt to validate the vast variety of dispersion models under the wide variety of atmospheric and topographical conditions encountered in actual field conditions. In other words, a certain amount of professional judgment has to be applied in any given application.

A BRIEF TUTORIAL IN AIR POLLUTION MODELING

Expressed in more scientific terms, the problem facing the smokestack engineer is to determine how much of the desired fuel will be burned per unit time and based on the typical gas and particle emissions of that fuel, calculate the mass of pollutant generated. Then given the rate of flow of combustion gases through a stack of fixed diameter, calculate the mass of pollutant emitted each second from the top of the stack. Then an appropriate air pollution dispersion model must be chosen to estimate downwind pollutant concentrations. These concentrations can then be compared to applicable air quality standards to evaluate the safety of the plume exposure of the downwind populations at any given distance. The model estimates will then determine the minimum safe stack height necessary to protect public health. If the cost of stack construction or even aesthetics are paramount considerations, this often overrides safety. The flattened ice-cream cone shaped plume in Figure 67 illustrates the most basic atmospheric dispersion model, called the *Gaussian Plume Model*. A Gaussian is a bell-shaped curve that is an idealized mathematical representation of the pollutant concentration horizontally and vertically from the plume centerline and is used to compute the plume concentration as a function of local wind speed and atmospheric turbulence as it travels downwind from the stack. The elliptical cross section of the cone in Figure 67 approximates a very irregular plume. Because there is a vertical density gradient in the atmosphere, i.e., the density of the air decreases with altitude, the axes of the ellipse will differ in the vertical direction from the horizontal direction as the plume travels downwind.

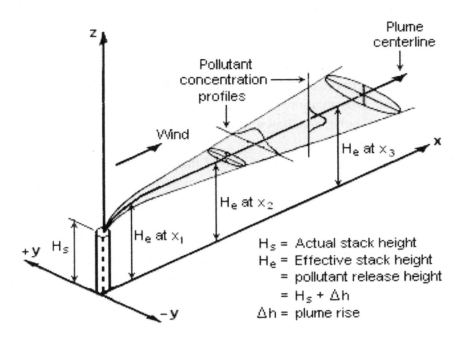

FIGURE 67. THE SMOKESTACK PLUME IDEALIZED AS AN ELLIPSOIDAL CONE WITH AN INCREASING CROSS SECTIONAL AREA AS IT TRAVELS DOWNWIND IN THE X DIRECTION. THE POLLUTANT CONCENTRATION PROFILES IN THE Y AND Z DIRECTIONS ARE SIMULATED BY BELL-SHAPED (GAUSSIAN) CURVES (TURNER, 1970). THE AXES OF THE ELLIPSE DIFFER IN THE VERTICAL (Z) AND LATERAL (Y) DIRECTIONS, AND INCREASE IN THE DOWNWIND DIRECTION AS THE PLUME PROPAGATES IN THE WIND DIRECTION (X). SO THE PLUME IS MORE CONCENTRATED CLOSE TO THE SMOKESTACK, AND IS LESS CONCENTRATED AS IT DISPERSES DOWNWIND.

The faster the wind blows, the further apart the pollutant molecules will be as they are carried downwind, and the lower the concentration of pollutant in the plume. So it is essential to know the variation in speed, direction, and frequency of local winds at the stack site. The amount of vertical and horizontal spread of the plume will also depend on the temperature and stability of the surrounding air. Temperatures vary from season to season, from day to night, and are also affected by sunlight, cloud cover, and precipitation. Also, there are many different dispersion models for the air pollution engineer to choose from, adding a further layer of complexity. The Faroe Islands are windy, cloudy and cool throughout the year with over 260 annual rainy days. The islands lie in the path of depressions moving northeast and this means that strong winds and heavy rain are possible at all times of the year. Sunny days are rare and overcast days are common. Knowing these local conditions is essential for accurately estimating air pollution dispersion of smokestack plumes.

In any case, no matter what model is chosen, it is vital to rely upon the historical record, i.e., the *local* meteorology over time. Unstable air is turbulent, causing the plume to spread rapidly and leads to wide excursions in pollutant concentration, while stable air allows the plume to retain its structure and results in a more uniform concentration. Put mathematically, the Gaussian plume model posits that pollutant concentration along the plume axis is directly proportional to the amount of pollutant mass that the chimney emits per second and is inversely proportional to the cross-sectional area of the plume times the wind speed. So, the pollutant concentration downwind will be a function of distance from the stack and atmospheric stability and is expressed in units of mass divided by volume, typically in micrograms per cubic meter. *Turner's Workbook* has tables of pollutant dilution factors incorporating these vertical and horizontal spreads, or plume parameters, for typical wind speeds. Plume rise can be estimated from plume temperature and momentum equations and the pollutant concentration on the ground incorporates both stack height and plume rise. It is vital to note that complications arise when there is complex terrain downwind, such as hills or tall buildings. Model uncertainty is much higher in such cases. *Modelers ignore this at their peril.*

Determining what wind speeds to use in the model requires the application of a local "wind rose." Wind roses give the historical ranges of wind frequency, wind direction, and wind speed on a seasonal or yearly basis, and are essential tools for airport operators and aircraft pilots as well as meteorologists. Wind roses are compiled by meteorologists who measure the wind parameters using recording anemometers, and are generally available in graphical, tabular, and digital form from government agencies concerned with aviation. Any modeler worthy of the name knows this.

The Tórshavn Wind Rose, overlaid on a schematic of the local community, is shown in Figure 68. It incorporates a great deal of local-scale information vital for air pollution modelers and is available in tabular form. The pictorial representation in this figure conveys a great deal of information to the experienced eye. This particular wind rose is divided into 12 sectors of compass bearing, each covering a thirty-degree (30°) arc. A series of concentric solid rings define the wind frequencies for each 30° pie-shaped sector from the stack and overlay the rectangular shapes that represent the inhabited structures at each distance from the stack. The ring labeled 10% refers to the frequency that the wind blows in that direction; the outermost ring is 20% for this wind rose. The radii of the dashed circles denote the horizontal distances of the buildings from the smokestack; the innermost purple circle is 50 meters distant, the red one next is at 100 meters, the yellow one is at 200 meters, and the blue outermost one is at 300 meters. The length of each pie-shaped wedge denotes the wind frequency blowing from a given compass sector. For example, the slices of pie labeled SSE and SSW (compass bearings south-southeast and south-southwest) denote wind frequencies of about 9% each, while the sector labeled S (south) is at 5.5%. Periods of calm (no wind) in this locale occur with a mere 0.5% frequency. The sharp tips of the sectors point in the direction that the wind blows. The Tórshavn wind rose indicates that when these winds blow respectively *toward* the NNW, NNE, and N directions, they directly impact the hilltop community. These winds, blowing *from* the SSE to the SSW directions, occur with a combined frequency of 23.5% of the time. The darkest gray sections of each of the 30° sectors represent wind speeds greater than 10 meters per second (m/s) i.e., greater than 22.4 miles per hour. The lighter gray portions of the sectors represent wind speeds ranging from 5 m/s to 10 m/s, and the white sections are wind speeds from 0.2 m/s to 5 m/s.

Further complicating the prediction of downwind plume aerosol concentrations is the degree of atmospheric turbulence, known technically as the "stability condition." This will determine the amount of plume spreading, and hence the downwind pollutant concentration. Air pollution meteorologists divide the stability of the atmosphere into six turbulence categories ranging from very unstable (*A* and *B*), to neutral (*C* and *D*), to very stable (*E* and *F*). The spread of the plume downwind as a function of distance is greatest for category *A* and least for *F*. Typically, strong sun and high winds are approximated by *A* and *B* stability, overcast conditions with intermediate winds by *C* and *D* stability, and nighttime conditions with low wind speeds by *E* and *F* stability categories.

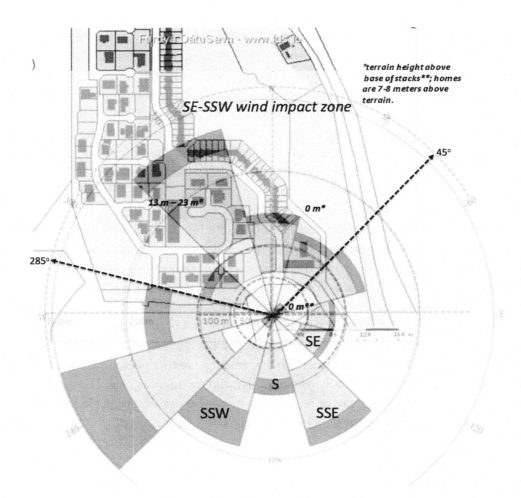

FIGURE 68. THE TÓRSHAVN WIND ROSE OVERLAID ON THE TOPOGRAPHY OF THE NEIGHBORHOOD. THE PIE-SHAPED SECTORS ARE CENTERED ON THE STACK SITE, AND SHOW THE DIRECTION, SPEED, AND FREQUENCY OF THE WINDS RELATIVE TO THE COMMUNITY. WINDS FROM THE SE TO SSW BLOW TOWARD THE HOMES BETWEEN 285° AND 45° IN COMPASS BEARING (BUILDING LAYOUT FROM AVERHOFF REPORT, WIND ROSE OVERLAY BY AUTHOR).

Then there is the question of how high the plume will rise above the downwind community. This can be estimated by the Holland Plume Rise Equation, by which the modeler can estimate the rise of plume as a function of distance from the stack. This equation posits that the smokestack plume rise is directly proportional to the increase in stack gas temperature above that of the ambient air, and inversely proportional to the wind speed. However, this equation is not recommended for use within the first few hundred meters from the stack since plume rise occurs over some distance downwind. Finally, the local topography and stack height must be taken into account.

Next, the modeler must take into account the quantity and nature of the specific emissions from the type of fuel burned, the stack width and height, the relative height of the stack compared to the height of the building from which it rises, the temperature of the stack gas, efficiency of stack-gas cleaning, if any, the temperature of the atmosphere, the wind direction, wind speed, the frequency of occurrence of each of the seven categories of atmospheric stability, the frequency of the presence or absence of precipitation and sunlight, as well as the height of the surrounding terrain, the distance of the target population from the smokestack, and the height of the buildings. This is at minimum, more than twenty possible variables to incorporate into a model. Each of these input variables has a margin of error. One might expect that experimental validation of any putative atmospheric dispersion model would be a very expensive and lengthy operation, given the variability of local atmospheric conditions. Thus it is rarely done comprehensively.

Moreover, it is very difficult to validate a model in "complex terrain," i.e., when there are hills and valleys of varying heights and depths surrounding the stack. The great number of input variables suggests to the physicist that the predictions of any outdoor atmospheric dispersion model must be taken *cum grano salis* – with a grain of salt. (This is in sharp contradistinction to the indoor Habitual Smoker model for secondhand smoke, which is usually accurate to within several percent.) I provided much of this discussion I give here for the benefit of the affected community, so that they could begin to grasp some of the factors involved in this mysterious business. Some of the residents were highly technically educated, so this effort was not wasted. And it set the scene for understanding the serial bungling that followed.

THE MODELERS BUNGLE THE JOB

So, to set the scene, the local community was within a few hundred meters distant from the stack. And – since this community was on the seacoast, and the proposed heating plant lay between the community and the sea, the stiff offshore sea breezes would tend to suppress plume rise downwind of the stack. Lynn's topographical map of the *Inni á Gota* community showed that the top of the stack was about the same height as the lowest point of ground level of the hilltop community, suggesting that I use an Occam's Razor approach and model the hilltop concentration using a stack height of zero. This is equivalent to a ground level emission. Being downwind from a campfire is a good example. If the stack height is less than the height of the downwind receptor community, a similar situation can occur. This is where Averhoff made four major blunders: first, for their own modeling convenience, they blindly assumed that the community was 20 meters (~66 feet) *below* the three smokestacks of the proposed heating plant. This was inexcusable. In fact, nearly every home in the community as well as the local elementary school, was located above the top of the stack (Figure 69).

FIGURE 69. VIEW FROM THE INNI Á GOTA KINDERGARTEN 100 METERS FROM THE PROPOSED HEATING PLANT STACKS. (PHOTO ART CREDIT, L. REVEAL, 2012).

Second, they used a single year of ancient wind rose data from 1976. Third, to add insult to injury, the wind rose was not local to the Faroe Islands, but from Kastrup Airport in Copenhagen on mainland Denmark, *1300 kilometers (~800 miles) distant from Hoyvik.* Fourth, there was an airport with *thirty years* of wind rose data readily available from the nearby town of Tórshavn, only a few kilometers distant from the affected community of Hoyvik. I grabbed for my metaphysical brass knuckles. My initial report, which incorporated local meteorology, assumed zero plume rise because of the frequency of strong sea breezes blowing onshore. I concluded that the stack gases from the proposed heating plant would violate the health-based World Health Organization (WHO) air quality guidelines for fine particulate matter ($PM_{2.5}$) and the acid gases sulfur dioxide (SO_2) and nitrogen dioxide (NO_2), endangering the health of residents of the hilltop community. Specifically, I estimated that $PM_{2.5}$ pollutant concentrations at 100 meters downwind would violate the WHO 24-hour guideline within ½ hour under nighttime or overcast day conditions, and within 1½ hours for conditions where there was strong sun, at a typical local wind speed of 8 meters per second, or a blustery 18 miles per hour. Such a high wind speed would tend to bend the plume horizontally, depressing the plume rise.

The community extended from 80 meters to over 400 meters distant from the proposed stack site. At 200 meters downwind from the stacks, my modeling showed that excessive pollutant exposures would occur within two to five hours. For SO_2, at 100 meters downwind, concentrations would violate the WHO 10-minute maximum exposure guideline within a mere 1 to 2 minutes, while at 200 meters, violations would occur within 6 minutes. For the WHO 24-hour guideline, at 100 meters downwind, violations would occur within 9 minutes, while at 200 meters, violations would occur within a half-hour. Finally, for NO_2, downwind concentrations would violate the WHO 1-hour guideline within 8 to 18 minutes, and at 200 meters, violations would occur within an hour. I concluded that it was vital for the protection of the health of community residents that the proposed plant be relocated to an uninhabited area.

THE OLESEN REPORT

Dr. H.R. Olesen, Senior Advisor at the Danish National Environmental Research Institute at Aarhus University, who performed his own analysis of the air pollution from the proposed heating plant, entitled: *Re: Planned distant heating facility in Tórshavn,* which I read in English translation provided by Lynn Reveal. Dr. Olesen's analysis, dated 26 July 2010, used the same OLM atmospheric dispersion model that Averhoff had used. Olsen agreed that Averhoff's analysis was flawed because it did not adequately take topography into account, and also because Averhoff used an inapplicable Danish regulatory guideline to evaluate the air pollution level.

Olesen concluded, as I had, that the proposed plant burning oil with 0.75% sulfur would not be environmentally acceptable. So far, so good. Olesen then decided that if low sulfur (0.1%) diesel oil was burned instead, the air quality impact would be environmentally acceptable. However, Dr. Olesen, repeating Averhoff's blunder, used the very same 1976 wind rose and meteorology from Kastrup airport in Copenhagen more than 800 miles distant. Olesen attempted to compensate for the use of non-local meteorology in lieu of local Faroese meteorology by raising the receptor height in his model in all directions surrounding the stacks. But then Olesen dismissed my calculations because I failed to incorporate plume rise.

OK, fair enough. Accordingly, I revised my calculations in a second report, dated September 11th 2012, to incorporate both plume rise and the low-sulfur light oil emission factors. In performing the revised calculations, I used the exact same parameters for stack geometry, buoyant flux, and stack gas temperature used by Olesen, adjusting for the lower acid gas and particulate emissions from the lighter low-sulfur oil. However, unlike Olesen, I used the local Tórshavn data tables for topography and meteorology as before. Then I carried it a step further, by comparing the single-year 1976 Kastrup wind rose on the Danish mainland, incorporated as a default in the OLM model used by both Averhoff and Olesen, to the 30-year results obtainable from the 1961 to 1990 Tórshavn wind rose on the Island of Streymoy. As I had suspected, this comparison revealed significant differences between the two wind roses. In particular, in the SSE wind sector, the Kastrup data underestimated the Tórshavn wind frequency by 23%, affecting 73 homes, or fully two-thirds of the residences in the *Inni á Gota* community. Moreover, in the crucial SSW to SSE wind sectors combined, Kastrup's highest category of wind speeds (>10 m/s), which would tend to depress the plume the most, showed a frequency of 0.4%, compared to 4.7% at Tórshavn, a nearly 12-fold difference. So, using the Kastrup Wind Rose was not kosher. It was very sloppy work indeed.

I continued to focus on the two most common local atmospheric stability conditions (*C* and *D* stability), and used the sea-breeze wind speeds and wind frequency blowing from the proposed power plant toward the hilltop community, as shown by the Tórshavn wind rose. Additionally, I considered the impact of the nighttime land-breeze down-slope winds upon the tall nearby Faroese Telecom building, which would suck plume gases into the fresh air intakes situated on its rooftop.

All dispersion models are similar in that they involve two basic characteristics of the stack effluent: (a) the speed and direction that the plume moves with the wind, and (b) the dispersion, i.e. lateral and vertical spread in directions orthogonal to the wind direction due to atmospheric turbulence and the vertical atmospheric density gradient. Although many sophisticated computer models such as the OLM incorporated multiple parameters that could improve precision relative to simpler models (like the basic Gaussian that I used), as the number of parameters these sophisticated models use increases, they often require data that is unavailable (or ignore data that is), introducing uncertainty and errors. In other words, using a sophisticated model with inadequate data won't improve accuracy relative to a simpler model with more accurate inputs. I observed that well-known common deficiencies in modeling plume dispersion include the lack of accurate, up-to-date, and local meteorological data, and failure to communicate the resulting uncertainty in the model predictions.

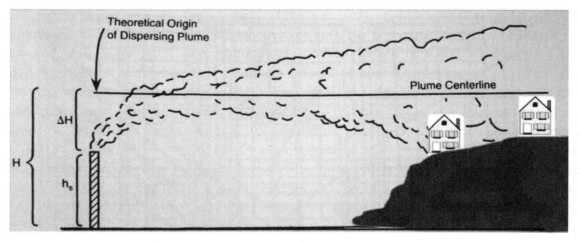

FIGURE 70. A PICTURE IS WORTH A THOUSAND WORDS. THIS IS THE PICTORIAL RESULT OF MY CALCULATIONS, AS PORTRAYED IN REPORT #2. H IS THE HEIGHT OF THE PLUME CENTERLINE, h_s IS THE STACK HEIGHT, AND ΔH IS THE PLUME RISE DUE TO MOMENTUM AND BUOYANCY. THE WIND BLOWS TOWARD THE RIGHT. AND YOU DON'T HAVE TO UNDERSTAND THE CALCULATIONS TO UNDERSTAND THE RESULT: IF THEY BURN, YOU WILL GET GASSED (REPACE, 2012).

I noted that the community lay from 80 meters to about 350 meters downwind of the stacks, and at a common local wind speed of 8 m/s, the estimated total plume rise due to buoyancy and upward momentum combined reached about 7 meters above the stack top at 80 meters downwind from the stacks, and about 11 meters above stack-top level at 137 meters downwind of the stacks. When local topography was factored in, at 80 meters downwind the plume *centerline* would be an estimated 117 meters altitude above sea level, 9 meters above the rooftops that reached only to 108 meters in altitude. But this did not consider the plume thickness: the lower plume boundary extended downward to 103 to 107 meters altitude, depending on distance from the stack, 1 to 5 meters <u>below</u> the rooftops, indicating that the plume would envelop those homes. Further downwind, at 137 meters distant from the stack, the situation was even worse. There, the estimated plume centerline altitude had increased to 121 meters, but the rooftop altitude lay 118 meters above sea level. Thus, the lower plume boundary would extend downward to 110 meters, which was actually at community ground level at that distance, indicating an even worse fumigation of those homes. Figure 70 displays a pictorial representation of the calculations in my report.

My calculations incorporating accurate local topography and meteorology plainly suggested that despite the substitution of low sulfur fuel oil, the new lower emissions would *still* violate WHO short-term air quality guidelines for the most frequently encountered local atmospheric conditions in Tórshavn. The punch line was that the obvious purpose of a 20-meter stack height was to ensure that the stack gases were released at a minimum of 20 meters above the highest point in the downwind community. This was plainly impossible when the community was already elevated 20 meters above the base of the stack. I reiterated my strong recommendation to relocate the plant to a safer location.

The local inhabitants of the Hoyvik community knew that I was correct in my assumption that the prevailing offshore winds would blow the stack gases horizontally from their own observations of the behavior of nearby electric power plant plumes, and even provided me with photos of those plumes that supported my conclusions. However, discounting the discredited Averhoff Report, the Umhvørvisstovan was still faced with two different reports from dueling experts, mine and Olesen's, which left them in a quandary. So, they decided to obtain yet a third opinion. And this time, they commissioned meteorologist Dag Tønnesen of The Norwegian Institute for Air Research (NILU) to review both reports, Olesen's and Repace's. Tønnesen decided to perform his calculations using a different complex dispersion model called CONCX. Tønnesen's results from the CONCX model differed from Olsen's OLM model by a factor of 2, despite using the identical inputs.

This glaring uncertainty did not faze him at all. Echoing Olesen, Tønnesen insisted that with the use of low sulfur oil, a 20-meter smoke stack was adequate to comply with Danish regulations for smoke stack emissions. Tønnesen asserted that his CONCX dispersion model was accurate, despite his factor of two difference with the OLM model, despite his use of Kastrup airport meteorology instead of local Tórshavn meteorology, repeating the same blunder that Averhoff and Olesen had committed. Plus, he ignored the plain fact that the ground level of the target population was level with the top of the stack. Further, adding insult to injury, Tønnesen deprecated my revised modeling effort, asserting that the "calculations done by J. Repace build on conditions about air movement and dispersion processes which are inadequate or unsubstantiated, and the results show concentration contributions, which in relation to amount of release, local wind and height of smoke stack, are way too high." [N.B., The NILU report is in Norwegian; English translation provided by Ms. Lynn Reveal.]

I was getting seriously pissed off and struck back with my third report. My new analysis focused on Tønnesen's flawed modeling. I demonstrated graphically that he had made several significant errors. I rebutted his criticisms and questioned the adequacy of his calculations in protecting the health of the community residents. I also disputed false claims by the Faroese Environmental Agency staff that I had ignored plume rise in my calculations for the low-sulfur oil emissions in my second report (which to give them the benefit of the doubt, Lynn thought might be due to their limited understanding of English). Søren Antoft, a Faroese professor of chemistry who resided in the hilltop community, carefully checked my calculations and fully endorsed them. Antoft agreed with me that Tønnesen had made several errors, concluding, as I had, that Tønnesen performed his emissions calculations for a *single* stack instead of *three* stacks, and in addition, Antoft discovered that Tønnesen had used a laminar flow model that would keep the plume from impacting the ground, which was inappropriate because the steep cliffs on which the community rested would cause turbulent flow. Antoft remarked in an email to me: "Our first criticism of the OML model was that the local landscape and buildings should be taken into the model. NILU has a very intelligent modeling program named Airquis, that does this. Why did [Tønnesen] use a model for flatland and industry areas? Second, local weather situations should be taken into [account]. [Tønnesen] doesn't do this and states that smoke only moves upwards with plume rise. Everyone living in Faroes driving by Sund and Brennistødi á hjalla [local power plants] knows that this is not the case in Faroese weather."

Comparison of Repace & NILU Models

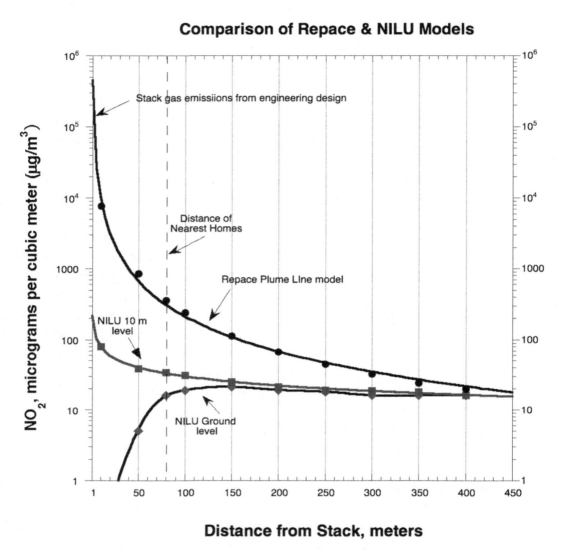

FIGURE 71. COMPARISON OF THE REPACE GAUSSIAN PLUME MODEL WITH TØNNESON'S NILU MODEL (REPACE REPORT #3, 2014). NOTE THAT THE CURVES, WHEN EXTRAPOLATED BACK TO THE ORIGIN, SHOULD APPROXIMATE THE 135,000 µg/m³ CONCENTRATION AT THE MOUTH OF THE STACK. THE REPACE MODEL YIELDS ~150,000 µg/m³, WHILE TØNNESON'S NILU MODEL YIELDS ~200 µg/m³.

My third report, dated May 15, 2014, attacked the NILU results as seriously erroneous. When I extrapolated Tønnesen's concentration vs. distance curve back to zero meters, I should have gotten a close approximation to the plume concentration at the top of the stacks, which according to Tønnesen's calculation, was 50,000 µg/m³. However, when extrapolated backward to the stack top, Tønnesen's concentration curve plotted as a function of distance yielded only about 200 µg/m³, a staggering 1% of expected as shown in Figure 71. So he was apparently calculating the plume concentration as if the community lay at the ground level of the plant. Furthermore, my calculations indicated that the emission from three stacks was 135,338 $\mu g/m^3$, almost three times as great as Tonneson's 50,000 $\mu g/m^3$. By contrast, when I performed the same extrapolation for the concentration vs. distance curve, my results were just 11% different from the actual design emissions for three stacks, at 150,000 $\mu g/m^3$. Antoft and I agreed that Tønnesen's calculations for a single stack had grossly underestimated the three stack emissions by 63%.

With respect to the meteorology, I noted that the Tórshavn wind rose indicates that at least 5% of the time, or 447 hours per year, the blustery winds will blow toward the hilltop community further at speeds greater than 10 to 30 meters per second (m/s) [22 to 67 miles per hour]. Tønnesen further blundered by excluding winds greater than 7 m/s, and moreover, unaccountably failed to specify the atmospheric stability conditions he actually used. Moreover, when standardized to the same stack emissions, the pollutant dilution factor in the NILU model and the Danish OLM model differed by a factor of 2.4. This difference alone should have indicated the necessity of including a large margin of safety. Finally, Tønnesen's petty complaint about the amount of work necessary to use Faroese meteorological data, when it was clearly available in digital form was a frankly unbelievable excuse. A community's health, safety, and air quality were at stake. The Faroese Health Department had paid him the equivalent of $20,000 for this shabby work… [My full reports are posted on Research Gate (Repace, 2010; 2012; 2014)].

On December 27th 2014, I received the following email from Lynn Reveal, in the Faroe Islands:

"Our delegation met with the mayor and told him we didn't care if they stored hot water on the site but we didn't want them to burn. As the city owns half the utility ... he had the power to ask [the heating company] to find another way. Their application has not been cancelled, so technically it and our appeal are still alive, but it looks good for us. The chairman of their board was interviewed on the news and said that they would honor the mayor's request not to burn. The environmental agency still thinks it is safe enough. So in the end, it was a political decision. We had gathered over 2000 signatures.

Best regards,
Lynn"

Vox Populi, Vox Dei.

CHAPTER 24

EPILOGUE

"It is impossible in the modern world for a man of science to say with any honesty, 'My business is to provide knowledge, and what use is made of the knowledge is not my responsibility.' ... everybody knows that the modern world depends upon scientists, and, if they are insistent, they must be listened to. We have it in our power to make a good world; and, therefore, with whatever labor and risk, we must make it."

BERTRAND RUSSELL, THE SOCIAL RESPONSIBILITIES OF SCIENTISTS. SCIENCE 131, 391 (1960).

As I reflect on the chapters of my life, I wonder – what if I had never made measurements of secondhand smoke in the hospitality industry? How long would it have taken for other researchers to accomplish that goal? What if I had not joined the EPA in the policy office, would EPA have gotten involved at all in the issues of indoor air pollution and secondhand smoke? Would its risk assessment of ETS ever been written? Although surely the epidemiological community in the wake of the papers of White and Froeb, Hirayama and Trichopoulos would have continued its study of passive smoking and lung cancer, would the Surgeon General and the NAS reports been written in the 1980's? Without our risk assessment of lung cancer from secondhand smoke, would the press have gotten so actively involved in covering this issue? Would the CDC have embraced cotinine studies as early as it did? Would the smoking ban on aircraft been passed in 1989? Would activist scientific opposition to the tobacco industry's junk science have arisen? Would ASHRAE have gotten involved in indoor air quality as soon as it did? Would tobacco industry propaganda and malign legislative influence have successfully delayed smoking bans for decades longer? The answers to these questions remain in the realm of speculation. What can be answered definitively is the impact of smoking bans on nonsmokers' exposure to secondhand smoke. Undeniably, EPA, and especially its 1993 Report on ETS, played a central and perhaps *the* central role in this drama. Let's explore that thesis a bit further.

The work of Repace and Lowrey (1980) implicating secondhand smoke as a major indoor air pollutant would not have had any societal impact without being able to compare our respirable particle (RSP) measurements to the air quality standards for total suspended particulates (TSP) previously set and enforced by the EPA based on earlier research by the scientific community into outdoor air pollution episodes. Those national standards not only helped control air pollution by quantifying it, they educated legislators, the press, and the public to its harms. Later epidemiological and clinical research led to the abandonment of the TSP standard which encompassed all particle sizes that can float in favor of the much smaller and more harmful inhalable particle size fraction, PM_{10} in 1987. (Particles in the size range from 10 to 50 microns, the largest size that will float, are filtered out by the hairs in the nose – that's what nostril hair is good for, in case you bush-beaks might have wondered.) The PM_{10} standard in turn would be eclipsed in 1997 by the

$PM_{2.5}$ standard, the most harmful particle size fraction, capable of penetrating deep into the lungs. (Particles between 3.5 microns and ten microns, called the coarse fraction, generally enter the lungs only of mouth breathers). $PM_{2.5}$ is nearly identical to the $PM_{3.5}$ that we had measured in our 1980 *Science* paper.

In 2006, the level of the $PM_{2.5}$ standard would be tightened and tightened again in 2012. To place our 1980 results in a modern health perspective, I've replotted them in Figure 72 using modern statistical analysis. In retrospect, these levels of fine particle air pollution, measured from 86 $\mu g/m^3$ to 697 $\mu g/m^3$ for the smoking venues in the late 1970's, viewed through the lens of EPA's 2013 Air Quality Index, ranged from Unhealthy to Significant Harm (Figure 73). So the impact of secondhand smoke on indoor microenvironments, viewed in hindsight, was far more harmful than we knew at the time. Even the outdoor air levels that we measured in the 1970's ranged from Moderately polluted to Unhealthy by current standards.

Repace and Lowrey (1980) had also suggested that due to the large number of carcinogens present in tobacco smoke, that the efforts of public health authorities to control public exposure to carcinogens in outdoor air, water, and food justified similar efforts to prevent involuntary exposure to ambient tobacco smoke indoors. Then the simultaneous publication of the paper by White and Froeb (1980) in the prestigious *New England Journal of Medicine*, cited as a note added in proof to our manuscript, reported that secondhand smoke pollution in the workplace measurably impaired the pulmonary function of nonsmokers, providing an important complement to our work. When the vitally important back-to-back papers of Hirayama (1981) and Trichopoulos (1981) implicating passive smoking as a cause of lung cancer appeared, the major publicity they received galvanized public attention. In turn, those crucial epidemiological studies enabled us to perform the quantitative risk assessment of passive smoking and lung cancer, estimating the number of lung cancer deaths from passive smoking (Repace and Lowrey, 1985). This in turn laid the groundwork for the cascade of the landmark reports by the Surgeon General and the National Academy of Sciences in 1986, followed by NIOSH CIB 54 in 1989, and then the seminal EPA Report on Environmental Tobacco Smoke at the end of 1992, all of which firmly established the carcinogenicity of secondhand smoke and affirmed that thousands of nonsmokers were dying from passive smoking every year. These reports, accelerated by the California ETS Reports in 1997 and 2006, collectively triggered the exponential increase in 100% smoke-free laws in the USA (Table 1), which endured until about 2008, slowing to a linear slope as the low-hanging fruit of the non-tobacco states was picked (Figure 74).

The tobacco industry's tooth-and-nail battle to prevent or delay smoke-free workplace laws in the U.S, although successful at the federal level by its sandbagging of OSHA, began to crumble at the grass-roots level. Gradually, as nonsmokers began to revel in smoke-free air in restaurants, local clean indoor air activists were able to defeat the industry's powerful lobbyists in city-by-city, state-by-state battles to enact clean indoor air laws, failing statewide mainly in the change-resistant Southern tobacco-growing regions.

Overall in the U.S. as of April 1, 2018, 25 states, along with the District of Columbia, Puerto Rico, and the U.S. Virgin Islands, had passed laws that required non-hospitality workplaces, restaurants, and bars to be 100% Smokefree (Table 1). These laws, along with local laws in the remaining states, protect 58.6% of the U.S. population up from a baseline of 0% in 1992 (ANRF, 2018). However, 25 states still do not cover non-hospitality workplaces. 21 states, along with Puerto Rico and the U.S. Virgin Islands, require all state-regulated gambling to be 100% smoke-free. Maine's Smoke-Free Gambling law only covers gambling facilities opened in July 2003 or later (ANRF, 2018).

These achievements resulted from scientists and physicians and nonsmokers' rights groups speaking out and capturing media attention, which in turn led to increased public demand for restrictions on smoking in restaurants, bars, and other workplaces, which resulted in political action.

DIVINING THE IMPACT OF SMOKE-FREE LAWS ON POPULATION EXPOSURE

An important scientific question arises: by how much has this mix of state and local laws reduced population secondhand smoke exposure? In October of 2012, Wayne Ott and I co-chaired a symposium, *Clearing the Air We Breathe: Progress Reducing Exposure to Pollutants in Ambient, Occupational, and Personal Settings,* at the 22nd Annual conference of the International Society for Exposure Science, and co-authored a presentation that addressed this very issue. It was titled, *ESTIMATED REDUCTIONS IN POPULATION PM$_{2.5}$ EXPOSURE FROM AMBIENT AIR POLLUTION AND SECONDHAND SMOKE, 1990 to 2010.* To put our results in perspective, we compared the reductions in U.S. population exposure from 1990 to 2010 from outdoor fine particulate matter in the 50 States due to EPA regulations, to the reduction in fine particle exposure from secondhand smoke made possible by state and local clean indoor air laws. We found that over this 20-year period, the annual average PM$_{2.5}$ ambient air concentrations nationwide, according to EPA's network of outdoor air pollution monitoring stations, had decreased by 38%, from ~16 μg/m^3 to 10 μg/m^3, as a result of EPA regulations governing mobile and stationary source emissions.

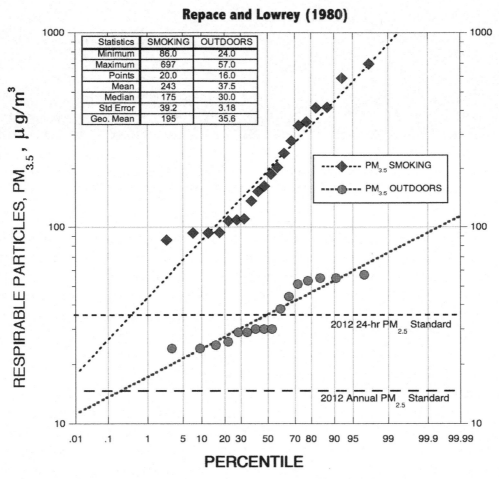

FIGURE 72. A REPLOT OF THE RSP DATA MEASURED BY REPACE AND LOWREY (1980) USING THE IMPROVED STATISTICAL ANALYSIS AFFORDED BY THE LOG-PROBABILITY PLOT. THE INDOOR PM$_{2.5}$ MEAN IS 6.5 TIMES OUTDOORS, SUGGESTING THAT 82% OF THE INDOOR RSP WAS DUE TO SECONDHAND SMOKE. ALTHOUGH THESE LEVELS ARE SHORT-TERM, NOT 24-HOUR AVERAGES, COMPARISON WITH THE 2012 STANDARDS (35 μG/M^3 FOR THE DAILY, AND 12 μG/M^3 FOR THE ANNUAL) INDICATES THE DEGREE OF POLLUTION JUDGED BY 21ST CENTURY STANDARDS. THE 24-HR NAAQS FOR TSP WAS 7 TIMES HIGHER IN 1980, AND IT LUMPED NON-RESPIRABLE PARTICLES IN WITH THE RESPIRABLE. (N.B., IN 2005, THE WHO 24-HR PM$_{2.5}$ GUIDELINE BECAME 25 μG/M^3, AND THE ANNUAL PM$_{2.5}$ GUIDELINE WAS PEGGED AT 10 μG/M^3).

Air Quality	Air Quality Index	PM$_{2.5}$ (µg/m³)	Health Advisory
Good	0-50	≤12	None
Moderate	51-100	13-35	Unusually sensitive people should consider reducing prolonged or heavy exertion.
Unhealthy for Sensitive Groups	101-150	36-55	People with heart or lung disease, older adults, and children should reduce prolonged or heavy exertion.
Unhealthy	151-200	56-150	People with heart or lung disease, older adults, and children should avoid prolonged or heavy exertion. Everyone else should reduce prolonged or heavy exertion.
Very Unhealthy	201-300	151-250	People with heart or lung disease, older adults, and children should avoid all physical activity outdoors. Everyone else should avoid prolonged or heavy exertion.
Hazardous	301-500	251-500	People with heart or lung disease, older adults, and children should remain indoors and keep activity levels low. Everyone else should avoid all physical activity outdoors.
Significant Harm Level	>500	>500	Imminent and substantial endangerment to public health

FIGURE 73. THE U.S. EPA AIR QUALITY INDEX [AQI] (2013). JUDGED BY THE 24-HR AQI, THE GEOMETRIC MEAN OF THE DATA MEASURED BY REPACE & LOWREY (1980) CORRESPONDED TO UNHEALTHY AIR QUALITY, AND THE TWO HIGHEST PREMISES WERE POLLUTED AT THE SIGNIFICANT HARM LEVEL DUE TO SECONDHAND SMOKE.

To estimate the reduction in populations exposure to SHS, our methodology utilized a Rosetta Stone equation relating the nicotine metabolite cotinine from CDC's NHANES study to the fine particles inhaled due to passive smoking. We derived the evidence supporting the contemporaneous reduction in PM$_{2.5}$ exposure due to smoke-free laws by plotting them against the temporal decrease in the U.S. population's serum cotinine levels. By comparison, over the same 20-year period from 1990 to 2010, we estimated that the U.S. population's personal exposures to PM$_{2.5}$ from SHS had decreased by 76%, from ~16 µg/m³ to 4 µg/m³, due to smoke-free laws and smoking restrictions. Epidemiologists, take note. We further estimated that a national smoke-free law would have decreased U.S. population PM$_{2.5}$ exposure by an additional 29%.

Our analysis showed that in 1990, exposure from secondhand smoke was as great as outdoor air pollution as a source of general population exposure to fine particles. However, by 2010, the decrement in personal exposure to PM$_{2.5}$ resulting from smoke-free laws was twice as large as that from controls on stationary and mobile sources. However, for both outdoor PM$_{2.5}$ and SHS PM$_{2.5}$ combined, the net reduction in total population exposure was 44%. That counts as significant progress. Of course, these reductions in general population SHS exposure did not apply to certain disenfranchised occupational groups, such as casino workers and bar staff, many of whom remained exposed to high levels of secondhand smoke.

We also examined the effect of statewide 100% smoke-laws by combining ANR's 100% smoke-free statewide law database with CDC's population-based serum cotinine database (courtesy of Tom Bernert, CDC), forming the plot in Figure 75. As the number of statewide smoke-free laws, whether comprehensive or not, increased from 2 states (4% of the total) in 1994 to 36 states (72% of the total), by 2010, the nonsmoking population's cotinine dose from secondhand smoke had decreased by 80%. How does this translate into lives saved? In 1990, Repace and Lowrey (1990) reviewed nine published risk assessments performed by US., Canadian, and U.K. researchers on secondhand smoke and lung cancer, collectively estimating that secondhand smoke caused an average of 5000 ± 2500 deaths from lung cancer (excluding one of the nine, which was Sterling's mole paper), and in 1992, the EPA estimated 3000 deaths annually from passive smoking, with a range from 800 to 7000. In 1994, Jud Wells estimated that secondhand smoke caused 62,000 deaths per year from ischemic heart disease. In 1997, the California EPA expressed its estimates for passive smoking induced lung cancer based on the U.S. EPA report as 3000 deaths per year, and heart disease as from 35,000 to 62,000 deaths per year reflecting estimates by Wells (1988 and 1994) and Glantz and Parmley (1991). Thus, as of the mid-1990's, taking an average of 48,500 heart disease deaths per year and 3000 lung cancer deaths per year there was a combined total of 51,500 estimated deaths from secondhand smoke annually. This reflected the state of smoke-free laws and workplaces as of the early 1990's.

TABLE 1. THE STATE OF U.S. SMOKE-FREE LAWS IN 2017 (ANRF, 2017).

ANRF AMERICAN NONSMOKERS' RIGHTS FOUNDATION

Defending your right to breathe smokefree air since 1976

Summary of 100% Smokefree State Laws and Population Protected by 100% U.S. Smokefree Laws
April 1, 2018

Population reflects only municipalities and states with ordinances or regulations that are *currently in effect* and do not allow smoking in attached bars or separately ventilated rooms and do not have size, age, or hours exemptions are listed here.

Type of Law	Number of States*	Population Covered by Local and State Laws	% of Population Covered by Local and State Laws
Workplaces[1] and/or Restaurants[2] and/or Bars[3] and/or Gambling[4]	36	260,056,801	81.6%
Workplaces[1] and Restaurants[2] and Bars[3]	25	186,739,457	58.6%
Workplaces[1] and Restaurants[2] and Bars[3] and Gambling[4]	17	141,506,477	44.4%
Workplaces[1]	30	234,764,621	73.7%
Restaurants[2]	35	246,728,013	77.5%
Bars[3]	30	209,780,442	65.9%
Gambling[4]	20	158,742,262	49.8%
Workplaces[1] and Restaurants[2]	29	221,464,802	69.5%

2015 population estimates were provided by RPM Consulting, LLC, using ESRI demographic data, with the exception of American Samoa CNMI, Guam, and USVI, which were sourced from the U.S. Census 2010, and Puerto Rico, which was sourced from the U.S. Census 2015.

[1]Includes both public and private *non-hospitality* workplaces, including, but not limited to, offices, factories, and retail stores.

[2]Includes any attached bar in the restaurant.

[3]Includes freestanding bars without separately ventilated rooms.

[4]Includes only state-regulated, non-tribal gambling facilities. Tribal gambling facilities are sovereign and not covered by state laws. States marked as having smokefree gambling facilities include at least one of the following types of gambling: Non-tribal casinos and racinos, card clubs, race tracks, and/or jai-alai centers.

[5] Smoking is not permitted in 100% of rooms in hotels, motels, and other lodging establishments.

[6] The use of e-cigarettes and other electronic smoking devices is not permitted in venues required to be 100% smokefree by state law.

^ Enactment date does not include date for e-cigarette use laws.

*Maine law requires state-regulated gambling facilities opened after July 1, 2003 to be 100% smokefree, but prior facilities may have a smoking room.

N/A = State-regulated gambling not permitted.

Altogether, there are 22,665 municipalities covered by either local or state 100% smokefree laws in at least one of the three main categories (non-hospitality workplaces, restaurants, and bars). Since some have 100% smokefree coverage in more than one category, the numbers are not mutually exclusive.

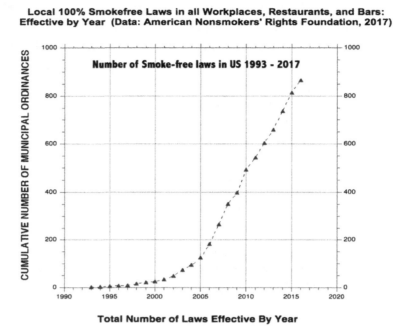

Local 100% Smokefree Laws in all Workplaces, Restaurants, and Bars:
Effective by Year (Data: American Nonsmokers' Rights Foundation, 2017)

FIGURE 74. SOURCE: J.L. REPACE & W.R. OTT, PAPER TuE2, 22ND ANNUAL MEETING OF THE INTERNATIONAL SOCIETY OF EXPOSURE SCIENCE, SEATTLE WASHINGTON, OCT. 28-NOV.1, 2012 [PLOT UPDATED TO 2017]. THE EPA REPORT APPEARED IN DECEMBER 1992.

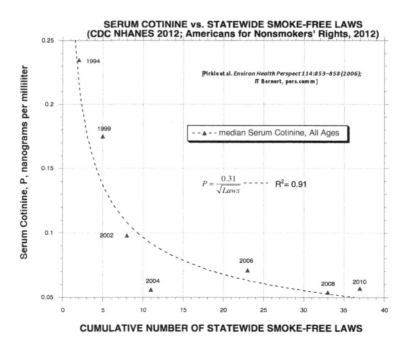

FIGURE 75. SOURCE: ESTIMATED REDUCTIONS IN U.S. POPULATION $PM_{2.5}$ EXPOSURE FROM AMBIENT AIR POLLUTION AND SECONDHAND SMOKE, 1990 TO 2010. J.L. REPACE & W.R. OTT, PAPER TuE2, 22ND ANNUAL MEETING OF THE INTERNATIONAL SOCIETY OF EXPOSURE SCIENCE, SEATTLE WASHINGTON, OCT. 28-NOV.1, 2012.

The National Academy of Science, on the basis of its review of the available experimental and epidemiologic literature in 2010, including relevant literature on air pollution and $PM_{2.5}$, concluded that there is a causal relationship between smoking bans and decreases in acute coronary events [NAS, 2010]. Given the best estimates of the contribution of secondhand smoke to lung cancer and heart disease mortality in 1994, based on the 80% decrease in population cotinine dose by 2012, it can be inferred that this estimated combined mortality impact of 51,500 U.S. nonsmokers' deaths per year in 1994 from passive smoking has been reduced by 80% to 10,300 deaths per year, for an estimated annual saving of nearly 41,200 nonsmokers' lives as a result of smoke-free laws enacted over this 19-year period. It is fair to assume that most of these lives were saved in the states and jurisdictions with the most stringent smoke-free laws, as shown in Figure 75.

THE EFFECT OF SMOKE-FREE AIR LAWS ON SMOKING PREVALENCE

Smoke-free workplace laws also work to reduce smoking prevalence. Table 2 shows that from 1995 to 2012, the number of adults aged 18 and over who were current smokers declined by 15% from 47 million to 40 million. Smoking prevalence made an even steeper decline. In 1995, the smoking prevalence was 24.7%; by the end of 2012, the smoking prevalence was 18.1%, a 26% decline. These 40 million smokers puffed about 264 billion cigarettes or about 19.5 cigarettes per smoker per day, down from 28.1 per day in 1995, a 31% decrease. Since the number of cigarettes smoked per day varied about the average by ± 2 cigarettes from 1965 to 1995, a reasonable inference is that the post-1995 decline in cigarettes smoked per day had everything to do with the increase in smoke-free workplace laws, which of course, suggests that the tobacco industry's fears of the impact of the secondhand smoke research that drove these laws were correct.

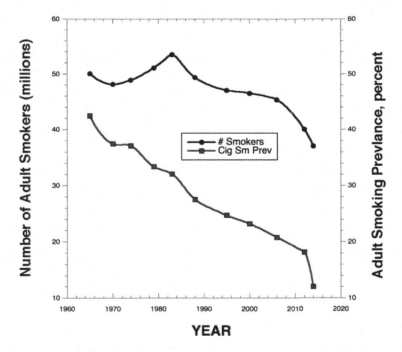

FIGURE 76. LEFT AXIS: (TOP LINE) NUMBER OF ADULT SMOKERS (AGED 18 YEARS AND OVER) FROM 1965 TO 2012. RIGHT AXIS: (BOTTOM LINE) SMOKING PREVALENCE FOR THE UNITED STATES OVER THE SAME PERIOD [CDC, 2016].

The cumulative toll that the smoking of the tobacco products manufactured by this amoral and science-denying industry has taken over the 50-year period from 1964 to 2014 has been enormous. An estimated *20 million* Americans sickened and died prematurely due to smoking, which remained the leading preventable cause of disease, disability, and death in the U.S. [MMWR, 2016]. Figure 76 plots the decline in the number of adult smokers (aged 18 years and over) from 1965 to 2012 (left axis, top line) and the decline in smoking prevalence for the United States (right axis, bottom line). The steady decrease in smoking prevalence from 1965 to 1985 was arguably largely due to government action to warn of the hazards of active smoking; from 1985 to 2017, it likely was mainly driven by increased smoking restrictions in workplaces.

As Figure 76 illustrates, US adult smoking *prevalence* has declined in an approximately linear fashion since its peak year in 1965. However, as the figure shows, the actual *number* of smokers increased from 1965 to 1983, as a result of vigorous industry marketing to children (more six-year-old children recognized Joe Camel than Mickey Mouse [DiFranza and Asquith, 1995]). After 1983, the number of smokers began to decline, but not as fast as smoking prevalence, due to the increase in the nonsmoking population. Table 2 shows that while there was a ~72% numerical decline in US adult smoking *prevalence* from 42.4% in 1965 to 12.0% in 2014, the decline in the *number* of US adult smokers from 1965 to 2014, from 50.1 million to 37 million was only 26%. And even when the peak year of 1983 is used as a referent, the 1983 to 2014 decrease in smokers was 13.5 million, or 25.2%, a little more than one-third of the decline in smoking prevalence. By 2014, Americans who were poor, uneducated, or lived in a rural area had far higher rates of cigarette smoking than the general population (Washington Post, 2017). Among people having only a GED certificate, smoking prevalence remained at more than 40%, the highest of any socio-economic status group (CDC, 2017).

So, the fortunes of the tobacco companies have not been impacted as severely as the decline in smoking prevalence would otherwise suggest, due to the 62% increase in total US population (all ages) over the same 47-year time period. In 2013, the US cigarette industry spent just under $9 billion on advertising and promotion [CDC, 2016; FTC, 2016; US Census 2016]. The struggle for tobacco-smoke-free air has made substantial progress but is far from over (Table 1). In 2015, according to the CDC, one out of four, or 58 million of the 232 million U.S. nonsmokers were exposed to secondhand smoke. However, this represents a sea change from the situation in 1980, when there were 175 million nonsmokers exposed to the fumes of 52 million smokers who were smoking 620 billion cigarettes. That was a time when smoke-free laws were only a dream, and virtually no workplaces, restaurants, or bars were smoke-free.

SMOKING RESTRICTIONS ABROAD

Abroad, according to the European Smokefree Partnership, all 27 EU Member States have some form of regulation aimed at limiting exposure to secondhand smoke, although the scope and character of these regulations differ widely from country to country. A number of EU member states have enacted strong smoke-free laws that ban smoking in virtually all indoor workplaces and public places, including bars and restaurants. On January 1st 2008, Portugal introduced a workplace smoking law banning smoking in hospitality venues, schools, shopping centers, hospitals, and other health care facilities. It followed Ireland, Norway, Italy, Malta, Sweden, Spain, Finland, Scotland, Belgium, France, and the UK.

WHO AVOIDS SMOKY RESTAURANTS AND WHY?

The tobacco industry's self-serving predictions and hospitality industry fears of economic doom resulting from workplace smoking bans never materialized; smoke-free laws have had a neutral or positive effect on businesses. Why was this? Lois Biener at the University of Massachusetts in Boston posed the question: Who avoided smoky bars and restaurants in Massachusetts, and why? (Biener, 1999). The smoking prevalence in Massachusetts in 1999 was just 19%. So adult nonsmokers outnumbered adult smokers in the state by five to one. Biener found that more nonsmokers avoided patronizing smoky venues *than there were smokers in the state*. This on balance, is why the economics of smoking bans are favorable. Table 2 shows that in 2014, only 1 out of 8 adults in the U.S. still smoked. Figure 72 shows that the number of smoke-free laws increased dramatically in the wake of the 1992 EPA risk assessment of passive smoking. Few public health investments have yielded such large public health gains in such a short period of time at so little cost.

THE SECONDHAND SMOKE WAR IS FAR FROM OVER

According to the National Cancer Institute, media communications play a key role in shaping attitudes toward tobacco, and current evidence shows that tobacco-related media exposure affects both tobacco use and prevention. Tobacco advertising and promotion in the United States totaled more than $13.5 billion in 2005 (in 2006 dollars), and media communications also continue to play an important role in tobacco control efforts and policy interventions [NCI, 2008]. In 2013, cigarette companies spent approximately $8.95 billion on cigarette advertising and promotion, down slightly from $9.17 billion they spent in 2012 (CDC, 2016).

World-wide, secondhand smoke exposure remains pervasive. There are about 1.1 billion smokers in the world, of whom roughly 80% dwell in low- and middle-income countries. Nearly two-thirds of the world's smokers live in 13 countries. China has 300 million of them, while India has 120 million. Sixty percent of Chinese adults are affected by smoking in the workplace, while thirty percent of Indian adults are (GATS China, 2010; GATS India, 2017). The percent of the population exposed to SHS ranges from 15% to as high as 70%. On July 18, 2018, Japan passed its first national tobacco control law. It banned smoking inside public facilities, but excluded many restaurants and bars, "and is seen as toothless." Most offices allow smoking only in designated lounges, and some cities restrict smoking in outdoor areas. However, according to government and WHO estimates, about 15,000 Japanese die annually due to secondhand smoke (Washington Post, 2018).

Globally, Big Tobacco remains the greatest obstacle to enacting comprehensive smoke-free policies, often by arguing that smoke-free policies harm businesses and cost jobs, against strong evidence to the contrary. Moreover, the tobacco industry continues to fund papers attempting to play down the injurious health effects of secondhand smoke. For example, a recent paper by the indefatigable Peter Lee, funded by Japan Tobacco Inc., asserts that, "The evidence does not convincingly demonstrate ETS causes nasopharynx cancer, head and neck cancer, various digestive cancers (stomach, rectum, colorectal, liver, pancreas), or cancers of endometrium, ovary, bladder and brain" [Lee et al. 2016]. However, for every 15 cigarettes a person smokes, there is DNA damage that could trigger carcinogenesis [Quit16.co.uk]. There is no known threshold for carcinogenesis. Tobacco smoke exposure at high doses is well-known to cause lung cancer, cancers of the mouth, nasal cavities, pharynx and larynx, stomach, kidney, bowel, liver, pancreas, ureter, esophagus, cervix, bladder and ovaries, plus myeloid leukemia (IARC, 2012), as well as breast cancer (Collishaw et al., 2009; Reynolds et al., 2009). These diseases also occur in nonsmokers, and because of an absence of a threshold for carcinogenesis, are likely to be increased in passive smokers as well. This remains an area for further epidemiological study.

The panoply of smoking-caused diseases includes cancer, heart disease, stroke, lung diseases, diabetes, and chronic obstructive pulmonary disease (COPD), which includes asthma, emphysema and chronic bronchitis. Smoking also increases risk for tuberculosis, certain eye diseases, and problems of the immune system, including rheumatoid arthritis, erectile dysfunction, facial wrinkles and tooth loss. In 2016 in the US, more than 16 million Americans were living with a disease caused by smoking (CDC, 2016).

As Figure 77 shows, in the states whose legislatures remain in thrall to Big Tobacco in 2017, comprehensive workplace smoke-free laws are absent, and nonsmokers are still breathing air polluted with tobacco smoke. The Northern Tier of States is mostly 100% smoke-free, as is the West Coast; California exempts non-hospitality workplaces with five or less workers, although most of its coastal cities do not. More than two-thirds of Californians reside in coastal counties. The rural areas of the West and South mostly do not have comprehensive smoke-free laws, although urban areas in many of these states do.

TABLE 2. POPULATION AND CIGARETTE SMOKING STATISTICS,
1965-2014 [CDC, 2016; FTC, 2016; US CENSUS 2016.

YEAR	US Population (millions)	No. Smokers (millions)	US Cigarette Consumption (billions)	Cigarettes per smoker per year	Cigarettes per smoker per day	US Adult Smoking Prevalence, %
1965	194.3	50.1	521	10401	28.5	42.4
1970	205.1	48.1	534	11106	30.4	37.4
1974	213.9	48.9	595	12157	33.3	37.1
1979	225.1	51.1	622	12168	33.3	33.4
1983	233.8	53.5	604	11282	30.9	32.1
1988	244.5	49.4	561	11350	31.1	27.5
1995	262.8	47.0	482	10260	28.1	24.7
2000	281.4	46.5	430	9247	25.3	23.2
2006	298.6	45.3	381	8411	23.0	20.8
2012	314.1	40.0	268	6693	18.3	18.1
2014	318.9	37.0	264	7135	19.5	12.0

Sources: US Census; US Federal Trade Commission; Centers for Disease Control & Prevention

WHAT REMAINS TO BE DONE?

Insofar as workers are concerned, according to the 2010 U.S. National Health Interview Survey, the prevalence of secondhand smoke exposure at work was highest for workers in the construction and extraction (31.4%) industries, in food preparation and serving (30.0%), in transportation and material moving (28.7%) and lowest in legal (11.8%), life, physical and social sciences (9.2%), management of companies and enterprises (9.4%), education services (9.7%), and education, training and library work (8.7%). Overall, the NHIS survey showed that secondhand smoke exposure among remaining workers still exposed to secondhand smoke in 2010 was 10%, which still left 12.5 million nonsmoking workers at risk. This compares to 62 million adult nonsmokers at risk in 1985 (Repace and Lowrey, 1985).

There were substantial regional differences in prevalence: workers in the Northeast had the lowest exposure prevalence at 8.1%, with the West second lowest at 9.3%, the Midwest at 9.8%, and the South at 11.6% of the workforce. As of 2010 there were no Southern states that had comprehensive smoke-free laws (Calvert et al., 2013). In 2013, current U.S. cigarette smoking ranged from a low of 10.3% (Utah) to a high of 27.3% (West Virginia). By comparison, the lung cancer mortality rate in Utah was 25.5 deaths per 100,000 persons in 2015, while in West Virginia, it was 77 per 100,000 (CDC, 2015). Do the math. During 2011–2013, current cigarette smoking declined significantly in 26 states: Arizona, Florida, Georgia, Hawaii, Illinois, Indiana, Kansas, Kentucky, Maine, Maryland, Michigan, Missouri, Montana, Nebraska, Nevada, New Hampshire, New Mexico, Oklahoma, Oregon, Rhode Island, South Dakota, Texas, Utah, Vermont, Wisconsin, and Wyoming. No significant changes were observed in any other states (CDC, 2015).

Worldwide, 40% of children and about 34% of adult nonsmokers were exposed to secondhand smoke in 2004. This exposure has been estimated to have caused 379,000 deaths from ischemic heart disease, 165,000 from lower respiratory infections, 36,900 from asthma, and 21,400 from lung cancer. An estimated total of 603,000 deaths were attributable to second-hand smoke in 2004, accounting for an estimated 1% of worldwide mortality. 47% of deaths from second-hand smoke occurred in women, 28% in children, and 26% in men. In 2004, an estimated 10.9 million years of healthy life were lost due to secondhand smoke; 61% of those lost years were in children. The largest estimated disease burdens were from lower respiratory infections in children younger than 5 years (5,939,000), ischemic heart disease in adults (2,836,000), and asthma in adults (1,246,000) and children (651,000) [Oberg, 2010].

Tobacco is estimated to have caused an astounding 100 million premature deaths in the 20th century. While smoke-free laws have proliferated worldwide since 2004, the situation remains grim. Each year, smoking and secondhand smoke combined continue to kill an estimated 6 million persons prematurely, a tribute to the ongoing sociopathy of tobacco industry executives and the massive failure of government institutions to punish them with criminal penalties. The annual global death toll could rise to more than eight million by 2030. Nearly 80% of these persons at risk live in low- and middle-income countries with poor or non-existent tobacco control laws. If current trends continue, tobacco smoking may cause one billion deaths in the 21st century (WHO, 2014).

According to the European Smoke Free Partnership: "Many EU countries are still failing to enact comprehensive smoke-free laws in indoor public places, workplaces and public transport, in spite of its legal obligation to do so under the Framework Convention on Tobacco Control (FCTC), the world's first public health treaty. Enacted in 2005, the FCTC treaty has been ratified by 179 countries; the holdouts are Cuba, Haiti and guess who, the United States of America.

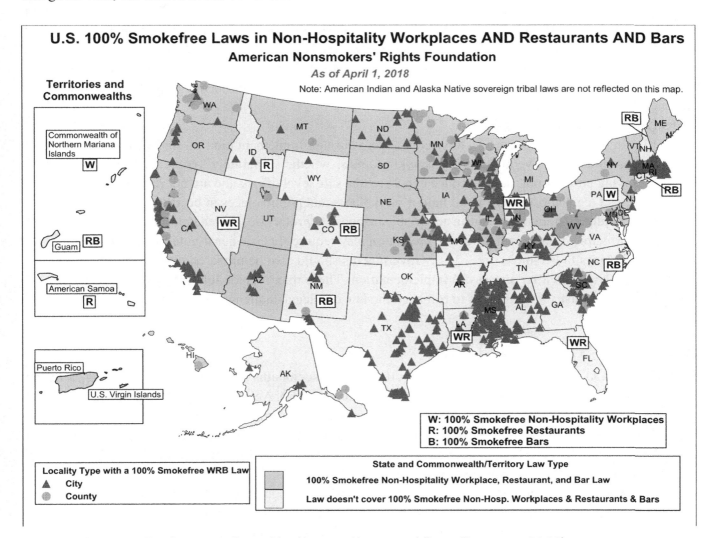

FIGURE 77. THE SMOKE-FREE STATES MAP (AMERICAN NONSMOKERS' RIGHTS FOUNDATION, 2018).

The burning of tobacco leaves indoors has exposed nonsmokers to indoor air pollution from tobacco combustion products containing many chemicals harmful to human health. Although society had long imposed quality standards for food, water, and outdoor air in the interest of public health, it has been slow to require that the indoor air be of a quality that would prevent morbidity and mortality. To put this into perspective, the same amount of contaminant deposited on the lung surface from the air that we breathe has greater potential for harm than an equal amount ingested from food or water, due to differences in absorption efficiency between the pulmonary and gastrointestinal membranes. For example, in a healthy adult, 5% of a gram of lead from a chip of accidentally ingested paint will be absorbed, while 95% of the same amount of lead inhaled as a fume from automobile exhaust will be absorbed. Secondhand smoke exposure can be a significant contributor to elevated blood lead. This is of particular concern for young children. Mannino et al. (2003) examined blood lead levels and passive smoking in a nationally representative sample of about 5600 U.S. children in the NHANES Survey (1988-1994), and found that geometric mean blood lead levels were 38% higher (95% CI 25–52%) in children with high cotinine levels compared with children who had low levels.

WHO reported that the proportion of the world's population covered by comprehensive smoke-free air laws was a mere 3.1 percent in 2007, according to *The WHO Report on the Global Tobacco Epidemic, 2009: Implementing smoke-free environments*. The report noted some progress: 22% of the 100 most populous cities in the world have smoke-free air laws, with 13 of those coming from city or state initiatives rather than through national efforts. By 2016, this had doubled to a still small fraction of 7% of the world's population covered by policies that protect people from secondhand tobacco smoke. In 2016, WHO reported that "Second-hand smoke (SHS) is one of the most important and most widespread exposures in the indoor environment. The link between SHS and several health outcomes, such as respiratory infections, ischaemic heart disease, lung cancer and asthma, has long been established."

WHO (2010) recommends, in part:

> 1. "Remove the POLLUTANT—tobacco smoke—through implementation of 100% smoke-free environments. … Ventilation and smoking areas, whether separately ventilated from non-smoking areas or not, do not reduce exposure to a safe level of risk and are not recommended.
> 2. Enact legislation requiring all indoor workplaces and public places to be 100% smoke-free …. Voluntary policies are not an acceptable response to protection. Under some circumstances, the principle of universal, effective protection may require specific quasi-outdoor and outdoor workplaces to be smoke-free. 3. … Governments should also be prepared to face challenges to the law even after successful implementation. These may include lobbying campaigns by tobacco industry front groups to roll back the law or a legal challenge in the courts. …"

HOW DOES BIG TOBACCO FARE TODAY?

Did the RICO lawsuit produce any lasting effect on the sociopaths who infest this rogue branch of the pharmaceutical industry like roaches? Although the Tobacco Control Act (TCA) signed into law in June 2009 gave the U.S. Food and Drug Administration (FDA) authority to regulate the manufacture, distribution, and marketing of tobacco products to protect public health, it specifically prohibited the FDA from banning an entire category of tobacco products, such as cigarettes, an ongoing tribute to the power of Big Tobacco to buy favorable legislation. The TCA's stated intent is to:

- Require new and more effective warning labels on tobacco products
- Educate consumers about the dangers of tobacco use, among other powers
- Establish and enforce restrictions on tobacco advertising and promotions
- Require tobacco companies to disclose what is in their products

- Review tobacco manufacturers' claims of "modified risk" products to prevent misleading claims.

On March 15, 2018, FDA published an advanced notice of a proposed rule to implement a rule regulating the maximum level of nicotine in combustible cigarettes.

However, with respect to secondhand smoke, these proposals have little to do with reducing exposure. According to the *New York Times*, the international tobacco cartel has enlisted moles in the U.S. Chamber of Commerce to combat WHO's anti-smoking efforts. Matt Myers, President of the Campaign for Tobacco-Free Kids, stated that the Chamber is "the tobacco industry's most formidable front group." Dr. Vera Luiza da Costa e Silva, the head of the Secretariat that oversees the Framework Convention on Tobacco Control, declared, "[The chamber] represent the interests of the tobacco industry, they are putting their feet everywhere where there are stronger regulations coming up." Largely hidden from public view, the industry's secretive influence has been global. "Around the world, the chamber lobbies with its foreign affiliates to defeat antismoking laws. Thomas J. Donohue, the chamber's chief executive, personally lobbied to defend the tobacco industry's ability to sue under future international treaties, notably the Trans-Pacific Partnership, the trade agreement proposed between the United States and several Pacific Rim nations." The chamber has had long-time relationships with the tobacco industry, and the top executive at the global tobacco giant Altria Group serves on the chamber's board. Philip Morris International plays a leading role in the global campaign to defeat international tobacco control efforts. The cigarette makers' payments to the chamber have not been disclosed. *The Times* editorialized, "some members of the chamber are probably not aware of every lobbying campaign the organization is running around the world. Now that it is clear what kind of pro-tobacco advocacy the chamber is carrying out, the organization's members, particularly in the health care industry, ought to speak out. Do they want their names associated with such a blatant attempt to stop governments in developing countries from enacting sensible public health policies?" [NY Times, 2015].

In 2011, the US Food & Drug Administration proposed striking images of the damaging effects of active and passive smoking to be imprinted on every pack of cigarettes. The industry sued to block these images of diseased lungs, rotted teeth, and the anguish of secondhand smoke poisoning, blatantly arguing that these images were "unconstitutional, and would make them a mouthpiece for the Government's emotionally charged anti-smoking message." A compliant federal judge, Richard J. Leon, granted the industry an injunction, incredibly stating that the images were "calculated to provoke" rather than disseminate "purely factual and uncontroversial information." In March 2013, the Obama administration failed to appeal the ruling (CBS News, 2013). *Et tu, Obama?*

In researching the past for this book, I ran into an item of note. In January 2015 – wait for it – R.J. Reynolds banned its employees from smoking in common areas of its workplaces. Workers may not smoke at their desks, in hallways and elevators, or while grabbing a cup of java in the break room. "We believe it's the right thing to do and the right time to do it, because updating our tobacco use policies will better accommodate both nonsmokers and smokers who work in and visit our facilities," RJR spokesperson David Howard told *Newsweek* [Dwyer 2014]. Hypocrisy, where is thy sting?

No Country For Old Scientists

On November 8th 2016, a date that will live in infamy, despite losing the popular vote by 3 million, the anti-science Donald J. Trump, was elected president of the U.S. by the anachronistic electoral college, which gives a voter in Wyoming, population 570,000, 3.7 times the electoral college voting power of a voter in California, population 40 million. According to Americans for Nonsmokers' Rights, at the time of his election, Trump owned between $500,001 and $1,000,000 worth of Altria (Philip Morris) stock in his Oppenheimer brokerage account. His Vice President, Mike Pence, has accepted campaign contributions from Big Tobacco. Moreover, Pence, when Governor of Indiana, cut funding for smoking cessation, and has written that he believes that "smoking doesn't kill" [ANR, 2016]. And Scott Pruitt, the recently fired Trumpist EPA Administrator, a died-in-the wool Anne Gorsuch clone who met the same fate, was a card-carrying agent of the fossil fuel industry. Pruitt shrouded his corrupt activities in a $43,000 secure telephone booth in his private office, and ridded EPA and its science advisory board of its troublesome academic scientists, replacing them with stooges for polluting industries. According to the Environmental Defense Fund, in his first 100 days he had "begun the process of abandoning the Clean Power Plan, taken aim at the Mercury and Air Toxics Rule lobbied the White House to withdraw from the Paris Climate Agreement shutting out neutral scientific advice attempted to enact a 31% budget cut at EPA, the largest of any federal agency stocking his agency with appointees with serious conflicts of interest (Gaby K, 2017).

Pruitt also used private jets for personal travel at government expense, travelled first class on scheduled airlines, had round-the-clock security protection, attempted to buy a bulletproof SUV and even a bulletproof desk and wanted to use flashing lights and sirens to cut through DC traffic to expedite local trips, and sidelined 5 EPA employees who questioned his extravagance according to *The Times* on April 5th, 2018. On April 18, 2018, *The New York Times* editorialized, "Despite stiff competition, Scott Pruitt, … is by common consensus the worst of the ideologues and mediocrities President Trump has chosen to populate his cabinet. Pruitt's self-aggrandizing and borderline thuggish behavior has disgraced his office and demoralized his employees." Although he is gone, his replacement was a former lobbyist for the coal industry and a former staffer for Sen. Jim Imhofe (R), OK. Inhofe is the author of the book, *The Greatest Hoax: How the Global Warming Conspiracy Threatens Your Future. Plus ça change, plus c'est la même chose.*

The fate of environmental science in the Age of Trump is of great concern to those of us who have been in the trenches for lo these many years. There are great parallels to the demonization of scientists who worked on combatting such issues as lead pollution, incineration, and secondhand smoke in earlier eras to what has happened to climate scientists today. At this writing, EPA remains in existence. However, its future survival is in grave jeopardy. My old friends in the environmental science community, Wayne Ott, Hal Levin, Matti Jantunen, Dave Mage, Kirk Smith, and many others, most of whom have remained active researchers, have looked on in horror at the wrecking ball the Trump Administration is applying to all we have worked so hard to build. It has been painful to watch.

THE AGE OF POT IS UPON US

According to *The Washington Post,* in 2016, support for marijuana smoking has hit an all-time high. A new survey by the AP-NORC Center for Public Affairs Research found that a record high percentage of Americans, 61%, support marijuana legalization. While I may agree it is foolish to criminalize marijuana possession, users who imagine that it is less harmful than cigarette smoking are delusional. Burning biomass at red heat whether it's tobacco, marijuana, or wood, produces toxic products of incomplete combustion. As Dr. Russell Martin of Baylor University said in 1979, as he related the results of his pulmonary lavage experiments on smokers: "marijuana smoking tears the hell out of your lungs." Potheads, take note.

Glantz and Springer (2015) observed,

"It will be non-controversial to legislate against 'driving while stoned' and the use of marijuana on the job. However, secondhand smoke presents another way for increased marijuana use to harm public health that may be less obvious to policy makers, due to rarity of studies that have explored these effects. … Because of their similar chemical composition, marijuana secondhand smoke and tobacco secondhand smoke are likely to have similar harmful effects on public health. … The similarity of the chemical composition of secondhand smoke from tobacco and marijuana, along with our observation that both kinds of smoke can impair blood vessel function, indicate that marijuana secondhand smoke is not harmless and that legal limitations on public exposure to secondhand smoke should apply to both tobacco and marijuana.

Wang et al. (2016) measured the effect of exposure to secondhand marijuana smoke for only one minute on flow meditated dilation (FMD) of the femoral artery in rats at levels similar to real-world conditions. They found that SHS from marijuana substantially impairs endothelial function in rats for at least 90 minutes, considerably longer than comparable impairment by tobacco SHS. Importantly they reported that impairment of FMD does not require cannabinoids, nicotine, or rolling paper smoke. Their findings in rats suggest that "SHS can exert similar adverse cardiovascular effects regardless of whether it is from tobacco or marijuana." To the extent that so-called 'medical marijuana' could benefit chronic pain sufferers, ingesting 'Alice B. Toklas Brownies' might be a better alternative.

AND A WORD ABOUT ECIGS

About that new way of getting a nicotine fix: The E-Cigarette. Although widely promoted as a way for adults to quit smoking tobacco cigarettes, these devices could also readily be used to circumvent existing smoke-free laws and sustain cigarette smoking among adults, as well as increase initiation and use of tobacco products among adolescents.

In October of 2013, I wrote a *Commentary: Indoor Air Pollution from E-cigarettes* and posted it on Research Gate. E-cigarettes vaporize a nicotine-containing liquid without combustion, and users inhale the vapors, but blow a visible aerosol into the air while exhaling. I noted that,

> "The growing popularity of e-cigarettes among smokers has led to increased availability with a number of new manufacturers entering the market every year. Also, these devices are being used in spaces where smoking has been banned, leading to increased indoor air pollution despite reductions in building air exchange rates. The few extant studies of Ecigarette emissions, although limited in the number of products tested, show that these devices pollute indoor air. Nevertheless, they are being promoted as "emitting only harmless water vapor," when studies show the emission of polluting VOCs, as well as heavy metals and fine and ultrafine particles. There is little or no quality control in, or government oversight of, the manufacture of E-liquids. If dozens of so-called "vapers" begin to frequent bars, restaurants, discos, offices, and these are permitted to fog the air on aircraft, decades of progress in cleaning up indoor air in workplaces and public access buildings is on the threshold of reversal. This is a very dangerous development."

A recent study by Tzortzi et al. (2018) supports my concern. In a controlled experiment, the authors concluded that the effect of a 30-minute passive exposure to Ecigarette emissions revealed immediate alterations in respiratory mechanics and exhaled inflammatory biomarkers.

These unregulated new sources of indoor air pollution are rapidly proliferating around the world and are obviously here to stay. E-cigarettes have divided the tobacco control community into two camps: the self-styled "harm reductionists" who view these as a safer alternative to smoking for adult smokers, to be promoted at any cost, and the misnamed "prohibitionists" who view them either as a new and uncontrolled source of indoor air pollution (I am obviously in this camp) or as a new gateway into nicotine addiction or as a means for cigarette smokers to circumvent smoking restrictions in indoor public places, all of which they clearly are. My view is that E-cigarette use should be prohibited everywhere that smoking is forbidden. Some progress has been made: In March 2016, the U.S. Department of Transportation banned E-cigarettes on all scheduled flights of U.S. and foreign carriers. The harm reductionists are premature in their confidence; in 2016, a Korean study compared the prevalence rates for asthma in South Korean high school students. Current users had more than doubled asthma prevalence compared to nonusers of Ecigs, (Cho & Paik, 2016). In another recent paper, the authors concluded that vaping E-cigarettes is associated with decreased expression of a large number of immune-related genes, which are consistent with immune suppression at the level of the nasal mucosa (Martin et al., 2016). Such studies are in their early phases, so the jury is still out on the degree of "harm reduction."

Moreover, there are manifold E-cigarette designs, and hundreds of manufacturers of these devices; some of them operating from garages in China, which suggests quality control is out the window. These fly-by-night manufacturers produce such a multiplicity of liquids, which contain many flavoring agents of variable composition, that it will be a Herculean task to characterize their emissions in a generalizable way. By January 2014 there were 466 brands (each with its own website) and 7764 unique flavours. They were increasing at a rate of increase of 10.5 brands and 242 new flavors per month (Zhu, 2014). This will prove to be a hugely expensive undertaking for any research body, and virtually impossible to be done on a small scale. This suggests that it is unlikely to get done. On May 5th 2016, The U.S. Food and Drug Administration (FDA) finalized a rule regulating all tobacco products, including vaporizers, vape pens, hookah pens, electronic cigarettes (E-Cigarettes), e-pipes, and all other electronic nicotine delivery systems (ENDS). FDA now regulates the manufacture, import, packaging, labeling, advertising, promotion, sale, and distribution of ENDS. This includes components and parts of ENDS but excludes accessories. According to FDA,

- More than 3 million middle and high school students were current users of e-cigarettes in 2015, up from an estimated 2.46 million in 2014.
- Sixteen percent of high school and 5.3 percent of middle school students were current users of e-cigarettes in 2015, making e-cigarettes the most commonly used tobacco product among youth for the second consecutive year.
- During 2011-2015, e-cigarette use rose from 1.5 percent to 16.0 percent among high school students and from 0.6 percent to 5.3 percent among middle school students.
- In 2013-2014, 81% of current youth e-cigarette users cited the availability of appealing flavors as the primary reason for use.
- In 2014, 12.6% of U.S. adults had ever tried an e-cigarette, and about 3.7% of adults used e-cigarettes daily or some days.

Glantz and Bareham (2018) in a review paper, concluded that:

"Since they appeared in the mid-2000s, some have embraced e-cigarettes as a safer alternative to conventional cigarettes and an effective way to stop smoking. While e-cigarettes deliver lower levels of carcinogens than conventional cigarettes, they still expose users to high levels of ultrafine particles and other toxins that may substantially increase cardiovascular and non-cancer lung disease risk, raising the possibility that e-cigarettes could be half as dangerous as conventional cigarettes. This is a high enough risk to lead to a net population harm. Rather than smokers switching from conventional cigarettes to less dangerous e-cigarettes or quitting all together, e-cigarettes are reducing smoking cessation and expanding the nicotine market by attracting youth who would be unlikely to initiate nicotine use with conventional cigarettes."

Finally, during the past 8 years since Ecigs have been available in the U.S., reports of explosions and fires caused the U.S. Department of Transportation to ban them in checked baggage on airlines. In addition, a recent report described an incident involving an 18-year old vaper whose Ecig exploded in his mouth, inflicting cuts, burns, and blowing out his front teeth [Rogér et al., 2016.] Apparently 92 events involving Ecigarette explosions occurred as of early 2016. Some events have resulted in life-threating injury, permanent disfigurement or disability, and major property damage [Rudy & Durmowicz, 2016].

SMOKING IN THE MOVIES

To ensure that there is a dependable supply of new smokers to replace the ones that die, the industry has long used a very effective recruitment tool: depictions of smoking on the silver screen. This normalizes smoking for children. This has been done with complicity from Hollywood and the independent film-makers, and now includes on-line content from video streaming companies. Polanski et al. (2017) wrote that

"In the last two decades, health researchers in more than a dozen countries have repeatedly confirmed what US tobacco companies have known since the late 1920s: movies sell cigarettes. In 2012, after reviewing the scientific evidence, the US Surgeon General concluded that exposure to smoking on screen causes kids to smoke.

Harm from film smoking | Exposure to on-screen smoking is a major factor in smoking initiation. Based on large-scale US studies of exposure effects, the US CDC estimated that films will recruit 6.4 million new US smokers from among today's children. Almost 90 percent of those recruited to smoke by on-screen exposure will start smoking before age 18. Two million of them will ultimately die from tobacco-induced diseases, including heart disease, lung cancer, stroke, and emphysema.

One million of these deaths will be from exposure to smoking in movies that the MPAA [the major film studios' trade association, the Motion Picture Association of America] rates as appropriate for youth (G/PG/PG-13).

… reducing kids' exposure to on-screen smoking will reduce kids' risk of smoking. In January 2014, the US Surgeon General reported that eliminating smoking from youth-rated films by R-rating future films with tobacco imagery would cut the impact on kids in half, reducing teen smoking rates by 18 percent. …

Only the proposed R-rating covering all companies, including the independents, and all films, whether low- or high-budget, will protect children and adolescents from the promotional effects of onscreen smoking."

SMOKING AND CHILD CUSTODY

When the unfortunate offspring of divorced or separated parents reside with a custodial parent who either smokes or otherwise allows smoking in the presence of the child, to the objection of the estranged nonsmoking parent, this can be a major factor affecting child custody. I'm proud of the three legal cases I've helped win on behalf of those beleaguered children in bitter child custody battles. These are *Baker v. Kelley* (1998) in New York, *Heagy v. Kean* (2005) in Indiana, and *Melton v. Melton* (2010) in Arkansas. In all three cases, to demonstrate secondhand smoke exposure, I arranged for cotinine tests before and after visits to the custodial parent and calculated the secondhand smoke air pollution levels using Rosetta Stone models. Many states are reluctant to take children away from their mothers on the grounds of smoking. In both *Baker* and *Heagy*, the courts denied custody to the nonsmoking fathers. However, the court ruled that the custodial smoking mothers were forbidden from continuing to expose their children to secondhand smoke. But in *Melton*, the nonsmoking father was granted sole custody.

Subsequently, in *Heagy*, the mother violated the trial court's injunction against exposing the child to secondhand smoke, and the nonsmoking non-custodial father appealed for sole custody. In 2007, an appellate court ruled in favor of the custodial parent but with the smoking restriction remaining in place. In *Baker*, there were three girls, aged 9, 13, and 15, who were exposed to their stepfather's smoking at home, in transit, and in restaurants, as well as to family friends who were smokers. The girls' non-custodial father, a physician, was extremely concerned for their health. Accordingly, I recommended cotinine tests. The girls' urine cotinine levels ranged from 5 to 6 ng/mL; this was four times higher than the mean of 1.4 ng/mL for US children in that age group in CDC's NHANES study, when expressed in urine cotinine equivalents of serum cotinine. These cotinine levels corresponded to an estimated annualized daily average fine particle exposure of 67 μg/m³, exceeding EPA's 12 μg/m³ health-based annual average air quality standard by a factor of 5.

A later study puts the cognitive damage done to children from secondhand smoke into perspective. Secondhand smoke contains lead, a cumulative poison affecting the central nervous system. Children with cotinine levels increased by just 1 nanogram per milliliter of blood have their blood lead increased by 38%, placing them at increased risk of impaired intelligence (Mannino et al., 2003). In the *Heagy* case, I developed a plot illustrating the cognitive decline in children as their cotinine increases (Figure 78).

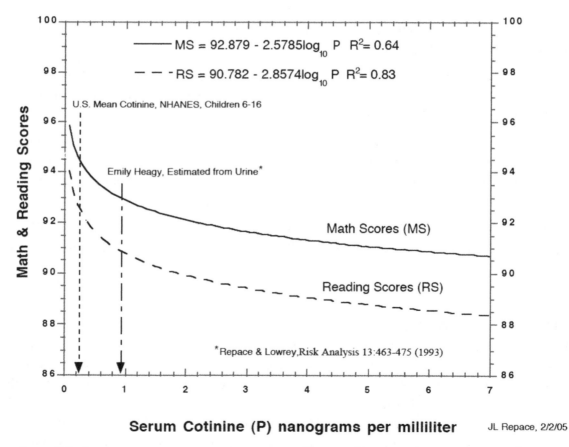

Serum Cotinine (P) nanograms per milliliter   JL Repace, 2/2/05

FIGURE 78. A GRAPH USED IN THE CHILD CUSTODY CASE, *HEAGY V. KEAN*, PLOTTED WITH DATA FROM YOLTON ET AL., EXPOSURE TO ENVIRONMENTAL TOBACCO SMOKE AND CHILD COGNITIVE ABILITIES. *ENVIRONMENTAL HEALTH PERSPECTIVES* 113:98-103 (2005).

In addition to shaving points off their IQ's, for smokers' children of all ages, those with high cotinine levels in the national survey had almost doubled incidence of wheezing apart from colds in the past year; doubled likelihood of six or more days of school absence in the past year; and lung function deficits of 2 to 6%. Moreover, 4-to-6 year-old children suffered a five-fold increased risk of asthma (Mannino et al., 2001).

To place these effects of secondhand smoke into perspective, consider the actual acute health effects the toddlers in my cases experienced. In *Heagy*, Emily, a three-year old, suffered multiple respiratory problems including chest congestion, otitis media, bronchitis, cough, pneumonia, sinusitis, decreased lung volume and asthma. Her cotinine test reached the 80th percentile for children aged 3-11 when compared to the *2nd Annual Report on Human Exposure to Environmental Chemicals*. Prolonged exposure would have resulted in significant cognitive decline (Figure 78). In *Melton*, Brilee, a two-year old, was gassed by secondhand smoke from *seven* smokers jammed into a double-wide mobile home. Brilee's cotinine level ascended to the 95th percentile for the *NHANES 1999-2002 cotinine survey for ages 3-11*, corresponding to an enormous 24-hour average fine particle air pollution exposure of 632 $\mu g/m^3$. This level is well beyond the "Very Hazardous" level of the EPA air quality index, reaching into the "Significant Harm" zone. Brilee suffered severe wheezing after these exposures and had to be treated with inhalers and antibiotics. But her lucky daddy prevailed. In January 2011, I received an email from Brilee's grandmother, Laurie: *"Mr. Repace, We just wanted to let you know that Brandon WON CUSTODY of Brilee!! Thank you so much for being part of saving a little girls life. God Bless you!"* Accompanying the email was a photo, which I treasure (Figure 79). Unfortunately, about two in five U.S. children aged 3–11 years (40.6%) remained exposed to secondhand smoke in 2012 (CDC, 2015).

THE ISES MEHLMAN AWARD FOR POLICY

The International Society of Exposure Science (ISES) "promotes and advances exposure science (methods, measurements, models) as it relates to the complex inter-relationships between human populations, communities, ecosystems, wildlife, and chemical, biological, and physical agents, and non-chemical stressors. ISES members have diverse expertise and training in biological, physical, environmental, and social sciences, as well as various engineering disciplines. According to the National Research Council, 'exposure science links human and ecological behavior to environmental processes in such a way that the information generated can be used to mitigate or prevent future adverse exposures.' The Society's multidisciplinary expertise and international reach make it the premiere professional society for practitioners associated with all aspects of exposure science (research, teaching, policy, communication, outreach)" (ISES 2015).

In October of 2015, the International Society of Exposure Science (ISES) conferred its Constance L. Mehlman award on Yours Truly. The award is given *"To recognize an ISES member who has made an outstanding contribution in exposure analysis research that helped shape a national or state policy or provided new approaches for reduction or prevention of exposures."* It was endowed in 1999 by Myron Mehlman, the Society's first President and former managing editor of the *Journal of Exposure Analysis and Environmental Epidemiology,* endowed a new ISEA award in honor of his late wife, Constance Mehlman, an environmental attorney, and it came with a grant of $2000. Instructively, Mehlman himself had been a former Mobil Oil Corporation toxicologist who was fired after advising a Mobil subsidiary in Japan to stop selling gasoline with hazardous levels of benzene, a known cause of human leukemia [Richter et al. 2002]. I was nominated for the Mehlman Award by Wayne Ott, seconded by Lance Wallace, and endorsed by eight other members, several of them former presidents of our society. This award from my research peers, presented at the ISES Annual Meeting in Henderson, Nevada, October 18-22, 2015, was extremely gratifying. The text of the award reads:

FIGURE 79. HAPPY FATHER WITH CHILD RESCUED FROM PASSIVE SMOKING (MELTON V. MELTON,).

"For over 35 years, James L. Repace has conducted original research measuring, and modeling human exposure to, and risk from, secondhand smoke (SHS) in a wide variety of locations where people live and work. His research, lectures, and testimony before the legislatures of many countries in North and South America, Europe, Asia, and the Pacific Rim has been a prime contributor to a worldwide effort to reduce the exposure of millions of people to SHS. His early research, published in 1980 in the journal *Science*, showed that $PM_{2.5}$ concentrations averaged six times higher in buildings where smoking was permitted than in nonsmoking buildings or outdoors, and this pioneering work had a major impact on the scientific community.

In 1985, he published the first health risk assessment of passive smoking and lung cancer in the journal *Environment International*, estimating 500 to 5000 US lung cancer deaths annually, and developed an exposure-response relationship demonstrating that ventilation could not control SHS exposures to within an acceptable level of risk. His research became the subject of numerous radio, television, and newspaper interviews and commentaries around the world. In 2004, he published an air monitoring study in *JOEM* comparing particle levels before and after a statewide smoking ban in six bars, a casino, and a pool hall in Delaware. It showed that 90 to 95% of $PM_{2.5}$ and particulate polycyclic aromatic hydrocarbon (PAH) levels were caused by SHS, and generated 650 million media impressions internationally, helping to persuade several countries to enact smoke-free workplace laws. This societal change cleaned the air in indoor spaces where people spent a significant portion of their time.

James Repace has explored a remarkably diverse set of projects on SHS and human exposure to SHS, ranging from exposure and doses of flight attendants in the smoky skies, of workers and patrons in smoky restaurants, bars, offices, factories, casinos and multi-unit housing, to levels of smoke in outdoor cafes, on cruise ships at sea, and on college campuses. He was one of the first investigators to use portable monitors to measure air pollutants indoors, and his field studies have included measurements of particulate matter, PAHs, nicotine, carbon monoxide, and air exchange rates. He has shown that it would take tornado-like levels of ventilation or air cleaning to control tobacco smoke pollution to de minimis levels of lung cancer and heart disease mortality risk in hospitality locations.

He has demonstrated a set of physical and pharmacokinetic equations for SHS correlating the SHS atmospheric markers nicotine, respirable particles, and carbon monoxide, to each other and with the SHS biomarkers cotinine in serum, saliva, and urine as well has hair nicotine. In collaboration with others, he has used this methodology to estimate levels of fine particle air pollution in bars from the urine cotinine of bartenders and patrons and compared them to the federal air quality index for outdoor air pollution alerts. These efforts have resulted in 48 peer-reviewed papers on secondhand smoke, in scientific, medical, engineering journals, earning over 3400 citations.

James Repace is presently a secondhand smoke consultant. He previously served as a research physicist at the Naval Research Laboratory and as a senior air policy analyst at the US EPA. He has earned several national awards, including The Surgeon General's Medallion, A Lifetime Achievement Award from the American Public Health Association, the Flight Attendant Medical Research Institute's Distinguished Professor Award, and the Robert Wood Johnson's Innovators Combating Substance Abuse Award. He has served as a Visiting Asst. Clinical Professor at the Tufts University School of Medicine, and as a Consultant to the Stanford University Department of Civil and Environmental Engineering."

Google Scholar is an on-line research tool that "provides a simple way to broadly search for scholarly literature, including articles, theses, books, abstracts and court opinions. Google Scholar ranks documents weighing, inter alia, where it was published, who authored it, and how often and how recently it has been cited in other scholarly literature. As of mid-June 2018, Scholar showed that 4417 research publications have cited my work, and that it had an h-index of 32. This indicates that 32 of my research papers received 32 or more citations. Hirsch (2005), a physicist who first proposed the index, noted that for faculty at major research universities, an *h* index of 20 after 20 years of scientific activity characterizes a successful scientist. Like many scientists, I have posted my entire body of work, as well as many slide presentations and selected legal cases, on *Research Gate*, where it is available for viewing or in some cases, direct downloading by researchers requesting reprints. In 2018, *Research Gate* reached 12 million members.

Figure 80 displays the citations per year to my research papers from 1982 to June 2018, ranging from 23 in 1982 to a high of 320 in 2009. It shows that research funding makes a difference. The $900 K in research grants from FAMRI and RWJF arrived in 2002, and the numerous research papers that it made possible had a discernable societal impact in subsequent years. As of late June 2018, the top four publications of mine in terms of citations were measurement papers: the *Science* paper of Repace and Lowrey (1980) with 438 citations, the *MMWR* paper reporting on measurements before and after New York's smoke-free law in Western New York bars and restaurants by Travers et al. (2004), which I co-authored, with 313 citations and the *JOEM* paper of Repace (2004) that measured particles and carcinogens before and after Delaware's state-wide smoke-free workplace law, with 282 citations. The fourth reported measurements of exposure and risk before and after Ireland's smoking ban by Mulcahy et al. (2005) in which I was a co-author, with 285 citations. A fifth measurement paper, in *BMC Public Health* by Repace et al. (2006) ranking 11th in my top citations, reported on measurements before and after Boston's smoking ban, earned 133 citations. Together, these five papers garnered 1451 citations, showing the importance of measurements of secondhand smoke concentrations. Harvard professor Jack Spengler once said, "It's not enough to be right. You have to publish your findings on something subject to controversy over and over and over again" [Davis, 2002].

In an additional modest effort to combat tobacco industry disinformation, I participated in five YouTube videos: *Merchants of Death – Bad Acts*; *Secondhand Smoke: The Case for Smoke-Free Casinos*; *Secondhand Smoke in Multi-Unit Housing* and *Fighting for Smokefree Air: James Repace on Ventilation* and *Comparison of Truck and Cigarette Air Pollution* [Repace, 2014; ANR 2013; Ott et al. 2015]. (Their combined views totaled 5810 as of late June 2018)

SMOKING JUST ONE CIGARETTE PER DAY...

Smoking just one cigarette a day can't be that harmful can it? Au contraire, mon amis. Striking new evidence has emerged indicating that a very steep non-linear dose-response relationship exists between inhalation of cigarette smoke and cardiovascular disease. It has profound significance for both active and passive smoking. A recent meta-analysis by Allan Hackshaw and colleagues (2018) of 141 prospective cohort studies from 21 countries and regions followed 5.6 million individuals for coronary heart disease (CHD) and 7.3 million persons for stroke. It included 110 000 new cases of CHD and 135 000 cases of stroke. Risks associated with one, five, and 20 cigarettes a day were modelled in each study for CHD and stroke, controlling for at least age and sex.

Smoking just one cigarette a day was associated with a 48% (all studies) to 74% (studies controlling for confounders in addition to age and sex) increase in the risk of coronary heart disease (CHD) in men, a 57% to 119% increase in CHD risk for women, and a roughly 30% increase in the risk of stroke for both men and women. In other words, smoking only one cigarette a day accounted for fully half of the excess CHD risk associated with smoking 20 a day in men and for one third of the risk in women. For stroke, one cigarette accounted for roughly one third of the risk associated with smoking 20 a day.

As Johnson (2018) editorialized:

"The high cardiovascular risk associated with very low cigarette use has major public health implications. Firstly, light smoking, occasional smoking, and smoking fewer cigarettes all carry substantial risk of cardiovascular disease. Secondly, passive smoking is essentially another form of low dose smoking that carries a substantial cardiovascular risk. Comprehensive smoke-free laws in public places, now common in high resource countries, result in large drops in hospital admissions (about 15%) for cardiac, cerebrovascular, and lung disease, and it would be prudent for low resource countries to follow suit.

Marijuana and sheesha (hookah) smoke are also of concern because incomplete combustion of organic substances produces many highly toxic chemicals, with similar serious adverse health consequences. Although e-cigarettes deliver reduced levels of carcinogens, they still expose users to high levels of ultra-fine particles and other toxins that may markedly increase cardiovascular risk. Somewhat lower emissions of many toxic substances from heat-not-burn cigarettes do not make these products safe. Regulatory approval of these products should be withheld. We cannot afford to wait several more decades to document the illness, disability, and deaths caused by new recreational tobacco and nicotine products. Thirdly, new tobacco products, such as e-cigarettes and heat-not-burn cigarettes, may carry substantial risk for heart disease and stroke."

POSTSCRIPT: MARTIN'S STORY

In early October 2017, an old friend, Martin Pion, President and cofounder of Missouri GASP, sent me a poignant email, whose burden he asked me to share with you. Missouri GASP was founded in 1984 after Martin hosted a fund-raiser for Paul Smith following the Smith v. Western Electric case, which I wrote about earlier.

Martin was born in London in 1936. In 1940, to escape the notorious London smog, his nonsmoking parents decamped for the clean air of the seaside town of Bournemouth. Martin, a lifelong nonsmoker, developed a smoke-sensitivity in his twenties. He fortunately had scant exposure to secondhand smoke in University, or at ITT's Central Research Lab where he later worked, partly in a semiconductor clean room. In early 1977, Martin accepted a transfer to ITT's new optical fiber facility in Roanoke, VA, and he and Joyce, his French wife, and their young son emigrated from England. In 1980, Martin left ITT to join McDonnell Douglas Astronautics Co. in St. Louis Missouri, to design and manage a new laser diode lab for a space program. They bought a home in a leafy part of the small city of Ferguson, in North St. Louis County.

Unfortunately, the only smoke-free area in his workplace was a room housing a mainframe computer. Martin was assigned a desk in an open area dubbed "the bullpen," about a dozen feet away from the department's chain-smoking secretary whose desk was outside the office of the smoking department manager. Later, when his group was assigned to cubicles, Martin smelled smoke from a false ceiling return vent near his desk whenever a co-worker lit up in a few cubicles away. Later in that decade, when company smoking rules made smoke-free more the norm, both the secretary and the co-worker, a senior engineer, continued to ignore them. Due to his sensitivity to secondhand smoke, he avoided attending meetings whenever possible, which were still held in smoking-permitted conference rooms. This negatively impacted his career.

From February 1988 through October 1989, Martin conducted a series of clandestine measurements of his SHS exposure using a passive nicotine monitor clipped to his lapel. This revealed significant exposure levels despite the company's smoking restrictions. He supplemented these results in 1989 by measuring fine particles with a borrowed Piezobalance, both in his workspace as well as numerous adjoining buildings, including immediately outside the executive suite in the HQ building. To establish a smoke-free control, he made comparison measurements over a holiday weekend, to compare with regular work shift readings with smokers present. He subsequently shared his results with management who objected to his "unauthorized behavior" which could "justify his being fired." Subsequently, the chain-smoking senior engineer who had been reporting to Martin was abruptly chosen to head up the new Opto-Electronics Group. She then excluded Martin on the grounds that he was "a trouble-maker" due to his smoke-free air efforts. In 1991 he departed McDonnell Douglas to become Vice President of a small scientific software company, working from his smoke-free home office. Martin, then 81 years old, related that he'd suffered from increasing hip pain for over a month, but an X-ray had failed to disclose any pathology. However, a follow-up CT scan revealed that he had late stage lung cancer. He was treated with immunotherapy, which failed to stem the tide. He passed away on March 27th 2018; Requiescat in Pacem.

Martin's tale is far from unique. This is what it was like for many nonsmokers in the Bad Old Days of smoker hegemony in the workplace. Like Martin Pion, the many tens of thousands of nonsmokers who suffered from secondhand smoke in the workplace have paid the full price for their managements' irresponsibility, fomented, aided, and abetted by Big Tobacco and all of its vile works. So. Has waging the war on secondhand smoke been worth it? *You bet your life it has.*

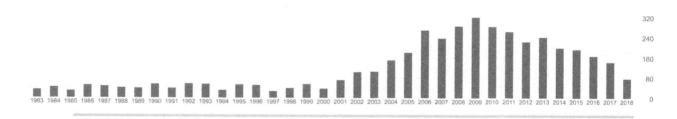

FIGURE 80. CITATIONS PER YEAR, DECEMBER 31, 1981 TO JUNE 26, 2018, REPACE AUTHORED OR CO-AUTHORED PAPERS, [GOOGLE SCHOLAR, 2017]. NOTE THE EFFECT OF THE BACK-TO-BACK AWARDS IN 2002 ON MY PRODUCTIVITY.

Finally, for the interested viewer, these are the URLs for the five YouTube videos that flesh out some of the issues discussed in this book:

https://www.youtube.com/watch?v=wsOxbTi12j4
Flight Attendants & Casino workers.

https://www.youtube.com/watch?v=FZbeI1RXn7w&t=8s
The case for smoke-free casinos.

https://www.youtube.com/watch?v=FrNzJ_spCqM&t=1s
Secondhand Smoke in Multiunit housing.

https://www.youtube.com/watch?v=I54XyduAy8Q&t=11s
Bad Acts. The Federal RICO lawsuit.

https://www.youtube.com/watch?v=uUo-fqjYEjM
Diesel exhaust vs. Cigarette smoke.

For those who wish to pursue the subject further, I can also highly recommend Richard Kluger's *Ashes to Ashes: America's Hundred-Year Cigarette War, the Public Health, and the Unabashed Triumph of Philip Morris*, Allen Brandt's *The Cigarette Century: The Rise, Fall, and Deadly Persistence of the Product That Defined America*, and Stan Glantz's *The Cigarette Papers*, which also discuss my efforts. Other important books involving Big Tobacco include Sharon Eubanks' memoir, *Bad Acts: The Racketeering Case Against the Tobacco Industry*, and Robert Proctor's *Golden Holocaust: Origins of the Cigarette Catastrophe and the Case for Abolition. Particles in the Air: The Deadliest Pollutant is One You Breathe Every Day*, by Doug Brugge.

ACKNOWLEDGEMENTS

I am grateful to Laura Oliver for her stimulating ten-week course on Memoir at St. Johns College, to Lance Wallace for his thorough reviews of a very rough first draft and a more polished 9th draft, to Wayne Ott, Jane McAteer, and Tom and Angela Murphy for helpful comments, and to Randy Ladenheim-Gil for editorial advice on the 3rd draft. In addition, I would like to express my deep appreciation to Clara Gouin, John O'Hara, and Willard Morris for contributing historical materials from the early days of the non-smokers' rights movement. Much of the detail on the tobacco industry would not be possible without the enormous contribution of Stanton Glantz in establishing the Legacy Tobacco Documents Library, at the University of California, San Francisco, now known as the Truth Tobacco Industry Documents website, which is a treasure trove of more than 14 million OCR searchable documents created by tobacco companies about their advertising, manufacturing, marketing, scientific research and political activities, hosted by the UCSF Library and Center for Knowledge Management. I would also like express my gratitude to Stan Shatenstein in Montreal for his indefatigable support and invaluable assistance with document retrieval.

APPENDIX A.

TESTIMONY OF TOM BLILEY, THE CONGRESSMAN FROM PHILIP MORRIS BEFORE THE HOUSE COMMITTEE ON ENERGY AND COMMERCE – HEALTH AND ENVIRONMENT SUBCOMMITTEE, HEARING ON ENVIRONMENTAL TOBACCO SMOKE, SERIAL NO. 103-51, JULY 31, 1993.

**"EPA AND ENVIRONMENTAL TOBACCO SMOKE:
SCIENCE OR POLITICS?**

(Preamble):

Mr. Chairman - I am testifying today in order to report to the Subcommittee the results of my extensive investigation of the EPA's handling of the controversy surrounding environmental tobacco smoke or 'ETS'. As you know, in the past the Oversight and Investigations [O and I] Subcommittee of this Committee has conducted hearings on EPA's abuses of government contracting requirements. So pervasive is the level of abuse that Chairman Dingell has characterized EPA's pattern of contract mismanagement as a 'cesspool'. EPA's Inspector General recently has confirmed that such abuses also have taken place in connection with a number of EPA contracts involving ETS, and the O and I Subcommittee's own investigation is continuing.

In addition to various contractual improprieties, however, my own investigation suggests that in its consideration of ETS, the Agency has deliberately abused and manipulated the scientific data in order to reach a predetermined, politically motivated result. EPA's risk assessment on ETS released in January of this year claims that ETS exposure is responsible for approximately 3,000 lung cancer cases per year in the United States. Analysis of the risk assessment reveals, however, that EPA was able to reach that conclusion only by ignoring or discounting major studies, and by deviating from generally accepted scientific standards.

EPA's willingness to distort the science in order to justify its classification of ETS as a 'Group A' or 'known human' carcinogen seems to stem from the Agency's determination early on to advocate smoking bans and restrictions as a socially desirable goal. EPA began promoting such policies in the mid-to late 1980s, ostensibly as part of its efforts to provide information to the public on indoor air quality issues. The Agency then decided to develop the ETS risk assessment to provide a scientific justification for smoking bans. The risk assessment thus was never intended to be a neutral review and analysis of the ETS science. Rather, it was intended from the start to function as a prop for the Agency's predetermined policy.

Not surprisingly, therefore, the process at every turn has been characterized by both scientific and procedural irregularities. In addition to the contracting violations mentioned at the outset, those irregularities include conflicts of interest by both Agency staff involved in preparation of the risk assessment and the members of the Science Advisory Board panel selected to provide a supposedly independent evaluation of the document. I will not itemize each and every one of these improprieties. Instead, I ask consent that a memorandum providing full details of the history of EPA's handling of ETS be included in the record. The memorandum summarizes the results thus far of my investigation into the Agency's handling of ETS and is based on publicly available documents, extensive correspondence between myself and former Administrator Reilly, and interviews conducted by my staff with the responsible EPA officials.

I. INTRODUCTION

With almost unprecedented fanfare, the Environmental Protection Agency ('EPA') released at a news conference on January 7, 1993, a risk assessment on tobacco smoke in the air – often referred to as environmental tobacco smoke ('ETS'). According to the EPA risk assessment, ETS is a 'Group A' or 'known human' carcinogen that is responsible each year for approximately 3,000 cases of lung cancer among nonsmokers residing in the United States. The risk assessment also claims that ETS is a cause of respiratory problems in infants living in homes in which one or both parents or some other family member smokes.

Not surprisingly, the claims contained in EPA's risk assessment on ETS generated substantial publicity, with most major newspapers, television news program and radio stations devoting substantial attention to EPA's conclusions. The publicity was, in part, a natural and expected response to the rather dramatic claims made in the EPA report. But EPA officials and staff, joined by Secretary Sullivan of the Department of Health and Human Services ('HHS'), also left no stone unturned to ensure heavy media coverage of the report. The EPA/HHS campaign was seeded by periodic 'leaks' of drafts of the report, and those leaks were followed with a heavily promoted press conference and individual interviews.

The EPA/HHS representatives made clear at their January press conference that they hoped that the EPA report would lead to additional smoking restrictions by private entities as well as by government at all levels. If the conclusions of the report are valid, that hope is certainly understandable. At the same time, however, if the claims made in the report are invalid, as appears to be the case, the likely consequence will be additional unjustified harassment of and discrimination against smokers – a consequence that received little attention at the January press conference.

The assumption that often is made is that smoking restrictions and other comparable measures are essentially costless. Increasingly, that assumption has been shown to be incorrect. Whether measured in terms of the number of people who are fired or are not hired because they smoke, by unjustified feelings of guilt among smokers or by the erosion of courtesy and tolerance, the campaign against smoking is not the no-lose proposition it is often portrayed as being.

In Washington, D.C., for example, which has adopted workplace smoking restrictions, the consequences of the ETS controversy are unmistakable. At all hours of the working day, people can be seen, even in the middle of winter, huddled near the doorways of office buildings smoking cigarettes. In fact, some employers – in Washington, D.C., and elsewhere – have gone so far as to require current and prospective employees to submit to a urine test, looking for the telltale sign of nicotine.

… The classification of ETS as a Group A carcinogen required substantial stretching by EPA. To reach that conclusion, the EPA report combined eleven spousal smoking studies from the United States in a so-called 'meta-analysis.' Of the eleven studies, however, ten reported no statistically significant increase in cancer among nonsmokers purportedly exposed to ETS. To ensure that the meta-analysis would produce the desired results, therefore, EPA had no choice but to manipulate the numbers.

Although in the past EPA and the scientific community have used a 95% confidence interval as a means of ensuring that study results did not occur by chance, EPA adjusted the confidence interval downward – to 90% – in its report on ETS. As James Enstrom, an epidemiology professor at the University of California, Los Angeles, explained, 'that doubles the chance of being wrong.'(5) To put it in lay terms, EPA's statistical maneuvering is the equivalent of moving the goal lines at a football game in order to score more touch-downs.

…

B. Early EPA Staff Initiatives Concerning ETS

EPA's policy of promoting restrictions on smoking seems to have begun with James L. Repace, an 'environmental protection specialist' in EPA's Indoor Air Division. In 1980, even before the first major ETS health claims appeared in the scientific literature, Repace wrote with A.H. Lowrey an article reporting on particulate matter in the air of various environments such as bars, restaurants and bingo parlors, without distinguishing whether these particulates were from ETS or other substance or activity.(11) The only 'office' measurements made by Repace were in an experimental, enclosed room in which thirty-two cigarettes were smoked in less than one hour, generating ETS levels grossly in excess of those encountered in the real world. Subsequent research has discredited both the methodology and conclusions of the 1980 Repace study.(12) On the basis of these observations, however, the article claimed that 'indoor air pollution from tobacco smoke presents a serious risk to the health of non- smokers * * * [that] deserves as much attention as outdoor air pollution.'(13)

459

A few years later, Repace published (again with A.H. Lowrey) an article purporting to show that ETS was riskier than 'all regulated industrial emissions combined.'(14) This second article by Repace and Lowrey, which represented a crude attempt at quantitative risk assessment, has been roundly criticized by both government and private sector scientists.(15)

Repace's extensive work with political advocacy organizations such as the Group Against Smoke Pollution ('GASP') and Action on Smoking and Health ('ASH') and his private and professional focus on smoking raise questions about Mr. Repace's ability to evaluate indoor air issues in a balanced manner. Since the 1970s, Mr. Repace also has been appearing as a paid witness in numerous lawsuits and testifying before various legislative bodies to support governmental restrictions on smoking. Consider in this regard Mr. Repace's statements to the press in reaction to the defeat of an antismoking legislative proposal in Maryland:

People aren't going to stand for this. Now that the facts are clear, you're going to start seeing nonsmokers becoming a lot more violent. You're going to see fights breaking out all over. Washington Star, April 5, 1980, p. D-1.

Based on my own experience with Mr. Repace, I do not find these accounts surprising. In 1991, at the invitation of EPA Administrator Reilly, my staff interviewed several EPA employees as part of my and the Oversight Committee's efforts to gather the facts about EPA's procedures in preparing ETS-related documents. When he presented himself in my office, however, Mr. Repace categorically refused to answer any questions. He was accompanied by John Banzhaf, ASH's Executive Director, and Mr. Nantkes of the EPA General Counsel's office. Both were said to be serving as Mr. Repace's attorneys. Within minutes after Mr. Repace left my office, my staff received inquiries from the media characterizing my efforts as 'intimidation.'

During the late 1980s, Mr. Repace became the driving force behind EPA's push to classify ETS as a 'Group A' carcinogen. He began by outlining plans for two reports designed to promote the elimination of ETS. Although his plans personally to draft a 'handbook' on the subject were not realized, Repace assumed primary responsibility for two long-term projects – an 'ETS literature compendium' and an 'ETS workplace smoking policy guide,' as well as a smaller project, an 'ETS fact sheet.' These projects were meant to further the agenda first announced in Repace's 1980 article.

Even as Mr. Repace expanded his activities within the Indoor Air Division, he was traveling around the world, at the invitation and expense of [anti]-smoking organizations, to appear at various conferences and media events to promote antismoking restrictions. For example, Mr. Repace traveled to New Zealand in 1990 to support antismoking legislation in that country. Press coverage there was typical of Mr. Repace's media appearances, including the identification of Mr. Repace as an EPA employee unaccompanied by the required disclaimer that his views did not then reflect an official EPA position.

In numerous media interviews, Mr. Repace has made the baseless assertion that 50,000 people in the U.S. die each year from exposure to ETS and has left the clear impression that these views reflect EPA's official position rather than his personal views. Such demonstrated bias would create a serious conflict of interest issue at any regulatory agency, apparently with the exception of EPA, most likely leading to the official's recusal from further involvement in the issue in question. In fact, Mr. Repace continued to play a key role in the preparation of documents for the public that were represented as neutral and dispassionate analyses of the facts pertaining to ETS despite the advocacy role he was playing in his private capacity.

C. How EPA Used Its Role In Indoor Air Research To Further An Antismoking Agenda

1. The ETS 'Fact Sheet'

In 1989, Repace prompted the Agency's publication of a 'Fact Sheet' on ETS. Despite its name, 'Indoor Air Facts Number 5' made extravagant health claims about ETS, going far beyond the conclusions of the 1986 reports of the National Academy of Science ('NAS') and the Surgeon General on the same subject. For example, it claimed that exposure to ETS was linked to heart disease, when both the NAS and Surgeon General had found that the available studies did not support that claim.

The 'Fact Sheet' also took certain statements in the 1986 Surgeon General's report out of context in order to claim a consensus that 'passive smoking significantly increases the risk of lung cancer in adults' (p. 1). Whereas the Surgeon General and NAS reports had emphasized critical limitations on their findings of a possible connection between exposure to ETS and lung cancer, the 'Fact Sheet' ignored those limitations and treated the purported relationship as irrefutable.

The 'Fact Sheet' also failed to note that even the limited conclusions of the Surgeon General and NAS reports had been strongly criticized and that other reviewers – including the World Health Organization's International Agency for Research on Cancer – had reached different conclusions based upon the same data. See, e.g., 'IARC Monograph on the Evaluation of the Carcinogenic Risk of Chemicals to Humans: Tobacco Smoking,' vol. 38, p. 308 (1986). Furthermore, a number of other studies and reviews published since 1986 contradicted the findings of the Surgeon General and NAS reports with respect to the purported relationship between ETS and lung cancer.(16) None of these was mentioned in the 'Fact Sheet.'

Finally, the 'Fact Sheet' characterized ETS as 'a major contributor of particulate indoor air pollution' (p. 2) while failing to mention the numerous studies showing that inadequate ventilation is the single most important cause of indoor air pollution. Significantly, no SAB panel or expert committee ever reviewed the 'Fact Sheet's' claims. Instead, the document was distributed freely to the public as if it contained the official, carefully considered policy of the U.S. government rather than simply the personal opinions of Mr. Repace. …

3. The ETS Technical Compendium

In November 1989, EPA released a draft ETS 'technical compendium,' the second of the Agency's documents concerning ETS. Conceived originally as a reference document, the compendium consisted of ten (later eleven) chapters on a variety of subjects not always directly related to ETS. With the exception of a draft chapter on 'Exposure Assessment of Passive Smoking' by Mr. Repace, the compendium articles were solicited from scientists and consultants outside the Agency. …

In addition to the chapter on trends in public attitudes, the compendium contained other articles on active smoking and on economic issues surrounding workplace smoking. The only unifying theme of the compendium is that, in the Agency's view, smoking and ETS are 'bad.' Like most of the Agency's outside contractors on ETS, many chapter authors for the compendium, including Stanton Glantz, Jonathan Samet, and, of course, James Repace – had long been active in the antismoking movement. …

Although styled (and later defended by the Agency) as a scientific reference document, the compendium was in fact designed as an advocacy document for smoking restrictions. The preface to the compendium indicated that it was intended to be distributed to scientists, public officials, legislators and those in the private sector who are or may be concerned about ETS. The overall purpose was to 'provide information necessary to allow the public, government agencies, and the building industry to make well-informed choices regarding exposure to ETS' (p. 2). The letter accompanying the draft compendium indicated that the compendium was an 'integral component of [EPA's] ETS strategy,' which was to include a separate 'policy-maker's guide' that in turn would be a simplified version of the compendium. ...

4. Bias In Preparing The Compendium

Although still in draft form and not reviewed by the SAB, the compendium received widespread media attention. Robert Axelrad, Director of the Indoor Air Division, had asserted unequivocally in a May 8, 1990, letter to The Tobacco Institute's counsel that EPA was 'not interested in promoting any media attention to the documents while they are in draft form and will do everything possible to assure that they are not construed as EPA policy.' Notwithstanding Mr. Axelrad's assurances, the compendium was leaked to the press and its more sensational claims openly publicized prior to any scientific review of the document's contents. According to a February 1993 report by the General Accounting Office ('GAO'), EPA staff in April 1991, before EPA had completed its own internal review of the document, improperly sent a draft of the compendium to several external reviewers, including Stanton Glantz. Glantz, an outspoken antismoking activist since the 1960s, immediately proceeded to provide a copy to an Associated Press reporter. According to the GAO, Glantz claims that his release of the report was simply a 'mistake.' ...

Most disturbing was the public dissemination of the chapter on cardiovascular disease. Glantz, one of the authors of that chapter, appeared in Boston – again with James Repace – at the World Conference on Lung Health in late May 1990 and gave both a presentation and news interviews on that chapter. Dr. Glantz used the occasion to repeat and underscore the unsupported claim that more than 30,000 nonsmoking Americans die of heart disease each year as a result of exposure to ETS.   ...

[m]uch of the controversy over the report had focused on the estimate of 37,000 heart disease deaths attributed to secondhand smoke. That section was written by Stanton Glantz and Dr. William Parmley of the University of California, San Francisco. 'Thirty-seven thousand may be a figment of Stan Glantz's imagination and William Parmley's imagination, or it may be a real estimate,' said Axelrad [Director of EPA's Indoor Air Division]. 'Any effort or any attempt to imply any kind of endorsement or acceptance by EPA' of the death estimates in the technical compendium 'is at this time totally inappropriate,' he said. ...

Equally disturbing, I have learned recently that, as the SAB considered the first draft of the risk assessment, Dr. Steven Bayard, the EPA staff member with principal responsibility for the document, was providing 'enthusiastic' support to a grant proposal by Dr. Stanton Glantz and his associates in California for a project designed explicitly to discredit any scientist who has consulted on the ETS issue for the tobacco industry and expressed critical views with regard to the risk assessment. As discussed earlier, Dr. Glantz prepared a chapter of the ETS technical compendium and is a well-known and vocal anti-tobacco activist. The grant proposal seeks to study '[t]he tobacco industry and scientific research.' The purpose of the study is to arrive at 'an understanding of tobacco industry tactics for influencing research on ETS' by identifying whether particular scientists are 'funded by the tobacco industry.' That Dr. Bayard's January

10, 1991, letter in support of that application offered to continue to cooperate actively with Glantz and his associates at a time when the risk assessment was still under SAB review raises questions about the EPA staff's approach to resolving legitimate scientific criticisms of their work. Rather than addressing those criticisms on the merits, Dr. Bayard's endorsement of the Glantz proposal creates the impression that he is more interested in silencing his critics.

Dr. Bayard's participation in this effort is even more alarming given his role in the selection of SAB panelists. Mr. Reilly repeatedly shunted aside bias concerns on the ground that the procedures for selecting SAB members are intended to ensure that members 'are free from legal and perceived conflict-of-interest.' Later on, however, I wrote to EPA asking for an explanation of how the ETS panel was being selected. In response, EPA informed me that the candidates were being selected by Dr. Bayard, with assistance from Robert Axelrad and James Repace. …

Together, EPA and the SAB have undermined the process by which risk assessments ought to be conducted: first, by ignoring the substantial scientific controversy about what the ETS studies actually show; and, second, by conducting the forum where that controversy should have been thoroughly aired as a mere rubber stamp proceeding. As a result, EPA's preparation and review of the risk assessment have given the appearance of a scientific show trial to legitimize a predetermined policy. …

(14) J.L. Repace and A.H. Lowrey, A Quantitative Estimate of Nonsmokers' Lung Cancer Risk From Passive Smoking, Env. Int., vol. 11, pp. 3-22, at 12 (1985). This study was not funded or sponsored by EPA. Repace apparently undertook the study on his own initiative. The source of his funding has never been revealed.

(15) Reviews critical of the Repace and Lowrey risk assessment, calling their methodology and conclusions into question, were completed by EPA's Carcinogen Assessment Group prior to publication of the Repace and Lowrey paper. See E. Anderson, Repace and Lowrey's Estimate of the Nonsmokers' Lung Cancer Risk From Passive Smoking (undated); H. Gibb, Repace and Lowrey's Estimate of the Non- smokers' Lung Cancer Risk From Passive Smoking (undated). In addition, the Repace and Lowrey paper was criticized by the Congressional Office of Technology Assessment in Passive Smoking in the Workplace: Selected Issues, pp. 21-22 (May 1986). Other scientific articles criticizing the Repace and Lowrey risk assessment as well as their earlier work on ETS include A. Gross, Risk Assessment Relating to Environmental Tobacco Smoke, Environmental Tobacco Smoke, Proceedings of the International Symposium at McGill University, D.J. Ecobichon and J.M. Wu, (eds.), Lexington Books, Lexington, Mass., pp. 293-302 (1990); N. Balter et al., Causal Relationship Between Environmental Tobacco Smoke and Lung Cancer in Non-Smokers: A Critical Review of the Literature, Proceedings of the 79th Annual Meeting of the Air Pollution Control Association (1986); A. Arundel et al., Nonsmoker Lung Cancer Risks From Tobacco Smoke Exposure: An Evaluation of Repace and Lowrey's Phenomenological Model, J. of Env. Sci. and Health, vol. 84(1), pp. 93-118 (1986); M. Lebowitz, The Potential Association of Lung Cancer With Passive Smoking, Env. Int., vol. 12, pp. 3-9 (1986); P. Burch, Health Risks of Passive Smoking: Problems of Interpretation, Env. Int., vol. 12, pp. 23-28 (1986)."

APPENDIX B.

THE REVISION OF STANDARD 62: WHAT A DIFFERENCE A DECADE MAKES

A Persily, National Institute of Standards and Technology, Gaithersburg, MD, USA Proceedings: Indoor Air 2002.

"ASHRAE approved the first version of Standard 62, titled Standards for Mechanical and Natural Ventilation, in 1973 (ASHRAE, 1977). It was republished as Ventilation for Acceptable Indoor Air Quality in 1981 (ASHRAE, 1981), with another revision in 1989 (ASHRAE, 1989). The approval of Standard 62-1989 was not without controversy, and it was felt that its revision should begin right away in anticipation of the time that might be required. A committee was formed in 1991 to develop the revised standard and met for the first time in January of 1992. It has been ten years since that first meeting; this paper summarizes what has been accomplished to date and what remains to be done. …

A complete draft revision was issued for public review in August of 1996. It received about 8000 public review comments, most of which were duplicates generated by organized efforts to express displeasure with various aspects of the draft. Despite the controversy, this draft did achieve the goal of a standard written in code-intended language that incorporated new research results and experience. … Addendum 62e removed a note to the table of minimum outdoor air requirements stating that these rates accommodated "a moderate amount of smoking." Since the 1989 publication of the standard, numerous public health and gov…ernmental authorities declared environmental tobacco smoke (ETS) to be a significant health risk. The committee removed this note based on the inconsistency between the stated purpose of the standard to 'minimize the potential for adverse health effects' and the presence of ETS. …

These addenda went out for public comment, as noted, in March 1998. A number of comments were received on each of them, and the committee attempted to resolve the issues raised by the commenters. Four of these five addenda were approved for publication in 1999. The publication of one, Addendum 62e, was appealed to the ASHRAE Board of Directors and ultimately to ANSI. These appeals were denied, and these four addenda became part of the standard when it was republished as ASHRAE Standard 62-1999. … A range of issues has impacted the approval of the addenda in the 1999 and 2001 revisions and continues to impact the development of the addenda … . Overlaid on these technical issues, there has been a layer of controversy, procedural changes and politics that has distracted the committee and ASHRAE during the revision process. …

Controlling ETS Exposure
As might be expected, a great deal of controversy has arisen as the committee has dealt with the issue of environmental tobacco smoke (ETS). The first step, described earlier, was the deletion of the note stating that the minimum ventilation rate requirements in the standard

accommodate a moderate amount of smoking. Two other proposed changes to the standard have been developed by the committee and are working their way through the approval process. The first, addendum 62g, contains requirements for separating smoking and non-smoking spaces such that the non-smoking spaces are sufficiently free of ETS that they can meet both the comfort and health requirements of the standard. This addendum would require depressurization of spaces where smoking is occurring and separation of ETS-exposed and 'ETS free' spaces.

The objective of these requirements is to prevent significant ETS transport into ETS free spaces, but they are not expected to prevent absolute separation such as what one is trying to achieve in some infectious disease wards in hospitals using airlocks. While the standard's purpose of providing health and comfort is inconsistent with the presence of ETS, designers still need to design spaces where smoking is allowed. The committee is attempting to develop guidance for determining ventilation rates in these spaces through addendum 62o, which provides a method for determining outdoor air ventilation rates in smoking-permitted spaces for odor control only. This guidance is proposed for inclusion in an informative appendix to the standard, which is not officially part of the standard and therefore need not be consistent with the health goals of the standard."

REFERENCES

[N.B. Documents from the University of California, San Francisco Industry Documents Library https://www.industrydocumentslibrary.ucsf.edu/tobacco/ can be accessed by Bates numbers entered into the search engine. Bates numbering is used in the legal, medical, and business fields to place identifying numbers or date/time-marks on images and documents as they are scanned or processed.]

PREFACE

Google Ngram. In the fields of computational linguistics and probability, an *n-gram* is a contiguous sequence of n items from a given sequence of text or speech. The items can be phonemes, syllables, letters, words, or base pairs according to the application. The n-grams typically are collected from a text or speech corpus. *[Wikipedia, 2016].*

Frankfurt, HG. *On Bullshit.* Princeton University Press, Princeton and Oxford, 2005.

Guardino SD, and Daynard RA (2007). Tobacco industry lawyers as "disease vectors" *Tobacco Control* 2007;16:224–228. doi: 10.1136/tc.2006.018390.

Glantz, Stanton A., John Slade, Lisa A. Bero, Peter Hanauer, and Deborah E. Barnes, editors The Cigarette Papers. Berkeley: University of California Press, ©1996. http://ark.cdlib.org/ark:/13030/ft8489p25j/.

Hansen J, 2009. *Storms of My Grandchildren: The Truth about the Coming Climate Catastrophe and Our Last Chance to Save Humanity.* Bloomsbury USA; 1st edition November 30, 2009.

Mann M, 2016. This is what the coming attack on science looks like. *Washington Post,* Sunday, 18 December 2016, Section B, p.1.

Marquis Who's Who, 2017. http://www.24-7pressrelease.com/press-release/james-l-repace-presented-with-the-albert-nelson-marquis-lifetime-achievement-award-by-marquis-whos-who-446638.php

Richter E, Soskolne CL, LaDou J, Berman, T. Whistleblowers in Environmental Science, Prevention of Suppression Bias, and the Need for a Code of Protection. *Investigating Research Integrity, Proceedings of the First ORI Research Conference on Research Integrity,* Eds. Steneck NH, and Scheetz MD. Office of Research Integrity, U.S. Dept. of Health and Human Services, 2002.

Russell B. The Social Responsibilities of Scientists. *Science* 1960; 131: 391-392.

San Francisco Examiner, 1997. Sullivan K. Dec. 2, 1997, p. A7. Smokers to appeal UCSF research suit – tobacco group had alleged Glanz misused funds; case was dismissed.

The Tobacco Atlas, 5th Edition, Eriksen M, Mackay J, Schluger N, Gomeshtapeh FI, Drope J. American Cancer Society & World Lung Foundation (2015).

TTID. Truth Tobacco Industry Documents Library, University of California, San Francisco (formerly Legacy Tobacco Documents Library or LTDL): **https://industrydocuments.library.ucsf.edu/tobacco/results/#q=Glantz&h=%7B%22hideDuplicates%22%3Afalse%2C%22hideFolders%22%3Afalse%7D&subsite=tobacco&cache=true&count=26272.**

WSJ, 1998. Hwang, Suein L. Tobacco Memos Detail Passive-Smoke Attack. *The Wall Street Journal*, April 28, 1998: B1, B8.

Chapter 1. When Smoking Was King

ALA Archive, 2000. http://archive.tobacco.org/Documents/dd/ddfrankstatement.html.

Barad CB. Smoking on the Job: The Controversy Heats Up. *Occupational Health and Safety* 48: 21–24.1979.

Cummings KM, Morley CP, Hyland A. Failed promises of the cigarette industry and its effect on consumer misperceptions about the health risks of smoking. *Tobacco Control* **11**, suppl 1, i110-i117, 2002.

DLPA, 2016. Digital Public Library of America, Internet Archive, David Goerlitz.

https://dp.la/item/f5642f809ac6e88c746508f18e0d6b39?back_uri=https%3A%2F%2Fdp.la%2Ftime-line%231991%2Ff5642f809ac6e88c746508f18e0d6b39

Haines v. Liggett Group, Inc., et al. C.A. 84-678 (D.N.J. 1992).

Herbert, 1993. In America; Tobacco Dollars. *The New York Times*, November 28, 1993.

Mintz M. Legal Battles Smolder Six Decades After 'the greatest health protection in Cigarette History – Fair Warning http://www.fairwarning.org/2013/10/legal-battles-smolder-six-decades-after-the-greatest-health-protection-in-cigarette-history/, accessed Sept. 23, 2006.

Proctor RN. The history of the discovery of the cigarette – lung cancer link: evidentiary traditions, corporate denial, global toll. *Tobacco Control* 2012 21: 87-91.

Roper Organization. *A Study of Public Attitudes Toward Cigarette Smoking and the Tobacco Industry*. Vol. 1, 1978.

Repace, 1985. James L. Repace, Risks of Passive Smoking, Chapter One, in *To Breathe Freely, Risk, Consent, and Air*, Mary Gibson, Ed., Maryland Studies in Public Philosophy, Rowman and Allenheld, 1985.

Repace JL, and Lowrey AH. Tobacco Smoke, Ventilation, and Indoor Air Quality.

ASHRAE TRANSACTIONS 88: Part I, 895-914 (1982).

Sharkey J. What flying was like before the smoke cleared. *The New York Times*, Business Day, Feb. 23, 2015.

Speer F. Tobacco and the Nonsmoker. *Archives of Environmental Health* 16: 443-446 (1968).

Szabo L. U.S. smoking warning made history, saved lives. *USA Today*, Jan 8, 2014.

Goodman J. 2005. *Tobacco in History and Culture: An Encyclopedia*. Jordan Goodman Ed. © 2005 by Thomson Gale, Scribners & Sons.

TTID T109020978. Letter from Kastenbaum (Tobacco Institute) to Abelson (Science Magazine Editor, April 10, 1980.

TTID. 100209946 The Problems of Passive Smoking, Harke, HP. (Carreras Rothmans Research Division).

TTID. 2024077063.

Vickers v. VA (1982). Lanny L. Vickers, Plaintiff, v. The Veterans Administration, et al., Defendants. No. C81-85V. United States District Court, W.D. Washington, August 31, 1982, 549 F. Supp. 85.

Wikipedia. Cigarette. https://en.wikipedia.org/wiki/Cigarette#History.

Chapter 2. The Brass Knuckle School of Physics

ACS, 2014. Herman Mark and the Polymer Research Institute.
http://www.acs.org/content/acs/en/education/whatischemistry/landmarks/polymerresearchinstitute.html].

Garfield, E, 1973, *Essays of an Information Scientist*, Feb. 1973.

Lung Association of Southern Maryland, *Lungs Are Lovely*, 1975.

National Academy of Sciences. *Facilitating Interdisciplinary Research*. Committee on Facilitating Interdisciplinary Research, National Academy of Sciences, National Academy of Engineering, Institute of Medicine National Academy Press, Washington, DC, 2005.

NSA, 2002. *Cryptologic Almanac 50th Anniversary Series*, The Effort to Create a Smokefree National Security Agency [Unclassified Document].

Wikipedia, 2016. *RCA Laboratories at Princeton, New Jersey.* **http://ethw.org/RCA_Laboratories_at_Princeton,_New_Jersey.**

Chapter 3. The Blue Plains Sludge War

Davis, 2002. Davis D. *When Smoke Ran Like Water – Tales of Environmental Deception and the Battle Against Pollution.* Basic Books, Perseus Books Group, New York, 2002.

Glantz SA, Slade J, Bero LA, Lisa A., Hanauer P, Barnes DE, *The Cigarette Papers,* p. 296, University of California Press.

Glantz SA, Barnes DE, Bero LA, Hanauer P, Slade J. Looking through a keyhole at the tobacco industry. The Brown and Williamson documents. *JAMA* 19;274(3):219-24 (1995).

Janssen JE. The History of Ventilation and Temperature Control, ASHRAE Journal, 47-52, September, 1999.

Layzer, 2012. *Open for Business: Conservative Opposition to Environmental Regulation. J.A. Layzer, MIT Press, 2012.*

Met Office, UK, 2015. The Great Smog of 1952. http://www.metoffice.gov.uk/learning/learn-about-the-weather/weather-phenomena/case-studies/great-smog

Repace, JL. Risks of Passive Smoking. In: *To Breathe Freely, Risk, Consent, and Air. Gibson M., Ed. Rowman & Allanheld, Totowa, NJ, 1985.*

TTID. LG 2002750. Letter from Patrick M. Sirrige, Shook, Hardy, and Bacon, to Joseph Greer Esq., Arnold Hanson, Esq., Alexander Holtzman Esq., Ernest Pepples Esq., Arthur J. Stevens Esq. S.B. Witt III Esq. Re: Dr. Theodor Sterling, March 1, 1982.

TTID. T10384-1202. Tobacco Institute Memo From Fred Panzer to Jack Mills on Indoor Air Pollution – NAS Study, September 3, 1981.

TTID. TI00430746, ASHRAE 62-1981 Briefing Book from Tobacco Institute Records.

[United States of America et al. vs. Philip Morris, et al. Amended Final Opinion, 503645463-5463 (US 29696)].

The Washington Post (2004). Anne Gorsuch Burford, 62, Dies; Reagan EPA Director. http://www.washingtonpost.com/wp-dyn/articles/A3418-2004Jul21.html.

Chapter 4. Where There's Smoke, There's Ire

Boca Raton News. Lawsuit 'Airlines could not rid planes of smoke,' Tuesday August 5, 1997.

Cain WS, Isseroff R, Leaderer BP, Lipsitt ED, HueyRJ, Perlman, Bergland LG, and Dunn JD. *VENTILATION REQUIREMENTS FOR CONTROL OF OCCUPANCY ODOR AND TOBACCO SMOKE ODOR: LABORATORY STUDIES FINAL REPORT*, April 1981. LBL-12589 UC-41. Lawrence Berkeley Laboratory, University of California, Energy & Environment Division.

CE&N, 2017. Isabella Karle dies at age 95. Crystallographer remembered for her pioneering contributions to solving molecular structures. https://cen.acs.org/articles/95/web/2017/10/Isabelle-Karle-dies-age-95.html.

Kloepfer, 1984, TTID. T10411-2063; Environmental Forum, 1985; *Deseret News*, Sunday, Sept. 26 2010.

Leaderer BP Cain WS, Isserof R, Berglund LC. Paper 81-22.6, presented at the 74th Annual Meting of the Air Polution Control Association, Philadelphia, PA, June 22-25, 1981.

Miesner EA, Rudnick SN, Hu F-C, Spengler JD, Preller L, Ozkaynak H, and Nelson W. Particulate and Nicotine Sampling in Public Facilities and Offices. *JAPCA* 39: 1577-1582 (1989).

New York Times (1982). Judge Rules Smoke Victim Legally Handicapped. *New York Times* from *AP*, Sept. 2, 1982.

PIALF: Webpages of the Potomac Institute and the Atlantic Legal Foundation; downloaded 4/25/2014].

Repace and Lowrey, 1980. Repace JL, and Lowrey AH. Indoor Air Pollution, Tobacco Smoke, and Public Health. Science 208: 464-474, (1980).

Repace JL. The Problem of Passive Smoking. *BULLETIN OF THE NEW YORK ACADEMY OF MEDICINE* 57: 936-946 (1981).

Repace and Lowrey, 1982. Repace JL, and Lowrey AH. Tobacco Smoke, Ventilation, and Indoor Air Quality. *ASHRAE TRANSACTIONS* 88: Part I, 895-914 (1982).

Repace, 1985. Repace, JL. Risks of Passive Smoking. Chapter 1 in *To Breathe Freely – Risk, Consent, and Air*. Gibson M, Ed. Center for Philosophy and Public Policy University of Maryland, College Park, Rowman & Allenheld Publishers, 1985.

Sem GJ (1976). *Methods and standards for environmental measurement, proceedings of the 8th Materials Research Symposium*. National Bureau of Standards, Gaithersburg, Maryland, September 20-24, 1976.

Shimp D, Blumrosen AW, Finifter SB. *How to Protect Your Health at Work: A Complete Guide for Making the Workplace Safe*." Environmental Improvement Associates, 1976.

TTID. 980066038-980066041. http://legacy.library.ucsf.edu/tid/dyf94f00/pdf.

TTID. 51271 6782. *Smoking in public: Let's separate fact from friction*, Bates #.

TTID. 621508026. Pride in Tobacco NEWSLINE, R.J. Reynolds Tobacco Company, Jan. 1984.

TTID. SK000600 09579307 10230264. *Second-Hand Smoke: The Myth and The Reality*.

TTID. TI 17720302. Internal tobacco institute memo, Susan Stuntz to Peter Sparber, March 11, 1987, Re: ASHA. http://legacy.library.ucsf.edu/tid/ord00g00. Bates #:.

Source Watch, 2014. Project Down Under – Group Presentation to Senior Management Friday, 870626 – SourceWatch; TTID. 2021502671.

USDOL, 2001. U.S. DEPARTMENT OF LABOR, Employees' Compensation Appeals Board. *In the Matter of LANNY VICKERS and VETERANS AFFAIRS, VETERANS ADMINISTRATION MEDICAL CENTER*, Seattle, WA, Docket No. 00-1159; Submitted on the Record; November 14, 2001.

Vickers v. Veterans Administration, 549 F. Supp. 85 (W.D. Wash. 1982), U.S. District Court for the Western District of Washington - 549 F. Supp. 85 (W.D. Wash. 1982) August 31, 1982.

Weiss, ST. Passive smoking and lung cancer, what is the risk? *American Review of Respiratory Disease* 133, #1, January 1986.

CHAPTER 5. PIONEERING INDOOR AIR POLLUTION AT THE EPA

Alli, W (2009). *Too Young for a Forgettable War*. Xlibris; Amazon Digital Services Ebook, 2009.

Garfinkel, L. (1981) Time trends in lung cancer mortality among nonsmokers and a note on passive smoking, *J. Natl. Cancer Inst.* 66, 1061-1066.

Hammond EC, Selikoff IJ. Passive smoking and lung cancer with comments on two new papers. *Environmental Research* 24: 4440452 (1981).

Hirayama, T. (1981). Non-smoking wives of heavy smokers have a higher risk of lung cancer: A study from Japan. *British Medical Journal*, 282.

Johnson K, Samet J, and Glantz S. A. Judson Wells, PhD (1917–2008): a pioneer in secondhand smoke research. *Tobacco Control* 17:1–2 (2008). doi:10.1136/tc.2008.025437.

Repace JL. The Effect of Ionizing Radiation on Mobile Ion Current Peaks in MOS Capacitors", IEEE TRANSACTIONS ON ELECTRON DEVICES ED-25: 492- (1978).

Repace JL and Goodman AM. The Effect of Process Variations on Interfacial and Radiation-Induced Charge in Silicon-on-Sapphire Capacitors. IEEE TRANSACTIONS ON ELECTRON DEVICES ED-25: 978- (1978).

Repace JL. Indoor Air Pollution. *Environment International* 8: 21-36 (1982).

Repace JL, Lowrey AH: A quantitative estimate of nonsmokers' lung cancer risk from passive smoking. *Environment International* 11: 3-22 (1985).

Repace JL, and Lowrey AH. A Rebuttal To Criticism of the Phenomenological Model of Nonsmokers' Lung Cancer Risk from Passive Smoking. *ENVIRONMENTAL CARCINOGENESIS REVIEWS (Journal of Environmental Science and Health)*, C(4) 225-235 (1986).

Spengler JD, Dockery DW, Turner WA, Wolfson JM, and Ferris BG. Long-term measurements of the respirable sulfates and particles inside and outside homes. *Atmospheric Environment* 1981: 15: 23–30.

Tobacco Institute, 1986. *Tobacco Smoke & the Nonsmoker Scientific Integrity at the Crossroads* [TTID. 2042356366].

Trichopoulos, D., Kalandidi, A., Sparros, L., and MacMahon, B. (1981). Lung cancer and passive smoking, *Int. J. Cancer* 27.

CHAPTER 6. INDOOR AIR POLLUTION, TOBACCO SMOKE, AND PUBLIC HEALTH

CIAR: Request for Applications 1989-1990 Research Agenda, Center For Indoor Air Research, 1099 Winterson Rd., Suite 280, Linthicum, MD 21090, May 1989.

Center for Indoor Air Research, personal communication.
Davis, 2002. Davis D. *When Smoke Ran Like Water – Tales of Environmental Deception and the Battle Against Pollution*. Basic Books, Perseus Books Group, New York, 2002.

EPA, 2018. *Health and Environmental Effects of Particulate Matter (PM)*
Health Effects. https://www.epa.gov/pm-pollution/health-and-environmental-effects-particulate-matter-pm. Accessed 8 Feb. 2018.

Garfield, 1990. The Most-Cited Papers of All Time, SCI 1945-1988. Current Comments. Essays of an Information Scientist: Journalology, KeyWords Plus, and Other Essays, Vol:13, p.45, 1990 Current Contents, #7, p.3-14, February 12, 1990. EUGENE GARFIELD INSTITUTE FORSCIENTIFIC INFORMATION, 3501 MARKET ST PHILADELPHIA PA 19104.

Google Scholar, accessed July 21, 2016.
https://scholar.google.com/citations?view_op=view_citation&hl=en&user=gy2WVfQAAAAJ&citation_for_view=gy-2WVfQAAAAJ:u5HHmVD_uO8C.

Medical World News, 1981. "On Passive Smoking: Cancer Society and Tobacco Institute in Rare Unity." July 6, 1981, p. 30.

New York Times, 1992. 'Tobacco' Its Middle Name, Law Firm Thrives, for Now
By David Margolick. November 20, 1992.

NRL LABSTRACTS, 30(2):8 -10 (1992), The top 100 NRL papers, 1973-1988.

Raeburn P. EPA smoking panel includes scientists linked to tobacco industry. *Associated Press*, Thurs. Nov 8, 1990.

Raeburn P. EPA abandons tobacco research in response to industry, critics charge. *Associated Press*, July 7, 1993.

Repace JL. Risks of Passive Smoking. Chapter 1, in *To Breathe Freely, Risk, Consent, and Air, Maryland Studies in Public Philosophy*, Edited by M. Gibson, Center for Philosophy and Public Policy, University of Maryland; Rowman and Allenheld, Totowa, N.J., 1985.

Repace JL. Tobacco Smoke Pollution. J.L. Repace, Chapter 7 in *Nicotine Addiction, Principles and Management,* T. Orleans and J. Slade, Ed.s, Oxford University Press, New York, 1993.

Repace JL, Lowrey AH. Issues and answers concerning passive smoking in the workplace: rebutting tobacco industry arguments. *Tobacco Control* 1:208-219 (1992).

RICO Trial Transcript vol. 21, 2004, [http://legacy.library.ucsf.edu/tid/hgg34e00/pdf; http://legacy.library.ucsf.edu/tid/ito08h00/pdf].

Stapf SE. A propaganda war against cigarettes. *The New York Times*. Business Section Sun Jan 4, 1987.

Spengler J. Personal communication.

Stolwijk J. personal communication.

TTID. 503947515. Tobacco Institute Press Release on Mantel, 1981.

TTID. 2504042040. Harris D. Memorandum, McGill University ETS Symposium, 1990.

U.S. Environmental Protection Agency Office of Research & Development Indoor Air Research Program FY 90, October 12, 1989.

Wikipedia, 2018. *The Washington Star.* Accessed Feb. 9, 2018. https://en.wikipedia.org/wiki/The_Washington_Star

Chapter 7. The Purge of the Ice Queen & The Rise of Joe Cannon

Bahura et al. v. SEW Investors, Inc., DC Superior Court, Civil Action No .1, 90 CA 10594, Judge Rufus King, III.

CCCP, 1985. Repace JL. Risks of Passive Smoking. Chapter 1, in *To Breathe Freely, Risk, Consent, and Air, Maryland Studies in Public Philosophy*, Edited by M. Gibson, Center for Philosophy and Public Policy, University of Maryland; Rowman and Allenheld, Totowa, N.J., 1985.

Crandall MS, Highsmith R, Gorman R, Wallace L. Library of Congress and US EPA indoor air quality and work environment study: environmental survey results. Proc. of the indoor air quality and work environment study: environmental survey results. *Proc. of the 5th International Conference on Indoor Air Quality and Climate, vol 4*, 597-602. Toronto, Canada, July 29-August 3, 1990.

JStor, 2017. https://www.jstor.org/stable/29500293?seq=1#page_scan_tab_contents.

Kessler, 2006. Final Amended Opinion, USA et al. Plaintiffs, v. Philip Morris USA, Inc. et al., Civil Action No. 99-2496 (GK), 2006.

McBride SJ, Ferro AR, Ott WR, Switzer P, Hildemann LM. Investigations of the proximity effect for pollutants in the indoor environment. *J Expo Anal Environ Epidemiol.* 1999 Nov-Dec;9(6):602-21.

Molotsky, Irvin. E.P.A. Study Links Deaths of Nonsmokers to Cigarette. Saturday, November 3rd, 1984, *The New York Times*.

Ozkaynak H1, Xue J, Spengler J, Wallace L, Pellizzari E, Jenkins P., Personal exposure to airborne particles and metals: results from the Particle TEAM study in Riverside, California. *Journal of Exposure Analysis and Environmental Epidemiology.* 6:57-78, 1996.

Repace JL, and Lowrey, AH. An indoor air quality standard for ambient tobacco smoke based on carcinogenic risk. *New York State Journal of Medicine*, 1985; 85:381-383.

Repace JL, and Lowrey AH. Risk Assessment Methodologies in passive smoking-induced lung cancer. RISK ANALYSIS, 10: 27-37, (1990).

Repace JL. Is the dose -response curve between tobacco smoke exposure and lung cancer really linear from active smoking to passive smoking?" (letter) Environment International 18: 427-429 (1992).

Repace JL, and Lowrey AH. An enforceable indoor air quality standard for environmental tobacco smoke in the workplace. *Risk Analysis*, 13:463-475 (1993).

Source Watch, 2016. Jacob Medinger & Finnegan. https://www.sourcewatch.org/index.php/Jacob,_Medinger_%26_Finnegan

Stanevich RS, Hern SC, Stetzenbach LD. Characterization of airborne microorganisms: two indoor case studies. *Proc. of the 5th International Conference on Indoor Air Quality and Climate*, vol 4, 677-682. Toronto, Canada, July 29-August 3, 1990.

Yin L, Yu K, Lin S, Song X, Yu X. Associations of blood mercury, inorganic mercury, methyl mercury and bisphenol A with dental surface restorations in the U.S. population, NHANES 2003-2004 and 2010-2012. *Ecotoxicol Environ Saf.* 2016 Dec;134P1:213-225.

CHAPTER 8. JUDGEMENT DAY FOR ETS

Arundel A, Irwin T, and Sterling T. NONSMOKER LUNG CANCER RISKS FROM TOBACCO SMOKE EXPOSURE: AN EVALUATION OF REPACE AND LOWREY'S PHENOMENOLOGICAL MODEL. *J. ENVIRON. SCI. HEALTH*, C 4 (l), 93-118 (1986).

Bero L, Glantz S. Tobacco industry response to a risk assessment of environmental tobacco smoke. *Tob Control*. 1993; 2:103–113.

Ecobichon DJ, Wu JM. Eds. *Environmental Tobacco Smoke, Proceedings of the International Symposium at McGill University 1989*. Lexington Books, D.C. Heath and Company, Lexington, MA and Toronto. 1990.

GAO, 1993. General Accounting Office Report "Plans in Limb o for Consolidated EPA, GAO/GGD 93-84. to the Chairman, Subcommittee on Oversight and Investigation, Committeee on Energy & Commerce, U.S. House of Representatives. Gori, GB. [http://en.wikipedia.org/wiki/Gio_Batta_Gori].

IARC Monographs On The Evaluation of the Carcinogenic Risk of Chemicals to Humans Tobacco Smoking Volume 38, IARC, Lyon, France, 1986.

Miesner EA, Rudnick SN, Hu FC, Spengler JD, Preller L, Ozkaynak H, Nelson W.
Particulate and nicotine sampling in public facilities and offices. *JAPCA,* 39:1577-82 (1989).

National Research Council 1986. *Environmental Tobacco Smoke: Measuring Exposures and Assessing Health Effects*. Committee on Passive Smoking, Board on Environmental Studies and Toxicology. National Academy Press, Washington, DC 1986.

Ozkaynak H1, Xue J, Spengler J, Wallace L, Pellizzari E, Jenkins P., Personal exposure to airborne particles and metals: results from the Particle TEAM study in Riverside, California. *Journal of Exposure Analysis and Environmental Epidemiology*. 6:57-78, 1996.

Repace JL. Invited Discussant: Healthy Buildings '88 Conference, Workshop W7, "Avoiding Health Problems in Low Energy Buildings; Workshop W8, "Benefits & Drawbacks of Natural & Mechanical Ventilation"; Workshop W14, "Consequences of Dramatic Changes in Outdoor Air Rates"; Stockholm, Sweden, Sept. 5-8, 1988.

Repace JL, and Lowrey AH. Risk Assessment Methodologies in passive smoking-induced lung cancer. *Risk Analysis* 10: 27-37, (1990).

Repace JL. Is the dose -response curve between tobacco smoke exposure and lung cancer really linear from active smoking to passive smoking?" (letter) ENVIRONMENT INTERNATIONAL 18: 427-429 (1992).

Repace JL. Flying the Smoky Skies: Secondhand Smoke Exposure of Flight Attendants. *Tobacco Control* 13(Suppl 1): i8-i19 (2004).

TI, 1989. News Release, *The Tobacco Institute, 1875 I Street, Northwest, Washington, DC 20006 (800)424-9876.* TOBACCO INSTITUTE COUNTERS EPA'S RELEASE OF UNSUPPORTABLE 'FACT SHEET' One-sided document scientifically deficient, contains inaccurate claims. FOR RELEASE: June 22,1989; CONTACT: Brennan Dawson, 202/457-4877 [TTID. TI1030-2729].

TTID. TI08530513. Rupp to Rosenberg Letter, 1989.

TTID. T108530511. Rosenberg to Rupp Letter, 1989.

Surgeon General, 1986. *THE HEALTH CONSEQUENCES OF INVOLUNTARY SMOKING, a report of the Surgeon General*, U.S. DEPARTMENT OF HEALTH AND HUMAN SERVICES, Centers for Disease Control, Office on Smoking and Health, Rockville, MD, 1986.

USA v. Philip Morris et al. Volume 21 Morning Session Transcript of Trial Record Before the Honorable Gladys Kessler United States District Judge, p. 4197. CA No. 99-2496 (GSK), Oct. 28, 2004.

Chapter 9. The Industry Strikes Back

ACS, 2003. *American Cancer Society Condemns Tobacco Industry Study for Inaccurate Use of Data. Study Part of Organized Effort to Confuse Public About Secondhand Smoke* American Cancer Society Press Release, May 15, 2003.

American Smoker's Journal. Vol I(1) 1992 Summer issue. United Smokers of America, Frankfort, KY.

Bliley, July 21, 1993. Statement of the Hon. Thomas J. Bliley, Jr. before the House Committee on Energy and Commerce Health and Environment Subcommittee, EPA AND ETS.

Ecobichon DJ, Wu JM. Eds. *Environmental Tobacco Smoke, Proceedings of the International Symposium at McGill University 1989.* Lexington Books, D.C. Heath and Company, Lexington, MA and Toronto. 1990.

Hansen J. *Storms of My Grandchildren,* Bloomsbury USA, 2009.

Houston Post, "Activists out to ban all smoking in public." Blum J. August 10, 1992, A1.

Jenkins RA, Palausky A, Counts RW, et al. Exposure to environmental tobacco smoke in sixteen cities in the United States as determined by personal breathing zone air sampling. *J Exposure Analysis & Environmental Epidemiology* 1996;6:473–502.

Lewtas J, et al. (1989). *Human Exposure and Dosimetry of Environmental Tobacco Smoke,"* [EPA/600/1-91/008, March 1989].

Needleman HL. Salem Comes to the National Institutes of Health: Notes from inside the crucible of scientific integrity. *Pediatrics* 90:977-981 (1992).

Repace JL, Lowrey AH. Editorial. Environmental tobacco smoke and indoor air quality in modern office work environments. *J Occup Med* 29: 628-629 (1987).

Repace JL, Lowrey AH. Issues and answers concerning passive smoking in the workplace: rebutting tobacco industry arguments. *Tobacco Control* 1:208-219 (1992).

Sterling TD, Collett CW, Sterling EM. Environmental tobacco smoke and indoor air quality in modern office work environments. *J Occup Med* 1987:29 :57-62.

TI, 1989. TOBACCO INSTITUTE COUNTERS EPA'S RELEASE OF UNSUPPORTABLE "FACT SHEET" One-sided document scientifically deficient, contains inaccurate claims. The Tobacco Institute, June 22, 1989 [TTID. TEMN 0125269].

TTID. TI2992-1778- 1780. TO: Regional Vice Presidents FROM: Diana Avedon. SUBJECT: CDC Study on Cotinine Levels in Nonsmokers.

The Virginian-Pilot and The Ledger-Star. Editorial, Secondhand smoke targeted by EPA. Sun Mar 31, 1991, Norfolk VA.

Chapter 10. The Waterside Mall Disaster

Banham R. Lawsuits Lend Visibility To Air Quality Issue. *Journal of Commerce*, Oct. 15, 1995. http://articles.chicagotribune.com/1995-10-15/business/9510150036_1_dupage-county-courthouse-sick-building-syndrome-healthy-buildings-international. Accessed July 20, 2017.

BOMA, 2017. Building Class Definitions. http://www.boma.org/research/pages/building-class-definitions.aspx. Accessed 2/05/2017.

Crandall MS, Highsmith R, Gorman R, Wallace L. Library of Congress and US EPA indoor air quality and work environment study: environmental survey results. *Proc. of the 5th International Conference on Indoor Air Quality and Climate*, vol 4, 597-602. Toronto, Canada, July 29-August 3, 1990.

Hirzy JW & Morison R (1991). Carpet/4-Phenylcyclohexene Toxicity: The EPA Headquarters Case. In *Advances in Risk Analysis,* Volume 9 1991. The Analysis, Communication, and Perception of Risk Editors: B. John Garrick, Willard C. Gekler
ISBN: 978-1-4899-2372-1 (Print) 978-1-4899-2370-7 (Online).

New York Times, 1992. Real Estate Section. Seeking Remedies For 'Sick Buildings', By David W. Dunlap, July 26, 1992

NIEHS, 2002. 4-Phenylcyclohexene [CASRN 4994-16-5], Review of Toxicological Literature National Institute of Environmental Health Sciences, Masten S, Haneke KE, July 2002.

Repace, 1996. INDOOR AIR POLLUTION AND MULTIPLE CHEMICAL SENSITIVITY. James Repace, Physicist, Center for Pollution and Source Guidance, Indoor Environments Division, Office of Radiation and Indoor Air United States Environmental Protection Agency, Washington, DC. (https://www.researchgate.net/publication/236211407_INDOOR_AIR_POLLUTION_AND_MULTIPLE_CHEMICAL_SENSITIVITY

TCM vs Chavez, 1977. TOWN CENTER MANAGEMENT CORPORATION, Appellant, v. Roy CHAVEZ, Appellee. No. 9805. District of Columbia Court of Appeals. Argued October 14, 1977. Decided May 3, 1977.

USEPA, 1997. *Leading by Example. Two Case Studies Documenting How The Environmental Protection Agency Incorporated Environmental Features into New Building.* EPA742-R-97-006 Pollution Prevention and Toxics December 1997.

Wallace L, Nelson CJ, Glen WG. Perception of indoor air quality among government employees in Washington, DC. *J Franklin Institute*: 1-16(1995).

Washington Post, 1992. Bias Suit nets $350,000, by Christine Spolar, May 28, 1992.

CHAPTER 11. THE BATTLE FOR SMOKE-FREE SKIES

Davis, 2002. Davis D. *When Smoke Ran Like Water – Tales of Environmental Deception and the Battle Against Pollution.* Basic Books, Perseus Books Group, New York, 2002.

EPA, 1990. *Environmental Tobacco Smoke: A Guide To Workplace Smoking Policies.* June 25, 1990; EPA/400/6-90/004.

EPA, 1990. *Current Federal Indoor Air Quality Activities.* US EPA, Air and Radiation, ANR-445, EPA 400/10-90/006.

Globe & Mail , Business Traveler: Jury still out on cabin smoke. Tues Sept 15, 1992.

Hirschhorn, N. Shameful science: four decades of the German tobacco industry's hidden research on smoking and health. *Tobacco Control* 2000; 9:242–247.

Hong M-K, Bero LA. How the tobacco industry responded to an influential study of the health effects of secondhand smoke. *BMJ* 325 14 DECEMBER 2002

Lee, PN. Environmental Tobacco Smoke and Health Effects of Passive Smoking, Notes on the symposium held in Oslo on 7th-10th October 1990; 23.10.90. [TTID. 40097331].

Repace JL, and Lowrey AH. Risk Assessment Methodologies in passive smoking-induced lung cancer. *RISK ANALYSIS* 10: 27-37, (1990).

Repace JL, and Lowrey AH. An Enforceable Indoor Air quality Standard for Environmental Tobacco Smoke in the Workplace. *RISK ANALYSIS* 13:463-475 (1993).

Repace JL. The dramatic changes in recommended outdoor air rates - what are the rational motives and consequences - workshop comments. *Proc. Healthy Buildings '88 Conference, Vol 4, Swedish Council for Building Research,* Stockholm, Sweden, pp. 132-133, June 1991.

Source Watch, 2017. Philip Morris Corporate Scientific Affairs. http://www.sourcewatch.org/index.php/Philip_Morris_Corporate_Scientific_Affairs Accessed Sept. 26, 2017.

[TTID. 2028361848] Note for Peters, Nancy, from Pages, Robert, re: FW Repace, Lowrey article.

Spengler JD, Dockery DW, Turner WA, Wolfson JM, Ferris BG, Jr. Long-term measurements of respirable sulfatea and particles inside and outside homes *Atmospheric Environment* 15(1):23-36,1981.

US Congress, 1989. To Ban Smoking on Airline Aircraft: Hearing Before the Subcommittee on Aviation of the Committee on Public Works and Transportation, House of Representatives, One Hundred First Congress, First Session, June 22, 1989.

Wolfe S, Douglas C, Wilbur P, Kirshenbaum M,McCarthy P, Basme A, and McKnew D. *ENVIRONMENTAL TOBACCO SMOKE: SCIENCE OR POLITICS?* July 21, 1993; *The Congressional Addiction to Tobacco: How the Tobacco Lobby Suffocates Federal Health Policy.* A Report by the Public Citizen Health Research Group and The Advocacy Institute. The Advocacy Institute, Washington, DC December 1992.

CHAPTER 12. EPA BRANDS ETS "GROUP A"

Associated Press, Money Awarded in Secondhand Smoke Death Case. *Washington Post*, December 16, 1995, p. A24.

Bliley, 1993. Statement of the Hon. Thomas J. Bliley, Jr. before the House Committee on Energy and Commerce Health and Environment Subcommittee, July 21, 1993. http://dengulenegl.dk/blog/wp-content/uploads/2009/11/the-bliley-statement-1993.pdf
Accessed July 20, 2016.

Boyse S, response by Repace JL and Lowrey AH, 1993. Passive smoking and the tobacco industry. *Tobacco Control* 1993; 2:56-57.

Flue-Cured Tobacco Cooperative Stabilization Corp., The Council for Burley Tobacco, Inc., Universal Leaf Tobacco Company, Inc., Philip Morris Inc., R.J. Reynolds Tobacco Co., and Gallins Vending Company vs. United States Environmental Protection Agency. Civil Action No. 6:93CV370, June 22, 1993, U.S. District Court, Greensboro, NC.

Glantz SA, Parmley WW. Passive smoking and heart disease, Epidemiology, physiology, and biochemistry. *Circulation*. 83:1-12 (1991).

Holcomb LC. Impact of environmental tobacco smoke on airline cabin air quality. *Env Tech Lttrs* 9:509-514 (1988).

Globe & Mail , Business Traveler: Jury still out on cabin smoke. Tues Sept 15, 1992.

Karr AR, Gutfeld R. OSHA inches toward limiting smoking. *Wall Street Journal,* Thurs Jan 11, 1992, B1.

Levin, 1997. Levin M. Tobacco Firms Battle Flight Attendant Suit. Law: Class-action case in Florida claims harm from secondhand smoke on airliners. Verdict could affect course of giant settlement plan. *Los Angeles Times*, Sunday, Sept. 28, 1997.
Mahood G, personal communication.

Muggli ME, Hurt RD, Becker LB. Turning free speech into corporate speech: Philip Morris' efforts to influence U.S. and European journalists regarding the U.S. EPA report on secondhand smoke. Prev Med. 2004; 39:568-80.

Public Interest Investigations, PowerBase http://powerbase.info/index.php/John_Luik, accessed 6/26i/2015].

Rabble.ca, Gutstein, D., Following the money: The Fraser Institute's tobacco papers
http://rabble.ca/news/2009/10/following-money-fraser-institute's-tobacco-papers.

Raeburn P. Secondhand smoke report could trigger avalanche of regulations. Associated Press Report., Jan 6, 1993.

Repace JL, and Lowrey AH. Issues and answers on passive smoking in the workplace: rebutting tobacco industry arguments. *TOBACCO CONTROL*, 1: 208-219 (1992).

Repace JL. Is the dose -response curve between tobacco smoke exposure and lung cancer really linear from active smoking to passive smoking?" (letter) *ENVIRONMENT INTERNATIONAL* 18: 427-429 (1992).

Source Watch (2016). Sharon Boyse. Center for Media and Democracy, Source Watch. http://www.sourcewatch.org/index.php/Sharon_Boyse

The New York Times. No right to cause death. Editorial, Sunday, Jan 10, 1993.

TTID. 325101390-93. Letter from The Fraser Institute ["Offering market solutions to public policy problems since 1974"] to Martin Broughton, Chairman of British American Tobacco, January 28, 2000.

TTID. 512682339 et seq. OSHA HEARING REPORT ALLEN R. PURVIS SHOOK, HARDY & BACON.

U.S. Dept. of Labor, Occupational Safety & Health Administration. 29 CFR Part 1910 (Docket # H-122) Occupational exposure to indoor air pollutants; request for information. Fed Reg 56 # 183, Fri Sept. 20, 1991 47892-47897.

U.S. Department of Labor Office of Information Press Release: Statement by Secretary of Labor Lynn Martin announcing commencement of rulemaking addressing hazards of occupational exposure to second hand smoke. Thurs Jan 14, 1993.

U.S. Environmental Protection Agency, Washington, DC. *Respiratory Health Effects of Passive Smoking: Lung Cancer and Other Disorders.* EPA/600/6-90/006 F (1993).

Wolfe S, Douglas C, Wilbur P, Kirshenbaum M,McCarthy P, Basme A, and McKnew D. ENVIRONMENTAL TOBACCO SMOKE: SCIENCE OR POLITICS? July 21, 1993; *The Congressional Addiction to Tobacco: How the Tobacco*

Lobby Suffocates Federal Health Policy. A Report by the Public Citizen Health Research Group and The Advocacy Institute. The Advocacy Institute, Washington, DC December 1992.

CHAPTER 13. BIG TOBACCO SANDBAGS OSHA

Associated Press. *Court reinstates flight attendant's suit against Northwest Airlines*, by Bob Egelko, Friday, April 07, 2000.

Baker F, Dye JT, Stuart R, Ainsworth MA, Crammer C, Thun M, Hoffmann D, Repace J, Henningfield J, Slade J, Pinney J, Shanks T, Burns B, Connally G, Shopland D. Cigar smoking health risks: state of the science. *JAMA* 284:735-740 (2000).

Barnes DE, Hanauer P, Slade J, et al. Environmental Tobacco Smoke - The Brown and Williamson Documents. *JAMA* 274:248-253 (1995).

Barnes RL, Hammond SK, Glantz SA. The Tobacco Industry's Role in the 16 Cities Study of Secondhand Tobacco Smoke: Do the Data Support the Stated Conclusions? Environmental Health Perspectives 114:1890–1897 (2006).

Coggins CRE. COMMENTS ON REPACE & LOWREY (1993) MODEL FOR ESTIMATING ETS LUNG CANCER RISKS. OSHA Docket H-122, August 1994, [TTID. 2046369181].

Dockery DW, Spengler JD. Personal exposure to respirable particulates and sulfates. *J. Air Pollution Control Assoc.* 31(2):153-15 (1981).

Fontham ET, Correa P, WuWilliams A, Reynolds P, Greenberg RS, Buffler PA, Chen VW, Boyd P, Alterman T, Austin DF, et al. Lung cancer in nonsmoking women: a multicenter case-control study *Cancer Epidemiol Biomarkers Prev.* 1991 Nov-Dec;1(1):35-43.

Glantz SA, Barnes DE, Bero L, Hanauer P, Slade J. Looking Through a Keyhole at the Tobacco Industry, The Brown and Williamson Documents. *JAMA* 274:219-224 (1995).

Glantz SA, Slade J, Bero L, Hanauer P, Barnes DE, Eds. *The Cigarette Papers.* University of California Press, 1998.

Helsing KJ, Sandler DP, Comstock GW, Chee E . Heart disease mortality in nonsmokers living with smokers. *Am J Epidemiol*, 127 (1988), pp. 915-922.

Kessler, David A. (2001). A Question of Intent: A Great American Battle with a Deadly Industry. Public Affairs. ISBN 1-58648-121-5.

Lebret, E., Boleij, J., and Brunekreef, B. (1990). Environmental tobacco smoke in Dutch homes. In Indoor Air '90: *Proceedings of the 5th International Conference on Indoor Air Quality and Climate vol. 2* (Walkinshaw D, ed.), pp. 263-268. Canada Mortgage and Housing Corp. Ottawa, Ontario.

Leaderer BP, Hammond SK. Evaluation of Vapor-Phase Nicotine and Respirable Suspended Particle Mass as Markers for Environmental Tobacco Smoke. *Environ. Sci. Technol.* 25: 770-775 (1991).

Maxwell, 1996. US Tobacco Companies' Shares of US Cigarette market. John Maxwell, *Tobacco Reporter*, March 1996, p.16.

Moghissi AA. Environmental Tobacco Smoke: Allegations of Scientific Misconduct. *Environment International* 22: 147-148 (1996).

New York Times, 1994. McDonald's Bans Smoking at All the Sites It Owns. February 24, 1994.

New York Times, 1995. U.S. Convenes Grand Jury to Look at Tobacco Industry. By Philip J. Hilts, July 26, 1995.

Persily A, (2002). THE REVISION OF STANDARD 62: WHAT A DIFFERENCE A DECADE MAKES. National Institute of Standards and Technology, Gaithersburg, MD, USA. Proceedings: Indoor Air 2002.

Philip Morris, 1994. OSHA Hearing Report, Background Report. TTID. 2501341198.

Phillips K, Bentley MC, Howard DA, Alvan G. Assessment of air quality in Stockholm by personal monitoring of nonsmokers for respirable suspended particles and environmental tobacco smoke. Scand J Work Environ Health 22:1-24 (1996).

Ravara SB, Calheiros JM, Agular P, Taborda Barata L. Smoking behaviour predicts tobacco control attitudes in a high smoking prevalence hospital: A cross-sectional study in a Portuguese teaching hospital prior to the national smoking ban. *BMC Public Health* 2011; http://www.biomedcentral.com/1471-2458/11/720].

Repace JL, and Lowrey AH. An enforceable indoor air quality standard for environmental tobacco smoke in the workplace. *Risk Analysis*, 13:463-475 (1993).

Repace JL, Lowrey AH. Environmental Tobacco Smoke: Allegations of Scientific Misconduct. *Environment International* 22: 268-270 (1996).

Repace JL. Exposure to Secondhand Smoke. Chapter 9, In: *Exposure Analysis,* W Ott, A Steinemann, and L Wallace, Eds. CRC Press (2007).

TTID. 2063890444. REGULATORY DECISION MAKING: Procedural Violations In the National Toxicology Program *Report on Carcinogen* Program. Multinational Business Services, Inc. 11 Dupont Circle, N.W. Suite 700 Washington,B.C. 20036. January 21, 1999. https://www.industrydocumentslibrary.ucsf.edu/pdf

TTID. 2505443955
TTID. PM3006639539
Wallace L. Indoor Particles: A Review. Air & Waste Manage. Assoc. 46: 98-126 (1996).

Washington Post, 1995. Smokers Get A Break in MD. C. Babington, 8 March 1995.

Chapter 14. Sparring With The Congressional Research Service

Beatty Al., Haight TJ, Redberg, RF. Associations between respiratory illnesses and secondhand smoke exposure in flight attendants: a cross-sectional analysis of the Flight Attendant Medical Research Institute Survey. *Environmental Health* 2011, **10**:81 doi:10.1186/1476-069X-10-81.

Drope J, Bialous SA, Glantz SA. Tobacco industry efforts to present ventilation as an alternative to smoke-free environments in North America. *Tobacco Control* 2004; 13(Suppl I): i41–i47.

Lowrey AH, Wallace LA, Kantor S, and Repace JL. Concentrations of combustion particulates in outdoor and indoor environments. Chapter 10 in *Combustion Efficiency and Air Quality,* T. Vidóczy and I. Hargittai, Eds. Plenum Publishers. N.Y. pp 175-211 (1995).

Physicians, 2000. Multinational Tobacco Companies and Legislation to Protect Workers and the Public From Second Hand Smoke. Submission to the Workers' Compensation Board of British Columbia, June 2000. PHYSICIANS FOR A SMOKE-FREE CANADA - MEDECINS POUR UN CANADA SANS FUMEE. www.smoke-free.ca.

Repace JL. Risk management of passive smoking at home and at work. *St. Louis University Public Law Review*, XIII (2) 763-785 (1994).

Repace JL, and Lowrey AH. A rebuttal to tobacco industry criticism of an enforceable indoor air quality standard for environmental tobacco smoke. *Risk Analysis* 15: 7-13 (1995).

Repace JL. Tobacco, history, and the AMA. (Letter) *The Lancet*, 19 August 1995.

Shopland DR, Hartman AM, Repace JL, and Lynn WR. Smoking behavior, workplace policies, and public opinion regarding smoking restrictions in Maryland. *Maryland Medical Journal* 44: 977-982 (1995).

TTID. 2080409207. Turpin JP. Where there's smoke, there's Ire. *Engineered Systems* January 2000, 92-98.

TTID. 2067453623. Pataskan GJ, Philip Morris USA Memorandum 5. U.S. expert claims 150 Irish bar workers per year will die from ETS, the Irish press reports, From: Satterfield MP, To: Andriot M, et al. Subject: FW: Important Message. Importance: High.

TTID. 526303357. TMA News: 14-Feb-2002 WORLD [7] Refusing to Butt Out, Minister Vows To Stub Out Smoking. Author: Sean McCarthaigh, BBS Ireland.

TTID. 2021180527. Fax from The Newman Partnership, to 1-212-298-9866596 (Steve Parrish/Office Philip Morris, Apr. 18, 1990. Repace JL, Lowrey AH. Risk Assessment Methodologies fro Passive Smoking-Induced Lung Cancer *Risk Analysis* 10: 1990.

TTID. 2048785823. Grren J, Lister C. Overview of Principal Europe-wide Threats to Public Smoking Involving Air Ouality Standards. Privileged and Confidential Attorney Work Product. July 26, 1995. Philip Morris Records.

BMJ 2003;327:503. Letters >> Passive smoking. Agreeing the limits of conflicts of interest. Richard Horton.

Redhead CS, Rowberg RE. *CRS Report for Congress, Environmental Tobacco Smoke and Lung Cancer Risk.* Congressional Research Service, The Library of Congress, 95-1115, Nov. 14, 1995.

CHAPTER 15. HAVE SLIDES, WILL TRAVEL

CALIFORNIA ENVIRONMENTAL PROTECTION AGENCY. (1997). *Health Effects of Exposure to Environmental Tobacco Smoke, Final Report.* Office of Environmental Health Hazard Assessment.

Doll R, Peto R, Wheatley K, Gray R, Sutherland I. Mortality in relation to smoking: 40 years' observations on male British doctors. *BMJ.* 1994;309:901-11.

Doll R, Peto R. Boreham J, Sutherland I. Mortality in relation to smoking: 50 years' observations on male British doctors *BMJ* 2004; 328 *BMJ* 2004;328:1519.

Eubanks SB, & Glantz SA, 2013. *Bad Acts: The Racketeering Case Against the Tobacco Industry.* (American Public Health Association) eBook ISBN: 978-0-87553-267-7; Print ISBN: 978-0-87553-017-8.

Gorini G, Antonio Gasparrini, Francesc Centrich, Maria Josè Lopez, Maria Cristina Fondelli, Elizabeth Tamang, Adele Seniori Costantini, and Manel Nebot. Environmental Tobacco Smoke (ETS) Exposure in Florence Hospitality Venues before and after the smoking ban in Italy. JOEM 47:1208–1210 (2005).

Hedley AJ, McGhee SM, Repace JL, Wong TW, Yu MYS, Chan AYW, Lam TH, Lo PCK, Tsang M, Wong LC, Chan ALN, Ng ESL, and Janghorbani M. Passive smoking and risks for heart disease and cancer in Hong Kong catering workers 2001. Report # 8, Hong Kong Council on Smoking and Health. < http://www.info.gov.hk/hkcosh/enew-index.htm>.

Hirschhorn, N. Shameful science: four decades of the German tobacco industry's hidden research on smoking and health *Tobacco Control* 2000;**9**:242–247.

Jaakkola MS, Samet JM. Occupational exposure to environmental tobacco smoke and health risk assessment. *Environmental Health Perspectives* 107, Suppl. 2: 829-835 (1999)
Jarvis MJ, Feyerabend C, Bryant A, Hedges, B and Primatesta P. Passive smoking in the home: plasma cotinine concentrations in non-smokers with smoking partners. *Tobacco Control* 2001 10: 368-374 doi: 10.1136/tc.10.4.368.

Kawachi I, et al. "Deaths from lung cancer and ischemic heart disease due to passive smoking in New Zealand." *The New Zealand Medical Journal* 102: 337-340 (1989).

Klepeis NE, Ott WR, and Repace JL. The effect of cigar smoking on indoor levels of carbon monoxide and particles. *Journal of Exposure Analysis and Environmental Epidemiology* 9:1-14 (1999).

Kuller LH, Garfinkel L, Correa P, Haley N, Hoffmann D, Preston-Martin S, and Sandler D. Contribution of passive smoking to respiratory cancer. *Environmental Health Perspectives* 70:57-69 (1986).

Landman A, Glantz SA. Tobacco Industry Efforts to Undermine Policy-Relevant Research. *AJPH* 99: 45-58 (1999).

Mattson ME, Boyd G, Byar C, et al. Passive smoking on commercial air flights.
JAMA 1989;261:867–72.

Mannino DM, Moorman JE, Kingsley B, Rose D, and Repace J. Health effects related to environmental tobacco smoke exposure in children in the United States. Data from the Third National Health & Nutrition Examination Survey. *Archives of Pediatric & Adolescent Medicine* 155:36-41 (2001).

Mannino DM, Caraballo R, Benowitz N, and Repace J. Predictors of cotinine levels in US children - data from the third national health and nutrition examination survey. *Chest* 120:718-724 (2001).

Muggli ME, Forster JL, Hurt RD, and Repace JL. The smoke you don't see: uncovering tobacco industry scientific strategies aimed against environmental tobacco smoke policies. *American Journal of Public Health* 91: 1419-1423 (2001).

National Research Council (1986). *Environmental tobacco smoke – measuring exposures and assessing health effects.* National Academy Press, Washington, DC.

National Toxicology Program. *9th Report on Carcinogens 2000*. U.S. Dept. of Health & Human Services, National Institute of Environmental Health Sciences, Research Triangle Park, NC.

NIOSH Current Intelligence Bulletin #54. *Environmental Tobacco Smoke in the Workplace, Lung Cancer and Other Health Effects*. U.S. Department of Health and Human Services, National Institute for Occupational Safety and Health, Cincinnati, OH June 1991.

NIOSH Pocket Guide to Chemical Hazards, U.S. Dept. Health & Human Services, Centers for Disease Control & Prevention, June 1994..

NRL's 100 Most-Cited Papers 1973-1988. NRL LABSTRACTS 30(2):8 -10 (1992).

Nagda et al. *Airliner Cabin Environment: Contaminant Measurements, Health Risks, and Mitigation Options*. U.S. Dept. of Transportation Report DOT-P-15-89-5, USDOT, Washington, DC, (1989).

Nagda NL, Koontz MD, Konheim AG, Hammond SK. Measurement of cabin air quality aboard commercial airliners. *Atmospheric Environment, Part A, General Topics* 26:2203-2210 (1992).

Ott WR. Mathematical models for predicting indoor air quality from smoking activity. *Env Health Persp* 107, suppl 2, 375-381 (1999).

Ott WR., Langan L, Switzer P. (1992). A time series model for cigarette smoking activity patterns: model validation for carbon monoxide and respirable particles in a chamber and an automobile. *J Exp Anal & Environ Epidemiol* suppl 2: 175-200.

Ott W, Switzer P, & Robinson J. (1996) Particle Concentrations Inside a Tavern Before and After Prohibition of Smoking: Evaluating the Performance of an Indoor Air Quality Model, Journal of the Air & Waste Management Association, 46:12, 1120-1134, DOI: 10.1080/10473289.1996.10467548.

Repace JL, Klepeis NE, Ott WR. National Cancer Institute. Chapter 5, Indoor Air Pollution from Cigar Smoke, in: *Smoking and Tobacco Control Monograph 9. Cigars - Health Effects and Trends*. National Institutes of Health, National Cancer Institute, Bethesda, MD (1998).

Repace J, Kawachi I, Glantz S. *Fact Sheet on Secondhand Smoke*, compiled for the International Union Against Cancer (UICC), Geneva, Switzerland, and presented at the 2nd European Conference on Tobacco or Health and the 1st Iberoamerican Conference on Tobacco or Health Canary Islands, Spain, 23-27 February 1999. https://www.researchgate.net/publication/253991606_Fact_sheet_on_secondhand_smoke.

Repace JL, and Lowrey AH. A Quantitative Estimate of Nonsmokers' Lung Cancer Risk from Passive Smoking. *Environment International* 11: 3-22 (1985).

Repace JL, and Lowrey AH. An enforceable indoor air quality standard for environmental tobacco smoke in the workplace." *Risk Analysis*, 13:463-475 (1993).

Repace JL, and Lowrey AH. An Indoor Air Quality Standard For Ambient Tobacco Smoke based on Carcinogenic risk. *N.Y. State Journal of Medicine* 85:381-383 (1985b).

Repace JL, and Lowrey AH. Indoor Air Pollution, Tobacco Smoke, and Public Health. *Science* 208: 464-474 (1980).

Repace JL, and Lowrey AH. Tobacco Smoke, Ventilation, and Indoor Air Quality. *ASHRAE TRANSACTIONS* 88: Part I, 895-904 (1982).

Repace JL, Consistency of Research Data on Passive Smoking and Lung Cancer *The Lancet* (ii): 3 March 1984, p. 506.

Repace JL, Jinot J, Bayard S, Emmons K, and Hammond SK. Air nicotine and saliva cotinine as indicators of passive smoking exposure and risk. *Risk Analysis* 18: 71-83 (1998)

Repace JL, Lowrey AH. Indoor Air Pollution, Tobacco Smoke, and Public Health, *Science* 208: 464-474 (1980).

Repace JL, Lowrey AH. Is the dose -response curve between tobacco smoke exposure and lung cancer really linear from active smoking to passive smoking? *Environment International* 18: 427-429 (1992).

Repace JL, Lowrey AH. Risk Assessment Methodologies in passive smoking-induced lung cancer. *Risk Analysis*, 10: 27-37, (1990).

Repace JL. Effects of passive smoking on coronary circulation. (letter) *JAMA*. 2002; 287 #3, January 16.

Repace JL. Indoor concentrations of environmental tobacco smoke: models dealing with effects of ventilation and room size", *Ch. 3, IARC Scientific Publications no.81, Environmental Carcinogens–Selected Methods of Analysis–Volume 9 Passive Smoking;* I.K. O'Neill, K.D. Brunnemann, B. Dodet & D. Hoffmann, International Agency for Research on Cancer, World, Health Organization, United Nations Environment Programme, Lyon, France, (1987).

Repace JL. Indoor concentrations of environmental tobacco smoke: models dealing with effects of ventilation and room size. Ch. 3, in *IARC Scientific Publications no.81, Environmental Carcinogens–Selected Methods of Analysis–Volume 9 Passive Smoking; O'Neill I, Brunnemann K, Dodet B, and Hoffmann D.* International Agency for Research on Cancer, World, Health Organization, United Nations Environment Programme, Lyon, France; 1987.

Repace JL. Indoor concentrations of environmental tobacco smoke: field surveys. Ch. 10, *IARC Scientific Publications no. 81, Environmental Carcinogens–Selected Methods of Analysis–Volume 9 Passive Smoking;* I.K. O'Neill, K.D. Brunnemann, B. Dodet & D. Hoffman, International Agency for Research on Cancer, World, Health Organization, United Nations Environment Programme, Lyon, France, (1987).

Repace JL. Ott WR, Klepeis NE. Indoor Air Pollution from Cigar Smoke. JL . In *Smoking and Tobacco Control Monograph 9. Cigars - Health Effects and Trends.* National Institutes of Health, National Cancer Institute, Bethesda, MD (1998).

Repace, JL, and Lowrey, AH (1985a). A quantitative estimate of nonsmokers' lung cancer risk from passive smoking. *Environment International* 11: 3-22.

Repace, JL, and Lowrey, AH. Tobacco Smoke, Ventilation, and Indoor Air Quality. *ASHRAE TRANSACTIONS* 88: Part I,895 (1982).

Samet JM, Wang SS. Environmental tobacco smoke. Ch. 10, in: *Environmental Toxicants, Human Exposures and their Health Effects.* M. Lippmann, Ed. John Wiley & Sons, New York, 2000.

Samet JM. Environmental Health Perspectives 107, Suppl. 2: 309 -312 (1999).

Siegel M, Skeer M. Exposure to secondhand smoke and excess lung cancer mortality risk among workers in the "5 B's": bars, bowling alleys, billiard halls, betting establishments, and bingo parlours. *Tobacco Control* 2003;12:333–338.

SCOTH 1998. *Report of the Scientific Committee on Tobacco and Health*, UK Department of Health The Stationery Office, 1998.

Spengler JD. Buildings operations and ETS exposure. *Environmental Health Perspectives* 107, Suppl. 2: 313-317 (1999).

Surgeon General. *The Health Consequences of Involuntary Smoking, A Report of the Surgeon General.* U.S. Dept. of Health and Human Services, Washington, DC (1986).

Surgeon General. *The Health Consequences of Involuntary Exposure to Tobacco Smoke, A Report of the Surgeon General.* U.S. Dept. of Health and Human Services, Washington, DC (2006).

Tancrede M, Wilson R, Zeise L, and Crouch EAC. The carcinogenic risk of some organic vapors indoors: a theoretical survey. *Atmospheric Environment* 21: 2187-2205 (1987).

Travers MJ, KM Cummings, A Hyland, J Repace, S Babb, T Pechacek, PhD, R Caraballo. Indoor Air Quality in Hospitality Venues Before and After Implementation of a Clean Indoor Air Law — Western New York, 2003. *MMWR* 53:1038-104 (2004).

TTID. T12567-0436; TTID. TI 22567-0429. *Connecticut Smoker Public Policy Issues Vol II*, published by the greater Bridgeport Area Smokers' Rights Association.

TTID. 2046557219. ASA GOES TO WASHINGTON! *ASA News* Spring 1995, An American Smokers' Alliance Publication, Vol VI Number 1.

TTID. TI 22567-0428. Letter from CT State Senator GL Gunther to Donald D'Errico, Regional Vice President, The Tobacco Institute, 25 march 1993.

U.S. Department of Health and Human Services. A report of the Surgeon General. *Reducing the health consequences of smoking.* Public Health Service, Washington, DC, 1989.

U.S. Dept. of Labor, Occupational Safety & Health Administration. 29 CFR Parts 1910, 1915, 1926, and 1928 Indoor air quality, proposed rule *Fed Reg* 59 # 65, Tues April 5, 1994, 15968-16039.

U.S. Environmental Protection Agency, Office of Health and Environmental Assessment, Office of Research and Development. *Respiratory Health Effects of Passive Smoking: Lung Cancer and Other Disorders.* Report No. EP-A/600/6-90/006F. Washington, DC, 1992.

Weiss ST. Passive smoking, what is the risk? *American Review of Respiratory Disease* 133:1-3, 1986.

Wigle DT, Collishaw NE, Kirkbride J, Mao Y. Deaths in Canada from lung cancer due to involuntary smoking. *CMAJ.* May 1;136(9):945-51(1987).

Zitting A, Husgafvel-Pursiainen K, Rantanen J. Environmental tobacco smoke — a major preventable cause of impaired health at work. *Scandinavian Journal of Work, Environment, & Health* (Vol. 28, supplement 2, 2002).

CHAPTER 16. 'TWAS LIKE A NOBEL FOR SMOKE

Jarvis M. Quantitative survey of exposure to other peoples' smoke in London for staff. London: Department of Epidemiology and Public Health, University College London, 2001.

Jenkins RA, Finn D, Tomkins BA, Maskarinec MP. Environmental tobacco smoke in the nonsmoking section of a restaurant: a case study. *Regulatory Toxicology and Pharmacology* 34: 213-20 (2001).

Kolb S, Bruckner U, Nowak D, Radon K. Quantification of ETS exposure in hospitality workers who have never smoked. *Environmental Health* 2010, 9:49.

Leavell NR, Muggli ME, Hurt RD, and Repace JL. Blowing Smoke – British American Tobacco's Air Filtration Scheme and the UK *Public Places Charter on Smoking.* BMJ 332;227-229 (2006).

Mulcahy M, Evans DS, Hammond SK, Repace JL, and Byrne M. Secondhand smoke exposure and risk following the Irish smoking ban: an assessment of salivary cotinine concentrations in hotel workers and air nicotine levels in bars. *Tobacco Control* 14: 384-388 (2005).

Nord E; Repace JL. Agreeing the limits of conflicts of interest. *BMJ* 2003; 327:503 (Published 28 August 2003).

Ott W, Switzer P, Robinson J. Particle concentrations inside a tavern before and after prohibition of smoking: evaluating the performance of an indoor air quality model. *Journal of the Air Waste Management Association.* 1996;46:1120-1134.

Repace JL. Respirable Particles and Carcinogens in the Air of Delaware Hospitality Venues Before and After a Smoking Ban. *Journal of Occupational and Environmental Medicine*, 46:887-905 (2004).

Repace JL. Exposure to Secondhand Smoke. Chapter 9, In: *Exposure Analysis,* W Ott, A Steinemann, and L Wallace, Eds. CRC Press (2007).

Repace JL, Hyde JN, Brugge D. Air pollution in Boston bars before and after a smoking ban. *BMC Public Health.* 2006:6, 266.

Repace, 2015. TESTIMONY OF JAMES L. REPACE BEFORE THE QUEBEC NATIONAL ASSEMBLY, ON BILL 44, AN ACT TO BOLSTER TOBACCO CONTROL. https://www.researchgate.net/publication/281495524_TESTIMONY_OF_JAMES_L._REPACE_BEFORE_THE_QUEBEC_NATIONAL_ASSEMBLY_ON_BILL_44_AN_ACT_TO_BOLSTER_TOBACCO_CONTROL

Repace and Johnson, 2006. Can Displacement Ventilation Control Secondhand ETS? *ASHRAE IAQ Applications* 7(4): 1-6.

Repace JL. 2003. *A Killer on the Loose. An Action on Smoking and Health Special Investigation into the threat of passive smoking in the U.K. workforce.* http://ash.org.uk/search/?q=Killer+on+the+loose; www.repace.com.

Repace JL, 1987. Indoor concentrations of environmental tobacco smoke: models dealing with effects of ventilation and room size", *Ch. 3, IARC Scientific Publications no.81, Environmental Carcinogens–Selected Methods of Analysis–Volume 9 Passive Smoking;* I.K. O'Neill, K.D. Brunnemann, B. Dodet & D. Hoffmann, International Agency for Research on Cancer, World, Health Organization, United Nations Environment Programme, Lyon, France, (1987).

Repace JL, Jinot J, Bayard S, Emmons K, and Hammond SK. Air nicotine and saliva cotinine as indicators of passive smoking exposure and risk. Risk Analysis 18: 71-83 (1998).

CHAPTER 17. THE INDUSTRY FALLS UNDER THE HAMMER

Hyland A, Travers MJ, Dresler C, Higbee C, Cummings KM. A 32-country comparison of tobacco smoke derived particle levels in indoor public places. *Tobacco Control* 17: 159–65 (2008).

Kessler, 2006. UNITED STATES DISTRICT COURT FOR THE DISTRICT OF COLUMBIA UNITED STATES OF AMERICA, :: Plaintiff, :: Civil Action No. 99-2496 (GK) v. :: PHILIP MORRIS USA, INC., : (f/k/a Philip Morris, Inc.), *et al.*, :: Defendants. : AMENDED FINAL OPINION.

New York Times, 2007. "A New Arena in the Fight Over Smoking: The Home." **http://www.nytimes.com/2007/11/05/us/05smoke.html?_r=0.**

Pope CA 3rd, Burnett RT, Turner MC, Cohen A, Krewski D, Jerrett M, Gapstur SM, Thun MJ. Lung Cancer and Cardiovascular Disease Mortality Associated with Ambient Air Pollution and Cigarette Smoke: Shape of the Exposure–Response Relationships *Environ Health Perspectives* 119:1616–1621 (2011).

Repace JL, and Lowrey AH. Is the dose-response curve between tobacco smoke exposure and lung cancer linear from active to passive smoking? *Environment International,* Vol. 18, pp. 427-429 (1992).

Repace JL. Flying the Smoky Skies: Secondhand Smoke Exposure of Flight Attendants. *Tobacco Control* 13(Suppl 1): i8-i19 (2004).

Repace JL. Indoor and outdoor carcinogen pollution on a cruise ship. *14th Annual Conference of the International Society of Exposure Analysis*, Philadelphia, PA. 17-21 October 2004.

TTID. 2023988627. "Donald Shopland Public Health Advisor, National Cancer Institute Shopland is the former Director of the Office of Smoking. He remarked in 1986 that "of all the issues, this [ETS] is the one that will propel the United States toward a smoke-free society." Author unknown.

CHAPTER 18. NOBODY FOOLS WITH RICO

ASHRAE, 2008. *Position Document on Environmental Tobacco Smoke* http://www.no-smoke.org/pdf/ASHRAE_PositionStatementonETS.pdf

Lee K, Hahn EJ, Pieper N, Okoli CTC, Repace J, and Troutman A. Differential Impacts of Smoke-Free Laws on Indoor Air Quality, *Journal of Environmental Health* (70: 24-30 (2008).

Leavell NR, Muggli ME, Hurt RD, and Repace JL. Blowing Smoke – British American Tobacco's Air Filtration Scheme and the UK *Public Places Charter on Smoking*. BMJ 332;227-229 (2006).

Hedley AJ, McGhee SM, Repace JL, Wong L-C, Yu YSM, Wong T-W, Lam T-H.

Risks for heart disease and lung cancer from passive smoking by workers in the catering industry. *Toxicological Sciences* 90: 539–548 (2006).

Hyde J, Brugge D, Repace J, Hamlett J, Rand W, and Haley N. Worker Exposure to Environmental Tobacco Smoke in Smoking-Restricted Restaurants and Bars. Ch. 14, In: *Passive Smoking and Health Research*. ISBN: 1-60021-382-0, Editor: N.A. Jeorgensen, pp. - © 2006 Nova Science Publishers, Inc.

Repace J, Hughes E, and Benowitz N. Exposure to Secondhand Smoke Air Pollution Assessed from Bar Patrons' Urine Cotinine. *Nicotine and Tobacco Research* 8:701-711 (2006).

Repace JL, Hyde JN, Brugge D. Air Pollution in Boston Bars Before and After a Smoking Ban. Open Acess, on-line journal: <http://www.biomedcentral.com/1471-2458/6/266>, *BMC Public Health* 2006, 6:266 (27 Oct 2006).

Repace JL, Al-Delaimy WK, Bernert JT. Correlating Atmospheric and Biological Markers in Studies of Secondhand Tobacco Smoke Exposure and Dose in Children and Adults. *JOEM* 48: 181-194 (2006).

Repace JL, Al-Delaimy WK, Bernert JT. Correlating Atmospheric and Biological Markers in Studies of Secondhand Tobacco Smoke Exposure and Dose in Children and Adults. JOEM 48: 181-194 (2006). Repace JL. and Johnson KC. Can Displacement Ventilation Control Secondhand ETS? Technical Feature, *ASHRAE IAQ Applications* 7:1-6 (Fall, 2006).

Repace JL. *Air Pollution in Virginia's Hospitality Industry.* A report prepared for Virginians for a Healthy Future 1001 E. Broad Street, Suite 225 Richmond, VA 23219.

Repace JL. *Air Pollution in Virginia's Hospitality Industry.* A slide presentation given to the Virginia State Board of Health, Richmond, VA. 3 February 2006.

CHAPTER 19. YOU BET YOUR LIFE

Daisey JM. Tracers for assessing exposure to environmental tobacco smoke: what are they tracing? *Environmental Health Perspectives Supplements.* Environmental Tobacco Smoke Exposure 107:Suppl. 2, May 1999; 319-328.

James HR, Barfield L, Britt JK, and James RC (2008) Occupational Hazards - Worker Exposure to Secondhand Smoke Evaluating a Prediction Model. *PROFESSIONAL SAFETY* SEPTEMBER 2008. 34-44 www.asse.org.

Lee PN, Fry JS, Forey BA. A review of the evidence on smoking bans and incidence of heart disease. *Regulatory Toxicology and Pharmacology*, 70 (2014) 7–23

Lee, P.N., Fry, J.S.. Reassessing the evidence relating smoking bans to heart disease. *Regulatory Toxicology and Pharmacology.* 61, 318–331 (2011).

National Academy of Sciences Institute of Medicine, *Secondhand Smoke Exposure and Cardiovascular Effects: Making Sense of the Evidence.* http://www.iom.edu/~/media/Files/Report%20Files/2009/Secondhand-Smoke-Exposure-and-Cardiovascular-Effects-Making-Sense-of-the-Evidence/Secondhand%20Smoke%20%20Report%20Brief%203.pdf.

Repace JL, Repace Associates, Inc., *Expert Report on the Empress Horseshow Casino, In The Matter of Januszewski et al., v. Horseshoe Hammond, USDC, NDIN, Hammond Div., 2:00CV352JM,* March 14, 2006.

Repace JL. APPLICATION OF THE ROSETTA STONE EQUATIONS TO CASINO WORKERS' SECONDHAND SMOKE EXPOSURE: AN ANALYSIS OF A NIOSH HEALTH HAZARD EVALUATION. ResearchGate.org, https://www.researchgate.net/publication/275714751_APPLICATION_OF_THE_ROSETTA_STONE_EQUATIONS_TO_CASINO_WORKERS%27_SECONDHAND_SMOKE_EXPOSURE_AN_ANALYSIS_OF_A_NIOSH_HEALTH_HAZARD_EVALUATION.

CHAPTER 20. YOU CAN'T FIGHT CITY HALL

Lee, K., Hahn, E.J., Okoli, C.T.C., Repace, J., Troutman, A. Differential impact of smoke-free laws on indoor air quality. *Journal of Environmental He*alth 70:24-70 (2008).

Raab, S. Longtime Numbers King of New York Goes Public to Clear His Name., *New York Times*, July 6, 1997.

Raab, S. Faxes Produce Numbers Arrest in Harlem Ring. *New York Times*, July 6, 1997.

RAYMOND MARQUEZ, Respondent, v. CITY OF NEW YORK et al., Appellants.

Appellate Division of the Supreme Court of the State of New York, First Department.

48 A.D.3d 241 (2008); 850 N.Y.S.2d 449. Decided February 7, 2008.

Repace JL. Benefits of smoke-free regulations in outdoor settings: beaches, golf courses, parks, patios, and in motor vehicles. *William Mitchell Law Review* 34(4):1621-1638 (2008).

CHAPTER 21. BEATING THE HOUSE AT ITS OWN GAME

Associated Press, March 29, 2008, by Susan Heigh, carried in *Indian Country News*.

Collishaw NE (Chair), Boyd NF, Cantor KP, Hammond SK, Johnson KC, Millar J, Miller AB, Miller M, Palmer JR, Salmon AG, Turcotte F. *Canadian Expert Panel on Tobacco Smoke and Breast Cancer Risk.* Toronto, Canada: Ontario Tobacco Research Unit, OTRU Special Report Series, April 2009.

Glantz SA, Gibbs E. Changes in ambulance calls after implementation of a smoke-free law and its extension to casinos. *Circulation.* 2013 Aug 20;128(8):811-3.

The Glouster County Times (2010). AC casino worker gets $4.5M settlement in cancer suit. December 3, 2010. http://www.nj.com/atlantic/index.ssf/2010/12/ac_casino_worker_gets_45m_settlement_in_cancer_suit.html.   Accessed 7/10/2016.

Jiang RT, Cheng K-C, Acevedo-Bolton V, Klepeis NE, Repace JL, Ott WR, and Hildemann LM. Measurement of Fine Particles and Smoking Activity in a Statewide Survey of 36 California Indian Casinos. *Journal of Exposure Science & Environmental Epidemiology*: 21, 31-41 (2010).

Nytimes.com. Casino Dismisses Worker Seeking Smoking Ban. N.Y./Region. New York Times, March 6, 2007. Accessed, July 10, 2016. http://www.nytimes.com/2007/03/06/nyregion/06smoke.html?_r=0.

Pope, C.A. III (2007) Mortality effects of longer term exposures to fine particulate air pollution: review of recent epidemiological evidence, *Inhalation Toxicology*, 19 (Suppl. 1), 33–38.

Pope CA 3rd1, Burnett RT, Krewski D, Jerrett M, Shi Y, Calle EE, Thun MJ. Cardiovascular mortality and exposure to airborne fine particulate matter and cigarette smoke: shape of the exposure-response relationship. *Circulation* (2009) Sep 15;120(11):941-948. doi: 10.1161/CIRCULATIONAHA.109.857888. Epub 2009 Aug 31.

Repace, J., Hughes, E. and Benowitz, N. (2006) Exposure to secondhand smoke air pollution assessed from bar patrons' urine cotinine, *Nicotine and Tobacco Research,* 8: 701–711.

Repace JL. Secondhand Smoke in Pennsylvania Casinos: A Study of Nonsmokers' Exposure, Dose, and Risk. *American Journal of Public Health* 99: 1478–1485 (2009).

Repace J, Zhang B, Bondy SJ, Benowitz N, Ferrence F. Air Quality, Mortality, and Economic Benefits of a Smoke-Free Workplace Law for Non-Smoking Ontario Bar Workers. *Indoor Air* 2013; 23: 93–104.

Shamo F, Wilson T, Kiley J, Repace J. Assessing the effect of Michigan's smoke-free law on air quality inside restaurants and casinos: a before-and-after observational study. *BMJ Open*, 2015, 5: e007530. doi:10.1136/bmjopen-2014-007530.

CHAPTER 22. BREATHING YOUR NEIGHBOR'S SMOKE

Bohac David L., Martha J. Hewett, S Katherine Hammond, David T. Grimsrud, (2004). Reduction of Environmental Tobacco Smoke Transfer in Minnesota Multifamily Buildings Using Air Sealing and Ventilation Treatments. Center for Energy and Environment 212 3rd Avenue North, Suite 560, Minneapolis, MN 55401.

Bohac David L., Martha J. Hewett, S Katherine Hammond, David T. Grimsrud. Secondhand Smoke Transfer and Reductions by Air Sealing and Ventilation in Multi-Unit Buildings: PFT and Nicotine Verification. *Indoor Air.* 2010 Jul 20. doi: 10.1111/j.1600-0668.2010.00680.x. [Epub ahead of print]

Dacunto PJ, Cheng K-C, Acevedo-Bolton V, Klepeis NE, Repace JL, Ott WR, Hildemann LM. Identifying and quantifying secondhand smoke in multiunit homes with tobacco smoke odor complaints. *Atmospheric Environment* 2013; 71:399-407.

Dacunto PJ, Cheng K-C, Acevedo-Bolton V, Jiang R-T, Klepeis NE, Repace JL, Ott WR, Hildemann LM. Identifying and quantifying secondhand smoke in source and receptor rooms: logistic regression and chemical mass balance approaches. *Indoor Air* 2013, Apr 30. doi: 10.1111/ina.12049. [Epub ahead of print].

Dacunto PJ, Cheng KC, Acevedo-Bolton V, Jiang RT, Klepeis NE, Repace JL, Ott WR, Hildemann LM. Real-time particle monitor calibration factors and PM2.5 emission factors for multiple indoor sources. Environ Sci Process Impacts. 2013 Jul 24;15(8): 1511-9. doi: 10.1039/c3em00209h.

Lstiburek J. BSD-110: *HVAC in Multifamily Buildings.* Building Science Corporation, Oct. 24, 2006.

Lstiburek J. BSD-109: *Pressures in Buildings.* Building Science Corporation, Jan. 15, 2014.

Habitat Magazine, March 2, 2016. The Price of Smoking in Co-ops Just Went Up. Way Up. New York City. http://www.habitatmag.com/Publication-Content/Building-Operations/2016/2016-March/Coop-Smoking

New York Magazine, March 2, 2016. Manhattan Co-op Ordered to Pay $120,000 to a Woman Affected by Secondhand Smoke, By Samuel Lieberman.
http://nymag.com/daily/intelligencer/2016/03/nyc-co-op-made-to-pay-over-secondhand-smoke.html.

Schoenmarklin S. Infiltration of Secondhand Smoke into Apartments, Apartments and Other Multi-Unit Dwellings. *A Law Synopsis by the Tobacco Control Legal Consortium, October 2009.*

Schuman v. Greenbelt Homes, Inc. (2013). David S. Schuman v. Greenbelt Homes, Inc., No. 2020, Sept. Term 2011. Court of Special Appeals of Maryland, June 27, 2013.

Schuman v. GHI, Inc. and Popovic (2010). IN THE CIRCUIT COURT FOR PRINCE GEORGE'S COUNTY MARYLAND Civil Division DAVID S. SCHUMAN) 11 Ridge Road, Unit Q Greenbelt, Maryland 20770) Plaintiff, vs. GREENBELT HOMES, INC. 25 Hamilton Place Greenbelt, Maryland 20770 vs. Greenbelt Development Corp. 25 Hamilton Place Greenbelt, Maryland 20770 and SVETLANA and DARKO POPOVIC, 11 Ridge Road, Unit R,Greenbelt, Maryland 20770) Defendants. COMPLAINT FOR MONETARY DAMAGES, DECLARATORY JUDGMENT PRELIMINARY INJUNCTION AND A PERMANENT INJUNCTION.

Steinemann A. Ten questions concerning air fresheners and indoor built Environments. *Building and Environment* 111: 279-284 (2017).

CHAPTER 23. THE FAROE ISLANDS FARRAGO

Repace JL. ANALYSIS OF THE AIR QUALITY IMPACT OF PROPOSED TÓRSHAVN POWER PLANT; APRIL 24, 2010, PART I, PART II SEPT. 11, 2012; PART III, MAY 15, 2014 (AVAILABLE ON RESEARCH GATE).

TURNER DB. *WORKBOOK OF ATMOSPHERIC DISPERSION ESTIMATES*, U.S. Environmental Protection Agency, Research Triangle Park, NC, Revised 1970. Also, 2nd Edition, 1994, CRC Press.

CHAPTER 24. EPILOGUE

ANR, Nov. 16, 2016. *"Change moves at the speed of trust" Stephen M.R. Covey.* Hallet C, Americans For Nonsmokers' Rights.

Biener L, et al. Who Avoids smoky restaurants and bars and why? J. Publ. Heath Mgt. & Practice 5: 74-78 (1999).

California Environmental Protection Agency 2005. *Health Effects of Exposure to Environmental Tobacco Smoke: Final Report*, APPENDIX III, PROPOSED IDENTIFICATION OF ENVIRONMENTAL TOBACCO SMOKE AS A TOXIC AIR CONTAMINANT AS APPROVED BY THE SCIENTIFIC REVIEW PANEL ON JUNE 24, 2005. https://oehha.ca.gov/media/downloads/air/report/app32005.pdf

Cho JH, Paik SY (2016) Association between Electronic Cigarette Use and Asthma among High School Students in South Korea. PLoS ONE 11(3): e0151022. doi:10.1371/journal.pone.0151022

CBS News, 2013. *FDA's graphic cigarette labels rule goes up in smoke after U.S. abandons appeal.* http://www.cbsnews.com/news/fdas-graphic-cigarette-labels-rule-goes-up-in-smoke-after-us-abandons-appeal/.

CDC, MMWR 64/No. 19, May 2015. *State-Specific Prevalence of Current Cigarette Smoking and Smokeless Tobacco Use Among Adults Aged ≥18 Years — United States, 2011–2013.*

CDC, 2016. Fact Sheet: *Tobacco Industry Marketing.* http://www.cdc.gov/tobacco/data_statistics/fact_sheets/tobacco_industry/marketing/

Centers for Disease Control and Prevention. *Vital Signs: Disparities in Nonsmokers' Exposure to Secondhand Smoke—United States, 1999–2012.* Morbidity and Mortality Weekly Report 2015;64(4):103–8. http://www.cdc.gov/mmwr/preview/mmwrhtml/mm6404a7.htm. [accessed 6/28/16].

CDC, 2016 - Fact Sheet - Fast Facts - Smoking & Tobacco Use. http://www.cdc.gov/tobacco/data_statistics/fact_sheets/fast_facts/ Accessed 6/30/16.

CDC, 2017. *Cigarette Smoking and Tobacco Use Among People of Low Socioeconomic Status.* https://www.cdc.gov/tobacco/disparities/low-ses/index.htm. Accessed 15 June 2017.

Cho JH, Paik SY (2016) Association between Electronic Cigarette Use and Asthma among High School Students in South Korea. *PLoS ONE* 11 (3): e0151022. doi:10.1371/journal.pone.0151022.

Collishaw NE, Boyd NF, Cantor KP, et al. Canadian Expert Panel on Tobacco Smoke and Breast Cancer Risk. Toronto, Canada: Ontario Research Unit; 2009. (OTRU Special Report Series).

Davis, 2002. Davis D. *When Smoke Ran Like Water – Tales of Environmental Deception and the Battle Against Pollution.* Basic Books, Perseus Books Group, New York, 2002.

DiFranza JR, Asquith BF. Does the Joe Camel campaign preferentially reach 18 to 24 year old adults? Tobacco Control 4: 367–371 (1995).

Dwyer, L., 2014. *At this Tobacco Company, Smoking at Your Desk Is Finally Off-Limits. Take Part* <At This Tobacco Company, Smoking at Your Desk Is Finally Off-Limits | TakePart>.

Eubanks SB and Repace JL, 2014. *Merchants of Death: BAD ACTS* July 15, 2014, https://www.youtube.com/watch?v=I54XyduAy8Q;

Gaby K, 2017. *EDF Voices: People on the Planet – Pruitt's first 100 days at the EPA: His most alarming actions so far.* Environmental Defense Fund, May 25, 2017.

GATS China, 2010. *Global Adult Tobacco Use Survey, Fact Sheet China: 2010.*

GATS India, 2017. *Global Adult Tobacco Use Survey, Fact Sheet India: 2017.*

Glantz SA, Bareham DW. E-CIGARETTES: USE, EFFECTS ON SMOKING, RISKS, AND POLICY IMPLICATIONS. In press. *Annual Reviews of Public Health;* Publication date: March 2018.

Habitat Board Operations, 2013. http://www.habitatmag.com/Publication-Content/Board-Operations/2013/2013-February/Recent-Secondhand-Smoke-Lawsuit#.Vtiw51srKJA.

Hackshaw A, Morris JK, Boniface S, Tang JL, Milenković D. Low cigarette consumption and risk of coronary heart disease and stroke: meta-analysis of 141 cohort studies in 55 study reports. *BMJ* 2018; 360: j5855.

IARC Working Group on the Evaluation of Carcinogenic Risks to Humans.
ARC Monogr Eval Carcinog Risks Hum. 2012; 100(Pt E):1-538.
Review Personal habits and indoor combustions. Volume 100 E. A review of human carcinogens.

Ingraham C. Support for Marijuana legalization has hit an all-time high. *The Washington Post Wonkblog*, March 25, 2016.

(ISES, 2015). International Society of Exposure Science – Science for Better Environmental Health. https://www.intl-exposurescience.org.

Johnson KC. Just one cigarette a day seriously elevates cardiovascular risk. *BMJ* 2018;360:k167 doi: 10.1136/bmj.k167 (Published 24 January 2018).

Lee, PN, Thornton AJ, Hamling JS. Epidemiological evidence on environmental tobacco smoke and cancers other than lung or breast, *Regulatory Toxicology and Pharmacology* (2016), doi: 10.1016/j.yrtph.2016.06.012.

Martin EM, et al. E-cigarette use results in suppression of immune and inflammatory-response genes in 2 nasal epithelial cells similar to cigarette smoke. *Am J Physiol Lung Cell Mol Physiol* (June 10, 2016). doi:10.1152/ajplung.00170.2016.

Mannino DM, Albalak R, Grosse S, Repace J. Second-hand smoke exposure and blood lead levels in U.S. children. *Epidemiology* 14: 719-727 (2003).

Mannino DM, Moorman JE, Kingsley B, Rose D, and Repace J. Health effects related to environmental tobacco smoke exposure in children in the United States. Data from the Third National Health & Nutrition Examination Survey. Archives of Pediatric & *Adolescent Medicine* 155:36-41 (2001).

Marquis Who's Who, 2017. http://marquispressreleases.com/press-release/james-l-repace-presented-with-the-albert-nelson-marquis-lifetime-achievement-aw

MMWR 65 (44): Nov. 11, 2016. *Great American Smokeout – November 17, 2016.*

MMWR, 2012, *Consumption of Cigarettes and Combustible Tobacco — United States, 2000–2011*, August 3, 2012 / 61(30);565-569.

The New York Times – International Business - U.S. Chamber of Commerce Works Globally to Fight Antismoking Measures, by D. Hakim, JUNE 30, 2015 http://nyti.ms/1KmEZa4.

The New York Times – EDITORIAL, Tarred by Tobacco, online, JULY 3, 2015.

NCI, 2008. National Cancer Institute. *The Role of the Media in Promoting and Reducing Tobacco Use. Tobacco Control Monograph No. 19*. Bethesda, MD: U.S. Department of Health and Human Services, National Institutes of Health, National Cancer Institute. NIH Pub. No. 07-6242, June 2008.

NCI, 2016. U.S. National Cancer Institute and World Health Organization. The Economics of Tobacco and Tobacco Control. *National Cancer Institute Tobacco Control Monograph 21.* NIH Publication No. 16-CA-8029A. Bethesda, MD: U.S. Department of Health and Human Services, National Institutes of Health, National Cancer Institute; and Geneva, CH: World Health Organization; 2016.

Oberg M, Jaakkola MS, Woodward A, et al. Worldwide burden of disease from exposure to second-hand smoke: a retrospective analysis of data from 192 countries. *Lancet* 2011; 377(9760): 139–146.

Polanski JR, Modisette D, Garci C, Glantz SA. Smoking in top-grossing US movies 2017.UCSF Center for Tobacco Control and Education, University of California, San Francisco. http://escholarship.org/uc/item/5939j0kd, March 2018.

Repace and Ott, 2012. Estimated reductions in population $PM_{2.5}$ exposure from ambient air pollution and secondhand smoke, 1990 to 2010. J.L. Repace & W.R. Ott, Paper TuE2, 22nd Annual Meeting of the International Society of Exposure Science, Seattle Washington, Oct. 28-Nov.1, 2012 [Plot updated to 2017].

Repace, 2012.
https://www.youtube.com/watch?v=FrNzJ_spCqM.

Repace, 2014. Fighting for Smokefree Air: *James Repace on Ventilation*, posted by Americans For Nonsmokers' Rights, https://www.youtube.com/watch?v=wsOxbTi12j4;

Repace, 2014. *Secondhand Smoke: The Case for Smoke-Free Casinos* May 28, 2014☐, https://www.youtube.com/watch?v=FZbeI1RXn7w;

Reynolds P, Goldberg D, Hurley S, Nelson DO, Largent J, Henderson KD, Bernstein L. Passive Smoking and Risk of Breast Cancer in the California Teachers Study.
Cancer Epidemiol Biomarkers Prev. 2009 Dec; 18(12): 3389–3398.
doi: 10.1158/1055-9965.EPI-09-0936

Richter E, Soskolne CL, LaDou J, Berman, T. Whistleblowers in Environmental Science, Prevention of Suppression Bias, and the Need for a Code of Protection. *Investigating Research Integrity, Proceedings of the First ORI Research Conference on Research Integrity,* Eds. Steneck NH, and Scheetz MD. Office of Research Integrity, U.S. Dept. of Health and Human Services, 2002.

Rogér et al., Oral Trauma and Tooth Avulsion Following Explosion of E-Cigarette.
J Oral Maxillofac Surg 74:1181-1185 (2016).

Rudy SF, Durmowicz. Electronic nicotine delivery systems: overheating, fires and explosions. *Tobacco Control* 2016; 0:1–9. doi:10.1136/tobaccocontrol-2015-052626.

Springer ML, and Glantz, SA. *Marijuana Use and Heart Disease: Potential Effects of Public Exposure to Smoke.* UNIVERSITY OF CALIFORNIA, SAN FRANCISCO, April 13, 2015.

Wang X, Derakshandeh R, Liu J, Le S, et al. Secondhand Marijuana Smoke Is Not Benign. Editorial. *J Am Heart Assoc.* 2016;5:e003858 doi: 10.1161/JAHA.116.003858).
Washington Post, 14 June, 2017, A4.

Wan, W. America's new tobacco crisis: The rich stopped smoking, the poor didn't. *Washington Post*. National, June 13, 2017. https://www.washingtonpost.com/national/americas-new-tobacco-crisis-the-rich-stopped-smoking-the-poor-didnt/2017/06/13/a63b42ba-4c8c-11e7-9669-250d0b15f83b_story.html?utm_term=.062cefcd17d1.

Washington Post, 2018. Japan OKs 1st anti-smoking law, but seen as lax and partial. Yamaguchi, M. July 18, 2018.

WHO, 2010. The World Health Organization Report, **Second-hand smoke,** *Assessing the burden of disease at national and local levels,* WHO Environmental Burden of Disease Series, No. 18, 2010.

WHO Fact Sheet 2014. Tobacco Fact Sheet N°339, Updated May 2014. http://www.who.int/mediacentre/factsheets/fs339/en/.

Zhu, SH, Sun JY, Bonnevie E, Cummins SE, Gamst A, Yin L, Lee M. Four hundred and sixty brands of e-cigarettes and counting: implications for product regulation. *Tob Control* 2014; 23:iii3–iii9. doi:10.1136/tobaccocontrol-2014-051670.

James L. Repace, Legal Cases, 1981-2013.

1. Office Worker. Gordon vs. Raven, D. C. Superior Court, Washington, D. C. 1981.

2. Civil Servant: Levinson & Communications Workers of America vs. State of NJ, Trenton, NJ, 1984.

3. Booking Agent: Irons & Teamsters Union vs. Pan American World Airways, NY, 1984.

4. Engineer: Smith vs. AT&T, Washington, DC, 18 June 1984.

5. Office Worker: Wilson & Public Service Alliance vs. Health & Welfare Canada, Ottawa, 1985.*

6. 6. Civil Servant: EEO Stiltner vs. U.S. Department of Commerce, Colorado, 1985.*

7. US Government Hearing: AFGE/AFLCIO vs. U.S. Dept. of Health & Human Services,. Washington, DC, 1988.*

8. Prisoner: Beeson vs. Johnson et al. U.S. District Court, Eastern District of North Carolina, Raleigh NC. 1989.*

9. Office Worker: Bettes and Canadian Auto, Aerospace, and Agricultural Implement Workers' Union vs. DeHavilland Aircraft. Toronto, Ontario, Canada 1989.*

10. Railroad: AMTRAK VS. CTWU, Washington, DC 1989.*

11. US Government: AFGE vs. VETERANS' ADMINISTRATION BEFORE THE FEDERAL SERVICE IMPASSE PANEL, Washington, DC 1989. (Arbitration)*

12. Railroad: Norfolk Southern Railway v. Communications Transportation Workers, Washington, DC, 1989.*

13. State education workers: Federation of State, County Education Personnel vs Commonwealth of Pennsylvania, Harrisburg, PA, 1990.*

14. Equipment Mfr.: Crenlo, Inc. vs United Auto, Agricultural Implement, and Aerospace Workers Rochester, MN 16 , 1990. (Arbitration)*

15. Industrial Electronics Mfr.: Allied Signal vs. International Association of Machinists and Aerospace Workers, Mission Kansas, 1990. (Arbitration)*

16. Teachers' Union: PENNSYLVANIA STATE EDUCATORS' ASSOCIATION vs PSEA Staff.

    Harrisburg PA. 1991. (Arbitration)*

17. U.S. Government: AFGE LOCAL 3480 AFL-CIO vs NIOSH.* before the FEDERAL LABOR RELATIONS AUTHORITY, Cinncinati, Ohio, 1991.

18. U.S. Government: National Treasury Employees Union, Chapter 230, vs. DEPARTMENT OF HEALTH & HUMAN SERVICES, Chicago, IL, 1991. (Arbitration)*

19. U.S. Government: National Treasury Employees Union Ch. 230 vs. U.S. Dept. of Health & Human Services, San Francisco, CA, 1991. (Arbitration)*

20. Nurse: Wiley v. RJR Nabisco, et al., Indianapolis, IN, 1998.

21. Railroad Worker: Thaxton v. Norfolk Southern, Chattanooga, TN, 1998.

22. Province. SOOKE RIVER HOTEL LTD. V. CAPITAL REGIONAL DISTRICT, S.C.B.C. # 98 1744 – VICTORIA REGISTRY, VICTORIA, BC, CANADA.

23. Child Custody: Baker v. Kelley Syracuse, NY, 1998.*

24. Casino Workers: Avallone v. American Tobacco et al.(NJ) + Badillo v. American Tobacco et al.(NV)} 1998.

25. Real Estate Appraiser: Leonard v. Rollette County, ND. 1998.*

26. Casino Workers: Mullen v. Treasure Chest, New Orleans, LA 1999.*

27. SECONDHAND SMOKE INFILTRATION. Sagatelian vs. South Lake et al. Pasadena, CA. 1999.

28. Casino Worker: Brook vs. Burswood Casino, Perth, Australia, 1999.

29. Restaurant Workers. Edwards et al., v. GMRI, Inc. (Red Lobster; Ruby Tuesday), et al., USDC, DKC, MD 97-4327.

30. State Government: State of California v. Philip Morris et al., San Diego, CA: 2000.*

31. Flight Attendants: Duncan v. Northwest Airlines, Seattle, WA: 2000.

32. Prisoner: Blackiston v. Horne, Philadelphia, PA: 2000.*

33. Prisoners: Johnson v. Robinson, USDC, MD, Southern Div. CASE NOS. PJM-94-2871, PJM-95-190, PJM-98-4109. Baltimore, MD, 2000.*

34. Prisoners: Warren v. Keane. New York: 2000.

35. Real Estate Appraiser. Leonard v. Rollette County, ND. 2000.*

36. Municipality: City of Anchorage v. Hooters: Anchorage AK, 2001.*

37. Prisoner: McLaurin v. Strack, New York: 2001.*

38. Prisoner: Reilly v. Grayson, Detroit: 2001.*

39. Flight Attendants: Routh v. Philip Morris et al., Dade County Circuit Court, 11th Judicial Circuit.

40. General Jurisdiction Division, Case # 00-3030 CA 27. 2002.

41. Office Worker: Raymond v. NCMA, Arlington, VA: 2001.*

42. Prisoner: Alamin v. Coefield, New York, 2002.*

43. Health Officer: Pelletier et al. v. Sarsfield & Northwestern Health Unit, Toronto, 2003.*

44. Prison Guards. Malpass, et al. v. Dept. of Corrections, Washington State, 2004.

45. Railroad Worker. Thaxton v. Norfolk Southern Railway, Atlanta, 2004.*

46. Child Custody. Kean vs. Heagy, Cause # 48D02-9901-JP-030, Superior Court, Madison County, Indiana.*

47. Prisoners. Shird et al., vs. Andrews, United States District Court, District of Maryland, Civil Action No.: PJM-03-249, 2005.

48. Casino Workers. Januszewski et al., v. Horseshoe Hammond, USDC, NDIN, Hammond Div., 2:00CV352JM. 2006.*

49. Railroad Conductor. HEPBURN V. LONG ISLAND RAILROAD. U.S. District Court, Eastern District of New York, Civil Action No. CV 04-4194.

50. Prisoner. MARQUEZ V. CITY OF NEW YORK AND NEW YORK CITY DEPARTMENT OF CORRECTION, Supreme Court of the State of New York, Index No. 123370/01. 2007.

51. Prisoners. ABDULLAH & WILLIAMS VS. DC DEPARTMENT OF CORRECTIONS, CA 02-1642 (JDB)(RMC), 2007.

52. Prisoner. SHEPHERD V. HOGAN ET AL. Supreme Court of the State of New York, Index No. 123370/01, No. 99 Civ. 1275 (N.D.N.Y. Aug. 15, 2006), 2007.

53. Prisoner. Boyd v. Walker et al. United States District Court, Southern District of Illinois Case # 06478 MJR, 2007.

54. SECONDHAND SMOKE INFILTRATION. Alberini v. Jenkins, Case Number 2008-CA-8659-B (D.C. Superior Court), 2008.

55. Child Custody. Brandon W. Melton v. Brandy Jean Melton, Sevier County Circuit Court Case No. DR 2010-35-2, Arkansas, 2010.*

56. Prisoner. King v. Sherry, Case # 2:07-CV-133, US Federal Court, Western District of Michigan, 2011.*

57. APARTMENT TENANT (OUTDOOR SWIMMING POOL). Birke (plaintiff) v. Oakwood Worldwide et al. Birke v. Oakwood Worldwide (2009), Cal.App.4th, [No. B203093. Second Dist., Div. Seven.], 2011.

58. SECONDHAND SMOKE INFILTRATION. Schuman v. Greenbelt Homes, Inc., et al. PG Circuit, CAL-10-6047. CIRCUIT COURT FOR PRINCE GEORGE'S COUNTY, MARYLAND, Upper Marlboro, MD, 2011.

59. SECONDHAND SMOKE INFILTRATION. Powers v. Tarkowski, Case Number 2012-CA-9112-B (D.C. Superior Court), 2012.*

60. SECONDHAND SMOKE INFILTRATION. Hershman v. Kaibni, Case Number 346968-V (Montgomery Circuit Court), 2012.*

61. SECONDHAND SMOKE INFILTRATION. Daggett v. Landini, Case Number 12-4603 (Alexandria Circuit Court). 2012/2013.*

62. SECONDHAND SMOKE INFILTRATION. Starr v. Pater-Rov, D.C. Superior Court 2012-CA-6487-B, 2012/2013.*

63. SECONDHAND SMOKE INFILTRATION. Eric Motley v. Wadsworth House Condominium Assoc. Inc, Case 2015-CA-000597B; Kimberly Smallis, & Lewis Bertorelli, Case 2013-CA-006831-B. Washington, DC, Superior Court, 2015.*

64. SECONDHAND SMOKE INFILTRATION. Samuel Himes v. Donald Balla, Travis Grooms, Erica Grooms. Fairfax County Circuit Ct. VA, Case # 2016-07618.*

65. SECONDHAND SMOKE INFILTRATION. Montgomery County Commission on 66. Common Ownership Communities. Linda Sen Usui v. Americana Finnmark Condominium Assoc. Inc. Case # 10-16. In process Aug 11.

Plaintiff prevailed.

GLOSSARY OF TECHNICAL TERMS

Bates Numbers. Search the Truth Tobacco Industry Documents Library by entering the Bates number, e.g., T109020978 in the search field, and checking the box labeled "Tobacco Collections," and hitting Return or the Magnifying Glass Icon.

Case-Control Epidemiological Study. A study comparing patients who have a disease (cases) with patients who do not have the disease (controls), and usually retrospectively compares the frequency of exposure to a risk factor present in each group to probe the relationship between the risk factor and the disease.

Clean Air Act. The Clean Air Act identifies six common air pollutants that are found all over the United States. These pollutants can injure health, harm the environment and cause property damage. EPA calls these pollutants "criteria air pollutants" because the agency has developed health-based criteria (science-based guidelines) as the basis for setting permissible exposure levels in the air we breathe. $PM_{2.5}$ is a criteria pollutant. EPA establishes national ambient air quality standards for each of the criteria pollutants.

Dose. The concentration of a substance absorbed by the body and present in body fluids such as blood, saliva, or urine. Dose is the product of exposure and absorption efficiency through membranes of the lung, intestine, or skin.

Environmental Tobacco Smoke. An older term for secondhand smoke. Environmental tobacco smoke (ETS) and secondhand smoke (SHS) refer to the constellation of tobacco smoke chemicals in the air liberated by smoking of cigarettes, pipes, and cigars. The terms passive smoking and involuntary smoking refer to a nonsmoker's inhalation of those chemicals. These terms began to appear in books around 1970, reflecting public concern, and by 2008, secondhand smoke (40%) and passive smoking (32%) were the most prominent terms in use, with environmental tobacco smoke at 27% and involuntary smoking at 1.4% [Google Ngram, 2015]. Passive smoking and involuntary smoking reached their peak popularity in 1992, secondhand smoke in 2004, and environmental tobacco smoke in 2002.

Exposure. The product of concentration and duration of contact with a substance.

Involuntary smoking. A Public Health Service term for passive smoking.

Micrograms per cubic meter ($\mu g/m^3$). The units of density, or concentration, in which air pollution in the air is usually expressed.

Mole. The term "mole" has been used in spy fiction to mean any long-term clandestine spy or informant within an organization, government or private. While the tobacco industry certainly had many of these, in this book, "mole" is used as a synonym for what Philip Morris termed "White Coats," whose job it was to purvey the industry's propaganda and junk science, in order to discredit the actual science of secondhand smoke. Moles were paid handsomely for their services through secret accounts kept by the industry, but industry lawyers carefully vetted their pronouncements to reflect Big Tobacco's policies. They often concealed industry funding, or if they were forced to disclose it, claimed that their views were "their own." Stan Glantz and I kept lists of moles as we discovered them. Moles pretended to be scientists independent of the tobacco industry, but in reality, had direct or indirect ties to the tobacco industry, its external law firms or its front organizations. Very few scientific moles conducted or published actual secondhand smoke research. The industry had moles in the traditional sense as well, and industry document showed there was at least one at EPA.

National Ambient Air Quality Standards (NAAQS). Standards established by the United States Environmental Protection Agency under authority of the Clean Air Act (42 U.S.C. 7401 et seq.) that legally apply for outdoor air throughout the USA. Primary standards are designed to protect human health in the general population, with an adequate margin of safety, including sensitive populations such as children, the elderly, and individuals suffering from respiratory diseases.

OSHA PELs. OSHA's PELs (permissible workplace exposure limits) were issued shortly after adoption of the Occupational Safety and Health (OSH) Act in 1970, and have not been updated since that time. OSHA has recognized that many of its permissible exposure limits (PELs) are outdated and inadequate for ensuring protection of worker health. Since 1970, OSHA issued new PELs for 16 agents, and standards without PELs for 13 carcinogens. OSHA states that industrial experience, new developments in technology, and scientific data clearly indicate that in many instances these adopted limits are **not** sufficiently protective of worker health. In general, the PELs for a given pollutant are far in excess of EPA NAAQS for the same pollutant. For example, the 24-hr NAAQS for fine particles is 35 $\mu g/m^3$, which for an 8-hr exposure would be 105 $\mu g/m^3$, while the 8-hr average OSHA PEL for fine particles is 15,000 $\mu g/m^3$, 143 times higher. The tobacco industry and its moles often cited OSHA PELs as evidence that secondhand smoke is safe to breathe. See TLVs.

Passive smoking. The inhalation of secondhand smoke from the air by a person or animal [dogs who lived with smokers were prey to nasal sinus cancer if they had long snouts, or lung cancer if they had short ones. https://www.sciencedaily.com/releases/2007/08/070831123420.htm

Particulate matter. The term for particles found in the air, including dust, dirt, soot, smoke, and liquid droplets. Particles can be suspended in the air for long periods of time. Particles less than 2.5 microns in diameter, or $PM_{2.5}$, are readily inhaled through the nose into the lung and are common combustion-related air pollutants in both indoor and outdoor air.

Prospective Cohort Epidemiological Study. A prospective cohort study begins with a cohort of disease-free persons and follows them during a prolonged study period looking for a specific disease outcome, and relates this to other factors such as suspected risk or protective factors. The cohort of subjects serves as their own controls. This type of study usually involves a large number of subjects and is far more expensive to conduct than the case-control type.

$PM_{2.5}$. Particles less than 10 micrometers in diameter (PM_{10}) pose a health concern because they can be inhaled into and accumulate in the respiratory system. Particles less than 2.5 micrometers in diameter ($PM_{2.5}$) are referred to as "fine" particles and are believed to pose the greatest health risks. Because of their small size (approximately 1/30th the average width of a human hair), fine particles can lodge deeply into the lungs.

Respirable particulates. The International Agency for Research on Cancer, and the World Health Organization (IARC and WHO) designate airborne particulates as a Group 1 carcinogen. Particulates are the deadliest form of air pollution due to their ability to penetrate deep into the lungs and blood streams unfiltered, causing permanent DNA mutations, heart attacks, and premature death. In 2013, a study involving 312,944 people in nine European countries revealed that there was no safe level of particulates and that for every increase of 10 $\mu g/m^3$ in PM10, the lung cancer rate rose 22%. The smaller PM2.5 were particularly deadly, with a 36% increase in lung cancer per 10 $\mu g/m^3$ as it can penetrate deeper into the lungs.

Risk Assessment. Health risk assessment is a process by which the nature and probability of adverse health effects in humans exposed to chemicals in contaminated environmental air, water, or food, now or in the future, may be estimated.

Secondhand smoke. Secondhand smoke is the smoke that comes from the burning end of a cigarette, cigar or pipe, plus the smoke that smokers breathe out (exhale). Secondhand smoke contains substances that irritate the lining of the lungs, eyes, nose, and throat. These substances cause changes that interfere with cells developing normally in the human body. These changes in cells increase the risk of heart disease, cancer, and respiratory conditions (see also environmental tobacco smoke).

Significant Risk. In its 1980 Benzene decision, the Supreme Court, stated its view of the boundaries of acceptable and unacceptable risk for OSHA. The Court stated: "It is OSHA's responsibility to determine what it considers to be a 'significant' risk. Some risks are plainly acceptable and others are plainly unacceptable. If for example, the odds are one in a billion that a person will die from cancer by taking a drink of chlorinated water, the risk clearly could not be considered significant. On the other hand, if the odds are one in a thousand that regular inhalation of … benzene will be fatal, a reasonable person might consider the risk significant and take steps to decrease or eliminate it. So a risk of 1/1000 (10^{-3}) is clearly significant. It represents the uppermost end of a million-fold range somewhere below which the acceptable versus unacceptable risk boundary must fall." The Court added, that significant risk determination is "not a mathematical straitjacket," and that "OSHA is not required to support its findings with anything approaching scientific certainty."

Smoker density. The number of smokers divided by the space volume.

Threshold Limit Values (TLVs). TLV's are *recommended* by the American Conference of Governmental Industrial Hygienists (ACGIH) and are not legally enforceable, whereas PELs are legally enforceable exposure limits set by OSHA. Although many PELs are based on TLVs. PELs and TLVs are 8-hour workplace air pollution exposure concentration guidelines for which it is believed that ***nearly*** all workers may be repeatedly exposed without adverse health effects. According to Castleman and Ziem AJIM 13:531-559 (1988), TLVs for many substances have revealed serious shortcomings in the process followed by the American Conference of Governmental Industrial Hygienists. Unpublished corporate communications were important in developing TLVs for 104 substances; for 15 of these, the TLV documentation was based solely on such information. Corporate representatives listed officially as "consultants" since 1970 were given primary responsibility for developing TLVs on proprietary chemicals of the companies that employed them (e.g, Dow, DuPont). See PELs.

EXPOSURE MODEL VALIDATION

The following discussion shows how Repace et al. (2006) finally validated the exposure model in the risk assessment of passive smoking and lung cancer by Repace and Lowrey (1985). The nicotine metabolite cotinine, is the biomarker of choice for tobacco smoke dose in body fluids. In 1993, Repace and Lowrey (1993) would publish a pharmacokinetic model which enabled relating cotinine in a person's blood to their dose of nicotine inhaled from secondhand smoke. By 1996, in CDC's NHANES national survey of US nonsmokers, Pirkle et al. (1996) reported measurements of cotinine in blood serum and reported a mean level of P = 0.93 nanograms per milliliter (ng/mL) for U.S. nonsmokers exposed both at work and at home. A simplified version of this model can be written as N (μg/m^3) = 167 P/ρH, where N is the nicotine concentration in air, ρ (rho) is the average respiration rate of a person, and H is the duration of a person's secondhand smoke exposure, and 167 is the factor converting cotinine P in units of ng/mL to nicotine N in (μg/m^3).

Table A1, adapted from Repace and Lowrey, (1985)				
Venue of Second-hand smoke exposure	Estimated Exposure Probability, % Of U.S. adult Population	Modeled RSP, in Venue, μg/day	Probability-Weighted Estimated RSP, μg/day	Probability-Weighted Estimated Nicotine, μg/day
Work + Home	39	2270	890	89.0
Neither Work nor Home	14	0.00	0.00	0.00
Home Only	23	450	100	10.0
Work Only	24	1820	440	44.0
Total	100%		1430	143

For a person exposed both at work and at home, if assume H = 16 hours per day, and an average respiration rate of ρ = 0.75 cubic meters (m^3)/hour as recommended by EPA, this yields: N = 167 P/ρH = (167)(0.93)/[(0.75)(16)] = 12.9 μg/m^3. Over a 16 hour day, then, a person would inhale (12.9 μg/m^3)(16 hours)(0.75 m^3/hour) = 155 micrograms of nicotine. From chamber studies performed by Leader and Hammond in the early 1980's we knew that the RSP-to-nicotine ratio was 10:1. From Table 1, we estimated the typical person would inhale 143 micrograms of nicotine, which is equivalent to 1430 micrograms of RSP. This compares to 1550 micrograms of RSP calculated from the NHANES study. So our 1985 estimates would eventually be shown to be in the ballpark.

As a graphic illustration, the figure below (Repace et al., 2006), used the pharmacokinetic (PK) model developed by Repace and Lowrey in 1993, to graphically compare the 1996 CDC result for the entire study cohort of US nonsmokers to our estimate of average and maximum exposure of typical nonsmokers from Repace and Lowrey (1985). Our estimate of exposures of the typical U.S. nonsmoker coincides with the peak and extreme values of the cotinine distribution, validating our physical intuition two decades earlier (Repace et al. 2006).

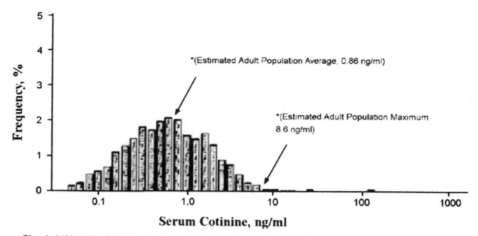

Fig. 1. NHANES III Distribution of Serum Cotinine in U.S. Nonsmoking population ≥4 years of age (1988–1991), exposed at home or at work[4] versus PK model predictions for typical and most-exposed persons in U.S. population using Equation 3.[8]

INDEX

Made in the
USA
Middletown, DE

77469107R00296